Lecture Notes in Computer Science 10056

Commenced Publication in 1973
Founding and Former Series Editors:
Gerhard Goos, Juris Hartmanis, and Jan van Leeuwen

More information about this series at http://www.springer.com/series/7409

Rosa Bottino · Johan Jeuring
Remco C. Veltkamp (Eds.)

Games and Learning Alliance

5th International Conference, GALA 2016
Utrecht, The Netherlands, December 5–7, 2016
Proceedings

 Springer

Editors
Rosa Bottino
Institute for Educational Technology
Genova
Italy

Johan Jeuring
Utrecht University
Utrecht
The Netherlands

Remco C. Veltkamp
Utrecht University
Utrecht
The Netherlands

ISSN 0302-9743   ISSN 1611-3349   (electronic)
Lecture Notes in Computer Science
ISBN 978-3-319-50181-9   ISBN 978-3-319-50182-6   (eBook)
DOI 10.1007/978-3-319-50182-6

Library of Congress Control Number: 2016959172

LNCS Sublibrary: SL3 – Information Systems and Applications, incl. Internet/Web, and HCI

Printed on acid-free paper

This Springer imprint is published by Springer Nature
The registered company is Springer International Publishing AG
The registered company address is: Gewerbestrasse 11, 6330 Cham, Switzerland

Preface

The 5th Games and Learning Alliance (GALA) Conference was held in Utrecht, The Netherlands, December 5–7, 2016. It was organized by the Serious Games Society and the Center for Game Research at Utrecht University.

The GALA series of conferences provides an excellent opportunity to discuss important themes and emergent topics within the growing field of serious games. The meeting involves academic researchers, industrial developers, teachers, and corporate decision makers.

GALA 2016 received 55 submissions. Each paper was reviewed by at least three Program Committee members. The Program Committee selected 27 of these papers for presentation at the conference, and 14 for presentation at a poster session at the conference. The majority of the authors are based in Europe, but all continents except for Australia were represented at the conference.

The conference started with a day of tutorials, at which various topics such as learner models, interactive virtual characters, addressing learners with different backgrounds, and gamification were discussed. European projects such as WATCHME, RAGE, and BODEGA contributed significantly to these tutorials.

It was an honor to have Jean-Marc Labat, Université Pierre et Marie Curie, France, and Yasmin B. Kafai, University of Pennsylvania, USA, as keynote speakers at GALA 2016. Jean-Marc Labat presented a meta-design perspective on enhancing the usage of educational games by teachers, and Yasmin Kafai spoke about connected gaming: what making video games can teach us about learning and literacy.

The conference featured eight paper presentation sessions. A number of paper presentation sessions discussed the relation between serious games and particular domains, namely, health, sustainability, management, maths and programming, and soft skills. Other sessions discussed game development and the assessment of games, the relation between games and learning, and mobile games.

As in previous years, selected best papers of the GALA Conference will be published in a dedicated special issue of the *International Journal of Serious Games*, the scientific journal managed by the Serious Games Society, which is a great reference point for academicians and practitioners to publish original research work on serious games and be informed about the latest developments in the field.

We thank the authors for submitting many interesting papers, the Program Committee members for reviewing these papers, and the Serious Games Society and the Center for Game Research at Utrecht University for organizing the conference.

October 2016

Rosa Bottino
Johan Jeuring
Remco C. Veltkamp

Organization

Games and Learning Alliance
5th International Conference, GALA 2016
Utrecht, December 5–7, 2016
Proceedings

GALA 2016 was organized by the Serious Games Society and the Center for Game Research at Utrecht University.

General Chair

Remco C. Veltkamp   Utrecht University, The Netherlands

Program Chairs

Rosa Bottino   ITD – CNR, Italy
Johan Jeuring   Utrecht University, The Netherlands

Demo Chair

Jannicke Baalsrud   BIBA, Germany/KTH, Sweden
Hauge

Tutorial Chair

Carolina Islas Sedano   University of Eastern Finland, Finland

Program Committee

Anissa All	University of Gent, Belgium
Alessandra Antonaci	ITD-CNR, Italy
Sylvester Arnab	Coventry University, UK
Jon Arambarri	Virtualwaregroup, Spain
Aida Azadegan	The University of the West Scotland, UK
Jannicke Baalsrud Hauge	BIBA, Germany
Per Backlund	Högskolan i Skövde, Sweden
Norman Badler	University of Pennsylvania, USA
Sylvie Barma	Université Laval, Canada
Francesco Bellotti	University of Genoa, Italy
Riccardo Berta	University of Genoa, Italy
Rafael Bidarra	TU Delft, The Netherlands

Wim Westera	Open University, The Netherlands
Antonie Wiedemann	University of Genoa, Italy
Peter Wolf	ETH Zürich, Switzerland
Josef Wolfartsberger	University of Applied Sciences Upper Austria, Austria
Su Ting Yong	University of Nottingham Malaysia Campus, Malaysia
Zerrin Yumak	Utrecht University, The Netherlands

Award Committee

Antonie Wiedemann	University of Genoa, Italy

Local Arrangements Committee

Heleen Groenendijk	Utrecht University, The Netherlands
Rita Jansen	Utrecht University, The Netherlands

Publications Chair

Riccardo Berta	University of Genoa, Italy

Communication and Promotion Chair

Francesco Bellotti	University of Genoa, Italy

Administrative and Financial Chair

Antonie Wiedemann	University of Genoa, Italy

Contents

Games and Soft Skills

Games and Management

Games and Learning

Game Development and Assessment

Mobile Games

Posters

Games and Sustainability

Sustainable Competence Development of Business Students: Effectiveness of Using Serious Games

Rink Weijs[1], Geertje Bekebrede[2]($\boxtimes$), and Igor Nikolic[2]

[1] Rotterdam Business School, Rotterdam University of Applied Sciences,
Kralingse Zoom 91, 3063 ND Rotterdam, The Netherlands
r.h.weijs@hr.nl
[2] Faculty of Technology, Policy and Management, Delft University
of Technology, Jaffalaan 5, 2628 BX Delft, The Netherlands
{g.bekebrede,i.nikolic}@tudelft.nl

Abstract. A transition towards a safer, healthier, more equitable and more sustainable world requires focused Sustainable Development education. While this is true for all forms of education, it is particularly vital for business education curricula, and here it is sorely lacking. The main problem is that teachers lack the methods to teach sustainability competences. Gaming is proposed as a suitable method, as it involves action, direct feedback and high motivation. In this research we used a pre-post tests research set up to measure the learning effects from three simulation games. These games were played with 160 2nd year business students. We conclude that simulation games have limited contribution to cognitive learning about SD. However, a majority of respondents see additional value of gaming within their education.

1 Introduction

According to UNESCO the 'development of a sustainable society should be seen as a continuous learning process, exploring issues and dilemmas, where appropriate answers and solutions may change as our experience increases' [1]. The debate about educating future business leaders about sustainable development highlights the role of business schools and other management education institutions [2, 3]. Management education has been accused of 'having failed to integrate reflections on ethical values, social responsibility and sustainability into the curriculum and to educate future decision-makers to act in the long-term interests of business and society' [4].

The lack of integration of ESD in business schools is caused by limited experience with pedagogical methods suitable for developing sustainability competences. Many researchers conclude that traditional teaching methods are insufficient [5, 6]. ESD, more than other domains, requires pedagogic methods that facilitate experiential learning [7]. Gaming is seen as a suitable method as it facilitates systemic understanding of sustainability through experiential learning. Furthermore, gaming is engaging because of direct experiences and contextualization of learning by applying knowledge in action.

© Springer International Publishing AG 2016
R. Bottino et al. (Eds.): GALA 2016, LNCS 10056, pp. 3–14, 2016.
DOI: 10.1007/978-3-319-50182-6_1

This paper evaluates the contribution of three selected simulation games to key sustainability competencies. A quasi-experimental research design was chosen for the games evaluation, in specific a pre-test post-test non-equivalent group design. About 160 students from the Rotterdam Business School, The Netherlands, played one of the three games and shared their experiences.

In the next section, we will discuss the main sustainability competences relevant for this research, namely normative competences, anticipatory competences and systems thinking. Section 3 discusses why gaming is expected to be a valuable instrument. In Sect. 4 the research approach is presented and the three games are introduced. The results can be found in Sect. 5 and the discussion and conclusions can be found in Sect. 6.

2 Sustainable Development Competences for Business Students

UNESCO [1] emphasizes that competency-based education offers great opportunities for re-examination and reorientation of educational policy towards sustainability. A competency is understood as an integrated set of knowledge, skills, values and attitudes [8] which enable successful task performance and problem solving [9, 10]. For new sustainability programs, key competencies are a critical reference point for developing the knowledge and skill profile of students as future problem solvers and change agents [11].

The following five competences have been identified in the literature [12]: systems-thinking, anticipatory competence, normative competence, strategic competence, and interpersonal competence'. However, the literature 'does not sufficiently operationalize the key competencies by listing specific learning outcomes and developing evaluative schemes and do not give information about the practical integration in the curriculum' [13].

For this research, the competencies; normative competency, anticipatory competency and systems thinking are selected as they are related to the course Business and Sustainability.

2.1 Normative Competence

Sterling [14] speaks of a 'normative ethical sensibility that for example extends the boundary of care and concern beyond the immediate and personal to a sense of solidarity with others, distant people, environments, species and future generations'. This capacity enables students to collectively assess the (un-)sustainability of current and/or future states of social-ecological systems, based on power relations, intra- and inter-generational equity, and democratic governance, and create sustainability visions for these systems.

2.2 Systems Thinking Competence

'Systems thinking competence is the ability to collectively analyze complex systems across different domains (society, environment, economy, etc.) and across different scales (local to global)' [13] It relates to problems of sustainable development like global warming, poverty and decline of biodiversity which are complex and cannot be solved in a simple way. Inherently, it requires students to think across different domains (people, planet and profit) and understand their interdependencies and boundaries.

2.3 Anticipatory Competence

Anticipatory competence is the ability to 'identify short and long term consequences of decisions or plans in the context of both immediate priorities as well as long term concerns' [15]. It involves placing value on the future, taking responsibility and ownership of our impacts on generations to come and promoting concepts of inter-generational equity. As such, society should 'reduce over-exploitation of resources and pressures on ecological systems so that natural resources and ecosystems are available for use and enjoyment into the future' [16].

3 Using Serious Games to Teach SD Competences

Tilbury and Wortman [17] indicate that there is a need for tools and educational models that promote systems thinking. Typical sustainability topics like externalities, management of common pool resources and economic growth vs. future needs require a more holistic, systemic and interdisciplinary approach that offers room for learner-centered knowledge construction next to absorbing factual information. Higher-order learning demands a different pedagogical method; one that experiential learning can offer, such as gaming.

Games in education are suitable tools to facilitate a systemic understanding of sustainability [18], practice with contextual and paradigm changes [19] and play a role in all four stages of Kolb's experiential learning cycle. Games stimulate the players to understand the subject matter based on participation and experimentation. Furthermore, games have the unique ability to model the essential structures of complex systems and present them to the player to experience and manipulate [20]. Finally games have the potential to motivate players and emotionally engage them in the game dynamics.

However, many curricula currently do not include games. Literature research shows very few articles that analyze games used in sustainability education. The existing publications focus on game characteristics like player mode, type of game [21] or describe their 'operating mechanisms' from a theoretical perspective [18, 22]. Evaluation of the learning process and outcomes of simulation games are rare [18]. In this paper we aim to contribute to amend this situation by showing the results of an evaluation study of using sustainability games in education.

4   Research Approach

In this research existing games were used to test within a classroom setting. First the selected games are introduced and linked to the SD competences, secondly the data collection is explained.

4.1   Selected Simulation Games

In total three simulation games were played: The Intergenerational Equity Game, The Fisheries Game and the Externalities Game (See Table 1). These games were selected based on criteria that met the target group, course context and time schedule for playing. These games have initially been developed by Sadowski et al. [23]. The materials where retrieved with permission from the EthicsCore Collaborative Online Resource Environment (https://nationalethicscenter.org/). The games were slightly adapted to the course context and several teachers were briefed to facilitate the game and observe the game play and behavior of the participants.

The learning objective of The Intergenerational Equity Game is to experience the results of resource usage for production and technology investments along three generations. Furthermore, the game demonstrates is the relation between production and the technological factor, based on work by Solow [24].

The Fisheries Game is a game developed with the learning objective to teach students about the Tragedy of the Commons [25].

Learning goal of The Externality Game is to experience the relationship between economic growth and negative externalities, in this case environmental impact of GHG-emissions. Players can act in their self-interest or choose to negotiate an alternative distribution of production that results in a higher benefit for all participants.

Table 1. Summary of relevant key sustainability concepts addressed within the simulation games

Game	Concepts
Intergenerational equity game	Human needs & welfare levels, future generations, inter- and intra-generational justice, natural and technical capital, resource capacity, just savings rate, wealth distribution, population size
Fisheries game	Short-term & long-term profit, population growth (exponential growth), renewable resources, carrying capacity and overexploitation, resource depletion, private gain vs. collective gain
Externalities game	Positive & negative externalities, climate change, CO_2-emissions (per unit of production), private & social costs, economic growth (GDP), market mechanisms and market failure, level playing field

4.2   Data Collection

A pre-post test research design was used to measure the effect of simulation games on acquiring the sustainability competence.

In January 2016 the games were tested by 9 classes. The classes consist of second year students, following the course Sustainability and Business, as part of the International Business Management Studies at the Rotterdam Business School. The groups were divided by class, which means each class played one of the three games. The games were randomly divided and finally each simulation game was played three times. The setup of the data collection was similar for each class and follows the following structure:

- One week prior to the game, students were asked to read the introduction materials, define their strategy and fill in a pre-game questionnaire to test pre knowledge. All information was provided within an online learning management system
- Game play for 75 min during class, where the gameplay was observed by other lecturers, and the game output was collected digitally
- After the game, students were asked to fill in a post-game survey about cognitive learning and assessing games as learning tools. As each game has different learning objectives, separate questions were used to test the cognitive knowledge of the students

5 Results

5.1 Respondents

In total 160 students participated in the simulation games experiment. After cleaning the data, 124 respondent results remained who had the complete set of data (pre- and post-test and game play). It is assumed that the classes are comparable as the students had the same background (Table 2).

Table 2. Overview of the participants

	Intergenerational equity game	Fishery game	Externalities game
Number of students	47	49	64
Complete data sets	38	37	49
Percentage male/female	53/47	61/39	63/37

5.2 The Intergenerational Equity Game

The learning objectives of the Intergenerational Equity Game was to understand the consequences of using resources now or leaving them behind for future generations. Three questions were asked to see the differences in understanding before and after game play (See Table 3).

The answers show a shift of preference towards taken into account more generations, with the majority choosing three generations. The second question tested their factual knowledge combined with strategic foresight (anticipatory competence), asking

Table 3. Learning outcomes The Intergenerational Equity Game

	Pre Test	Post test	Post-Pre Test
1. How many generations should we take into account?			
None		3%	3
One (20 years)	8%	3%	-5
Two (40 years)	28%	6%	-22
Three (60 years)	32%	52%	20
Four (80 years)	12%	13%	1
Five (100 years)	16%	16%	0
Six (120 years)	4%	6%	2
2. Which is a positive accumulation scenario in the graph underneath?			

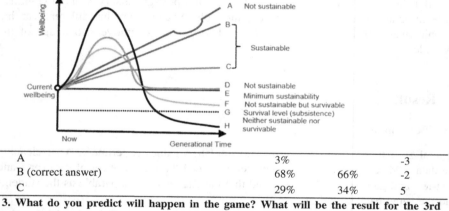

	Pre Test	Post test	Post-Pre Test
A	3%		-3
B (correct answer)	68%	66%	-2
C	29%	34%	5
3. What do you predict will happen in the game? What will be the result for the 3rd generation after all rounds?			
Accumulation	21%	21%	0
Collapse	5%	10%	5
Low-nature, high-tech	61%	34%	-27
Similar to current generation	10%	13%	3
Survival level	3%	21%	18

which possible well-being scenario shows a positive accumulation scenario. Most respondents scored correct (option B) both times, however during the post-test the score was one respondent lower. To test their anticipatory competency further, the respondents were asked to predict the most likely scenario at the end of the game. Remarkable is that the low-nature, high-tech option scored significantly lower and that all teams managed to stay in the game without collapse. Similar to current generation would have been the correct answer, but just 4 students predicted this scenario and afterwards just 5 chose it as correct scenario.

In conclusion, the majority of respondents stressed that we should pass on more environmental resources to the next generation in comparison to what we inherited during the pre-test. This ethical position towards intergenerational equity is reflected in the strategies used by the different generations that played the game.

5.3   The Fishery Game

The fishery game had the objective to teach systems thinking and especially the concept of the tragedy of the commons. Six questions test their factual knowledge and normative competences and two test participant's anticipatory competences.

Table 4 shows that the knowledge of the participants was already high at the start of the game, except for question 3, where a significant change can be observed. After the game, the score on the right answer was significantly higher. In total 26 from the 37 students predicted that the game would go beyond the maximum sustainable yield (question 7). Most changes can be seen in their definition of a winning strategy where the answer 'Cooperation' saw an increase of 6 respondents. 'Invest in a pond' proved better with hindsight just as 'Cooperate and cheat' which showed higher scores of respectively 4 and 2 respondents. 'Waiting until the fish regenerates' or 'Government intervention' both were chosen less after playing the game.

It is clear that playing the game did not create a strong improvement with regards to the theoretical constructs tested. In the pre-test the question 'Who should regulate how much fish is caught in the oceans?' was answered with 'The International Federation of Fishermen' or 'The government' by the majority. Judging from the game scores and the apparently inevitable collapse in all games, this answer gives some insight into the perspective of the players: someone else should regulate.

Table 4. Learning outcomes The Fishery Game

	Pre Test	Post test	Post-Pre Test
1. The concept Tragedy of the Commons means:			
It is due to consumer societies becoming disconnected from the natural environment	5%	2,5%	-2,5
It is environmental degradation in which self-interest of people results in the destruction of common or shared resource (correct answer)	95%	95%	-
The common people go through tragedies through environmental problems	0	2,5%	2,5
2. What is an example of the Commons			
Higher education	3%	3%	-
National parks	27%	24%	-2
The Pacific Ocean (correct answer)	68%	71%	3

3. Which point is the Maximum Sustainable Yield in the diagram underneath?

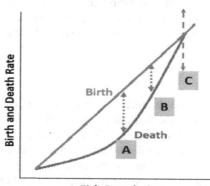

A	59%	30%	-29
B (correct answer)	16%	62%	46
C	24%	8%	-16

4. What is a potential solution for the Tragedy of the Commons according to Gareth Hardin?

Improve the carrying capacity of the commons	5%	8%	3
Increase collective responsibility	16%	24%	8
Increase individual responsibility	8%	3%	-5
Privatization (correct answer)	70%	65%	-5

5. What is the most important factor influencing the Commons according to Hardin?

Amount of natural capital available	8%	5%	-3
Population growth (correct answer)	76%	70%	-6
Renewable rate of resources	16%	14%	-2
Technological efficiency		11%	11

6. The number of individuals that a particular place can support indefinitely is called the

All of the answers below	11%	5%	-6
Carrying capacity (correct answer)	86%	85%	-1
Population life cycle		5%	5
Sustainability factor	3%	5%	2

7. Which scenario do you forecast will happen during the game?

Optimal scenario (equal to MSY)	14%	11%	-3
Sub-optimization (lower then MSY)	16%	19%	3
Tragedy of the Commons (beyond MSY)	70%	70%	-

8. What is a winning strategy

Cooperation	17%	28%	11
Cooperate and cheat	0%	6%	6
Cooperation but impossible due to cheating	0%	3%	3
Governmental Regulation	11%	0%	-11
Maximum fishing	33%	31%	-2
Invest in pond	6%	16%	10
Start slow and keep increasing	11%	6%	-5
Wait until fish regenerate	22%	9%	-13

5.4 The Externalities Game

This game focuses on externalities, and the survey contained seven questions to test knowledge about it. See Table 5 for the results.

The questions showed hardly any improvement in the answers on question 1, 2, and 5. Question 6, the correct responses even went down in the post-test. In question 3, and question 4 showed an improvement in the right answer. The last question targeting their strategic forecast of the gameplay shows an inconsistency between their previous predication and what they remembered to predict. 'More equal distribution of costs and benefits' was chosen more than before, with an increase from 19 to 23 respondents.

In general, the game stimulated the students to discuss the game rules and ask questions to clarify these. Playing the game resembled somewhat the challenge of the Paris climate summit (COP21) which was used as example during debriefing. The relevance of the game and the link with real-life were thereby very clear and understandable.

Table 5. Results of the Externalities Game

	Pre Test	Post test	Post-Pre test
1. Which does NOT cause positive externalities?			
Education & Training	2%	2%	-
Free cosmetics samples (correct answer)	89%	92%	3
Historical places	4%	4%	-
Medical industry	6%	2%	-4
2. How are negative externalities included in market prices?			
All answers	61%	55%	-6
Business raising their products prices	2%	4%	2
Consumers making compensation	5%	8%	3
Governments taxes (correct answer)	33%	33%	-
3. Which of the following diagrams underneath shows the social costs correctly?			

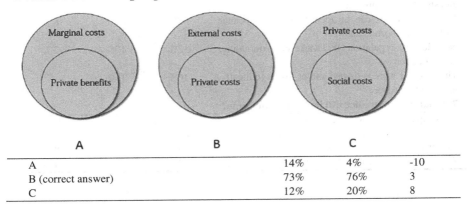

	A	B	C
A	14%	4%	-10
B (correct answer)	73%	76%	3
C	12%	20%	8

4. Which area in the diagram underneath shows the social costs?

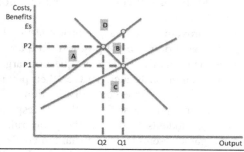

A	16%	8%	-8
B (correct answer)	61%	80%	19
C	8%	2%	-6
D	14%	10%	-4

5. The production costs grow linear, the externality costs exponential. At what point is the highest gain?

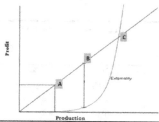

A	4%	4%	-
B (correct answer)	63%	71%	8
C	30%	22%	-8
A	4%	4%	-

6. What is NOT a reason for market failure?

It is not clear who exactly bears the consequences and should be compensated	12%	22%	10
Market outcomes can be identified and associated with a value (correct answer)	59%	51%	-8
No rules and regulations that make the externalities accounted for	12%	10%	-2
The value of what is gained and/or lost is (ethically) difficult to measure	16%	16%	-

7. What do you predict will happen in the game?

More equal distribution of costs & benefits	39%	47%	8
Poorer becoming rich, richer will be poor	4%	8%	4
Richer become richer, poorer poorer	45%	37%	-8
Zero-score (balance between costs & benefits)	12%	8%	-4

5.5   General Observation

The findings show that the cognitive learning outcomes for the simulation games are relatively small, even though the concept was described in the compulsory preparation materials. The findings also show that there is not much improvement before and after playing. In some cases the scores are even lower on the knowledge questions.

Except from reaching the learning objectives, we also looked at the acceptance of the use of gaming in the classroom to teach SD competences. The students scored the games positively on the fun aspect (TIG: mean 7, sd 1,3; TFG: mean 6,1 sd 2; TEG: mean 6,3 sd 2,2) and suitability for learning SD competences (TIG: mean 7,1, sd 1,7; TFG: mean 6,4 sd 2,2; TEG: mean 5,6 sd 2,3). They also agree that the games have to be played next year. This is interesting as the learning effects are limited.

The results of the contribution to learning effects and suitability of the methods are confirmed by the observers of the game play sessions.

6   Conclusion and Discussion

Based on this research the educational value of using simulation games to contribute to cognitive learning in sustainable development is questionable. The results show that although some improvements are seen, the number of correct answers on other theoretical questions declined, albeit not significantly. The same holds for the normative and anticipatory competences. Surprisingly however, a majority of respondents indicate that they see additional value of games here within their education. The inherent attractiveness of gaming proves favorable within this experimental setting.

The research also shows several aspects which can be improved and could positively contribute to learning. First aspect is retention. The post test was taken directly after the game and students indicated that they will remember the experienced lessons longer. By testing this competences after a longer period, it could be validated if the competences indeed stay on a higher level. The second factor is the time of play. The game was scheduled in one lecture. We know that time for playing is an important factor and to run Kolb's learning cycle multiple times could improve the outcomes. Playing longer or more often would be an advice in the future. From the observations we learned that most students played by trial-and-error. Considering the fact that one has to be conscious of the rules and options within a game to devise a strategy, this shows a lack of opportunity for the players to really get into the game and 'master' it.

References

1. UNESCO: United Nations Decade of Education for Sustainable Development (2004–2015): Draft International Implementation Scheme. UNESCO, Paris (2005)
2. Starkey, K., Hatchuel, A., Tempest, S.: Rethinking the business school: a European perspective. J. Manag. Stud. **41**(8), 1521–1531 (2004)
3. Khurana, R.: From Higher Aims to Hired Hands. The Social Transformation of American Business Schools and the Unfulfilled Promise of Management as a Profession. Princeton University Press, Princeton (2010)

4. Currie, G., Knights, D., Starkey, K.: Introduction: a post-crisis critical reflection on business schools. Brit. J. Manag. **21**, S1–S5 (2010). Issue Supplement
5. Dale, A., Newman, L.: Sustainable development, education and literacy. Int. J. Sustain. High. Educ. **6**(4), 351–361 (2005)
6. Steiner, G., Posch, A.: Higher education for sustainability by means of transdisciplinary case studies: an innovative approach for solving complex, real-world problems. J. Cleaner Prod. **14**(9–11), 877–890 (2006)
7. Sipos, Y., Battisti, B., Grimm, K.: Achieving transformative sustainability learning: engaging head, hands, and heart. Int. J. Sustain. High. Educ. **9**(1), 68–86 (2007)
8. Rychen, D.S., Salganik, L.K.: Key Competencies for a Successful Life and a Well-Functioning Society. Hogrefe & Huber, Göttingen (2003)
9. Spady, W.G.: Outcome-Based Education: Critical Issues and Answers. American Association of School Administrators, Arlington (1994)
10. Baartman, L.K.J., Bastiaens, T.J., Kirschner, P.A., Van der Vleuten, C.P.M.: Evaluation assessment quality in competence-based education: a qualitative comparison of two frameworks. Educ. Res. Rev. **2**, 114–129 (2007)
11. McArthur, J.W., Sachs, J.: Needed: a new generation of problem solvers. Chronicles High. Educ. **55**(40), 64–66 (2009)
12. Wiek, A., Withycombe, L., Redman, C.: Key competencies in sustainability: a reference framework for academic program development. Sustain. Sci. **6**(2), 203–218 (2011)
13. Lambrechts, W., Mulà, I., Van den Haute, H.: The integration of sustainability in competence based higher education. Using competences as a starting point to achieve sustainable higher education. In: Proceedings of the 6th Conference 'Environmental Management for Sustainable Universities (EMSU)', Delft, The Netherlands, 29 October 2010
14. Sterling, S.: Education in change. In: Huckle, J., Sterling, S. (eds.) Education for Sustainability, pp. 18–39. Earthscan, London (1996)
15. Crofton, F.: Educating for sustainability: opportunities in undergraduate engineering. J. Cleaner Prod. **8**(5), 397–405 (2000)
16. Frisk, E., Larson, K.L.: Educating for sustainability: competencies & practices for transformative action. J. Sustain. Educ. **2**, 1–20 (2011)
17. Tilbury, D., Wortman, D.: Engaging People in Sustainability. IUCN, Gland, Switserland and Cambridge, UK (2004)
18. Fabricatore, C., López, X.: Sustainability learning through gaming: an exploratory study. Electron. J. e-Learn. **10**(2), 209–222 (2012)
19. Dieleman, H., Huisingh, D.: Games by which to learn and teach about sustainable development: exploring the relevance of games and experiential learning for sustainability. J. Cleaner Prod. **14**(9), 837–847 (2006)
20. Duke, R.D., Geurts, J.L.A.: Policy Games for Strategic Management: Pathways into the Unknown. Dutch University Press, Amsterdam (2004)
21. Katsaliaki, K., Mustafee, N.: A survey of serious games on sustainable development. In: Simulation Conference (WSC), Proceedings of the 2012 Winter IEEE, pp. 1–13 (2012)
22. Liarakou, G., Sakka, E, Gavrilakis, C., Tsolakidis, C.: Evaluation of serious games, as a tool for education for sustainable development. Eur. J. Open Distance E-Learn. **15**(2) (2012)
23. Sadowski, J., Seager, T.P., Selinger, E., Spierre, S.G., Whyte, K.P.: An experiential, game-theoretic pedagogy for sustainability ethics. Sci. Eng. Ethics **19**(3), 1323–1339 (2013)
24. Solow, R.M.: A contribution to the theory of economic growth. Q. J. Econ. 65–94 (1956)
25. Hardin, G.: The tragedy of the commons. Science **162**(3859), 1243–1248 (1968)

The Design of an Augmented Reality Collaborative Game for Sustainable Development

Alysson Diniz dos Santos[1,2(✉)], Francesco Strada[1], and Andrea Bottino[1]

[1] Dipartimento di Automatica e Informatica, Politecnico di Torino, Torino, Italy
{francesco.strada,andrea.bottino}@polito.it
[2] Instituto Universidade Virtual, Universidade Federal do Ceara,
Av. Humberto Monte, s/n, bloco 901, 60.440-554 Fortaleza, Brazil
alysson@virtual.ufc.br

Abstract. In spite of recent efforts, there is still a demand for tools facilitating sustainability instruction. To this end, serious games offer remarkable possibilities to foster learning in this area. However, evidences suggest that these potentialities have not been fully leveraged yet. In particular, it is challenging to design games representing the different domains (ecology, economics, politics, and culture) and social structures (individuals, families and communities) involved by sustainability issues. This work explores the mix of augmented reality, collaborative gaming and theoretical guidelines in the design of Sustain, an educational game focused on raising awareness on sustainability topics. The paper details Sustain design decisions, highlighting their relation with the chosen methodology. Our aims are: (i) to exemplify the use of a not yet adopted theoretical background, and (ii) to present reflections concerning its use.

Keywords: Sustainability · Educational games · Augmented reality · Collaborative games

1 Introduction

The concept of *sustainable development*, or sustainability, was first introduced in 1987 in the report of World Commission on Environment and Development (Brundtland Commission) [2]. Sustainable development has been defined as the search of significant shifts in technologies, techniques or infrastructure, meeting today demands, without compromising future generations' needs. In order to improve people's capacity of addressing sustainability, it is critical to disseminate information towards environment and development issues [15]. Nevertheless, such task is not trivial. Sustainability has specific requirements, that can be summarized in two aspects: (i) the framing of issues contemplating individuals, families, communities and the society, and (ii) the representation of several interrelated domains, such as ecology, economics, politics and culture [14].

© Springer International Publishing AG 2016
R. Bottino et al. (Eds.): GALA 2016, LNCS 10056, pp. 15–23, 2016.
DOI: 10.1007/978-3-319-50182-6_2

In this context, recent research [3,6] suggests that serious games, *i.e.* those that do not have entertainment as their primary purpose, offer unique possibilities for creating educational tools towards sustainability. Serious games allow experimentation in controlled environments, useful for instance for simulating future scarcity scenarios. They can be used as persuasive tools to influence players ideas and behaviors. They can provide compelling experiences helping to create engagement towards sustainability. However, at the same time, there are evidences that the approaches developed so far often fail to fully leverage such potentialities [6] and several research questions remain open. Which are the design models most suited to guarantee that these serious games can achieve their pedagogical goals? Since collaboration among users is a relevant dimension for learning, which are the design elements and the technological tools that can foster such cooperation? How innovative user interaction paradigms can be exploited to improve the expected outcomes of sustainability serious games?

This work tries to provide some preliminary answers to these questions through the description of *Sustain*, a collaborative game focused on raising awareness on sustainable development issues. The aim of Sustain is to engage the players in the management of a city, being responsible for creating and maintaining infrastructures towards environmental awareness. To ground the theoretical aspect of Sustain, the game design has been based on a model specifically proposed for driving the development of game-based sustainability learning by Fabricatore and Lopez in 2014 [7]. Immersion and collaboration among players are fostered by allowing co-located users to interact in augmented reality (AR) with a virtual scenario, which is also projected on a screen to facilitate result discussion and decision making.

Concerning the related works, the approaches most related to Sustain are the games EnerCities [10] and Futura [1], which aim to engage the players in city management mechanics. Qualitative and quantitative evaluation support the success of both games in offering enjoyable experiences and increasing awareness concerning sustainability issues [1,10]. In addition, some recent products coupled augmented reality with sustainable games. As an example, in 2013 McDonalds Germany released the mobile app McMission, in which visitors, by playing AR mini-games, receive information related to the societal and environmental projects in which the company is involved [11].

To the best of our knowledge, this work is the first to base its game design on the Fabricatore and Lopez model, and also the first to merge, in a sustainability serious game, multiplayer collaboration, augmented reality interaction and city management mechanics. Therefore, although the implementation is still in its early stage, we think this work exemplifies the use of the adopted tools and, thus, might allow to start a discussion about how to enhance their effectiveness.

2 Theoretical Background

The model proposed by Fabricatore and Lopez for game-based sustainability learning [7], on which the design of Sustain was based on, is grounded on theoretically solid research, *e.g.* [13,14], and is the result of a thorough analysis of 30 sustainability games, which were used to offer practical examples of the framework's concepts. According to its authors, alongside the assimilation of domain-specific knowledge, sustainability requires promoting learning to deal with *complex systems* [7], whose main characteristics are:

- *Emergence*, *i.e.* changes in the system happen independently of external action, and their origins cannot be traced back entirely;
- *Uncertainty*, *i.e.* the impossibility of full predicting the outcomes of actions on the system, and;
- *Non-linearity*, *i.e.* depending on the actual context, the interactions among the various elements of the system can develop according to different patterns.

Thus, to cope with such complex systems, the game design should consider four main aspects. First, it is important to design for *contextualization* of the game activity. In order to facilitate the transfer of game-based learning to real-world contexts, the background story, gameplay and objectives should be coherent with the sustainability values to target. Second, the game should *empower* the players, who should be able to exert control on the game system by acting as freely as possible. The rationale is that empowered players are likely to be more easily engaged in the gameplay experience. Third, the game should foster *adaptivity*, *i.e.* force players to adapt to non-player-planned disruptions in system dynamics, which is an attitude that can help them better understanding the complexity involved in sustainability scenarios. Finally, the introduction of meaningful *social* interactions among players, and between players and artificial-intelligence-based agents, can (again) help engaging the players and harnessing their knowledge acquisition.

3   Sustain Game

Following the definitions of Fabricatore and Lopez model, the educational goal of Sustain is not to provide direct instruction to players, but to engage them in a complex system representing an urban area environment. The game aims at increasing awareness on both immediate and long-term consequences that policy-makers decisions' can generate.

Although the current version of Sustain is a prototype, it employs all the features that enable the discussion of the adopted theoretical framework, hardware platform, augmented reality interaction and collaborative gameplay. In the following subsections, we thoroughly discuss the design and implementation of Sustain. Section 4 relates the actual game design with the Fabricatore and Lopez model, and outlines future extensions of the game.

3.1   The Game Design

Sustain is a city management game for three players, whose goal is to expand the population of an urban area, exploiting a set of resources (coal, oil and money). The game rules aim at guaranteeing the relevance of sustainability practices, since a non-sustainable city causes unsatisfied citizens to leave, thus leading players to defeat.

Players can take action in the scenario by assuming one of three roles: mayor, ministry of energy, and ministry of agriculture. Every role has a specific set of actions, which are progressively made available to the player as the game advances. These roles can be summarized as follows:

- The mayor can take decisions related to the construction of houses, factories, public transportation and leisure areas. He can also call for laws that influences the population energy consumption and food habits.
- The ministry of energy can decide for an energy matrix based on renewable sources (wind and solar) or not (coal, gas or nuclear fusion). He can also take action on the oil consumption of the urban area.
- The ministry of agriculture chooses mainly for the food production of the urban area, that can be turned to numbers increase, or to convince people to consume in a healthier way.

The roles are chosen by the players in the beginning of the game. They are balanced to be attractive to game audience, in order to foster game re-playability (thus players are hopefully willing to re-play with different characters). Sustain is intended for players of minimum 10 years old, who are able to understand the environmental impact of their decisions, and to handle the mechanics of managing diverse aspects in real time.

3.2   The Interaction Design

The game scenario is composed of two interrelated areas, the city and the farm. Each area is composed by a grid of 3 × 3 blocks. Players interact with these areas through a tablet, thus being free to move inside the physical game environment. By clicking on any block, the player sees the actions that he/she can take at that specific time, according with his/her role. In the farm area, the actions are related with the production of food and energy, and with resources collection. The city area actions deal with the consumption of the resources provided by the farm area, and also with offering housing, employment, developing public transportation and leisure activities for the population. Visualization and interaction with the game scenario exploit marker-based Augmented Reality (AR).

The rationale of leveraging on AR is that it allows the customization of players' view, according to their specific role. For example, when the ministry of energy focuses the city area, the rooftops of the buildings glow when it is possible to install solar panels on them. If the mayor points at the same area, the view highlights areas available for constructing houses and factories. Therefore, in Sustain, AR enhances the representation of different points of view over the same problem, a feature that is a concrete challenge to face in sustainability games [6].

The marker used to register the augmented view is a large image representing an urban area and its suburbs, printed on a A0 paper (84.1 × 118.9 cm), and fixed on a table (80×160 cm). These dimensions intend to offer adequate physical space for three players, and to allow a consistent and stable marker tracking from various distances and view angles. Figure 1 shows an example of the 3D view of the game scenario and, in the background, the marker defining the game area.

Fig. 1. View of the augmented scenario on the tablet screen, from the city point of view.

Sustain features as well a projected virtual environment (Fig. 2). This screen shows the overview of the urban area, and the information regarding the game objective (population number), the available resources (money, coal and oil) and the sustainability status (energy level and environment friendliness). The projected screen aims at further enhancing players' collaboration by offering, during debriefing sessions after each game turn, a shared understanding of what has been achieved and how far they are from the objective, thus facilitating discussion and decision making processes.

3.3   The Gameplay

Sustain is played on 5 turns. Each turn corresponds to six months in the game time, thus a match spans 2,5 life years of the fictional urban area. During a turn, the players can take collectively 5 actions, with a maximum of two actions per player. This means that every round all the players are required to act, but one of the players has only one action. This intends to foster players reflection on which actions are the most important at every specific moment, highlighting the importance of the cooperation among different roles. The turns have no time limit, and the end of a turn is decided when the five actions are taken.

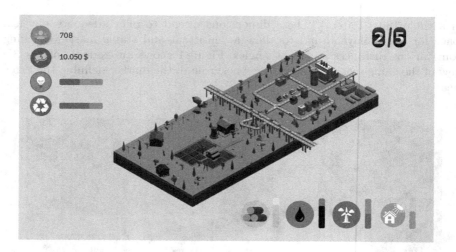

Fig. 2. An image of the projected scenario, displaying as well population number, available money, energy and environment friendliness levels (top left), the number of turns (top right) and coal and oil resources, and renewable energy production (bottom right).

Once that the turn is finished, each players' action is executed and its aftermath can be evaluated. This is the moment when players focus on the shared screen, which displays the influence of their actions on the three main game variables: (i) resources production and consumption, (ii) sustainability status (energy level and environment friendliness), and (iii) quantity of population of the city. The values of these variable are also reflected in the representation of game scenario. For example, the environment can get polluted (and displayed as such) when the environment friendliness level is low, or get darker due to the lack of public illumination when the energy level decreases.

After the second turn, the list of available actions per player starts to include what we called "critical" actions, *i.e.* actions introducing both relevant advantages and severe consequences. Examples of such actions are the construction of a nuclear plant (ministry of energy) or of an industrial park (mayor), and the alleviation of environmental policies in agriculture to increase the production and reduce costs (ministry of agriculture). Since these actions are critical for the environment, players willing to activate them must (mandatorily) find an agreement with their peers, who should grant explicit permission with their tablet. This game rule avoids any player to issue disruptive policies in a non-democratic way and is meant again to increase the in-game collaborative activities.

After the 5 game turns have been played, the win or lose conditions are related to the number of actual city dwellers. In case of defeat, a motivational message is displayed to encourage players to try again building a "better" city.

3.4   Implementation Details

Concerning the technical aspect, Sustain has been implemented into Unity 3D, a cross-platform game engine, which offers advanced lighting and rendering options, built-in support for spatialized audio, physics management, complex animations, multitasking, pipeline optimization and networking. Multiplayer collaborative interaction has been managed implementing a client-server architecture, in which the server handles the simulation state and controls the projected screen and the clients are the players' tablets. Finally, we used as AR engine Vuforia, a software library that can be integrated into Unity, thus supporting the game deployment on different mobile platforms (Android, iOS, Windows Phone and Tizen).

4   Results and Discussion

Being in its development stage, a systematic evaluation of Sustain is not possible at the moment. However, to obtain some preliminary indications, we can comment some of the feedbacks received by our alpha testers, which seem to suggest the appreciation of a gameplay combining both multiplayer collaboration and augmented reality interaction. Players readily understood the need to collaborate, which means that the game mechanics and platform were successful in promoting collaborative behaviors. Players also expressed overall enjoyment in playing the game, specially towards the use of augment reality to display the interactive areas.

One aspect we deemed interesting to analyze is how the four keypoints of the Fabricatore and Lopez model described in Sect. 2 influenced the game design. In the following, we analyze separately each of these keypoints.

Contextualization. Three main design elements have been introduced to contextualize the game thematic with environmental issues: (i) the Sustain virtual scenario, which resembles real-life ones and where players perform real-life roles; (ii) the gameplay and game rules, which guarantee that the adoption of non-sustainable practices leads to player (collective) defeat; (iii) the game platform, where the shared screen and the tablets have been introduced with the purpose of adequately representing the interrelations of elements in a complex urban environment.

Empowerment. The possibility to differentiate the players' role is the fundamental feature related with empowerment. Every player has a unique skill-set, which requires her/him to negotiate with peers and to explore alternative ways to fulfill their common tasks. Players also freely decide which action to take, driving the non-linearity of the gameplay. Indeed, although the game main objective is clearly defined, the possible paths that lead to a positive conclusion are numerous and cannot be shaped as an algorithm. Finally, visually displaying in the shared environment the aftermath of players' actions aims to deliver what Sweetser [13] calls third order emergence, *i.e.* changes on a global scale rising from dynamics happening at a local scale.

Social. The social dimension highlighted by Fabricatore and Lopez and the verbal interaction among players are stimulated by several design elements: (i) players sharing the same physical space, (ii) the possibility to debrief each game turn sharing a common view, through the projected screen, (iii) the game-play rules that require synchronized coordination, and (iv) the voting system, for enabling critical actions, which requires reaching an agreement over relevant development policies.

Adaptivity. Players' adaptivity is fostered by the division in turns of a game. After having performed their actions, players have to adapt to the new situation created. Furthermore the introduction of novel actions that can be performed in each new turn, force the player to mentally adapt to the new features available. Despite that, we believe that the adaptivity aspect has not been fully developed in Sustain, as also partially confirmed by our testers.

4.1 Further Extensions

Since Sustain is in its development stage, there is still plenty room for introducing improvements to its design. The first is related to reviewing and enhancing the features related with the adaptivity dimension. One possibility we are considering is the introduction of *crisis*, events related to players action (for example, cities with high dependence of fossil fuels, can face a depletion of the resources) or independent from them (a natural disaster). The players will be offered novel sets of actions to deal with the crisis, which should be activated in a short time. Inadequate response to the crisis would lead to a massive escape from the city and defeat in the game.

In addition, we are planning to (i) extend the number of blocks in the interactive scenario in order to provide a higher diversification of the game areas and, thus, more challenges for the players, and (ii) introduce novel problems to deal with, such as trash recycling and water management.

Another point we are planning to investigate in further details is related to a question arose during the development process: *how to guarantee the transfer of game-based learning to real-world contexts?*

Fabricatore and Lopez link game-based learning transfer to the contextualization aspect. Although there are scientific evidences supporting this statement [5], we found hard to assess whether the contextualization features of Sustain effectively improved the players' understanding of real-life sustainability issues. We think that a deeper game evaluation with players is needed to enlighten this question.

5   Conclusions

In this work we presented the design and (initial) development of Sustain, a collaborative AR-based multiplayer game aimed at supporting sustainability learning. The game design is based on a sound theoretical model, which helped us to identify the main elements for improving the expected educational outcomes of the game. Preliminary evaluation sessions indicate the game success in immersing the players in a collaborative experience.

As future work, we are planning to complete the implementation of Sustain, introducing as well some improvements to the current design (as detailed in Sect. 4.1). We are also planning to perform a thorough evaluation of the game, exploiting both quantitative and qualitative approaches. Such evaluation would allow assessing the efficacy of the chosen reference framework in guiding the design of sustainability educational games.

References

1. Antle, A.N., Tanenbaum, J., Bevans, A., Seaborn, K., Wang, S.: Balancing act: enabling public engagement with sustainability issues through a multi-touch tabletop collaborative game. In: Campos, P., Graham, N., Jorge, J., Nunes, N., Palanque, P., Winckler, M. (eds.) INTERACT 2011. LNCS, vol. 6947, pp. 194–211. Springer, Heidelberg (2011). doi:10.1007/978-3-642-23771-3_16
2. Burton, I.: Report on reports: our common future: the world commission on environment and development. Environ. Sci. Policy Sustain. Dev. **29**(5), 25–29 (1987)
3. Coakley, D., Garvey, R.: The Great, the Green: sustainable development in serious games. In: ECGBL2015-9th European Conference on Games Based Learning: ECGBL2015, vol. 135 (2015)
4. Crookall, D.: Serious games, debriefing, and simulation/gaming as a discipline. Simul. Gaming **41**, 898–920 (2010)
5. Dieleman, H., Huisingh, D.: Games by which to learn and teach about sustainable development: exploring the relevance of games and experiential learning for sustainability. J. Clean. Prod. **14**, 837–847 (2006)
6. Fabricatore, C., Lopez, X.: Sustainability learning through gaming: an exploratory study. Electron. J. e-learn. **10**(2), 209–222 (2012)
7. Fabricatore, C., Lopez, X.: A Model to identify affordances for game-based sustainability learning. In: Busch, C. (Ed.), Proceedings of the 8th European Conference on Game Based Learning, p. 99109, Reading (2011)
8. Huber, M.Z., Hilty, L.M.: Overcoming the limitations of persuasive technologies. In: Aebischer, B., Hilty, L.M. (eds.) ICT Innovations for Sustainability. AISC, vol. 310, pp. 367–385. Springer International Publishing, Heidelberg (2015)
9. Katsaliaki, K., Mustafee, N.: Edutainment for sustainable development a survey of games in the field. Simul. Gaming **46**(6), 647–672 (2015)
10. Knol, E., De Vries, P.W.: EnerCities-a serious game to stimulate sustainability, energy conservation: preliminary results. In: eLearning Papers (2011)
11. https://www.youtube.com/watch?v=laIqVPTXT88. Accessed July 2016
12. Santos, A.D., Fraternali, P.: A comparison of methodological frameworks for digital learning game design. In: De Gloria, A., Veltkamp, R. (eds.) GALA 2015. LNCS, vol. 9599, pp. 111–120. Springer, Heidelberg (2016). doi:10.1007/978-3-319-40216-1_12
13. Sweetser, P.: Emergence in Games. Cengage Learning, Boston (2008)
14. Tilbury, D.: Rising to the challenge: education for sustainability in Australia. Aust. J. Environ. Educ. **20**(02), 103–114 (2004)
15. UNESCO United Nations Conference on Environment, Development: Agenda 21 1992 (2011)
16. Van Krevelen, D.W.F., Poelman, R.: A survey of augmented reality technologies, applications and limitations. Int. J. Virtual Real. **9**(2), 1 (2010)

Designing Virtual River: A Serious Gaming Environment to Collaboratively Explore Management Strategies in River and Floodplain Maintenance

Robert-Jan den Haan[1(✉)], Vivian Juliette Cortes Arevalo[2],
Mascha van der Voort[1], and Suzanne Hulscher[2]

[1] Design Department, University of Twente,
Postbus 217, 7500 AE Enschede, The Netherlands
{r.j.denhaan, m.c.vandervoort}@utwente.nl
[2] Department of Water Engineering and Management, University of Twente,
Postbus 217, 7500 AE Enschede, The Netherlands
{v.j.cortesarevalo, s.j.m.h.hulscher}@utwente.nl

Abstract. Dutch river management is in transition from a phase of intervention and implementation to a phase of maintenance. In light of this transition, we discuss initial results towards the development of a serious gaming environment where river and floodplain management actors can collaboratively explore intervention and maintenance strategies. We introduce the design approach of a serious gaming environment based on qualitative interviews with river and floodplain maintenance actors. Based on these interviews, we identified two key variables to explore strategies for river and floodplain maintenance: maintenance intervals and floodplain scaling. We proceed with presenting the Virtual River; a concept for a serious gaming environment. In this environment, actors can play out intervention and maintenance scenarios around these two key variables over time using simplified hydrological, morphodynamic and vegetation models.

1 Introduction

Serious games are finding their way more and more in river management as tools for training, for raising awareness as well as for creating shared understanding [1–8]. This is not surprising as river management is an inherently complex socio-technical system and serious games are well suited to address such systems [9, 10]. A particular complex socio-technical river system is the Dutch Rhine-Meuse Delta. This delta area is prone to flooding[1], inhabits a large percentage of the Dutch population and is vital to the Dutch economy[2]. Currently, river management in the Rhine-Meuse Delta is entering a phase of maintenance following the (near) completion of many large-scale riverine projects [11]. As these projects transitioned river management to forms of adaptive (co-)management

---

[1] Over 60% of the Netherlands is prone to flooding from either the sea or rivers.
[2] For example, the Waal river, a Rhine branch, is the main shipping route from the Rotterdam harbor to the industrial Ruhr region in Germany.

© Springer International Publishing AG 2016
R. Bottino et al. (Eds.): GALA 2016, LNCS 10056, pp. 24–34, 2016.
DOI: 10.1007/978-3-319-50182-6_3

[12], this maintenance phase bears the challenge of sustaining this adaptive approach to river management.

In response to these developments, our research focuses on developing a serious gaming environment where actors can collaboratively explore management strategies in river and floodplain interventions and maintenance. In this paper, we present preliminary results of our research and a concept for the serious gaming environment based on identifying key variables in river and floodplain maintenance. In Sect. 2, we briefly introduce the context of river management in the Netherlands and discuss the implications of the upcoming maintenance phase. In Sect. 3, we review serious games applications in river management according to two identified categories. Next, we use this review as well as the river management context to frame the approach for our serious gaming environment. In Sect. 4, we present and discuss the interview method we are using to explore possible directions for the serious gaming environment. In Sect. 5, we present key variables identified in on-going interviews with river management actors. In Sect. 6, we describe the concept of our serious gaming environment, Virtual River, based on these identified variables. Finally, we conclude with remarks for the next steps in the development of Virtual River.

2 Dutch River Management: Room for the River

That the Rhine and Meuse rivers both nearly flooded in both 1993 and 1995 took the Netherlands by surprise and renewed the focus on river management. River management can be described as the continuous activities of human intervention in river systems in order to produce or retain some defined objective(s) in regard to river functions such as water safety, navigation, nature development or agriculture. The 1993 and 1995 events sparked the 'Room for the River' (RvdR) program; a combination of riverine projects in the Dutch Rhine-Meuse delta aimed at increasing flood safety by creating space for water [13]. With the emphasis on space for water, secondary objectives towards for example nature, housing, recreation and business were included in the projects under the guise of 'enhancing spatial quality'. The RvdR program transformed flood prevention in river management from 'resistance' to 'resilience' [13]. This river management transformation can be considered a transition to adaptive (co-)management [12]; a form of management that explicitly links learning – both experiential and experimental – and collaboration in order to facilitate effective governance [14, 15].

Given that all RvdR projects are (nearly) completed, Dutch river management is now transitioning to a post-RvdR maintenance phase. New dilemmas are emerging within this transition, especially in the floodplains of the rivers. As the name suggests, floodplains are an integral part of flood protection. However, since nature was a specific focus point within RvdR, many floodplains were converted into protected areas in cooperation with nature organizations to establish 'self-regulating nature areas' [16]. Many of these areas are now 'Natura 2000' areas; protected nature areas subjected to EU policy objectives.

In recent years, concerns have started to arise among water managers whether these self-regulating nature areas would severely affect the discharge capacity of the river system. Vegetation in the floodplains – especially thicket and forest areas – adds friction and obstruction to the water flow, lowering the amount of water that can safely be discharged. In response and in anticipation of RvdR's completion, the main Dutch water authority initiated the 'Streamline' program [16]. In this program – in execution at the time of writing – a large amount of vegetation in the Dutch floodplains is removed and 'reset' back to the norms of 1997, around the time when RvdR was initiated.

These combined developments have resulted in the so called 'nature-safety dilemma' where flood protection objectives are conflicting with nature objectives [16, 17]. Our research therefore focuses on developing a serious gaming environment where actors can collaboratively explore strategies in river and floodplain interventions, in particular those focusing on maintenance. In the next section, we review serious games applications in river management and frame the approach for our serious gaming environment.

3 Serious Gaming in River and Delta Management

A recognized strength of serious games is their ability to combine technical complexity with social complexity [9, 10]. It is therefore not surprising that serious games are increasingly used in river management as rivers are inherently complex socio-technical systems [18]. From this socio-technical perspective, two types of serious games in river management can be distinguished based on their relation to water. First are games where water is considered a (non-infinite) resource that can be used – e.g. for irrigation – and the use of water has an effect at the system level. Examples of such games are Aqua Republica [1], River Basin Game [2], PIEPLUE [3] and LASY [4]. In the second type, water is considered a boundary condition – e.g. low or high river discharges – leading to possible events – e.g. imminent droughts or floods. Examples of this type of games are the Sustainable Delta Game [5], STORM [6], FloodSim [7], and SimDelta [8].

The serious gaming environment we are developing falls under this second type and the mentioned serious games show similarities to our approach. For example, in the Sustainable Delta Game, players are presented with a non-existing, typical Dutch river basin and develop strategies to limit the probabilities of both floods and droughts occurring [5]. This way, players learn about the complex interplay between water management, climate change and changes in society. The STORM role-play game stimulates a dialogue between relevant stakeholders in a planning process of the Dutch Rhine and its floodplains [6]. As such, players are demonstrated with relevant stakeholder interests, the interaction between these interests, the types of conflict that might occur and the effects of human intervention to the physical system. In SimDelta, players are presented with interactive maps of scenarios. Each scenario describes problems and solutions which intend to explain the complexity of the Rhine-Meuse Delta [8]. The main objective of SimDelta is to provide this explanation faster and more intuitively than reports and presentations.

Although many differences can be noted, a major difference between these examples and our serious gaming environment approach is that we explicitly include monitoring and maintenance in river management over purely focusing on planning intervention measures. In particular, actors collaboratively explore integral strategies – from planning to maintenance – in the envisioned serious gaming environment as river management requires the coordination of resources not only for implementation, but also for monitoring and maintaining the functions of intervention measures [19].

Given this approach, our serious gaming environment can be characterized as serious gaming for self-organization based on Mayer et al.'s frame reflective discourse analysis [20]. In this category, actors expand their knowledge and understanding through interactions with others who may have different perceptions and ideas. Serious games in this frame therefore aim to affect the ways in which people organize and interact [20].

Serious gaming for self-organization can be linked directly to adaptive (co-)management; Olsson et al. include the *"self-organized process of learning-by-doing"* in their adaptive (co-)management definition [14]. A main driver in adaptive (co-)management is therefore social learning; *"a change in understanding that goes beyond the individual to become situated within wider social units or communities of practice through social interactions between actors within social networks"* [21]. Games, in particular role-playing games, have been recognized as a successful way to support social learning [9, 18] and many scholars have reported that gaming is indeed successful to establish social learning processes [22–24].

However, to facilitate social learning processes, a deeper understanding of context, power dynamics and values is needed that influence the ability of people and organizations to collaborate [25]. In the next section, we explain the method we used to gain this deeper understanding in search of concept directions.

4   Qualitative Interview Approach

We conducted interviews to gain a deeper understanding of the context of river and floodplain management as well as explore key variables that actors would like to able to experiment with in our serious gaming environment. We chose face-to-face qualitative interviews based on a semi-structured protocol as interviews are well suited to tap into motivations, perceptions, wishes and needs of participants [26].

We set up the interviews using a human-centered design approach to analyze use scenarios based on moving from remembering and experiencing to imagining and envisioning [27]. Within this approach, we used Dervin's sense-making methodology as a guide for our questions [28]. Dervin's sense-making methodology is based on the notion that a person, embedded in a context-laden *situation*, is faced with a *gap* (or a *sensemaking need*) which prevents him/her from moving towards a *desired outcome*. To reach this outcome, the gap needs to *bridged*.

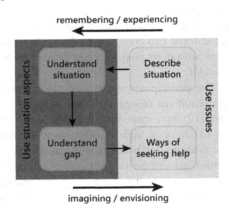

Fig. 1. Interview approach schematization based on Van der Bijl-Brouwer [27] and Dervin and Foreman-Wernet [28].

The interviews were set up semi structured and questions were divided into four phases following the schematization of Fig. 1: (1) introductory questions related to their work activities in order to describe the situation; (2) contextual questions related to a challenging situation in order to understand the situation; (3) specific questions regarding the participant's concerns, struggles and questions they had in the challenging situation in order to understand the gap; and (4) envisioning questions regarding preferred outcomes and help they would have liked in the challenging situation.

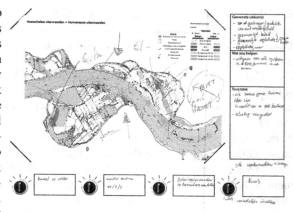

Fig. 2. Example of materials and results of the envisioning phase of the interview.

Throughout the second, third and fourth phase, we used maps – vegetation and satellite maps of river segments – to assist participants in reflecting on their challenging situation. Furthermore, we used a paper canvas around the maps for each phase. These paper canvasses served three functions: (1) as a guide for the interview and the structured questions; (2) as material for participants to provide direct feedback – writing or drawing –; and (3) as an initial verification of the notes we wrote down in relation to their responses. Figure 2 shows an example of the interview results including the map of the challenging situation, identified by the participant, and the fourth phase's paper canvas. The text boxes on the right related to questions on desired outcomes; what would help them achieve this and what would help them if they had a magic wand (no constraints). In the bottom of the fourth phase's canvas are four text boxes with dials next to them. These text boxes related to the identification of the key variables.

The participants we invited were contacted based on the criteria that they: (1) are representatives of organizations who are active in Dutch river and floodplain mainte-nance; (2) have more than five years of experience in river and floodplain maintenance; and (3) have a high position in their organization. The participants were part of organizations for water management (main Dutch water authority and regional water boards), governmental (ministries, provinces and municipalities), nature conservation (Dutch state forestry agency, regional landscape organizations and nature development organizations) and agriculture (agricultural nature organizations and farmers). As this is work in progress, 11 interviews were analyzed within the scope of this paper. We conducted all interviews at the offices of the participants. The interviews all lasted between 60 and 110 min and were recorded for transcription and coding. All partici-pants were men.

5 Key Variables

Below, we present the initial results of our interviews in the form of two key variables for experimentation identified by multiple participants. We present and discuss the key variables and their background based on information obtained during the interviews. We used these key variables to develop our initial concept, which we discuss in the Sect. 6.

5.1 Key Variable 1: Maintenance Intervals

Both water managers and nature managers mentioned the exploration of the variable of maintenance intervals, albeit for very different reasons. In anticipation of the post-RvdR maintenance phase, the main Dutch water authority initiated the 'Streamline' program. This program effectively removes vegetation from the floodplains in order to increase water safety as vegetation lowers the river's discharge capacity. In parallel to this program, the Dutch water authority developed the so-called 'Vegetation layer': a categorized vegetation map of all floodplains of the Rhine and Meuse branches. Based on this map, maintenance concerning vegetation – e.g. removing fast growing vegetation – is executed at specified time intervals to keep all areas within the floodplain to their mapped category.

Nature managers stated that the Streamline program and the Vegetation layer are a thorn in the side as (1) they had just spent years developing nature in the floodplains as part of the RvdR program; and (2) they did not consider mapping and categorizing areas of the floodplains as nature development or conservation, but as – in their words – "gardening". Combined, the nature managers felt the two developments would undo many promising nature development results and severely limit the possibilities to meet previously defined nature objectives. At the same time, the nature managers acknowledged that water safety is leading in floodplain maintenance.

The nature managers were convinced that extensive maintenance measures with longer intervals in between would be more cost-effective. In addition, this approach would allow "surprises in nature to develop" as floodplain conditions constantly vary. These surprises would be beneficial for the biodiversity of floodplains.

The water managers also mentioned the maintenance interval variable with cost-effectiveness in mind, albeit from a perspective of mapping and monitoring. The water managers explained that to develop the Vegetation layer, they used aerial photographs to map all floodplains. This mapping process was both costly and time-consuming (nine months). Therefore, this process is a problem in relation to (bi-)yearly maintenance as: (1) mapping each year is too costly; and (2) by the time mapping is completed, the resulting map is already outdated.

In light of this variable, both water and nature managers wondered what measures would be needed if interventions were only performed every five, ten or twenty years. They also asked what the extensiveness and costs of such measures would be and when it would be necessary to act in between maintenance intervals.

5.2 Key Variable 2: Floodplain Scaling

The variable of floodplain scaling was brought forward by both governmental actors and nature managers, but again for different reasons. Dutch floodplain maintenance is currently rather fragmented [16] as: (1) the mapping of vegetation in the floodplains is categorized on a local scale; and (2) the floodplains are owned by some 15,000 land owners [11]. Floodplain maintenance is therefore performed at a local level as opposed to on the level of a larger river segment. Even two opposing floodplains, divided only by the river itself, are monitored and maintained separately.

The nature managers stated that it is therefore very well possible that maintenance in floodplain A would be executed even though it is not needed as maintenance measures in opposing floodplain B were effective enough to reach the combined water safety objective for the river segment. A more integral approach of combining monitoring and maintenance of floodplain A and B could lead to more flexibility. From their perspective, this flexibility could be more cost-effective and would enable them to leave specific areas untouched when surprising nature developments occur.

Multiple governmental actors would also like to explore the floodplain scaling variable to establish cost-effective maintenance. Because of the fragmented ownership, there is very little coordination in maintenance activities. The local mapping and monitoring contributes to this lack of coordination. As a response, the governmental actors proposed forming coalitions between organizations involved in floodplain management in order to pool resources and coordinate maintenance efforts in a river segment. The floodplain scaling variable for the provincial government is therefore the length of the river segment in relation to the size – the amount of actors – of such coalitions.

Regarding the floodplain scaling variable, the governmental actors and nature managers stated that they would like to explore the benefits of looking at floodplains on a larger scale. Questions they put forward related to what the ecological flexibility would be at this larger scale, how they should approach monitoring and how floodplain maintenance at a larger scale can be organized.

6 Virtual River Concept

In our serious gaming environment concept, titled Virtual River, we combine the maintenance interval and floodplain scaling variables. In Virtual River, players – river management actors – can collaboratively explore management strategies while explicitly taking river and floodplain maintenance into account. To achieve this, we present players with a digital environment, a river stretch including floodplains, where they can play out management scenarios over time. We include simplified hydrological, morphodynamic and vegetation models to Virtual River in order to present players with realistic feedback on their actions in regard to the river's discharge capacity and vegetation development.

At the start, players join the game on their own console as a representative of a specific river management actor; either all players take on the role that they also have in reality or all players take on a role different from their traditional role. In the first level,

maintenance measures

score feedback

specific feedback (water safety)

date and pause/play

side-channel planning

side channel specifications: depth and profile

Fig. 3. Virtual River concept's main surface where a side-channel is drawn as a maintenance measure in the floodplain.

players are presented with a single floodplain area on a main surface where certain water safety and nature objectives have to be met (Fig. 3). Players are given the challenge to collectively develop strategies to meet these objectives. However, players also have individual objective(s) based on their roles. For example, a water manager could have the objective of limiting the maintenance costs to a given amount while a nature manager might have to objective to leave a certain area in the floodplain untouched. Based on their respective role, players also have their own resources. Water managers for example have a large budget available to them while nature managers have access to flocks of horses to graze the floodplains. Resources can also be very specific to their role; water managers for example have access to other monitoring options (e.g. aerial photographs) than nature managers (e.g. network of volunteers). Of course, such resources cannot be deployed limitlessly.

Collectively, players can look into possible intervention measures and their extensiveness based on the maintenance intervals. Measures are performed once per interval – e.g. digging a side-channel for the river (Fig. 3) – or continuous – e.g. horses grazing the floodplains to limit vegetation growth. Using the main surface, intervention measures and maintenance strategies are collectively discussed and planned. During this planning, the game provides players with some initial predictions on the effects towards water safety and nature objectives. Once the measure is put in place, players look into monitoring options and decide who is responsible for monitoring. At the same time, they also need to decide the conditions under which intervention is necessary in between maintenance intervals; there is an inherent level of uncertainty attached to riverine measures and perhaps a measure is not as effective as planned. Afterwards, time is started and players can use their consoles to monitor development, manage their own resources and request resources or actions from other players.

While exploring management scenarios, players can track their progress in relation to water safety and nature objectives as well as costs. As players put more extensive maintenance measures in place, thus increasing the maintenance interval, they experience that this has a positive effect on the nature objectives as less intervention provides more opportunities for nature. However, longer intervals have a negative effect on water safety as these add more uncertainty to the floodplain's development over time. In the end, players notice that reaching both the water safety and nature objectives is difficult and requires trade-offs. If players do not reach both objectives, they may choose either to explore other management strategies or to collectively adjust the flood safety and/or nature objectives and/or the budget in such a way that the objectives can be met.

In the second level, players are presented with a similar situation as the first level, with the main exception that now they are dealing with a river segment containing up to four separate floodplain areas. They are still provided with specific water safety and nature objectives, but can reach these objectives by combining measures in multiple floodplain areas. Similar to the first level, players experience that their decisions cause trade-offs between water safety and nature.

As players play out such maintenance scenarios over time, they experience (1) the trade-offs made between water safety and nature; (2) the uncertainty attached to the river system; and (3) the objectives of other river and floodplain management actors.

7 Concluding Remarks and Next Steps

In this paper, we set out to present a concept for a serious gaming environment in regard to river management based on identifying key game variables. Our interviews revealed two key variables that are interesting to pursue further as multiple participants mentioned these for different reasons. Moreover we presented Virtual River, a concept for our serious gaming environment, which plays into the unique opportunity to contribute to collaboration in a transition of river management phases in the Netherlands. Within Virtual River, players can play out river management scenarios over time and learn about trade-offs between water safety and nature, uncertainties attached to the river system and objectives of other actors.

However, Virtual River as presented here is still conceptual. After concluding the interviews, the next step in our research is therefore to iteratively develop Virtual River further together with actors in a particular case study as 'show case'. First, we will use paper prototyping in co-design sessions in order to (1) explore the key variables together with participants in-depth; and (2) explore how participants would like to work with these variables in the gaming environment. A focus point in these co-design sessions is to explore the options and feedback participants would like to have while playing in the game – e.g. the incorporated hydrological, morphodynamic and vegetation models – and at what level of detail. Following these co-design sessions, an early prototype will be developed and evaluated on usability.

Acknowledgements. Research for this paper was conducted as part of the program RiverCare: towards self-sustaining multifunctional rivers, funded by the Technology Foundation STW (Grant Number P12-P14). In addition, the authors would like to thank all interview participants for their participation and cooperation.

References

1. Chew, C., Lloyd, G.J., Knudsen, E.: Capacity building in water with serious games. In: Sourina, O., Wortley, D., Kim, S. (eds.) Subconscious Learning via Games and Social Media, pp. 27–43. Springer, Singapore (2015)
2. Hoekstra, A.Y.: Computer-supported games and role plays in teaching water management. Hydrol. Earth Syst. Sci. Discuss. **9**, 1859–1884 (2012)
3. Barreteau, O., Abrami, G.: Variable time scales, agent-based models, and role-playing games: the PIEPLUE river basin management game. Simul. Gaming **38**, 352–361 (2007)
4. Valkering, P., et al.: Modelling cultural and behavioural change in water management: an integrated, agent based, gaming approach. Integr. Assess. **9**(1), 19–46 (2009)
5. Valkering, P., et al.: A perspective-based simulation game to explore future pathways of a water-society system under climate change. Simul. Gaming **44**(2-3), 366–390 (2013)
6. Ubbels, A., Verhallen, A.J.M.: The use of role-playing in integrated water management. In: Proceedings of the International Assembly of Hydrological Sciences, pp. 191–197, Maastricht, The Netherlands (2001)
7. Rebolledo-Mendez, G., et al.: Societal impact of a serious game on raising public awareness: the case of FloodSim. In: Proceedings of the 2009 SIGGRAPH Symposium on Video Games, pp. 15–22. ACM (2009)
8. Rijcken, T., Stijnen, J., Slootjes, N.: "SimDelta" - inquiry into an internet-based interactive model for water infrastructure development in The Netherlands. Water **4**(2), 295–320 (2012)
9. Mayer, I.S.: The gaming of policy and the politics of gaming: a review. Simul. Gaming **40**(6), 825–862 (2009)
10. Bekebrede, G.: Experiencing complexity: a gaming approach for understanding infrastructure systems. Dissertation TU Delft, Delft University of Technology (2010)
11. Fliervoet, J.M., Van der Born, R.J.G.: From implementation towards maintenance: sustaining collaborative initiatives for integrated floodplain management in the Netherlands. Int. J. Water Resour. Dev., 1–21 (2016)
12. Pahl-Wostl, C.: The importance of social learning in restoring the multifunctionality of rivers and floodplains. Ecol. Soc. **11**(1) (2006). Article No. 10, http://www.ecologyandsociety.org/vol11/iss1/art10/
13. Warner, J., Edelenbos, J., Van Buuren, A.: Making space for the river: governance challenges. In: Warner, J., Van Buuren, A., Edelenbos, J. (eds.) Making Space for the River: Governance Experiences with Multifunctional River Flood Management in the US and Europe, pp. 1–14. IWA Publishing, London (2013)
14. Olsson, P., Folke, C., Berkes, F.: Adaptive comanagement for building resilience in social–ecological systems. Environ. Manag. **34**(1), 75–90 (2004)
15. Armitage, D.R., et al.: Adaptive co-management for social–ecological complexity. Front. Ecol. Environ. **7**(2), 95–102 (2009)
16. Fliervoet, J.M., et al.: Combining safety and nature: a multi-stakeholder perspective on integrated floodplain management. J. Environ. Manag. **128**, 1033–1042 (2013)
17. Vreugdenhil, H.S.I.: Pilot projects in water management: practicing change and changing practice. Dissertation TU Delft, Delft University of Technology (2010)
18. Pahl-Wostl, C.: Transitions towards adaptive management of water facing climate and global change. Water Resour. Manag. **21**(1), 49–62 (2007)
19. Pratt Miles, J.D.: Designing collaborative processes for adaptive management: four structures for multistakeholder collaboration. Ecol. Soc. **18**(4) (2013). Article No. 5, http://www.ecologyandsociety.org/vol18/iss4/art5/

20. Mayer, I., Warmelink, H., Zhou, Q.: A frame-reflective discourse analysis of serious games. Br. J. Educ. Technol. **47**(2), 342–357 (2016)
21. Reed, M., et al.: What is social learning? Ecol. Soc. **15**(4) (2010). http://www.ecologyand society.org/vol15/iss4/resp1/
22. Barreteau, O., Bousquet, F., Attonaty, J.: Role-playing games for opening the black box of multi-agent systems: method and lessons of its application to Senegal River Valley irrigated systems. J. Artif. Soc. Soc. Simul. **4**(2), 5 (2001)
23. Duijn, M., et al.: Gaming approach route 26: a combination of computer simulation, design tools and social interaction. J. Artif. Soc. Soc.Simul. **6**(3) (2003). Article No. 7, http://jasss. soc.surrey.ac.uk/6/3/7.html
24. Hummel, H.G.K., et al.: Scripted collaboration in serious gaming for complex learning: effects of multiple perspectives when acquiring water management skills. Br. J. Educ. Technol. **42**(6), 1029–1041 (2011)
25. Keen, M., Brown, V.A., Dyball, R.: Social Learning in Environmental Management: Towards a Sustainable Future. Routledge, Abingdon (2005)
26. Erlandson, D.A.: Doing Naturalistic Inquiry: A Guide to Methods. SAGE Publishing, Thousand Oaks (1993)
27. Van der Bijl-Brouwer, M.: Exploring usability. Design for dynamic and diverse use situations. Dissertation University of Twente, The Netherlands (2013)
28. Dervin, B., Foreman-Wernet, L.: Sense-Making Methodology as an Approach to Understanding and Designing for Campaign Audiences. SAGE Publishing, Thousand Oaks (2012)

Games for Math and Programming

A Game-Based Approach to Examining Students' Conceptual Knowledge of Fractions

Manuel Ninaus[1,2(✉)], Kristian Kiili[3], Jake McMullen[4],
and Korbinian Moeller[1,2,5]

[1] Leibniz-Institut für Wissensmedien, Tuebingen, Germany
{m.ninaus,k.moeller}@iwm-tuebingen.de
[2] LEAD Graduate School, Eberhard-Karls University, Tuebingen, Germany
[3] TUT Game Lab, Tampere University of Technology, Pori, Finland
kristian.kiili@tut.fi
[4] Centre for Learning Research, University of Turku, Turku, Finland
jamcmu@utu.fi
[5] Department of Psychology, Eberhard Karls University, Tuebingen, Germany

Abstract. Considering the difficulties many students and even educated adults face with reasoning about fractions, the potential for serious games to augment traditional instructional approaches on this topic is strong. The present study aims at providing evidence for the validity of a serious game used for studying students' conceptual knowledge of fractions. A total of 54 Finnish fifth graders played the math game on tablet computers using tilt-control to maneuver an avatar along a number line for a total of 30 min. Results indicated that most of the hallmark effects of fraction magnitude processing as identified in basic research on numerical cognition were successfully replicated using our serious game. This clearly suggests that game-based approaches for fraction education (even using tilt-control) are possible and may be effective tools for assessing and possibly promoting students' conceptual knowledge of fractions.

1 Introduction

Fractions are among the most difficult relations to learn and even adults frequently fail to process them correctly ([9, 29] for a review). However, understanding of fractions seems crucial for math education (e.g. [2] and later life prospects [25]. Not only does high school students' fraction knowledge correlate with their mathematics achievement (r > .8), fraction knowledge in fifth grade also predicts future algebra and overall mathematics achievement in high school (e.g., [1, 2]). Given the widespread difficulties many adults and children face with reasoning about fractions, traditional instructional methods may be reconsidered and complemented by new tools for fostering fraction knowledge.

Games or game-based applications have the potential to provide such new, engaging, and innovative ways of training children as well as adults in mathematics. Recently, the use of games in cognitive training, learning and educational interventions has increased considerably (for a systematic review see [3]) because of their ability to keep users motivated to play and thus to interact with the learning content [6, 23]. Studies even

© Springer International Publishing AG 2016
R. Bottino et al. (Eds.): GALA 2016, LNCS 10056, pp. 37–49, 2016.
DOI: 10.1007/978-3-319-50182-6_4

indicate that the use of game-based tasks or the implementation of game elements in conventional cognitive tasks can not only increase motivation and engagement of users but also their cognitive performance (e.g. [22]; for a review see [17]). Game-based tasks have proven to be an effective approach for learning in the domain of mathematics education, in particular, to engage and motivate users (for reviews see [4, 19]). Thus, in the present work we studied the usefulness of our game-based rational number research engine called "Semideus" in assessing students' conceptual knowledge of fractions.

1.1 Fractions and Number Line Estimation Task

The processing and learning of fractions is one of the most challenging problems in mathematics education as identified by the National Mathematics Advisory Panel of the US [20]. On the other hand, conceptual knowledge of fractions and processing of fractions is important for mathematics education. A crucial part of fraction knowledge is the successful representation of fraction magnitude (reflecting the relation between numerator and denominator). The concept of a mental number line is often used metaphor to describe our mental representation of number magnitude. Accordingly, the number line estimation task, in which participants have to indicate the spatial position of a target number on a number line with only its endpoints specified (e.g., where goes 38 on a number line ranging from 0 to 100), is a popular approach to measure and train individuals' representation of number magnitude (e.g., [16]). Recent research studies emphasized that children's mental representation of number magnitude can be fostered by training to map numbers onto space as in the number line estimation task (e.g. [30]). Most of the time conventional computer tasks or paper-pencil versions are used to train individuals' representation of number magnitude. However, in recent years new methods of training numerical skills were developed such as embodied trainings [16] with interactive whiteboards [7], dance mats [8] as well as game-like versions of the number line task (e.g. [14]).

According to conceptual change theories, children form an initial conception of numbers as counting units before they encounter fractions, and later they draw heavily on this initial understanding to make sense of rational numbers [5]. As such, misconceptions about rational numbers tend to originate in children's erroneous belief that properties of whole numbers can be applied to rational numbers. According to DeWolf and Vosniadou [5] this is detrimental for children's understanding of fractions as it implies that they tend to treat numerators and denominators as two separate whole numbers instead of considering their relation. From this conceptualization they often infer that the value of a fraction increases when either the numerator or the denominator increases. For example, 3/8 (0.375) is smaller than 2/5 (0.4) although its numerator 3 is larger than 2 and the denominator 8 is larger than 5. This phenomenon is referred as a *whole number bias* [21].

This whole number bias has been found to cause difficulties in reasoning about the size of fractions (e.g. [10]). Interestingly, even educated adults and mathematics experts have been shown to be slower to respond on tasks in which whole number features are incongruent with rational number features ([24, 32]). Importantly, however, successful understanding of the magnitude of fractions was found to be an important precursor of later knowledge of rational numbers, such as the density of rational numbers [18] and arithmetic operations with rational numbers [11].

Other difficulties and affordances with fraction magnitude processing are of interest in examining how a serious game can capture students' conceptual knowledge of the numerical magnitude of fractions. Successful representation of fraction magnitude as the relation between numerator and denominator can be conceptualized as and assessed by being able to localize fraction magnitude on a number line estimation task for the number range 0 to 1. Applying such fraction knowledge in a magnitude comparison task would allow for further information on the representation of fraction magnitude. From basic research on numerical cognition it is known that the so-called *distance effect* (i.e., longer and more error prone comparisons of fractions that are closer in magnitude than for fraction further apart in magnitude) indicates a successful representation of fraction magnitude (e.g., [27]).

1.2   Present Study

The present study is a part of an ongoing project in which we are developing a game-based rational number research engine called Semideus. The gameplay is based on recent findings on numerical development and fraction processing (e.g. [18, 28]). The main purpose of the current study was to demonstrate the validity of our game-based research engine to assess students' fraction knowledge. More specifically, we investigated pros and cons of using a game as a research and assessment tool for investigating students' biases in conceptual fraction knowledge.

In order to successfully apply the Semideus research engine for future research and training studies, we need to demonstrate that the game-based solution provides similar effects (e.g. whole number bias and distance effect) as reported with conventional and non-game based assessment measures. Thus, in the current study we investigated 5th graders' accuracy and speed of comparison of fraction magnitudes while playing the Semideus Exam game on a tablet with the tilt control. The use of tilt control is based on pilot testing, which indicated that this sort of control provides a more gameful experience for the users than touch or click controls. Moreover, the concept of embodied cognition suggests that bodily experiences such as using tilt-control support the training of numerical concepts (e.g. [16]).

Initially, a *general demonstration* of participants' *ability to master the user interface* (including tilt-control supporting embodied cognition) within the first few trials is necessary before any form of assessment can be validly performed. Following this, we assume that students' performance will be defined by their understanding of fraction magnitude and not general game mechanics. In order to evaluate this statement, we set up five hypotheses. Hypotheses are based on previous research on numerical cognition. Thus, this approach provides important information about the validity and usefulness of the Semideus games as an assessment and research tool.

Previous research has shown that fractions that are consistent with whole number ordering are mastered better than fractions that are inconsistent with whole number ordering due to what is called the whole number bias [11, 32]. Thus, we expect that students solve consistent tasks better (*Hypothesis 1a*) and faster (*Hypothesis 1b*) than inconsistent tasks. Moreover, we expect to observe a standard distance effect for fraction comparisons with fraction pairs with a small distance being more difficult (*Hypothesis 2a*) and taking longer to be compared than pairs with larger distances (*Hypothesis 2b*).

Both number line estimation and magnitude comparison tasks reflect understanding of fraction magnitudes and thus we expect (*Hypothesis 3*) that there is a reliable correlation between performance in these tasks like previous research has shown (e.g. U.S. students in [31]).

2   Method

2.1   Participants

Three Finnish fifth grade classes participated in the study. Fifty-six students were involved in the study, from which 54 followed the designed playing protocol and were included in the study. Of the participants 28 were females, 19 males, whereas the rest did not specify their sex. Mean age was 11.26 years (SD = 0.48 years).

2.2   Description of the Semideus Research Engine

Semideus is a fraction research engine that can be used to create games that aim at supporting the development of children's conceptual fraction knowledge. The engine was used to configure a game (a research instrument), Semideus Exam, which was used in this study. The gameplay is founded on tasks that require working with number lines implemented as walkable platforms of a mountain. In the game the user controls a character, called Semideus, who tries to collect gold coins that Kobalos the Goblin has stolen from Zeus. Semideus has discovered the locations of the hidden coins, encrypted in mathematical symbols, and must race the goblin to retrieve the coins from trails of Mount Olympos.

Several fraction processing tasks can be included in Semideus games (e.g. number line estimation, magnitude comparison, magnitude ordering, and density awareness). Figure 1 shows examples of estimation and comparison tasks that were used (for more details see also https://youtu.be/rhl88VvGCvI). In the number line estimation tasks the user tries to locate a gold coin based on a given number. In comparison levels, the user has to compare two stones with values on them by arranging the stones in ascending order with regard to the numerical magnitudes depicted on them. The exact spot on the number line (ranging from smaller numbers on the left to larger numbers on the right) does not matter as long as the order of the stones is correct. The user can also pile the stones up when he or she thinks that the magnitudes are equivalent.

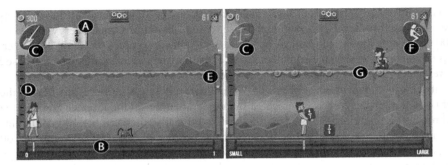

Fig. 1. Examples of number line estimation (left) and magnitude comparison tasks (right); (A) Number to estimate (i.e. location of the hidden coin); (B) Number line (in this case ranging from 0 to 1); (C) Answer button to dig up the coin in an estimation task or to check the order of the stones in a comparison task; (D) Progress bar that visualizes the progress towards the mountain top (E); Health bar that shows how much energy is left and the limit to earn a star based on energy; (F) Button for lifting and dropping stones; (G) Number of available coins are shown. User will earn all the coins that the goblin does not manage to dig up before user's answer.

The Level Structure and Configuration the Semideus Exam Game. The Semideus Exam game was a web based application played through an iPad browser. The game world consisted of seven levels (see Fig. 2 for structure of the game). The first two levels were designed for onboarding in order to familiarize users with the basic rules, controlling mechanics, and to set expectations for what the game exam is about. From an assessment perspective this phase is important, because we can not assume that all users master the user interface right from the beginning. In the first three items of the whole number estimation tasks (Level 1) the correct answer was indicated by a coin (see Fig. 2: Level 1). With this a user should immediately understand that the correct solution indicates the position of the coin on the number line. Moreover, the first three items are used to evaluate how well users master the tilting user interface. The actual exam consisted of five levels (Levels 3–7). The third level included ten fraction estimation tasks and Levels 4–7 included seven fraction comparison tasks per level.

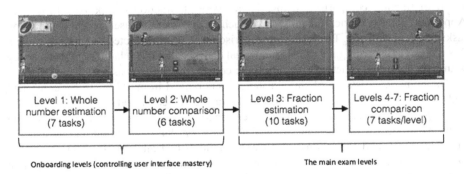

Fig. 2. The level structure of the Semideus Exam game world

The game was configured in a way that each participant could play all the seven levels once starting from level one. Although a user could run out of virtual energy in a level (100 units energy in the beginning), he or she is still able to complete the level. However, if users run out of energy they did not receive a bonus at the mountain top, which is based on remaining energy. Within levels users were allowed only one answer to each task. Feedback was shown after each answer. When the location was estimated accurately the right position of the coin was indicated by a green marker on the number line and the estimation accuracy percentage was shown. Additionally, the user got 100–500 coins depending on the degree of correctness (over 98% correct = 500 coins; 95–98% = 300 coins; 92–94% = 100 coins). For inaccurate estimations the user lost 15 units of energy and the right place of the coin was shown with a green marker. After feedback, the user progressed to the next platform (i.e., faced the next task). In the comparison tasks the number of coins awarded to the user depended on the time taken to answer (under 9 s = 500 coins; 9–12 s = 400 coins; 12–16 s = 300 coins; 16–20 s = 200 coins; over 20 s = 100 coins; wrong answer = 0 coins and 20 units energy loss).

After completing a level (reaching the top of the mountain) a user got additional feedback: 1–3 stars and earned coins were shown (i.e., possibility to get one star for completing the level, one star for collecting enough coins, and one star from accuracy reflecting that enough energy was left). Additionally, a bonus was given based on remaining energy (energy % * 500 coins).

The Semideus character's movement was controlled by tilting the device to the left or right. Movement speed depended on the angle of tilting with a steeper angle resulting in higher speed. Importantly, the possibility to alter walking speed on tablets was required as the tilting interface with appropriate static speed was not precise enough (based on earlier pilot studies) and slower pace allowed fine tuning of an estimation answer.

The Tasks of the Semideus Exam Game. The onboarding phase (cf. Fig. 2: Onboarding Levels) included seven whole number estimation items (Level 1: number line ranging from 0 to 100) and six whole number comparison items (Level 2: three digit numbers). The exam phase (cf. Fig. 2: Main Exam Levels) started with ten fraction estimation items (Level 3: number line ranging from 0 to 1) in order to study their relation to fraction comparison performance. The order of the fraction estimation items was randomized. The second and the major part of the exam phase (Levels 4–7) consisted of fraction comparison items. There were 28 fraction comparison tasks (see Appendix). The numerical magnitude of each of the fractions used in the comparison tasks was less than one. The fraction comparison task was conducted as a within-subject 2 × 2 design discerning the factors numerical distance (small vs. large) and consistency with whole number ordering (fraction type: consistent vs. inconsistent).

The numerical distance of small distance pairs ranged from .07 to .18 for consistent and .10 to .24 for inconsistent items. The average distance of both conditions was .14. For large distance pairs numerical distance ranged from .30 to .42 for consistent and from .31 to .43 for inconsistent items. The consistent large condition had an average distance of .36 and the inconsistent large condition had an average distance of .37. Overall the consistent condition had an average distance of .25 and the inconsistent condition had an average distance of .26. Moreover, the fraction comparison tasks were designed to have pairs that were on different sides of ½ (6 pairs/condition), the same side of ½ (6 pairs/condition), and include ½ (2 pairs/condition). These factors were equated across conditions and counterbalanced so that half of the time the larger fraction stone appeared on top of the smaller stone and the other half time the smaller fraction stone appeared on top of the larger stone.

2.3 Procedure

Students were tested in three groups during a regular school day. First, the experimenters introduced the game and explained the progress of the game exam to the students. Second, the students got their personal passwords for the game that was used to record playing behavior. After that, each student got an own iPad and they played the game individually. Students were not allowed to discuss about the game tasks with other students during the playing session. They got 30 min to complete the game.

2.4 Analysis

Prior to analyses, response times were log10-transformed to normalize distributions. For the analysis of Hypothesis 1a, 1b, 2a, and 2b, performance in the fraction comparison task was analysed by a 2×2 ANOVA with the factors type (consistent, inconsistent) and numerical distance (small, large). The expected associations between fraction estimation accuracy and fraction comparison performance (Hypothesis 3) was evaluated using correlation analysis. ANOVAs and correlations were conducted using R [26] and the R packages Ez (Anova; [15] and corrplot (Correlations; [33]). For data visualization the package ggplot2 was used [34].

3 Results

3.1 Onboarding Phase - Descriptive Statistics

In order to study the adoption of the user interface we explored users' performance during the onboarding phase (Whole Number Estimation & Whole Number Comparison). During the first three whole number estimation task items a coin indicated the correct position of the whole number on the number line. Students achieved an accuracy of 98.87% ($SE = 0.09\%$). When the tutorial elements (a coin indicating the correct solution) were no longer available whole number estimation accuracy decreased (i.e., items 4–7: mean accuracy = 92.74%, $SE = 0.7\%$). Nevertheless, accuracy rates of >90% clearly indicated students' ability to handle user interface and tilt control. In line with this claim, students' performance in whole number comparison ($M = 96.60\%$, $SE = 1.02\%$), as indicated by correctly solved comparisons, was very good. The accuracy of the first two comparison tasks were 94.44% (SE = 2.16%) and at the end, i.e. last two comparisons, of the onboarding phase the accuracy increased to 97.22% (SE = 1.57%). In order to explore reasons for mistakes made in the last two whole number comparison tasks, users' answers were analyzed. The analysis revealed that all the mistakes were wrong because users ordered the stones from largest to smallest. We assume that this is a common careless error that happens also in paper based ordering tasks. Nevertheless, this finding indicates that the students could handle the stone carrying user interface.

3.2   Exam Phase - Fraction Comparison and Estimation

Comparison Accuracy: The ANOVA revealed a significant main effect of numerical distance [Hypothesis 2a: $F(1,53) = 62.07, p < .001$] indicating that accuracy was lower for items with a small numerical distance ($M = 71.03\%$, $SE = 2.42\%$) as compared to items with a large numerical distance ($M = 85.71\%$, $SE = 2.11\%$). Neither the main effect of fraction types (Hypothesis 1a, inconsistent: $M = 77.51\%$, $SE = 2.87\%$ vs. consistent: $M = 79.23\%$, $SE = 1.77\%$) nor the interaction was significant (see Fig. 3 Left).

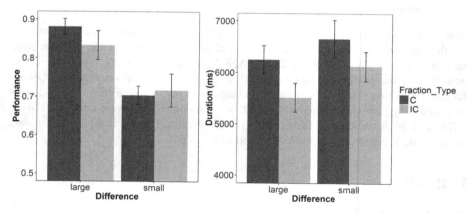

Fig. 3. Left: Mean performance for distance (small, large) and comparison condition (C = Consistent; IC = Inconsistent); Right: Mean duration in ms for distance (small, large) and comparison condition (C = Consistent; IC = Inconsistent). Error bars depict the standard error of the mean.

Comparison Speed: The ANOVA revealed significant main effects of numerical distance [Hypothesis 2b: $F(1, 53) = 12.45, p < .01$] and fraction type [Hypothesis 1b: $F(1, 53) = 18.11, p < .001$]. In line with our hypothesis, this indicated that responses were slower for items with a small as compared to a large numerical distance ($M = 6394$ ms, $SE = 231$ ms vs. $M = 5887$ ms, $SE = 199$ ms). However, contrary to our expectations inconsistent items were responded to faster than consistent items ($M = 5824$ ms, $SE = 201$ ms vs. $M = 6456$ ms, $SE = 228$ ms). The interaction between the fraction type and numerical distance was not significant (see Fig. 3 Right).

Association of Fraction Comparison and Fraction Estimation Performance: In line with our expectations (Hypothesis 3) the correlation analysis indicated that there was a high positive association between fraction comparison and fraction estimation tasks [$r(52) = 0.69$, $p < 0.001$, $R^2 = 47.62\%$].

4 Discussion and Future Work

The goal of this study was to examine whether a game created with rational number game research engine (Semideus) with tilt control can be used successfully to assess users' conceptual fraction knowledge. The present findings corroborate this claim. Our findings were in line with most of our hypotheses regarding the processing of fraction magnitude as derived from basic research on numerical cognition. In particular, the present data indicated that in-game measures provided valid information about students' conceptual fraction knowledge. The current data show the potential of using a game with a tilting user interface to assess fraction knowledge and that it can be used in basic research to study numerical cognition.

Students Adoption of the User Interface: Descriptive analysis of the onboarding phase indicates that the participants were well able to handle the user interface including the tilt control of the Semideus Exam game (with accuracy >90%). While this appears trivial, appropriate handling of such a new and innovative user interface is not guaranteed and is an absolute necessity to perform valid assessment of students' performance. Based on these results we argue that the user interface of the game is appropriate for studying students' conceptual fraction knowledge. To further explore whether Semideus provides valid data for the assessment of users' conceptual fraction knowledge 5 hypotheses were derived from previous basic research on numerical cognition. In the following, we will discuss the results in light of each of these hypotheses in turn.

Fraction Magnitude Comparison Performance: Hypotheses 1a, 1b, 2a, and 2b specifically addressed the comparison of fraction magnitude and the influence of (i) fraction type (i.e., the inconsistency of the fraction's magnitude with its whole number components) as well as (ii) numerical distance. With respect to the *fraction type*, it is known that fraction processing seems to be biased by the numerical values of numerators and denominators (e.g., the erroneous assumption that ¼ may be larger than ⅓ because 4 is larger than 3). Accordingly, we expected that students perform worse and slower when comparing fraction magnitudes for which the magnitudes of numerators and denominators are inconsistent with whole number ordering as compared to fractions pairs for which the magnitudes of numerators and denominators are consistent with whole number ordering (Hypothesis 1a). However, no effect of fraction type was found on comparison accuracy. In fact, participants were faster when solving inconsistent items as compared to consistent ones, which is in contrast to what we expected (Hypothesis 1b). Recent studies, however, revealed inconsistent results regarding the whole number bias on fraction magnitude comparison. For instance, DeWolf and Vosniadou [5] observed a regular whole number bias for adult participants from the United States (i.e., inconsistent comparisons were responded to less accurately and slower). Yet, the authors also found that participants from Greece showed the opposite result pattern (i.e., a reversed consistency effect as in the current study on Finnish students). Importantly, the origin of these inconsistent results are still not resolved. One line of research, suggests that depending on their educational background (e.g., US psychology students vs. Greek computer science students, [5] or the stimulus set used [12] participants may use differing strategies to compare the magnitude of fractions.

With respect to the expected *distance effect* our results were consistent with our Hypotheses 2a and 2b. We observed a significant distance effect in the fraction comparison task. Children's performance was more accurate and faster when distances between two fractions were large as compared to when they were small. This result suggests that students estimated or calculated and then compared the two fractions' overall numerical magnitudes utilizing a holistic processing strategy (e.g., [13]. Together with the results concerning Hypothesis 1a and 1b, this indicates that these students compared the magnitude of the fractions based on a combination of holistic and componential strategies (see also e.g. [27]).

Relation Between Number Line Estimation Accuracy and Magnitude Comparison Performance: In line with our expectation that number line estimation as well as magnitude comparison tasks require an understanding of fraction magnitudes, a high correlation ($r = 0.69$) between number line estimation accuracy and magnitude comparison performance was observed (Hypothesis 3).

4.1   Theoretical and Practical Implications

Taken together, these results indicate that a game-based assessment of students' conceptual knowledge of fractions using the Semideus game engine is capable of replicating relevant empirical findings from basic research. This indicates that students' performance while playing Semideus provides meaningful information on students' fraction knowledge. Moreover, this provides evidence about the usefulness of the game engine as a research and assessment tool. As well, these findings extend our understanding of the nature of fraction knowledge suggesting that within multiple contexts, including paper-and-pencil (e.g. [18]), computer-based basic tasks (e.g. [32]), and now game-based number line tasks, students face similar difficulties with understanding fraction magnitudes. Importantly, this even holds when students use tilt-control to maneuver on the number line.

The confirmation of Semideus as a valid instrument for examining students' fraction knowledge also provides the possibility that it may be used as a diagnostic tool for uncovering deficits in students' knowledge across a range of issues related to the development of conceptual fraction knowledge. Such game-based assessment is not only less anxiety-inducing, but can also provide teachers with specific diagnostic information about students' performance in order to apply targeted support. The possibilities to align gameplay with a particular student's specific difficulties suggests that Semideus may be a potentially powerful tool for assessing and training conceptual fraction knowledge.

4.2   Limitations and Future Work

The current study yielded promising results regarding the use of a mathematics learning game as a research and assessment tool. However, there are some limitations that should be taken into account in future studies. The present study does not examine students' fraction knowledge using a standardized curricular test. Such a measure would be valuable for further validation of the game. Moreover, examining differences in students' motivation and math or test anxiety during gameplay and on traditional paper-and-pencil tasks would be desirable to better understand the specific benefits of game-based learning and assessment. Furthermore, the study was not designed as an intervention study to evaluate how gameplay improved students' actual knowledge about fraction magnitudes. In more controlled studies, online processes of engagement and motivation should also be taken into consideration in order to further examine the nature of the gaming effects on students' performance and learning.

5   Conclusions

In summary, the current study aimed at evaluating whether students' conceptual fraction knowledge can be assessed by a game using a tilting user interface. We used game-based fraction number line estimation and fraction magnitude comparison tasks implemented with the game engine. This novel implementation of these tasks raised the question of whether these tasks yield valid measures of fraction magnitude understanding. The present results indicate that this is the case as relevant findings from basic research on fraction knowledge were replicated using the Semideus game engine. This provides first evidence suggesting that game-based assessment can provide valid knowledge about students' conceptual fraction knowledge.

Acknowledgments. The current research was supported by the Leibniz-Competition Fund (SAW) supporting Manuel Ninaus (SAW-2016-IWM-3) and Academy of Finland supporting Kristian Kiili.

Appendix: Fraction Comparison Pairs

See Table 1.

Table 1. Fraction comparison pairs separated by fraction type and distance.

	Consistent			Inconsistent		
Small distance	1/2	vs.	4/7	2/5	vs.	1/2
	2/3	vs.	4/5	2/3	vs.	4/9
	5/9	vs.	3/8	2/9	vs.	1/3
	3/7	vs.	1/4	3/7	vs.	2/3
	4/7	vs.	2/5	5/8	vs.	3/4
	9/10	vs.	7/9	7/11	vs.	10/19
	3/11	vs.	5/12	6/19	vs.	5/12
Large distance	1/2	vs.	8/9	1/9	vs.	1/2
	2/5	vs.	5/7	3/9	vs.	3/4
	1/3	vs.	3/4	3/4	vs.	4/9
	6/11	vs.	11/13	3/9	vs.	2/3
	13/18	vs.	4/11	7/8	vs.	8/15
	8/17	vs.	1/16	12/22	vs.	11/12
	4/11	vs.	13/18	10/11	vs.	11/23

References

1. Bailey, D.H., et al.: Competence with fractions predicts gains in mathematics achievement. J. Exp. Child Psychol. **113**(3), 447–455 (2012)
2. Booth, J.L., Newton, K.J.: Fractions: could they really be the gatekeeper's doorman? Contemp. Educ. Psychol. **37**(4), 247–253 (2012)
3. Boyle, E.A., et al.: An update to the systematic literature review of empirical evidence of the impacts and outcomes of computer games and serious games. Comput. Educ. **94**, 178–192 (2016)
4. Cohen Kadosh, R., et al.: Interventions for improving numerical abilities: present and future. Trends Neurosci. Educ. **2**(2), 85–93 (2013)
5. DeWolf, M., Vosniadou, S.: The representation of fraction magnitudes and the whole number bias reconsidered. Learn. Instr. **37**, 39–49 (2015)
6. Erhel, S., Jamet, E.: Digital game-based learning: impact of instructions and feedback on motivation and learning effectiveness. Comput. Educ. **67**, 156–167 (2013)
7. Fischer, U., et al.: Full-body movement in numerical trainings: a pilot study with an interactive whiteboard. Int. J. Serious Games **2**(4), 23–35 (2015)
8. Fischer, U., et al.: Math with the dance mat: on the benefits of embodied numerical training approaches. In: Lee, V. (ed.) Learning Technologies and the Body: Integration and Implementation in Formal and Informal Learning Environments, pp. 149–163. Routledge, Abingdon-on-Thames (2014)
9. Gigerenzer, G.: Calculated Risks: How to Know When Numbers Deceive You. Simon and Schuster, New York (2002)
10. Van Hoof, J., et al.: Are secondary school students still hampered by the natural number bias? A reaction time study on fraction comparison tasks. Res. Math. Educ. **15**(2), 154–164 (2013)

11. Van Hoof, J., et al.: In search for the natural number bias in secondary school students' interpretation of the effect of arithmetical operations. Learn. Instr. **37**, 30–38 (2015)
12. Huber, S., et al.: Adaptive processing of fractions — evidence from eye-tracking. Acta Psychol. (Amst) **148**, 37–48 (2014)
13. Ischebeck, A., et al.: The processing and representation of fractions within the brain: an fMRI investigation. Neuroimage **47**(1), 403–413 (2009)
14. Kucian, K., et al.: Mental number line training in children with developmental dyscalculia. Neuroimage **57**(3), 782–795 (2011)
15. Lawrence, M.A.: ez: Easy analysis and visualization of factorial experiments. R package version 4.3 (2015). https://cran.r-project.org/package=ez
16. Link, T., et al.: Walk the number line - an embodied training of numerical concepts. Trends Neurosci. Educ. **2**(2), 74–84 (2013)
17. Lumsden, J., et al.: Gamification of cognitive assessment and cognitive training: a systematic review of applications and efficacy. JMIR Serious Games **4**(2), e11 (2016)
18. McMullen, J., et al.: Modeling the developmental trajectories of rational number concept(s). Learn. Instr. **37**, 14–20 (2014)
19. Moeller, K., et al.: Computers in mathematics education – training the mental number line. Comput. Hum. Behav. **48**, 597–607 (2015)
20. National Mathematics Advisory Panel: The final report of the national mathematics advisory panel. Foundations **37**(9), 595–601 (2008)
21. Ni, Y., Zhou, Y.-D.: Teaching and learning fraction and rational numbers: the origins and implications of whole number bias. Educ. Psychol. **40**(1), 27–52 (2005)
22. Ninaus, M., et al.: Game elements improve performance in a working memory training task. Int. J. Serious Games **2**(1), 3–16 (2015)
23. Ninaus, M., et al.: Neurofeedback and serious games. In: Connolly, T.M., et al. (eds.) Psychology, Pedagogy and Assessment in Serious Games, pp. 82–110. IGI Global, USA (2013)
24. Obersteiner, A., et al.: The natural number bias and magnitude representation in fraction comparison by expert mathematicians. Learn. Instr. **28**(July), 64–72 (2013)
25. Parsons, S., Bynner, J.: Does Numeracy Matter More?. NRDC, London (2006)
26. R Core Team: R: a language and environment for statistical computing. R Foundation for Statistical Computing (2016). https://www.r-project.org/
27. Schneider, M., Siegler, R.S.: Representations of the magnitudes of fractions. J. Exp. Psychol. Hum. Percept. Perform. **36**(5), 1227–1238 (2010)
28. Siegler, R.S., et al.: An integrated theory of whole number and fractions development. Cogn. Psychol. **62**(4), 273–296 (2011)
29. Siegler, R.S., et al.: Fractions: the new frontier for theories of numerical development. Trends Cogn. Sci. **17**(1), 13–19 (2013)
30. Siegler, R.S., Ramani, G.B.: Playing linear numerical board games promotes low-income children's numerical development. Dev. Sci. **11**(5), 655–661 (2008)
31. Torbeyns, J., et al.: Bridging the gap: fraction understanding is central to mathematics achievement in students from three different continents. Learn. Instr. **37**, 5–13 (2015)
32. Vamvakoussi, X., et al.: Naturally biased? In search for reaction time evidence for a natural number bias in adults. J. Math. Behav. **31**(3), 344–355 (2012)
33. Wei, T., Simko, V.: corrplot: visualization of a Correlation Matrix. R package version 0.77 (2016). https://cran.r-project.org/package=corrplot
34. Wickham, H.: ggplot2: Elegant Graphics for Data Analysis. Springer, New York (2009)

EyeMath: Identifying Mathematics Problem Solving Processes in a RTS Video Game

Aura Hernández-Sabaté[1,2], Lluís Albarracín[3,4(✉)],
Daniel Calvo[1,2], and Núria Gorgorió[3]

[1] Computer Vision Center, Universitat Autònoma de Barcelona, Barcelona, Spain
[2] Department of Computer Science, Universitat Autònoma de Barcelona,
Barcelona, Spain
aura.hernandez@uab.cat
[3] Department of Didàctica de la Matemàtica i de les Ciències Experimentals,
Universitat Autònoma de Barcelona, Barcelona, Spain
[4] Serra Húnter Fellow, Universitat Autònoma de Barcelona, Barcelona, Spain
lluis.albarracin@uab.cat

Abstract. Video games are promising tools in educational environments since they have features that can promote learning in a playful environment. Formerly, we identified mathematics learning opportunities in a real time strategy video game. Going further, in order to precisely understand which information the students use to solve the challenges provided by the video game, this paper presents an eye tracker based tool to identify processes of mathematics problem solving while playing the game. The first preliminary results show the potential of the tool to further identify metacognitive and mathematics problem solving processes.

Keywords: Mathematics education · Problem solving · Eye-tracker · Image processing · Tower defense

1 Introduction

Video games have appealing features that, at the same time, endow a great potential as instruments for promoting learning and developing specific strategies for knowledge acquisition [1]. In this sense, according to [2], the essential features that endow video games as tools in educational environments are competition, presence of objectives, rules well defined and decision making needs.

From the perspective of mathematics education we realize that video games have not been fully exploited as educational tools. We claim that to full benefit from the most of the characteristics of video games as educational tools we should profit everything that make them attractive and align learning objectives to the objectives of the game. Following this perspective, in an exploratory work [3], we identified mathematics problem solving processes while students, aged from 10 to 12 years old, were playing a real time strategy (RTS) video game of Tower defense genre in which challenges for players constantly arise. In our study we identified

© Springer International Publishing AG 2016
R. Bottino et al. (Eds.): GALA 2016, LNCS 10056, pp. 50–59, 2016.
DOI: 10.1007/978-3-319-50182-6_5

that the activity of players includes interwoven problem resolution cycles formed by processes of "Observation - Planning - Decision Making", where mathematical concepts of numerical and geometrical content and functional relation among variables intervene.

Our aim is to precisely understand which information the students use to take decisions, how they take them and which elements are important at each moment. For that, in the former study, to force explicit mentions of the decisions and strategies adopted while playing, students played in pairs. This allows to explore the relation between the discussion and agreements about game strategies the students did and the actions they performed. However, this method is slow and limited. On the one hand, to analyze all the collected data takes a huge time, since each game play took between 26 and 68 min. On the other one, the speech of the students is limited due to their age and the nature of the game.

To overcome these limitations, in this paper we propose the use of an eye tracker to create an automatic tool that not only gives the position the player is looking at, but for combining it with the actions taken in the game process itself, reflected in the screen. For that, we create several areas of interest, derived from the previous study, and we intersect them with the gaze of the user. The result is a video of the recorded game play enhancing the area of interest the user is gazing in the screen at every moment. The preliminar results obtained from the analysis of some of these videos show the potential of the proposed tool. We can observe that it either allows the assertion of mathematics learning opportunities previously identified in our previous work [3], or the finding of new learning opportunities that are so intangible to be drawn from the speech recorded while playing.

2   Related Work

2.1   Video Games as Educative Tools

Video games have proven to be an educative attractive tool for two main aspects. On the one hand, they are designed from specific rules and objectives. On the other one, the nature of human-machine interaction allows players an immediate response of their actions [4]. In a systematic revision of the literature, the authors in [5] identified those studies that provide empirical evidence of the positive impact of video games on different aspects of school learning. In their work they found evidence of improvement in motor and perceptual skills as well as cognitive skills such as mental rotation, memory or problem solving in a broad sense. The authors in [6] use mini games as a player's challenge to discover or investigate real context details in 3D digital environments.

In the specific field of Mathematics Education there are some studies aimed at determining the impact of the use of video games for learning mathematical content. In the research described in [7] several video games that propose challenges and puzzles to students were used. These video games foster students to work with mathematical content such as numerical sequences, addition and subtraction problems, estimation and recognition of geometric figures.

The results of this study show an increase in student motivation during class-room work, showing an increase in cooperation and verbal interaction between students. Also, participating students significantly improved their results in a test of mathematical knowledge to a higher level than students in the control group who did not use video games.

A study [8] analyzing the behavior of students playing some mini games specifically designed for learning mathematics, the author highlights that a key design aspect of these games is the relationship between the game objectives and the learning ones, which usually not match. This fact is supported by the work in [9] that show that one of the main challenges in game design oriented to learning is to integrate or incorporate learning content in the game and its narrative mechanics.

In a recent study [10], the authors used two video games in the same didactic proposal with students of the first courses of primary education. The video games used, *Semideus* and *Wuzzit Trouble*, have been designed from a dynamic visual representation of particular mathematical constructs (the line of numbers and the integer arithmetic, respectively) to build a video game around them. In this way, to solve the puzzles and challenges of the game it is necessary to understand and solve the mathematical problem underlying the raised situation. The results of this study show an improvement in the results about numerical aspects among students who followed the teaching proposal. Meanwhile, the authors in [11] complement this study by analyzing the strategies developed by the students while playing *Wuzzit Trouble*. These authors noted that the video game forces students to constantly review the strategies used, even to develop complex conceptual aspects such as the factorization of natural numbers and combine them to solve the proposed challenges.

2.2 Eye Tracking on Game-Based Learning

In the recent years, eye tracking has been used in several fields like psychology, psycholinguistics, visual systems, market research, product design and gaze based interactions [12,13]. In the last years, it has also reached the field of video games with several aims such as interaction tool [14] or evaluation of game experiences [15]. The study of gaze behavior can provide insight about the visual attention of players and thus assist game designers in identifying problems with game play.

Focusing on game-based learning, to the best of our knowledge, the studies done with eye trackers neither go beyond improving the educational games interfaces by means of user experience perception, without forgetting their value to the educative community. The authors in [16] analyzed different attention skills during the interaction of the users with a set of puzzle games. They concluded that gaze patterns allow them to determine some "hot areas" where to put the most relevant contents. The study carried on in [17] explored story comprehension in comic books and video games, finding that comprehension of narrative may be greater in game players than in comic readers. Kiili et al. [18] also claim that eye tracking can provide very deep and objective information about human-game interaction design and layout, although the results interpretation can not be only based on fixation counts and hot spot maps.

We propose going one step further since in our project, the importance lies in extracting information that actually is not directly reflected in eye tracker data. Using image processing techniques and the data obtained from the eye tracker we propose a tool that merge the information given by the eye tracker with the own game solving for simplifying data analysis to identify the mathematical learning processes of the players.

3   External Tools

This section presents the external tools used in this work, the video game and the eye tracker.

The Vector Tower Defense 2. The video game used in the previous and present studies is Vector Tower Defense 2 [19], a RTS video game. The goal is to prevent enemy units (called vectoids), who arrive in waves, from crossing the map. To achieve this, defense towers have to be built to assault vectoids as they pass. Vectoids move along a specific path, and players have a large variety of towers, upgrades and bonus points, boosting them to exploit their strategic skills to the limit. Strategic considerations are based on the choice and placement of the towers and resource management. The game provides the players with many information such as the game map, score, available funds, tower types and their characteristics, like their cost, the damage they inflicts in each attack and their bonus points expressed in percentages.

The Eye Tracker. The Eye tracker employed in monitoring the player's eye actions is SMI RED 500 by SensoMotoric Instruments [20]. It can be mounted on a monitor size that ranges from 19 to 60 inches and can be controlled remotely from the workstation PC using software provided by SMI.

The SMI iViewX is a software installed on a workstation PC that uses infrared illumination and computer based image processing to calibrate and record eye data. This software remotely controls the eye tracker. It has variable manual calibration and automatic and fast calibration modes.

The SMI Begaze is the software used to replay, visualize, analyze and export raw data recorded with the eye tracker. It has the AOI editor that helps in drawing Area Of Interest points on the gaze replay video and then export data corresponding to the AOIs. Several metrics can be defined to the data sets and the required data sets alone can be extracted. The data exported from BeGaze can then be analyzed for further research.

4   EyeMath: Automatic Identification of Key Game Actions

In this section we present the EyeMath, the tool we have developed to contribute to the identification of the elements that determine the type of mathematical learning opportunities when playing a Tower Defense game. Figure 1 shows the pipeline of the process. First of all, the user sits in front of the screen where he/she will play the video game. The binocular eye tracker is placed below the screen. While the user is freely playing the game match, the eye tracker records the fixations, saccades and blinks of the user. Besides, the SMI iViewX collects the data recorded by the eye tracker together with the video of the game match and the positions of the mouse clicks done by the user. After that, an automatic process of the data collected is carried on to analyze what happens in the screen and fuse that information with the actions and fixations of the user. The result is a new video of the game match with the mouse path and the enhancement of the area where the user is gazing at each moment that allow the easy detection of relevant events.

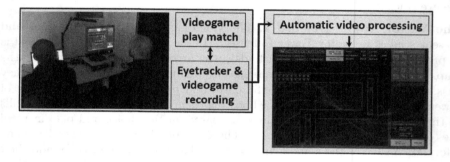

Fig. 1. Pipeline of the resource creation

Eye Tracking and Game Play Recording. In the first step a remote eye tracker records eye movements while students play. The eye tracker tracks the eye movements by the infrared light that causes visible reflections in the cornea when it is directed towards the pupil. As we explained before, the software SMI iViewX tracker remotely controls the eye tracker, calibrates the system, and records eye data. It also records screen and mouse click events.

Automatic Data Processing. Once all the relevant data is recorded, the automatic data processing starts. First of all, we split the screen in eight Areas Of Interest (AOI), based on critical times detection in our previous study [3]. These areas are shown in Fig. 2 and are summarized down below: Send the vectoids button, game details such as lives, money, interest, bonus, etc., tower selection, information about the tower selected, tower upgrade information, tower selling information, current and upcoming enemies information, game play area and background.

From the segmentation of the screen, we create a mask of the AOI and we intersect it with the fixations information given by the eye tracker. In the case of game play area, since it is too large and we are really interested in knowing if the user is looking at the vectoids or not, we create a dynamic mask of the vectoids (whenever they appear in the screen) at each frame by means a background subtraction between the path of a known image without vectoids and the path

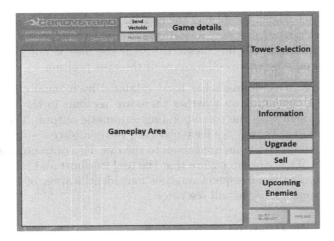

Fig. 2. Screen segmentation in static areas of interest

of the current frame of the video. Figure 3 shows the process of background subtraction of the reference frame and a frame under study. First of all, a mask of the path is multiplied by each frame. The resulting images are subtracted and a convex hull of the result is computed to create the mask of vectoids. This dynamic mask is considered another AOI, so it is added to the AOIs list.

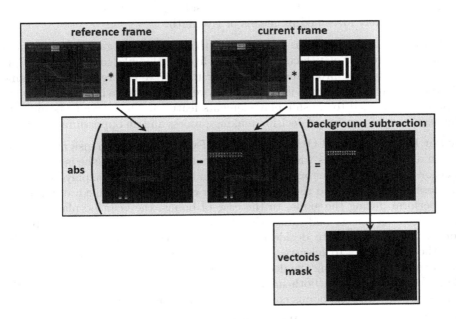

Fig. 3. Background subtraction Process

Finally, at each frame, the gaze of the user is intersected with the corresponding AOI. In the case of game play area, if the user is looking at the vectoids, the former computed mask will be enhanced, but if the user is not looking at the vectoids, it will only be enhanced a range of the eyes position.

Validation. The dynamic mask has been validated by manually labeling 3600 frames as 0 or 1 depending on whether there are vectoids in the screen or not and comparing them with the corresponding automatic output. The results are a 100% of reliability. As well, we have observed the complete resulting videos of 4 game plays and we have compared them to the raw data obtaining also a 100% of true positives. Thus, we can ensure that the tool is robust and reliable, so that it serves to help in the subsequent analysis and identification of mathematical learning opportunities, as we will see below.

5   Preliminar Results

In this section we describe the qualitative aspects the EyeMath allows to identify from the observed game plays. In this first approximation, we have analyzed the videos obtained from the game matches of two players aged 13 and 15 years during 37.51 and 34.03 min, respectively. In both cases, we recorded the second match they played, since the first time served to show them the game mechanics. As we describe in [3], the process of the Vector Tower Defense 2 is compared to a mathematics problem solving activity, due to the identified processes, the observed complexity and the mathematical content covered. In this way, we appreciate the following findings as problem solving aspects and processes that can be exclusively identified by means of EyeMath.

Data Read in the Screen. Players read the data with regard to towers and enemies features or play facts (remaining lives, accumulated resources). The identification of that processes should allow to observe differences in the game play between experts and novices players, as well as to observe in which moments expert players need to consult play elements features. These moments indicate the beginning of a reasoned decision making process and an opportunity to learn.

Tower Placement and Other Elements. EyeMath allows an insightful observation of the screen areas where a player is looking at when he/she is taking the decision of placing a tower or using a bonus. In the case of towers, players observe the possible positions and the area that tower covers to determine if it will properly perform during the game. In the case of bonus, they can be placed in the same boxes as towers and affect the towers in a neighborhood of the placed bonus. The player has to decide the optimal position to squeeze its potential and the tool allows to observe in which concrete aspects the player focus on the time he/she is making the decision. Figure 4 shows an example of a decision about bonus placing. In both images, the player is looking (green box) at the borders of the area the bonus covers to decide its optimal position.

Anticipating Processes. We observe that players anticipate to the game actions in some circumstances and with different aims. From the point of view of

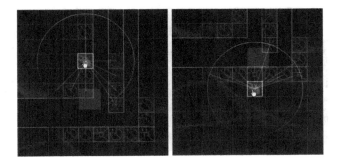

Fig. 4. Example of bonus placement (Color figure online)

mathematics learning, this advance denotes the need of achieving data to analyze the play situation. We have observed several types of advance processing:

- Players look at screen areas where there is no tower cover yet, even they do not place any tower immediately after this fixation. We think they evaluate the chances of placing them in a future.
- Players follow the vectoids as they move forward in the screen but they deviate the gaze to the positions the vectoids will occupy in an immediate future to estimate if the placed tower will be enough to kill them. Given the play features, each type of enemy is differently affected by the different types of tower. Thus, the chances of killing the enemies are substantially different in each round. We have observed that novices players do not advance to the vectoids movement in the first rounds but they do as soon as they observe these difficulties. Thus, players intuitively learn that the power of towers depends on their features according to the enemies ones. We consider that this fact could be explicit if there would exist a way of visualizing the amount of damage a tower can causes in each round, e.g. with the inclusion of damage plots. Figure 5 shows an example of an anticipating process. The image on the left shows that the player is following the vectoids, while the image on the right, which occurs 10 seconds later, shows that the player is looking at another area of the path where the vectoids still have to reach.

Decision Making in Risk Moments. In those moments when a situation opposite to the player concerns occurs and he/she needs to react fast, the tool allows to clearly observe the objects the player follows to try to solve the issue. This situation is a clear further learning opportunity since actions taken in these circumstances can not be supported in reasoning, given the short time margin, but they can be mathematically studied later.

Successful Play Habits. We have observed that both players achieve the habit of checking the available resources and the costs of the next available towers at the beginning of each round. We think that this process of anticipation allows the players to take decisions more effectively and faster in risk moments. From experience failing in these moments due to a bad planning or a lack of

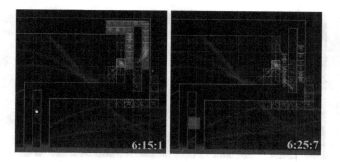

Fig. 5. Example of an anticipating process. (Color figure online)

crucial information to answer the challenges provided by the game, players ultimately acquire this habit. We think that this process highlight metacognition
during the game and it could be exploited in education environments due to its
great potential and adaptability in other contexts and circumstances.

6   Conclusions and Further Work

In this paper we present an analysis tool, the EyeMath, that allows to identify
mathematics problem solving aspects in a RTS video game. In particular, we
have shown its potential by highlighting, not only some aspects previously identified in a previous work [3], but also some others that hardly will be expressed
by players. Consequently, a range of possibilities to analyze processes that could
not be analyzed so far opens up. In particular, the EyeMath allows to identify
game processes, such as how the users interpret screen data, mathematics problem solving processes, like the way the users place the towers in the field, and
metacognitive ones such as anticipating processes. All of them should be further
explored since this potential opens the door to understand in more detail the
relation between play activity and mathematical content addressed. As well, it
should be a key support to determine classroom activities for boosting mathematics work and suggest some new designs for the development of a new educational version of the game.

References

1. Gros, B.: Digital games in education: the design of games-based learning environments. J. Res. Technol. Educ. **40**(1), 23–38 (2007)
2. Charsky, D.: From edutainment to serious games: a change in the use of game
   characteristics. Games Cult. **5**(2), 177–198 (2010)
3. Hernández-Sabaté, A., Joanpere, M., Gorgorió, N., Albarracín, L.: Mathematics
   learning opportunities when playing a tower defense game. Int. J. Ser. Games
   2(4), 57–71 (2015)

4. Dickey, M.D.: Engaging by design: how engagement strategies in popular computer and video games can inform instructional design. Educ. Technol. Res. Dev. **53**(2), 67–83 (2005)
5. Connolly, T.M., Boyle, E.A., MacArthur, E., Hainey, T., Boyle, J.M.: A systematic literature review of empirical evidence on computer games and serious games. Comput. Educ. **59**(2), 661–686 (2012)
6. Bellotti, F., Berta, R., De Gloria, A., Zappi, V.: Exploring gaming mechanisms to enhance knowledge acquisition in virtual worlds. In: Proceedings of the 3rd international conference on Digital Interactive Media in Entertainment and Arts, pp. 77–84. ACM (2008)
7. Rosas, R., Nussbaum, M., Cumsille, P., Marianov, V., Correa, M., Flores, P., Grau, V., Lagos, F., López, X., López, V., et al.: Beyond nintendo: design and assessment of educational video games for first and second grade students. Comput. Educ. **40**(1), 71–94 (2003)
8. Ke, F.: A case study of computer gaming for math: engaged learning from gameplay? Comput. Educ. **51**(4), 1609–1620 (2008)
9. Clark, D.B., Martínez-Garza, M.: Prediction and explanation as design mechanics in conceptually integrated digital games to help players articulate the tacit understandings they build through game play. In: Games, learning, and society: Learning and meaning in the digital age. Cambridge University Press (2012)
10. Kiili, K., Devlin, K., Perttula, T., Tuomi, P., Lindstedt, A.: Using video games to combine learning and assessment in mathematics education. Int. J. Ser. Games **2**(4), 37–55 (2015)
11. Pope, H., Mangram, C.: Wuzzit trouble: the influence of a digital math game on student number sense. Int. J. Ser. Games **2**(4), 1–18 (2015)
12. Mele, M.L., Federici, S.: Gaze and eye-tracking solutions for psychological research. Cogn. Process. **13**(1), 261–265 (2012)
13. Khushaba, R.N., Wise, C., Kodagoda, S., Louviere, J., Kahn, B.E., Townsend, C.: Consumer neuroscience: assessing the brain response to marketing stimuli using electroencephalogram (EEG) and eye tracking. Expert Syst. Appl. **40**(9), 3803–3812 (2013)
14. Ekman, I.M., Poikola, A.W., Mäkäräinen, M.K.: Invisible eni: using gaze and pupil size to control a game. In: CHI 2008 Extended Abstracts on Human Factors in Computing Systems, pp. 3135–3140. ACM (2008)
15. Yan, S., El-Nasr, M.S.: Visual attention in 3d video games. In: Proceedings of the 2006 Symposium on Eye Tracking Research and Applications, pp. 42–42. ACM (2006)
16. Frutos-Pascual, M., García-Zapirain, B., Mehdi, Q.H.: Where do they look at? Analysis of gaze interaction in children while playing a puzzle game. In: 2015 IEEE Computer Games: AI, Animation, Mobile, Multimedia, Educational and Serious Games (CGAMES), pp. 103–106 (2015)
17. Kinzer, C.K., Turkay, S., Hoffman, D.L., Gunbas, N., Chantes, P., Chaiwinij, A., Dvorkin, T.: Examining the effects of text and images on story comprehension: an eye-tracking study of reading in a video game and comic book. In: Literacy Research Association Yearbook, vol. 61, pp. 259–275 (2012)
18. Kiili, K., Ketamo, H., Kickmeier-Rust, M.D.: Eye tracking in game-based learning research and game design. Int. J. Ser. Games **1**(2), 51–65 (2014)
19. Vector Tower Defense 2. http://www.arcadeboss.com/game-1823-9-vector-td-2.html. Accessed 25 July 2016
20. SMI Vision. http://www.smivision.com/en/gaze-and-eye-tracking-systems/products/red250-red-500.html. Accessed 25 July 2016

Building Arduino-Based Tangible Serious Games for Elementary Mathematics and Physics

Luca Mollo, Francesco Bellotti[✉], Riccardo Berta,
and Alessandro De Gloria

Elios Lab, DITEN, University of Genoa, Genoa, Italy
luca92mollo@hotmail.it, {franz,berta}@elios.unige.it,
alessandro.degloria@unige.it

Abstract. This paper concerns the development of new tangible game tools for learning basic mathematic concepts. The prototypes can be easily implemented by exploiting new open source electronic hardware technologies, such as Arduino and related sensors and actuators, combing simplicity, wide diffusion and low cost. Two simple proof of concepts are presented. First, a music game, in which children collaborate to create a melody composed by different sounds controllable by changing the hand's distance in a theremin-like approach. The second project intends addressing the concepts of distance and alignment. In both cases, they are not closed-box fully automatic games, but tools freely usable by an educator (e.g., a teacher or a parent) with children. The experience shows that several alternative configurations are easily implemented, calling for the possibility of developing a hardware/software component library for development/assembly of various types of tangible games also by non experts.

1 Introduction

Despite the obvious importance of scientific and technological education, the number of university students in these areas is decreasing, and not only because of the demographic winter in Western countries. It becomes thus ever more important to investigate new, complementary educational methodologies, particularly studying new tools that can be help to show relevance of math and science in real world, possibly also combining artistic aspects.

This paper presents some first steps in this direction, implementing elementary tangible games for early primary school students, the main requirements being feedback, precision, pleasant experience and participation of students and educators. The system is in an early implementation stage, where the goal is to identify and verify what the main functionalities for a tangible game system could be to support learning in some basic scientific areas. Thus, the focus of this paper is not yet on Human-Computer Interaction or insertion in a real classroom environment.

The first project concerns a music game, in which children collaborate to create a melody composed by different sounds. The second addresses the concepts of distance and alignment. In both cases, they are not closed-box fully automatic games, but tools freely usable by an educator (e.g., a teacher or a parent) with children.

© Springer International Publishing AG 2016
R. Bottino et al. (Eds.): GALA 2016, LNCS 10056, pp. 60–69, 2016.
DOI: 10.1007/978-3-319-50182-6_6

2 State of the Art

High quality tools and products have been recently deployed in the market to support scientific learning through smart objects able to sense the context, compute and communicate. Outstanding examples include micro:bit[1] and robot cubelets[2]. Cubelets are a groundbreaking robot construction system designed for budding young innovators. Some tools (e.g. Lego Mindstorm[3], Code Combat[4]) specifically target programming. While this area looks well developing, we also see a need for lower cost tools for a general school audience. This is already addressed with software serious games for mathematics, that are increasingly being used especially to exercise computation in elementary schools [1, 2]. Cyberchase 3D Builder is an iPad game that allows children to turn 2D shapes into 3D structures in the cartoon world of the television series Cyberchase [3]. We think that real-world toys and tangible games [4–7] could allow a better coverage and comprehension of scientific (particularly geometry and physics) concepts, by enlarging the offer and supporting more extensive body interactions [8]. As a valuable example, Vuzik is a promising new application where the user manipulates, arranges, and composes music with painting interaction akin to that used when standing at an easel, to a traditional, GUI based musical interface [9]. Tangible interfaces look also suited to enhance collaborative learning experiences [10], which could be another motivating factor for pupils.

New open source electronic hardware technologies, such as Arduino and related sensors and actuators [11, 12], can significantly help in this research direction, especially by providing an effective prototyping environment combing simplicity, wide diffusion and low cost [13].

3 The "Orchestra" Prototype

The orchestra project intends to make children collaborate in creating nice sounds/melodies using physical concepts such as distance and illumination.

Music is often related to mathematics, thus lends itself well to the learning of certain concepts. Musical theory divides notes into octaves, series of eight notes (Fig. 1). An octave includes twelve semitones. The frequency of the i-th semitone is proportional to the frequency of its predecessor, according to the following rule. In this way we see that each octave doubles its starting frequency.

$$F_i = f_{i-1} * \sqrt[12]{2}.$$

---

[1] https://www.microbit.co.uk/.

[2] http://www.modrobotics.com/cubelets/.

[3] http://www.lego.com/mindstorms/.

[4] https://codecombat.com.

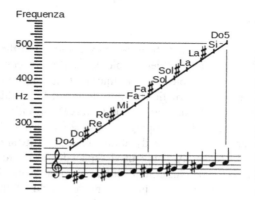

Fig. 1. Scale of the fourth octave

3.1 Notes and Distance

The idea is to exploit ultrasound sensors and photoresistors, that provide immediate quantitative feedback about a physical phenomenon or concept such as distance. A first example is to choose a set of notes (e.g., an octave's 7 main notes) and make them play by a child. The frequency of the played note will be proportional to the distance of the hand from sensor, as synthetized in Table 1, where the extreme values have been set to 5 and 100 cm respectively, and the others computed through a line equation.

Table 1. Correspondence among notes, frequency and distance.

Scale							
Note (It)	Do	Re	Mi	Fa	Sol	La	Si
Note	C	D	E	F	G	A	B
Freq	262	294	330	349	392	440	494
Distance (cm.)	5	18	33	41	58	78	100

3.2 Notes and Time

Another educational goal is learning the length of time. For this, a child could keep his hand still to play the note for a certain time and then remove it. Feedback is provided with different tones (or melodies, in a simpler, discrete approach) according to the measured difference from the target values.

3.3 Notes and Luminosity

Another physical phenomenon of interest is represented by light, and simple photoresistors can be used for a quantitative evaluation.

A first sample game involves keeping a torch fixed and varying its light intensity. Then, the child may move the torch in the space. In both cases, the system will play different notes or different sound intensity according to the measured light intensity.

The system may be used like the one based on ultrasounds, but looks more complicate with respect to the distance of the hand. An easier game could involve time intervals, asking the child to switch on/off the light at the right moment (i.e., after a certain number of seconds). The feedback is given as said above.

Another variation consists in rotating the light source around the sensor, while keeping the same distance and light intensity. This would lead to a change in the perceived light (due to a certain directionality of the sensor), thus in a different note feedback, as if the child changed light source distance or intensity.

3.4   Theremin

The tool created with the ultrasound distance sensor is inspired by the theremin music instrument, created by Lev Sergeevič Termen in 1919. The theremin can be played by only moving hands, without any physical contact, as the perceived distance is translated into a music sound. The difference is that theremin exploits electromagnetic waves [14]. Moreover, the hand's position influences intensity and frequency of the note, which is fixed and comes from the variation of the produced electromagnetic field, while in our case the played note is programmable.

3.5   Game System

In the current version, the prototype involves of three Arduino Uno bases, constituting two musical instruments and one orchestra director. The goal of the director is to allow defining, through two simple potentiometers, the length of the playable notes and of the pause among them. The first instrument plays different sounds based on the player's hand distance (ultrasound sensor). The second instrument can be played through hands (lowering the environment light) or, better, a light source.

At least two children can play together. An educator can assess the orchestra performance based on quantitative (meeting the constraints set by the director) and qualitative (the quality of the produced sounds) aspects.

3.6   System Architecture

Figure 2 shows the reference flowchart for the programme wrt the Director and one of the two instruments.

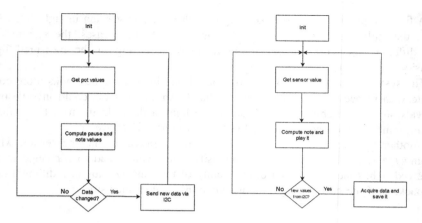

Fig. 2. Flowchart of the director and of an instrument

The sequence diagram is provided in Fig. 3.

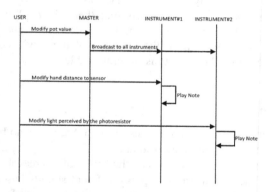

Fig. 3. Generic sequence diagram for the Orchestra prototype

Figure 4 shows an elementary prototype implementation schema for the three instruments, for simplicity placed on the same breadboard and with an I2C bus communication. The utilized electronic components include:

Director: 1 Arduino Uno, 2 10 kΩ potentiometers, 2 4.7 kΩ resistors, 4 330 Ω. Resistirs, 4 red leds;

Luminosity instrument: 1 Arduino Uno, 1 photoresistor (with a 500 value dynamic range measured in the application), 1 10 kΩ resistor, 1 680 Ω resistir, 1 330 Ω resitior, 1 audio speaker;

Ultrasound device:1 Arduino Uno, 1 SRF-02 sensor (with a 18 cm–2.5 m range, with a 40° –3 dB angle), 1 330 Ω.resistor, 1 100 μF, 1 audio speaker.

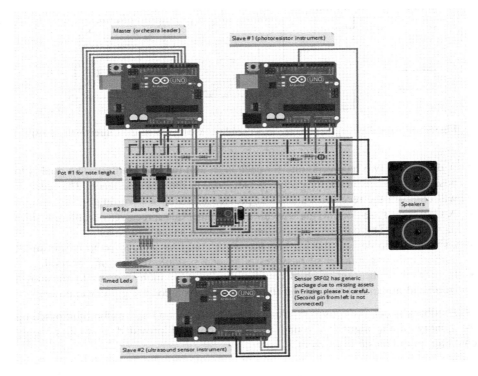

Fig. 4. Breadboard schema of the Orchestra prototype

4 The "Row" Prototype

A second example developed addresses the concept of alignment. The system involves several box-shaped devices that a player should align and place at equal distance from each other. Devices are properly cased, in order to leave the openings for the infrared (IR) transmitters and receivers in parallel with the orientation of the box (Fig. 5a). Figure 5b shows two examples, the first one very directional, the second one more like a traffic-light case.

In lab, we have tried several different game experiments, such as the following.

- Every device has a transmitter on one side and a receiver on the other. The player's goal is to align as many devices as possible. For counting, serial IR communication is exploited, with the first device (not receiving any signal from a previous one) transmitting a "1", and the others transmitting the received value increased by 1.
- Like the previous case, but adding the concept of distance, programmable via software and/or tunable with a potentiometer. The distance could be subsequently doubled, with a feasibility limit of 50 cm, for our sensor.

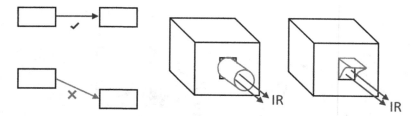

Fig. 5. Right and wrong alignment (a); Possible box cases to support directionality (b)

- A device has two receivers, one for each side, and two transmitters. The goal is to position one transmitter for each receiver side, at the same distance. The receiver will compare the received values and provide a feedback accordingly.
- A variation of the domino game, with a transmitter and a receiver on different sides of the tessel. The correct composition will have a snake-like shape.
- Using a single device, the led and transistor could be aligned so to create an IR barrier, counting number of passages (e.g., of a pendulum) and time interval.
- In another application, a child could control one or more buttons to transmit a command associated to a button (like a remote) or a code (e.g., Morse coding).

Feedback is currently given by three coloured leds acting as a traffic light based on the quality of the signal. A sound feedback could be provided as well, possibly enabling a new music instrument.

4.1   System Architecture

Figure 6 shows a system configuration with a device with two receivers and two devices with a transmitter each. Correct alignment is notified on a four led color scale (red, yellow, green, blue).

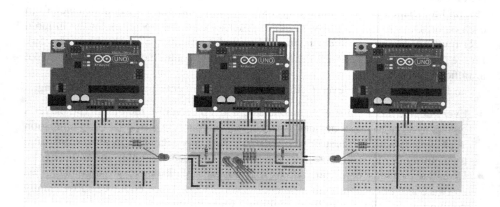

Fig. 6. Circuit schema (Color figure online)

The receiver circuit include salso a feedback emission part (four leds connected through resistors to the Arduino's 2–5 outputs). The LTR 301 infrared receiver is a transistor, whose basis captures the IR light. Thus, its collector is connected to the power with a 10 kΩ resistor and the emitter to the ground. The output is given by the collector-ground voltage, which is sent to the Arduino's analogic input pin. Components include:

Transmitter: 1 Arduino Uno, 2 330 Ω resistor, 1 LTE 302 IR.
Receiver: 1 Arduino Uno, 2 10 kΩ. resistor, 4 330 Ω resistor, 2 LTR 301 IR transistor, 4 leds.

Figure 7a shows the receiver's flowchart.

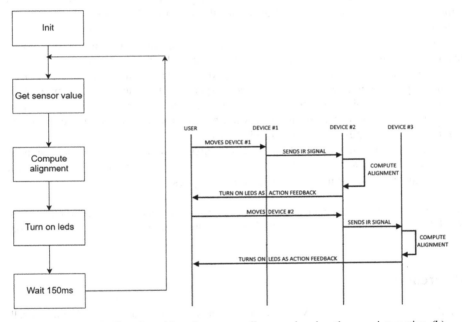

Fig. 7. Receiver's flowchart (a) and sequence diagram showing the user interaction (b)

The sequence diagram in Fig. 7b shows the user interaction in the configuration case of devices with one receiver and one transmitter each. The user's moving of device 1 will make the alignment change. Once computed the distance, device 2 will switch on the led to provide feedback (devices are interchangeable).

The feedback computation happens as it follows: if the values read by the two receivers are below 750 (about 3.65 V), alignment is maximum, and the blue led is switched on. Red light is for the 900 (4.4 V) case. Beyond this threshold no light is provided.

According to the datasheets, both the led transmitter and transistor receiver have an opening angle of 40°, which allows signal detection even in case of misalignment. Using the cases in Fig. 5, it is possible to increase the distance to 15 cm.

5   Conclusions

There is a lively community around the Arduino platform and little of this is described in scientific papers, probably because of lack to scientific evaluation of such systems. With this work, we intend to bring to the attention of the academic world the possibility of exploiting the benefits of the open source hardware technologies to build a platform for prototyping educational games, enabled by the Internet of things technologies.

Beside pre-defined-path games, the system supports also open interactions between children and educators. This could also path the way to collaborative design of new games.

The experience shows that several alternative configurations are easily implemented from the technological point of view. This calls for the possibility of developing a hardware/software component library for easy development and deployment of various types of tangible games also by non experts. In this view, the presented work can be a starting point for activities involving different disciplines, particularly pedagogy experts to improve learning effectiveness. The artistic value (particularly for the "orchestra" prototype) should be considered as well.

Next steps of our work will also include integration with smartphones for more extended feedback and user interaction, and network connectivity to provide cloud computing services, for instance for learning analytics.

Acknowledgments. The authors would like to thank the anonymous reviewers, whose insightful and constructive comments have helped to improve the quality of the final manuscript.

References

1. Kiili, K.J.M., Devlin, K., Multisilta, J.: Editorial: is game-based math learning finally coming of age? Intl. J. Serious Games **2**(4) (2015)
2. Kiili, K.J.M., Devlin, K., Perttula, A., Tuomi, P., Lindstedt, A.: Using video games to combine learning and assessment in mathematics education. Intl. J. Serious Games **2**(4) (2015)
3. Doherty, E., Templeton, M., Kleinman, M., McCarthy, B., Tiu, M.: Cyberchase 3D builder: a new way to look at geometry. In: Proceedings of the 12th International Conference on Interaction Design and Children (IDC 2013). ACM, New York (2013)
4. Feaster, Y., Farha, A., Hallstrom, J.O.: Serious toys: teaching the binary number system. In: Proceedings of the 17th ACM Annual Conference on Innovation and Technology in Computer Science Education (ITiCSE 2012), pp. 262–267. ACM, New York (2012). http://dx.doi.org/10.1145/2325296.2325358

5. Khandelwal, M., Mazalek, A.: Teaching table: a tangible mentor for pre-k math education. In: Proceedings of the 1st International Conference on Tangible and Embedded Interaction (TEI 2007), pp. 191–194. ACM, New York (2007). http://dx.doi.org/10.1145/1226969. 1227009

6. Yingying, S., Liyan, G., Zuyao, Z.: Researches and development of interactive educational toys for children. In: International Conference on Artificial Intelligence and Education (ICAIE) (2010)

7. Berta, R., Bellotti, F., van der Spek, E., Winkler, T.: A tangible serious game approach to science, technology, engineering, and mathematics (STEM) education. In: Nakatsu, R., Rauterberg, M., Ciancarini, P. (eds.) Handbook of Digital Games and Entertainment Technologies, pp. 1–22. Springer, Heidelberg (2016)

8. Caon, M., Angelini, L., Mugellini, E., Matassa, A., Bianchi-Berthouze, N., Singh, A., Tajadura-Jiménez, A.: Third workshop on full-body and multisensory experience. In: Proceedings of the 2016 ACM International Joint Conference on Pervasive and Ubiquitous Computing: Adjunct (UbiComp 2016), pp. 962–967. ACM, New York (2016)

9. Ichino, J., Pon, A., Sharlin, E., Eagle, D., Carpendale, S.: Vuzik: the effect of large gesture interaction on children's creative musical expression. In: Proceedings of the 26th Australian Computer-Human Interaction Conference on Designing Futures: The Future of Design. ACM, New York

10. Scarlatos, L.L., Landy, S.S.: Experiments in using tangible interfaces to enhance collaborative learning experiences. In: CHI 2001 Extended Abstracts on Human Factors in Computing Systems (CHI EA 2001). ACM, New York (2001)

11. Badamasi, Y.A.: The working principle of an Arduino. In: 11th International Conference on Electronics, Computer and Computation (ICECCO) (2014)

12. Mellodge, P., Russell, I.: Using the arduino platform to enhance student learning experiences. In: Proceedings of the 18th ACM Conference on Innovation and Technology in Computer Science Education (ITiCSE 2013), pp. 338–338. ACM, New York (2013). http://dx.doi.org/10.1145/2462476.2466530

13. Esposito, W.J., Mujica, F.A., Garcia, D.G., Kovacs, G.T.A.: The Lab-In-A-Box project: an Arduino compatible signals and electronics teaching system. In: Signal Processing and Signal Processing Education Workshop (SP/SPE) (2015)

14. Liu, T.-C., Chang, S.-H., Hsiao, C.-Y.: A modified Quad-Theremin for interactive computer music control. In: International Conference on Multimedia Technology (ICMT) (2011)

Database Engineering Game

Markus Siepermann[(⊠)]

Technische Universität Dortmund,
Otto-Hahn-Str. 12, 44227 Dortmund, Germany
markus.siepermann@tu-dortmund.de

Abstract. Database engineering consists of several tasks like database modelling and SQL. Usually, these tasks are taught and practiced separately. This paper presents a game based e-learning system that combines these tasks of database engineering so that students can experience the later consequences of their work in earlier steps. Several tools are provided that check the students' solutions and give hints what is done well and what has to be improved.

Keywords: Database engineering · Data modelling · SQL

1 Introduction

Modern information systems (IS) are based on a database, usually a relational database. For students of many different disciplines it is therefore crucial to be taught in the design and handling of databases. The main problem is that database design (DBD) is some kind of a creative process that does not result in one best solution. Instead, there are often several solutions that solve some parts of the problem differently well but exclusive of a single best solution. In addition, two solutions may solve a given problem and lead to the same result but one solution solves the problem in a more general and flexible way and should therefore be preferred. Only if the database engineer is experienced enough s/he can judge which modelling alternative should be used for a certain application.

In classic exercises, students usually get a description of a problem that has to be solved. Then, they model a database schema that is either corrected by an instructor or an intelligent tutoring system (ITS) or they compare their solution against a reference solution on their own. If we let students practice DBD like this, the main issue is that problems of their solution are discussed but they do not really experience the consequences of their database schema and learn which problems their solution bears for the operation of the IS. For example, some schemata do not allow saving information A before saving information B but in reality information B is often not known or known after A. An experienced database engineer would avoid such situations but students who are new to the subject have to experience these issues so that they know why to choose a certain modelling alternative.

In this paper, we introduce a game based intelligent tutoring system for database engineering that tries to overcome the aforementioned issues. Students play the role of a database engineer and administrator who is instructed to build a new IS for a firm. According to the given application, students have to model the database schema as the

R. Bottino et al. (Eds.): GALA 2016, LNCS 10056, pp. 70–79, 2016.
DOI: 10.1007/978-3-319-50182-6_7

basis for the IS. Then, they implement the database and have to perform several typical tasks with the IS they have built. While coping with these tasks, they usually encounter several problems due to issues of their data schema. Therefore, they can reiterate the design process to improve their database schema so that the typical tasks can be performed better. During this process, several supporting tools are provided by the ITS that help to improve the database design.

The remainder of this paper is organised as follows. The next section gives an overview about the related literature in the field of e-learning systems for DBD and SQL. In Sect. 3, the problem of database design is explained more deeply so that the problem itself becomes clearer. Section 4 describes the Database Engineering Game. In Sect. 5, the marking and grading of students' solutions is described. The paper closes with a conclusion in Sect. 6 that summarises the results, reports some limitations and gives an outlook towards future developments.

2   Literature Review

This paper contributes to several e-learning streams. First of all, we use a graphical modelling technique that must be checked automatically. This stream of research started in 2002 with a framework for e-assessments [24]. Thomas presented an idea how to mark diagrams for a quite specialised application [20]. The work of Waugh et al. is based on this approach but does not describe precisely how the method is working exactly [25]. Instead, different results of experiments with their system are presented [22]. Siepermann introduced the concept of graph covering [18]. A student's solution is automatically marked by covering the graphical model with correct parts of the reference solution and wrong parts of already marked students' solutions, so-called patterns. Not recognised parts of the student's solutions have to be corrected by instructors. Then, those parts can be used as part solutions during the marking of other student solutions. Thomas et al. also mentioned the usage of patterns [23]. Later, they switched from ER-diagrams to sequence diagrams [21]. Prados et al. do not use patterns but alternative reference solutions that are compared with the student's solution [14]. In Siepermann et al. model checking was used as an alternative method for the marking instead of graph covering [19].

The second stream of research concerns the database language SQL. After students have modelled their solutions, regardless if these are checked for syntax and semantics, the models are transformed via database language commands into a database. This can either be done automatically or must be done by students themselves in order to practice SQL. After that, students have to solve additional tasks to test their database design.

Because of the usual problems reported when teaching SQL, [6] several authors presented different teaching systems. Dekeyser et al. and Cigas and Kushan give an overview of most of the systems [4, 6].

Dietrich et al. developed the tool WinRDBI [7]. It is a standalone application that has to be installed on a computer. Students can practice with predefined databases by executing their own SQL commands. WinRDBI visualises the data schemata and data sets and returns the results of the SQL commands executed.

Kearns et al. introduced esql [10]. Even if esql provides a complete database to students where the typical commands can be executed, the system focuses on the explanation and visualisation how the SELECT command works. Kearns et al. developed a sophisticated algorithm that shows step by step how a user defined SELECT command is executed by a database.

SQLT-Web is the web based version of SQL-Tutor [12, 13]. Both systems focus on the feedback task. They provide exercises that have to be solved by students. The student's SQL commands are parsed and analysed syntactically and with limitations also semantically. The analysis is based on more than 600 rules that are problem independent but use a reference solution that solves the exercise correctly. With the help of the reference solution, the system gives hints to students what they did wrong or what is still missing.

The tools SQLator [17] and AsseSQL [15] do qualitatively the same. Both systems provide exercises to students. The students' solutions are then tested against the normal database and a second test database that is not visible to students. If the output of the students' solutions and of the reference solution equal, one can usually assume that the exercise was solved correctly. Sadiq et al. report a rate of 95% of successful evaluations [17]. Dekeyser et al. enlarge this approach with their tool SQLify [6]. In addition to the heuristic of SQLator and AsseSQL, they use the fact that in the class of conjunctive queries it is possible to decide whether two queries are equivalent.

Grillenberger and Brinda developed eledSQL, a system especially designed for secondary school level [9]. They criticise that the existing systems are pure learning environments that mostly provide predefined and unchangeable databases but neglect the need of working with databases. They claim the need of different roles for teachers and pupils that functions can be turned on and off, that the system must be adoptable to a schools requirements etc.

Brusilovsky et al. as well as Brusilovsky et al. focus on the integration of different learning systems into one platform [1, 2]. One part of their open platform is SQL-Knot that generates different exercises based on predefined databases and templates individually for each student. The student's solution is then tested as in SQLator and AsseSQL.

The aforementioned tools are of great help for online learning and providing learning environments to students when teaching database modelling or SQL. However, they do not connect these two separate tasks. The database design process is regarded apart from SQL and vice versa. The game based system that we introduce in the next sections provides this link between the process of designing a database and using it. Here, students cannot only try if their SQL commands work, they can also experience if their database designs is good or bears some issues that they still have to solve.

3   Database Modelling, SQL and E-Learning

The main purpose of graphical modelling techniques is to formalise given facts of the real world by using graphical symbols with fixed meanings with respect to a fixed number of modelling rules that depend on the modelling technique used that is used.

The modelling is done with regard to certain objectives. In the case of database modelling, the purpose is to structure the information that should be worked with and have to be stored in an IS. Depending on the application, the informational objects have to be identified and characterised by their properties. In addition, the relations between the objects have to be defined [5, 16]. There exist several graphical modelling techniques that can be used to define a data schema. The most popular one is the Entity Relationship Model (ERM) introduced by Chen [3]. Also class diagrams of the Unified Modelling Language can be used or the Structured Entity Relationship Model of Ferstl and Sinz [8], a further development of the ERM. What modelling technique ever is used, when teaching and practising database design, two questions have to be answered:

1. Is the use of the modelling technique correct?
2. Does the student solution meet all requirements in content?

The first question deals with the syntax of the modelling technique. The syntax of a modelling technique is based on simple rules. For example, when using the ERM, two different entity types are not allowed to be connected via edges, they can only be adjacent to a relationship type with which the relation between the entity types can be modelled and stored in the database. Such modelling rules concern graph theory and can usually be checked with a simple depth first search [18].

The second question deals with the semantics of the student's solution. That means does the solution comprise every fact that is given within the task description or does it neglect some facts? These questions are quite difficult to be checked automatically because even for human instructors it is often quite difficult to interpret the meaning of a student's solution. Approaches to cope with this problem are introduced in [14, 18–23, 25]. In addition, these approaches also try to check another requirement of DBD:

3. The smartness of a solution.

Even if syntax and semantics are correct and the model leads to correct results the modelling of a solution may contain faults. These faults usually concern the flexibility and practical use of a solution. The database schema should be as precise as possible so that anomalies during the operation time are suspended ex ante and as flexible as possible so that the IS is prepared for new requirements in the future. Information should not be stored redundantly as long as the advantages do not outweigh its disadvantages, e.g. when inserting, updating, or deleting a data set this usually should not be done twice or more but aggregated data that are often used should be stored separately so that it does not have to be calculated each time that it is requested [5, 16]. Thus, two solutions may serve a given purpose equally well, but one solution is more flexible and more general than the other. Therefore, the more flexible and more general solution is to be preferred.

The balancing of these different aspects usually requires experience acquired by working with IS and cannot be taught using solely paper and pencil. Students must practice with databases using real life problems to learn how to find a balance between redundancy and data parsimony, flexibility and accuracy etc. But existing ITS usually just check the syntax of a student's solution and to a certain degree the semantics. Then, the student is told what was done correctly and where there are mistakes in the solution.

In this paper, the syntax and semantics checks are also provided, but in addition, we go a step further. The game based ITS at hand let students work with their solutions so that they can experience what is solved well and what is solved badly and has to be improved. This must be done using the database language SQL.

4   The Database Game Concept

In the game, the user (he in the following) takes the role of a database engineer. In the first step, the user can choose between different orders that he can fill. The number of orders is not fixed but can be extended gradually by instructors. The difficulty level of an order depends on the database that has to be designed and the supporting tools that can be used within the order. If he accepts an order, he is contracted to design, construct and administer the database of a new IS for his customer (she in the following). Depending on the difficulty level, he can earn more or less virtual money. Each order consists of several tasks. Once the user accepts an order, he is obliged to fulfil the different tasks of the order within a given time. If he fails to do so, he must pay a virtual contract penalty. If he succeeds, he will be credited depending on the quality of his solution.

The first task of each order is to design the conceptual database schema with the use of a database model. The user gets a description of the IS that has to be designed. All necessary information are given in the description. With the help of these information, the user models the database schema. Figure 1 depicts the user interface for this task.

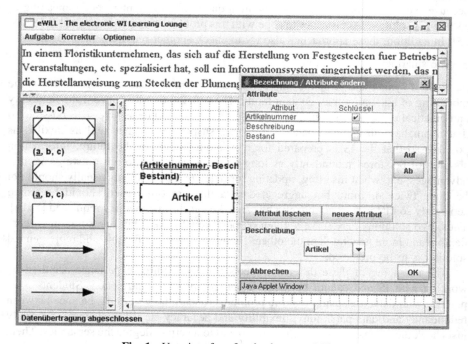

Fig. 1. User interface for database modelling

Depending on the game mode, the first task is finished after modelling the database schema or there are several supporting tools that can be used to check the user's solution. The syntax checker checks if the database schema that was modelled violates any modelling rule. If so, any mistake is listed and the user can correct his database schema. The semantic checker tries to verify if the database schema meets all requirements concerning the content. (The functioning of this check is described in Sect. 5.) Again, the user can correct potential issues by changing his solution.

The second task is to implement the database according to the database schema using SQL. Again depending on the game mode, this can either be done automatically by the system, then the user has nothing to do, or he has to do the SQL commands himself. If the latter one, there are potentially differences between the database schema and the database definition done with SQL. To find these differences, the user can use the definition checker that finds and lists all mistakes that the user made when converting the database schema into the database. Again, the user can correct his SQL commands according to the report of the definition checker.

The third task consists in filling the database with data sets and working with the data stored in the database. During this task, the user has to fulfil several sub-tasks like placing orders, invoicing etc. For this, he has to store data in the database that he created, update or delete some data. If he is not able to accomplish these tasks, there may be two reasons:

1. His knowledge of SQL is not good enough.
2. The database he created has some issues that do not allow for storing these data.

In the first case, he will not get the full amount of virtual money that can be earned. In the second case, he can step back to the first task and redesign the database by changing the database schema in order to improve the IS. If he accomplishes all tasks correctly in the given time, he gets the full amount of virtual money that can be earned. For each (sub-)task that was not solved, the earned sum is reduced.

In addition to the operational tasks, new requirements and extensions to the database must be implemented to test the flexibility of the student's solution. If his current solution does not allow simple modifications or extensions, he has to reiterate the DBD phase. In the worst case, he has to re-perform already solved daily tasks because he had to redesign his schema so that old data must be reorganised.

Each time, the user has to step back into the modelling phase and redesign parts of his schema, he is charged with additional costs (e.g. for his employees) so that his revenue will be reduced. The same applies if the user uses the different supporting tools (syntax checker, definition checker, etc.) provided by the system.

5   Marking and Grading

The main problem for the definition of orders is to define what is a correct solution concerning the database schema in the first task. In order that the system can mark and grade a solution, it must be able to judge if parts of a user's solution are correct or wrong. For this, the system uses the approach of graph covering [18]. Graph covering is based on a reference solution (RS) that contains all elements that have to be modelled within the database schema. Usually, there is not always only one correct solution but several ones that can be qualitatively worth the same. In addition, the alternative solution may qualitatively differ. For this, the best reference solution is divided into different parts so-called patterns. These patterns together build a feasible correct solution. Let us assume that there is another correct solution (AS) that differs in some parts from the initial reference solution. One difference may concern one pattern of the reference solution or several patterns. If only one pattern P is affected, the part of the alternative solution AS that is different from RS defines a new pattern AP that can be used alternatively to P and is inserted into the set of patterns as an alternative pattern. Let $P_1, \ldots, P_n$ be the patterns of RS that are affected by one part of the alternative solution. Then, this affecting part is divided into n patterns $AP_1, \ldots, AP_n$ such that any AP_i affects only one pattern P_i of the reference solution. The new patterns are then inserted into the number of patterns of the reference solution as alternative pattern. Figure 2 shows how the reference solution is extended by an alternative solution (less valuable) and how old patterns are divided into several new patterns.

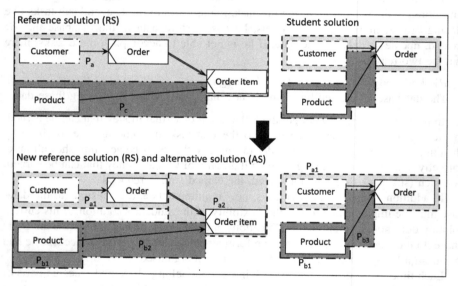

Fig. 2. Extension of reference solution and pattern representation

With the help of these patterns, the solution of a user can be covered. If a user's solution cannot be covered completely, an instructor must mark the parts that are not recognised as correct or incorrect. These parts are then inserted into the set of patterns. As we can see, the reference solution does not only consist of one best solution but of many alternatives. In addition, also wrong patterns are part of the reference solution so that wrong parts of the user's solution can easily be identified and marked. Each pattern can be weighted such that it corresponds to coins of the virtual money that can be earned. If the alternative solution is qualitatively not the same, its patterns have less weight than the patterns of the best alternative of the reference solution.

The second problem that occurs during modelling is the definition and recognition of properties. Usually, many synonyms exist that can be used as captions so that it can be quite difficult to judge if the user's solution contains all information. Several solutions for this problem are conceivable. In the system described here, a user cannot choose his own captions but only captions provided in a list of possible captions. This list may contain synonyms or useless captions but should contain any caption that is necessary. Usually, all meaningful words of the order description are provided as captions.

The third problem concerns the recognition if the user has transformed his database schema correctly into SQL commands. This can easily be done by comparing the tables that he created with the tables that must be created when automatically deriving the database from the user's database schema.

The fourth problem concerns the SQL tasks that the user has to perform. For this, all user commands are recorded. If data sets should be inserted into the database, it is easy to check if the user's commands contain any information provided. If data sets shall be deleted, it can easily be checked how many tables are used and if this corresponds with the correct solution. After execution of the user's deleting commands, the information that should be deleted should not exist in the database anymore. If data sets should be updated, it can be checked if the updated information is stored in the database or not.

As we can see, for any task that has to be fulfilled by the user, we can check if it was done correctly or not. Each task is associated with coins of the virtual money. If the task was done well, the user earns the according money. If the task was solved but alternative was less good than the optimal solution, the user is paid less according to the weight of the alternative solution. All users compete on a leaderboard showing how much they earned, differentiated after each order.

6 Conclusion

In this paper, we presented a game concept for teaching and practicing database engineering. The user takes the role of a database engineer who has to fill different orders. The game combines the tasks of database design, definition and operation. In the first step, the structure of the database must be designed resulting in a database schema. Then, this schema must be converted into a database. After this, several tasks have to be solved using SQL. When solving these tasks, users usually experience several issues with their database schema. Because of this, they can step back to the database design and resolve these issues.

The advantages of the system are obvious. Instead of focusing only on one task of database engineering at one time, now these tasks are combined such that students can really experience the consequences of their design decisions. If they do a careless design, they have to do much more work in later steps. If they thoroughly design their databases, only little must be done in later steps. If desired, a user gets feedback in each step of the design process. Students can practice when, where and how long they want to. This self steered learning is one of the most efficient ways of learning [11].

However, some limitations remain. First of all, the captions that can be used in the system for naming objects and properties are given in fixed list. Even if the list contains synonyms or captions that are traps, the list contains parts of the correct solution and therefore may reveal important information to users. Secondly, the database schema can sometimes be marked only with the help of a human instructor. This usually happens in the beginning after a new order was defined. The more students have filled the order, the more patterns are stored in the reference solution so that the automatic marking process needs a decreasingly number of instructor's interventions. However, to the best of our knowledge, there is no approach that can cope better with the problem of marking database schemata until now.

In the next steps, the list of predefined captions will be replaced by a phonetic comparison of student defined captions and the captions of pattern solutions. In addition, the SQL tasks will be completed by SELECT commands that are not implemented yet for an automatic marking and grading.

References

1. Brusilovsky, P., Sosnovsky, S., Lee, D.H., Yudelson, M., Zadorozhny, V., Zhou, X.: An open integrated exploratorium for database courses. ACM SIGCSE Bull. **40**(3), 22–26 (2008)
2. Brusilovsky, P., Sosnovsky, S., Yudelson, M.V., Lee, D.H., Zadorozhny, V., Zhou, X.: Learning SQL programming with interactive tools: from integration to personalization. ACM Trans. Comput. Educ. TOCE, **9**(4) (2010). Article 19
3. Chen, P.P.S.: The entity-relationship model—toward a unified view of data. ACM Trans. Database Syst. (TODS) **1**(1), 9–36 (1976)
4. Cigas, J., Kushan, B.: Experiences with online SQL environments. J. Comput. Sci. Coll. **25** (5), 251–257 (2010)
5. Date, C.J.: An Introduction to Database Systems, 8th edn. Addison-Wesley Educational Publishers Inc., Reading (2003)
6. Dekeyser, S., de Raadt, M., Lee, T.Y.: Computer assisted assessment of SQL query skills. In: Proceedings of the Eighteenth Conference on Australasian Database, vol. 63, pp. 53–62. Australian Computer Society Inc. (2007)
7. Dietrich, S.W., Eckert, E., Piscator, K.: WinRDBI: a windows-based relational database educational tool. ACM SIGCSE Bull. **29**(1), 126–130 (1997)
8. Ferstl, O.K., Sinz, E.J.: Grundlagen der Wirtschaftsinformatik. Band 1, 7. Aufl., De Gruyter Oldenbourg, München (2013)
9. Grillenberger, A. Brinda, T.: eledSQL: a new web-based learning environment for teaching databases and SQL at secondary school level. In: Proceedings of the 7th Workshop in Primary and Secondary Computing Education. ACM, pp. 101–104 (2012)
10. Kearns, R., Shead, S., Fekete, A.: A teaching system for SQL. In: Proceedings of the 2nd Australasian Conference on Computer Science Education, pp. 224–231. ACM (1997)
11. Kerres, M., Jechle, T.: Didaktische Konzeption des Telelernens. In: Issing, L.J., Klimsa, P. (eds.) Information und Lernen mit Multimedia und Internet, pp. 267–281. BeltzPVU, Weinheim (2002)
12. Mitrovic, A.: Learning SQL with a computerized tutor. ACM SIGCSE Bull. **30**(1), 307–311 (1998)

13. Mitrovic, A.: An intelligent SQL tutor on the web. Int. J. Artif. Intell. Educ. **13**(2), 173–197 (2003)
14. Prados, F., Boada, I., Soler, J., Poch, J.: A web-based tool for entity-relationship modeling. In: Gavrilova, M., Gervasi, O., Kumar, V., Tan, C.J.K., Taniar, D., Laganá, A., Mun, Y., Choo, H. (eds.) ICCSA 2006. LNCS, vol. 3980, pp. 364–372. Springer, Heidelberg (2006). doi:10.1007/11751540_39
15. Prior, J., Lister, R.: The backwash effect on SQL skills grading. In: Proceedings of ITiCSE 2004, Leeds, UK, pp. 32–36 (2004)
16. Rob, P., Coronel, C., Morris, S.: Database Systems - Design, Implementation, and Management, 10th edn. Cengage Learning, Boston (2012)
17. Sadiq, S., Orlowska, M., Sadiq, W., Lin, J.: SQLator: an online SQL learning workbench. ACM SIGCSE Bull. **36**(3), 223–227 (2004)
18. Siepermann, M.: Lecture accompanying E-learning exercises with automatic marking. In: Richards, G. (Ed.). Proceedings of E-Learn 2005, Chesapeake, USA, pp. 1750–1755 (2005)
19. Siepermann, M., Lackes, R., Börgermann, C.: Using model checking to automatically mark graphical E-learning exercises. In: Luca, J.; Weippl, E.R. (Eds.), Proceedings of ED-MEDIA 2008 World Conference on Educational Media, Multimedia, Hypermedia and Telecommunications, Chesapeake, pp. 5302–5307 (2008)
20. Thomas, P.: Grading diagrams automatically. Technical report, Computing Department, Open University, UK (2003)
21. Thomas, P., Smith, N., Waugh, K.: Automatic assessment of sequence diagrams. In: 12th International CAA Conference: Research into e-Assessment, Loughborough University, UK (2008)
22. Thomas, P., Waugh, K., Smith, N.: Experiments in the automatic marking of ERDiagrams. In: 10th Annual Conference on Innovation and Technology in Computer Science Education, Monte de Caparica, Portugal, pp. 27–29 (2005)
23. Thomas, P., Waugh, K., Smith, N.: Using patterns in the automatic marking of ERDiagrams. In: 11th Annual Conference on Innovation and Technology in Computer Science Education, Bologna, Italy, pp. 26–28 (2006)
24. Tsintsifas, A.: A framework for the computer based assessment of diagram based coursework. Doctoral thesis, Nottingham (2002). http://www.cs.nott.ac.uk/~cah/pdf/azt-phd.pdf
25. Waugh, K., Thomas, P., Smith, N.: Toward the automated assessment of entity-relationship diagrams. In: Second Workshop of the Learning and Teaching Support Network - Information and Computer Science) TLAD (Teaching, Learning and Assessment of Databases), Edinburgh, Scotland (2004)

Games and Health

Effects of a 3D Virtual Reality Neurofeedback Scenario on User Experience and Performance in Stroke Patients

Silvia Erika Kober[1,2(✉)], Johanna Louise Reichert[1,2],
Daniela Schweiger[1], Christa Neuper[1,2,3], and Guilherme Wood[1,2]

[1] Department of Psychology, University of Graz,
Universitaetsplatz 2/III, 8010 Graz, Austria
{silvia.kober,johanna.reichert,daniela.hofer,
christa.neuper,guilherme.wood}@uni-graz.at
[2] BioTechMed-Graz, Krenngasse 37/1, 8010 Graz, Austria
[3] Laboratory of Brain-Computer Interfaces, Institute of Neural Engineering,
Graz University of Technology, Stremayrgasse 16/IV, 8010 Graz, Austria

Abstract. Learning to control one's own brain activity using neurofeedback can cause cognitive and behavioral improvements in healthy individuals and neurological patients. However, little is known about the impact of feedback design. Therefore, we investigated the effects of traditional two-dimensional and three-dimensional virtual reality based feedback modules on training performance and user experience in stroke patients. Neurofeedback performance was comparable between conditions. Interest, perceived feeling of control, and motivation were higher in patients using the virtual reality application compared to the two-dimensional feedback condition. In contrary, patients who performed the virtual reality training showed higher values in incompetence fear and lower values in mastery confidence compared to the traditional training group. These results indicate that neurofeedback can be improved with the implementation of virtual reality scenarios, especially with regard to patients' interest and motivation. However, stroke patients might be more skeptical concerning virtual reality technique and less self-confident in using it.

1 Introduction

Neurofeedback (NF) is a modality of biofeedback in which voluntary control over one's own brain activity can be learned by means of real-time feedback of specific neuronal responses, leading to cognitive as well as behavioral improvements [1]. In such applications, healthy, age appropriate brain activity is rewarded with visual, auditory or even tactile stimulation while undesirable patterns of activity are ignored or even punished. Brain activity is recorded for instance by using the electroencephalogram (EEG), relevant features of the neurophysiological signal are extracted in real-time (e.g. specific EEG oscillations) and translated online into an output signal (visual/auditory feedback) that is fed back to the participants to alter the targeted brain activity as required. There is evidence that NF can be used as neurological rehabilitation tool to improve cognitive functions after brain lesions, e.g. stroke [2–4], by

© Springer International Publishing AG 2016
R. Bottino et al. (Eds.): GALA 2016, LNCS 10056, pp. 83–94, 2016.
DOI: 10.1007/978-3-319-50182-6_8

directly modulating brain activation patterns underlying cognitive functions. However, to obtain cognitive or behavioral improvements, a large number of repeated NF training sessions are mandatory. Depending on the target behavior or cognitive function, up to 50 training sessions with a duration of 30-50 min each are recommended to achieve significant improvements [5–8]. Such a high number of repeated NF training sessions can make NF users bored and tired, and even result in high costs [5]. Furthermore, successful NF performance requires top-down cognitive control [9–13], so that the user can stay focused and concentrated on the NF task over a long training period. In this context, the feedback modality might play an important role. Generally, auditory (e.g. a tone changes its volume or pitch in dependence on the brain activity level) and/or two-dimensional (2D) visual (e.g. simple bars or circles increase/decrease in size in dependence on the brain activity level) feedback is provided to the participants. Such monotonous feedback methods might not attract users to focus on them [14], leading to decreased motivation, interest, concentration, and finally to a lower NF performance and success rate [15]. Therefore, in the present study we investigated whether a three-dimensional (3D) virtual reality (VR) based NF training scenario might increase user experience and psychological factors such as motivation, mood, concentration, interest, feeling of control, anxiety, probability of success, or challenge as well as NF training performance compared to more traditional 2D feedback modalities. Some prior NF training studies used 2D game-like feedback displays to increase the level of interest and motivation during repeated NF training sessions (e.g. pacman-like game scenarios, flying space ships, soccer applications, [8, 14, 16–18]). A few brain-computer interface (BCI) studies classified brain activation patterns during mental imagery to control VR scenarios [19–22]. There are also studies comparing the effects of VR based NF training with traditional 2D feedback screens [5, 14, 23–25]. However, effects of these game or VR scenarios on user experience, psychological variables and training performance have not been evaluated in more detail before.

Generally, the purpose of using VR in neurorehabilitation is to construct a virtual environment with natural interactivity and to create a real sensation from multi-modality, tailored for the individual needs of neurological patients [26]. 3D VR is much more attractive and interesting than most 2D environments [27]. Virtual rehabilitation can spur patients' motivation, especially in connection with video game-based therapeutic approaches [28]. However, the clinical acceptance of virtual rehabilitation is low since studies examining the medical efficacy and comparability with classical rehabilitation approaches are lacking [28]. Additionally, some kind of technology gap, which is strongly pronounced in older people, increases resistance to computer based applications. Older individuals are generally not familiar with computer technology [29]. In some cases, interacting in VR can cause side-effects including ocular problems, disorientation, and nausea, which is called simulator sickness or cybersickness. About 25% of participants interacting in VR report such sickness symptoms, which can potentially confound data [30].

Rehabilitation scenarios using VR technology might directly impact brain structures, which are affected by stroke [31]. In this context, several VR systems have been developed and evaluated for the rehabilitation of motor deficits following stroke, with particular emphasis on the rehabilitation of the upper extremities. These studies demonstrated the potential of engaging stroke patients in task-oriented neuromotor rehabilitation. Virtual limbs are used since there is evidence that movement observation also affects motor areas in the brain by recruiting the mirror neuron system probably boosting the rehabilitation success [32–34].

In the case of neurofeedback, where users learn to modulate their own brain activation in a desired direction, depicting changes in brain activity is not as intuitive as limb movements, since brain activity is generally not consciously perceived. There are somatic receptors, which convey information on the hemodynamic brain activity in specific brain regions to associative learning systems. But there are no somatic receptors to register the electrical brain activity as measured by the EEG. Hence, VR can be used to provide the NF user with explanatory feedback, informing the user about what is going on in his/her brain, as well as with engaging and entertaining feedback [24]. In our first approach, we decided to present a human body on the feedback screen, whose organs (brain, heart and vascular system) changed in appearance depending on the feedback training results. The virtual body provided an anatomically realistic visualization of the NF process. Successful EEG based NF training performance was rewarded by visual modulations of this human body. Hence, changes in the brain activity due to NF training could be illustrated directly to the participant by showing these changes in the virtual body. The direct illustration of electrophysiological changes in the brain due to NF training may lead to a better understanding of what is happening in the brain during NF training and might foster the training outcome. There are already some prior attempts to visualize the brain activity on 3D brain models used in BCI or NF studies [19, 24, 35, 36].

In the present study, we investigated the potential value of 3D VR based NF training in the context of neurological rehabilitation. We compared the effects of a traditional 2D feedback scenario with a 3D VR feedback scenario on (i) NF training performance as well as on (ii) user experience and psychological constructs such as training motivation, mood, interest, challenge, anxiety, mastery confidence, perceived control and level of concentration during NF training in stroke patients.

2 Methods

2.1 Participants

We recruited $N = 9$ stroke patients with first-time stroke for this study. Table 1 summarizes patient specific data. Seven patients performed a traditional 2D NF training (vertically moving bars) during their stationary stay in a rehabilitation clinic and formed the 2D control group (CG). Two patients (patient A and B) performed the 3D VR based NF training. These patients were outpatients and performed the 3D VR based NF training in our lab at the University of Graz. Because of logistic issues it was not possible to assign patients randomly to the groups. Exclusion criteria were: drug treatment that interferes with the vigilance state, visual hemi-neglect, dementia (MMSE < 24, [37]), psychiatric disorders such as depression or anxiety, concomitant neurological disorders, e.g. Parkinson disease or visual-reflex epilepsy, aphasia, insufficient motivation and cooperation. Furthermore, all participants had normal or corrected-to-normal vision and hearing. The study was approved by the local ethics committee of the University of Graz and was in line with the code of ethics of the World Medical Association, Declaration of Helsinki.

2.2 Neurofeedback

For the NF training the EEG signal was recorded using a 10-channel amplifier (NeXus-10 MKII, Mind Media BV) with a sampling frequency of 256 Hz, the ground was located at the right mastoid, the reference was placed at the left mastoid. Patients performed up to ten NF training sessions on different days three to five times per week. The number of training session per patient can be found in Table 1. One NF training session lasted approximately 45 min and consisted of seven runs á 3 min each. The first run was a baseline run in which no real-time feedback was provided. In the consecutive six feedback runs patients got visual feedback about their EEG activity (either 2D or 3D). Three different feedback protocols were used in which patients should either learn to voluntarily increase their SMR (sensorimotor rhythm, 12–15 Hz) or UA activity (upper alpha, 2 Hz above the individual alpha frequency [38]), or they had to decrease their T/B ratio (theta 4–7 Hz/beta 13–21 Hz). Stroke patients were assigned to the different NF training protocols depending on their most prominent cognitive deficits as assessed before the start of the NF training [2, 3, 39]. There is evidence that the success in voluntarily modulating these different EEG frequency bands is comparable [2, 3]. Cz was used as feedback electrode for the SMR and T/B training, Pz was used for UA training.

Table 1. Patient description (Bt, bilateral; F, female; Lt, left; M, male; MMSE, mini-mental state examination; and Rt, right).

Code	Number of NF training sessions	Trained EEG frequency	Sex	Age	ICD-10 diagnosis	Lesion location	Time since onset (days)	MMSE
CG 1	5	SMR	M	48	I63.5	Rt arteria cerebri media	785	29
CG 2	10	T/B	F	49	I63.9	Bt arteria cerebri posterior, Medulla Oblongata, Cerebellum	2998	29
CG 3	10	T/B	M	62	I64	Rt arteria cerebri media, arteria cerebri posterior	847	29
CG 4	6	T/B	M	76	I63.5	Bt arteria cerebri media, arteria vertebralis	66	26
CG 5	10	T/B	M	67	I63.9	Rt occipital-parietal	2182	30
CG 6	10	T/B	F	37	I66.0	Rt arteria cerebri media	203	29
CG 7	10	T/B	M	63	I64	Rt arteria cerebri media	5025	30
Pat A	6	UA	M	73	I63.3	Lt arteria cerebri media	2111	29
Pat B	10	UA	F	52	I63.9	Brainstem	693	29

The traditional 2D visual feedback screen showed three vertically moving bars on a conventional computer screen [2, 3]. A larger bar in the middle of the screen changed its size depending on the EEG amplitude of the trained EEG frequency (either SMR, UA, or T/B, see Fig. 1). The patients' task was to move this bar in the desired direction (up for SMR and UA, down for T/B). Two further moving bars were placed on the left and on the right side of the screen, which should be kept as low as possible. These two bars were control bars that increased when ocular or movement artifacts were too strong. When patients were successful in voluntarily modulating the trained EEG frequency in the desired direction while keeping artifacts low, they got reward points indicated with a reward counter placed at the bottom of the screen and the moving bars changed their color from red to green.

To provide 3D visual feedback, a commercial BenQ 3D Vision stereoscopic 24" display was used. For the stereoscopic effect, a lightweight pair of stereoscopic glasses was used. On the 3D display, patients saw a virtual 3D semi-transparent stereoscopic render of a human body, which was developed with Unity3D and whose organs (brain, heart and vascular system) changed in appearance depending on the NF training results. Additionally, a lightbulb was included in the scene to reinforce the feedback effect. When patients successfully modulated the trained EEG frequencies while keeping artifacts low, the virtual brain was tinted green and the lightbulb got brighter. Otherwise the brain became red and the lightbulb darker. On the left lower corner of the feedback screen small moving bars could be additionally seen. During the training, a reward counter acting as a score (shown as a large number) increased when the goals of the training were achieved. Figure 1 illustrates example pictures of the 3D VR visual feedback during the baseline run and the feedback runs.

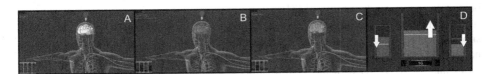

Fig. 1. Visual feedback screens. Virtual 3D semi-transparent stereoscopic render of a human body during the baseline run (A), and during the feedback runs while receiving positive (B) or negative (C) feedback. Traditional 2D visual feedback screen showing vertically moving bars (D). (Color figure online)

EEG data analysis was performed offline using the Brain Vision Analyzer software (version 2.01, Brain Products GmbH, Munich, Germany). Artefacts (e.g. eye blinks/movements, muscle activity) were rejected by means of a semi-automatic artefact rejection (criteria for rejection: >50.00 μV voltage step per sampling point, absolute voltage value $> \pm 100.00$ μV). To analyze the feedback training data, absolute power values of the trained EEG frequencies were extracted using the Brain Vision Analyzer's built-in method of complex demodulation, averaged separately for each 3-minute feedback run of each session, and z-transformed for better comparability between patients.

2.3   Questionnaires and Rating Scales

Mood and motivation of stroke patients were assessed during the NF training sessions (first, middle, and last NF training session) using a visual analogue scale (VAS) ranging from 0–100 and a standardized motivation questionnaire, the Questionnaire on Current Motivation (Fragebogen zur Erfassung Aktueller Motivation, FAM, [40]). The FAM uses 18 items to measure four motivational factors in either field or laboratory learning and achievement situations: *Incompetence Fear* (anxiety), *Mastery Confidence* (probability of success), *Interest*, and *Challenge*. Furthermore, each patient ranked his/her perceived control over the visual feedback and the subjective level of concentration during the NF training on a rating scale from 0 (= no control, bad concentration) to 10 (= high control, very good concentration).

The Simulator Sickness Questionnaire (SSQ) was used to determine whether patients using the VR NF paradigm experienced cybersickness symptoms [41]. The short SSQ was completed before and after each VR based NF training session.

2.4   Statistical Analysis

In order to analyze the NF training performance, we determined the time course of the trained EEG frequencies averaged over the NF training sessions across the six feedback runs using linear regression analysis. In addition, a one-sample t-test against 0 was calculated for the CG to verify the consistency of the learning effects. The slopes of the regression line of the single stroke patients that performed the 3D NF task were statistically compared to the slopes of the 2D CG by applying single-case analysis methods [42]. These methods enable the assessment of the probability that test scores and test score discrepancies of a single patient and a modest-sized control sample belong to the same distribution [43].

To analyze whether there is a significant change in motivation, mood, the FAM subscores, feeling of control, and level of concentration, as assessed with questionnaires and rating scales in the 2D control group, univariate repeated-measures analyses of variance (ANOVA) with the within-subjects factor session (first vs. middle vs. last NF training session) were calculated. Again, single case analysis methods [43] were used to compare the results of the single patients that performed the 3D NF task with the results of the 2D control group.

3   Results

3.1   Neurofeedback Performance

The 2D CG as well as the single stroke patients performing the 3D NF task showed a linear increase in the trained EEG frequency bands over the feedback runs, indicating successful NF training [44] (Fig. 2). The one-sample t-test revealed that the slopes of the CG significantly differed from zero ($p < 0.01$). All significance tests on differences between single patients' slopes and the control sample were not significant (all $p > 0.05$). Hence, the NF training performance was comparable in the 2D and 3D VR feedback condition.

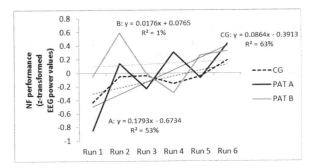

Fig. 2. Neurofeedback training performance. Time course of EEG feedback frequencies over the six NF training runs, averaged over all NF training sessions, presented separately for the 2D control group and patient A and B who performed the 3D VR NF training. The results of the regression analysis and the regression slopes are added as well. Note that the results of patients of the CG who performed the T/B NF training were inversely transformed.

3.2   Questionnaire and Rating Scale Data

When analyzing possible changes in the questionnaire and rating scale data of the 2D control group across the NF training course, the ANOVA models revealed a significant main effect of session ($F(2,12) = 13.0$, $p < 0.01$, $\eta^2 = 0.72$) for the FAM subscore *Mastery Confidence*. Posttests indicated that mastery confidence was significantly higher during the middle and last session compared to the first NF training session in the 2D control group (Table 2). Although the main effect of session slightly failed the significance level for the rating scale *Feeling of Control*, there was a trend showing an increasing level of feeling of control across the NF training sessions in the 2D control group (Table 2).

Single case analysis revealed that motivation was higher in patients performing the 3D NF task than in the 2D CG, although these differences were only statistically significant for patient B during the middle session. Patient B showed a significantly lower mood during the first session compared to the CG. The results of the FAM indicate that the patients who performed the 3D VR NF training showed higher values in *Incompetence Fear* and lower values in *Mastery Confidence* compared to the 2D patient CG. In contrary, *Interest* was higher in patients performing the 3D VR training compared to the 2D CG. No statistically significant differences in *Challenge* were observed. The perceived *Feeling of Control* was higher in patient A compared to the 2D control group, but lower in patient B. This is in line with the results of the NF training performance since patient A also showed descriptively a better NF performance than patient B. The *Concentration* level did not differ between participants (Table 2).

Patient A and B, who performed the 3D VR NF task, showed no cybersickness symptoms after the VR based NF training compared to the values before the start of the VR based NF training as assessed with the SSQ (Table 3).

Table 2. Results (means and SE) of questionnaire and rating scale data, presented separately for the 2D control group (CG) and patient A and B who performed the 3D NF scenario for the first, middle, and last NF training session. Significant differences between single cases and group data are marked with asterisks ($*p < 0.10$, $**p < 0.05$).

	2D CG			PAT A			PAT B		
	Means (SE)			Single raw values			Single raw values		
	First session	Middle session	Last session	First session	Middle session	Last session	First session	Middle session	Last session
Motivation (%)	78.8 (5.4)	76.1 (2.9)	65.5 (5.8)	89.0	85.0	87.0	76.0	89.0*	68.0
Mood (%)	70.6 (5.2)	63.8(10.2)	69.2 (6.7)	84.0	89.0	87.0	45.0*	68.0	45.0
Mastery confidence (raw score)	19.3 (1.1)	22.7 (1.1)	21.8 (1.7)	12.0**	15.0**	13.0*	13.0**	14.0**	21.0
Incompetence fear (raw score)	9.8 (1.4)	7.2 (0.7)	11.0 (2.2)	12.0	8.0	5.0	12.0	12.0**	26.0**
Interest (raw score)	27.0 (2.8)	25.7 (3.3)	25.8 (2.4)	26.0	34.0	35.0*	35.0	33.0	33.0
Challenge (raw score)	22.3 (1.8)	22.8 (1.7)	22.2 (2.0)	19.0	18.0	19.0	28.0	28.0	28.0
Feeling of control (raw score)	4.6 (1.0)	6.4 (0.8)	7.2 (0.4)	9.0*	10.0*	10.0**	3.0	7.0	7.0
Concentration (raw score)	7.4 (0.7)	7.4 (0.5)	8.7 (0.5)	9.0	9.0	10.0	5.0	7.0	7.0

Table 3. Results of the SSQ, assessed before (pre) and after (post) the first, middle, and last VR based NF training session, presented separately for patient A and B.

	PAT A						PAT B					
	First session pre	First session post	Middle session pre	Middle session post	Last session pre	Last session post	First session pre	First session post	Middle session pre	Middle session post	Last session pre	Last session post
Nausea	9.5	9.5	0.0	0.0	0.0	0.0	38.1	38.1	28.6	9.54	19.0	9.54
Oculo-motor problems	37.9	30.3	22.7	22.7	22.7	22.7	45.4	37.9	37.9	37.9	30.3	30.3
Disorientation	69.6	55.6	27.8	27.8	27.8	27.8	27.8	13.9	13.9	13.9	27.8	13.9
Total score	26.1	26.1	11.2	11.2	11.2	11.2	29.9	29.9	22.4	18.7	18.7	14.9

4   Discussion

In the present NF training study we examined the effects of traditional 2D visual feedback and 3D VR based visual feedback on the NF training performance and user experience in stroke patients. The NF training results were comparable between the two single patients receiving VR feedback and the 2D patient control group. The patients were able to linearly modulate the trained EEG frequencies in the desired direction. Hence, the VR interface did not improve the NF training performance compared to a traditional feedback modality. Prior NF training studies that investigated the effects of VR feedback scenarios on NF performance reported heterogeneous results [5, 14, 23–25]. Cho et al. (2004) and Gruzelier et al. (2010) found that NF training performance was by trend higher in 3D VR feedback conditions compared to simple 2D feedback [5, 23], while Mercier-Ganady et al. (2014) and Bayliss (2003) did not find any differences in performance between 2D and 3D conditions [24, 25]. Generally, it is assumed that VR approaches might spur motivation and interest especially when NF training has to be performed over a long training period (e.g., up to 50 training sessions), which might consequently affect the NF training performance [5, 28]. However, 3D VR feedback might be more complex than 2D feedback. Probably, users need more time to get used to the VR feedback and to understand how it works [24]. Consequently, a maximum of ten NF training sessions might not have been enough to reveal such positive effects of VR feedback on NF training performance. Unfortunately, in the present proof-of-concept study we were not able to perform more than ten NF sessions because patients at the clinic and outpatients were not available for longer time periods. Furthermore, differences in availability of patients were also the reason why not all patients performed ten NF sessions, which might have influenced the present findings.

In line with the literature, patients using the 3D VR NF model were more motivated during the training than the 2D patient control group. This indicates that new and innovative VR applications have the potential to attract and motivate users more than classical 2D feedback screens [14, 28].

The results of the FAM indicated that the patients who performed the VR training showed higher values in incompetence fear and lower values in mastery confidence compared to the 2D patient group. Patients who performed the more complex VR based training were probably more skeptical concerning the VR technique and less self-confident. Mercier-Ganady et al. (2014), who used an augmented reality paradigm, in which the own brain activity was processed in real-time and displayed on the mirrored head of the user, also compared NF training effects between this augmented reality scenario and a standard visualization (2D moving bars). Although the users particularly appreciated the innovation and originality of this novel augmented reality approach as assessed with questionnaires, participants rated the augmented reality condition as less simple and less clear [24]. In this context, there might be some kind of technology gap, which is generally stronger pronounced in older people, increasing resistance to or fear of computer based applications, especially of "unusual" computer techniques such as VR. Studies on people over 40 years old provide evidence that as age increases, attitudes toward computer technique tend to become more negative and increasing age is associated with increased computer anxiety. Older people have more negative emotional reactions to making errors using computers [45] and are generally not familiar with VR interfaces [29], which might explain the increased incompetence fear in stroke patients using the VR system compared to the 2D group. In contrary, interest and challenge were higher in patients performing the VR training compared to the 2D group. Hence, the VR application fostered to some extent the interest in the NF training and the challenge to perform well, which might increase adherence to the training. Yan et al. (2008) also investigated effects of VR based feedback scenarios. Although the authors did not directly assess the level of interest and motivation of the participants during VR based NF training, they mentioned that most of their participants admitted that VR was more interesting and attractive than traditional 2D graphical feedback presentations used in previous studies [14].

The perceived feeling of control was higher in patient A, who performed the 3D VR training, compared to the 2D group. This result goes along with the NF training performance of patient A, since he descriptively showed the best NF training performance.

Interacting with the VR feedback scenario led to no side effects such as cyber-sickness. Hence, the results were not confounded by sickness symptoms.

The small sample size, the fact that it was not possible to assign patients randomly to the groups and the differences in the number of training sessions are limitations of this proof-of-principle study.

Nevertheless, these preliminary results indicate that NF training modules can be improved by the implementation of VR scenarios, especially with regard to patients' interest and motivation, providing the user with explanatory and engaging feedback [24]. One has to keep in mind that VR technology might be more complex than traditional simpler feedback modalities, which might lead to incompetence fear and lower values in mastery confidence. This might be particularly the case for older individuals who are not used to such an advanced technology. Thus, it is essential to consider these factors when using VR based NF in neurorehabilitation.

Acknowledgments. This work was partially supported by the European STREP Program – Collaborative Project no. FP7-287320 – CONTRAST and by BioTechMed-Graz, Austria. Possible inaccuracies of information are under the responsibility of the project team. The text reflects solely the views of its authors. The European Commission is not liable for any use that may be made of the information contained therein. The authors are grateful to T-Systems ITC Iberia for technical support.

References

1. Gruzelier, J.H.: EEG-neurofeedback for optimising performance. I: a review of cognitive and affective outcome in healthy participants. Neurosci. Biobehav. Rev. **44**, 124–141 (2014)
2. Hofer, D., Kober, S.E., Reichert, J., Krenn, M., Farveleder, K., Grieshofer, P., Neuper, C., Wood, G.: Spezifische Effekte von EEG basiertem Neurofeedbacktraining auf kognitive Leistungen nach einem Schlaganfall. Ein nutzvolles Werkzeug für die Rehabilitation? Lernen und Lernstörungen **3**, 1–19 (2014)
3. Kober, S.E., Schweiger, D., Witte, M., Reichert, J.L., Grieshofer, P., Neuper, C., Wood, G.: Specific effects of EEG based neurofeedback training on memory functions in post-stroke victims. J. Neuroeng. Rehabil. **12**, 107 (2015)
4. Reichert, J.L., Kober, S.E., Schweiger, D., Grieshofer, P., Neuper, C., Wood, G.: shutting down sensorimotor interferences after stroke. a proof-of-principle SMR neurofeedback study. Front. Hum. Neurosci. **10**, 110 (2016)
5. Cho, B.-H., Kim, S., Shin, D.I., Lee, J.H., Lee, S.M., Kim, I.Y., Kim, S.I.: Neurofeedback training with virtual reality for inattention and impulsiveness. Cyberpsychol. Behav. **7**(5), 519–526 (2004). The Impact of the Internet, Multimedia and Virtual Reality on Behavior and Society
6. Arns, M., de Ridder, S., Strehl, U., Breteler, M., Coenen, T.: Efficacy of neurofeedback treatment in ADHD: the effects on inattention, impulsivity and hyperactivity: a meta-analysis. Clin. EEG Neurosci. **40**(3), 180–189 (2009)
7. Tan, G., Thornby, J., Hammond, D.C., Strehl, U., Canady, B., Arnemann, K., Kaiser, D.A.: Meta-analysis of EEG biofeedback in treating epilepsy. Clin. EEG Neurosci. **40**(3), 173–179 (2009)
8. Strehl, U. (ed.): Neurofeedback Theoretische Grundlagen - Praktisches Vorgehen - Wissenschaftliche Evidenz. Kohlhammer, Stuttgart (2013)

9. Ninaus, M., Kober, S., Witte, M., Koschutnig, K., Stangl, M., Neuper, C., Wood, G.: Neural substrates of cognitive control under the belief of getting neurofeedback training. Front. Hum. Neurosci. **7**(914), 1–10 (2013)

10. Ninaus, M., Kober, S., Witte, M., Koschutnig, K., Neuper, C., Wood, G.: Brain volumetry and self-regulation of brain activity relevant for neurofeedback. Biol. Psychol. **110**, 126–133 (2015)

11. Wood, G., Kober, S.E., Witte, M., Neuper, C.: On the need to better specify the concept of "control" in brain-computer-interfaces/neurofeedback research. Front. Syst. Neurosci. **8**, 171 (2014)

12. Emmert, K., Kopel, R., Sulzer, J., Brühl, A.B., Berman, B.D., Linden, D.E., Horovitz, S.G., Breimhorst, M., Caria, A., Frank, S., Johnston, S., Long, Z., Paret, C., Robineau, F., Veit, R., Bartsch, A., Beckmann, C.F., van de Ville, D., Haller, S.: Meta-analysis of real-time fMRI neurofeedback studies using individual participant data: How is brain regulation mediated? NeuroImage **124**, 806–812 (2016)

13. Gaume, A., Vialatte, A., Mora-Sánchez, A., Ramdani, C., Vialatte, F.B.: A psychoengineering paradigm for the neurocognitive mechanisms of biofeedback and neurofeedback. Neurosci. Biobehav. Rev. **68**, 891–910 (2016)

14. Yan, N., Wang, J., Liu, M., Zong, L., Jiao, Y., Yue, J., Lv, Y., Yang, Q., Lan, H., Liu, Z.: Designing a brain-computer interface device for neurofeedback using virtual environments. J. Med. Biol. Eng. **28**(3), 167–172 (2008)

15. Kleih, S., Nijboer, F., Halder, S., Kübler, A.: Motivation modulates the P300 amplitude during brain–computer interface use. Clin. Neurophysiol. **121**(7), 1023–1031 (2010)

16. Harris, K., Reid, D.: The influence of virtual reality play on children's motivation. Can. J. Occup. Ther. **72**(1), 21–29 (2005)

17. Benedetti, F., Catenacci Volpi, N., Parisi, L., Sartori, G.: Attention training with an easy–to–use brain computer interface. In: Shumaker, R., Lackey, S. (eds.) VAMR 2014. LNCS, vol. 8526, pp. 236–247. Springer, Heidelberg (2014). doi:10.1007/978-3-319-07464-1_22

18. Aart, J. v., Klaver, E., Bartneck, C., Feijs, L., Peters, P.: EEG headset for neurofeedback therapy - enabling easy use in the home environment. In: Proceedings of the Biosignals - International Conference on Bio-inspired Signals and Systems, Funchal, pp. 23–30 (2008)

19. Lécuyer, A., Lotte, F., Reilly, R.B., Leeb, R., Hirose, M., Slater, M.: Brain-computer interfaces, virtual reality, and videogames. Computer **41**(10), 66–72 (2008)

20. Ron-Angevin, R., Daz Estrella, A., Reyes-Lecuona, A.: Development of a brain-computer interface (BCI) based on virtual reality to improve training techniques. In: Applied Technologies in Medicine and Neuroscience, pp. 13–20 (2005)

21. Leeb, R., Lee, F., Keinrath, C., Scherer, R., Bischof, H., Pfurtscheller, G.: Brain-computer communication: motivation, aim, and impact of exploring a virtual apartment. IEEE Trans. Neural Syst. Rehabil. Eng. **15**(4), 473–482 (2007). A Publication of the IEEE Engineering in Medicine and Biology Society

22. Friedman, D., Leeb, R., Guger, C., Steed, A., Pfurtscheller, G., Slater, M.: Navigating virtual reality by thought: what is it like? presence Teleoper. Virtual Environ. **16**(1), 100–110 (2007)

23. Gruzelier, J., Inoue, A., Smart, R., Steed, A., Steffert, T.: Acting performance and flow state enhanced with sensory-motor rhythm neurofeedback comparing ecologically valid immersive VR and training screen scenarios. Neurosci. Lett. **480**(2), 112–116 (2010)

24. Mercier-Ganady, J., Lotte, F., Loup-Escande, E., Marchal, M., Lecuyer, A.: The Mind-Mirror: see your brain in action in your head using EEG and augmented reality. In: 2014 IEEE Virtual Reality (VR), Minneapolis, MN, USA, pp. 33–38 (2014)

25. Bayliss, J.D.: Use of the evoked potential P3 component for control in a virtual apartment. IEEE Trans. Neural Syst. Rehabil. Eng. **11**(2), 113–116 (2003). A Publication of the IEEE Engineering in Medicine and Biology Society

26. Rose, F.D., Brooks, B.M., Rizzo, A.A.: Virtual reality in brain damage rehabilitation: review. Cyberpsychol. Behav. **8**(3), 241–262 (2005). The Impact of the Internet, Multimedia and Virtual Reality on Behavior and Society

27. Marzbani, H., Marateb, H.R., Mansourian, M.: Neurofeedback: a comprehensive review on system design, methodology and clinical applications. Basic Clin. Neurosci. **7**(2), 143–158 (2016)

28. Burdea, G.: Virtual rehabilitation: benefits and challenges. Methods Inf. Med. **42**(5), 519–523 (2003)

29. Morganti, F.: Virtual interaction in cognitive neuropsychology. Stud. Health Technol. Inform. **99**, 55–70 (2004)

30. Brooks, J.O., Goodenough, R.R., Crisler, M.C., Klein, N.D., Alley, R.L., Koon, B.L., Logan Jr., W.C., Ogle, J.H., Tyrrell, R.A., Wills, R.F.: Simulator sickness during driving simulation studies. Accid. Anal. Prev. **42**(3), 788–796 (2010)

31. Cameirão, M., Bermúdezi Badia, S., Zimmerli, L., Oller, E.D., Verschure, P.: A virtual reality system for motor and cognitive neurorehabilitation. Chall. Assist. Technol. **20**, 393–397 (2007)

32. Rizzolatti, G., Craighero, L.: The mirror-neuron system. Annu. Rev. Neurosci. **27**, 169–192 (2004). doi:10.1146/annurev.neuro.27.070203.144230

33. Mulder, T.: Motor imagery and action observation: cognitive tools for rehabilitation. J. Neural Transm. **114**(10), 1265–1278 (2007)

34. Sollfrank, T., Hart, D., Goodsell, R., Foster, J., Tan, T.: 3D visualization of movements can amplify motor cortex activation during subsequent motor imagery. Front. Hum. Neurosci. **9**, 463 (2015)

35. Hwang, H.-J., Kwon, K., Im, C.-H.: Neurofeedback-based motor imagery training for brain–computer interface (BCI). J. Neurosci. Methods **179**(1), 150–156 (2009)

36. Arrouet, C., Congedo, M., Marvie, J.E., Lamarche, F., Lécuyer, A., Arnaldi, B.: Open-ViBE: a 3D platform for real-time neuroscience. J. Neurother. **9**(1), 3–25 (2005)

37. Kessler, J., Markowitsch, H.J., Denzler, P.: Mini Mental Status Examination MMSE. German Version. Beltz, Weinheim (1990)

38. Klimesch, W.: EEG alpha and theta oscillations reflect cognitive and memory performance: a review and analysis. Brain Res. Brain Res. Rev. **29**(2–3), 169–195 (1999)

39. Bounias, M., Laibow, R.E., Bonaly, A., Stubblebine, A.N.: EEG-neurobiofeedback treatment of patients with brain injury: part 1: typological classification of clinical syndromes. J. Neurother. **5**(4), 23–44 (2002)

40. Rheinberg, F., Vollmeyer, R., Burns, B.D.: FAM: Ein Fragebogen zur Erfassung aktuller Motivation in Lern- und Leistungssituationen. Diagnostica **47**(2), 57–66 (2001)

41. Kennedy, R.S., Lane, N.E., Berbaum, K.S., Lilienthal, M.G.: Simulator sickness questionnaire: an enhanced method for quantifying simulator sickness. Int. J. Aviat. Psychol. **3**(3), 203–220 (1993)

42. Crawford, J.R., Garthwaite, P.H.: Statistical methods for single-case studies in neuropsychology: comparing the slope of a patient's regression line with those of a control sample. Cortex **40** (3), 533–548 (2004). A Journal Devoted to the Study of the Nervous System and Behavior

43. Crawford, J., Garthwaite, P.H.: Investigation of the single case in neuropsychology: confidence limits on the abnormality of test scores and test score differences. Neuropsychologia **40**, 1196–1208 (2002)

44. Kober, S.E., Witte, M., Stangl, M., Valjamae, A., Neuper, C., Wood, G.: Shutting down sensorimotor interference unblocks the networks for stimulus processing: an SMR neurofeedback training study. Clin. Neurophysiol. **126**(1), 82–95 (2015)

45. Wagner, N., Hassanein, K., Head, M.: Computer use by older adults: a multi-disciplinary review. Comput. Hum. Behav. **26**(5), 870–882 (2010). Advancing Educational Research on Computer-supported Collaborative Learning (CSCL) through the use of gStudy CSCL Tools

Looking for Metacognition

A Knowledge Taxonomy for Psychotherapeutic Games

Priscilla Haring[1(✉)] and Harald Warmelink[2]

[1] Independent Media Psychologist, Witte de withstraat 20HS,
Amsterdam, The Netherlands
priscillaharing@hotmail.com
[2] HKU University of the Arts Utrecht,
Lange Viestraat 2b, Utrecht, The Netherlands
harald.warmelink@hku.nl

Abstract. Most of scientific literature on computer games aimed at offering or aiding in psychotherapy has little information on how the game exactly relates to the relatively recent development of the 'third wave' of behavioural psychotherapy, which includes metacognition. This paper first introduces metacognition and subsequently studies five cases of psychotherapeutic games (Personal Investigator, Treasure Hunt, Ricky and the Spider, Moodbot and SuperBetter) by looking at them through the lens of Blooms' Revised Taxonomy of Knowledge. The paper offers design recommendations for future (metacognitive) psychotherapeutic games.

1 Introduction

Over the past decade we have observed the emergence of a modest amount of psychotherapeutic games. With the term psychotherapeutic games, we refer to computer games aimed at offering or aiding in therapy for a range of psychological disorders or conditions (most often the precursors of e.g. depression or anxiety). The use of psychotherapeutic board games as well as existing, entertainment computer games during therapy is already widely regarded as good practice in many situations [1]. Innovative game- based therapy has shown a higher chance of engaging mostly younger target audiences than traditional conversational and 'paper-based' methods [2]. It is therefore surprising to find only a limited number of newly designed and researched psychotherapeutic games, at least in the scientific literature [2, 3].

Cognitive Behavioural Therapy (CBT) has advanced to what some call the 'third wave'. The first wave of therapy is attributed to the 1950s and applied classical conditioning and operant learning. The second wave applied information processing and brought CBT to its worldwide status. Currently, a third wave of psychotherapies is establishing itself which "… comprise a heterogeneous group of treatments, including acceptance and commitment treatment, behavioural activation, cognitive behavioural analysis system of psychotherapy, dialectical behavioural therapy, metacognitive therapy, mindfulness-based cognitive therapy and schema therapy." [4]. Such third wave therapies have already amassed enough evidence to be considered empirically

© Springer International Publishing AG 2016
R. Bottino et al. (Eds.): GALA 2016, LNCS 10056, pp. 95–106, 2016.
DOI: 10.1007/978-3-319-50182-6_9

supported [4]. This third wave builds upon the current research in psychology and reflects the changes and ongoing insights of the field, for example by building on the exploration of metacognition.

Our objective with this paper is to demonstrate that this 'third wave' is as yet a largely missed opportunity in most psychotherapeutic games, specifically looking at addressing metacognition. We will demonstrate this by analysing five psychotherapeutic games. These five games have been specifically selected, since they have been published about scientifically in sufficient detail for us to perform an analysis. In other words, given the limited amount of publications concerning psychotherapeutic games overall, these were the only five games for which we could find enough material to perform the analysis. We chose not to uphold any further case selection criteria. Doing so would not have served our objective. Moreover, having found only five games after quite an extensive literature search, we had to conclude that this is still a young field. Dismissing one or more games when the field is so young would more likely harm the field's development rather than stimulate it. Having said that, we acknowledge that we have not included psychotherapeutic Virtual Reality (VR) games [5, 6] in our analysis. Given the much more immersive and physical experience of VR, we feel that psychotherapeutic VR games are of a completely different genre and deserve an in-depth analysis in their own right, after which the results might still be compared to the ones presented here.

In the following section we first introduce metacognition and a knowledge taxonomy that provides an analytical framework with which we can offer brief case studies of the five games: Personal Investigator, Treasure Hunt, Ricky and the Spider, Moodbot and SuperBetter.

2 On Metacognition

Metacognition is often referred to as the 'thinking about thinking' level of cognition. Although a helpful intuitive concept, this definition falls somewhat short. "Metacognitive knowledge includes knowledge of general strategies that might be used for different tasks, knowledge of the conditions under which these strategies might be used, knowledge of the extent to which the strategies are effective, and knowledge of self" [7]. The process of achieving and adapting metacognitive knowledge is a constant feedback cycle [8]. Strategy selection and application of strategy is seen as part of metacognitive skills related to monitoring and control of ones' own cognition [7]. Training metacognitive skill in a therapeutic game environment should improve the awareness of this level of cognition and its' use.

The concept of metacognition as well as its emergence might be clarified by relating it to the Bloom's Taxonomy of knowledge. Bloom's original Taxonomy [9] stems from the field of education and consisted of categories for Knowledge, Comprehension, Application, Analysis, Synthesis and Evaluation. Research has since shown that students who are aware of their own thinking learn better [10]. Such research and other developments in the field of cognitive psychology has led to the Revised Blooms taxonomy [7]. This revised taxonomy differentiates between a

Knowledge dimension - which has the new subcategory of Metacognitive Knowledge - and the Cognitive Process dimension. Both dimensions have a hierarchical nature.

2.1   Blooms Revised Taxonomy

Knowledge dimension

1. Factual Knowledge - The basic elements that students must know to be acquainted with a discipline or solve problems in it.
   (a) Knowledge of terminology
   (b) Knowledge of specific details and elements
2. Conceptual Knowledge - The interrelationships among the basic elements within a larger structure that enable them to function together.
   (a) Knowledge of classifications and categories
   (b) Knowledge of principles and generalizations
   (c) Knowledge of theories, models, and structures
3. Procedural Knowledge - How to do something; methods of inquiry, and criteria for using skills, algorithms, techniques, and methods.
   (a) Knowledge of subject-specific skills and algorithms
   (b) Knowledge of subject-specific techniques and methods
   (c) Knowledge of criteria for determining when to use appropriate procedures
4. Metacognitive Knowledge - Knowledge of cognition in general as well as awareness and knowledge of one's own cognition.
   (a) Strategic knowledge
   (b) Knowledge about cognitive tasks, including appropriate contextual and conditional knowledge
   (c) Self-knowledge

Cognitive Process dimension

1. Remember - Retrieving (recognizing, recalling) relevant knowledge from long-term memory.
2. Understand - Determining (interpreting, exemplifying, classifying, summarizing, inferring, comparing, explaining) the meaning of instructional messages, including oral, written, and graphic communication.
3. Apply - Carrying out (executing) or using (implementing) a procedure in a given situation.
4. Analyse - Breaking material into its constituent parts and detecting how the parts relate to one another and to an overall structure or purpose (differentiating, organizing, attributing).
5. Evaluate - Making judgments (checking, critiquing) based on criteria and standards.

   Create - Putting elements together (generating, planning, producing) to form a novel, coherent whole or make an original product.

   Pintrich combines these two dimensions and all subcategories in a table that provides an overview to look at educational content [7]. In the remainder of this paper we offer brief case studies of five psychotherapeutic games. After these studies, we position the discussed specific therapeutic gameplay actions in Pintrich's table, thereby using the taxonomy as a lens to understand each game's therapeutic aspects.

3   Case #1: Personal Investigator

Personal Investigator is a game based on Solution Focused Therapy (SFT) and aimed at adolescent psychological patients. Coyle et al. [11] present SFT as 'a structured rather than a freeform therapeutic model', similar to CBT The game is meant to help adolescent patients go through five different conversational steps with their therapists. These five steps are translated into five main areas in the 3D game world, where the player interacts with non-playing characters. Initial trials proved promising, but further trials would be required to further test the game's validity [11].

The game is a single-player 3D computer game with role-playing characteristics. In the game the player becomes the personal investigator that 'hunts for solutions to personal problems', keeping a notebook along the way to keep a record of the hunt and the solutions found. It is played over roughly three therapy sessions, taking just over half of the one-hour session each time. During the sessions, the player plays the game on the computer, while the therapist observes and offers explanations if requested.

- *PI1: The Introduction Area - Setting Goals.* In this first area the player meets the principal of the Detective Academy, who guides the player through the first 'Setting Goals' conversational strategy. The player is then asked to identify the goals that lie underneath the problems he/she is facing. Which we identify as an *analysis* on a *conceptual knowledge* level. The player needs to be able to approach his/her situation as one in which different factors (event, personality traits) lead to a classification, i.e., a problem. Subsequently, this step requires the player to *create* new *conceptual knowledge*, i.e., the identification of the goals underlying the perceived problem.
- *PI2: The Evidence Area – Recognising Exceptions.* The player meets a forensic scientist who asks him/her to look back and identify times when his/her problem was less prevalent or non-existent, as well as what of his/her behaviour was different at the time and what goals could be set to repeat that behaviour more often, again an *analysis* on a *conceptual knowledge* level. The player needs to be able to look back in his/her life and frame situations as ones without the problem, mostly based on a difference in one main factor: his/her own behaviour. Subsequently, this step requires the player to again *create* new *conceptual knowledge*.
- *PI3: The Finding Clues Area – Coping.* The player meets a detective who asks him/her to write in the notebook about how he/she copes with difficult situations, encouraging to focus on the positive, active ways of coping that draw on his/her strengths and interests. Asking the player to *analyse* on a *procedural knowledge* level. He/she needs to be able to identify certain behaviour in the past as coping behaviour. Subsequently, he/she is asked to *analyse* on a more *conceptual knowledge* level, as the player reviews the list of coping and connects it to positive aspects of his/her personality.

- *PI4: The Backup Area – Identifying Resources.* The player meets a New York policeman who explains the need for backup when the police are in trouble. The policeman then asks the player to write down in his/her notebook who in his/her life could help out, and to think about his/her own internal strengths. In this step we argue that the patient is asked to first *remember* on a *factual knowledge* level, as the player will likely recall immediate acquaintances, friends, neighbours, family or colleagues. Then the player is asked to *understand* on a more *conceptual knowledge* level, as he/she needs to fathom his/her own strengths in relation to needing help.

- *PI5: The Detecting Solutions Area – The Miracle Question.* The player meets the final detective who poses the 'miracle question', 'Imagine you woke up tomorrow and the problem was solved, how would your life be different?', and asks him/her to depict the answer in the form of a simple drawing in the notebook. The detective also asks how close he/she is to achieving this future on a scale of 1 to 10, allowing the therapist to judge the confidence and optimism of the player. In this final step, the patient is clearly asked to *create* on a *conceptual knowledge* level and to *evaluate* this again a *conceptual knowledge* level.

4 Case #2: Treasure Hunt

Treasure Hunt is a game meant to support CBT for children with both internalizing (e.g. depression, anxiety) and externalizing (e.g. oppositional defiant disorder, conduct disorder) psychological disorders [2]. It specifically supports therapy 'by offering electronic homework assignments and rehearsing basic psychoeducational parts of treatment' [12]. Players experience the CBT support by going through six levels during gameplay, each corresponding to a certain step of the therapy. Again, initial tests proved promising, but further rigorous trials would be required to test the game's validity [12].

The game is a single-player, 2.5D adventure computer game on a old ship inhabited by Captain Jones, Felix the ship's cat and Polly the ship's parrot. The captain has found an old treasure map that he needs to decipher. The player helps by completing tasks to obtain sea stars, which will eventually allow him/her and the captain to read the map. Finally, after receiving a certificate signed by the captain and the therapist and summarizing what he/she has learnt, the player will find the treasure. The player plays one level per therapy session, lasting roughly 20 min.

As mentioned, the game consists of six levels (corresponding with six employed steps of CBT) that can be grouped into four types:

- *TH1: Thoughts, Feelings and Behaviour | Thoughts Influence our Feelings | Four Basic Feelings.* During the first three levels, the basic psychological foundations of CBT are laid out:
  - one's personality is made up of thoughts, feelings, and behaviour;
  - one's thoughts influence one's feelings;
  - four basic feelings can be distinguished, i.e., anger, fear, happiness and sadness. We argue that these three levels all ask the player to *understand factual* and *conceptual knowledge*.

- *TH2: Helpful and Unhelpful Thoughts.* During the fourth level the game helps the player understand that there are helpful and unhelpful thoughts, both in general and specific to the player him-/herself. Again the player is asked to *understand conceptual knowledge*, but the player is also asked to *analyse* on a *conceptual knowledge* level, when he/she is asked to think of his/her own specific helpful and unhelpful thoughts.
- *TH3: Chasing Away Unhelpful Thoughts, Replacing them with Helpful Ones.* During the fifth level the game demonstrates the cognitive exercise of identifying unhelpful thoughts and conceptualizing helpful thoughts. This level essentially asks the player to *apply procedural knowledge*.
- *TH4: Recapitulation.* During the sixth and final level, all previous exercises are revisited. As a recapitulation, this level is purely repeating what has been covered. Thus the player is only asked to recall or *remember* all the *factual, conceptual* and *procedural knowledge* covered in the previous levels.

5   Case #3: Ricky and the Spider

Ricky and the Spider is a game based on CBT for treating obsessive compulsive disorder (OCD) amongst children. Brezinka presents the game as 'not a self-help game' but one that 'should be played under the guidance of a therapist' [13]. The game's design foundation is a 'child-friendly metaphor' for understanding both OCD and the CBT approach, thereby combining 'psycho-education, externalizing techniques and exposure with response prevention'. Players experience the therapy by going through eight levels during gameplay. Data gathered from therapists and patients who purchased the game revealed promising results, but further, rigorous trials would be required to test the game's validity more convincingly [13].

The game is a single-player, 3D adventure computer game. In the game the player is confronted by Ricky the Grasshopper and Lisa the Ladybug who (without saying it explicitly) suffer from OCD and need to confront The Spider who has been making demands that they cannot meet. They ask Dr. Owl for advice, who in turn requires the player's help. In eight levels of gameplay in which Dr. Owl, Ricky and/or Lisa explain certain theories and tools and give certain tasks that the player must apply and fulfil. The first four levels are all psycho-educational. The latter four levels are focused on exposure tasks that are called 'courage tasks' in the game. With the therapist observing, the player plays one level at the beginning of a therapy session, which takes approximately 15 min, and recounts the content of the level after which the therapy session continues from there.

As mentioned, the game counts eight different levels that represent in total four different kinds of steps in the CBT approach for OCD treatment:

- *RS1: Subtle Beginnings of OCD & Thought Filter.* In the first level, Ricky and Lisa explain the subtle beginnings of their disorder and how they follow the Spider's orders because of their fear of the Spider. Ricky explains that his OCD is getting worse and that he needs help from Dr. Owl. Dr. Owl explains peoples' streams of thoughts which follows an established cognitive model of OCD. 'In our stream of thoughts, there is a thought filter that prevents absurd thoughts from passing through. Unfortunately, the Spider has damaged Ricky's and Lisa's thought filters and they are aware of every absurd thought, while others can ignore them' [13]. Clearly the player is asked in these two levels to *understand conceptual knowledge*.

- *RS2: Tools that help fight OCD, Externalizing Strategies.* In the third level, Dr. Owl presents a four-leaf clover representing four strategies to fight against the Spider: being kind to oneself, the courage to change, patience and a helper. Subsequently, Dr. Owl encourages the player to come up with silly nicknames for the Spider. In this level, the player is asked to do multiple things. First, he/she is asked to *understand* mostly *procedural knowledge*, in this case concerning four strategies for confronting demands that the player cannot or should not fulfil. Second, he/she is asked to *analyse, evaluate,* but mostly *create conceptual knowledge*, by conjuring up silly nicknames. then evaluates its silliness.

- *RS3: Creating the Compulsion Map.* In the fourth level, Ricky and Lisa gather the Spider's demands and rate the difficulty of not obeying them on a scale of 1 to 10. Since they need courage to not obey these demands, they call the tasks 'courage tasks', forming together a compulsion map. Subsequently, the player needs to make his/her own compulsion map of courage tasks. Here the player is asked to *evaluate procedural knowledge*, since the act of not obeying a demand is evaluated on its difficulty.

- *RS4: Exposure Tasks.* In the fifth level, Dr. Owl helps Ricky and Lisa to simplify some of the courage tasks and instructs them to carry out the easiest one. While Lisa is eager to try, Ricky is more hesitant to follow. Dr. Owl then encourages the player to find his/her easiest courage task and practice doing it several times each day. In the next two levels, first Lisa gets additional courage tasks and then Ricky gets more as well. They are encouraged to not give up and not put off doing the courage tasks, though warned by Dr. Owl not to rush ahead before having mastered the previous courage task. Here the player is asked to *apply* and *evaluate procedural knowledge*. After all, the courage tasks are being applied, while the player regularly needs to evaluate whether that courage task is being applied well and whether it is time to pick up another one.

6   Case #4: Moodbot

Moodbot is a game for adult psychological patients recovering from conditions such as psychosis and attempts to prevent them from relapsing [14]. As such the game is not tied to a single form of psychotherapy, but is a more general psychotherapeutic aid. As a relapse prevention aid, the game is based on two assumptions. The first is that 'communication between a patient and his/her healthcare worker about the patients' mental state is important for the patient's path towards recovery'. The second is that patients exhibit various, unique signs that indicate whether they are likely to relapse that need to be recorded in so-called 'alert schemes' so that they may be used to help prevent relapse. Moodbot is therefore primarily a way of identifying and communicating mental states and any indicative signs from a patient to his/her therapist between therapy sessions. The game is apparently being trialled in professional psychothera-peutic practice. As yet, there is no further information available to ascertain the game's validity.

The game is an online, multiplayer 2D computer game, although the interaction with other players is indirect (similar to well-known online, social games such as FarmVille). In the game the player is on board a highly imaginative ship (a large fish) and has to help keep it moving and steer it towards certain islands [15, 16]. The player can overview all the rooms of the ship and visit individual rooms where he/she can perform specific actions that might earn him/her points ('dustbunnies') that can be spent to get the ship moving and to steer it towards an island. The game is played daily for approximately five to ten minutes per day [14]. In doing so the player offers daily updates of his/her mental state as well as signs that could be indicative of a relapse that the therapist can access in a backend interface at any time.

In Moodbot players have several activities that they can choose to perform at any time:

- *MB1: Mood Expressions.* Players can express how they feel that day in three different ways:
  - by adjusting their 'moodbot', which is a robot that lives in their own room onboard the ship. The moodbot's facial expression and posture can be adjusted, and players can type in a short text that the moodbot then expresses;
  - by adjusting the wallpaper and background music of their 'moodtube', basically a television that offers a small set of pictures and music samples from which to choose;
  - by setting sliders that have been pre-defined with their therapists based on their personal goals and alert schemes (e.g. level of tiredness, fear or aggression).

  Doing this the player is asked to first *evaluate factual knowledge*, i.e., what the player is actually feeling. Subsequently, the player needs to *evaluate* and *create procedural knowledge*, i.e., he/she needs to evaluate what available manners of expression in Moodbot are suitable in order to express him-/herself.
- *MB2: Helping Others.* Players can visit each other's rooms and leave advice or tips if they see the moodbots suggesting a negative feeling with its facial expression and posture. Here the player is asked to *evaluate* and *create conceptual* and/or *proce-dural knowledge*, depending on whether the player will leave knowledge on the other patient's emotional state or actual practical tips or techniques.
- *MB3: Challenges.* Players are offered a number of real-world challenges related to their own personal, positive coping styles, defined by the therapist. After com-pleting a certain amount of challenges (and after three of the player's supervisors have checked each challenge completion) players will have grown a plant that they can plant on an island that they can visit. Here the player is clearly asked to *evaluate* and *apply procedural knowledge*.
- *MB4: Spending Action Points.* Players gain action points with all of the above activities. These can be spent in different rooms of the ship to make it go forward or change its direction, thereby providing the opportunity to visit specific islands. This action is purely an extrinsic motivation for the other actions. Hence interpreting it cognitively using our analytical framework serves no purpose.

7   Case #5: SuperBetter App

Superbetter is a game (or gamified platform) that is available as a web-based tool and an app for mobile devices. It appropriates game mechanics in order to provide a new narrative for accomplishing challenging health and wellbeing related goals [17]. Superbetter is not specifically designed as a psychotherapeutic game. However, in a random controlled trial Superbetter proved itself effective on decreasing depressive symptoms in comparison with a waitlist group [18].

In Superbetter players give themselves a superhero-secret-identity based on their 'favourite heroes'. Players then select a goal to work toward and are awarded 'resilience points' throughout the game (physical, mental, emotional and social resilience) and level up. Gameplay ends when the goal is achieved and can be continued by setting new goals. Players can take steps towards achieving their goal by performing Quests; actions that share a common theme. Superbetter has predetermined Quests that players can select, or design their own or select Quests designed by other players. Players can also undertake mood-enhancing activities (power-ups), which are simple and instantly possible actions such as drinking a glass of water or hugging yourself. The platform provides Bad guys to battle. These Bad guys belong to certain Quests or can be copied from other players or designed by the player. Finally, players gather social support (invite allies). Players can invite friends through the Superbetter platform to help them. Superbetter offers a mail contact form and a Facebook plug-in to do this. The system sends the text "SuperBetter is a site to help people who are recovering from an injury or illness or striving to achieve a personal health goal. As an Ally, you'll play a special part in helping [Player name] reach their Epic Win: [stated goal]" along with a link to a short video explaining how to be an Ally. If the friend becomes an Ally they have access to the players' Quests, Power ups and Bad guys and can suggest new ones. An Ally can also view the players' Activity, Achievements and Resilience scores.

In Superbetter players can undertake the following actions:

- SB1: Pick a superhero secret identity. This means the player uses conceptual knowledge of classifications and categories and creates a name.
- *SB2: Epic win.* Here the player uses *conceptual knowledge* as he/she is exploring a relationship between concepts and *self-knowledge* without guidance of a therapist or a more rigid game-structure, and is *creating* new content – the epic win to be achieved – without yet demonstrating any procedural knowledge of how to achieve it.
- *SB3: Quests.* The player uses different knowledge levels depending on the design of the Quest – if the player uses Quests designed by the system or other players than he/she is *evaluating* the available Quests *using knowledge of theories, models and structures*. If the player is designing his/her own quests *procedural knowledge* and/or *self-knowledge* are also needed for *creation*. Performing the quests shows *execution* of *procedural knowledge*.
- *SB4: Power Ups.* A player demonstrates *evaluation* based on *conceptual knowledge* when selecting a Power up provided by Superbetter or other players and demonstrates *self-knowledge* if *creating* a Power up. Performing Power ups shows *execution* of *procedural knowledge*.

- *SB5: Battle bad guys*. If a player uses Bad guys designed by the system or other players than he/she is *evaluating* given Bad guys by *using knowledge of theories, models and structures*. If the player is designing his/her own Bad guys, than *procedural knowledge* and/or *self-knowledge* is needed for *creation*. Battling the Bad guys shows *execution* of *procedural knowledge*.
- *SB6: Invite allies*. A player selects from their social circle someone they see fit as an Ally. Players' have to understand the *concept* of what being an Ally means and *apply* this to the people they know.

8   Taxonomy Table

In the Table 1 below we provide an overview of what levels of knowledge and cognitive processing are addressed in our use cases. The table follows Pintrich's table and is filled with references to the game actions discussed in the previous sections.

Table 1. Pintrich's (2002) knowledge taxonomy table.

	Remember	Understand	Apply	Analyse	Evaluate	Create
Factual knowledge	PI4, TH4	TH1, TH2			MB1	
Conceptual knowledge	TH4	PI4, TH1, RS1	SB6	PI1, PI2, PI3, TH2, RS2	PI5, RS2, MB2, SB3*, SB4*, SB5*	PI1, PI2, PI5, RS2, MB2, SB2
Procedural knowledge	TH4	RS2	TH3, RS4, MB3, SB3, SB4, SB5	PI3	RS3, RS4, MB1, MB2, MB3	MB1, MB2, SB1
Metacognitive knowledge						SB2, SB3*, SB4*, SB5*

Depending on the design of the game-element
PI = Personal Investigator (with a total of five actions); TH = Treasure Hunt (with a total of four actions); RS = Ricky and the Spider (with a total of four actions); MB = Moodbot (with a total of four actions); SB = Superbetter (with a total of six actions)

9   Conclusion and Design Recommendations

From the analysis we see that most of the game content addresses the *analysis, evaluation and creation of conceptual knowledge* and/or the *application, evaluation and creation of procedural knowledge*. In all but one type of game-element the metacognitive knowledge level is not necessarily addressed by the psychotherapeutic games. This is in line with using the second wave CBT as a therapeutic model in game design for it addresses specific cognitions, procedures and behaviours without necessarily addressing the more abstract level of cognition. The table seems to indicate that the psychotherapeutic games under analysis here have not yet found the 'third wave' of cognitive behavioural therapies and are therefore not at the frontier of cognitive science, where it may take better advantage of the latest (empirically proven) insights [4].

Metacognitive knowledge is only addressed in our case studies when players are asked to create their own game components targeting their own behaviour. When this is done without strict guidance by a therapist or a rigid game structure (e.g. with a pre-selected set of options) self-knowledge must be brought to the table. The rest of the metacognitive row in the table (remember, understand, apply, analyse, evaluate) remains devoid of game content.

These conclusions shape the following design recommendations:

1. To use the Revised Blooms taxonomy as a lens to look at the design of a psychotherapeutic game and the knowledge levels it must address, judging by the actions a player undertakes.
2. One way to address metacognition would be to facilitate players in creating (unstructured) parts of the gameplay that reflect on the players' own cognitions and/or behaviour.
3. Finding the 'third wave'. Although second wave CBT is effective and a widely accepted form of therapy, insights from the fields of cognitive psychology and behavioural therapy continue to develop. Addressing metacognition is just one of the insights that might be used to good advantage by game designers.

10   Limitations and Future Research

We are aware that every assignment in a game *could* be approached from a higher knowledge level, a deeper understanding and a more overt strategy compared to where we allocated them in the taxonomy table. The role of a therapist might be in guiding these processes one way or another. However, we judged the game content for what knowledge levels and processes where *necessary* to fulfil its' assignment and can therefore be predicted.

We are also aware that the current discussion of these games is a first overview and not an in-depth analysis where knowledge and actions during gameplay might be more minutely described and categorized. Although this analysis is by no means exhaustive, we believe that this first level of analysis can already be helpful to game designers or practitioners in the field of psychotherapeutic gaming. One very interesting future research direction would be to perform a more in-depth and minute analysis of several psychotherapeutic games. This would ideally include observing gameplay and interviewing both the player and the therapist. Moreover, as already mentioned, this analysis can and should also be extended to include psychotherapeutic VR games.

References

1. Ceranoglu, T.A.: Video games in psychotherapy. Rev. Gen. Psychol. **14**(2), 141–146 (2010). doi:10.1037/a0019439
2. Brezinka, V.: Computer games supporting cognitive behaviour therapy in children. Clin. Child Psychol. Psychiatry **19**(1), 100–110 (2014). doi:10.1177/1359104512468288

3. Fovet, T., Micoulaud-Franchi, J.-A., Vaiva, G., Thomas, P., Jardri, R., Amad, A.: Le serious game: applications thérapeutiques en psychiatrie. L'Encéphale (n.d.). https://doi.org/10. 1016/j.encep.2016.02.008

4. Kahl, K.G., Winter, L., Schweiger, U.: The third wave of cognitive behavioural therapies: what is new and what is effective? Curr. Opin. Psychiatry 25(6), 522–528 (2012)

5. Glanz, K., Rizzo, A.(Skip), Graap, K.: Virtual reality for psychotherapy: current reality and future possibilities. Psychother.: Theory Res. Pract. Training 40(1–2), 55–67 (2003). https://doi.org/10.1037/0033-3204.40.1-2.55

6. Parsons, T.D., Rizzo, A.A.: Affective outcomes of virtual reality exposure therapy for anxiety and specific phobias: a meta-analysis. J. Behav. Ther. Exp. Psychiatry 39(3), 250–261 (2008). https://doi.org/10.1016/j.jbtep.2007.07.007

7. Pintrich, P.R.: The role of metacognitive knowledge in learning, teaching, and assessing. Theory Pract. 41(4), 219–225 (2002)

8. Kuhn, D.: Metacognitive development. Curr. Dir. Psychol. Sci. 9(5), 178–181 (2000)

9. Bloom, B.S., Engelhart, M.D., Furst, E.J., Hill, W.H., Krathwohl, D.R.: Taxonomy of Educational Objectives: Handbook I: Cognitive Domain. David McKay Co., Inc., New York (1956)

10. Bransford, J.D., Brown, A.L., Cocking, R.R.: How People Learn: Brain, Mind, Experience, and School. National Academy Press, Washington, D.C. (1999)

11. Coyle, D., Matthews, M., Sharry, J., Nisbet, A., Doherty, G.: Personal investigator: a therapeutic 3D game for adolecscent psychotherapy. Interact. Technol. Smart Educ. 2(2), 73–88 (2005). doi:10.1108/17415650580000034

12. Brezinka, V.: Treasure Hunt-a serious game to support psychotherapeutic treatment of children. In: Andersen, S.K. (ed.) eHealth Beyond the Horizon – Get IT There, vol. 136, pp. 71–76. IOS Press, Amsterdam (2008)

13. Brezinka, V.: Ricky and the spider - a video game to support cognitive behavioural treatment of children with obsessive-compulsive disorder. Clin. Neuropsychiatry 10(3) (2013). http://www.clinicalneuropsychiatry.org/pdf/01Brezinka.pdf

14. Hrehovcsik, M., van Roessel, L.: Using Vitruvius as a framework for applied game design. In: Schouten, B., Fedtke, S., Bekker, T., Schijven, M., Gekker, A. (eds.) Games for Health, pp. 131–152. Springer Fachmedien Wiesbaden, Wiesbaden (2013). http://link.springer.com/10.1007/978-3-658-02897-8_10

15. Gainplay Studio. Moodbot (2016). http://www.gainplaystudio.com/moodbot/. Accessed 30 Sept 2016

16. ALTRECHT/HKU/IPPO. Moodbot (2013). http://moodbot.nl/. Accessed 30 Sept 2016

17. Roepke, A.M., Jaffee, S.R., Riffle, O.M., McGonigal, J., Broome, R., Maxwell, B.: Randomized controlled trial of SuperBetter, a smartphone-based/internet-based self-help tool to reduce depressive symptoms. Games Health J. 4(3), 235–246 (2015)

18. McGonigal, J.: SuperBetter: A Revolutionary Approach to Getting Stronger, Happier, Braver and More Resilient. Penguin Press, New York (2015)

Evaluating a Gaming System for Cognitive Screening and Sleep Duration Assessment of Elderly Players: A Pilot Study

Costas Boletsis[✉] and Simon McCallum

Norwegian University of Science and Technology,
Teknologivegen 22, 2815 Gjøvik, Norway
Konstantinos.Boletsis@sintef.no, simon.mccallum@ntnu.no

Abstract. Using serious games for cognitive screening can provide a motivating and entertaining alternative to traditional cognitive screening methods. Cognitive decline is usually measured by tests of mental processing, however age-related changes in sleep may also reveal signs of cognitive decline among older individuals. The current work presents and evaluates a gaming system for cognitive screening and sleep duration assessment of the elderly. The gaming system consists of an original serious game for cognitive screening (Smartkuber) and a smartwatch (Basis Peak). A pilot study is conducted to identify and improve the weaknesses of the gaming system and to evaluate the gaming system as to its usability and the game experience it offers for elderly players, assesing its suitability for a large-scale study. The pilot study lasted for 6 weeks and 101 gaming sessions were recorded from 5 elderly players. Elderly players were entertained by the game, while they were impressed by the smartwatch's performance. Limitations of the study and future directions are discussed.

Keywords: Cognitive screening · Serious games · Smartwatch

1 Introduction

Cognitive impairment is often associated with the normal ageing processes; they can however signal early onset dementia [4,6,21]. Unfortunately, cognitive impairment is still under-recognised and under-diagnosed [6,11,23,25,28]. Cognitive screening represents the initial step in the assessment process for dementia and can help identify potential cases for assessment, thus leading to early diagnosis [4,6,21].

Serious games for cognitive screening are presented as an alternative to traditional, pen-and-paper and computerised cognitive screening tests, potentially motivating and engaging the user to regularly perform cognitive screening tasks, increasing the recognition of cognitive impairment [4,6,17,29]. Cognitive screening serious games can address the limitations of the traditional, pen-and-paper cognitive screening tests [6]. They can be economical of time and cost, provide

© Springer International Publishing AG 2016
R. Bottino et al. (Eds.): GALA 2016, LNCS 10056, pp. 107–119, 2016.
DOI: 10.1007/978-3-319-50182-6_10

accurate and frequent response recording, eliminate learning effects (due to dynamically updated content), be self-administered or require little training, provide a pleasant experience and reduce the psychological stress caused by the regular screening processes [4,6,18]. Moreover, cognitive screening serious games - when consisted of accredited cognitive exercises - can provide an indicative measurement of the player's cognitive performance through the game score [6,16,27]. They can be validated against established tests used in clinical practice and consequently provide the players with constant monitoring of their cognitive health, in an entertaining, motivational and engaging way [4,6,30].

Even though, cognitive screening practices mainly focus on examining the performance of mental processes, there are also other indicators of cognitive decline, one of the most strongly associated being sleep quality [1,22]. Detrimental changes in sleep duration and quality are more common with increasing age. Age-related changes in sleep may contribute to cognitive decline among older individuals, with intermediate sleep durations (>6–9 h/night) exhibiting significantly higher cognitive scores than individuals with short sleep (0–6 h/night) or long sleep duration (>9 h/night) [12,14]. Associations between sleep duration and cognitive function measures have been shown to be U-shaped with poorer cognitive function scores at the short and long ends of the sleep distribution [12].

The measurement of sleep duration and sleep quality is a challenging issue. Many studies utilise subjective, self-report measures (such as the Pittsburgh Sleep Quality Index [10]), as objective measures of sleep quality present several challenges mostly due to the obtrusive character of the measurement instruments, such as encephalogram (EEG) head sets. However, the recent advances in smartwatches provide the ability to record sleeping habits [7]. Naturally, their accuracy - compared to formal medical practices - is being actively researched, while devices like the Basis Peak, or Apple Watch smartwatch, provide an opportunity to test low-cost, unobtrusive, objective measurements of sleep quality, for simple indicative results and correlation effects [7].

The current work presents, examines, and studies a gaming system for cognitive screening and sleep duration assessment of the elderly. The pilot study aims to (1) identify and improve the weaknesses of the gaming system, (2) evaluate the gaming system as to its usability and the game experience it offers to a small sample of elderly players, from a qualitative point of view, and finally, (3) assess the suitability of the system for a large-scale study. The gaming system consists of an original serious game for cognitive screening, namely Smartkuber, and the Basis Peak smartwatch (Fig. 1). Smartkuber is a cognitive screening mobile game, addressing the cognitive and motor skills of the players by utilising an interaction technique based on Augmented Reality (AR) and the manipulation of tangible, physical objects (cubes). The game has been analysed in a previous study and has demonstrated high concurrent validity with the MoCA test, high level of internal consistency, satisfying levels of predictive and content validity, and no learning effects [6]. This article presents the next step of the project, building on the design and evaluation of the cognitive screening game, described in the previous study [6]. In our attempt to further improve the specificity and

Fig. 1. The cognitive screening gaming system: the Smartkuber setup (left) and the Basis Peak smartwatch (right).

sensitivity of the game, the smartwatch device is integrated, in order to perform sleep duration assessment, thus creating a gaming system. The ultimate goal of the project is a system that will triangulate its measurements (by measures of cognitive skills, motor skills, and sleep duration/stages) in order to trigger reliable referrals for a more comprehensive assessment, when cognitive decline is indicated, thus playing an intermediary role between the (potential) patient and the medical expert, and leading to early treatment.

2   Materials and Methods

2.1   Gaming System

The cognitive screening gaming system utilises the Smartkuber game - as its main component - for stimulating the cognitive and motor skills of the players, and the Basis Peak smartwatch for providing unobtrusive and - as reliable as possible - measurements of sleep duration (Fig. 1). The measurements coming from both instruments are stored in a database (namely the "Cognitive Passport"), which essentially constitutes a user profile, tracking the player's performance over time.

2.2   Cognitive Screening Game

Smartkuber is a collection of cognitive mini-games of preventative health purpose and is targeting elderly players (60+ years old), mild cognitive impaired players and, secondarily, healthy adults, with an interest in video gaming. The stimulating cognitive training with Smartkuber is aiming to screen the cognitive abilities of the players on a frequent basis (even daily).

The main components of Smartkuber's interaction design are: the tangible, physical objects, which serve as input mechanisms - i.e. the cubes - and the Augmented Reality technology, for real-world recognition and content verification purposes. The interaction technique of Smartkuber features the player using a tablet device to load the game tasks and then manipulating the cubes to perform those tasks [6]. The gaming session can take place in a small space, while the

Table 1. The titles and the descriptions of the Smartkuber mini-games.

1.	**Reconstruct the flag:** The player has to memorise the flag and use the cubes to reconstruct it
2.	**Reconnect old friends:** The player has to memorise the friends' faces and use the cubes to form the right pair of friends
3.	**Repeat the pattern:** The player has to memorise a shape pattern and use the cubes to form it
4.	**Numerical calculation:** The player has to do a numerical calculation and use the cubes to form the right answer
5.	**Find the word:** The player is given a word quiz and uses the cubes to form the right answer

whole system is quite portable; it consists of 6 cubes of 4.4 cm/edge with game content on every side (e.g. letters, numbers, colours, faces, shapes), and a board on which the cubes are placed, to create a uniform background for Augmented Reality content verification purposes [6].

Smartkuber consists of 5 different cognitive mini-games (Table 1), addressing various cognitive abilities, like Attention, Memory, Motor skills, Visual and Spatial processing, Language, and Executive functions: problem solving, decision-making, working memory, flexibility, and response inhibition. The order of the mini-games remains always the same, however the levels of each mini-game are chosen randomly from a "pool" of levels, in order to address learning effects, while the difficulty level is tweaked to a challenging, yet "normal" level [6].

Smartkuber's scoring is related to the successful completion of the cognitive task and is also inversely related to the level completion time, therefore the faster the player completes each level's task, the more points he/she scores. The game features a leaderboard with all the players' scores (Fig. 2) [6].

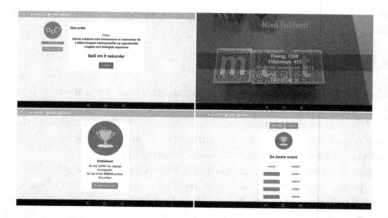

Fig. 2. Playing the "Find the word" mini-game (upper part), finishing the session and checking the Smartkuber high scores (lower part).

2.3 Smartwatch

The smartwatch chosen for our gaming system is the Basis Peak (Fig. 1). Its choice over several competitors was based on the several metrics captured by the sensors, as well as the simple user interaction required. The charging and uploading-data (syncing) process of the Basis Peak is straight-forward (by just connecting it to an external device, e.g. laptop or mobile), while it is able to automatically recognise the user's activity state (e.g. sleeping) without the user pressing any button to mark the start or end time of the activity (which is the case with many similar smartwatches) [7]. The Basis Peak translates the user's biosignals into metrics on how everyday activities affect the body [7]. Its sensors include: optical blood flow sensor, 3D accelerometer, body temperature, ambient temperature reading, and galvanic skin response. The sleep analysis attempts to recognise the sleep stages (REM, light, and deep sleep) and records the sleep duration for each stage, as well as total sleep duration [7]. A measurement of unknown stage is also recorded and calculated in the total duration, when the device is not able to identify the sleep stage. Since the Basis is not a medical device, there is the issue of the validity and accuracy of the physical health data [7]. However, the Basis smartwatch has been shown to provide valuable and reliable data for the home-based dementia care [7], and also that the sleep analysis algorithm of the smartwatch demonstrated excellent agreement with polysomnography data for sleep duration and sleep staging [20].

2.4 Database

The game scores, game times, the sleep stages, and the sleep duration measurements of each player are stored in a database, called the "Cognitive Passport" (coming from the concept of the Biological Passport [26]). The database constitutes the players' user profiles with the player's cognitive-related measurements and performance, over time (Fig. 3). The Cognitive Passport sets each player's baseline performance and provides the opportunity to detect changes related to the individual performance, rather than just measuring performance against population means.

2.5 Study Design

A qualitative methodological approach, enhanced by quantitative methods, was followed for the usability and game experience evaluation of the gaming system. The focus of the pilot study was on qualitative observations related to usability and game design issues.

The study design was divided into two stages. The first stage consisted of weekly, open-ended, and semi-structured interview sessions, which were taking place with each one of the five elderly players, addressing the negative and the positive points of their experience with the gaming system. The weekly interview sessions would take place until the reported technical, interaction, and game design or experience issues were solved, since the current study follows the

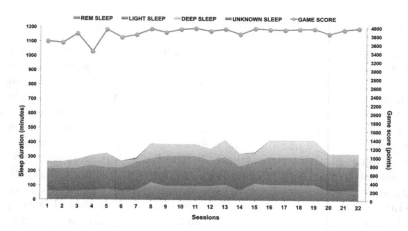

Fig. 3. A stacked visualization of a player's game scores and sleep duration measurements (22 sessions), as stored in the Cognitive Passport database.

concept of data saturation [15]. In this case, data saturation was defined as the point where the collection of new data regarding technical and game design issues would not shed more light on the system's usability and the game experience it offered.

The data saturation point was estimated at approximately 8 weeks, based on the fact that the Smartkuber game was already evaluated and has succeeded in providing an entertaining, engaging, and motivating gaming experience to elderly players at a previous study [6]. The study's sample size was determined, based on the experience we have acquired from previous related testings and studies [3,5] and the notion that iterative sessions would take place, naturally, targeting data saturation.

The second stage of the study's methodology took place during its last week and it deployed a multi-analytical standpoint. At first, the iGEQ and SUS surveys were administered. Then, the overview of the system was further discussed at a final, open-ended, semi-structured interview session, where the players' overall remarks were documented. The quantitative methods (the iGEQ and SUS surveys) were used in a "triangulation" context, further evaluating the qualitative analysis and the results coming from the final interview, thus verifying the data saturation process.

The methodology supported the examination of the game experience and the usability of the system after addressing all the technical and game design issues that were discovered during the first weeks and which may have heavily affected the game experience and, therefore, skewed the results.

2.6 Participants

A sample of five older adults (n = 5) was recruited between July and December 2015. The inclusion criteria stated that the participants should be ≥60 years old, independently performing activities of daily living (ADL), not have been diagnosed with any kind of dementia, be familiar with technology (i.e. using or having used laptop, tablet PC, smartphone, et al.) and video games (i.e. playing or having played video games before). The inclusion criteria addressed the technology-use and video-gaming biases, which can be present in game studies when participants are asked to use systems that have no experience or interest in [6]. All participants gave consent and agreed to participate in the study.

2.7   Procedures

Demographic data were collected at the initial stage of the study. Afterwards, the components of the gaming system were given, along with instructions on their functionality. The gaming system was tested under realistic conditions, therefore the participants were allowed to take Smartkuber with them and play it at their own place of will (e.g. home, office, et al.), for as many sessions as they wanted (a frequency of 2 game sessions/week was proposed, but not forced). The participants wore the smartwatch during the study period. Minor technical problems, which were reported and could be addressed remotely, were solved within 1–12 h. The two stages of the study followed (as described in Sect. 2.5).

2.8   Measures

Demographic data included age, sex, level of education attainment, frequency of technology use ("never", "rarely", "most days", "everyday"), and experience with technology (participants listing devices they own and use).

The players' game experience was measured by asking participants to fill out the In-Game Experience Questionnaire (iGEQ) [19]. The iGEQ contains 14-items, rated on a five-point intensity scale ranging from 0 ("not at all") to 4 ("extremely"), distributed in pairs between seven dimensions of player experience: (1) Immersion, (2) Flow, (3) Competence, (4) Tension, (5) Challenge, (6) Negative affect and (7) Positive affect. The iGEQ is the shorter and reliable in-game version of the Game Experience Questionnaire (GEQ), and it was chosen so as not to tire the participants [5,13].

The usability of the system is measured using the System Usability Scale (SUS) [8]. The System Usability Scale is an instrument that allows usability practitioners and researchers to measure the subjective usability of products and services. Specifically, it is a 10-item survey that can be administered quickly and easily, and it returns scores ranging from 0–100. SUS has been demonstrated to be a reliable and valid instrument, robust with a small number of participants, and to have the distinct advantage of being technology agnostic, meaning it can be used to evaluate a wide range of hardware and software systems [2,5,9].

3   Results

In total, 5 participants (mean age: 72, SD: 10.15, male/female: 4/1) were recruited for the pilot study. Four participants have completed tertiary education and one has completed secondary. All of the participants were using technology on an everyday basis, using a laptop or desktop PC and at least one mobile device (tablet, smartphone, or e-reader). The participants had some degree of experience with video games (two of them playing video games "rarely" and the other three "frequently"). All participants successfully completed the study, playing the game at an open and free rate. 101 gaming sessions (mean number of sessions/player: 20.2, SD: 1.48) were recorded from the 5 participants.

The period of study was 6 weeks. The first stage of the study (i.e. the weekly interview sessions) lasted for 5 weeks until we reached and verified data saturation. The second stage of the study (iGEQ-SUS surveys and the final interview) took place during the last 6th week, when the gaming system's performance was formally evaluated.

The weekly interviews resulted in the discovery of a main technical issue related to the Basis Peak smartwatch's syncing process (i.e. uploading users' data to the database). The syncing process was too slow and it was confusing to four out of five users. The issue was addressed by providing technical instructions for a better syncing process (via Bluetooth) and the device's firmware was updated. The issue was solved by the third week. Several Smartkuber bugs (mostly concerning user-interface and device-compatibility issues) were reported via e-mail and they were fixed instantly or within 1–12 h. On the positive side, participants enjoyed playing the Smartkuber game and competing with each other, while the interaction technique was simple and did not cause any issues. Furthermore, the elderly participants enjoyed using the smartwatch, as well as reading their sleep-related performances. Even though, the technical issues and the positive observations were collected and addressed by the third week, we decided to let the players have two more weeks of gameplay (and interview sessions), in order for them to have a more complete gaming experience and for us to be able to verify data saturation.

During the second stage of the study, all participants completed the iGEQ questionnaire, displaying high values of Flow, Positive Affect, Immersion, and Competence, moderate values of Challenge, and low values of Negative Affect and Tension (Fig. 4).

The data acquired by the SUS survey provided extra insight on the usability of the system and, especially, the integration of the smartwatch and the use of Tangible Augmented Reality (TAR). The average SUS score for the gaming system was 84 (SD: 6.75, range: 77.5–95), placing its percentile ranking around 93 %, according to the percentile rankings of SUS scores [2,24]. The SUS score of 84 is placed at the top 10 % of scores and it indicates that the gaming system has a higher usability score than approximately 93 % of all applications tested.

The final interview session was focused on the overall positive and negative points of the gaming system and it resulted in the following qualitative results/remarks, presented in Table 2. The remarks were further organised and are listed according to their frequency of occurrence (top to bottom, top being the most frequently occurring remark).

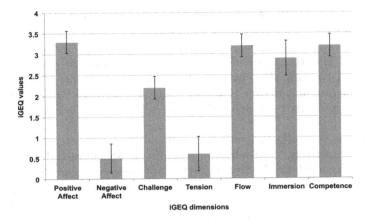

Fig. 4. The iGEQ mean scores (with SD bars) across the seven dimensions of Game Experience, for the gaming system.

Table 2. The elderly player's remarks as collected from the final interview session.

1.	The Smartkuber high score competition was motivating and entertaining
2.	The smartwatch presented a technical, syncing problem, which was solved later on
3.	The fact that the game score and the sleep duration/stages measurements over time - as stored in the Cognitive Passport database - were available, provided useful feedback and motivated for better performances
4.	The Smartkuber game was quick, stimulating, and fun
5.	The TAR interaction and the cubes provided a user-friendly interaction technique
6.	The smartwatchs seamless functionality, in combination with the accurate sleep duration measurements were impressive to the users
7.	The smartwatch felt like a regular wristwatch and it was not interfering with ADL

4   Discussion

The examination of the cognitive screening gaming system showed promising results. Overall, the two stages of the pilot study helped us not only to evaluate the gaming system, but also to improve it. The first stage allowed us to collect and address all the system's issues, as well as document its positive points. The second stage provided a formal evaluation of the gaming system's usability and game experience, utilising both quantitative and qualitative tools. The fact that the pilot study was based on data saturation, having an open timeframe and a relatively small sample size, allowed us to optimise the system over time, as well as "build" a meaningful collaboration with the elderly players and involve them in the design process.

As documented in Remark #4 (Table 2) and supported by the high iGEQ value of Positive Affect (Fig. 4), elderly players considered the gaming system to be entertaining, while they felt extrinsically motivated by the competitive nature of Smartkuber and by playing against other elderly players (Remark #1). The gaming system's feedback, also, managed to tap into the players' intrinsic motivators and their individual need to always want to perform better - as reported in Remark #3 - by providing their game scores and sleep duration/stages measurements over time, through the Cognitive Passport database. The remarks can also be supported by the high iGEQ Flow and Immersion values.

The gaming system managed to offer challenging content and to stimulate the players cognitively. Naturally, the cognitively stimulating features of the gaming system come from the Smartkuber cognitive screening properties, leading to a quick, stimulating game experience (Remark #4). The challenging and stimulating character of the gaming system can be potentially revealed by the high iGEQ values of Immersion and Challenge.

The evaluation of the gaming system's usability was one of the main goals of the current pilot study. Overall, the interaction of the gaming system proved to be user/elderly-friendly, scoring high at the System Usability Scale, while presenting high iGEQ Competence and Positive Affect and low Negative Affect and Tension values. The Smartkuber interaction technique, utilising Augmented Reality and tangible objects, was considered to be user-friendly for the elderly (Remark #5). The Basis Peak smartwatch performed satisfactorily. Even though there was a technical problem during the first sessions (Remark #2), its low complexity, seamless performance and accuracy were impressive to the elderly users (Remarks #6 and #7).

Undoubtedly, the gaming system's main component is the Smartkuber game. The findings related to Smartkuber agreed with the ones of the previous study [6]. Furthermore, the smartwatch's integration was beneficial for the gaming system, with the elderly players being impressed by the fact that a device that looks and feels like a regular wristwatch can provide so much information about their sleeping habits. Within the context of the gaming system's current version, the use of the smartwatch is not related with the game mechanics, since we wanted to have a clear picture of the device's usability performance, without being affected by extrinsic game motivators. Naturally, the next step for the smartwatch is highlighting its role in the system as an active gaming component, by gamifying its use frequency, thus adding extrinsic motivation around the smartwatch's use and sleep duration assessment.

The present small-scale pilot study was limited by the inclusion criteria and the fact that the technology-use and video-gaming biases were addressed, restricting the target population of the cognitive screening and sleep duration assessment process. In the study, the motor skills of the players - even though stimulated - were not directly measured, since the technical implementation is a challenging task, which falls into the future-work timeframe.

5   Conclusion

The gaming system for cognitive screening and sleep assessment described herein managed to provide stimulating cognitive challenges, user-friendly interaction, as well as an entertaining and motivating gaming experience. The pilot study was of great significance for improving and evaluating the gaming system from a user-centered perspective and preparing it for the next research step, which will focus on utilising a larger sample size and evaluate the sleep duration assessment as for its concurrent validity against the Smartkuber score. From a game design and development perpective the smartwatch's use will be gamified, the measurement of motor skills will be technically implemented, and the Cognitive Passport database will be utilised to develop a user platform with the players' performance profiles.

Acknowledgements. The authors would like to thank the staff and volunteers of Seniornett Norge (Oslo) for their support and participation in the study, as well as Tore Langemyr Larsen and Joop Cuppen for establishing this meaningful collaboration. The authors also thank Dr. Brynjar Landmark for his significant contribution to the smartwatch's use and the game's design, development, and evaluation processes.

References

1. An, C., Yu, L., Wang, L., Jin, G., Song, M., Zhu, Q., Jia, H., Liu, K., Wang, M., Wang, X.: Association between sleep characteristics and mild cognitive impairment in elderly people. Neurophysiology **46**(1), 88–94 (2014)
2. Bangor, A., Kortum, P.T., Miller, J.T.: An empirical evaluation of the system usability scale. Int. J. Hum.-Comput. Interact. **24**(6), 574–594 (2008)
3. Boletsis, C., McCallum, S.: Augmented reality cube game for cognitive training: an interaction study. Stud. Health Technol. Inform. **200**, 81–87 (2014)
4. Boletsis, C., McCallum, S.: Connecting the player to the doctor: utilising serious games for cognitive training & screening. DAIMI PB **597**, 5–8 (2015)
5. Boletsis, C., McCallum, S.: Augmented Reality cubes for cognitive gaming: preliminary usability and game experience testing. Int. J. Serious Games **3**(1), 3–18 (2016)
6. Boletsis, C., McCallum, S.: Smartkuber: a cognitive training game for cognitive health screening of elderly players. Games Health J. **5**(4), 241–251 (2016)
7. Boletsis, C., McCallum, S., Landmark, B.F.: The use of smartwatches for health monitoring in home-based dementia care. In: Zhou, J., Salvendy, G. (eds.) DUXU 2015. LNCS, vol. 9194, pp. 15–26. Springer, Heidelberg (2015). doi:10.1007/978-3-319-20913-5_2
8. Brooke, J.: SUS-a quick and dirty usability scale. In: Usability Evaluation In Industry, pp. 189–194. Taylor & Francis, Abingdon-on-Thames (1996)
9. Brooke, J.: SUS: a retrospective. J. Usability Stud. **8**(2), 29–40 (2013)
10. Buysse, D.J., Reynolds, C.F., Monk, T.H., Berman, S.R., Kupfer, D.J.: The Pittsburgh sleep quality index: a new instrument for psychiatric practice and research. Psychiatry Res. **28**(2), 193–213 (1989)
11. Connolly, A., Gaehl, E., Martin, H., Morris, J., Purandare, N.: Underdiagnosis of dementia in primary care: variations in the observed prevalence and comparisons to the expected prevalence. Aging Mental Health **15**(8), 978–984 (2011)

12. Ferrie, J.E., Shipley, M.J., Akbaraly, T.N., Marmot, M.G., Kivimaki, M., Singh-Manoux, A.: Change in sleep duration and cognitive function: findings from the whitehall ii study. Sleep **34**(5), 565–573 (2011)
13. Gamberini, L., Fabregat, M., Spagnolli, A., Prontu, L., Seraglia, B., Alcaniz, M., Zimmerman, A., Rontti, T., Grant, J., Jensen, R., Gonzales, A.: Eldergames: videogames for empowering, training and monitoring elderly cognitive capabilities. Gerontechnology **7**(2), 111 (2008)
14. Gildner, T.E., Liebert, M.A., Kowal, P., Chatterji, S., Snodgrass, J.J.: Associations between sleep duration, sleep quality, and cognitive test performance among older adults from six middle income countries: results from the study on global ageing and adult health (sage). J. Clin. Sleep Med. **10**(6), 613–621 (2014)
15. Glaser, B.G., Strauss, A.L.: The Discovery of Grounded Theory: Strategies for Qualitative Research. Transaction Publishers, New Brunswick (2009)
16. Hanna-Pladdy, B., Enslein, A., Fray, M., Gajewski, B.J., Pahwa, R., Lyons, K.E.: Utility of the NeuroTrax computerized battery for cognitive screening in Parkinson's disease: comparison with the MMSE and the MoCA. Int. J. Neurosci. **120**(8), 538–543 (2010)
17. Hansen, D.: Fighting dementia with brain health assessment. Games Health J. **3**(1), 10–12 (2014)
18. Ismail, Z., Rajji, T.K., Shulman, K.I.: Brief cognitive screening instruments: an update. Int. J. Geriatr. Psychiatry **25**(2), 111–120 (2010)
19. Neistadt, M.: A critical analysis of occupational therapy approaches for perceptual deficits in adults with brain injury. Am. J. Occup. Ther. **44**(4), 299–304 (1990)
20. Patel, S., Ahmed, T., Lee, J., Ruoff, L., Unadkat, T.: Validation of Basis Science Advanced Sleep Analysis: Estimation of Sleep Stages and Sleep Duration. Basis Science (2014). http://www.mybasis.com/wp-content/uploads/2014/04/Validation-of-Basis-Science-Advanced-Sleep-Analysis.pdf. Accessed 6 July 2016
21. Persson, J., Nyberg, L., Lind, J., Larsson, A., Nilsson, L.G., Ingvar, M., Buckner, R.L.: Structure-function correlates of cognitive decline in aging. Cereb. Cortex **16**(7), 907–915 (2006)
22. Potvin, O., Lorrain, D., Forget, H., Dube, M., Grenier, S., Preville, M., Hudon, C.: Sleep quality and 1-year incident cognitive impairment in community-dwelling older adults. Sleep **35**(4), 491–499 (2012)
23. Prince, M., Bryce, R., Ferri, C.: World Alzheimer report 2011: the benefits of early diagnosis and intervention. In: Alzheimer's Disease International (ADI) (2011)
24. Sauro, J.: A practical guide to the system usability scale: background, benchmarks & best practices. CreateSpace Independent Publishing Platform (2011). http://www.measuringu.com/products/SUSguide. Accessed 6 July 2016
25. Scanlon, L., O'Shea, E., O'Caoimh, R., Timmons, S.: Usability and validity of a battery of computerised cognitive screening tests for detecting cognitive impairment. Gerontology **62**(2), 247–252 (2016)
26. Sottas, P.E., Robinson, N., Rabin, O., Saugy, M.: The athlete biological passport. Clin. Chem. **57**(7), 969–976 (2011)
27. Tong, T., Yeung, J., Sandrakumar, J., Chignell, M., Tierney, M.C., Lee, J.: Improving the ergonomics of cognitive assessment with serious games. Proc. Int. Symp. Hum. Factors Ergon. Health Care **4**(1), 1–5 (2015)
28. Waldemar, G., Phung, K., Burns, A., Georges, J., Hansen, F.R., Iliffe, S., Marking, C., Rikkert, M.O., Selmes, J., Stoppe, G., Sartorius, N.: Access to diagnostic evaluation and treatment for dementia in Europe. Int. J. Geriatr. Psychiatry **22**(1), 47–54 (2007)

29. Zucchella, C., Sinforiani, E., Tassorelli, C., Cavallini, E., Tost-Pardell, D., Grau, S., Pazzi, S., Puricelli, S., Bernini, S., Bottiroli, S., et al.: Serious games for screening pre-dementia conditions: from virtuality to reality? A pilot project. Funct. Neurol. **29**(3), 153–158 (2014)
30. Zygouris, S., Giakoumis, D., Votis, K., Doumpoulakis, S., Ntovas, K., Segkouli, S., Karagiannidis, C., Tzovaras, D., Tsolaki, M.: Can a virtual reality cognitive training application fulfill a dual role? Using the virtual supermarket cognitive training application as a screening tool for mild cognitive impairment. J. Alzheimers Dis. **44**(4), 1333–1347 (2015)

Introducing the Fling – An Innovative Serious Game to Train Behavioral Control in Adolescents: Protocol of a Randomized Controlled Trial

Wouter J. Boendermaker[1]([✉]), Remco Veltkamp[2], Robbert Jan Beun[2],
Rens van de Schoot[3], and Margot Peeters[1]

[1] Department of Interdisciplinary Social Sciences, Utrecht University, Utrecht,
The Netherlands
{w.j.boendermaker,m.peeters1}@uu.nl
[2] Department of Information and Computing Sciences, Utrecht University,
Utrecht, The Netherlands
{r.c.veltkamp,r.j.beun}@uu.nl
[3] Department of Social Sciences: Methodology and Statistics, Utrecht
University, Utrecht, The Netherlands
a.g.j.vandeschoot@uu.nl

Abstract. Behavioral control weaknesses are a strong predictor of problematic behaviors in adolescents, such as heavy alcohol use. Heavy alcohol use at this young age can lead to health and school-related problems and is a severe societal problem. Strengthening of cognitive control mechanisms through computerized training has been shown to have positive effects on behavior, but is often perceived as a tedious exercise. Applying novel serious gaming techniques to evidence-based training paradigms may offer a solution to this motivational problem. This paper describes the design and analysis plan that will be used to evaluate an innovative Serious Game called The Fling, aimed specifically at increasing cognitive control over impulses in adolescents. The game will be evaluated in a randomized controlled trial (RCT) among adolescents between 15–18 years in mainstream and special education.

Keywords: Serious games · Cognitive training · Adolescents · Motivation · Inhibition

1 Introduction

Heavy alcohol use among adolescents is a severe societal problem that can lead to health problems and academic underperformance, as well as addictive behaviors later in life [1]. Weaknesses in behavioral control (e.g., the ability to plan behavior, inhibit inappropriate responses, and consider alternative response options) are a strong predictor of alcohol use [2–5]. Experimenting with risky behaviors such as alcohol use is a relatively normative development often associated with the onset of puberty. Some adolescents, however, have difficulties to withstand the feelings of temptation and craving, associated with some of these behaviors (e.g. alcohol, smoking, drug use [6]),

© Springer International Publishing AG 2016
R. Bottino et al. (Eds.): GALA 2016, LNCS 10056, pp. 120–129, 2016.
DOI: 10.1007/978-3-319-50182-6_11

resulting in a shift from relatively innocent experimental behavior to more uncontrolled and compulsive behavior. Weaknesses in behavioral control increase the chance that adolescents will develop an uncontrolled and problematic drinking style.

Recently, several effective, evidence-based cognitive training paradigms have been developed that can increase behavioral control [e.g., 7, 8], and thus help adolescents to control their drinking behavior. By applying these training paradigms, we may be able to withhold adolescents from developing an unhealthy drinking pattern. An important aspect of these cognitive training paradigms is that they are often seen as long and boring [9]. Many interventions aimed at reducing adolescents' alcohol use focus on changing the outcome behavior and not so much on motivating participants to complete the training. Moreover, risk groups that could benefit the most from interventions aimed at controlling drinking behavior, are often groups that have difficulties with concentration and attention [2]. This characteristic increases the likelihood of inefficient training in this particular group. It is therefore of vital importance to develop a training that matches the needs and motivates participants in the best way. This is where the use of serious gaming techniques may offer a solution. Serious games have been shown capable to increase participants' motivation to complete training [e.g., 10]. They provide a safe training environment, tailored to adolescents' individual level of development, against a competitive and arousing game background, which connects well to the perceptions of adolescents [11].

In line with recent developments in the application of serious games to induce behavioral change [12, 13], we have adapted one of these training paradigms by integrating it in a serious game, called *The Fling*. Two mechanisms are targeted using evidence based training principles [e.g., 7, 14–16]: delay of gratification (withstanding immediate rewards in favor of bigger long term rewards) and response inhibition (the ability to suppress or delay automatic responses or impulses that might be inappropriate or irrelevant in a given context).

There are two similar paradigms that are most frequently used for training response inhibition: the go/no-go (GNG) and the stop-signal (SST) paradigm [17]. Both can be used to train response inhibition by consistently pairing certain stimuli with a go-response and others with a no-go or stopping response. The difference between a no-go-cue and a stop-cue is subtle. Both cues indicate that a response should be withheld, but a no-go cue represents the instruction to withhold a response immediately when it is presented, whereas a stop-cue first appears as a go-cue, and then turns into a stop-cue after a brief interval (e.g., 300 ms). The latter thus makes it more difficult to withhold a response as a motor response to the initial go-cue may already be underway. As such, the SST paradigm is believed to target executive processes at the motor level [18].

Another aspect relevant to inhibition is the differentiation between automatic response inhibition and controlled response inhibition [17]. Controlled response inhibition is a top-down process that can be used to actively inhibit a response, whereas automatic response inhibition is a bottom-up process that can develop when a certain stimulus is consistently paired with a no-go or stopping response [19]. Repeated exercise with such stimulus-cue combinations can strengthen the ability to develop automatic inhibition [19]. For example, Houben and colleagues [7] used a GNG training that consistently paired alcohol-related cues with a no-go response to strengthen the ability to inhibit responses to alcohol-related stimuli in heavy drinking college students. A more indirect strategy can be to strengthen controlled response inhibition in a more general context. For example, Dovis and colleagues [20] successfully improved controlled response inhibition in children with ADHD through a gamified training inhibition training based on the SST paradigm.

Dovis and colleagues [20] also suggest that for the purpose of training controlled response inhibition, the GNG may be less appropriate compared to the SST. The way the GNG task is designed makes that it interacts with other processes, such as selective attention, and has a relatively low load on inhibition [21]. Verbruggen and colleagues [19] also showed that a controlled response inhibition training at the motor level with the SST paradigm can translate specifically to a decrease in risky behavior (assessed with a monetary gambling task). The SST paradigm may thus show better transfer of cognitive control improvements to other cognitive domains [19, 22] whereas the go/no-go paradigm appears to be more suitable to train domain specific behavioral control (e.g., [7]). Therefore, the training task used as a basis for The Fling is based on the SST paradigm.

The aim of the current study is to see whether a general controlled response inhibition training can help adolescents to gain more control over their risk behavior. The cognitions involved in behavioral control are still maturing during mid and late adolescence [23, 24], making this period particularly suitable for training. In the current article we will describe the design process and elaborate on our plans to evaluate The Fling in an upcoming randomized controlled trial (RCT) among regularly developing adolescents between 15–18 years in a mainstream education setting.

2   Methods

2.1   The Fling: Concept and Development

The target population for The Fling consists of typically developing adolescents between 15–18 years of both sexes. As such, the game elements used were aimed specifically at adolescents in that age group. In The Fling, the player is presented with a brief introduction to a lighthearted 'boy-meets girl' love story. After the brief cut-scene, the first of five training levels can be started. During each training level a song is played, presenting a musical rhythmic pattern that coincides with the presentation of the go- and stop-cues. Besides fitting the atmosphere of the game, the music is also intended to make the tendency to respond to the cues more potent: after several go-cues are presented to the rhythm of the song, when a stop-cue appears to the rhythm, the impulse to keep tapping the response key may be higher, thus creating a stronger response conflict, which may lead to a stronger training effect [25, 26]. Figure 1 depicts The Fling during training. The camera flies along a ribbon through a colorful scene that connects to an overarching story arc. Along the way, and on the rhythm of the accompanying music, the cues show up in a neutral color (grey), turning either green (signaling a go-cue) or green followed by red (signaling a stop-cue) at 1000 ms in front of the camera. The cues are placed randomly on one of three lanes on the ribbon. In the first levels the three lanes all correspond to one response key on the keyboard (the [SPACEBAR]). Later in the game, two additional response keys become active, where each key represents a different lane (the [Q], [SPACEBAR], and [P] keys, respectively).

Fig. 1. The stop-signal paradigm incorporated into the fling game, used in the active and placebo game training conditions. Green cues signal go-responses and green cues that have turned red signal stop-responses. The scene depicts a lighthearted boy-meets-girl scene while the ribbon flows through the tree. The horizontal white line signals the optimal reaction time. (Color figure online)

To keep participants challenged throughout the game, the speed with which the cues approach varies slightly over the course of each level, based on performance, as well as the time it takes for the stop-cue to turn red. Additionally, from level 4 onwards, blue cues sometimes appear in place of green cues signaling that the player should keep the correct button pressed for 500 ms, giving an extra bonus score. This cue serves no purpose beyond other go-cues, other than adding diversity to the game. To motivate the player to also respond quickly, but not too fast, the number of points awarded for each correct go-response increases the closer the cue moves to the camera. This 'optimal reaction time' is also visualized through a horizontal bar overlaying the ribbon, as well as the cue itself becoming brighter. If the response was correct, this is signaled by an increase of points. When an incorrect response is given (either the wrong or no key on a go-cue, or any key on a stop-cue), the screen briefly gives a little shake (emulating the force feedback feature found in many console games). In both cases a text message also appears, indicating whether the response was correct or incorrect, too late or too fast. Doing well on the training also affects the background of the level during play, e.g., the first level (depicted in Fig. 1) features a lighthearted boy-meets-girl scene while the ribbon flows through the tree. Doing well makes the tree change color to reveal fresh green leaves and flowers, whereas incorrect responses turn the tree into a darker, autumn-like color. After finishing each level, another brief cut-scene is shown that shows how the love story progresses, usually in a slightly comical way (e.g., after singing his song underneath the tree, the boy is devastated to see the girl he's trying to impress still leaves him there - upon which a meteor falls down from above and destroys the entire scene, comically reflecting the boy's feelings).

The game is currently designed to be played twice over four play sessions: once in story mode and another time where one can skip the cut-scenes and focus on getting high scores. Specifically, during the first session, the first two levels can be played; during the second session, levels 3, 4 and 5 are played, and the special blue go-cue is introduced. In the third session, levels 1 through 3 are played again, but this time the difficulty is increased a bit by introducing the additional response keys. During the fourth session, levels 4 and 5 are played again, as well as a new sixth level, which is an 'endless' level, allowing players to keep going until they want to quit, or until the time limit is reached. This free play time will be used as a behavioral measure of motivation to play the game.

2.2   Study Design and Procedure

The study will include three experimental groups ($N = 150$): *The Fling* with active training elements (the Game-training condition); *The Fling* without training elements as a control measure for the training aspect (the Placebo condition, using only go-cues) and a standard non-game control training to evaluate the added value of the game elements (the Non-Game training condition). The training will be divided over four ten-minute sessions spread over four weeks. Immediately before the first training session a baseline assessment will take place for 20 min. Following the last training, another assessment will take place for 20 min. All training sessions will take place at schools and are performed under the guidance of trained research assistants. The training and assessments are individually completed on notebooks and each participant has a headphone. A brief (one minute) three-month follow-up assessment will be presented through email. Passive informed consent will be obtained from the adolescents' parents through letters sent by the schools two weeks before the first session. The adolescents will be informed that participation in the study is entirely voluntary and that no information will be shared with their school. Before they start, the adolescents will also give active consent to their participation in the study. They can earn a ten Euro gift voucher to be used in a large online store, when they complete the entire training and follow-up assessment. The Ethical Review Board of Utrecht University has approved the study, protocol number #FETC16-064, and the study has been registered at The Netherlands National Trial Register (registry number forthcoming).

The effectiveness of *The Fling* will be evaluated based on its ability to increase behavioral control and subsequently reduce of adolescents' drinking behavior, as well as being fun to play, as measured by self-reported questionnaires and actual play time. It is expected that participants in the Game- and Non-game training conditions will show an increase in behavioral control, and in effect a reduction in alcohol drinking, over time, whereas participants in the Placebo condition do not. The Placebo and the Game training are expected to be more fun to do than the Non-game training.

2.3   Sample

For this study we will target students in mainstream education, specifically in the vocational tracks as these children tend to show most attention and concentration related problems [27] and for that reason may benefit most from the motivating game elements.

Because of these problems, these are also children that typically are at risk of developing heavy alcohol drinking habits [2, 27]. The children will be 15–18 years old and we aim towards an equal distribution between boys and girls. Power analyses based on effect sizes found by Prins and colleagues [13] suggest a sample size of $N = 51$ students per condition. Since we have clear expectations about the directions of the effects, analyzing our data using inequality constrains [28] will allow us to include fewer participants (<30% in our study), meaning roughly 40 participants for each condition (see Table 1 in [29]), while maintaining power and effect size. Expecting at least some level of drop-out in the study, the aim is to include up to 50 participants per condition.

2.4 Materials

Questionnaires. At baseline, demographic information (e.g., age, sex, level of education) will be assessed, as well as month and year prevalence of alcohol use, and frequency of smoking behavior and cannabis use (conf. [30, 31]). Both before and after training, the recent level of alcohol use will be assessed using a quantity by frequency measure (i.e., drinking days during the week and weekend multiplied by average drinks on a drinking day in the weekend and/or during the week). As a measure of inhibitory control, the 13-item Brief Self-Report Scale (BSCS) [32] will be conducted both before and after the training. After training, we will inquire about experience with computer games in general and evaluate the (game or non-game) training with a number of questions specifically developed for this project.

Assessment Tasks. To ascertain the effect of the training on cognitive control, two measures will be used. First, a Stop-Signal Task [SST; 18] will be used to measure inhibitory control before and after training (and an extra assessment after two training sessions). In this task, participants are instructed to respond as quickly and accurately as possible to the direction (left or right) of a green arrow. However, when the green arrow turns red (a stop signal), they are instructed to withhold their response. A Stop-Signal Reaction Time (SSRT) can be calculated from this task, indicating the adolescent's ability to inhibit certain responses. As delay of gratification also relates to working memory [33] and is an important aspect of behavioral control (cf. [3]), a computerized version of the Self-Ordered Pointing Task (SOPT; [34]) will be used to assess working memory capacity (WMC). The SOPT presents participants with a grid of pictures of concrete or abstract objects with the instruction to click on each picture only once. After each click, the pictures are shuffled and presented again, until the number of responses matches the number of pictures presented in the grid. The task starts with a practice block of 4 pictures, followed by several test blocks with increasing numbers of pictures. The total number of unique pictures selected can be used as a measure of WMC.

Training Tasks. The training tasks used in this study, including The Fling, are based on the stop-signal paradigm. Participants are presented with a minimum of 200–300 training trials per level, depending on the duration of the song. 75% of the trials are go-trials and 25% stop trials. In contrast, while being visually and procedurally similar to the Game condition, the Placebo condition will feature only go-signals. This essentially makes the

PG-training somewhat easier and, most importantly, not focused on inhibition. Finally, the Non-Game condition will be a stop-signal training more closely matched to the original paradigm, without music or game elements. The amount of training is matched in terms of training time, rather than number of trials, but should be roughly equal between conditions. Figure 2 shows a trial in the Non-Game version of the training.

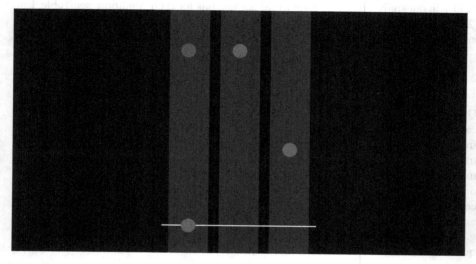

Fig. 2. The stop-signal paradigm as used in the active non-game training condition. Green cues signal go-responses and green cues that have turned red signal stop-responses. (Color figure online)

3 Conclusions and Future Work

The study described in this paper aims to evaluate a new cognitive training game called *The Fling*. The Fling aims to offer adolescents a motivating environment to increase their levels of cognitive control, without stigmatizing messages about the negative effects of alcohol use. Effectivity of the game in terms of motivation and cognitive improvement will be evaluated in the upcoming study.

While serious games have certainly gained in popularity over the last few years, it remains important to include a firm scientific basis in the design process. One way to safeguard this is to describe the development process of serious games as well as the theoretical basis which is the guiding principle of the serious game. We hope that this paper may give insight into some of the challenges and opportunities serious game development has to offer, specifically when it involves cognitive training.

In addition to the study described in this paper we plan to continue development of *The Fling* into a mobile app to test it among a broader audience with fewer limits on play time. That way we can ascertain the possibly beneficial effects of prolonged training, but also determine if fatigue may start to play a role. A central question in serious game development is for how long games can manage to raise levels of motivation beyond that observed in regular training. Indeed, a recent study [35] showed that when participants' motivation to play drops after some time, it may even go below that found in a non-gamified counterpart, which can potentially have negative effects. As such, extensive evaluation of any serious game is to be advised, preferably using a randomized-controlled study design. Finally, it should be noted that, in theory, using games to prevent problematic alcohol use could lead to problems related to addictive gaming in some participants. Although the current, small number of supervised training sessions with game elements seems very unlikely to be sufficient to elicit, or even trigger, addictive gaming behavior, we have included several measures of the amount of gaming activity.

The current study emphasizes the importance of presenting interventions in a form that adolescents can relate to, without losing scientific integrity [12]. Serious games may be uniquely suitable to bridge the gap between an evidence-based training paradigm and an attractive, motivating training environment.

Acknowledgments. The authors wish to thank our collaborators at Shosho Amsterdam, Harold de Groot and Frank van Vugt in particular, for their invaluable contributions to the game's design and development. This research was supported by the Utrecht University Strategic Theme *Dynamics of Youth* grant #SM.DoY.2015.6.T, awarded to Margot Peeters.

References

1. Steinberg, L.: Risk taking in adolescence new perspectives from brain and behavioral science. Curr. Dir. Psychol. **16**, 55–59 (2007). doi:10.1111/j.1467-8721.2007.00475.x
2. Peeters, M., Janssen, T., Monshouwer, K., Boendermaker, W., Pronk, T., Wiers, R., Vollebergh, W.: Weaknesses in executive functioning predict the initiating of adolescents' alcohol use. Dev. Cogn. Neurosci. **16**, 139–146 (2015). doi:10.1016/j.dcn.2015.04.003
3. Fernie, G., Peeters, M., Gullo, M.J., Christiansen, P., Cole, J.C., Sumnall, H., Field, M.: Multiple behavioural impulsivity tasks predict prospective alcohol involvement in adolescents. Addiction **108**, 1916–1923 (2013). doi:10.1111/add.12283
4. Nigg, J.T., Wong, M.M., Martel, M.M., Jester, J.M., Puttler, L.I., Glass, J.M., Adams, K.M., Fitzgerald, H.E., Zucker, R.A.: Poor response inhibition as a predictor of problem drinking and illicit drug use in adolescents at risk for alcoholism and other substance use disorders. J. Am. Acad. Child Adolesc. Psychiatry **45**(4), 468–475 (2006). doi:10.1097/01.chi. 0000199028.76452.a9
5. Khurana, A., Romer, D., Betancourt, L.M., Brodsky, N.L., Giannetta, J.M., Hurt, H.: Working memory ability predicts trajectories of early alcohol use in adolescents: the mediational role of impulsivity. Addiction **108**, 506–515 (2013). doi:10.1111/add.12001
6. Crone, E.A., Dahl, R.E.: Understanding adolescence as a period of social-affective engagement and goal flexibility. Nat. Rev. Neurosci. **13**, 636–650 (2012). doi:10.1038/nrn3313
7. Houben, K., Nederkoorn, C., Wiers, R.W., Jansen, A.: Resisting temptation: decreasing alcohol-related affect and drinking behavior by training response inhibition. Drug Alcohol Depend. **116**, 132–136 (2011). doi:10.1016/j.drugalcdep.2010.12.011

8. Houben, K., Wiers, R.W., Jansen, A.: Getting a grip on drinking behavior: training working memory to reduce alcohol abuse. Psychol. Sci. **22**, 968–975 (2011). doi:10.1177/0956797611412392

9. Beard, C., Weisberg, R.B., Primack, J.: Socially anxious primary care patients' attitudes toward cognitive bias modification (CBM): a qualitative study. Behav. Cogn. Psychother. **40**, 618–633 (2012). doi:10.1017/S1352465811000671

10. Dovis, S., van der Oord, S., Wiers, R.W., Prins, P.J.M.: What part of working memory is not working in ADHD? Short-term memory, the central executive and effects of reinforcement. J. Abnorm. Child Psychol. **41**, 901–917 (2013). doi:10.1007/s10802-013-9729-9

11. Granic, I., Lobel, A., Engels, R.C.: The benefits of playing video games. Am. Psychol. **69**, 66–78 (2014). doi:10.1037/a0034857

12. Boendermaker, W.J., Prins, P.J.M., Wiers, R.W.: Cognitive bias modification for adolescents with substance use problems – can serious games help? J. Behav. Ther. Exp. Psychiatry **49**, 13–20 (2015). doi:10.1016/j.jbtep.2015.03.008

13. Prins, P.J.M., Dovis, S., Ponsioen, A., Ten Brink, E., Van der Oord, S.: Does computerized working memory training with game elements enhance motivation and training efficacy in children with ADHD? Cyberpsychol. Behav. Soc. Netw. **14**, 115–122 (2011). doi:10.1089/cyber.2009.0206

14. Antrop, I., Stock, P., Verté, S., Wiersema, J.R., Baeyens, D., Roeyers, H.: ADHD and delay aversion: the influence of non-temporal stimulation on choice for delayed rewards. J. Child Psychol. Psychiatry **47**, 1152–1158 (2006). doi:10.1111/j.1469-7610.2006.01619.x

15. Bickel, W.K., Yi, R., Landes, R.D., Hill, P.F., Baxter, C.: Remember the future: working memory training decreases delay discounting among stimulant addicts. Biol. Psychiatry **69**, 260–265 (2011). doi:10.1016/j.biopsych.2010.08.017

16. Jones, A., Field, M.: The effects of cue-specific inhibition training on alcohol consumption in heavy social drinkers. Exp. Clin. Psychopharmacol. **21**, 8–16 (2013). doi:10.1037/a0030683

17. Verbruggen, F., Logan, G.D.: Automatic and controlled response inhibition: associative learning in the Go/No-Go and stop-signal paradigms. J. Exp. Psychol. Gen. **137**, 649–672 (2008). doi:10.1037/a0013170

18. Logan, G.D., Cowan, W.B.: On the ability to inhibit thought and action: a theory of an act of control. Psychol. Rev. **91**, 295–327 (1984). doi:10.1037/0033-295X.91.3.295

19. Verbruggen, F., Adams, R., Chambers, C.D.: Proactive motor control reduces monetary risk taking in gambling. Psychol. Sci. **23**, 805–815 (2012). doi:10.1177/0956797611434538

20. Dovis, S., van der Oord, S., Wiers, R.W., Prins, P.J.M.: Improving executive functioning in children with ADHD: training multiple executive functions within the context of a computer game. A randomized double-blind placebo controlled trial. PLoS ONE **10**(4), e0121651 (2015). doi:10.1371/journal.pone.0121651

21. Rubia, K., Smith, A.B., Brammer, M.J., Taylor, E.: Right inferior prefrontal cortex mediates response inhibition while mesial prefrontal cortex is responsible for error detection. Neuroimage **20**, 351–358 (2003). PMID:14527595

22. Spierer, L., Chavan, C.F., Manuel, A.L.: Training-induced behavioral and brain plasticity in inhibitory control. Front. Hum. Neurosci. **7**, 427 (2013). doi:10.3389/fnhum.2013.00427

23. Blakemore, S.J., Choudhury, S.: Development of the adolescent brain: implications for executive function and social cognition. J. Child Psychol. Psychiatry **47**, 296–312 (2006). doi:10.1111/j.1469-7610.2006.01611.x

24. Luna, B., Garver, K.E., Urban, T.A., Lazar, N.A., Sweeney, J.A.: Maturation of cognitive processes from late childhood to adulthood. Child Dev. **75**, 1357–1372 (2004). doi:10.1111/j.1467-8624.2004.00745.x

25. Veling, H., Aarts, H.: Unintentional preparation of motor impulses after incidental perception of need-rewarding objects. Cogn. Emot. **25**, 1131–1138 (2011). doi:10.1080/02699931.2010.524053

26. Veling, H., Holland, R.W., van Knippenberg, A.: When approach motivation and behavioral inhibition collide: behavior regulation through stimulus devaluation. J. Exp. Soc. Psychol. **44**, 1013–1019 (2008). doi:10.1016/j.jesp.2008.03.004

27. Kepper, A., van den Eijnden, R., Monshouwer, K., Vollebergh, W.: Understanding the elevated risk of substance use by adolescents in special education and residential youth care: the role of individual, family and peer factors. Eur. Child Adolesc. Psychiatry **23**(6), 461–472 (2014). doi:10.1007/s00787-013-0471-1

28. van de Schoot, R., Hoijtink, H.J.A., Dekovic, M.: Testing inequality constrained hypotheses in SEM models. Struct. Equ. Modeling **17**, 443–463 (2010). doi:10.1080/10705511.2010.489010

29. Vanbrabant, L., Van De Schoot, R., Rosseel, Y.: Constrained statistical inference: sample-size tables for ANOVA and regression. Front. Psychol. **5**, 1–7 (2015). doi:10.3389/fpsyg.2014.01565

30. Peeters, M., Monshouwer, K., van de Schoot, R., Janssen, T., Vollebergh, W.A.M., Wiers, R.W.: Automatic processes and the drinking behavior in early adolescence: a prospective study. Alcohol. Clin. Exp. Res. **37**(10), 1737–1744 (2013). doi:10.1111/acer.12156

31. Peeters, M., Wiers, R.W., Monshouwer, K., Van de Schoot, R., Janssen, T., Vollebergh, W.A.M.: Automatic processes in at-risk adolescents: the role of alcohol-approach tendencies and response inhibition in drinking behavior. Addiction **107**, 1939–1946 (2012). doi:10.1111/j.1360-0443.2012.03948.x

32. Tangney, J.P., Baumeister, R.F., Boone, A.L.: High self-control predicts good adjustment, less pathology, better grades, and interpersonal success. J. Pers. **72**, 271–324 (2004). PMID:15016066

33. Hinson, J.M., Jameson, T.L., Whitney, P.: Impulsive decision making and working memory. J. Exp. Psychol. Learn. Mem. Cogn. **29**(2), 298–306 (2003). PMID:12696817

34. Petrides, M., Milner, B.: Deficits on subject-ordered tasks after frontal-and temporal-lobe lesions in man. Neuropsychologia **20**, 249–262 (1982). PMID:7121793

35. Boendermaker, W.J., Sanchez Maceiras, S., Boffo, M., Wiers, R.W.: Attentional bias modification with serious game elements: evaluating the shots game. J. Med. Internet Res.: Serious Games (in press)

Games and Soft Skills

Social Agents for Learning in Virtual Environments

Agnese Augello[1], Manuel Gentile[2(✉)], and Frank Dignum[3]

[1] ICAR - National Research Council of Italy,
Viale delle Scienze - Edificio 11 - 90128 Palermo, Italy
augello@pa.icar.cnr.it
[2] ITD - National Research Council of Italy,
Via Ugo La Malfa 153, 90146 Palermo, Italy
manuel.gentile@itd.cnr.it
[3] Utrecht University, Princetonplein 5, De Uithof, 3584 CC Utrecht, The Netherlands
F.P.M.Dignum@uu.nl

Abstract. Several serious games have been proposed to practice communication strategies in formal contexts. Intelligent virtual agents (IVA) can be used to show the player the effects of a conversational move. In this paper we discuss the key role of using social context for the virtual agents in these serious games. Social practices are exploited to bundle social interactions into standard packages and as a basis to model the deliberation processes of IVAs. We describe a social practice oriented IVA architecture used in the implementation of a serious game for the practicing of communication in medical interviews.

Keywords: Social practice · IVAs · Serious games · Conversational agents

1 Introduction

In the present day society social skills become more and more important. A growing body of research considers the possession of adequate interpersonal, social and communicative competences as necessary for ensuring social, psychological and occupational well-being [1]. Moreover, the role of social skills as a predictive factor for academic or professional success has been broadly acknowledged. People are more assertive and also in many professional situations traditional power ascribed to roles no longer exists to the same extent. This means that professionals in many occupations have to train their social skills to cope with this new situation. E.g. policemen in the street have to be able to stay calm and quiet down quarrels and fights between groups of people and doctors have to learn to talk to their patients in a respectful and empathetic way.

Several researchers underline the importance of the observational learning for training strategies aimed at social skills acquisition [2,3]. In particular, Bandura [2] hypothesizes that "behavioural, cognitive, and affective learning from

© Springer International Publishing AG 2016
R. Bottino et al. (Eds.): GALA 2016, LNCS 10056, pp. 133–143, 2016.
DOI: 10.1007/978-3-319-50182-6_12

direct experience can be achieved vicariously by observing people's actions and the consequences for them". Through "role playing" it is possible to practice the desired behaviours in a controlled setting [1]. However, this approach can be difficult and expensive; often actors are used to train students, but each student can only practice a limited number of times in these realistic settings. Serious games can be exploited as an innovative and valid approach and virtual agents can be used to bring social elements of interactions into simulations [4,5]. The players can interact with the agents to experience the social effects of a conversation [6] and also to better understand how the social structure, the social practice and the social agents involved in a social interaction determine the actual conversation and the utterances that are used [6]. Therefore, virtual conversational agents seem perfect to provide learners with a continuous feedback about the social effects of conversational choices on the interlocutors [7]. However, the most of serious games for communicative skills training use scripted scenarios where the user's choices are limited according to an instructional design approach so that the scenario will be known after a few runs [7]. Although the efficacy of behavioural approach is proved, a greater degree of freedom during the interaction could support the user in a knowledge construction process according to a constructivist approach. Moreover, despite of an increased attention for the development of "more social" conversational agents [8], having a social identity [9] and being able to recognize the social attitude of their interlocutors [10], to the best of our knowledge, little has been done to put social context at the basis of the deliberation in conversation. Including social context could lead to adding excessive complexity to dialogue management: all the conditions that characterize the state of the conversation, and the effects of the choices on different variables related to the state of the dialogue and the interlocutor must be handled at every dialogue move, complicating the writing of the knowledge base of a conversational agent.

In a previous work [14], we proposed the use of *social practices* [11] as a way to bundle social interactions into standard packages. Social practices are used by people as well to direct and limit the interactions and set expectations. Thus we recognize social chitchat, bad news conversations and formal meeting dialogues. Each come with a set of rules that are usually followed, with actors that play a certain role in them and each have some predefined purpose. While in the previous architecture we focused only on the process of context analysis and choice of the proper social practice, in this work we deeply discuss the role of social practices in the serious games formalization, proposing a new architecture and a prototype of a game designed for medical students aimed at practicing social and communicative skills.

2   Role of Social Context in Serious Games: A Case Study in the Medical Context

Nowadays several serious games have been proposed to practice communication strategies especially in a medical context [7]. These games often exploit intelligent virtual agents to simulate a conversation with virtual patients. In this kind of games, it is important to correctly manage the social context in order to obtain a realistic behaviour for the agent and a proper evaluation of the player's abilities. At the same time, it is important to put the students in a complex learning path where the student has to cope with different situations in order to sense others feelings and perspectives, taking active interest in their concerns as well as recognizing one's emotions and their effects. A role play strategy where students experience different roles and scenarios, could lead to a better understanding of the worries of the patients and experiment what are the situations that lead to a greater openness in the conversation. The approach also fosters abstraction and reflection processes thus improving the effectiveness of medical patient dialogue [1]. In addition to the doctor role, players can act as patients and family members, observing from time to time, the reactions of patients in different social situations. As an example, the player can experience the difference in the patient behaviour if he plays the role of the personal doctor of the patient or if he plays the role of a substitute doctor that must gain the patient trustfulness. This implies a modelling of different behaviours and plans of actions for the agent, according to the specific social situation that involve specific social roles, plans, expectations and so on. Let us suppose that the agent acts as a patient usually having a strong headache. In a practice of consultation with his personal doctor, that is already aware of his situation and the symptoms that come with it, the patient's expectation is to quickly obtain the medicine prescription, therefore his plan consists of a sequence of actions related to the conversational protocol that he will soon carry out to obtain the therapeutic treatment. In an unexpected practice of consultation with un unknown doctor the agent expectation is that the doctor properly introduces himself and explains the reason of this substitution. Moreover, the conversation plan changes because the patient must give to the doctor all the required information about his health history. Different situations lead to different goals and plans of actions and also to different reactions of the interlocutor to the same event. As an example, if the substitute of the doctor recommends the patient to further examine his situation by making a CAT scan, the patient is confused and worried. He does not trust this doctor enough to understand that maybe a further check of his health situation can be a good thing. His reaction would certainly have been different if the request had come from his own doctor or if he deliberately went for a visit with an unknown specialist. Therefore in the waiting room he could start a conversation with other patients in order to obtain some useful information and to have some psychological support. As consequence, the virtual agents must be able to adapt itself to the different situations and at the same time the player behaviour must be evaluated according to the different scenarios designed in the game.

3   The SALVE Game

In this section we describe the initial steps in the implementation of a serious game for practicing communication in the medical context. SALVE stands for

"Social Agents for Learning in Virtual Environments" and it is a dialogue-based serious game in which the player can experiment different scenarios and act in different roles. We choose the Italian term "salve" to highlight the importance of social context in communication, because it is an appropriate greeting in various social circumstances. The game allows the player to practice his skills by interacting with a virtual agent. The aim is to offer the player a realistic simulation where he can observe the effects of his conversational choices on the dialogue progress, the reactions of the patients and where he can obtain a final evaluation that summarizes his social, communicative and professional skills. At the beginning of the game the player can select a specific scenario to practice. At the moment we have implemented an "anamnesis scenario" where the player acts as the personal doctor of the virtual agent, but future scenario will allow the player to act as a substitute of the personal doctor, a relative or another patient with similar health problems. Moreover, he can select the skills that he wants to asses during the game. The game offers the possibility to obtain an evaluation of social, emphatic, communicative and professional skills. The core of the game is a social context management according to the social practice theory, that drives the formalization of the agent processes of knowledge representation, understanding and deliberation.

3.1   Social Context Management

We use the theory of social practices in order to support the management of social context in serious games. A social practice refers to a routinized type of behaviour typically and habitually performed in a society. The sociological theory studies the behaviour of groups of people and their interactions according to social practices [11]. In [13], the theory is analyzed from an individual perspective in order to incorporate it into an agent architecture. The aim of the model is to provide a representation scheme that allows the implementation of cognitive agents able to use the social practice as a first-class construct in the agent deliberation process [13]. According to this model a social practice is characterized by a *Physical Context* describing resources, actors and places involved in the practice, and a *Social Context* indicating their social interpretation within the practices: actors will have *Roles*, the involved elements a *Social Interpretation* and proper *Norms* identify the rules that are expected to be followed inside the social practice. The model is also characterized by the *Activities* that an agent can perform in the practice, where the activities have a specific *Meaning* and require some *Competences* from the agent to perform them. The actors build *Plan Patterns* to reach a specific goal in the practice; a *Plan Pattern* is a sequence of expected scenes, where each scene is associated with a subgoal. The achievement of a goal triggers the transition to the next scene. The actors can force the transition to other scenes. In this case there is not a correct observance of the social practice, some goals cannot be fulfilled and this has consequences for the reaction of the interlocutor and on the final scores. (e.g. closing the conversation before properly explaining the proposed treatment).

The formalization of the game according to social practices has several advantages. A social practice gives the context to properly interpret the games events and their effect on a set of dimensions of interest. Putting social practice at the base of the agent's deliberation simplifies considerably its formalization, as discussed in [13–15]. In fact, in this way the analysis of an event is correctly managed and differentiated according to the current practice, the current scene inside the practice and finally the game state inside that scene. Among the dimensions of interest, it is possible to consider the agent's emotions and some dimensions related to the player behaviour that can be used to evaluate his final score. The patient's expectations change according to the social situation and the fulfilment or not of these expectations leads to specific emotions. In this sense social practices are useful to define in a simple manner the emotional reactions of the agent. Another advantage concerns the player evaluation, since his behaviour and in particular the observance of social practices allows for an implicit evaluation of social and professional skills, as will be further discussed into the Sects. 3.2 and 4.

3.2 Player Skills Relevant for the Game

The game is aimed at the evaluation of a set of skills that are important for a physician. In the literature several models have been proposed to assess social and communicative skills either in general but also in the specific context of medical consultations [16–18]. For example, a physician must have enough motivation, the ability to give convincing information to the patient, showing empathy and controlling bad emotions. Indeed, these features are fulfilled if the doctor follows the correct practice of consultation. Therefore, starting from a correct model of the social practices involved in the medical context it is possible to assess many of these skills analyzing the observance of the player of the practices. We therefore consider some main skills that correspond to specific scores in the game and that can be chosen by the player at the beginning of the game. The first is the *Social Interpersonal Behaviour*, the ability to assess and follow correctly the different social situations and medical protocols. As an example, consider an anamnesis scenario where the observance of the social practice of consultation with an unknown patient requires a correct greeting and introduction of the doctor, a properly conducted interview to deepen his health history and the current health problem, a proper information giving phase, and a detailed explanation of the therapy. Another important skill is the *Emotion Elicitation*, that we consider as the ability to elicit positive emotions in the patient, avoiding negative ones. According to the specific social situation the actors of a practice have expectations that, if confirmed or not, generate specific emotions. Therefore, the emotional internal state of the agent depends on how the dialogue flow confirms his expectations in a practice. A proper model to formalize the elicitation of emotions in the agent is the OCC model, and in particular the revisited model of Steunebrink et al. [19]. The model summarizes in a hierarchical structure the conditions that elicit emotions and the variables that affect their intensities. The emotion, classified in 22 types, can be a consequence of events, actions of other agents or aspects or objects that appear in the environment. Another important skill for a physician is showing *Empathy*, the ability to be aware of the needs of the patient, understanding his feelings, concerns and perspectives. Communication events have been classified in [18] according to the expressed empathy. This classification has been made analyzing a set of transcripts of medical consultations, considering the physicians answers to what is called an *Empathic Opportunity* and verbal expressions of emotions by patients that create an opportunity for an *Empathic Response*. An empathetic opportunity can be direct or potential if it is possible to infer an underlying emotion. The empathy skill of the player is therefore evaluated by checking if the player misses the empathetic opportunities in the course of the game or if he uses these opportunities properly. Finally, we consider also the evaluation of *Communicative Skills*, consisting of the ability to listen to the interlocutor, keeping his attention, giving feedbacks, answering in time and choosing appropriate wordings. Another skill that could be considered in future work is the evaluation of a *Self-awareness and regulation skill*, consisting in the ability to properly recognize one's own attitudes and preferences, select the appropriate skills and manage the internal impulses.

3.3   The SALVE Architecture

Let us consider that the agent has already identified the current social practice [14]. This identification influences the agent's beliefs and drives the understanding of the dialogue and its conversational choices. This is accomplished by the main module of the architecture, named *Interaction* and *Representation and Interpretation* (R&I) module (see Fig. 1). The game architecture considers also

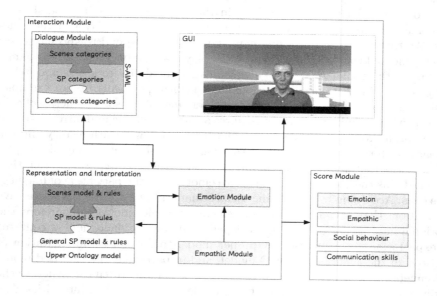

Fig. 1. The SALVE game architecture

a score module used to assess the player abilities. The following sections describe these modules in more detail using the anamnesis practice as example. The practice takes place inside the doctor's office at a visiting schedule time and involves two actors, assuming respectively the roles of the personal doctor of the patient and the patient itself. In the following sections we refer to a plan associated to this practice aimed to the arrangement of a health care path for the patient. The plan assumes the accomplishment of dialogue activities such as *greetings*, *health problem description* and *therapy acquisition*.

Interaction Module. The interaction module is composed of a graphical interface where an avatar is used to express the emotions and reactions of the patient, and a *dialogue* sub-module that allows the agent to manage the conversation, interpret the utterances of the players and recognize events. The dialogue sub-module is implemented by means of the S-AIML technology [20], an extension of the AIML language [21], that allows to bind the categories to specific practices and their activities. The S-AIML language and its relative processor, are enhancements of the traditional dialogue engine of Alice that allows the chatbot to manage the dialogue according to a specific social practice and to interact with the resoning module. The language is used to describe possible question-answer modules, called categories, that can be matched during the conversation. The categories can be matched in different practices (*Common Categories*), or can be organized according to the current social practice (*SP Categories*) by means of a *social practice* tag or more specifically according to a scene of the practice (*Scenes Categories*) by means of the (*scene* tag). Moreover it is possible indicate specific preconditions that have to be matched using the (*precondition* tag). The category shown in Fig. 2a allows for an interpretation of a greeting as the accomplishment of the subgoal associated to the *greeting* scene, and as result throws a *GreetingsReceived* event.

```
<scene name="greetings">
  <category>
    <pattern><set>greetings</set></pattern>
    <template>Hello!
      <insert packageName="sp.anamnesi.greetings"
typeName="GreetingsReceived" />
    </template>
  </category>
```

```
<category>
  <pattern>why are you here</pattern>
  <template>
<insert packageName="sp.anamnesi.health_problem"
typeName="HealthProblemAsked" />
    I'm experiencing one of my usual
    <getDroolsTemplate />. It's quite strong.
  </template>
</category>
```

(a)   (b)

Fig. 2. S-Aiml examples

The category shown in Fig. 2b allows for a transition to the next scene of the practice. When the player asks the agent the reason of the appointment, there is a transition to the *health problem* scene and the querying of the R&I module to get the specific health problem of the scenario. The answer of the agent will be: *I'm experiencing one of my usual headaches. It's quite strong.*

```
rule "GreetingsReceivedInTime"
when
    $startScene:EnterScene(scene.name=="greetings")
    $g:GreetingsReceived(this after[0ms,20000ms] $startScene )
then
    OCCHappenedEvent he=new OCCHappenedEvent();
    don(he,DesirableEvent.class);
    don(he,ProspectedRelevantEvent.class);
    insert(he);
    insert(new ChangeOfSceneFromGoal());
end
```

(a)

```
rule "DesirableProspectedEventHappened"
when
    $d:OCCHappenedEvent(this isA ProspectedRelevantEvent,
this isA DesirableEvent)
    $agent:Emotion(this isA Agent)
then
    $agent.setSatisfaction($agent.getSatisfaction()+1);
end
```

(b)

Fig. 3. Rules examples

Representation and Interpretation. This module organizes the knowledge and the rules required by the agent to correctly interpret the events recognized by the interaction module. Similarly to the previous module, there is a distinction between a more general knowledge and the knowledge specific for the social practices. The general knowledge is related to the agent beliefs and it also includes the formalization of the social practice module, its main components, the rules for starting and closing the practices and to choose and perform a plan pattern. A specific social practice carries implicit knowledge, therefore, depending on the social practice, the agent updates its social interpretation of the elements with which it interacts. The knowledge carried by a practice includes the agent's beliefs and expectations in a practice, the rules for the generation of plans and the analysis of possible norm violations. The rules embedded in a practice are used as a kind of short cuts in the deliberation of the agent. The events, generated by the conversational choices of the player, are analyzed according to the dimensions of interest in the game, in particular according to their influence on the agent emotions or the empathy transmitted by the player. As a specific example, a greeting received in time is interpreted an expected desirable event according to the OCC classification (Fig. 3a) and will elicit positive emotions (Fig. 3b).

Other rules are specific for the assessment of the player's skills, such as the empathy. E.g. a description of the headache by the agent generates an *Empathetic Opportunity* (Fig. 4a). Therefore, if the player underestimates the patient's prob-

```
<category>
  <pattern>How is your pain today</pattern>
  <template>
  It is very strong.
    <insert packageName="empathic"
typeName="EmpathicOpportunity" />
  </template>
</category>
```

(a)

```
<category>
  <pattern>Don't be exaggerated</pattern>
  <that>It is very strong</that>
  <template>Yes, it's really that bad..
    <insert
packageName="sp.anamnesi.health_problem"
typeName="DoctorUnderestimatesPain"/>
  </template>
</category>
```

(b)

```
rule "DoctorUnderestimatesPain"
when
    $e:EmpathicOpportunity()
    DoctorUnderestimatesPain(this after $e)
then
    EmpathicOpportunityTerminator ee=new
EmpathicOpportunityTerminator();
    insert(ee);
end
```

(c)

```
rule "EmpathicOpportunityMissed"
when
    $p:EmpathicOpportunity()
    EmpathicOpportunityTerminator(this after $p)
    $agent:Agent
then
    $agent.setEmpathicState("empathic
opportunity missed");
end
```

(d)

Fig. 4. Empathic flow example

lem (Fig. 4b) the *Empathetic Opportunity* is declared terminated (Fig. 4c and d) because the statement of the doctor moves the dialogue away from the expressed emotion.

4   Gaming

In the previous sections we have explained how the conversations with the trainee are managed using social practices. In this section we will discuss how this app-roach supports the creation of a conversation *game*. In the Communicate! plat-form [7], that was the primary inspiration for our work, the conversations were predesigned as a kind of tree structures and trainees have to make a choice at each state for the possible move they make next. In this set up it is easy to associate a score with each possible move in a positive or negative sense. We claim that th predetermined conversations are too limited and showed a way to give the trainee more initiative and freedom in the conversation. However, the consequence of this flexibility is that we cannot associate a score on fore-hand with every possibde move of the trainee (as they are not all known on forehand). Our approach using social practices and mental states of the agents suggests a scoring approach that is not tied to the actual conversation moves, but rather to the mental states that the agents maintain and the deviations or confirmation of the social practice that is followed. As we have shown, the trainees conversational moves lead to changes in e.g. the emotional state of the patient depending on the specific content of that move. Thus the target of the trainee is to communicate in a way to optimize the score of the patient's mental state. In a naive approach one might than say that a move that makes a patient angry, worried or impatient is bad (leads to a decrease in score). However, it is not always possible to avoid negative emotions in a patient in e.g. the anamnesis scenario. If the doctor finds out that the patient most likely has a brain tumor that causes his frequent headaches he needs to tell this and this might create all kinds of negative emotions in the patient. The training should be geared to how to cope with these emotions and use the conversation to decrease these emotions in some way in the way patient. If a patient is both worried and angry it can be best to first alleviate his worries and after that on his anger, but if they are tackled in the reverse order it might still work in the end. Thus scores should not be given to single states, but rather to sequences of states. E.g. a trainee gets a negative score if the anger of the patient stays above a certain level more than five or ten moves and even gets a very negative score if the patient is still angry at the end of the conversation. So, rather than scoring individual states we can give rules on the sequences of states that appear and their influence on the score. A second issue is that there are several aspects that play a role in the conver-sation and that the trainee should try to control. We have mentioned empathy with the patient in our context. Because the (felt) empathy is modelled as a separate aspect of the state of the patient it can get a separate score. Having to handle combinations of aspects the trainee now has to try to maximize the scores on all aspects, which often cannot be done at the same time (i.e. in one move). By attaching the scores to rules over state sequences it is now easily possible to show that some orders of conversational moves lead to better scores than other ones without limiting the conversation to some predetermined order(s). So, we get more flexibility and more accurate scoring of the trainee's performance. The social practice is used for the scoring as this practice gives a context in which the interaction takes place and it therefore also indicates the expected (range of) mental states of the participants during the conversation. Thus we can use these mental states as a kind of target values for the trainee to achieve. Thus scores become relative to a social practice rather than some absolute values, which makes the scoring more realistic. E.g. a patient should never be angry in a regular check-up meeting with his doctor, but he can be expected to become angry in a bad news conversation. Thus the patient becoming angry is not always bad, but is bad in certain contexts.

5   Conclusion

In this work we analyse the importance of a social context management in serious games, proposing an architecture for social agents modelling based on the social practice theory. The architecture puts social practice at the heart of the deliberative process of an agent, allowing for a more accurate interpretation of user sentences. According to the specific social practice, the choices of the player have a different effect on the agent's state and on his final score. It is important to highlight that the changes are not only on single question answer exchanges, but the activation of a social practice determines meaningful changes also on the entire dialogue path. It determines the activation of both knowledge and plans, and the correct understanding of the player sentences by means of the activation of a subset of S-AIML categories. Without a social practice approach there is a need to encode a lot of social and communication rules and heuristics into the game characters, while with the proposed approach the knowledge becomes modularized and efficiently used. Nevertheless, social practice is not a rigid structure; the agent acts according to its expectations into the practice, but his choices are consequence of a constant analysis of the dialogue state. We discussed about some preliminary steps in the implementation of what we called SALVE game. Future work will regard the development of other scenarios and the setting of specific trials to prove the educational effectiveness of the game.

References

1. Segrin, C., Givertz, M.: Methods of social skills training and development. In: Greene, J.O., Burleson, B.R. (eds.) Handbook of Communication and Social Interaction Skills. Lawrence Erlbaum Associates Inc., Mahwah (2003)
2. Bandura, A.: Social cognitive theory of personality. In: Theory and Research, Handbook of Personality, pp. 154–196 (1999)
3. Hodgson, R.: Review of T. L. Rosenthal, and B. J. Zimmerman 'Social Learning and Cognition'. Behav. Psychother. **10**, 124 (1982)
4. Swartout, W., Artstein, R., Forbell, E., Foutz, S., Lane, H.C., Lange, B., Morie, J., Noren, D., Rizzo, S., Traum, D.: Virtual humans for learning. AI Mag. **34**(4), 13–30 (2013)

5. Babu, S.V., Suma, E., Hodges, L.F., Barnes, T.: Learning cultural conversational protocols with immersive interactive virtual humans. Int. J. Virtual Reality **10**, 25–35 (2011)
6. Fairclough, N.: Analysing Discourse: Textual Analysis for Social Research. Psychology Press, Abingdon-on-Thames (2003)
7. Jeuring, J., Grosfeld, F., Heeren, B., Hulsbergen, M., IJntema, R., Jonker, V., Mastenbroek, N., Van Der Smagt, M., Wijmans, F., Wolters, M., Van Zeijts, H.: Demo: communicate! - a serious game for communication skills. In: Proceedings EC-TEL 2015: 10th European Conference on Technology Enhanced Learning (2015)
8. Klüwer, T.: "I like your shirt" - dialogue acts for enabling social talk in conversational agents. In: Vilhjálmsson, H.H., Kopp, S., Marsella, S., Thórisson, K.R. (eds.) IVA 2011. LNCS (LNAI), vol. 6895, pp. 14–27. Springer, Heidelberg (2011). doi:10.1007/978-3-642-23974-8_2
9. Cassell, J.: Social practice: becoming enculturated in human-computer interaction. In: Stephanidis, C. (ed.) UAHCI 2009. LNCS, vol. 5616, pp. 303–313. Springer, Heidelberg (2009). doi:10.1007/978-3-642-02713-0_32
10. Carofiglio, V., De Carolis, B., Mazzotta, I., Novielli, N., Pizzutilo, S.: Towards a socially intelligent ECA. IxD&A **5**, 99–106 (2009)
11. Reckwitz, A.: Toward a theory of social practices a development in culturalist theorizing. Eur. J. Soc. Theory **5**(2), 243–263 (2002)
12. Minsky, M.: A framework for representing knowledge. In: Computation & Intelligence, pp. 163–189. American Association for Artificial Intelligence (1995)
13. Dignum, V., Dignum, F.: Contextualized planning using social practices. In: Ghose, A., Oren, N., Telang, P., Thangarajah, J. (eds.) COIN 2014. LNCS (LNAI), vol. 9372, pp. 36–52. Springer, Heidelberg (2015). doi:10.1007/978-3-319-25420-3_3
14. Augello, A., Gentile, M., Dignum, F.: Social practices for social driven conversations in serious games. In: De Gloria, A., Veltkamp, R. (eds.) GALA 2015. LNCS, vol. 9599, pp. 100–110. Springer, Heidelberg (2016). doi:10.1007/978-3-319-40216-1_11
15. Augello, A., Gentile, M., Weideveld, L., Dignum, F.: Dialogues as social practices for serious games. In: Proceedings of the 22nd European Conference on Artificial Intelligence, ECAI 2016 (2016, to appear)
16. Elksnin, L.K., Elksnin, N.: Teaching social skills to students with learning and behavior problems. Interv. Sch. Clinic **33**(3), 131–140 (1998)
17. Street Jr., R.L.: Interpersonal communication skills in health care contexts. In: Greene, J.O., Burleson, B.R. (eds.) Handbook of Communication and Social Interaction Skills, pp. 909–933. Lawrence Erlbaum, Mahwah (2003)
18. Suchman, A.L., Markakis, K., Beckman, H.B., Frankel, R.: A model of empathic communication in the medical interview. JAMA **277**(8), 678–682 (1997)
19. Steunebrink, B.R., Dastani, M.M., Meyer, J.-J.C.: The OCC model revisited. In: Reichardt, D. (ed.) Proceedings of the 4th Workshop on Emotion and Computing - Current Research and Future Impact. Paderborn, Germany (2009)
20. Augello, A., Gentile, M., Weideveld, L., Dignum, F.: A model of a social chatbot. In: Pietro, G., Gallo, L., Howlett, R.J., Jain, L.C. (eds.) Intelligent Interactive Multimedia Systems and Services 2016. SIST, vol. 55, pp. 637–647. Springer, Heidelberg (2016). doi:10.1007/978-3-319-39345-2_57. ISBN 978-3-319-39345-2
21. Marietto, M.D.G.B., de Aguiar, R.V., Barbosa, G.D.O., Botelho, W.T., Pimentel, E., Frana, R.D.S., da Silva, V.L.: Artificial intelligence markup language, a brief tutorial. arXiv preprint (2013). arXiv:1307.3091

EscapED: Adapting Live-Action, Interactive Games to Support Higher Education Teaching and Learning Practices

Samantha Clarke[✉], Sylvester Arnab, Helen Keegan,
Luca Morini, and Oliver Wood

Disruptive Media Learning Lab, Coventry University, Coventry, UK
{ab4588, aa8110, ab7942, ac2009, ab5576}@coventry.ac.uk

Abstract. Game-based learning (GBL) is often found to be technically driven and more often than not, serious games for instance, are conceptualised and designed solely for digital platforms and state of the art technologies. To encourage a greater discussion on the potential benefits and challenges of a more holistic approach to developing GBL, that promote human centred interactions and play for learning, the authors present the Game Changers initiative. The Game Changers initiative is discussed and focus is drawn to one of its programmes titled; escapED, for developing non-digital GBL approaches within the context of Science, Technology, Engineering and Mathematics combined with Arts (STEAM) education. EscapED, aids the design and creation of educational Escape Rooms and Interactive Gaming Experiences for staff and students in further/higher education settings. The authors present the escapED theoretical framework as a tool to aid future design and development of on-site interactive experiences, in order to provide engaging alternatives for learning and soft skills development amongst higher education staff and students.

1 Introduction

The paradigm of adopting games and play as systems for representing real-life conditions, imparting knowledge and moral teachings, and generally nurturing social evolution, now referred to as game-based learning (GBL), has existed for thousands of years. Evidence of early board games, date back to the Predynastic burial tombs in Egypt, c. 3500 BC, where examinations of ancient burial frescos have revealed the oldest known game to man; Senet (Piccione 1980). The identification of Senet and other early examples of board games, found in various cultures and societies throughout history, emphasizes the fascination and value that humankind has had, and continues to have regarding the nature of games and play, so much so, that they are deeply embedded into our history as a civilization (Parlett 1999). Equally so, the significance of play for learning can be exhibited throughout the animal kingdom with one particular given example of; 'social play' (Bekoff and Allen 1998), that is used by most living mammals for developing practical skills and experiences needed for later adult life. The "classic" argument from Huizinga (1938) reverses the chronology, in that culture and civilization themselves arise in and from play. Similarly, Bateson (1955) argues that sociality and meaningful communication in animals arise from play.

© Springer International Publishing AG 2016
R. Bottino et al. (Eds.): GALA 2016, LNCS 10056, pp. 144–153, 2016.
DOI: 10.1007/978-3-319-50182-6_13

Whilst it is therefore evident that traditional games and play have always existed and have had their place within the context of life and society on earth, the 20th century led the way into something new that would change games and play forever, the rise of the digital revolution. The onset of the digital revolution brought with it computer based technologies that quickly became openly available to everyone. Video games, simulations and the internet followed these technologies, and offered exciting and novel ways of connecting and engaging with people of all ages, genders, cultures and races across the globe. Still, even further down the line into the 21st century, humankind's obsession with technology has not waned, as developments into new ways to experience the world through the use of technology such as; Location-Based Experiences, Smart Phone Technologies, VR, 3D, Augmented Reality and 360 video to name a few, has continued to grow and become central features or provide functional assistance within everyday living. Perhaps one of the most note-worthy aspects of humanities pursuit of technological ascendancy however, is in the endeavor to adopt these technologies for the purposes of games and play.

The appeal and engagement of video games has long been documented, and statistics produced by Newzoo and GlobalCollect (2014) confirmed their far reaching popularity, when they estimated that there were thought to be at least 1.78 billion gamers worldwide as of August 2014. Due to the high uptake of computer games throughout society, particularly amongst children and young adults, researchers and educators have championed the potential reach and use of computer games, simulations and their related technologies, as instructional delivery systems for various learning and behavior change endeavors (Tobias et al. 2014). As such GBL, began to take on a whole new identity which highlighted technology as a central theme (Gee 2006; Kafai and Resnick 1996; Salen 2007). In 2001, Prensky (2007) defined the term; Digital Game-Based Learning, which may have helped influence how the academic world developed and perceived the required conditions of GBL, particularly in relation to the requirement of technology. As such, the premise of GBL has since, subsequently developed predominantly within academic practice, to mean the theory of adopting digital games and technology as a method for delivering learning materials through play and study of in-game components (Squire 2011; Tang et al. 2007; Whitton 2014). Tang et al. (2009) offer the following definition of GBL:

> Games-based learning takes advantage of gaming technologies to create a fun, motivating, and interactive virtual learning environment that promotes situated experiential learning (Tang et al. 2009).

As such, most of the current research that has been conducted concerning the practice of GBL, centers on the adoption of using various technologies and digital gaming preferences as a means to delivering educational content and exploring techniques of maintaining motivation and engagement of varying user types. Whilst it is assumed that a larger proportion of GBL research has been aimed at digital gaming and technology, it has been recognized within the academic community that GBL can mean the adoption of non-digital examples such as tabletop, card or board games (Baker et al. 2005; Cook and Hazelwood 2002; Whitehead 2012). However, research into the design, development and evaluation of non-digital GBL applications still remains much scarcer than research surrounding their digital counterparts.

To challenge the current inclination towards adopting digital games and technologies as the leading method of delivering GBL, the authors present and review the holistic methods to game design and development offered by the Game Changers program. The Game Changers program and one of it's project's titled; escapED are discussed and theorized as to how these examples could be adopted and built upon to promote a return to human centered interaction and play within GBL, rather than the trending technology focused approach as of late.

2 The Game Changers Programme

The Game Changers Programme (gamify.org.uk) was set up to explore, experiment and exploit game design thinking in fostering creative problem solving and cross-disciplinary design collaboration. The overarching pedagogical construct of the initiative is motivated by 'learning by designing', which is a project-based inquiry approach, exploiting the characteristics of a design process that is non-linear, iterative, generative and creative. Design thinking as a domain has crossed over to learning, where it is a *"way of finding human needs and creating new solutions using the tools and mindsets of design practitioners"* (Kelley and Kelley 2013).

Game-making skills are emphasised as pathway to Science, Technology, Engineering and Mathematics (STEM) learning by existing initiatives, such as the Annual National STEM Video Game Challenge in NYC (Inaugural Challenge, 2010) aiming at combining creativity and STEM Skills through video game design. Games Design is also an extremely useful context for developing computational thinking and digital creativity (Nesta 2013), where computational thinking is taking an approach to solving problems, designing systems and understanding human behaviour that draws on concepts fundamental to computing (Wing 2006). Games present worlds with defined rules, clear objectives and often more than one possible solution to a problem, which enhances the context of both design and computational thinking.

Designing, developing and playing games has the potential to deepen content knowledge, strengthen collaborative skills, combine arts and technology, and build appreciation for the talents of others. According to the Science Education for Responsible Citizenship EU Report, *"innovative ideas emerge at the margins of disciplines"*, and the transition from STEM to STEAM (STEAM combined with Arts), including Arts and Humanities, means embracing the latter disciplines capacity for creativity, engagement and critical thinking. Creating games (digital/non-digital), as an activity on the edge of the diverse fields of Art, Narrative, Science, Computation and Engineering can be a fertile ground to cultivate these mind-sets, and to provide a place for them to meet and learn how to fruitfully cooperate.

The programme thus focuses on a holistic approach to design and development of games (analogue or digital) or gamified activities by adopting a more user and problem centred approach, which informs the type of gaming/gamified approach and technology the solution will consider. The programme provides open contents and resources to assist and guide participants and organise open sessions (workshops, speakers, etc.) throughout the process. The pilot has produced GBL resources, which includes non-digital initiatives such as the escapED project.

3   The EscapED Project

The philosophy and purpose of escapED, is to conceptualize interactive experiences and aid other educational facilitators in creating their own, live-action games for the purposes of education and positive behavior change in higher/further education settings. Based upon the design and experience of traditional entertainment Escape Rooms, escapED is adapted to incorporate educational themes, tangible learning objectives and behavior change metrics, to offer a new approach to human centered GBL. A study conducted by Nicholson (2005) on the growing phenomena of Escape Rooms defined them as:

> "live-action team-based games where players discover clues, solve puzzles, and accomplish tasks in one or more rooms in order to accomplish a specific goal (usually escaping from the room) in a limited time" (Nicholson 2005).

Traditional entertainment focused Escape Rooms, are growing in popularity worldwide, with rooms now available across most continents including Europe, America and Asia. Nicholson (2005) observes that the earliest well-documented example of an Escape Room, was run by the Scrap company in Kyoto, Japan in 2007 which facilitated teams of around 5–6 players. From there on, these live, interactive games have grown to become more elaborate and multi-faceted in their own quest to produce the most engaging and enjoyable experiences to accommodate small teams of a few people, to thousands of players participating in event settings.

Themes and narratives for entertainment Escape Rooms have ranged from horror (zombies, murderers, haunted houses) to mystery and adventure (detective, Indiana Jones). These themes and narratives, set the games atmosphere and lay the foundations of emotional investment and curiosity within the player. Based on live-action role-play (LARP) games such as Dungeons and Dragons (DND) (Gygax and Arneson 1974), the players essentially take on roles of different characters, although usually the same role such as a hostage, detective etc., within the Game Masters (Escape Room facilitator's) story. A sense of urgency and risk is usually maintained throughout the experience through the methods of time management, actors and props and outside influences, to generate a passionate response and investment from the players into completing the challenge in time.

Data collected from a survey of 175 Escape Rooms from around the world, conducted by Nicholson (2005), found that the demographic data of these Escape Rooms players, indicated some noteworthy discussions. Nicholson found that the demographic data from these rooms, exhibited an equal draw of players from both genders. Of the player groups of these rooms, it was reported that 71% were mixed genders, 15% were all male and 14% were all female. If Escape Rooms and other interactive, LARP games attract a balanced gender pool of player types, then GBL designers should consider and ask, what are the elements that make these experiences truly appealing to both genders?

Based on the growing market and the documented engagement levels that Escape Rooms seem to have generated within their diverse types of players, the authors selected to test the appeal and educational value of these forms of games within a University setting and developed a prototype experience of escapED for a University staff training event. The educational objective of the prototype was for players to develop soft skills such as communication, leadership and teamwork throughout their experience. The theme of the prototype was based around disarming a bomb, which was done through releasing an engineer hostage. Players were tasked to solve the riddles and tests to find the key code that would release the hostage's locks (Figs. 1 and 2).

Fig. 1. EscapED prototype: room 1 (bomb room)

Fig. 2. EscapED prototype: room 2 (hostage room)

On the day of the event, members of staff signed up to time slots and were put into teams no larger than 6 players. 3 teams participated in the game, with an overall total of 13 players taking part in the event. Each event lasted around 30 min, 10 min for introduction and rules, and 20 min for the game. A key feature of the design of the prototype was that the teams were split into two groups and placed into two adjoining rooms. One room held the bomb, and the other held the hostage. Riddles and clues were then split between the two rooms and relied on the communication of the players to describe and put the pieces together from both rooms. Players were not allowed to go between rooms and could only communicate via two laptops that were connected to skype, of which one was assigned to each room. Players could not move or touch the laptops, but could bring clues and puzzles to the laptop to show their teammates based in the other room. A first year drama student was employed to play the part of the hostage and to provide time awareness and clues to the players throughout the game. Most of the players were not aware/had not heard of Escape Room games before the event,

All players were observed by the author via their own connection to skype, and were monitored to observe player engagement and progress within the game. Each team was observed to display a similar method of entering and familiarizing themselves with the room, displaying conservative behavior but quickly figuring out where the laptops were placed and whether the other room could hear them. All players of each of the three teams displayed a high level of engagement throughout the experience, although this diminished somewhat when the players knew they had less than a minute left to complete the room. One team, was observed to develop a strategy in which they had a designated main communicator who would be responsible for relaying the information to the other room. None of the teams successfully completed the room, however a prize was offered to the team that came closest to completing the challenge (Fig. 3).

Fig. 3. EscapED prototype: player interacting with a puzzle

After the experience, each player was asked to fill in a short feedback sheet that asked four exploratory questions about their experience and perceptions of escapED that are detailed below:

1. Do you think escapED has any educational value?
2. Would you consider using the escapED program in your lesson plan?
3. What was good about the escapED prototype session?
4. What could we improve?

From the 13 participant players, a total of 8 feedback sheets were returned with all questions answered. All written feedback exhibited a positive theme throughout in regards to the experience itself. The words; 'Fun', 'Innovative' and 'Engaging' were repeated throughout the feedback and some player's indicated that they did not realize that 20 min had passed. All 8 feedback sheets stated that they could see the educational value of escapED, especially if the puzzles and theme of the experience, were worked into their taught subject matter. All feedback sheets indicated that the players would consider using escapED in their lesson plans but were unsure how to facilitate it. A few responses indicated that they thought the experience would be good as an induction into their lessons to encourage getting to know other students. One concern brought up through a number of the feedback responses was that the participants were curious to see how the experience would work with larger groups of players. None of the feedback received suggested that there were improvements that could or should be made to the experience.

Concluding on the prototype trial of escapED, the authors believe that from the behavior observed within the participating players throughout the live game experience, and from the follow up feedback gathered, that there are significant reasons to explore these type of LARP games for GBL purposes further. It is observed by the authors that from the varied backgrounds of the staff members that took part in the testing of the escapED prototype, the program could be used to create and facilitate cross-disciplinary teaching and learning scenarios. This would be particularly interesting to see developed for teaching and learning in the STEAM subjects, that is focused on bringing staff and students together from across these disciplines to work and pool their knowledge together to solve and contribute to something greater.

4   The EscapED Framework

Presented in Fig. 4 is the theoretical framework for escapED, which was used to design the prototype experience for the University staff training event.

Six main areas were considered whilst developing the prototype that consisted of; Participants, Objectives, Theme, Puzzles, Equipment and Evaluation. These areas were influenced and chosen, based on previous works conducted by Arnab and Clarke (2016), on the considerations of creating trans-disciplinary GBL experiences. Each of these areas were further broken down into specific segments that were needed in order to create an educational version of an Escape Room. Future works will look to develop more experiences adopting this method, that can be used to evaluate and expectantly validate the use of the escapED framework for creating engaging and educational versions of interactive, live-action games and experiences.

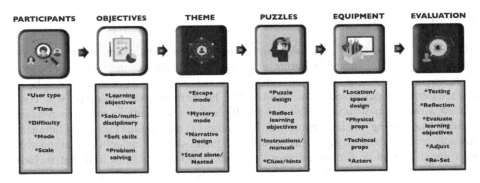

Fig. 4. EscapED framework

5 Conclusions

Game design thinking is a way to structure an iterative design process, and demonstrates how it is possible to frame a problem by considering game-play mechanics, dynamics and aesthetics so that the solutions we come out with are understandable, fun and engaging. It uses the idea of creating a a game/gamification product/resources, with an explicit process of brainstorming, finding out the needs of the audience, design, development, testing, sharing, and more. Design thinking can help students and teachers break out of the lecture/test model and showcase what young learners can do, rather than tests that try to catch them at what they can't do. It's a place for students to use different problem-solving styles, to add their own flair to the learning process, and to think about the impact they could have on the world.

Whilst this pilot has only considered University Lecturers who would be responsible for implementing such a learning style within their subject matter, the authors acknowledge that more trials need to be carried out with students to observe reactions and gain feedback relating to learning, acceptance and perceptions. Since lecturers may be more open to including new learning experiences such as live-action game-based learning, this may have been reflected within their feedback. Therefore it is essential that we gain feedback on this process from students to assess the overall valididy of this method within a university setting.

The Game Changers process has allowed us to look at the learning process from the perspective of experience design, which is key to ensuring that serious outcomes are fostered. Taking escaped project as an example, the holistic approach demonstrates transition from technology driven focus to a highly empathetic and experience-centred approach, which has also emphasised on the potential of arts and creativity in the enhancing the teaching and learning of STEM subjects. escapED showcases an approach that will inform the design of a more contextually immersive learning experience, which can be adopted and adapted in various learning contexts. The approach taps into our natural tendencies to learn by playing.

6 Future Works

The authors acknowledge the small sample size of player participation and feedback of the prototype test for escapED. Future works will include developing more experiences with larger samples of participants for more detailed data of experience, player engagement and perceived educational value. Furthermore, .the prototype was conducted with players who were University staff members. The authors intend to conduct similar trials using student participants to observe any similarities or differences towards reactions and engagement towards the game. A more indepth evaluation will be formed to explore further questions not picked up in this pilot trial that include concepts concerning learning styles and delivery times. Future experiences of escapED also intend to develop more subject specific puzzles and learning outcomes related to STEAM subjects.

References

Arnab, S., Clarke, S.: Towards a trans-disciplinary methodology for a game-based intervention development process. Br. J. Educ. Technol. (2016)

Baker, A., Navarro, E.O., Van Der Hoek, A.: An experimental card game for teaching software engineering processes. J. Syst. Softw. **75**(1), 3–16 (2005)

Bateson, G.: A theory of play and fantasy. Psychiatric Research Reports (1955)

Bekoff, M., Allen, C.: Intentional communication and social play: how and why animals negotiate and agree to play. In: Animal Play: Evolutionary, Comparative, and Ecological Perspectives, pp. 97–114 (1998)

Cook, E.D., Hazelwood, A.C.: An active learning strategy for the classroom—"who wants to win… some mini chips ahoy?". J. Acc. Educ. **20**(4), 297–306 (2002)

Gee, J.P.: Are video games good for learning. Nord. J. Digital Literacy **3**(10) (2006)

Gygax, G., Arneson, D.: Dungeons and dragons Tactical Studies Rules Lake Geneva, WI (1974)

Huizinga, J.: Homo ludens: Proeve fleener bepaling van het spel-element der cultuur. Tjeenk Willink, Haarlem (1938)

Inaugural Challenge (2010): National STEM video game challenge. http://stemchallenge.org/about/

Kafai, Y.B., Resnick, M.: Constructionism in practice: designing, thinking, and learning in a digital world Routledge (1996)

Kelley, T., Kelley, D.: Creative confidence: unleashing the creative potential within us all crown business (2013)

Nesta: Game design to develop computational thinking, 17 October 2013. http://www.nesta.org.uk/blog/game-design-develop-computational-thinking

Newzoo, G.: Number of video gamers worldwide in 2014, by region (in millions) (2014). http://www.statista.com/statistics/293304/number-video-gamers/

Nicholson, S.: Peeking behind the locked door: a survey of escape room facilities. White Paper (2005). http://scottnicholson.com/pubs/erfacwhite.pdf

Parlett, D.S.: The Oxford History of Board Games. Oxford University Press, Oxford (1999)

Piccione, P.A.: In search of the meaning of senet archaeological institute of America (1980)

Prensky, M.: Changing paradigms. Educ. Technol. **47**(4), 1–3 (2007)

Salen, K.: Gaming literacies: a game design study in action. J. Educ. Multimedia Hypermedia **16** (3), 301 (2007)

Squire, K.: Video games and learning: teaching and participatory culture in the digital age. In: Technology, Education–Connections (The TEC Series). ERIC (2011)

Tang, S., Hanneghan, M., El Rhalibi, A.: Introduction to Games-Based Learning. Games Based Learning Advancements for Multi-sensory Human Computer Interfaces. IGI Global, New York (2009)

Tang, S., Hanneghan, M., El-Rhalibi, A.: Pedagogy elements, components and structures for serious games authoring environment. In: 5th International Game Design and Technology Workshop (GDTW 2007), Liverpool, UK, pp. 26–34 (2007)

Tobias, S., Fletcher, J.D., Wind, A.P.: Game-based learning. In: Michalspector, J., Davidmerrill, M., Elen, J., Bishop, M.J. (eds.) Handbook of Research on Educational Communications and Technology, pp. 485–503. Springer, New York (2014). doi:10.1007/978-1-4614-3185-5_38

Whitehead, N.: Teaching use case modelling using fluxx® (2012)

Whitton, N.: Digital games and learning: research and theory routledge (2014)

Wing, J.M.: Computational thinking. Commun. ACM **49**(3), 33–35 (2006)

Parsifal a Game Opera

Experiential Learning in Gameful Performance Art

Rens Kortmann[1(✉)] and Arlon Luijten[2]

[1] Faculty of Technology, Policy, and Management,
Department of Multi-Actor Systems, Section Policy Analysis,
Delft University of Technology, Jaffalaan 5, 2628 BX Delft, The Netherlands
L.J.Kortmann@tudelft.nl
[2] Independent Theatre Maker, Parsifal Playingfields, and Operadagen
Rotterdam, Rotterdam, The Netherlands
AEMLuijten@gmail.com

Abstract. Richard Wagner's *Parsifal* was recently rewritten and performed as a 'game opera'. We used observations, questionnaires, and interviews to study how the 700+ audience were facilitated to experientially learn about the show's main themes: compassion and collaboration. This case study contributed to our understanding how performance art may improve games for learning and training purposes, many of which now are notoriously 'boring'. We concluded that performance art's main contribution, in particular to games discussing fundamental values such as compassion, is to captivate players and 'lure' them into their natural behaviour. Thus the Parsifal game opera emotionally confronted its audience with their – callous and selfish – behaviour and intensified their learning through embodied experiences. However, some players lacked time and support to (collectively) reflect on their experiences and lacked catharsis. Therefore, we recommend using gameful performance art for learning and training purposes, provided that all activities in experiential learning are sufficiently facilitated.

Keywords: Real-life games · Performance arts · Interactive drama · Experiential learning · Informal learning · Game-based learning · Professional training

1 Introduction

Many games for learning and professional training are notoriously boring. Often, such games fail to deliver an embodied learning experience [3]. At the same time, one of the greatest merits of the performance arts is to create intense experiences that captivate their audiences. Could the performance arts help to improve games for experiential learning and training in, for instance, schools or companies? We studied how a *gameful* theatre performance facilitated experiential learning [5, 6] and drew lessons from it.

Interactive drama exercises have been used before as instruments for experiential learning, for instance in management education [1]. Our work differs from these approaches in the sense that we studied a performance that was primarily of an artistic nature. Such work is generally not intended to be an instrument for formal, *intentional*

© Springer International Publishing AG 2016
R. Bottino et al. (Eds.): GALA 2016, LNCS 10056, pp. 154–164, 2016.
DOI: 10.1007/978-3-319-50182-6_14

learning activities such as a school lesson or corporate training. Therefore, the answer to the question above could simply be 'no'. However, we imagine that gameful performance art could be used for *unintentional* or *informal*, experiential learning [2] much in the way that social media platforms may facilitate informal learning processes [9]. Do audiences in gameful performances learn unintentionally by observing the environment, acting in it, and reflecting upon their actions, quite similarly to how children learn informally in everyday life by observing and 'pitching in' [10]? If so, how is the learning facilitated?

In the remainder of this paper we focus on one such gameful theatrical performance: the *Parsifal Game Opera* (from here on abbreviated as 'the Parsifal game'). Starting with the classic work by Richard Wagner, director Arlon Luijten and his team aimed to provide their audience with an experience that could trigger them to reflect upon the main themes of the work: compassion and collaboration. Although artistic quality was the foremost aim for the makers, they hoped that the performance would also raise questions and spark discussion about the need for compassion and collaboration to enable the transition of our society to a sustainable future [7].

To evaluate how the Parsifal game facilitated experiential learning for its audience we observed players' behaviour during the shows. After the shows we conducted questionnaires and held interviews with players and makers. This mixed-method approach provided, first, narratives about how the game facilitated the audience to experience and reflect upon the main themes in the performance. Second, these narratives are substantiated quantitatively after analysing the response to the questionnaire.

In Sect. 2, we provide some background to the theory on experiential learning in order to frame our problem space. Then, in Sect. 3, the Parsifal game design and performance are outlined. Based on the theory on informal, experiential learning, the game is then evaluated in Sect. 4, after which conclusions are drawn in Sect. 5 about the use of gameful performance art for experiential learning and training.

2 Experiential Learning

The concept of experiential learning has been defined in detail by Kolb and co-workers [5, 6]. It is often associated with informal learning which is often viewed as a process of making sense of experiences [2]. Kolb defined the experiential leaning cycle as consisting of four steps as shown in Fig. 1. The four consecutive steps are: abstract

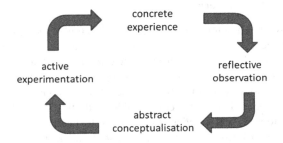

Fig. 1. The experiential learning cycle according to Kolb [5].

conceptualisation (the learner forms hypotheses of how her surroundings will respond to her actions, *e.g.*, 'If I give my mother a present, she will be happy'); active experimentation (the learner acts upon the environment to reach a certain aim based on her hypotheses, *e.g.*, 'I give my mother a present'); concrete experience (the learner senses (changes in) her environment as a result of her actions, *e.g.*, 'My mother shouts at me.'); reflective observation (the learner evaluates the experience to falsify or corroborate the hypotheses she made before, *e.g.*, 'My mother was not happy when I gave her a present.'). After the reflective observation step, the learner returns to the abstract conceptualisation step to update her hypotheses made before (*e.g.*, 'If I give my mother a present *that is not a dead mouse*, she will be happy.') and continues the cycle. After iterating the cycle several times, the learner will start to understand from experience how her surroundings work.

3   The Parsifal Game – Design and Performance

The Parsifal game was created as the second part of the theatre show *Parsifal the Grand Opera* that was performed during the International Rotterdam Opera Festival in the Netherlands in May 2016. The show consisted of three parts that were staged in different venues and attracted over 700 attendants (about 100 per game session).

3.1   Wagner's Parsifal

Wagner's Parsifal is based on the 13th century epic poem Parzival. The story, which is set in the Middle Ages, is about the innocent fool Parsifal who ventures out on an epic mission to retrieve a Holy Spear from the magical garden of the evil wizard Klingsor. The Spear is needed to heal Parsifal's king Amfortas who is mortally wounded and whose state induced a crisis amongst his people. In the magical garden lives Kundry, a cursed woman who is forced to sexually seduce all men that enter the Garden until one of them is able to withstand her advances. In the Garden, Parsifal felt compassion for his king and, therefore, Kundry was not able to seduce him. As a consequence, Parsifal could take the Holy Spear, return it to heal Amfortas, and thus bring salvation to his people. Moreover, Kundry was freed from her enslavement.

3.2   Parsifal the Grand Opera

In the current show, the director took a somewhat different stance towards the original story above. First, he could not relate to Parsifal acting as a solitary (anti)hero and saving his compatriots all by himself. Instead, the director felt that no person alone may save our current society from the many challenges it is facing. In fact, he believed it requires a common effort by all members of society to change it for the better in the long term. Second, he did not feel comfortable with the sexuality theme that the original story used to represent the vices of mankind. Instead, he considered other traits such as callousness and selfishness as larger threats to a sustainable future.

As a consequence, the director chose to remove Parsifal from the script. Where in the original work the community in crisis and Parsifal are introduced to the audience in the first act, the current show started with a director in crisis because of his main actor – Parsifal – not showing up. By the end of the first act the director concludes that Parsifal is not coming. Instead he invites the audience to become Parsifal themselves: to venture into the city, like Parsifal travelled to Klingsor's magical garden in act two, and find the 'Holy Spear'. Then, the audience was guided to the second venue.

After arrival in act two, Klingsor's magical garden, the audience were separated into eight teams and were assigned a game table and game coach (singer/performer). The aim of the game was to build a tower of ten building blocks that could be purchased with coins earned in the so-called 'coin rooms'. Coins could also be spent on weapons to attack other teams and to defend against them. Finally, teams could invest coins in developing new weapon technologies or in shares at a stock market. In order to provide players with a total embodied experience which induced not only thought, entertainment, and learning but also a catharsis as we find it in the theatre, we immersed them with live music (string quartet and live electronics responding to the players' behaviour), video, singing, and performance by the game-coaches.

The game was played in rounds that consisted of several phases. Each phase was announced and timed by the 'umpire' who also acted as game commentator. In phase 1 the team members were sent to the coin rooms to earn coins; in phase 2 all coins earned were spent on purchasing building blocks, weapons, shares, etc. Each game coach entered their team's choices into a mobile app that was custom-built for the show. In phase 3, the game coaches enacted a 'shoot-out' between the teams (see Fig. 2). Also, the umpire announced the battle results to the rhythm of the music played by a string quartet and supported by electronic samples. In phase 4 the umpire spun a wheel of fortune to simulate the stock market. Finally, in phase 5, the game coaches provided feedback to their teams about the results from the previous round.

Fig. 2. Impression of the parsifal game with game hosts performing a 'shoot-out'. Photo: bart visser. More impressions can be found on www.parsifal-playingfields.nl

In collaboration with local organisations, such as Erasmus University Rotterdam, the City of Rotterdam, and Codarts University for the Arts, about ten coin rooms were installed. The coin rooms discussed the show's themes: compassion and collaboration. For instance, one coin room discussed an important *Leitmotiv* from the original Wagner score where Kundry sings about compassion leading to salvation. Players that recognised the correct Leitmotiv received coins. Another coin room awarded coins to players that succeeded in playing collaborative mini-games. Finally, one coin room did not reward compassion or collaboration, but, as a counterweight, taught 'The Art of War' as developed by the ancient Chinese general Sun Tsu (500 BC).

The game's sustainable-future theme was represented in the magical garden modelled as a common resource pool [4]. Building blocks and weapons were built from the garden's resources, with weapons drawing more heavily upon the resource pool than building blocks did. When a healthy number of resources was maintained, the pool would replenish itself through natural growth. However, with declining numbers of resources, replenishment slowed down as well. A resulting scarcity of resources caused higher resource prices. Players could replenish resources by investing in 'eco science' at the stock market. Notably, this was the least profitable fund which resulted in a prisoner-dilemma type of game with defectors gaining a higher profit while benefiting from those who complied with investing in eco science.

Where Wagner's Parsifal saw compassion and abstinence as a prerequisite to save Amfortas' community, the Parsifal game, instead, aimed for its players to think about compassion and collaboration as enablers for the transition to a sustainable society. For this, the character Kundry played an important role. As in Wagner's Parsifal, Kundry is Klingsor's slave in the game. She is forced to seduce teams to play callously and selfishly. Also, parallel to the opera, she will not be free until all teams will withstand her advances and play compassionately after all. For instance, in round 3 she must offer a box to the team that built the smallest tower so far. In the box are a button and a note saying: "Inequality is the main threat to our current society. You can cure society by pressing the button in the box. The highest tower will then be removed from the game". If the team that is offered the box decides to press the button, the game is paused, sound samples of sirens and collapsing buildings are played, and the lights flash. The umpire then announces that the team that owned the highest tower has fallen victim to a terrorist attack and will need to start again from scratch.

In the game narrative, Kundry developed an alternative, compassionate way to find the Spear, which she inconspicuously encourages all teams to follow. For this she drops notes and cautiously shows players certain writings on her arms and legs. Players that pick up her hints will understand that the original Parsifal game, *i.e.*, Klingsor's game of building a tower to take the Spear, allows for and even *awards* callousness and selfishness: it is generally cheaper to steal building blocks from other teams than to purchase them. Instead, Kundry offers all teams a way to collectively build the Spear. Through a series of clues the players obtain a mould of a spear that needs to be filled with building blocks of all teams. Only if all teams decide to act compassionately and to collaboratively build the alternative spear, Kundry's way can be completed and Klingsor will be defeated. However, if one or more teams defect all is lost and all players become Klingsor's slaves as is enacted in the game's epilogue.

4   Evaluation

About 108 visitors (15%) responded to our online questionnaire through which we measured game experience and learning effects. The completion rate was 59%. Based on our observations, our sample of respondents represented the full population well. For our analyses we divided the sample in groups along the background variables (see Table 1) and compared their responses. For instance, we compared responses of the group of respondents below the age of 50 to the responses of the group above the age of 50. To compare averages between the groups shown above we used an independent-samples Student t-test.

Table 1. Background variables and groups of respondents.

Background variable	Grouping value	N	N (%)
Age	<50 years old	38	45%
	>=50 years old	70	55%
Gender	Female	61	56%
	Male	47	44%
Education	Non-academic	51	47%
	Academic	57	53%
Gaming frequency	Less than weekly	67	63%
	Weekly or more often	39	37%
Frequency of visits to theatre performances	Less than monthly	63	59%
	Monthly or more often	44	41%

Because of the statistical dependencies found between background variables, we defined another two groups as shown in Table 2. We found a weak but significant negative Pearson correlation between age and education ($r = -.21$; $p = .029$; $N = 108$) and a weak but significant positive Pearson correlation between age and the frequency of visits to theatre performances ($r = .25$; $p = .010$; $N = 107$).

To compare the responses of the groups shown in Table 2 we used a non-parametric Mann-Whitney U-test due to the relatively small sample sizes.

Table 2. Additional groups used in the analysis of the results.

Background variables	Grouping value	N	N (%)
Age and education	<50 years old and academic	27	40%
	>=50 years old and non-academic	40	60%
Age and frequency of visits to theatre performances	<50 years old and less than monthly	26	45%
	>=50 years old and monthly or more often	32	55%

Learning from the Gameful Performance. In our questionnaire we asked the players to what extent the show encouraged them to think about its main themes: compassion and collaboration. A majority of 63% of all respondents replied 'much' to 'very much' on a 5-point Likert scale. A similar percentage (58%) responded likewise when asked to what extent playing a game (as opposed to watching a theatre show) contributed to them thinking about the themes. When comparing groups, we found the largest differences between the averaged response from younger players (<50) that less often visit a theatre (<monthly) (N = 19) and the response from the older players that more often visit theatre performances (N = 20). Both groups found the game mind-capturing but to the former group's opinion the game was significantly more mind-capturing than to the latter (U = 113; p = .21).

We also asked our respondents what insights they had gained while playing the game and when these insights emerged. A majority responded that they had learned about the importance of compassion and collaboration as prerequisites for society to move towards a sustainable future. In addition, many reported about the difficulties they experienced to actually practice compassion and to collaborate in an environment that seemed to award callousness and selfishness. These insights emerged mostly 30 to 50 min after the start of the game. This period coincides with the time that Kundry started to encourage teams to play Kundry's way. Therefore, Kundry's way encouraged many players to think more about the main themes in the performance. Also, it stimulated the emergence of important insights in their minds.

Facilitation of Experiential Learning. How did the game facilitate experiential learning for its players? Could the facilitation be improved? To answer these questions we first aimed, in Table 3, to map the main activities in the Parsifal game to the four phases of Kolb's cycle (as introduced in Sect. 2). Then, we critically studied how each phase was facilitated by the game.

From the mapping above we deduct that players in the Parsifal game indeed spun the experiential learning cycle. Doing so, they discovered the mechanics of the game and, more importantly, started thinking about compassion and collaboration.

First, we found that the game provided ample time and space for the phase 'Concrete experience': players went through a rollercoaster of experiences as described in the table above. The game dedicated by far the most time for this phase and many game materials were developed for it. With the game being part of a theatrical art work, this emphasis on experience was expected and confirmed by the players. Most players enjoyed and were immersed by the overwhelming amount of stimuli, although we also received reports of a substantial number of players who got lost because of it. Second, the game facilitated the phase of 'Active experimentation'. Some significant time and a lot of materials were devoted to this phase (game table and board pieces, mobile app, Kundry's box, various materials for Kundry's way, etc.) but not as much as for the previous phase. Finally, the 'Abstract conceptualisation' and 'Reflective observation' phases were the least facilitated by the game. Although in every round of play some time was scheduled for feedback on the previous round's decisions, it was often no more than a short clarification by the game coach after which players needed to rush to a coin room. Few discussions were triggered by the feedback. Also, after visiting the coin rooms, players needed to hurry back to the game tables to invest their coins,

Table 3. Mapping of the phases in Kolb's experiential learning cycle [5] to the main activities in the parsifal game

Phase	Game activities
Abstract conceptualisation	Teams or players form hypotheses about: the activities on the game table (attacks, tower building, hacking, etc.) planned by other teams; the consequences of joining Kundry's way vs. remaining in Klingsor's game; the reasons and consequences of declining resources in the garden; ways to replenish resources in the garden; how to convince other players to join Kundry's way; the consequences of pressing the button in Kundry's box; the consequences of playing Kundry's split or steal
Active experimentation	Teams spend coins on building blocks, weapons, stocks, etc.; A player presses the button in Kundry's box; Teams play Kundry's split or steal; Teams buy Eco Science stocks to replenish the resources in the garden; Players decide to follow Kundry's way or, instead, remain in Klingsor's game; Players try to convince other players to join them in following Kundry's way; Teams negotiate with other teams about playing split or steal; players visit a coin room
Concrete experience (and between brackets the form in which the experience took place)	Teams capture building blocks from or lose them to other teams (shoot-out performance); Teams win or lose money in the stock market (spinning the wheel of fortune); The number of resources lowers or grows (announcement by the umpire); One or more other teams joined Kundry's way or, instead, remained in Klingsor's game (observation by players); A tower is blown up by Kundry's box (AV effects and announcement by the umpire); A natural disaster occurs due to resource scarcity; One or more teams complete their towers; All teams played split or, instead, one or more teams played steal in Kundry's split or steal; All teams complete Kundry's way (all announcements by the umpire); players experience a coin room (mini-game, lecture, performance)
Reflective observation	Players listen to their game coach who clarifies the results of their game table activities (attacks, building block transports, hacks, etc.); players interpret and discuss the game rules posted on the wall; players reflect on their experiences (coin rooms, interaction with Kundry, etc.) in solitude or together with other players

leaving very limited time for contemplation about their game room experiences and sharing them with fellow players. In particular players who indicated that they had not enjoyed the game, responded that there was not enough time for them to digest their experiences and discuss plans for new actions because they felt rushed and not in control of the game. However, many other players reported that they found time for reflection and conceptualisation 'in between scenes'.

Altogether, the Parsifal game very intensely facilitated the action-oriented phases of the experiential learning cycle ('active experimentation' and 'concrete experience'), whereas the phases that were mainly oriented towards thinking and communication ('Abstract conceptualisation' and 'Reflective observation') were facilitated much less.

The Added Value of Performance Art. To learn how performance art could add value to games for learning and training purposes, we analysed our video recordings and conducted interviews with makers and players. No strict protocol was used due to the exploratory nature of the work.

The video recordings showed many examples of players that were emotionally involved with the game. For instance, we noticed heated debates around the game tables about how to spend the team's coins. Some players argued ferociously to attack other teams in order to capture their building blocks whereas other held a passionate pacifist stance and argued against violence. In two game sessions, a player grabbed a microphone and pleaded for abandoning Klingsor's game and following Kundry's route instead. Finally, when one or more teams played 'Steal' in the final Split or Steal round, a general outcry of indignation was heard from the other teams.

From the interviews and questionnaire response we derived that players felt they were lured into their natural, callous and selfish, behaviour. The quick pace of the game and the overwhelming amount of sensory input encouraged them to play no other role than their natural self. Mostly, this meant that they made choices that were most highly rewarded by the game environment: to steal building blocks from other teams rather than purchasing them yourself; to eradicate another tower by pressing the button in Kundry's box rather than following Kundry's route; to buy funds that invested in weapon technology rather than 'eco-science'; etc. When the players were confronted with this behaviour, many felt ashamed about it. They felt they had not been faithful to their own values and norms and experienced a sense of guilt because of it.

5   Discussion and Conclusions

The players in the Parsifal game opera learnt to appreciate the difficulty of practicing compassion and working collaboratively in an environment that rewarded the opposite. An important contributing factor was the captivating, 'enchanting' nature of the art work. Players reported they were 'lured' into their natural behaviour. The art work provided them with a mirror to reflect on their callousness and selfishness. As a result many players felt 'ashamed' about their behaviour and felt the urge to change it for the better. Therefore, this case study taught us that performance art's main contribution to improving games for learning and training purposes may be catharsis: first beguile the players, then emotionally confront them with their undesirable behaviour, and thus create a sense of urgency for them to start learning. The confrontation and resulting sense of urgency become more significant when the issues at stake become more significant and personal. Therefore, performance art has the potential to provide game players with an intensified embodied experience that prepares them for learning; in particular when the learning concerns fundamental values (compassion, openness, authenticity, etc.) related to one's personality and the important choices in life.

It should be noted, however, that in earlier work [7] we heard similar responses from the players even though no performance arts were involved then. Therefore, does it really require a performance arts maker to design a game that generates as intense embodied experiences as in the Parsifal game opera? We suspect that in certain cases the performing arts play an indispensable role, but it requires further research to understand when and how. Therefore, to follow up on this research we suggest to study a stripped-down version of the Parsifal game, *i.e.*, a version in which all theatrical and musical elements (actors, costumes, song and dance, orchestras, lighting, etc.) are removed. It would be worthwhile to compare the latter version to the game opera in an effort to estimate the added value of the performance arts in the game.

In addition, the Parsifal game facilitated its players to learn from experience about the importance of the show's main thematic concepts: compassion and collaboration. A majority of players indicated that the performance, and in particular the game format, triggered them to think about these concepts. Also, many players have reported to have gained insights about the importance of these concepts for the transition of our society towards a sustainable future. In particular the action-oriented phases of Kolb's experiential learning cycle [5] (experimentation, experiencing) were well supported by the game's design and the game materials. The phases that are more related to thinking and verbal interaction between players (conceptualisation, reflection) were less well supported. This conclusion leads to an interesting design dilemma. On the one hand, the facilitation of the latter phases could be improved relatively easily by allocating more time and more game materials to them. It would benefit players whose learning styles focus on these phases. On the other hand, doing so could harm the game experience as well as the artistic, musical flow of the performance for other, more action-oriented players, thus preventing catharsis for them to take place. Therefore, in order to fully exploit the added value of the performance arts for learning and training, future research should focus on the extent to which the four phases in experiential learning are facilitated to achieve catharsis and embodied experiences for all players, irrespective of their learning styles.

References

1. Boggs, J.G., Mickel, A.E., Holtom, B.C.: Experiential learning through interactive drama: an alternative to student role plays. J. Manag. Educ. **31**(6), 832–858 (2007)
2. Davies, L.: Informal Learning: A New Model for Making Sense of Experience. Gower, Aldershot (2008)
3. Egenfeldt-Nielsen, S.: Third generation educational use of computer games. J. Educ. Multimedia Hypermedia **16**(3), 263–281 (2007)
4. Hardin, G.: The tragedy of the commons. Science **162**(3859), 1243–1248 (1968)

164   R. Kortmann and A. Luijten

5. Kolb, D.A.: Experiential Learning: Experience as a Source of Learning and Development. Prentice Hall, Upper Saddle River (1984)
6. Kolb, A.Y., Kolb, D.A.: Learning to play, playing to learn: a case study of a ludic learning space. J. Organ. Change Manag. **23**(1), 26–50 (2010)
7. Kortmann, R., van Daalen, E., Mayer, I., Bekebrede, G.: Veerkracht 2.0: embodied interactions in a servant-leadership game. In: Meijer, S.A., Smeds, R. (eds.) ISAGA 2013. LNCS, vol. 8264, pp. 44–51. Springer, Heidelberg (2014). doi:10.1007/978-3-319-04954-0_6
8. Loorbach, D.: Transition management for sustainable development: a prescriptive, complexity-based governance framework. Governance **23**(1), 161–183 (2010)
9. Madge, C., Meek, J., Wellens, J., Hooley, T.: Facebook, social integration and informal learning at university: "it is more for socialising and talking to friends about work than for actually doing work". Learn. Media Technol. **34**(2), 141–155 (2009)
10. Paradise, R., Rogoff, B.: Side by side: learning by observing and pitching in. Ethos **37**(1), 102–138 (2009)

Games and Management

Design Considerations for Building a Scalable Digital Version of a Multi-player Educational Board Game for a MOOC in Logistics and Transportation

Heide Lukosch[1(✉)], Shalini Kurapati[1], Geertje Bekebrede[1],
Simon Tiemersma[2], Daan Groen[3], Linda van Veen[3],
and Alexander Verbraeck[1]

[1] Faculty of Technology, Policy and Management,
Delft University of Technology, Jaffalaan 5, 2628 BX Delft, The Netherlands
{H.K.Lukosch, S.Kurapati, G.Bekebrede,
A.Verbraeck}@tudelft.nl
[2] Gamelab TU Delft Delft University of Technology,
Jaffalaan 5, 2628 BX Delft, The Netherlands
S.A.Tiemersma@tudelft.nl
[3] InThere, The Hague, Saturnusstraat 60, 2516 AH The Hague, The Netherlands
{daan, linda}@inthere.nl

Abstract. With more flexible and large-scale learning environments, new design requirements for games emerge. Massive Open Online Courses (MOOCs) are one of the most important innovations in the learning field. Still, it is a challenge to motivate learners and to keep them motivated in such huge learning environments. To address this challenge, we redesigned a board game targeting at an integrated view on disruption and communication management in an intermodal transportation situation. From the redesign, we have learned that an online game works better with fewer roles, requires immediate feedback, and an engaging way of challenge to keep players motivated. Our findings can inform the design of games for large groups of players in an online environment.

1 Introduction

MOOCs or Massive Open Online Courses represent a new dimension of 21st century learning environments. MOOCs enable long distance learning to an extensively distributed audience and are widely discussed to be alternatives to traditional classroom learning [1]. In traditional classroom settings, only a few people benefit from the learning environment offered, whereas MOOCs are able to reach a diversity of learners, especially those who are not able to attend high-quality formal learning courses, because of location, time and costs. Although MOOCs have unique advantages such as the ability to reach a broader audience, provide easy accessibility, high flexibility, open and often free course materials, they are often affected by high dropout rates [2]. One reason for this could be seen in the fact that most MOOCs are still based on basic text-based materials, video lectures and interactions in forums [3]. MOOCs face the

© Springer International Publishing AG 2016
R. Bottino et al. (Eds.): GALA 2016, LNCS 10056, pp. 167–176, 2016.
DOI: 10.1007/978-3-319-50182-6_15

challenge of designing learner-centered online courses, rather than just providing open access to static educational resources [4]. As they provide a huge opportunity for self-organized learning, there is a clear need to support learner's motivation and engagement by innovative and sophisticated instructional design, personalization and adaptability of the course [2]. We therefore propose a gamification of MOOCs in the sense of an integration of game elements and complete simulation games in the online learning process. The integration of simulation games is considered to have the potential to improve learner's motivation [2]. However these ideas are theoretical, and there are onle a few examples of simulation games successfully implemented in MOOCs yet [2, 3].

As an answer to this challenge, we started to develop a new MOOC called "Innovation in Logistics". This MOOC will represent a 5-weeks course targeting at students on a master level as well as professionals from the transportation domain. Innovative logistical concepts like automation, synchromodality, and management of big data will be discussed. Up to now, it is only a small group of students who are able to follow teaching programs dedicated to Transport and Logistics all over the world, while the societal and economical role of this domain is still growing. The new MOOC will support explorative learning approaches to motivate and engage a large group of learners. Simulation games and game elements will form an integrated part of this learning experience within the MOOC. As one element of this new course, we redesigned an existing and evaluated board game known as the "Container terminal disruption management game" that was focused on the development of Situational Awareness (SA) in integrated planning of container terminal operations. SA is considered to be a pre-requisite for good decision making [5, 6]. The game is built on simulation gaming methods to research and train problem solving capabilities in relation to SA [7, 8]. The board game has been successfully designed, tested and implemented in classroom settings and professional institutions [9, 10]. For the integration in the new MOOC, we redesigned the board game into an online version. The redesign of the game was based on lessons learned from a first prototype of a mobile version of the game.

The key contribution of this paper is to analyze the design process that started with a board game, which was then transformed to a scalable mobile game and finally redesigned towards an online game to be integrated in the MOOC. We provide insights in the lessons learned from this transition process, and into advantages as well as pitfalls that come with the technology change of the game.

2 The Container Terminal Disruption Management Board Game

Container transportation is a multi-modal system of transporting goods bundled into steel containers aimed at cost-effectiveness, safety and quicker service times [11]. Container terminals are crucial hubs in the global transportation network of goods that act as coupling and decoupling points for the transfer of containers from sea to land and vice-versa. The storage area of the terminal is called the yard, where containers are stored in stacks, thus facilitating the decoupling of seaside and landside operations [12].

Planning and aligning all functions in a container terminal is a difficult task [13]. All planning activities of e.g. berth location and timing of deep-sea vessels, and the sequence of containers to be (un)loaded, are interrelated, and changes in one plan have a big influence on other plans [14]. Moreover, container terminals are often affected by a wide range of disruptions like common equipment failures, sudden demand shocks, weather conditions, conflicts and political unrest, or even terrorism [6]. Each of the disturbances, disruptions or risks, described for instance in [15, 16] can have debilitating ripple effects on the container terminal, causing financial, operational, or collateral losses and in rare cases affecting human operator safety [17]. Therefore, important challenges for container terminals are related to integrated planning, effective disruption and information management. These challenges form the basis for the learning objectives of an educational board game to train participants in problem solving.

The Container terminal disruption management game, henceforth referred as the *game,* is a tabletop 5 player board game representing a setting of a container terminal. The game was designed based on the triadic game design approach of balancing the game aspects reality, meaning and play [18]. The game consists of five different roles (berth planner, vessel planner, control tower operator, resource planner and sales), each responsible for specific planning and operational tasks in the container terminal. They also need to maintain healthy levels of three main key performance indicators (KPIs) of the terminal namely Safety, Customer Satisfaction and Performance. See [9] for detailed description of the roles and rules of the game. As the game unfolds, disruptions start occurring that drastically affect individual operations as well as the operation of the entire organization. Three disruption scenarios each with varying levels of severity have been modelled in the game.

With each round of the game, the event complexity increases and the disruption situation escalates, unless some action by the players is taken. In order to make the 'right' decision and 'win' the game, participants need to manage information, communicate and coordinate if necessary, monitor the effects of disruptions and take the necessary actions at the right time to mitigate the negative effects. The game has three difficulty or complexity levels. In every successive level a new disruption unfolds in addition to the existing disruptions creating a more complex scenario for information exchange, coordination, effect control and decision-making.

The game was tested among several groups of 80 students and 25 professionals, all from the field of transport and logistics, to assess its usefulness as a learning method for disruption management in container terminals. The game play was observed along pre-described observers' guidelines and by the use of a post-test survey. An overview of the study including the analytical methods can be found in [9, 10]. From the survey data on the learning effect due to the game play, about 16% responded that it would be *very helpful,* 37% of the participants felt that the learning experience from the game would be *helpful,* and 38% felt that it would be moderately helpful, 9% answered slightly helpful to better prepare them to handle real world disruptions. Not even one participant responded that it would be not helpful.

Most of the participants (80%) stated that they learnt that communication and information sharing are extremely important for disruption management container terminals [9]. Descriptive answers from the survey highlighted learning aspects imparted from the game by participants. Following this, the game represents a good exercise to understand the importance of disruption management in transportation and supply chains. It also shows that it is difficult to pre-determine a perfect or optimal solution to manage disruptions, and that decision-making during disruption management is more complex and inter-dependent than one thinks. Communicating the right information at the right time is very important, as well as integrating the different pieces of information to make good decisions.

The results from the above mentioned sessions demonstrate that helpful learning experience in the field of disruption management of container terminal operations has been created with the use of the board game. While these positive results are encouraging, we observed several obstacles to adopt the board game as a scalable teaching tool as described below. First, the board game always requires an experienced human game master to be present in order to control the complex game processes. Secondly, the distribution and scalability of the game is limited to a small group of participants. Thirdly, in the board game only the human memory is available for debriefing, thus the learning experience is also limited as not all user interactions and decisions are tracked. Fourthly, the board game requires all players to be present in a single room at the same time. While this fosters a common game experience, it imposes an unrealistic situation, as in reality the different persons would be distributed across the port [19]. Based on before mentioned limitations of the board game, we aimed at further developing the board game to a more scalable and distributable version. We chose to re-develop it into a mobile game, which will be explained in the following sub-section.

3   The Mobile Version of the Board Game

The mobile version of the board game was developed in a platform called ARLearn. Subsequently the game can be downloaded as an Android application in all Android supported smartphones [19]. The instructional content of the mobile game is similar to that of the board game but some modifications have been made in the redesign for the sake of playability. The 5 roles in the board game have been consolidated to 3 roles (berth planner, controller and sales) to reduce waiting times of players due to communication delays. Every participant can choose a role to play.

The ARLearn game engine automatically updates the game state, evaluates player decisions and distributes information. Game rules, processes, decisions and all other game resources are encoded as game design script in ARLearn [19]. The mobile devices provide a realistic scenario, as the players use communication means similar to their daily activities as the game interaction is based on mobile devices. Users receive messages and interact with question items. Players don't need to be in one location but can be mobile [20]. In spite of the promising nature of the mobile game with respect to scalability, our initial and internal tests taught us some lessons regarding the usability and feasibility of the mobile game as a teaching tool for a large audience. Although it addresses some of the limitations of the board game, the main reasons for not considering this version of the game for the MOOC environment are related to the mobile technology used. First, the mobile game is not versatile as it can only be installed on

Android supported mobile devices. Secondly, although the mobile version provides a more scalable version than the board game, it is not a good alternative for a MOOC where students have flexible learning times, and not always have access to smart mobile devices. Thirdly, students in MOOCs are distributed geographically and it is difficult for 3 students to synchronize their timings and organize themselves to play a game that is supposed to be a fun learning instrument and not a burden. Technology glitches, connection issues might also arise. Fourthly, the platform doesn't have a 'digital game master' that can assign students to groups of 3 players, so that if two groups are playing simultaneously they will be aware who they are playing against and in which group they belong. Fifthly, all the actions in the game are text based, which might not contribute to player motivation in a massive online learning environment.

Given the above reasons, we decided to completely redesign the board game into an online game by keeping in mind the special and novel environment of MOOCs to integrate simulation games.

4   Redesign Towards a Scalable Online Version for a MOOC

In order to support the learning process and to foster motivation of the students, design requirements for the online game have been drawn from the specific learning situation within a MOOC. For certain aspects, this meant to radically change the initial design of the board game, also based on the lessons learned from the development of the mobile game in between.

4.1   Design Requirements and Challenges

Before starting developing the scalable online version of the game, we especially discussed the game design requirements within a team of experienced game designers. Again the triadic game design philosophy [18] was used as starting point for the redesign. Starting from the lessons we had learned from the mobile game, we identified four main requirements for the redesign of the game. First, it should motivate communication between players, even in situations where players are distributed amongst space and time. Secondly, the game should provide immediate and clear feedback to player actions to keep them motivated within the MOOc environment. Thirdly, information about other players' actions should be given to enable social learning. Fourthly, the online game should include less roles than the board game for better playability.

The second set of requirements came from the feedback of the professionals in the field of transport and logistics who had played the board game. Their feedback was that, despite the limited choices in the game, it was realistic and a good representation of a disruption. Therefore, little adaptations had to be done for the digital version, resulting in following requirements. The game should allow for realistic actions, decisions and ways of communication as in the board and mobile game. Secondly, the game should be based on realistic scenarios, which are based on the board game scenarios and our own experience from working together with deep-sea container terminals. A scenario where people are spotted in the yard replaced the scenario of the equipment failure from the board game, as this requires more communication amongst different roles. The resulting scenarios for the online version are a trucker's strike, an injury/fatality due to an accident, and people spotted near rails in a shunting yard.

Playing a game within a MOOC means additional implications for the design of a game, especially for the meaning part addressing the learning experience, and the way participants are involved in game play and feedback. We analyzed the requirements from the specific MOOC environment very carefully, leading to following design considerations. Due to the various backgrounds of students and their individual learning situations, the game should be playable on any computer or laptop, using different types of browsers (Firefox, Safari, Chrome). Due to the distribution of students in time and place, the game should not only be playable on separate locations, but additionally, an automated game master or game system should be included, which can guide the process of play. The game should also provide feedback after every level. Furthermore, we decided for a quasi-multi player game set up, with two of the roles played by the game itself. Players can choose any role, while the other two are automated. The participants need to change their role in every level, to experience the different decision making perspectives. As MOOCs are usually divided in short elements, the game play cannot take too long. The time for playing one level of a scenario is about 10 min. The look and feel of a game (as opposed to an exclusively text-based experience) should foster the motivation of the players. For the same reason, a clear in-game explanation of the learning context (SA, disruption management) and instructions of the game have to be included. The instructions should clearly explain the roles, objectives, rules and constraints, which are mainly the same as in the board game. For research purposes, game results should be logged.

Related to the aims of the redesign, all requirements contribute to immediate and clear feedback to the players, building a strong relation between learners and learning environment, getting information about player's actions and including multiple roles. The question how to motivate communication between players and between players and teachers, while the game being a single player activity, remains a challenge for the design.

4.2   Technical Specifications and Related Challenges

The game is built using Unity 3D, a game software creation tool that enables quick development and easy export possibilities. Because the game has a large amount of choices and information, the main system behind the game is a decision tree. The tree allows for scalability. Further disruption scenarios based on decision trees could be added quickly. One of the challenges in building the digital game was the creation of believable artificial intelligences (AI). The AI should make choices like real players would, which is necessary to give the player the idea that he or she is really communicating with other stakeholders of the disruption. The AI makes choices based on objective factors, but there is always a chance they make mistakes or communicate badly. The game will be published and hosted on the White box platform, developed by InThere, a Dutch game developing company. This system enables consistent user profile use and easy data collection.

4.3   First Design

For an internal test of the game, several mockup versions of the game interface have been developed that included the basic functionalities of the game. The design options were discussed with a group of 5 game designers and researchers from the field of game design and transportation research. Given the requirements for the game as defined above, we decided for an interface that should clearly show the roles involved, the information available and the choices a player can make. Tests with the first design of the game made clear that for a feeling of challenge, the decreasing time available to make a choice in the game should be as clear as the decrease in available communication resources of a player. A player is thus forced by the design to act quickly, as he or she would have to do in a case of a disruptive situation, and still care for the value of communication options and time, which is also important when managing a disruption. We found that the scoring system of the prototype still seemed not fair for every choice made. The right choice made, based on the right information, would sometimes give a lower score (a higher reduction of the KPI's) then the wrong score. In the initial version of the game, the player gets immediate feedback from the game. A general debriefing moment on how the player performed and the choices he or she made, is not yet included and has to be decided upon.

4.4   Second Design

Based on our observations, we decided to improve the interface design of the game as well as the feedback provided at the end of one game session. The player will get some feedback on his and her choices, together with an overview of the choices of the AI players. That should illustrate how the choices of the other actors influenced the result, too. The interface design shows different areas now, as illustrated in Fig. 1.

Fig. 1. Final interface design for the online game

The roles included in the game are illustrated by pictograms on the right. Below that, the player is able to view the key performance indicators (KPIs) for his role, in the example customer satisfaction and performance. Also the communication resources available are shown. In the middle, information available is shown in a scrollbar. The player can choose whether the information was useful or not, and whether it should be shared with whom. Based on the information received, the player has to make a certain decision, e.g. contacting an external party for help, to finish the round. After that, feedback is provided on the decisions and their impact on the KPIs.

5 Discussion and Conclusion

From the redesign process starting from a board game involving a lot of direct interaction towards an online game in a massive online learning environment, we came across several challenges and collected lessons learned.

To start with, we have learned from the experts in the field of transport and logistics, that a realistic set-up is a prerequisite for a valid learning game, no matter whether it is low or high tec. Similar to the realistic actions and decisions in the board game, the scenarios in the online game are realistic, and developed together with subject-matter experts. The functional fidelity of both game versions is thus very high and appreciated by the target group. The dynamics of the game situation on the opposite is really different in the two game versions. In the initial board game, players have to communicate directly. There is a tension between individual and general goals, and the facilitator introduces surprising disruptions as well as provides feedback on player's actions and decisions. This holistic approach results in a high involvement of the players. For the online version, we wanted to design a similar experience of involvement. We decided for the design of a quasi-multiplayer game to guarantee the involvement of the players. All roles involved in the game are visible for the player. Feedback is provided by points, but also by more or less happy faces of the artificial roles in the game. Automated feedback is thus the mechanism we decided for to address the engagement of players. In addition to this, the roles also support the narrative of the game, which enhances the learning effect [21].

In general, the development of the mobile version of the game was a useful step towards the final design as it forced us to think about the decision tree already, which was again used for the online version. We also learned that the mobile version would be useful for more informal learning situations, but that an enhanced version with more possibilities for interaction and feedback would be needed in a MOOC setting.

For challenging the player, we introduced a certain time pressure into the game. This is one element that has still to be validated by the target group, as we are not sure yet whether this is realistic. Even in situations of disruptions, a quick decision might not always be the most desired one.

In summary, our experiences with designing a simulation game for a MOOC can throw some light on the requirements, possibilities and challenges related to integrating a simulation game in a MOOC. We observe that the same game design steps can be followed, however the boundaries of a MOOC already define some design choices, like distributed place and time independent game set up, preferable single player, short playing time. In our future work, we will explore how to design effective debriefing mechanisms for simulation games in MOOCs. Simulation games provide rich feedback in the form of interaction data that can be used for detailed analytics. They also provide a supportive narrative context missing from bare simulations, making user decisions have consequences beyond simple grades [21]. We will soon test our design with students and our future work will inform the results of our simulation game design with respect to effectiveness of learning and levels of engagement.

Acknowledgments. The Dutch Institute for Advanced Logistics (DINALOG-TKI) funded this research initiative.

References

1. Kafai, Y.B., Peppler, K.A.: Beyond small groups: new opportunities for research in computer-supported collective learning. In: Spada, H., Stahl, G., Miyake, N., Law, N. (eds.) Connecting Computer-Supported Collaborative Learning to Policy and Practices: CSCL11 Community Events Proceedings, vol. 2, Short Papers & Posters, pp. 910–911. International Society of the Learning Sciences, Hong Kong (2011)
2. Bakki, A., Oubahssi, L., Cherkaoui, C., George, S.: Motivation and engagement in MOOCs: how to increase learning motivation by adapting pedagogical scenarios? In: Conole, G., Klobučar, T., Rensing, C., Konert, J., Lavoué, É. (eds.) EC-TEL 2015. LNCS, vol. 9307, pp. 556–559. Springer, Heidelberg (2015). doi:10.1007/978-3-319-24258-3_58
3. Romero, M., Usart, M.: Serious games integration in an entrepreneurship massive online open course (MOOC). In: Ma, M., Oliveira, M.F., Petersen, S., Hauge, J.B. (eds.) SGDA 2013. LNCS, vol. 8101, pp. 212–225. Springer, Heidelberg (2013). doi:10.1007/978-3-642-40790-1_21
4. Voulgari, I., Sampson, G.D.: Massive open online courses (MOOCs) and massively multiplayer online games (MMOGs): synergies and lessons to be learned. In: Sampson, G. D., Ifenthaler, D., Spector, M.J., Isaias, P. (eds.) Digital Systems for Open Access to Formal and Informal Learning, 41–56. Springer, Heidelberg (2014)
5. Endsley, M.R.: Toward a theory of situation awareness in dynamic systems. Hum. Factors: J. Hum. Factors Ergon. Soc. **37**, 32–64 (1995)
6. Verbraeck, A., Kurapati, S., Lukosch, H.: Serious games for improving situational awareness in container terminals. In: Zijm, H., Klumpp, M., Clausen, U., ten Hompel, M. (eds.) Logistics and supply chain innovation. LNL, pp. 413–431. Springer, Heidelberg (2016). doi:10.1007/978-3-319-22288-2_25
7. Perla, P.P., Markowitz, M., Nofi, A.A., Weuve, C., Loughran, J.: Gaming and shared situation awareness. DTIC Document (2000)
8. Lo, J.C., Meijer, S.A.: Gaming simulation design for individual and team situation awareness. In: Meijer, S.A., Smeds, R. (eds.) ISAGA 2013. LNCS, vol. 8264, pp. 121–128. Springer, Heidelberg (2014). doi:10.1007/978-3-319-04954-0_15
9. Kurapati, S., Lukosch, H., Verbraeck, A., Brazier, F.M.T.: Improving resilience in intermodal transport operations in seaports: a gaming approach. EURO J. Decis. Process. **3**, 375–396 (2015)
10. Kurapati, S., Groen, D., Lukosch, H., Verbraeck, A.: Microgames in practice: a case study in container terminal operations. In: The Shift from Teaching to Learning: Individual, Collective and Organizational Learning Through Gaming Simulation, pp. 333–346 (2014)
11. Muller, G.: Intermodal Freight Transportation. Eno Transportation Foundation, Washington, DC (1989)

12. Steenken, D., Voss, S., Stahlbock, R.: Container terminal operation and operations research-a classification and literature review. OR Spectr. **26**, 3–49 (2004)
13. Brinkmann, B.: Operations systems of container terminals: a compendious overview. In: Bose, J.W. (ed.) Handbook of Terminal Planning. Operations Research/Computer Science Interfaces Series, vol. 49, pp. 25–39. Springer, New York (2011)
14. Bose, J.: General considerations on container terminal planning. In: Bose, J. (ed.) Handbook of Terminal Planning. Operations Research/Computer Science Interfaces Series, vol. 49, pp. 3–22. Springer, New York (2011)
15. Behdani, B.: Handling disruptions in supply chains: an integrated framework and an agent-based model. Delft University of Technology (2013)
16. Harrington, L.H., Boyson, S., Corsi, T.: X-SCM: The New Science of X-Treme Supply Chain Management. Routledge, New York (2010)
17. Gurning, S., Cahoon, S.: Analysis of multi-mitigation scenarios on maritime disruptions. Marit. Policy Manag. **38**, 251–268 (2011)
18. Harteveld, C.: Triadic Game Design: Balancing Reality, Meaning and Play. Springer Science & Business Media, Heidelberg (2011)
19. Klemke, R., Kurapati, S., Lukosch, H., Specht, M.: Transferring an Educational Board Game to a Multi-user Mobile Learning Game to Increase Shared Situational Awareness. In: Zaphiris, P., Ioannou, A. (eds.) LCT 2015. LNCS, vol. 9192, pp. 583–594. Springer, Heidelberg (2015). doi:10.1007/978-3-319-20609-7_55
20. Klemke, R., Kurapati, S., Lukosch, H., Specht, M.: Lessons learned from creating a mobile version of an educational board game to increase situational awareness. In: Conole, G., Klobučar, T., Rensing, C., Konert, J., Lavoué, É. (eds.) EC-TEL 2015. LNCS, vol. 9307, pp. 183–196. Springer, Heidelberg (2015). doi:10.1007/978-3-319-24258-3_14
21. Freire, M., del Blanco, Á., Fernández-Manjón, B.: Serious games as edX MOOC activities. In: IEEE Global Engineering Education Conference (EDUCON), pp. 867–871 (2014)

SOA Applied: Engineering Software as Processing Unit of a Serious Game

Daniel Schwarz[2(✉)], Heinrich Söbke[3(✉)], Andreas F. Hofmann[1(✉)], Gerald Angermair[1], Lars Schnatmann[2], and Jörg Londong[3]

[1] tandler.com Ges. für Umweltinformatik mbH, Buch am Erlbach, Germany
{andreas.hofmann,gerald.angermair}@tandler.com
[2] takomat GmbH, Cologne, Germany
{dan,lars}@takomat.com
[3] Bauhaus-Institute for Infrastructure Solutions (b.is),
Bauhaus-Universität Weimar, Weimar, Germany
{heinrich.soebke,joerg.londong}@uni-weimar.de

Abstract. A mechanistic model is an essential component of any simulation game. The development of such a model, including its elementary components, their relations and calculation rules, is a demanding, costly and fault-prone task. This task becomes even more complex if very realistic models are required, as it is mostly the case for serious games. Alternatively, proven simulation software can be integrated into the serious game, turning the game into an easy to use and motivating user interface, and the simulation program into a verified processing unit. In this article, we present a serious game dealing with water infrastructure planning, which interfaces to an engineering simulation software for necessary calculations. After motivating the combination of game and simulation software in this special case of water infrastructure planning, we focus on the characteristics of the software architecture and the development process. Data availability and data aggregation are identified as issues central to a successful implementation of the presented architecture. This case study thus reveals advantages and challenges of serious games employing service-oriented architectures (SOA).

Keywords: Service oriented architecture · Transition path · Water infrastructure · Rating system · Serious game · Engineering software

1 Introduction

Planning and management of urban infrastructure is a technically complex task and requires expert knowledge as well as an ability to understand complex systems. This is especially relevant, when various groups of stakeholders are involved: Unlike engineers—who are experts in the field—citizens (public participation, e.g. [1]), politicians, and laymen decision makers (e.g. as members of honorary boards) might not have the necessary expert knowledge to overview and fully grasp the systemic impacts of planning decisions. Acting as virtual prototypes, video games can provide ways to experiment with complex systems without risking real world consequences. Games of this nature can play an important role for acceptance and spread of innovations [2]:

© Springer International Publishing AG 2016
R. Bottino et al. (Eds.): GALA 2016, LNCS 10056, pp. 177–186, 2016.
DOI: 10.1007/978-3-319-50182-6_16

stakeholders are more likely to accept an innovative technical solution, when they can experience its inner workings and mechanisms first hand via simulation [3].

Using video games for real-world planning can be carried out in diverse ways. The two main approaches are: first, a commercial off-the-shelf (COTS) game offers a cost-efficient approach. In the context of infrastructure mainly city builder games (e.g., *SimCity* [4]) or management games (e.g., *Railroad Tycoon* [5]) are discussed [6–9]. However, commonly mentioned main drawbacks of these games in serious contexts are their simplified simulation and data models. COTS are optimized for entertainment purposes; they are not designed to process real-world data. They cannot cope with the requirements of real-world planning: D'Artista and Hellweger analyzed the short-comings of *SimCity* in the sector of water infrastructure [10]. The second approach is the development of specific serious games. Although such games require in general many development resources, there are some successful examples. In the context of traffic infrastructure *Mobility* [11] is an excellent example of a widely used serious game, having provided exiting gameplay even in non-serious contexts. A further example in this sector is discussed by van den Hoogen, et al. [12]. In the area of energy infrastructure *Energetika* [13] is a publicly available serious game with more than 280.000 online game sessions; players created more than 2.200 valid sustainable energy strategies for Germany.

The design and production costs of such serious games are higher than comparable simulations for mere entertainment. Based on the experience of 14 serious games in diverse topics, *takomat* estimates the costs for a serious game twice as high than the production costs for a comparable entertainment game. The additional effort is caused by the integration of expert knowledge and real-world data in the game design and game assets (e.g. realistic measures and complexity of game objects), the programming of more complex game mechanics to represent real-world phenomena and a higher effort in balancing the game between gameplay fun and accuracy of the simulation.

The inherent challenge of financing this additional effort in serious games calls for a different strategy, which mainly aims at improving the efficiency of the development process. In recent years, game engine technology has improved considerably years: State-of-the-art commercial game engines are available at reasonable prices (e.g. *Unity3D* [14] or *CryEngine* [15]). Serious game companies like *takomat* have built their own simulation frameworks for serious games on the basis of these existing game engines using their basic components (e.g., Scene Graph, real-time rendering pipeline, etc.).

A further strategy to mitigate development efforts is the combination of already existing software packages or services. For military applications the coupling of systems using middleware is prevalent [16]. There are also attempts to employ middleware in virtual environments [17]. Applying service oriented architecture (SOA), these systems build game-like simulator environments. Generally, combining various resources to create a serious game is a promising strategy to reduce development costs and effort [18].

Building on the above ideas, we present a case study of a serious game in the application field of water infrastructure systems (WIS). The serious game uses SOA to interface to a commercial engineering software package, which acts as a modelling template and calculation engine.

2 Background and Prerequisites

In the following paragraphs we present specific requirements and conditions, which frame the design and development of the game. The game was developed within the research project TWIST++ (www.twistplusplus.de), which focused on design strategies in the context of transitions between different types of WIS. One of the objectives of TWIST++ was to develop a multi-criteria based rating system for WIS. Also a commercial engineering and planning software was extended to work with novel types of WIS within the TWIST++ project.

Area of Application and Game Content. The topic of the game are transition pathways between different types of WIS [19]. WIS, e.g. sewers and wastewater treatment plants (WWTP), usually are both extremely expensive and long lasting. Therefore, the value of such systems, both in financial terms and in terms of services provided, has to be considered over long periods of time. In the presence of changing boundary conditions, such as climate change and demographic changes, so-called transition paths have to be developed. Not only the target state of such a system is important, but a functional system has to be guaranteed during the complete transition from the initial state to the goal state. Employing the multi-criteria evaluation system provides an absolute rating of all states along the transition pathway.

These properties of a real-world WIS can be mapped onto the key features of a simulation game [3]: A functional system is propagated forward in time. At any point in time a rating or scoring of the current game state can be calculated and provides a goal-oriented feedback to the player.

Rating System. A major result of TWIST++ is the design of a rating system for WIS [20]. Common, established rating systems for WIS focus purely on economic aspects. The TWIST++ rating system introduces the dimensions of sustainability in order to measure overall sustainability. In the game, this rating system for sustainability is represented by the three points accounts *Economy*, *Ecology* and *Social Affairs*. The goal of the game is to keep these three points accounts in balance and to prevent that one of the points accounts falls to zero. If the player manages to accomplish this game challenge over the course of game time his planning solution is sustainable by definition. The game computes 36 indicators of urban water management with a multi-criteria assessment and maps these variables onto the three points accounts of sustainability. For example, it considers energetic gains and recovered resources. Based on those 36 input criteria and using a suitable weighting and aggregation scheme on various abstraction levels, a final score between 0 and 1 can be assigned to any WIS and any transition state between different types of WIS.

The TWIST++ rating system has been fully integrated into the game. It is used to calculate overall gaming scores, as well as to provide comprehensive feedback on the player's actions. Therefore, the rating system works as a guideline for decision making and assessment. It has been developed - based on an extensive literature research – in expert workshops. The main result of these workshops was the selection of criteria and their underlying attributes. In the rating system, criteria can be weighted according to preferences of various stakeholders. The game uses an exemplary set of weights which has been compiled in the TWIST++ project as well.

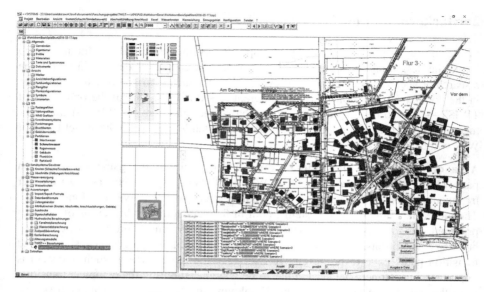

Fig. 1. ++SYSTEMS: User Interface

Commercial Engineering Software. *++SYSTEMS* [21] is a sanitary environmental engineering software package, which stores localized data and therefore is a type of geographical information system (GIS). Figure 1 gives an impression of its graphical user interface (GUI). Main features are hydraulic calculation of pipe networks, material flow analyses (pollutant loads) and storm water flood simulations. The implementation of these features required detailed knowledge and considerable effort. Their (even simplified) reproduction within the game would have been substantially costlier than implementing an interface between the engineering software and the game.

The engineering software simulates the functioning of a given WIS system at one point in time, calculates all necessary sustainability criteria and sends them for scoring and visualization purposes to the game via an interface. As the WIS system is changed over time by the player's actions, those changes are sent back to the engineering software, where the WIS model is changed and sustainability criteria are calculated again. In this fashion, the interplay between game and engineering software propagates a changing WIS system through time and calculates gaming scores along the way.

Simulation Game Framework. Development and usage of specific simulation frameworks as an amendment of a game engine is an effective measure to increase efficiency of serious game development. Thus we used takomat's simulation framework *epigene* here. It has evolved during the production of more than 14 different serious games in very different subject areas like Energy, Geography, Physics, Biology, etc. This framework has been implemented using different underlying commercial game engines and frameworks (e.g. *Havok Vision Engine* [22], *Unity3D* [14], *Flash* [23],). *epigene* supports serious game development by a broad existing set of algorithms and game mechanics to model dynamic systems in general.

3   Implementation

Architecture and Components. Service-oriented architectures (SOA) are a well-known approach in the field of military training systems [16, 17] and have recently been discussed in the field of serious games [24]. Potential candidates for services are software components from the field of genuine educational technology, e.g. survey- and assessment tools. In our case we have integrated engineering software as a service. Two main components have to communicate with each other (see Fig. 2): the game software—based on Unity3D and the *epigene* framework—and the engineering software –given by the core modules of *++SYSTEMS*. The communication is handled by a custom TCP/IP-based interface. Figure 2 illustrates the components and their projected distribution on hardware.

Simulation Model. Game and calculation back end both have to rely on coherent simulation models: the game visualizes the results of the calculation engine. The development of this simulation model has been guided significantly by the requirements of the rating system. The rating system is based on criteria attributes, which must be reflected in the simulation model. Therefore, a mapping between state variables and parameters in the engineering software's simulation model and respective rating system criteria has to be developed. For all well-defined, quantitative criteria, such a mapping is possible and the game can receive respective values from the engineering software. However, the rating system also includes qualitative parameters which are not represented in the engineering software – for those types of criteria the game itself needs to provide suitable calculation mechanisms.

Interface between Game and ++SYSTEMS-Server. Technically, the communication between game and server is based on TCP sockets. Semantically, a proprietary protocol using the JSON format [25] has been implemented. A list of commands and their appropriate parameters has been defined. The following example illustrates the command send to the engineering software as a result of a player's action:

```
{ "command": "addConstruction",
 "construction": { "id" :"E0011_GreywaterFilter",
"area_id": 42}
}
```

While the game works as a continuous simulation, calculations by the engineering software are only performed at discrete points in time. The commands are issued, while the player has activated a so-called *Build-Mode* in the game. During this mode, all build actions are recorded. To more seamlessly integrate necessary computational time of the engineering software into the flow of the game, multiple actions of the player are grouped: after leaving this mode, the commands are submitted to the server. Then the server applies these actions to the model in the engineering software. After it has been synchronized with the game model, a recalculation of the model is triggered. The results are returned to the game, which visualizes them and uses them to calculate game scores.

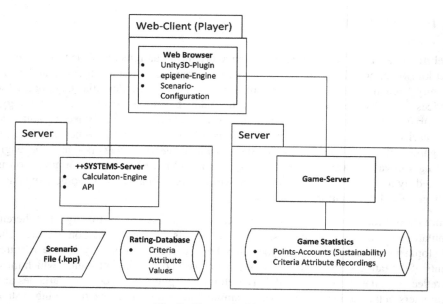

Fig. 2. Target Architecture

Data Distribution and Aggregation. The server holds detailed real-world data. During the implementation the development team discussed which data has to be locally available for the game and if it has to be aggregated or not. Performance and fluid gameplay demanded that some scoring criteria be calculated directly by the game. The interface to the engineering software is only used in cases where local calculation of criteria in the game is impossible due to the simplified game model. Only if the scenario has changed due to model changes, a new set of calculated values is transmitted to the game client. An example that refers to maintenance costs: a pipeline section ages by time in the simulation, thus each section has an attribute *Class of Damage*. The player needs to know this attribute in order to decide if rehabilitation is necessary. Alternatively, there will be an automated rehabilitation, if a pipeline section reaches a certain *Class of Damage*. Therefore, each pipeline section can become a target of player action. So the pipeline-section itself and its attribute *Class of Damage* is required in the game. In contrast, the criteria attribute *Emission of Total Organic Carbon (TOC,* a non-specific indicator of water quality) is a system-wide property. Its value is derived from the scenario and its wastewater streams and is calculated by the server. Therefore, no game-local attribute *TOC* for each wastewater stream is needed. The aggregated scenario global value is required. So, the simulation model of the game is designed such that all information necessary for implemented game actions is contained.

Game Design. The integration of the calculation engine offers new choices for the game dynamics. We adhered to the **general rule** that the calculation engine is used to determine a static status of the model, whenever a structural update of the model is done. All other calculations are processed by the game engine. Following time-based adjustments of the simulation model in the game are accomplished by linear updates. Changes to boundary conditions as of the demographic development or water prices are given by player definable simulation options (e.g. *Relative Decrease/Increase per Year*) in the game. These settings are processed in the game itself at regular intervals and do not cause a call of the engineering software backend.

Important components of the dynamics of gameplay are events. While the calculation engine does not originate any kind of event, the game itself causes three kinds of events: Random **System Events** are abrupt changes of boundary conditions, which partly influence the simulation model. An example is the increase of heavy precipitation events. This event requires a recalculation, because it impacts the total emission of *TOC* in a non-linear way. **Parameter-based Events** are triggered when limit values are exceeded. For example, if a pipeline reaches a certain *Class of Damage*, an automatic rehabilitation is started. Thus parameter-based events can trigger recalculation. When the player starts an action like building a WWTP, so-called **Action-based Events** are fired. Events themselves do not cause a recalculation directly, but events can trigger secondary actions which might require recalculation by the back end.

Player statistics have a prominent position in a simulation game. In our case, player statistics are based on the rating system, which is available in ++SYSTEMS as well. To foster easy understanding and captivating gameplay, player statistics here have been reduced to three categories in the top level of criteria (Ecology, Economy, and Social Issues). The rating system, however, is available on demand in full detail for the interested player.

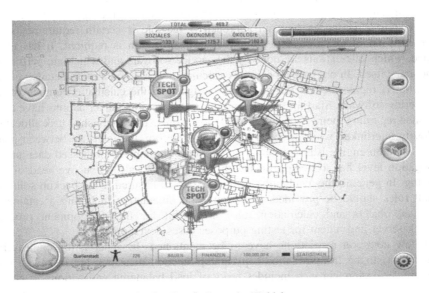

Fig. 3. Game: Scenario *Wohlsborn*

The Use Case *Wohlsborn*. The application of the software to a concrete scenario, i.e. a playable city or village, requires preparation work. The basic data is available as a corresponding *++SYSTEMS* file. An export file for the game has to be created and imported into the game. There it is visualized as a geographical map (see Fig. 3.). Depending on envisioned game actions for the city or village in question, some components might have to be predefined in both game and engineering software. This approach keeps the communication effort between game and *++SYSTEMS* as simple as possible. A consequence is a configuration file for the game: technologies and facilities, which are buildable, have to be defined. Additionally, so called *Tech Spots* have to be defined. These are short descriptions—containing photographs—of the most urgent problems considering WIS. They serves as a kind of mission briefing for the players.

The game has been implemented and tested using a model of Wohlsborn, a small village of 500 citizens in Thuringia (Germany). Model scenarios of this size can be calculated in the engineering software back end within seconds. Larger scenarios require more time. At a certain size a precalculation of most probable states could be necessary.

4 Discussion, Conclusions and Outlook

This case study presents a serious game, which employs a SOA approach and relies on online calculation results of a commercial engineering software package. Its most apparent benefit is the outsourcing of complex calculations to specialized software. This considerably reduces design and implementation efforts. A further advantage of this approach is that often an engineering simulation model already exists. It can act as a raw template for the game simulation model; thus the design effort is lowered.

From our experiences such an approach is feasible if certain requirements are observed. First of all, a clear definition of task allocation is required. It has to be defined, which calculations are done by the service software and which are performed in the game itself. In our case all complex calculations based on a more detailed model than what is represented in the game, are assigned to the calculation engine of the engineering software. Starting from learning targets, possible player actions have to be evaluated regarding their effects on recalculation events. The established task allocation is closely interlinked with the data allocation. Therefore, the interface between game and calculation engine is an important component. The kind of processed data and its aggregation level has to be specified with regard to the calculation overhead of this coupling. In general, the availability of data has to be ensured. As a backup solution, default rules should be provided. A thorough documentation including a catalog of attributes, objects and calculation rules is helpful for the development process. A mock-server and -client for testing purposes eases development.

A few common restrictions have to be mentioned. In general, the engineering software has to be licensed; thus copyright protection measures are involved. Furthermore, provision via web includes tasks of load balancing and actions to ensure reentrant software instances. Currently, two model files have to be kept updated.

Our future work includes—besides a profound evaluation of the efficacy of the game itself— establishing a web-accessible version of the game. The notion of a single source scenario has to be developed in order to remove error-prone manual synchronization work. Further investigations are needed to formalize this process of creating a serious game as simplified front-end using engineering software as back end.

Acknowledgements. The activities described in this article have been supported by the German Federal Ministry of Education and Research (BMBF) under the grant agreement FKZ 033W011E. The authors gratefully acknowledge this support. Furthermore, the authors thank the anonymous reviewers for their valuable comments.

References

1. Poplin, A.: Playful public participation in urban planning: a case study for online serious games. Comput. Environ. Urban Syst. **36**, 195–206 (2012)
2. Rogers, E.M.: Diffusion of Innovations. Free Press, New York (2003)
3. Söbke, H., Londong, J.: Promoting innovative water infrastructure systems: simulation games as virtual prototypes. In: Lohaus, J. (ed.) Proceedings of 17th International EWA Symposium "WatEnergyResources – Water, Energy and Resources" European Water Association, Hennef (2014)
4. Wright, W.: SimCity. www.simcity.com
5. Meier, S.: Railroad Tycoon. http://www.2kgames.com/railroads/
6. Devisch, O.: Should planners start playing computer games? Arguments from SimCity and second life. Plan. Theory Pract. **9**, 209–226 (2008)
7. Minnery, J., Searle, G.: Toying with the city? Using the computer game SimCityTM4 in planning education. Plan. Pract. Res. **29**, 41–55 (2013)
8. Rehm, M.: Do gamers change attitudes towards economics through playing manager games? Zeitschrift für Ökonomische Bild. **1**, 162–176 (2013)
9. Foster, A.N.: The process of learning in a simulation strategy game: disciplinary knowledge construction. J. Educ. Comput. Res. **45**, 1–27 (2011)
10. D'Artista, B.R., Hellweger, F.L.: Urban hydrology in a computer game? Environ. Model. Softw. **22**, 1679–1684 (2007)
11. Brannolte, U., Harder, R.J., Kraus, T.J.: Virtual city and traffic simulation game based on scientific models. In: Zupančič, B., Karba, R., Blažič, S. (eds.) EUROSIM 2007: Proceedings of the 6th EUROSIM Congress on Modelling and Simulation, Ljubljana, Slovenia, vol. 1 (2007)
12. van den Hoogen, J., Meijer, S.: Gaming and simulation for railway innovation: a case study of the Dutch railway system. Simul. Gaming. **46**, 489–511 (2015)
13. takomat: Energetika (2010). http://www.wir-ernten-was-wir-saeen.de/energiespiel/
14. Unity Technologies: Unity - Game Engine (2015). https://unity3d.com/
15. Crytek GmbH: CryEngine (2015). http://cryengine.com/
16. Noseworthy, J.R.: The test and training enabling architecture (TENA) supporting the decentralized development of distributed applications and LVC simulations. In: 12th IEEE/ACM International Symposium on Distributed Simulation and Real-Time Applications, DS-RT 2008, pp. 259–268 (2008)
17. van Oijen, J., Vanhée, L., Dignum, F.: CIGA: a middleware for intelligent agents in virtual environments. In: Beer, M., Brom, C., Dignum, F., Soo, V.-W. (eds.) Agents for Educational Games and Simulations. LNCS, vol. 7471, pp. 22–37. Springer, Heidelberg (2012). doi:10. 1007/978-3-642-32326-3_2

18. Stănescu, I.A., Stefan, A., Kravcik, M., Lim, T., Bidarra, R.: Interoperability strategies for serious games development. In: Internet Learning, pp. 33–40. DigitalCommons@APUS (2013)

19. Maier, K., Söbke, H., Londong, J.: Principles of transition paths: purposeful conversion of water infrastructure systems to multi stream variants. In: Memon, F.A. (ed.) Proceedings of the Water Efficiency Conference 2015, pp. 359–368. WATEF Network/University of Brighton, Exeter (2015)

20. Nyga, I., Alfen, H.W.: Ganzheitliche Bewertung von Wasserinfrastrukturen im Zuge von Transformationsprozessen. In: Steinmetz, H., Dittmer, U. (eds.) 5. Aqua Urbanica und 90. Siedlungswasserwirtschaftliches Kolloquium, Stuttgarter Berichte zur Siedlungswasserwirtschaft, Band 225, pp. 289–294. DIV Deutscher Industrieverlag, Stuttgart (2015)

21. tandler.com: ++SYSTEMS - IT im Dienste der Umwelt. http://tandler.com/kommunale_gis/siedlungswasser/umweltsoftware.htm

22. Havok: Vision Engine 8.2 Brings 3D Technologies Cross-Platform. http://www.havok.com/vision-engine-8-2-brings-3d-technologies-cross-platform/

23. Adobe Systems Incorporated: Flash Developer Center. http://www.adobe.com/devnet/flash.html

24. Carvalho, M.B., Bellotti, F., Hu, J., Hauge, J.B., Berta, R., De Gloria, A., Rauterberg, M.: Towards a service-oriented architecture framework for educational serious games. In: IEEE International Conference Advanced Learning Technologies, vol. 4 (2015)

25. Json.org: Introducing JSON. http://json.org/

Serious Gaming in Airport Management: Transformation from a Validation Tool to a Learning Environment

Sebastian Schier, Maria Freese$^{(\boxtimes)}$, and Thorsten Mühlhausen

German Aerospace Center (DLR), Institute of Flight Guidance,
Lilienthalplatz 7, 38108 Braunschweig, Germany
{Sebastian.Schier,Maria.Freese,
Thorsten.Muehlhausen}@dlr.de

Abstract. Traditional methods to model airport management for e.g. research or training are primarily simulations. These methods lack the ability to model social behavior in collaborative decision making. Serious gaming is an approach to fill this gap. Therefore, the German Aerospace Center (DLR) introduced the serious game D-CITE for research purpose. This paper describes its advancement to a training tool and the results of a first training session with different airport stakeholders. Their feedback emphasizes the importance of a strong communication culture.

1 Serious Gaming in Airport Management

Using conventional methods of real-time simulations in airport management is a long tradition. According to the European Operation Concept Validation Methodology (E-OCVM) [1], this kind of simulation is relevant to providing humans experience in a controlled environment (extensive training required) as well as for the validation of concepts. But real-time simulations are also limited, because the focus is not often on the social behavior of individuals. Furthermore, they are complex systems, which are difficult to set up [2]. One further possibility for analyzing human decision-making is the serious gaming approach. For some years the use of games focusing not only on entertainment, but also on aspects of education or training aspects has increased [3]. This is because serious games can be used to show complex decision-making processes (or other complex situations) in abstracted simplified environment [4]. They are easier to setup and participants can focus on the learning aspect rather than complex technical user interfaces.

The present paper deals with decision-making of airport managers and the question of whether it is possible to train for collaborative decision-making and awareness of information-sharing. Therefore, in the first section, an overview of airport management as well as the use of serious games in this area is given. The second main section deals with theoretical methods. Results of an experimental set-up are presented in the third key section. Finally, future conclusions and future directions are deviated.

© Springer International Publishing AG 2016
R. Bottino et al. (Eds.): GALA 2016, LNCS 10056, pp. 187–196, 2016.
DOI: 10.1007/978-3-319-50182-6_17

1.1   Airport Management

An Airport is a complex transportation system, where planning activities of different stakeholders are connected. These stakeholders are for example airlines, airport authorities, air traffic service providers, and ground-handlers. Especially the coordination of their interrelations is a challenge on account of divergent goals and different interests. A further problem is that the involved stakeholders focus only on their own business cases and are not interested in sharing information and knowledge [5] to keep a competitive advantage. But especially the collaborative decision-making process might be helpful in times with increasing challenges in airport management (e.g. rising traffic [6]). As a first step in this direction, the A-CDM (Airport Collaborative Decision-Making, [7]) focuses on using a common database, which is visible for all stakeholders. The goal is to improve the process of sharing information to have a common understanding of operations [6, 8]. Studies already have shown that using the concept of A-CDM leads to positive effects (e.g. reduction in ground delay). Through the use of A-CDM the accuracy of flight departures can be increased [9]. A further concept, developed on the basis of A-CDM is TAM (Total Airport Management). It consists of two key elements. The first element is the APOC (Airport Operation Center), where different stakeholders come together (real or virtual) to plan, to monitor, and to control airport-based processes [8, 10]. The second element is the AOP (Airport Operation Plan), which is an operational plan for a certain time horizon. This plan is collaboratively agreed and contains information about flights processes as well as weather constraints. As mentioned above, there are two methods to analyze the collaborative decision making process, human in the loop (HITL) simulations are built around the tools, which are used in this domain. As these are very heterogeneous, it is a high effort to integrate them and build a common simulation environment. Furthermore, the users need to be used to them before taking the next step and collaborate with the other stakeholders. Therefore, serious games have been developed, which allow an abstract implementation of the airport and its processes. By using them, it is possible to focus on the collaborative aspects without knowledge or restrictions of A-CDM tools. That said, the present paper focuses on using serious games for analyzing collaborative decision making processes.

1.2   Serious Gaming

In this sub-chapter an overview of the literature as well as previous research in the area of airport management is given. After this, the serious game D-CITE (*D*ecisions based on *C*ollaborative *I*nteractions in *TE*ams; [11]), which is used as a method including the game and learning mechanics, will be explained.

During the last years the focus on using serious games in the aviation context has increased. There are several serious games for training skills of pilots and air traffic controllers. In contrast to this development, serious gaming has rarely been used in the area of airport management. But the Netherlands Aerospace Centre (NLR) has already focused on using serious games in this area. They developed a number of paper-based games for training purposes (e.g. Skyboard [12] or Aerogame [13]).

D-CITE (see Fig. 1) is designed for simulating decision-making on the one hand and analyzing potential influence factors on decision-making processes on the other hand. For that reason, the German Aerospace Center (DLR) developed a computer-based multiplayer game, modelling the influences of airport operations, airlines and ground handling. Being able to conduct flights, open security lanes and transporting passengers to their aircraft a virtual airport world was implemented. The unique feature of D-CITE is, that it includes the individual interest of each stakeholder group and integrates them in the collaborative decision making process at airports. After using D-CITE successfully as a research instrument for validation, it was questioned if D-CITE can also be used as training and learning environment for airport stakeholders.

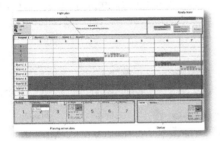 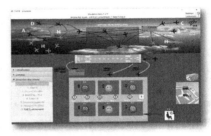

Fig. 1. Screenshots of D-CITE: planning phase (left) and simulation phase (right) (DLR intern, 2016).

Therefore, in the following sections, the game and learn mechanics are depicted. [14] developed a game and learning mechanics framework according to a modified model of Boom's Digital Taxonomy, which consists of higher (creating) and lower (retention/remembering) thinking skills (see Fig. 2, first row). Each category consists of different sub-categories, which are associated with key learning verbs (see Fig. 2, second and third row). A selection of these key verbs will be the basis in the present study, whereas as firstly the game, secondly the learning, and thirdly the mechanics according to D-CITE are presented.

Game Mechanics. In general game mechanics are rule-based systems, which motivate the player to explore and to learn. The defined framework is divided into six sections (from retention to creating) (see Fig. 2). For each section a selection of game mechanics according to the implementation in D-CITE is depicted.

Fig. 2. Overview of Game Mechanics [adapted from 14].

190   S. Schier et al.

Learning Mechanics. For each section of the framework a selection of learning mechanics (see Fig. 3) according to the implementation in D-CITE is presented.

Guidance	Participation	Competition	Analysis	Reflect	Planung
Explore	Time Pressure	Cooperation	Feedback	Motivation	Responsibility
Retention	**Under-standing**	**Applying**	**Analysing**	**Evaluating**	**Creating**

Fig. 3. Overview of Learning Mechanics [adapted from 14].

Mechanics According to D-CITE. The above mentioned mechanics are implemented in D-CITE. In Fig. 4 both groups of mechanics and concrete examples of D-CITE are visible.

Learning by Doing	Get to know the interdependen-cies	Competition of different teams	Feedback about the team-score	Reflection phase after the rounds	Planing
Guidance	Participation	Competition	Analysis	Reflect	Planing
Explore	Time Pressure	Cooperation	Feedback	Motivation	Responsibility
Retention	**Under-standing**	**Applying**	**Analysing**	**Evaluating**	**Creating**
Information	Role-play	Cooperation	Meta-Game	Resource Management	Design
Story	Tutorial	Time Pressure	Feedback	Collaboration	Strategy
Optimize the business of an airport	Interactive tutorial during training	Variation of the duration of the rounds	Feedback via Team-Score (financial)	Limited Resources (e.g., buses)	Airport-based setting

Fig. 4. Overview of Game (lower area) and Learning Mechanics (upper) area according to the implementation in D-CITE (orange background) [adapted from 14]. (Color figure online)

On the base of the presented literature about airport management, serious gaming and game as well as learning mechanics, the following research questions result.

1.3   Research Questions

1. Which changes need to be applied to a serious gaming validation tool to use it for training of airport management?
2. Is the validation tool accepted by the users as a learning tool?
3. To what extent are game mechanics involved in learning/relevant for learning?

2   Methods

Transferring D-CITE to a learning tool, demands for a structured analysis of the requirements. One method to perform this analysis can be taken from the fields of computer supported collaborative learning (CSCL). This research area focusses on supporting learning groups within their collaborative process by computer tools. Regarding the airport management decision process as the learning object, D-CITE is the tool to conduct this collaborative learning sessions. Analyzing requirements for CSCL tools, a distinct requirement analysis is suggested by K. Almendinger [15]. In the following section an overview of this analysis, including the necessary adaptions is given.

2.1   Tailored Change Requirement Analysis for CSCL Tools

To answer the first research question (Which changes need to be applied to a serious gaming validation tool to use it for training of airport management?), the CSCL requirement analysis suggested by K. Almendinger aims on defining requirements for a new CSCL tool. This analysis is performed in the following phases:

1. Analysis of learning objectives
2. Target group analysis
3. Requirement specification
4. Selection of technical basis
5. Cost-Benefit-Analysis

This approach must be tailored to the demand of the D-CITE transformation process. As D-CITE already exist it is not necessary to select a technical basis. Moreover, the cost-benefit analysis can be eliminated due to this study focusing on technical feasibility and acceptance rather than financial aspects.

Additionally, the analysis of the target group needs to be defined in details. As the special focus of the airport management and the decision making process is the interaction of the airport stakeholders, it is necessary to analyze their relations.

The stakeholders at the airports are influenced in their relations and decisions by multiple aspects. Primarily they represent a certain organization or company to whom goals and strategies they need to comply. Secondarily they take a certain role in the decision making process depending on the resources they manage (e.g. airport as the infrastructure provider managing stands and terminals). Finally, the stakeholders take part in the airport management as persons with their experiences and abilities. Summarizing these circumstances, the following adapted analysis procedure was derived:

1. learning objective analysis
2. target group analysis
   (a) person-role-organization (PRO)-analysis [16]
   (b) relationship analysis
   (c) analysis of learning dimensions [17]
3. requirement specification

Learning Objective Analysis. The learning objective analysis relies on two gap analysis performed in airport management. [5] as well as [18] performed interview sessions with multiple actors at an airport. Both studies come to the result that: "Missing, unprecise or delayed information threaten the coordination of the process steps" (cited and translated from [16, p. 6). Out of this statement the learning objectives come clear:

1. D-CITE must enable the users to learn what information for the current decision making step are necessary.
2. D-CITE must enable the users to learn when this information is provided optimally.
3. D-CITE must enable the users to learn how this information is provided optimally.

Target Group Analysis. The target group analysis consists of the three areas: (a) person-role-organization (PRO)-analysis, (b) relationship analysis and (c) analysis of learning dimensions.

The PRO-analysis was conducted on basis of [5, 20]. While generating a full picture of all airport stakeholders, it was defined that the airline agent(s), the airport agent, the ground handler agent and the air traffic controller need to be trained.

The relationship analysis among those four stakeholders showed that due to competition issues, airline and ground handler need to be included at least with two players each in D-CITE.

The analysis of the learning dimensions revealed multiple requirements such as training time (which can be from one day to one week duration), the function of the coach (who can operate as a facilitator or an instructor) or examples of current and future air traffic need to be encountered.

Requirement Specification. Concluding the tailored CSCL requirements analysis, the defined learning objectives and target group analysis was compared with the possibilities of D-CITE. Thereby it was noticed that D-CITE offers a gap at the participating stakeholders. On one hand air traffic control is missing. On the other hand including only one ground handler does not introduce the existing competition between multiple ground handlers at the airport. Therefore, it was decided that D-CITE needs to be extended with atc and a second ground handler.

Regarding the defined learning objectives on the information process, it was noticed that D-CITE in principle implements all possibilities to exchange the information in each phase of the decision making process, but the stakeholders are not forced to exchange their perspectives. Therefore, it was decided to include a change of roles and Debriefing sessions into the learning process. Thereby stakeholders can make the experience what information a certain role (they do not know in detail) misses or can not only encounter if delivered in a certain way.

Summarizing these findings, the following changes on D-CITE were recommended (see Table 1).

In the first experimental set-up the improved cost model, the role change as well as the intermediate debriefing sessions was applied.

Table 1. Recommended changes on D-CITE

Changes	Description
Improved cost model	To better integrate the profit orientation of the stakeholders
Role change	Determining that limitations to the own view leads to decreased collaborative performance, roles will be changed throughout the game
Intermediate Debriefing sessions	To determine joint procedures and behaviors within the collaboration
Integration of a second ground handler	To generate competition effects on the ground handling
Integration of an ATC	To broaden the influence area of the decision making process, ATC will provide airside boundary conditions to the collaborative process

2.2   Experimental Set-up

A first experimental set-up (for further details see [21]) with four airport managers (female = 1, male = 3; mean age = 43.5 years, standard deviation [SD] = 6.03 years, Range [R] = 35–49 years) focused on role change and the relevance of debriefing.

Therefore, the experts had the task to play a certain number of rounds of D-CITE (they did not know about the final number of rounds). After the second round, the first debriefing took place. The goal was firstly to analyze the problem of the last two rounds, secondly to talk to the other players about his or her own planning activities and thirdly to derive measures for a better game play. A second and final debriefing was conducted after finishing the third and last round of D-CITE. The focus was on the comparison of the rounds before and after the initial debriefing. After this, the team score was analyzed and the managers had the task to discuss about the role change.

3   Results

Detailed Results for the familiarity, the feedback and design of D-CITE and special observations are depicted in [21]. In the following the results of the second research question (Is the validation tool accepted by the users as a learning tool?) will be presented. With the already mentioned changes or new implementations of D-CITE, the focus on learning was the most relevant part. Therefore, in a first step the attitude toward serious games in general was measured before and after playing the game. It could be shown, that the attitude has changed positively toward serious games after playing D-CITE. Secondly, the debriefing was a strong learning mechanics. In Table 2 the discussed main points during the debriefing are depicted. According to the statements of the airport managers, especially the interaction with the other stakeholders was the most important point.

In addition to this, the behavior is another relevant factor. Therefore, it is necessary to understand, what the players learned during the game-play and debriefing and what they will realize in their daily working-life. The experts gave the following positive comments about the relevance of collaboration [21, p. 8]:

Table 2. Discussion points during debriefing session [20]

Main points	Detailed description/measurements
Analyze the problem of the last two rounds	Not only information exchange between Airlines or Airport and Ground-Handler, new developed interaction-model
Talk to the other players about his/her own planning activities	Give an overview about the decision-making competencies and action possibilities of his/her own role
To derive measures for better game play	Focus more on passenger contentment (relevant for long-term aspects)

1. *"The strengthening of collaborative work from round to round and especially after the debriefing was remarkable."*
2. *"The debriefing is really important for a better understanding and for creating a better common information base."*
3. *"It is surprising how much you can improve through communication."*

These comments illustrate the relevance of collaboration in this area.

For answering the third research question (To what extent game mechanics are involved in learning/relevant for learning?) a selection of the in D-CITE implemented game mechanics are discussed. First of all, a collaborative game-based learning situation was developed. During the multiplayer game-play the players have the chance to learn the relevance of information-sharing as well as the benefits of collaborative team-work. Therefore, the airport managers have to decide, which solution is the most efficient one for the whole team. During the game-play a common data base (A-CDM), limited resources and feedback were only three examples of mechanics, which should be considered by the players. Furthermore the time for playing one round was varied. Coming to the most important learning aspect, especially the role change was discussed by the airport managers. The players enjoyed it for a better understanding of the other working positions.

4   Conclusions and Future Directions

Having conducted the first learning session with D-CITE, we were able to observe improved collaborative airport performance in teams. Thereby the unique feature of D-CITE to integrate individual interest in collaborative decision making processes at airports foster the transfer to real situations. Especially through the role change an efficient communication and collaborative team-work can be trained. This is transferable to each area, in which different team members have to work together.

Currently, these learning effects are validated on a statistical basis. Moreover, the use of a second ground handler as well as an ATC is planned for a next training session.

While it was possible to learn effective interactions and personal behavior with D-CITE, two requirements of the learning analysis could not covered by the game itself. First, the handling of new systems is not trainable in D-CITE. Second, effects cannot be shown on real traffic examples.

However, these missing features of D-CITE can be covered by a joint learning environment with the DLR A-CDM simulation [19, 22]. This human in the loop simulation platform allows simulating airport management with real traffic scenarios and the integration of new tools. Thereby D-CITE and DLR A-CDM simulation can provide a most advanced training environment.

References

1. EUROCONTROL: European Operational Concept Validation Methodology (E-OCVM) (Version 3.0) (2010). https://www.eurocontrol.int/sites/default/files/publication/files/e-ocvm3-vol-1-022010.pdf. Accessed 11 June 2016
2. Barreteau, O.: The joint use of role-playing games and models regarding negotiation processes: characterization of associations. J. Artif. Soc. Soc. Simul. **6**(2), 1–20 (2003)
3. Abt, C.: Serious Games: The Art and Science of Games that Simulate Life. Viking Press, New York (1970)
4. Kriz, W.C.: Creating effective learning environments and learning organizations through gaming simulation design. Simul. Gaming **34**(4), 495–511 (2003)
5. Papenfuss, A., Carstengerdes, N., Günther, Y.: Konzept zur Kooperation in Flughafen-Leitständen. 57. FAS DGLR L6.4 Anthropotechnik, 25.–26.11.2015, Rostock (2015)
6. Mensen, H.: Handbuch der Luftfahrt [handbook of aviation], 2nd edn. Springer, Heidelberg (2013)
7. EUROCONTROL: Airport CDM Operational Concept Document (2006). http://www.euro-cdm.org/library/cdm_ocd.pdf. Accessed 11 June 2016
8. Günther, Y., Inard, A., Werther, B., Bonnier, M., Spies, G., Marsden, A., Temme, M., Böhme, D., Lane, R., Niederstrasser, H.: Total Airport Management (2006). http://www.bs.dlr.de/tam/Dokuments/TAM-OCD-public.pdf. Accessed 11 June 2016
9. Ball, M.O., Hoffman, R.L., Knorr, D., Wetherly, J., Wambsganss, M.: Assessing the benefits of collaborative decision making in air traffic management, Paper at 3rd USA/Europe Air Traffic Management R&D Seminar, Napoli, Italy (2000)
10. Jipp, M., Depenbrock, Suikat, R., Schaper, M., Papenfuß, A., Kaltenhäuser, S., Weber, B.: Validation of multi-objective optimization for total airport management. In: Proceedings of the 8th Asian Control Conference (ASCC), Kaohsiung (Taiwan) (2011)
11. Freese, M., Drees, S., Meinecke, M.: Between game and reality: using serious games to analyze complex interaction processes in air traffic management. In: Kaneda, T., Kanegae, H., Toyoda, Y., Rizzi, P. (eds.) Simulation and Gaming in the Network Society. Translational Systems Sciences, vol. 9, pp. 275–289. Springer, Heidelberg (2015)
12. Netherlands Aerospace Centre (NLR): Collaborative Learning & Serious Game Development (2014). http://reports.nlr.nl:8080/xmlui/bitstream/handle/10921/935/TP-2013-580.pdf?sequence=1. Accessed 15 June 2016
13. Maij, A., Nieuwenhuisen, D., Aalmoes, R., Faber, E.: Serious games to advance change in ATM, Paper at Air Transport and Operations Symposium 2015, Delft, The Netherlands, July 2015
14. Suttie, N., Louchart, S., Lim, T., Macvean, A., Westera, W., Brown, D., Djaouti, D.: Introducing the serious games mechanics: a theoretical framework to analyse relationships between game and pedagogical aspects of serious games. Poster presented at the "VS-Games 2012", Genoa, Italy (2012)

15. Allmendinger, K.: Bedarfsanalysen. In: Haake, J., Schwabe, G., Wessner, M. (eds.) CSCL-Kompendium 2.0: Lehr-und Handbuch zum computerunterstützten kooperativen Lernen, pp. 301–302. Walter de Gruyter (2012)
16. Filbert, W.: Die PRO-aktive Rollenanalyse. Coaching-Tools, pp 156–162 (2008)
17. Niegemann, H.M.: Selbstkontrolliertes Lernen und didaktisches Design. In: Lernen mit Medien: Ergebnisse und Perspektiven zu medial vermittelten Lehr-und Lernprozessen, pp 121–140. Weinheim (1998)
18. Schulze Kissing, D., Eißfeldt, H.: ConCent: Eine Simulationsplattform zur Untersuchung kollobarativer Entscheidungsprozesse in Leitzentralen. In: DGLR-Bericht 2015-01, 2015 (01), Seiten 157-170. 57.FAS DGLR L6.4 Anthropotechnik, 25.–26. November 2015, Rostock (2015). ISBN 978-3-932182-83-9, ISSN 0178-6362
19. Piekert, F., Schier, S., Marsden, A., Carstengerdes, N., Suikat, R.: A high-fidelity artificial airport environment for SESAR APOC validation experiments. In: Air Transport Research Society World Conference 2015, Singapore, July 2015
20. Schaar, D., Lance S.: Analysis of airport stakeholders. In: Integrated Communications Navigation and Surveillance Conference (ICNS), 2010. IEEE (2010)
21. Freese, M.: Game-based learning – an approach for improving collaborative airport management. In: 10th European Conference on Games Based Learning, Scotland, October 2016
22. Schier, S., Pett, T., Mohr, O., Yeo, S. J.: Design and evaluation of user interfaces for an airport management simulation. In: AIAA Modelling and Simulation Conference 2016, 13–17 June 2016, Washington D.C., USA (2016)

Games and Learning

Using Comparative Behavior Analysis to Improve the Impact of Serious Games on Students' Learning Experience

Dominique Jaccard, Jarle Hulaas[(⊠)], and Ariane Dumont

School of Business and Engineering, University of Applied Sciences of Western Switzerland, Avenue des Sports 20, 1401 Yverdon-les-bains, Switzerland
{dominique.jaccard,jarle.hulaas,
ariane.dumont}@heig-vd.ch

Abstract. In the last decade, the use of serious games as a teaching and learning tool has steadily increased in many disciplines. Nevertheless, serious games are still facing crucial challenges, such as their integration in the global learning process. On the other hand, with the increased adoption of online applications and courses, it is becoming possible to collect and centralize large amounts of trace data generated by players. Such data may be used to produce statistics on students' behaviors inside pedagogical serious games, both as individuals and aggregated as groups (e.g., classrooms). In this paper we propose a classification of potential uses of statistics in serious games and give new insights into how statistical analysis of groups' behavior may impact positively on the learning process. We also present experimental results obtained during a large-scale game deployment using the Wegas platform, our open source platform for game authoring and execution.

Keywords: Serious games · Statistics · Comparative behavior analysis · Classroom orchestration · Teacher empowerment · Learning analytics · Competency management · Deep learning

1 Introduction

The professional world is becoming more and more volatile, uncertain, complex and ambiguous. According to the World Economic Forum [25], students therefore need more than traditional academic learning: they must also develop new skills through education technology such as serious games (SGs). The use of SGs for pedagogical purposes has indeed become more widespread, from the health sector to engineering or management education, with some positive impacts reported (see e.g., [4]). Interactive teaching strategies have also proven to increase student attendance and engagement [7] and to foster higher performance [11]. But there are still many challenges to take up for effective acceptance of SGs in the educational process [12], such as how to promote deep learning [9] and trigger the higher levels of Bloom's taxonomy of learning [3] while integrating SGs in different teaching strategies.

Since SGs are used more and more in networked environments, it is becoming possible to centralize trace data that reflect students' behavior while they are playing.

© Springer International Publishing AG 2016
R. Bottino et al. (Eds.): GALA 2016, LNCS 10056, pp. 199–210, 2016.
DOI: 10.1007/978-3-319-50182-6_18

This in turn enables the aggregation of datasets with different scopes. Analysis of such statistics may lead to the definition of strategies for improving the learning process. The activity of collecting, analyzing and reporting data about learners and their contexts is called *learning analytics* [10]. In this paper, we are mainly interested in tracking and comparing players' behaviors, in particular their decision making, as opposed to more synthetic scores such as examination grades.

Whereas learning analytics has been previously studied as a means to follow, assess and predict student performance [1, 2, 18], in this paper we argue that behavioral statistics will help address other important challenges that are preventing the larger adoption of SGs. More precisely, we propose to compare behaviors inside games by categories of players, such as by different years, backgrounds (e.g., management or engineering), levels (e.g., undergraduate or postgraduate studies), environments (e.g., academic or professional) and teachers. The comparative analysis of such statistics has the potential of impacting the learning process in a positive way while supporting different pedagogical approaches. The same principle may also be leveraged to obtain better real-life decisions in companies or organizations.

In the following section, we propose a classification of the potential uses of statistical behavior analysis, with a special focus on SGs with pedagogical objectives. Following this, we present a study that took place in the frame of a project management game, which we use to validate the idea of comparing behavioral statistics in SGs. Then we discuss the significance of these results as well as their limitations. The paper concludes with some perspectives on possible extensions and future research directions.

2   A Classification of Statistics in Serious Games

Many SGs already make their statistics available to players and teachers. A promising but lesser studied field of learning analytics is to determine which aggregation levels are relevant and to which stakeholders this information will make sense. The purpose of this section is to provide an overview of these questions.

2.1   Stakeholders of Serious Games in Education

Many stakeholders are involved in the use of SG for educational purposes, including not only students and teachers, but also educational program chairs, SG designers, pedagogues, educational quality managers and instructional designers. All of these stakeholders have specific interests and questions about the use and results achieved with SGs. Decision makers outside of the educational setting, like human resource managers, may also be interested in using SGs as a support for their decisions.

2.2   Levels of Data Aggregation

Trace data may be aggregated with different scopes to produce meaningful statistics. The following scopes seem to be the most relevant to students' learning experience:

1. Single game play: e.g., individual statistics about each student, such as the percentage of correct answers or decisions he or she made throughout the game.
2. Classroom session: e.g., global statistics on the distribution of choices made inside a game played in parallel by several participants, such as in a classroom.
3. History of sessions for a specific course: e.g., statistics on the same course throughout a number of years.
4. Sessions of different categories of players: e.g., statistics comparing classrooms with different profiles that have played the same SG.

2.3   The Stakeholder/Scopes View

The use of learning analytics in SGs has previously been studied along 3 axes: what, when and where to evaluate [18]. In this paper we focus more on the potential applications of data aggregations and therefore are more interested in the question of what aggregations are useful, as well as for whom and why data are collected and analyzed.

The following table suggests which data aggregations may be relevant to the different classes of stakeholders. It embodies the intuitive idea that increased scopes of data aggregation will be of interest to a larger number of stakeholders because the additional information will contribute to answering more questions. Additionally, in order to introduce some structure in the list, we distributed stakeholders into three levels (micro, meso and macro) according to the size of their primary population of interest, but the boundaries between these levels are not strict (Table 1).

Table 1. The stakeholder/scopes view

	Micro level		Meso level		Macro level	
	Learner	Teacher	Educ. program manager	Game designer	Researcher	Other decision maker
1. Single game play	x	x				
2. Classroom session	x	x	x	x	x	x
3. History of sessions (same course)	x	x	x	x	x	x
4. Different categories of players	x	x	x	x	x	x

Micro Level: Learner and Teacher. At the micro level, both teachers and learners may benefit from all types of statistics.

Learner. The learner (possibly a player team, depending on the SG) is interested in how she has performed in a given game, where she has competence gaps and how she performed in comparison to other players or teams. A dashboard with relevant statistics is therefore useful to learners because it allows them to judge their own learning experience [16], although a teacher might be helpful in interpreting the results correctly. Following our gradation of aggregations, here are additional examples:

1. Single game play: the percentage of correct answers is already available in many SGs along with a trace of the game play, which is needed for identifying and understanding one's own errors (self-assessment) [2, 20].
2. Classroom session: these data enable a detailed comparison with other players in the same class. Such statistics are often available in massive online games.
3. History of past sessions (same course): a player's history enables comparison to previous players of equivalent expertise.
4. Comparison to sessions with different categories of players: the learner can examine what specialists would have done in the same situation and—in a more differentiated way than a simple score—how far she is from an expert status in the given subject field. Active learning may thus be promoted by providing students with a comparison between their own behavior and an expert behavior.

Teacher. The teacher's concerns are twofold: how to monitor and assess students and how to improve her teaching strategies in the longer run. Research shows that well-implemented targeted instructions can significantly improve student learning outcomes [13]: trace data and resulting statistics from SGs may be very helpful in this regard.

1. Single game play statistics are helpful for computer-assisted learner assessment and identification and for coaching of students at risk (see e.g. [2]). To support this, high-level game variables must be accessible to the teacher in order to enable openness, trust and customization; in other words, the SG should not be a black box [21]. More generally, the teaching-learning cycle (e.g., as found in [5]) begins with an identification of each student's learning needs, informed by data. Such data help teachers with pacing of the provision of appropriate resources.
2. Classroom session traces will enable the teacher to monitor global progress during play and to provide additional instructions in time if the dashboard reveals problems at specific places in the SG. They may reveal whether a complementary lecture is required. After the game, statistics can also serve as a tool for adapting the assessment to the average of the class [21].
3. With detailed statistics of past sessions of the same course, the teacher can gradually develop performance standards, improve her teaching in a targeted way and measure the impact of these adjustments. Such statistics will also help in developing predictive success/failure patterns [1].
4. By comparing sessions played by different categories of learners, the teacher can better tailor her course to a given target audience. During or right after the playing, the classroom's performance can be compared to traces previously generated by specialists; this will empower the teacher with concrete examples that she can give to the students to better illustrate which behavior was actually expected.

Meso Level: Program Manager and Game Designer. As we move away from the micro level, we suggest that stakeholders' interests will essentially focus on the wider data scopes.

Program Manager. Designers and managers of educational programs want to identify subject fields to be included in a given course and preliminary competencies to be required from the participants. For postgraduate or professional training, their questions are: what are the learning outcomes and which competencies are needed to perform a specific activity, what is the specific training needed by a new employee, is the content different if the new employee has a scientific academic background or a managerial education, etc.

1. Single game play: weakly informative without other data to compare to.
2. Classroom session: if student backgrounds are not homogeneous, session statistics may pinpoint insufficient prerequisites in certain pathways.
3. History of past sessions (same curriculum): these data allow adjustment of course content and complexity to the evolution of player results.
4. Comparison by categories of learners: the definition of a training program may be based on statistical comparison of behaviors in a specific SG, with analysis of differences between a cohort of experts (the control group) and a typical learner following the training program. It might also be possible to check whether there are fewer differences with the expert control group at the end of the program than before.

Game Designer. Developers and designers of SGs are interested in improving the design or contents of existing games and in developing new games that are more captivating and effective in terms of learning.

1. Single game play: weakly informative without other data to compare to.
2. Classroom session: to identify significant playability/usability issues in new games.
3. History of past sessions (same game scenario): to validate and improve game ergonomy and interest, e.g., if no player ever went through a given branch of the scenario, that branch should probably be made more attractive or else suppressed. Performance standards inside the game may also be adjusted on the basis of statistics.
4. Comparison by categories of learners: this may constitute a benchmark enabling automatic recognition of a player's profile. When the game identifies a player with little expertise in a given subject field, it may propose additional exercises.

Macro Level: Researcher and Decision Maker

Researcher. Researchers in pedagogy may be interested in the real impact of SGs and have questions such as how effective a specific SG really is and which competencies are developed inside a given game. They are also concerned with how the impact of an educational program or of different pedagogical approaches can be measured.

1. Single game play: weakly informative without other data to compare to.
2. Classroom session: comparison of learning paces among students in the same class may help devise a range of effective teaching strategies to be taken up by teachers.
3. History of past sessions (same course or curriculum): data on game play over time may help in building up a clear and comprehensive knowledge of students' needs in

order to enhance pedagogical methods. On the other hand, emerging new technologies for tracking psychophysiological signals may reveal how efficient the learning process is inside an SG and how engaging a game really is [18]: the availability of historical data will contribute to establishing more reliable correlations between player behavior, learning outcomes and neurophysiological traces.

4. Comparison by categories of learners: this may help researchers understand and improve the effectiveness of pedagogical methods (including SGs) for various professional sectors, using the SG to assess the acquisition of knowledge. This may help them understand when instructional methodologies need to vary in order to accommodate differences in student learning outcomes.

Other Decision Makers. This is a category of decision makers who may use statistics of behaviors inside the virtual world in order to support decisions made in the real world.

1. Single game play: weakly informative without other data to compare to.
2. Classroom session: from an HR perspective, behavioral statistics can be used to help decide between candidates competing for the same position.
3. History of past sessions (same category of players):

- HR department: to assess and improve employee competency.
- Academic managers (faculty or institution-level): to follow global student performance through the years and increase accountability [2].

4. Comparison by categories of learners:

- HR department: to sort employees by level of expertise and to optimize deployment of human resources.
- Academic managers: to adjust curricula and ensure they fit the needs of the labor market.
- Policy makers: to compare performances of schools or institutions [6].

3 A Study Using the Wegas Platform

Wegas is our web-based serious game authoring and execution platform[1]. Based on several years of experience in education in diverse environments, Wegas has been designed with a strong focus on scenario definition capabilities, in order to allow educators to customize content to learning objectives and to the participants' specific subject fields. The platform supports both hybrid on-site classroom learning and remote e-learning.

Wegas serves as the basis for a broad range of games, essentially of educational nature, of which the most popular is the Project Management Game (described below), a simulation tool for budding project managers that is actively used in many

---

[1] Project home page: http://www.albasim.ch/
The platform is open source and can be downloaded from https://github.com/Heigvd/Wegas.

universities in Switzerland and France. Wegas includes a teacher dashboard offering a real-time overview of player positions in the game, which helps identify students in difficulty. The dashboard also enables the teacher to inspect or impact player sessions, such as by giving advice inside the game as if it were coming from one of the virtual characters.

The generation of trace data is integrated in the platform, which systematically logs all choices made by the player (i.e., answers to questions or decisions made inside a game) as well as all values taken by numeric variables defined inside the game (representing e.g. game phases or player performance indexes).

3.1   The Project Management Game

The Project Management Game (PMG) was designed as a complete educational concept for teaching project management in a team-based approach that fosters collaborative skills [17]. This concept combines a simulation game with ex-cathedra theory and real-world activities such as presentations to a project management office.

In PMG, players take the role of project managers and have to choose among proposed actions. An important aspect of the game is the absence of judgment: there is no explicit feedback after each action to tell if it was a good or a bad choice. Instead, some general performance indicators will be updated from time to time and messages will arrive from virtual stakeholders inside the game (clients, colleagues, company executives, etc.). Learners therefore have to evaluate by themselves the impact of their actions and to conceptualize on their own the knowledge that could be built on this experience [14]. Following the principles of experiential learning [15, 19], the game teaches them to learn and to experiment with their new knowledge inside the simulation.

3.2   The Study

Over the course of one year, trace data were collected from PMG as it was used by 5 different teachers in 10 different courses. A typical classroom comprised 5 teams of 4 students each. For the study, a new interface was developed that enables the selection of up to four "groups" (aggregations of training sessions) and the display of statistical comparisons between the corresponding cohorts.[2]

For example, for a decision about doing a market analysis at the very beginning of the PMG game, we observed similar behavior in three classes of students who had mainly an engineering background (bachelor in media engineering, certificate of advanced studies in energy management, diploma in project management). Less than 30% of them decided to perform a complete market analysis, and a majority chose to do only a partial market analysis in order to preserve their budget and timeline. When the same question was given to different classes of students enrolled in management

---

[2] As of this writing, some of the functionality is only available to a restricted set of users until most usability and privacy protection issues have been addressed.

curricula (bachelor in management), we observed a similarly consistent behavior, but this time with a majority of them deciding on a complete market analysis and no more than 30% choosing a partial analysis. We found an analogous correlation among students in business administration (MBA).

In Fig. 1, players with similar backgrounds are grouped in order to compare typical behaviors of students with an engineering profile (blue bars), a management profile (red bars) and an MBA (yellow bars). In this graphic, one can clearly observe that students enrolled in engineering curricula are less likely to perform market analysis than students in management studies. The graphic also indicates that students in an MBA program tend to behave like students of management, even if these MBA students have an engineering background.

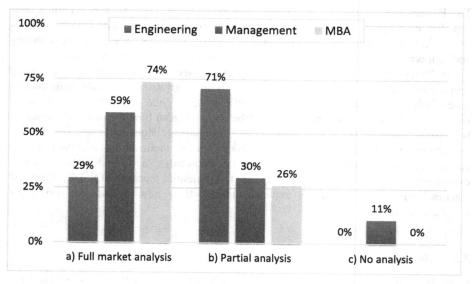

Fig. 1. Comparing decision making among three cohorts with different backgrounds. (Color figure online)

4 Discussion

We have proposed a classification of stakeholders of SGs and of the data scopes that we believe might be of interest to them. We developed an extension to the Wegas platform in order to experiment with these statistics, using a significant amount of data generated during one year by different categories of players in the PMG game. We observed that the comparative analysis of behaviors may bring excellent opportunities for pushing the adoption of SGs in the learning process, improving existing games and supporting decisions based on behaviors observed in SGs.

4.1   Improving Education Management

The comparison of different groups of learners may have a positive impact on decisions in the professional world or when designing training programs. By this means, it becomes possible to answer questions like "in this specific situation, what are the differences in behavior between an engineer and someone with a managerial background?" or "what should be included in an MBA program for engineers in order to give them a managerial behavior?"

4.2   Use in Professional Assessment

Comparative statistics also enable the detection of situations in which senior professionals have different behaviors than junior professionals or bachelor students. This may impact business decisions like "what kind of qualifications are needed for this kind of activity: expert, senior or junior?" Then, one can identify players that have a behavior similar to recognized experts but are less expensive to hire. One could more easily find new positions where valuable collaborators can be relocated inside a company by fitting their player statistics into specific categories. Thus the target audience of such analytics may be widened to HR specialists of competency management, whereas the traditional audience is composed of teachers and learners [6, 23].

4.3   Pedagogical Impact

With Wegas the teacher has the opportunity to present comparative statistics to the students and to highlight places in the SG where they behaved differently than actual expert-level players. Feedback based on previous cohorts constitutes a complete Learning Analytics Cycle, as recommended in [6]. Wegas makes this concept even more effective, as it enables the teacher (1) to prepare striking comparisons by selecting classrooms of different levels of expertise and (2) to provide illustrated feedback immediately after the playing session, which probably is the best moment to explain the reasoning behind an expert behavior. Emphasis may thus be placed on comparing reasoning instead of final scores, which warrants the pedagogical value of the feedback. Moreover, research shows that immediate feedback is beneficial to the learning process [8]. This way, the teacher can provide a significant added value in comparison to a situation in which statistics would simply be made available to the learner as a self-service.

4.4   Limitations and Perspectives

This article describes work in progress. Our goal was to identify and to classify useful statistics for various kinds of stakeholders, but we do not claim to be exhaustive at this stage. Whereas comparative statistics have been employed to enhance lectures using the Wegas platform and to make game scenarios more relevant, it's still necessary to quantify more generally the impact of such statistics on the learning experience.

Recent research already brings evidence that the provision of immediate feedback promotes student engagement in the learning process [8].

We have currently only tested our approach on the comparison of answers to closed questions. It is important to limit the number of possible answers, because this enables more reliable and objective comparisons. In the comparative approach, we are indeed mainly concerned with how close a player's performance is to that of various control groups. In order to extend this work, we may study the chronology and speed of action sequences and try to compare them. In addition, we have not tried to take into account communication patterns between players (chats, forums, etc.). This topic, which may reveal players' level of interest or a possible need for help, is already studied in [24].

A few requirements have to be fulfilled to make statistical comparisons reliable:

- A sufficient number of sessions must be played and logged beforehand.
- Game sessions should be organized with consistent player profiles in order to enable their classification into distinct categories. On the other hand, such categories do not necessarily have to be known a priori: one interesting research direction would be to apply data mining techniques on the statistics in order to elicit novel clusterings and comparison criteria after the game is played.
- Game scenarios and content must remain sufficiently stable across versions: comparisons are currently only allowed on choices that have the same internal identifier (chosen by the scenarist). This constraint will have to be relaxed, since new game versions will necessarily be published in order to correct errors, but also to observe new aspects of players' behaviors or to encompass teachers' customization requests.

Regarding privacy protection, complete playing traces are indeed collected and processed internally, but nominative data are only accessible to the player who produced them and to the relevant teacher. No personal information is made visible by the new statistics modules, except that teachers might be identified indirectly by cross-checking. Nevertheless, data protection issues in SGs need to be further investigated [22], especially as broader data aggregations will affect a larger number of persons and might be governed by legislations of multiple institutions and countries.

Finally, usability is an important requirement: the SG platform has to make statistics easily accessible to ensure that they will actually be employed by stakeholders such as teachers and students.

5 Conclusion

In this paper we proposed a vision of learning analytics that focuses on data aggregation levels and on their usefulness to main stakeholders. A systematic classification revealed a number of useful statistical comparisons that we have not found elsewhere in the literature. We extended our Wegas platform with a new aggregation and comparison module, which was fed with a significant amount of trace data collected during one year from different categories of players of our project management game. This experience confirmed that player profiles are relatively homogeneous inside each pathway and that complementary schooling allows players to improve their behavior in comparison to their initial weaknesses. Comparative statistics enable teachers to provide striking feedback based on expert cohorts in order to reinforce the impact of serious games on students. Outside the educational setting, businesses and organizations can compare cohorts of employees in order to appoint them to optimal roles.

Acknowledgments. The authors would like to express their gratitude to all developers of the Wegas platform as well as to the teachers who gave their feedback on the tool.

References

1. Arnab, S., et al.: Towards performance prediction using in-game measures. In: Proceedings of the Annual Meeting of the American Educational Research Association, Chicago, USA (2015)
2. Arnold, K.E.: Signals: applying academic analytics. EDUCAUSE Q. **33**, 1 (2010)
3. Bloom, B.S., et al.: Taxonomy of Educational Objectives: The Classification of Educational Goals. Handbook I: Cognitive Domain. David McKay Company, New York (1956)
4. Boyle, E.A., Connolly, T.M., Hainey, T.: The role of psychology in understanding the impact of computer game. Entertain. Comput. **2**, 69–74 (2011)
5. Bybee, R.W.: Achieving Scientific Literacy: From Purposes to Practice. Heinemann, Portsmouth (1997)
6. Clow, D.: The learning analytics cycle: closing the loop effectively. In: Proceedings of the 2nd International Conference on Learning Analytics and Knowledge - LAK 2012 (2012)
7. Deslauriers, L., Schelew, E., Wieman, C.: Improved learning in a large-enrollment physics class. Science **332**(6031), 862–864 (2011)
8. Dumont, A., Berthiaume, D.: La pédagogie inversée, De Boeck, Louvain-la-Neuve, Belgium (2016)
9. Entwistle, N.: Understanding classroom learning. Hodder and Stoughton, London (1987)
10. Ferguson, R.: Learning analytics: drivers, developments and challenges. Int. J. Technol. Enhanced Learn. **4**(5/6), 304 (2012)
11. Freeman, S., et al.: Active learning increases student performance in science, engineering, and mathematics. Proc. Natl. Acad. Sci. **111**, 8410–8415 (2014)
12. GALA R&D Roadmap on Serious Games no. 3, Deliverable no. 1.7 (4th year) of the Game and Learning Alliance (GaLA) (2014). http://www.galanoe.eu/index.php/documents
13. Goddard, Y., Goddard, M.: A theoretical and empirical investigation of teacher collaboration for school improvement and student achievement in public elementary schools. Teach. Coll. Rec. **109**(4), 877–896 (2007)
14. Jaccard, D., Riboni S.: Simprojet: an innovative simulation platform for experiential learning in project management. In: Proceedings of the 2nd International Conference on Computer Supported Education, Valencia, Spain, pp. 471–477 (2010)
15. Kolb, D.A.: Experiential learning: experience as the source of learning and development. J. Organ. Behav. **8**(4), 359–360 (1984). Prentice Hall, NJ
16. Marsh, C.J.: Key concepts for understanding curriculum. Falmer Press, London (1997)
17. Michaelsen, L., Sweet, M., Parmelee, D.: Team-based learning: small group learning's next big step. New Dir. Teach. Learn. **116** (2009). Jossey-Bass, San Francisco
18. Moreno-Ger, P., et al.: Learning Analytics for SGs, Deliverable no. 2.4 (4th year) of the Game and Learning Alliance (GaLA) (2014). http://www.galanoe.eu/index.php/documents
19. Rogers, C.R.: Freedom to Learn: A View of What Education Might Become, pp. 111–114. C.E. Merrill Pub. Co., Columbus (1969)

20. Sanchez, E., Ney, M., Labat, J.-M.: Jeux sérieux et pédagogie universitaire: de la conception à l'évaluation des apprentissages. Revue Internationale des Technologies en Pédagogie universitaire, Pédagogie Universitaire Numérique **8**(1–2), 48–57 (2011)
21. Serrano-Laguna, A., Torrente, J., Moreno-Ger, P., Fernández-Manjón, B.: Tracing a Little for Big Improvements: Application of Learning Analytics and Videogames for Student Assessment. In: 4th International Conference on Games and Virtual Worlds for Serious Applications (2012)
22. Slade, S., Prinsloo, P.: Learning analytics: ethical issues and dilemmas. Am. Behav. Sci. **57**(10), 1510–1529 (2013)
23. Verbert, K., et al.: Learning analytics dashboard applications. Am. Behav. Sci. **57**(10), 1500–1509 (2013)
24. Verbert, K., et al.: Learning dashboards: an overview and future research opportunities. J. Pers. Ubiquit. Comput. **18**(6), 1499–1514 (2014). Springer
25. World Economic Forum: New Vision for Education: Fostering Social and Emotional Learning through Technology (2016)

Immersion's Impact on Performance in a Spatial Reasoning Task

Laura Freina[⊠], Rosa Bottino, Mauro Tavella,
and Francesca Dagnino

National Research Council – Institute for Educational Technologies,
via de Marini, 6, 16149 Genoa, Italy
{Freina,Bottino,Tavella,Dagnino}@itd.cnr.it

Abstract. The present paper presents the results of a first experiment aimed at assessing if different levels of immersion can affect performance in a Spatial Perspective Taking (SPT) task. Since SPT is an embodied skill, the hypothesis was that the more immersive a tool is, the better the performance should be. Ninety-eight students from a local primary school have played with three different versions of a game: immersive using a Head Mounted Display, semi immersive played on a computer screen and non-immersive in which no movement was possible for the player. Results do not support the initial hypothesis: no significant impact from the immersion level has been found on performance.

1 Introduction

According to the European Union, there is evidence of skills shortages in STEM (Science, Technology, Engineering, and Mathematics) fields, while around 7 million new jobs are forecast until 2025 in this sector. Therefore, there is a strong need to prepare young people for a future that will require good scientific knowledge and a good understanding of technology [1]. A positive start, at an early stage is crucial for the subsequent formation of positive attitudes towards science [2]. Furthermore, the development of some basic abilities, among which spatial reasoning, has been proved to have a positive correlation with success in mathematics and science [3].

Newcombe [4] reports several different longitudinal studies that started back in the fifties by following the development of a large number of American children from nursery school all the way to adulthood. These studies have shown a close correlation between spatial reasoning skills and school results in STEM subjects; furthermore, having good spatial skills increases the probability to undertake STEM related jobs.

Supporting the development and consolidation of spatial reasoning in primary school children can thus have a positive and long lasting impact on their lives. Spatial reasoning is a complex skill, made of many components, among which Spatial Perspective Taking (SPT). SPT is the ability of imagining how the world looks like from another person's point of view, which is important for orientation in space. As Uttal et al. have shown [5], spatial reasoning can get better with a specific training, with durable and transferable results.

© Springer International Publishing AG 2016
R. Bottino et al. (Eds.): GALA 2016, LNCS 10056, pp. 211–220, 2016.
DOI: 10.1007/978-3-319-50182-6_19

According to Surtees et al. [6], SPT is an embodied process: when people are asked to state what another person sees, they actually imagine moving to the new position in space and then they reconstruct the view from there, activating, while doing so, those parts of the brain that are involved with movements in space. Due to this characteristic, training in an immersive virtual world may have a positive impact on performance. Virtual worlds can offer different levels of "immersion", by surrounding the users to make them feel as if they were "really there". An experiment has been set up to investigate if a higher immersion actually makes the SPT task easier.

"In Your Eyes" is a game taking place in a virtual living room where a Non-Player Character (NPC), after putting some objects on a table, moves to one of the four sides of that table. Four pictures on the wall show the scene from the four sides and the player has to pick the picture that shows the table from the NPC's point of view. The game is available in three different versions: completely immersive using a Head Mounted Display (HMD), semi-immersive where the virtual world is seen through a computer screen and non-immersive with a fixed view on the virtual room.

The SPT skill, according to Newcombe [4], completes its development in the first years of primary school; therefore, an experiment has been set up with a group of children between the age of 8 and 10. In our hypothesis, better performance should be measured in the complete immersive version of the game since having the possibility to "dive" into the virtual world allows the players to:

- Understand the task more easily by exploring the scene and testing the hypothesis;
- Better build a mental model of the scene and the involved objects by freely moving around the table and examining the objects from all the possible perspectives;
- Manage by themselves the amount of help needed: it is always possible, at any time of the game, to move to the other side of the table and see what the scene looks like;
- Increase their motivation and involvement in the game by exploring freely the virtual world.

However, using a HMD can be tiring and it can cause sickness to some players; a greater effort in managing an interface the players are not used to may be needed. Furthermore, the presence of a virtual environment in which to move and explore, can draw the attention away from the main task and therefore influence performance negatively.

A first analysis of the collected data shows that with the non-immersive version of the game the worse results are obtained, while with the other two versions small differences are found in favour of the completely immersive one. Apparently, better results are obtained when the players have the possibility to move around the table and check their answer, while full immersion seems not have a significant impact.

2 Spatial Perspective Taking and Virtual Worlds

Newcombe and Frick [7] define SPT as the ability to correctly identify the position and rotation of a person in space and understand that their perspective can be different from ours. It is the ability to imagine ourselves in the place of another person and be able to predict what will be seen after the corresponding movement in space. It involves occupying the place of the other person and understanding the relative position of objects.

SPT and its development in children has been investigated by Piaget [8], according to whom its complete development does not take place before the child is ten. Later studies [9] seem to demonstrate that the ability actually develops some years earlier. According to Surtees et al. [6], there are two different levels of SPT skills: the first level, which usually develops in children when they are about five, allows understanding if a given object can be seen from a different point of view. The second level, which usually develops some years later, between six and eight, makes it possible to imagine how a given scene would look like from a different perspective. Mayer et al. [10] have found a big difference in mathematical reasoning skills between second and third graders: up to grade two they are closely related to language skills, starting from grade three spatial reasoning can predict both mathematical reasoning and numerical operations skills. Due to these studies, the best moment for a specific intervention aimed at potentiating spatial reasoning appear to be in the last years of primary school.

Virtual reality is defined as an artificial environment that is experienced by the player through sensory stimuli and with which it is possible to interact in a natural manner using electronic tools. In virtual reality, the concepts of "spatial immersion" and "presence" are often used and sometimes there is confusion between the two. While "spatial immersion" is defined as an objective property that refers to the technical capability of the system to deliver a surrounding and convincing environment, "presence" is the human response to such an environment. Presence is therefore the extent to which participants believe they are somewhere different from their actual physical location [11].

Due to the embodied component of the SPT skill, an immersive virtual environment may be the best environment to practice it. As Dalgarno and Lee state "3-D Virtual Learning Environments can be used to facilitate learning tasks that lead to the development of enhanced spatial knowledge representation of the explored domain. (p. 18)" [12]. Furthermore, learning in a virtual world that is recognized as authentic by the learner makes learning transfer to the real world easier [13]. In the virtual world, the players can actually make the physical movements that are characteristic to the abilities that they are practising, supporting a kinaesthetic approach to learning.

3   Description of the "In Your Eyes" Game

The "In Your Eyes" game [14] takes place in a virtual living room, with a table in the middle and some objects on it. Four screens on the wall show the pictures of the table taken from the four sides, the coloured frames of the screens are used to identify them easily. In the room, a virtual friend (the NPC) welcomes the players and helps them along the whole game. Before starting the game, the players are free to move in the room so that they can see the table and the objects from every possible perspective.

The goal of the game is to train the players to recognize the screen that shows the table from the NPC's perspective. Each correct answer gives the player a maximum of 9 points, which are decreased by 3 at each error and by 1 at each exploration out of the play area. At each mistake, the wrong answer is blackened (the screen is switched off), and a brief hint is given.

At any moment, the players are free to move, they can go behind the NPC to check what the table looks like from there. This allows them to decide autonomously how much help they need. In this manner, as scaffolding theories state [15], the players are provided with all the support they may need to solve a problem that is a little beyond their capabilities without any help. As their skills improve, the quantity of help they will ask will decrease up to the moment when they will be able to play by themselves.

A fixed sequence of twelve different scenes has been defined, with one, two or three objects on the table. The number of scenes has been limited by the need to keep the play sessions rather short: Nicols [11] suggests that keeping the length of each play session around 10 min can limit sickness issues.

The assignment of the correct answer to a coloured screen on the wall is random so that it changes each time the scene is played to minimise the risk that the children would just remember the sequence of the correct answers from one session to the next (Fig. 1).

Fig. 1. The virtual room of the "In Your Eyes" game.

Special attention has been paid to the instructions given to the player. It is possible to solve the given task in two different ways: imagining either to move to the NPC's position and reconstructing the scene from there, or to turn the table round until the side where the NPC sits is in front of us. The two different approaches involve two different abilities: SPT in the first case and Object Rotation ability in the second. The two skills are different and performance can vary a lot in the same subjects. Inagaki et al. [16] have demonstrated that just by giving different instructions, with the same experimental setting, it is possible to stimulate the participants to use one skill or the other.

We wanted the children to use the SPT skill, therefore, the NPC asks the player to "imagine you are by my side and tell me what the table looks like from here". Furthermore, Tversky found that "… The mere presence of another in the scene with the potential for action elicits taking that person's perspective. (p. 125)" [17]. The NPC's body sitting at the tableside and looking at the scene promotes the use the SPT skill.

The game, which has been developed using Unity 3D[1] with Oculus Rift[2] in its SDK2 version, is available in three different versions, addressing different immersion levels:

- Immersive (Im-version): using a HMD, the player feels as if he actually is inside the living room where he can freely move around as he wishes.
- Semi-immersive (SI-version): the player can still move freely, he sees the virtual living room on a normal computer screen, he can explore but the feeling of actually "being there" should be reduced.
- Non-immersive (NI-version): there is a fixed view on the living room showing the table, the NPC and the pictures on the wall. No exploration is possible.

3.1   The Experiment

In order to assess if, and to what extent, immersion actually supports better performance in the SPT task, an experiment has been set up with six classes from a local primary school in Genova (Italy). The main research question was to assess if there is a correlation between the immersion level of the game and performance in the SPT task.

Six elementary classes have been chosen: four third grade classes (8–9 year olds) and two fourth grade classes (9–10 year olds). A meeting has been organized with the families to present the project and show them the three game versions. Informed consent was then signed and the authorized children were enrolled in the experiment.

The participants were 101, 60 boys and 41 girls aged from 8 years and 2 months to 10 years and 7 months, with an average age of 9 years and 1 month at the beginning of the experiment. Three participants dropped out before the end of the experiment leaving 98 participants.

Participants' ability in the SPT task has been measured at the beginning of the project using a paper based pre-test created following literature in the field [18]. Balanced groups with respect to the specific skill, sex and age have been made in order to counterbalance results and avoid order effects. A repeated measures design was chosen for the experiment, so that each child used all the three versions of the game with the same fixed sequence of scenes.

Each participant played three times, one for each game version available. The three sessions have been separated by a period of at least two weeks to minimize the memorization of the sequence of scenes.

One of the objectives of the experiment was to assess if a higher level of immersion would generate a higher feeling of presence. For this, a short questionnaire with the same three questions used by Slater [19] measuring a self-reported subjective feeling of

---

[1] https://unity3d.com/.

[2] https://www.oculus.com/en-us/.

presence in the virtual world has been defined. The questions have been translated into Italian and are measured on a seven-point Likert rating scale.

- Q1: Did the game make you feel as if you were physically inside the living room? (not at all – very much)
- Q2: Were there times during the game when the living room became real and you nearly forgot about the real world? (never – nearly always)
- Q3: The living room seemed more like (a place I saw – a place I visited)

Q3 was dropped after the first play session since many participants misinterpreted it thinking whether the virtual living room reminded them of a real room they had visited.

Each participant played with the game individually, always in presence of a researcher, leaving the class for the play session. At the end of the session, the presence questionnaire was filled in and the child returned to class. After the last session, each participant was asked, "Which version of the game did you like best? Which one do you think works better?"

4   Results and Discussion

Eleven participants (11.22% of the sample) stopped playing with the Im-version before the end of the session, because of sickness issues. Thus, 87 participants have been considered for the data analysis.

As far as the personal enjoyment of the game is concerned, at the end of the last play session 67.24% of the participants have answered that they preferred the Im-version, another 28.74% had no preference. Only 2.87% preferred the SI-version while 1.15% (one person only) preferred the NI-version. To be noted that, even if not considered in these percentages, some participants who stopped playing with the Im-version because they were sick, still preferred it to the other ones. Apparently, immersion can be good for motivating students, even though all participants were at their first or second trial of an immersive device and they were enthusiastic about the novelty as such.

4.1   Immersion Level and Performance

Game scores from the three play sessions have been considered as a measure of the participants' performance and they have been analyzed using the repeated measures ANOVA[3]. No significant influence has been found on performance from the immersion level alone [$F(2.85) = 2.233$, p = n.s.].

There is a slight difference in the average score of the NI-version (78.03), which is a little lower than the other two versions (Im-version: 80.72; SI-version: 80.57). This can easily be explained with the fact that both the SI-version and the Im-version allow players to move near the NPC and see the table from his point of view, while this is not possible in the NI-version.

---

[3] Data have been analysed using the IBM SPSS software.

Scores have then been analysed with a repeated measures MANOVA with the group as between subject factor. The group variable reflects the sequence in which the game versions have been used by participants. In this case, a significant immersion effect has been found [F(2.80) = 3.375, P = 0.039] as well as the interaction between immersion and sequence [F(2.80) = 2.231; p. = 0.018]. No effect is related to the order by itself.

The Post-hoc analysis showed that the significant effect is due to the results of the NIS group [F = 6.812(2.80); p = 0.002]; there is a significant difference between the NI-version score (M = 72, SD = 5.75) and the other two scores: SI-version (M = 83.72, SD = 5.03) and Im-version (M = 84.54, SD = 4.69) (Fig. 2).

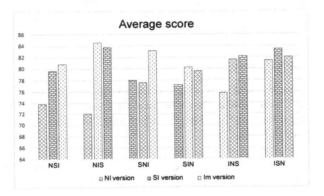

Fig. 2. Group average score for the three versions. The name of the groups shows the order in which the versions have been used: the three letters N, S and I are the initials of the three versions.

Group NIS used the NI-version in session one, followed by the Im-version in session two and the SI-version in session three. As for all the other cases, scores in session one are slightly lower than the following sessions, probably because the players still have to fully understand the task. In particular, when the NI-version is used in the first session, scores are even lower since the players cannot move, and this makes it more difficult to understand the task, thus confirming the initial hypothesis that the fully immersive version of the game better facilitates task understanding than the others.

4.2 Subjective Feeling of Presence

After each play session, the players answered the two questions about their subjective feeling of presence in the virtual room. Figure 3 shows the histograms of the answers to the two questions. As it can be seen, Im-version obtained an outstanding number of 7-answers to both questions. In Q1, the difference is greater, showing that immersion has an important impact of the feeling of being physically present in the virtual world.

Interestingly in Q2, especially for the SI-version and the NI-version, there is a high number of 1-answers. This is because these versions are experienced on the computer screen, and the surrounding world can be seen all the time during game play. While Q1 measures the physical involvement in the game, Q2 measures how much the players forgot about the real world, which is more difficult when it can be seen all the time.

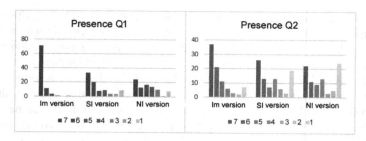

Fig. 3. Presence questions: Q1: Did the game make you feel as if you were physically inside the living room? (not at all – very much); Q2: Were there times during the game when the living room became real and you nearly forgot about the real world? (never – nearly always).

4.3   The Egocentric Error

In each play session, the first two scenes asked the players to select the screen that showed the objects on the table as they saw them (in these cases, the NPC sits near the players and they have the same view on the table). In all the other scenes, the NPC sits at a different side of the table.

An egocentric error happens when the players select their own view instead of the NPC's, and usually a very high egocentric error rate is expected, especially with respect to the first answers. According to Epley [20], the egocentric error is very frequent also in adults: they have simply learnt to correct the error better and in a shorter time. Epley states that adults tend to use themselves as standard when evaluating others, and they share with children an automatic egocentric default in perspective taking. Adults, with time, practice and experience have become better at correcting when necessary.

Our data confirms this expectation: The graph in Fig. 4, for each scene reports the first answers, showing the percentage of the correct answers, the egocentric errors and the other mistakes. Overall, in average, only 49.74% of scenes had no error, while 35.33% of first answers were egocentric errors and only 14.93% were other errors.

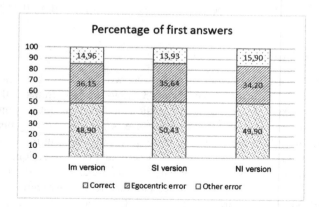

Fig. 4. The percentage of first answers that are correct, egocentric errors and other types of errors.

More surprising is data coming from the first two scenes: 19.44% of children in scene one and 18.06% in scene two had difficulty in recognizing the picture representing the scene in front of them. This will be further investigated.

5 Conclusions

An experiment has been organized with the aim of assessing if a higher immersion in a virtual world has a positive impact on a SPT task, which refers to the ability to imagine how the world would look like when seen from another person's point of view. The initial hypothesis was that performing a SPT task in a virtual world that is felt as if it was real would be easier than in other less immersive conditions. If that was the case, participants would make fewer errors and gain better scores when playing in an immersive virtual environment world rather than with other less immersive conditions.

In the experiment, three different versions of a game, with three different levels of immersion are tested with a group of elementary children. A repeated measures design was chosen for the experiment, balanced groups have been defined based on a paper based pre-test in order to counterbalance order effects.

Results do not fully support our hypothesis: only little differences have been found related to the level of immersion itself and they are statistically not significant. Nevertheless, the NI-version tends to have lower scores, while the SI-version and the Im-version score equally. Immersion and presence do not influence people's performance in a SPT task, but having the possibility to move in the virtual worlds and checking what the scene looks like from the NPC's point of view seems to have a positive impact. It is worth highlighting that the immersion level statistically affects performance only when the Im-version (immersive condition) follows the NI-version (non-immersive condition). This result, of course, deserves to be further explored.

Immersion presents a couple of other drawbacks. 11.22% of our players did not manage to use the HMD for sickness reasons, and this is, at the current state of the art, a drawback for an extensive training intervention. Furthermore, the HMD completely isolates the player from the surrounding world, limiting real life cooperation in the task. Finally, the limited availability of the tools and their costs make it very difficult to use them in formal educational contexts.

Acknowledgments. The authors wish to thank the Istituto Comprensivo "Sampierdarena" for the participation in the project, the help and support of all the teachers and the school headmistress.

References

1. OECD: Evolution of Student Interest in Science and Technology Studies – Policy Report; Global Science Forum (2006). http://www.oecd.org/science/sci-tech/36645825.pdf
2. Rocard, M., Csermely, P., Jorde, D., Lenzen, D., Walwerg-Heriksson, H., Hemmo, V.: Science Education NOW: A Renewed Pedagogy for the Future of Europe. European Commission, Brussels (2007)

3. Sinclair, N., Bruce, C.D.: New opportunities in geometry education at the primary school. ZDM **47**(3), 319–329 (2015)
4. Newcombe, N.S.: Picture this: increasing math and science learning by improving spatial thinking. Am. Educ. **34**(2), 29 (2010)
5. Uttal, D.H., Meadow, N.G., Tipton, E., Hand, L.L., Alden, A.R., Warren, C., Newcombe, N.S.: The malleability of spatial skills: a meta-analysis of training studies. Psychol. Bull. **139**(2), 352 (2013)
6. Surtees, A., Apperly, I., Samson, D.: The use of embodied self-rotation for visual and spatial perspective-taking. Front. Hum. Neurosci. **7**, 698 (2013)
7. Newcombe, N.S., Frick, A.: Early education for spatial intelligence: why, what, and how. Mind Brain Educ. **4**(3), 102–111 (2010)
8. Piaget, J., Inhelder, B.: The Child's Conception of Space, Trans. F. J. Langdon and J. L. Lunzer. Routledge and Kegan Paul, London (1956)
9. Newcombe, N.: The development of spatial perspective taking. Adv. Child Dev. Behav. **22**, 203–247 (1989)
10. Meyer, M.L., Salimpoor, V.N., Wu, S.S., Geary, D.C., Menon, V.: Differential contribution of specific working memory components to mathematics achievement in 2nd and 3rd graders. Learn. Individ. Differ. **20**(2), 101–109 (2010)
11. Nichols, S., Haldane, C., Wilson, J.R.: Measurement of presence and its consequences in virtual environments. Int. J. Hum.-Comput. Stud. **52**(3), 471–491 (2000)
12. Dalgarno, B., Lee, M.J.: What are the learning affordances of 3-D virtual environments? Br. J. Educ. Technol. **41**(1), 10–32 (2010)
13. Rose, F.D., Attree, E.A., Brooks, B.M., Parslow, D.M., Penn, P.R.: Training in virtual environments: transfer to real world tasks and equivalence to real task training. Ergonomics **43**(4), 494–511 (2000)
14. Freina, L., Canessa, A.: Immersive vs desktop virtual reality in game based learning. In: ECGBL 2015 – 9th European Conference on Games Based Learning: ECGBL 2015, p. 195. Academic Conferences and Publishing Limited, September 2015
15. Bottino, R.M., Ott, M., Tavella, M.: Scaffolding pedagogical planning and the design of learning activities: an on-line system. Gov. Commun. Innov. Knowl. Intensive Soc. 222 (2013)
16. Inagaki, H., Meguro, K., Shimada, M., Ishizaki, J., Okuzumi, H., Yamadori, A.: Discrepancy between mental rotation and perspective-taking abilities in normal aging assessed by Piaget's three-mountain task. J. Clin. Exp. Neuropsychol. **24**(1), 18–25 (2002)
17. Tversky, B., Hard, B.M.: Embodied and disembodied cognition: spatial perspective-taking. Cognition **110**(1), 124–129 (2009)
18. Frick, A., Möhring, W., Newcombe, N.S.: Picturing perspectives: development of perspective-taking abilities in 4-to 8-year-olds. Front. Psychol. **5**, 386 (2014)
19. Slater, M., Usoh, M., Steed, A.: Depth of presence in virtual environments. Presence: Teleoperators Virtual Environ. **3**(2), 130–144 (1994)
20. Epley, N., Morewedge, C.K., Keysar, B.: Perspective taking in children and adults: equivalent egocentrism but differential correction. J. Exp. Soc. Psychol. **40**(6), 760–768 (2004)

On the Impact of the Dominant Intelligences of Players on Learning Outcome and Game Experience in Educational Games: The TrueBiters Case

Pejman Sajjadi[✉], Eman El Sayed, and Olga De Troyer

Department of Computer Science, WISE,
Vrije Universiteit Brussel, Pleinlaan 2, 1050 Brussels, Belgium
{Ssajjadi, Eman.el.sayed, Olga.DeTroyer}@vub.ac.be

Abstract. This paper presents a digital educational game, TrueBiters, developed in order to help students practice the use of the truth tables to compute the truth-value of logical expressions in proposition logic. Next to improving the pass rate of our logic course, we also use the game to investigate whether there is a difference in learning outcome and game experience for students with different dominant types of intelligences. The results of a pilot study show that the use of TrueBiters resulted in an improvement of the learning outcome for logically-mathematically intelligent players. The results of a pilot study on game experience show differences for kinesthetically intelligent and logically-mathematically intelligent players with respect to certain game experience aspects. The number of participants was too small to draw definitive conclusions, but the results are an indication that the dominant types of intelligences do matter for the effectiveness of an educational game.

1 Introduction

The logic course in the 1st Bachelor Computer Science at our university is since years a stumbling stone for the students. On average less than 30 % succeed in the exam on the first try. Dealing with the formal and abstract language of logic is hard for most students. They easily lose interest and exhibit procrastination, and after a while they are completely lost. We tried to remedy this behavior in different ways but didn't succeed. Since educational games are commended as an enjoyable and effective way for learning and given our own research interest in games for learning, we decided to develop an educational game for the course.

We decided to first focus on practicing the truth tables of proposition logic, as a good knowledge of the truth tables is essential for understanding more complex topics introduced in the course. The TrueBiters game is a two-player game, inspired by a card game called "bOOleO" on Boolean logic[1]. We adapted the game to proposition logic and digitized it. Since most of our students have a smartphone and playing games on

---

[1] https://boardgamegeek.com/boardgame/40943/booleo.

© Springer International Publishing AG 2016
R. Bottino et al. (Eds.): GALA 2016, LNCS 10056, pp. 221–231, 2016.
DOI: 10.1007/978-3-319-50182-6_20

smartphones is popular among youngsters, we decided to develop a game for which they could use their smartphone with typical gesture-based interactions.

In addition, we wanted to use the TrueBiters game as a case study for our research on player-centered serious game design. We are investigating whether taking individual differences among players into consideration during game design can be beneficial for the game and/or learning experience [1, 2]. One direction that we explore is the use of the theory of Multiple Intelligence (MI). According to the theory of MI [3] the intelligence of a human being is multi-dimensional, in contrast to the commonly known one-dimensional Intelligence Quotient (IQ). In MI, eight distinct intelligence dimensions are proposed, each representing a different way of thinking, problem solving and learning. These dimensions are: visual-spatial, bodily-kinesthetic, logical-mathematical, linguistic, interpersonal, intrapersonal, musical, and naturalist. Everyone possesses every intelligence but to different degrees and all dimensions work together in an orchestrated way. We recognize that there are controversies about this theory. Opponents (e.g. [4–6]) criticize the lack of strong empirical evidence for the existence of the dimensions, while proponents [7] that the value of such a theory is rather in the contributions it could make to understanding and practice in the field. Therefore, we deem researching whether this theory can be used in understanding players' behavior and attitude worthwhile.

We used the TrueBiters game as a case study to investigate whether there would be a difference in learning outcome and game experience for students with different dominant types of intelligences. The results of a pilot study show that the use of TrueBiters resulted in an improvement of the learning outcome for logically-mathematically intelligent players. The results on game experience show that bodily-kinesthetically intelligent and logically-mathematically intelligent players demonstrate different experiences with respect to certain game experience aspects. The number of participants in the pilot study was too small to draw definitive conclusions but the results are a strong indication that the dominant types of intelligence do matter for the effectiveness of an educational game. Therefore, in the context of player-centered serious game design it may be important to take the intelligences of the target players into consideration when designing a learning game.

The paper is organized as follow: in Sect. 2 we review other educational games related to teaching logic or applying MI. Section 3 explains the TrueBiters game. Section 4 discusses the evaluation of TrueBiters both from a learning point of view and a game experience point of view, and Sect. 5 concludes the article.

2 Related Work

One of the first educational games related to logic is Robky's Boots (RB) [8]. In this game the players are introduced to the basic operations of logic, which they can use to construct arguments modeled as "machines", which is a composition of different logical gates and different electrical components. The objective of the game is to build a machine that can be turned on and off. In 1982 when this game was first introduced, it was perceived as intrinsically enjoyable and interesting by its players.

In [9] a serious game for learning and practicing propositional logic was introduced and evaluated. The game can be played with multiple users, collaboratively, cooperatively or competitively. The game is composed of eight modes (similar to levels) where each mode represents a different type of instruction and practice. The logical concepts are taught in a very abstract way using formulas, exactly as in textbooks on logic. Moreover, the practicing takes place through multiple-choice questions at the same abstract level. The results of the evaluations of this game indicate that it was perceived as easy to use, helpful, fun and motivating.

In [10] a prototype of a narrative-based interactive learning environment aimed at providing a rich and engaging learning experience for teaching binary arithmetic and logic gates was introduced and evaluated. The environment uses a fantasy narrative to contextualize the learning and domain knowledge. There is a computer on a ship that acts as the tutor to the player and then tests the player's understanding through a series of tasks. The results of the evaluation on learning using pre and post-tests and a control group showed that the game improved the test scores of the players in the post-test. Furthermore, the game was perceived as enjoyable by the players.

With respect to non-digital games, "bOOleO" is a strategy card game that employs the principles of Boolean algebra. It is a two player competitive game, and the goal is to reduce a list of bits by building a pyramid using Boolean operators and logical gates. Similarly, in [11] a (non-digital) board game, "The Logic Game", was proposed with the objective of providing students an effective way to understand and remember logical operators. An experiment with students taking a logic course showed that playing this game had a significant impact on their skills and understanding of logic.

On similar grounds, but from a more theoretical and pedagogical point of view, the research in [12] investigated the role of games as a tool in developing the logical-mathematical intelligence of MI. It was concluded that educational games in general will help players develop their logical reasoning abilities, since educational games push players to constantly analyze and solve problems.

To the best of our knowledge there are hardly any researches investigating the relationship between MI and learning outcome or game experiences in the context of serious games.

3 TrueBiters

TrueBiters is a digital two-player game for practicing the basic logical operators of propositional logic. It is played over two smartphones and a tablet. The game is inspired by the card game "bOOleO". While bOOleO is using Boolean logic, we applied its principles to proposition logic and digitized the game, which allows for an automatic verification of the rules of proposition logic. The game has a common area composed of tiles (i.e. the board - Fig. 1. (b)), which is rendered on a tablet. The different propositional operators are applied and displayed on the tiles. Furthermore, the game uses two smart phones, each operated by a player and containing a stack of cards representing logical operators that can be used by a player to perform an action on the common area. The three physical components are connected and synched using Bluetooth technology; the tablet is the master and the two smartphones are the slaves.

The game is using five logical operators represented by symbols representing fictive animals that can eat bits (Table 1). As is common in logic, the bit 1 represents TRUE and the bit 0 represents FALSE. Each binary logical operator (AND, OR, IMPLY, and EQUIVALENT) comes in two versions: one that results in a 1-bit and one that results in a 0-bit. For instance, the OR operator takes two bits as input and can either result in 0 or in 1 (depending on the input values). Next to these symbols, there are two error symbols, the invalid-symbol to indicate that an action cannot be applied to a tile because one or both inputs are not yet defined, and the wrong-symbol to indicate an incorrect action, e.g. the 1-version of the AND operator used on two 0-bits (which is incorrect according to the truth table of the AND operator).

Table 1. TrueBiters symbols

Logical operator symbols			
	OR		IMPLY
	AND		EQUIVALENT
	NOT		
Error symbols			
	WRONG		INVALID

Once the game commences each player receives a list of six bits. The values of these six bits are randomly generated. One player receives this list and the other player receives the inverted version of the list (Fig. 1(b)). Each player has to reduce his list of bits to a single bit being the right most bit of his list. The first player that achieves this is the winner. To do so, the player should use the correct logical operator cards that he has available on his mobile phone. For instance, he can reduce a 0-bit and a 1-bit into a 0-bit by using the 0-version of the AND operator. The players play alternately. If a player doesn't have a suitable operator at his disposal he has to skip his turn. The reduction process is guided by filling a pyramid of tiles. Each player has his own pyramid (Fig. 1(b)). The players select the tile they want to fill on the tablet by tapping on that tile, and swiping the desired card from their smartphone to that tile. If the action was allowed and correct the corresponding symbol will show up on the tile, otherwise the appropriate error symbol is displayed. By making a correct move, the player will earn a point; by making a mistake, he will lose one. Each player, at their turn, can only make one move. The version of the operator used determines the value of the tile, i.e. a 1-card version results in a 1-bit tile and a 0-card version results in a 0-bit tile. In this way, the tiles can be used as input for future operators. For example, in Fig. 1(b) the player using the top side of the board has chosen the AND operator with output value 0, to reduce the two rightmost bits (0 and 0) into a 0-bit.

Moreover, each player has the possibility to switch one of the initial bits with the corresponding bit of the other player. To do this, the player should have a NOT operator card available on his smartphone. He then selects the bit to be switched by tapping on it and swipes the NOT card to the board. This action will invalidate the results of that branch for both players, potentially resulting in extra work for the opponent. The opponent can directly cancel this action by also using a NOT card.

Each player starts with four randomly chosen operators in their card stack and can browse through them by swiping left or right. Selecting a card (i.e. use the card for the selected tile) is done by swiping up. When a card is used, it is removed from the card stack and replaced by a new card. A player can skip his turn by discarding a card. This is done by not selecting a tile on the board and swiping the desired card up, upon which a new card will be added to his stack.

The game also allows for self-training in order to become familiar with the game and to learn the different operators. The only difference is that in the self-training mode only one pyramid is shown (see Fig. 1(a)) and only one smartphone is needed.

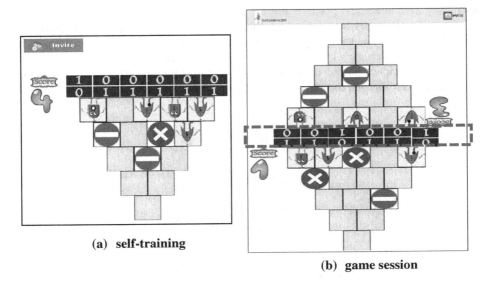

(a) self-training

(b) game session

Fig. 1. TrueBiters' board

4 Evaluation

4.1 Learning Outcome Evaluation

Before rolling out the game in our logic course, we first performed a pilot study to investigate the potential learning outcome of the game as well as the game experience. We invited those students from our logic course that failed their exam in the first session to participate. Because those students clearly didn't manage to master the course, they would be a good audience to test the effect of the game on. Although the students were incentivized through a gift and were assured complete anonymity, only four students (male) (out of 38) volunteered to participate.

In order to see to what degree the participants would improve after playing TrueBiters, we used a "pre-test[2]" and a "post-test[3]". The two tests were different in questions but we made sure to maintain the same level of difficulty. In the tests, the students had to resolve some questions requiring the use of the truth tables for the standard logic operators. During the course, they did similar exercises.

In order to see whether the differences in their learning outcome, if any, could be attributed to differences in intelligence dimensions, we measured their intelligence levels using the Multiple Intelligences Profiling Questionnaire (MIPQ) [13].

Before the players start the game, they were asked to do the pre-test and fill out the MIPQ. Afterwards, the game was explained and they were given 10 min for self-training. Next, they played the game (in the form of a tournament). After the play sessions, the participants were asked to do the post-test and fill-out a game experience questionnaire, 33 statements to be rated on a scale of 0 to 4 (0: not at all and 4: extremely) (see [14, 15] for more information). This questionnaire measured the participants' experiences in terms of their competence, immersion, flow, tension, challenge, negative affect and positive affect.

Since TrueBiters is a two-player game, in order to avoid any potential negative influence caused by a weak player, we organized the gameplay sessions in form of a tournament in which each of the four players played against each other. Therefore, in total each participant played three times and we had a total of six games. The comparison between the pre and post-test results are depicted in Fig. 2.

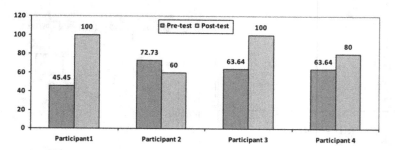

Fig. 2. Results of the pre and post-test (maximum score is 100)

The results of the post-test were significantly better for all participants except for participant two. To try to understand why participant two didn't improve (in fact he did worse), we investigated the results of the MI questionnaire. The results of this

---

questionnaire indicated that all participants expect participant two exhibit the **logical-mathematical** intelligence as one of their dominant intelligences. Participant two on the other hand, exhibits the **linguistics** intelligence as his dominant one. The logical-mathematical intelligence is defined as the capacity to conceptualize logical relations among actions or symbols, while the linguistic intelligence is defined as sensitivity to the meaning, order, sound, rhythms, inflections, and meter of words [16]. This difference may explain why participant two didn't make the same improvement as the three other participants in the same amount of time. Whether he would be able to improve after more practicing or he would never be able to master the topic within a reasonable time cannot be derived from this pilot study. We will investigate this with a more large-scale study lasting over a complete academic year.

4.2 Game Experience Evaluation

Since the results of our pilot study showed that dominant MI dimensions might be an influencing factor in the learning outcome, we wonder whether it would also influence the game experience of the participants. Therefore, in addition to the game experience results of our four participants in the pilot study, seven more participants (six male and one female) played the game. These participants were students from the second year Bachelor in Computer Science who already passed the exam of the logic course. The intelligences of these participants and their game experience were measured in the same way as in the previous evaluation. They were also given 10 min for self-training before playing the game. We didn't do the pre and post-test as we expected that they would already have a good knowledge of the logic operators and therefore most likely would show no improvement. These participants played the game twice. For these participants, the focus was purely on the game experience.

The results of the MIPQ of all 11 participants (4 from the first study and the 7 additional participants) showed that 82 % (9 players) of our population had the logical-mathematical intelligence as one of their dominant intelligences (which is not surprising as these are all students in Computer Science). A comparison between the game experience results of the logically-mathematically dominant participants and the others is shown in Table 2. We see that the logically-mathematically dominant participants were experiencing more challenge, more competence, immersion and flow. This suggests that TrueBiters is providing a proper balance between challenge and competence for the logical-mathematical dominant participants, as they are more immersed in the game and experiencing the flow state [17] more than the rest of the participants. A good game experience can potentially result in an increase of attention and motivation that may ultimately result in increased learning outcomes [18, 19]. However, they were slightly feeling more tension, slightly less positive affect, and more negative affect. This could be due to the fact that the interaction modality of TrueBiters is inherently kinesthetic, i.e. gesture-based. Therefore, we decided to see what percentage of our population was highly kinesthetic and how these highly kinesthetic participants experienced the game compared to the rest. The results of the MIPQ showed that 36 % (4 players) of our population had the kinesthetic intelligence as one of their dominant intelligences. As shown in Table 2 these participants were experiencing less tension and less negative affect. This can be explained by the fact that the gesture-based interaction better suits this group and can explain why the participants who do not have kinesthetic intelligence as one of their dominant ones score lower on these aspects. Therefore, we analyze TrueBiters based on its mechanics and their relation to these two intelligence dimensions using the recommendation tool introduced in [1]. This tool provides an evidence-based mapping between the MI dimensions and game mechanics; it indicates for each MI dimension which mechanics are appropriate (i.e. have a positive correlation with the dimension), are inappropriate (i.e. have a negative correlation), and for which no clear recommendation can be given (marked as "dubious"). The results are given in Table 3.

Table 2. Game experience results

	Logical	Rest	T-test	Kinesthetic	Rest	T-test
	Mean	Mean	Sig. 2-tailed	Mean	Mean	Sig. 2-tailed
Competence	2.37	1.9	0.54	2.05	2.42	0.54
Immersion	2.15	1.1	0.02	1.65	2.14	0.23
Flow	1.88	1.6	0.57	1.95	1.77	0.68
Tension	0.4	0.33	0.89	0.16	0.52	0.4
Challenge	1.35	1.2	0.7	1.2	1.4	0.54
Negative affect	0.58	0.25	0.4	0.5	0.53	0.91
Positive affect	2.71	2.8	0.83	2.55	2.82	0.4

Table 3. Analysis of TrueBiters in terms of mechanics and their relation to MI dimensions

Mechanic	Kinesthetic Intelligence	Logical-mathematical Intelligence
Motion	✓ positive	-
Repeat Pattern	✓ positive	✓ dubious
Memorizing	✓ negative	-
Submitting	✓ positive	-
Points	✓ positive	✓ positive
Quick feedback	✓ dubious	✓ positive
Modifier	✓ dubious	✓ positive
Disincentives	✓ negative	✓ negative
Companion gaming	✓ positive	✓ positive
Tutorial/first run scenarios	✓ dubious	✓ positive
Logical thinking	-	✓ positive
Strategizing	-	✓ positive
Browsing	-	✓ negative
Choosing	-	✓ negative

From this analysis we can conclude that TrueBiters employs a lot of game mechanics that are appropriate for the logical-mathematical dimension, i.e. *logical thinking, strategizing, modifier, points, quick feedback,* and *tutorials. Repeat pattern* is "dubious" for this MI dimension meaning that positive as well as negative correlations were found earlier. Some of these mechanics are also correlated (positive or dubious) with the kinesthetic dimension: repeat pattern, points, quick feedback, modifier, and tutorial. However, the mechanics browsing and choosing are negatively correlated to the logical-mathematical dimension and the mechanic disincentives (i.e. lose points) is negatively correlated with both MI dimensions. This analysis might explain why the logical-mathematical participants were feeling tension and negative affect while experiencing the flow state at the same time. It could also explain why the kinesthetic participants were experiencing less competence, immersion and challenge: the key gameplay mechanics (*strategizing* and *logical thinking*) are logical-mathematical oriented, and there is a negative correlation for the bodily-kinesthetic intelligence with the *memorizing* mechanic (i.e. remembering the truth tables, which is vital for being successful). These results are an indication that the dominant intelligences of players do play a role in the effectiveness of a learning game. It is also an indication that the popularity of game mechanics and interaction modes (e.g. gesture-base interaction) is not necessarily a guarantee for success.

It is important to mention that, due to the small number of participants used, analyzing if the differences for the different game experience aspects among the different groups of players were significant or not in unlikely to lead to interesting results. Nevertheless, based on a T-test analysis for each aspect of game experience between all groups, we observe that the experienced "immersion" by the logically-mathematically intelligent players was significantly higher than for the rest ($P < 0.05$).

5   Conclusions and Future Work

We presented an educational game developed in order to help students practicing the use of the truth tables to compute the truth-value of logical expressions in proposition logic. Although the number of participants used for the evaluation of the learning outcome in our pilot study was small, the results of our pilot study were promising: 3 out of 4 participants performed better in a logic test after playing the game compared to their result of a similar test taken before playing the game. The common denominator of the participants who showed improvement, with respect to the theory of MI, seems to be their dominant logical-mathematical intelligence. Furthermore, it was also observed that the dominant intelligence is also a contributing factor for the game experience. It was shown that for TrueBiters, which employs mostly mechanics positively correlated to the logical-mathematical dimension, the game experience of players with a high logical-mathematical intelligence was higher than for the other players (at least significantly with respect to immersion). We also observed a negative influence on some game experience aspects from the use of some negatively correlated game mechanics for these players. This is an indication that it is important to take the dominant intelligence of the target audience into consideration when designing a learning game.

In future work we will try to replace the negatively correlated game mechanics for the logical-mathematical dimension by better ones (or allow for a choice) and investigate whether this gives different results for the affected game experience aspects. Furthermore, a more large-scale experiment involving a control group, running over a longer period will be performed in the coming academic year. This is needed, since due to the low number of participants, we are not able to make generalizable conclusions at this point. Moreover, the quantitative research approach used need to be complemented with qualitative measures (i.e. interviews, observations) in order to gain a deeper understanding of the game experiences of the players, and their gained level of knowledge.

References

1. Sajjadi, P., Vlieghe, J., De Troyer, O.: Evidence-based mapping between the theory of multiple intelligences and game mechanics for the purpose of player-centered serious game design: VS-Games 2016. In: 8th International Conference on Games and Virtual Worlds for Serious Applications (2016, forthcoming)
2. Sajjadi, P., Vlieghe, J., De Troyer, O.: Relation between multiple intelligences and game preferences: an evidence-based approach. In: 10th European Conference on Games Based Learning: ECGBL2016 (2016, forthcoming)
3. Gardner, H.: Frames of Mind: The Theory of Multiple Intelligences. Basic Books, New York (2011)
4. Brody, N.: Geocentric theory: a valid alternative to Gardner's theory of intelligence. In: Howard Gardner Under Fire Rebel Psychol. Faces His Critics, pp. 73–94 (2006)
5. Waterhouse, L.: Multiple intelligences, the mozart effect, and emotional intelligence: a critical review. Educ. Psychol. **41**(4), 207–225 (2006)
6. Waterhouse, L.: Inadequate evidence for multiple intelligences, Mozart effect, and emotional intelligence theories. Educ. Psychol. **41**(4), 247–255 (2006)
7. Chen, J.: Theory of multiple intelligences: is it a scientific theory? Teachers Coll. Rec. **106**(1), 17–23 (2004)
8. Burbules, N.C., Reese, P.: Teaching logic to children: an exploratory study of Rocky's Boots. In: Assessing the Cognitive Consequences of Computer Environments for Learning (ACCCEL), no. 4, pp. 1–12 (1984)
9. Schäfer, A., Holz, J., Leonhardt, T., Schroeder, U., Brauner, P., Ziefle, M.: From boring to scoring – a collaborative serious game for learning and practicing mathematical logic for computer science education. Comput. Sci. Educ. **23**(2), 87–111 (2013)
10. Waraich, A.: Using narrative as a motivating device to teach binary arithmetic and logic gates. ACM SIGCSE Bull. **36**(3), 97–101 (2004)
11. Hicks, D.J., Milanese, J.: The logic game: a two-player game of propositional logic. Teach. Philos. **38**(1), 77–93 (2015)
12. Jing, L., Sujuan, M., Linqing, M.: The study on the effect of educational games for the development of students' logic-mathematics of multiple intelligence. Phys. Procedia **33**, 1749–1752 (2012)
13. Tirri, K., Nokelainen, P.: Multiple intelligences profiling questionnaire. In: Tirri, K., Nokelainen, P. (eds.) Measuring Multiple Intelligences and Moral Sensitivities in Education, pp. 1–13. Springer, Berlin (2011)

14. IJsselsteijn, W., Van Den Hoogen, W., Klimmt, C., De Kort, Y., Lindley, C., Mathiak, K., Poels, K., Ravaja, N., Turpeinen, M., Vorderer, P.: Measuring the experience of digital game enjoyment. In: Proceedings of Measuring Behavior, pp. 88–89 (2008)
15. IJsselsteijn, W., De Kort, Y., Poels, K., Jurgelionis, A., Bellotti, F.: Characterising and measuring user experiences in digital games. In: International Conference on Advances in Computer Entertainment Technology, vol. 620, pp. 1–4 (2007)
16. The Components of MI. http://multipleintelligencesoasis.org/about/the-components-of-mi/. Accessed 16 Mar 2016
17. Csikszentmihalyi, M.: Flow: The Psychology of Optimal Experience. Harper Perennial, New York (1991)
18. Webster, J., Trevino, L.K., Ryan, L.: The dimensionality and correlates of flow in human-computer interactions. Comput. Hum. Behav. 9(4), 411–426 (1993)
19. Graesser, A.C., D'Mello, S.K., Craig, S.D., Witherspoon, A., Sullins, J., McDaniel, B., Gholson, B.: The relationship between affective states and dialog patterns during interactions with AutoTutor. J. Interact. Learn. Res. 19(2), 293 (2008)

Game Development and Assessment

Care management and assessment

The RAGE Advanced Game Technologies Repository for Supporting Applied Game Development

Atanas Georgiev[1], Alexander Grigorov[1,6], Boyan Bontchev[1],
Pavel Boytchev[1], Krassen Stefanov[1(✉)], Wim Westera[2], Rui Prada[3],
Paul Hollin[4], and Pablo Moreno Ger[5]

[1] Faculty of Mathematics and Informatics,
Sofia University "St. Kliment Ohridski", Sofia, Bulgaria
{atanas,alexander.grigorov,
bontchev,boytchev,stefanov}@fmi.uni-sofia.bg
[2] Open University of the Netherlands, Heerlen, Netherlands
Wim.Westera@ou.nl
[3] University of Lisbon, Lisbon, Portugal
rui.prada@tecnico.ulisboa.pt
[4] The University of Bolton, Bolton, UK
pahl@bolton.ac.uk
[5] Universidad Complutense de Madrid, Madrid, Spain
pablom@fdi.ucm.es
[6] Institute of Mathematics and Informatics, Bulgarian Academy of Sciences,
Sofia, Bulgaria
grigorov@math.bas.bg

Abstract. This paper describes the structural architecture of the RAGE repository, which is a unique and dedicated infrastructure that provides access to a wide variety of advanced technologies (RAGE software assets) for applied game development. These software assets are reusable across a wide diversity of game engines, game platforms and programming languages. The RAGE repository allows applied game developers and studios to search for software assets for inclusion in applied games. The repository is designed as an asset life-cycle management system for defining, publishing, updating, searching and packaging for distribution of these assets. The RAGE repository provides storage space for assets and their artefacts. It will be embedded in a social platform for networking among asset developers and other users. A dedicated Asset Repository Manager provides the main functionality of the repository and its integration with other systems. Tools supporting the Asset Manager are presented and discussed. When the RAGE repository is in full operation, applied game developers will be able to easily enhance the quality of their games by including advanced game technology assets.

Keywords: Software assets · Serious games · Asset repository · Asset development · Taxonomy tools · Metadata editor · Applied games · Reuse

R. Bottino et al. (Eds.): GALA 2016, LNCS 10056, pp. 235–245, 2016.
DOI: 10.1007/978-3-319-50182-6_21

1   Introduction

Applied gaming is highlighted as one of the main priorities in Horizon2020, the Research and Innovation Programme of the European Commission. Policy makers of the European Commission envision a flourishing applied games industry that helps to address a variety of societal challenges in education, health, social cohesion and citizenship, and equally one that stimulates the creation of jobs in the creative industry sector.

Although applied or serious games have been successfully employed in education and training settings across a wide and varied range of application domains, seizing the full potential of applied games has been challenging. In contrast, the leisure games industry is an established industry dominated by large international hardware vendors (e.g. Sony, Microsoft and Nintendo) and large publishers and retailers. Conversely, the applied game industry is fragmented across a large number of small independent businesses with limited interconnectedness and knowledge exchange [1, 2].

The RAGE project [3] aims to stimulate the applied game industry by making available a set of advanced reusable game technology components (software assets) that game studios can easily integrate in their game development projects. Applied game studios would benefit from using state-of-the-art technologies, while incorporating complex pedagogic technical functionality would become easier and quicker, and the cost of development would be reduced. The software assets cover a variety of functionalities including game analytics, emotion recognition, assessment, personalised learning, game balancing and player-centric adaptation, procedural animation, language technologies, interactive storytelling, and social gamification.

While the main research goal of the RAGE project is to support the applied game industry by making available a large set of reusable, advanced software components (applied gaming assets), this paper focuses on the design of the repository infrastructure that supports the processes of development, reuse and sharing of applied gaming assets. This paper presents the asset repository architecture and the associated asset development methodology. We first present the related work efforts, then discuss our approach (research method), describe the software asset concept, provide details of the design and implementation of the back-end repository system architecture and corresponding front-end tools, and we conclude with a brief description of first experiments with the infrastructure, analysis and identification of further development and research efforts.

2   Related Work

Asset-based software development relies on reusing well documented and cohesive software artefacts and, therefore, it is inconceivable without a platform for storing and accessing assets. An asset repository as a software tool is defined by Ackerman and colleagues [4] for storing and retrieving reusable assets and managing asset access control for asset producers and consumers, according to the phases of the asset life cycle. They introduce the IBM Rational Asset Manager (RAS) repository, which handles tasks and activities of software asset producer, consumer and subscriber roles, while offering reduced production costs and improved software quality. In order to facilitate cross-project reuse of assets, the Rational Asset Manager model provides monitoring of asset categorization and usage together with multi-platform compliance management.

Another example for a RAS-based asset repository is the Atego Asset Library [5], which is a scalable Web-based repository for reusable software engineering artefacts. It is based on OMG RAS and integrates Unified Modelling Language (UML) and Systems Modelling Language (SysML) in order to facilitate asset reuse at design time. Currently, the tool is supported as PTC Integrity Asset Library[1] and, besides the publishing, finding and reuse of assets, provides services as interest registry and notification, automatic file interrogation, traceable links and reuse metric dashboard.

Extensions of the OMG RAS have been proposed for designing open source Web-based asset repositories providing advanced classification, search and utilization of reusable software assets of various types. The OpenCom asset repository was created as a supporting tool of Shanghai Component Library [6] based on an extension of OMG RAS profile aiming at collaborative creation of knowledge by web users. The Lavoi free source asset repository [7] was developed based on an extension of the component profile of OMG RAS broadening the categories about classification, solution, usage and related assets.

Within the computer games domain, the *asset* concept is often reserved for media files to be incorporated in a game. For example, the Intel® XDK HTML5 Cross-platform Development Tool [8] offers an asset manager for game development in conjunction with several game platforms. Here assets are often considered audio-visual game objects to be included in a project. In RAGE the focus is on software assets, reusable components adding specific (pedagogic) functionality for applied game development.

A similar attempt related to using a digital repository of metadata resources for education, combined with a portal for the respective community of practices build around the repository, is described in [9]. Other approaches to endowing digital libraries with adaptability capabilities in order to scaffold and enhance end user experience are presented in [10]. Similar attempts inside GALA Network of Excellence are the SoA framework for SGs [25] and the repository for exchange of game resources [26].

3   RAGE Software Assets

A RAGE asset as a self-contained software component related to computer games, intended to be reused and or repurposed across different game platforms. Its formal definition is compliant with the asset definition of the W3C ADMS Working Group [11], which refers to abstract entities that reflect some "intellectual content independent of their physical embodiments". In principle, not all assets are required to include software, however this paper focusses on software assets.

The RAGE asset is designed to contain advanced game technology (software), as well as value-adding services and attributes that facilitate their use, e.g. instructions, tutorials, examples and best practices, instructional design guidelines, connectors to

---

[1] http://www.ptc.com/model-based-systems-engineering/integrity-modeler/asset-library.

major game development platforms, test plans, test scripts, design documents, data capacity, and content authoring tools/widgets for game content creation.

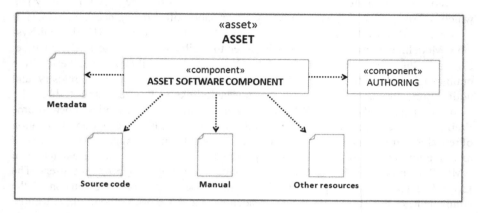

Fig. 1. Conceptual layout of a RAGE Asset

Figure 1 presents the general layout of a RAGE asset. Its software architecture is component-based and has been described and validated in [12]. It addresses both the internal workings of an asset and the level of interaction of assets with the outside world, including the mutual communications between assets. The RAGE architecture avoids dependencies on external software frameworks and minimises code that may hinder integration with game engines. It relies on a limited set of standard software patterns and well-established coding practices. Each RAGE asset contains metadata, which describe its content and functionality. RAGE metadata model in the domain of applied gaming was designed for defining the asset's metadata and for enabling the proper implementation of the RAGE Asset repository system architecture [13].

4   Our Approach

The research methodology for this study is based on the Rapid Application Development model [14]. We performed an extensive needs assessment study [15], including asset developers, educators and game producers. We have identified the services to be supported through the repository and other related tools and, in parallel, designed the RAGE metadata model to fit the specified domain of reusable gaming components (RAGE software assets). It was clear that we could not reuse any existing solution, but needed to design and implement our own software repository, targeting the identified needs and characteristics of the applied game domain.

In the next stage we provided the initial design of the RAGE asset as a software component, and the architecture of the RAGE software repository, aimed at supporting the development, storage, sharing and reuse of assets. In the next stage we provided details on the technical implementation of the software repository. We performed several interactions between these two stages until we reached a stable and more or less complete solution. In the last stage we analysed the first use case scenarios of the repository through several client tools, arranged first evaluations of the repository, and collected ideas for its improvement in the next cycle.

We will present the results of each stage in the next sections.

5   The Asset Repository System Architecture

Metadata is a key part of the information infrastructure necessary to help create order and provide a solid foundation for providing various information services such as descriptions, classifications, organizations, store, search, creation, modification and aggregation of information [16]. Rather than merely a software archive, the asset repository is viewed as a system for managing the lifecycle of an asset. In the repository the asset's artefacts are collected and conceptually tied together by defining the metadata. In addition, the repository allows for publication, updating, packaging for distribution and quality assurance, while accommodating different end-user tools.

The RAGE asset software repository is at the core of the asset development infrastructure. It is used to store and manage access to: (1) reusable game assets, (2) artefacts (resources within game assets), (3) metadata for game assets and artefacts, and (4) relationships between assets – dependencies, related assets, etc.

The Asset software repository leverages the discovery, development reuse and repurpose of game assets and artefacts. It will help both game asset developers and consumers in all the activities relating to the game asset lifecycle.

The main functions of the RAGE Asset software repository are as follows:

- Searching, finding and browsing assets/artefacts
- Creating, updating, publishing, deleting and downloading assets/artefacts
- Versioning support, source code import from GitHub and integration with IDEs

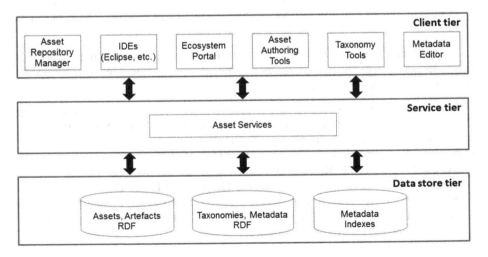

Fig. 2. Asset repository architecture

- Harvesting of external repositories for game assets and metadata using the Open Archives Initiative - Protocol for Metadata Harvesting (OAI-PMH)
- Reviewing and rating assets/artefacts

In order to implement these functions, we designed the asset repository infrastructure in three tiers (Fig. 2): client, service and data store tiers.

6 Implementation of the Asset Repository System Architecture

The main result from the second stage – Acting, is the implementation of the Asset repository. Fedora [17] is used for storing assets, metadata and artefacts; Sesame [18] for managing RDF data and supporting classification and entities; and Solr [19] for indexing and searching the repository. The data store tier consists of these three components and is used to store game assets, artefacts, metadata, taxonomies and indexes:

- **Fedora** stores the game assets, artefacts and metadata using RDF as primary data format. When the repository is updated by creating, modifying or deleting resources, it generates specific events so that the Fedora indexer copies RDF from the repository to an external triple store to keep it synchronized with the repository. Fedora is flexible, well established and it ensures scalability and durability (the complete repository can be rebuilt at any time).
- **Sesame** is an architecture for the efficient storage and expressive querying of large quantities of metadata in RDF and RDF Schema. This includes creating, parsing, storing, inferencing and querying over such data. Sesame RDF triple store contains metadata from Fedora and classification taxonomies/vocabularies.
- **Solr** is an open source platform optimized for searching. Its major features are full-text search, sophisticated faceted search, almost real-time indexing, dynamic clustering of data, etc. It is used for creating full text indexes on the RAGE metadata fields, as well as for realizing full text search and faceted search.

The service tier is used for access and preservation of the assets and artefacts. For the implementation of this tier, we developed the following services that provide access to the underlying data store tier:

- **Fedora Services**. Fedora provides a general RESTful HTTP API for accessing repository resources through HTTP methods. It supports OAI-PMH [20] requests on content and metadata in the repository.
- **Sesame Services**. Sesame offers a RESTful HTTP interface supporting the SPARQL Protocol for RDF. It is a superset of the SPARQL and supports communication for Update operations and the Graph Store HTTP Protocol [21].
- **Solr Services**. Apache Solr exposes Lucene's Java API as REST-like API's which can be called over HTTP. The RESTful endpoints allow CRUD style operations to be performed on the repository resources.

In addition, for the service tier to provide access to the client tier, we developed **Asset Services** for composition and execution of workflows over RAGE Game Assets.

The client tier includes web-based applications, plug-ins for integrated development environments (IDEs), and software components from the RAGE ecosystem that uses the services supported by Asset Repository Infrastructure. It includes:

- **The Asset Repository Manager** – we developed a web-based application embodying main functionalities for lifecycle management of assets and artefacts.
- **IDE Plug-ins** – we developed rich clients consuming services from the Asset Repository service tier, which thus allows developers to manage assets from within their integrated development environment (IDE).
- **Other Software Components from the RAGE Ecosystem**, such as the Ecosystem Portal (EP), which harvests assets and metadata through an OAI-PMH service provider from Asset Repository Service tier.

The Asset Repository services constitute an open interface for creating, modifying, deleting, and searching RAGE assets. They are realised on top of REST APIs, JSON, JSON-LD [22] and RDF, using Software as a Service (SaaS) model in the cloud. Based on the functionality exposed by these services, they can be grouped as:

- **Asset Access Services** defining an open interface for accessing assets within the RAGE Asset Repository allow for retrieving asset packages and metadata, and to search and browse for assets using keywords and metadata fields. The search interface provides both full-text search and semantic search. Full-text search enables performing of natural language queries using keywords and phrases occurring in any of indexed asset's metadata elements. The semantic search is using SPARQL for querying on asset metadata and SKOS taxonomies data represented as RDF triples.
- **Asset Management Services** defining an open interface for administering assets, including creating, modifying, and deleting, provide an abstract level of the operations, thus hiding the complexities of the internal formats, protocols and procedures for storing an asset in the Asset Repository.
- **Taxonomy Services** defining an open interface for managing classification taxonomies and controlled vocabularies used in RAGE Asset Metadata Model [13] to classify and describe an asset in educational and gaming contexts. For representation and storing Asset Repository adopts SKOS standard [23].
- **Authentication and Authorization Services** provide access for organisational needs. These services are implemented on top of Fedora Authentication and Authorization framework [17].

7 Usage Scenarios

In order to observe how the asset repository together with related client tools can support the asset developers and other users, and how effective and useful the services are, which it is offering, we have designed various usage scenarios. Also, asset developers and game developers have been involved for evaluating the functioning and usability of the repository. In this section we will present the scenarios, and in the next section will present the main conclusions based on the observations of real users.

To populate the repository with metadata we used four usage scenarios. The first scenario is publishing/updating a game asset through the web-based interface offered from the Asset Manager. The asset developer signs in, creates/selects an asset, enters/updates metadata and uploads artefacts or a packaged asset (see Fig. 3).

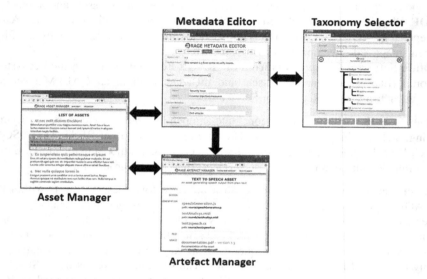

Fig. 3. Using the RAGE asset and artefact managers, the RAGE metadata editor and the RAGE taxonomy selector to populate the repository

The second scenario is publishing/updating a game asset from GitHub. The asset developer again should sign in the Asset Manager, creates/selects an asset, provides the GitHub repository identifier and credentials (if required). The files (artefacts) and metadata from GitHub are automatically harvested and published in the RAGE Asset Repository (using the GitHub API [24]). The user should also supply the rest of the required metadata.

In the third scenario, we tested publishing/updating a game asset from an IDE. For this scenario we developed an Eclipse IDE plugin. The asset developer opens the asset project in the Eclipse IDE; using the plugin the developer creates/updates the asset in RAGE Asset Repository within the IDE, providing credentials and needed metadata.

The fourth scenario: Asset consumers can search for a game asset using full text or advanced search, browse the repository, view assets metadata and download assets or artefacts for reuse.

At the moment, the repository is populated with the metadata of 12 currently developed Assets in RAGE project.

8   Scenario Evaluation

An evaluation of the usage scenarios was carried out by involving a group of 9 end users, viz. asset developers from the RAGE project. Preliminary findings of this user panel support the relevance of the repository system. Comments about the first version of the repository and related client tools can be summarized as follows:

- Users can easily work with basic services such as searching, downloading or uploading assets to the repository.
- Users need more specific instructions how to populate the repository with metadata.
- The metadata editor improved the process of populating the repository for users.
- Users encounter problems to identify the source of the information related to some of the metadata fields, like keywords and others.
- There is a need to automate further the definition of metadata fields.

While the evaluation is preliminary and relatively informal, the initial acceptance is positive, and confirms the viability of this first step within the RAGE Project.

9   Conclusions and Future Work

In this paper, we presented a unique software architecture supporting the lifecycle of reusable software components for applied gaming. The main innovation is related to the combination of RAGE Asset Model and RAGE Asset Metadata Model, backed up with server-side infrastructure (repository and services) and many end user tools. The software architecture plays a pivotal role within the RAGE Ecosystem, developed for the RAGE project and is considered of strategic importance for the domain of applied gaming.

The repository as the content core system of the RAGE Ecosystem allows for flexible design and development of RAGE game assets and future search, packaging and exchange. The current architecture guarantees both scalability and durability and the approach. It also provides a high level of flexibility across different taxonomies and standards.

Future work is planned on improving the architecture by providing support for Quality Assurance, asset development workflows, harvesting of assets from external systems and stores, social functions and for specific targeted support for the gaming community. A first provisional launch of the repository integrated in the RAGE social platform is expected in 2017.

Acknowledgements. This work has been partially funded by the EC H2020 project RAGE (Realising an Applied Gaming Eco-System); http://www.rageproject.eu/; Grant agreement No 644187.

References

1. García Sánchez, R., Baalsrud Hauge, J., Fiucci, G., Rudnianski, M., Oliveira, M., Kyvsgaard Hansen, P., Riedel, J., Brown, D., Padrón-Nápoles, C.L., Arambarri Basanez, J.: Business modelling and implementation report 2, GALA network of excellence. www.galanoe.eu
2. Stewart, J., Bleumers, L., Van Looy, J., Mariën, I., All, A., Schurmans, D., Willaert, K., De Grove, F., Jacobs, A., Misuraca, G.: The potential of digital games for empowerment and social inclusion of groups at risk of social and economic exclusion. Joint Research Centre, European Commission, Brussels (2013). ftp.jrc.es/EURdoc/JRC78777.pdf
3. RAGE: Project Web site (2015). http://www.rageproject.eu
4. Ackerman, L., Elder, P., Busch, C.V., Lopez-Mancisidor, A., Kimura, J., Balaji, N.A.: Strategic reuse with asset-based development. IBM RedBooks (2008). http://www.redbooks.ibm.com/redbooks/pdfs/sg247529.pdf
5. Kattau, S.: Atego launches RAS-based asset repository. SD Times Magazine, 13 February 2013. http://sdtimes.com/atego-launches-ras-based-asset-repository/#ixzz3wwMlvLJ8
6. Hong-min, R., Zhi-ying, Y., Jing-zhou, Z.: Design and implementation of RAS-based open source software repository. In: Proceedings of the Sixth International Conference on Fuzzy Systems and Knowledge Discovery, vol. 2, pp. 219–223 (2009)
7. Moura, D.S.: Software Profile RAS: estendendo a padronização do Reusable Asset Specification e construindo um repositório de ativos, Master's thesis, Univ. Federal do Rio Grande do Sul, Brasil (2013). http://www.lume.ufrgs.br/handle/10183/87582
8. Hilliar, G.: Developing Cross-Platform Mobile Apps with HTML5 and Intel XDK, in Dr. Dobb's Journal, UBM plc. (2014)
9. Böhm, T., Klas, C.-P., Hemmje, M.: Supporting collaborative information seeking and searching in distributed environments. In: Proceedings of the LWA 2013 Conference, Bamberg, Germany, pp. 16–20 (2013)
10. Stefanov, K., Nikolov, R., Boytchev, P., Stefanova, E., Georgiev, A., Koychev, I., Nikolova, N., Grigorov, A.: Emerging models and e-infrastructures for teacher education. In: 2011 International Conference on Information Technology Based Higher Education and Training ITHET 2011, IEEE Catalog Number: CFP11578-CDR, ISBN: 978-1-4577-1671-3 (2011)
11. Dekkers, M.: Asset Description Metadata Schema (ADMS). W3C Working Group (2013)
12. Van der Vegt, G.W., Westera, W., Nyamsuren, N., Georgiev, A., Martinez Ortiz, I.: RAGE architecture for reusable serious gaming technology components. Int. J. Comput. Games Technol. **2016** (2016), http://dx.doi.org/10.1155/2016/5680526
13. Georgiev, A., Grigorov, A., et al.: The RAGE software asset model and metadata model. In: Marsh, T., Ma, M., Oliveira, M.F., Baalsrud Hauge, J., Göbel, S. (eds.) JCSG 2016. LNCS, vol. 9894, pp. 191–203. Springer, Heidelberg (2016). doi:10.1007/978-3-319-45841-0_18
14. Martin, J.: Rapid Application Development. Macmillan, Indianapolis (1991)
15. Hollins, P., Westera, W., Manero Iglesias, B.: Amplifying applied game development and uptake. In: Proceedings of 9th European Conference on Game-Based Learning ECGBL 2015, pp. 234–241. Steinkjer, Norway (2015)
16. Duval, E., Hodgins, W., Sutton, S., Weibel, S.L.: Metadata principles and practicalities. D-lib Mag. **8**(4), 16 (2002). doi:10.1045/april2002-weibel
17. Woods, A.: Fedora 4.3 Documentation. https://wiki.duraspace.org/display/FEDORA43/
18. Broekstra, J., Kampman, A., Harmelen, F.: Sesame: a generic architecture for storing and querying RDF and RDF schema. In: Horrocks, I., Hendler, J. (eds.) ISWC 2002. LNCS, vol. 2342, pp. 54–68. Springer, Heidelberg (2002). doi:10.1007/3-540-48005-6_7

19. Smiley, D., Pugh, E., Parisa, K., Mitchell, M.: Apache Solr 4 Enterprise Search Server. Packt Publishing, Birmingham (2014). ISBN: 9781782161363
20. Lagoze, C., Van de Sompel, H.: The open archives initiative protocol for metadata harvesting (2015). https://www.openarchives.org/OAI/openarchivesprotocol.html
21. SPARQL 1.1: SPARQL 1.1 Overview, W3C Recommendation (2013)
22. JSON-LD 1.0: A JSON-based Serialization for Linked Data. W3C Recommendation (2014)
23. SKOS: Simple Knowledge Organization System Reference. W3C Recommendation (2009)
24. GitHub API: GitHub Developer Guide (2016). https://developer.github.com/v3/\
25. Carvalho, M.B., Bellotti, F., Berta, R., De Gloria, A., Gazzarata, G., Hu, J., Kickmeier-Rust, M.: A case study on service-oriented architecture for serious games. Entertain. Comput. **6**, 1–10 (2015). doi:10.1016/j.entcom.2014.11.001
26. Gloria, A., Bellotti, F., Berta, R., Lavagnino, E.: Serious games for education and training. Int. J. Ser. Games **1**(1), 100–105 (2014)

A Semantic Frame Approach to Support Serious Game Design

Manuel Gentile[1]([✉]), Giuseppe Città[1], Simona Ottaviano[1], Dario La Guardia[1], Valentina Dal Grande[1], Mario Allegra[1], and Aki Jarvinen[2]

[1] ITD - National Research Council of Italy,
Via Ugo La Malfa 153, 90146 Palermo, Italy
{manuel.gentile,giuseppe.citta,simona.ottaviano,dario.laguardia,
valentina.dalgrande,mario.allegra}@itd.cnr.it
[2] Sheffield Hallam University, City Campus, Howard Street, Sheffield S1 1WB, UK
a.jarvinen@shu.ac.uk

Abstract. This paper proposes a methodological framework to support the design of educational games based on a semantic frame analysis. Starting from a Frame Semantics point of view, the authors provide a deepen analysis of game mechanics definitions using the key concept of verb. To demonstrate the advantages of the proposed model an example is reported to illustrate how we can explicit the game mechanics used in a management/construction game by means of FrameNet and WordNet ontologies.

Keywords: Serious games design · Game mechanics · Semantic frame

1 Introduction

The aim of this work is to define a methodological framework that can support designers, scholars and educators in the analyzing and designing Serious Games. The educational point of view adds a dimension of analysis that makes the design of game for education not a trivial task. To fulfill this aim, we firstly ask a few questions:

- How should the educational aspect of games be taken into account during the design?
- More specifically, what are the game elements that allow a designer to connect game with the educational aspects?

The literature reports some previous works with the same goal [1–3] that support the idea that game mechanic is a key concept in the serious game design. As an example, the study of Arnab et al. [3] describes a tool for analyses designed to support the specification of the link between game mechanics and learning mechanics. The study provides a list (not exhaustive) of game mechanics and learning mechanics accompanied, in the form of tables, by a methodology and tools for the analysis that allows the elements belonging to the two domains to be

© Springer International Publishing AG 2016
R. Bottino et al. (Eds.): GALA 2016, LNCS 10056, pp. 246–256, 2016.
DOI: 10.1007/978-3-319-50182-6_22

linked. Anyway, the literature in the sector underlines the need of an additional level of specification in order to clarify the role and function of game mechanics in the design process.

Jarvinen [4] proposes the following definition, based on his theory of games as systems that are made up of particular game elements. In his theory, game mechanics are a specific element category. Their essential characteristic is in being compound elements that combine elements from other classes into one another. These combinations are put forward by players, within what the system affords them, i.e. game mechanics are the means of producing input to the system, given to the players by a game's designers. Consequently, from a system perspective, executing game mechanics is what players do when they play a game, e.g. by taking a character (that represents a component element) and moving it within a game level (an environment element). In other words, game mechanics as play actions take part in operating the game system, thus giving birth to the temporal phenomenon of game play.

In this paper, we recall the statements of the Jarvinen's work [4] in order to clarify the classes of elements that compose a game and to describe the relationships among them and above all, the idea of game mechanics as elements of the game that allow players to "interact" with the game itself. According to this point of view, in the following sections we propose a representation of game mechanics as verbs that leads us to a serious game design methodological framework based on a semantic frame analysis.

2   Game-Mechanics as Verbs

In a systemic view, game mechanics operate as external inputs to the system that are able to influence the dynamics of the game; therefore, game mechanics are generally identified by lexical verbal units, also according to other researchers [5]. Nevertheless, Jarvinen proposed game mechanic definitions in order to further clarify the context and dynamics of use of them, specifying the role of the verbs linked to the game mechanic. In our opinion, it is necessary to provide an additional level of specification in order to better clarify the concept of game mechanic. In the following sections we will consider the concept of game mechanics in more depth, starting from a specific view of verbs. Through verbs we aim to verify, in the light of Frame Semantics, if and how the introduction of the frame concept can support us in this process and in the end, whether it could help the designer to naturally link a game to the educational context. According to a Cognitive Linguistics perspective [6], verbs are more than linguistic elements. Beyond the linguistic aspect, they and their meanings are cognitive elements that constantly involve and stimulate higher-level processes such as e.g. reasoning, action planning, decision making [7]. Pinker efficaciously refers to them as a window into the human mind [8]. They can be defined as conceptual representations of events and states [7] and happenings [9], dynamic words that instantiate a process within which an element changes state or location along the time axis

[10]. That is, verbs profiles actions and processes that are defined as a set of relational components [11] sequentially scanned in their temporal evolution [12]. Referring to this representation of verbs, we suggest considering verbs as the most suitable elements for describing and managing game-mechanics as actions. A verb, conceived as described above, is an element that, thanks to its cognitive character, plays a role that goes beyond mere linguistic aspects since its meaning evokes a conceptualization of concrete experiences and constantly improves knowledge construction. Similarly, if we conceive of game-mechanics as elements that instantiates complex relations as actions and processes that evoke different and diverse aspects of knowledge, we are able to point out the cognitive potential of each game-mechanic, the basic and higher order skills it involves and their direct and indirect effects on learning. Within this perspective game-mechanics/verbs and their meanings emerge as cornerstones of larger contexts of knowledge, the frames, that come into play in different ways both when we are learning to handle new slices of knowledge and when we are managing pieces of previously acquired knowledge.

3 Toward an Empirical Semantics of Game-Mechanics

Our position is the result of exchanges between the perspectives on game-mechanics mentioned above and two areas of the linguistic field of Semantics: Lexical Semantics (LS) [13] and Frame Semantics (FS) [14–16]. According to the point of view that considers game-mechanics as players actions our perspective manages them as elements instantiated by lexical units belonging to the class of verbs. In order to achieve this purpose we will briefly describe below some key concepts we take into account from LS and FS. LS deals with the study of the meanings of words and the ways these meanings affect the composition and the interpretation of a clause (or proposition, sentence) [17]. It can be concisely and operationally defined as the study of what and why a lexical item means, how these features can be represented and where the whole meaning of a clause comes from [18]. Lexicon, in this perspective, is the core element in which the essential semantic and syntactic information is coded. It is not a collection of linguistic items (function and content words) plus a set of useful rules to combine them, but rather a system of lexical units in a continuum of several heterogeneous relationships [19,20]. A word in a sentence is in close relationship with the surrounding words, and its meaning semantically and syntactically contributes to create the whole meaning of the clause [21,22]. It is not merely an element inside a linguistic chain of independent symbols [23] but it is part of compositional patterns that represent the sentence as a structure of symbols temporally and contextually combined [24]. Therefore, contextual relationships of a word (its semantic relationships with other words) and contextual variations of the meaning of a word are the core of a Lexical Semantics perspective [13,25]. Although an LS perspective and its core assumptions allow us to analyse and manage lexical units and their mutual relationships within a phrasal context, it is essential to deal with the meaning of a word by taking into account some cognitive aspects that go beyond mere textual or contextual analyses. The inclusion of the cognitive dimension allows us to make the link between verbs and game-mechanics clearer. FS is the theoretical framework which can support cognitive aspects of our vision. FS, as a research program, focuses on the relationship between language and experience emphasizing their continuities [26]. Within this perspective a word and its meaning represent a categorization of experience [27]. In other words, FS deals with the relation between lexical semantic relationships from a cognitive point of view [13]. The FS core ideas are, in a nutshell, as follows: *"A word's meaning can be understood only with reference to a structured background of experience, beliefs, or practices, constituting a kind of conceptual prerequisite for understanding the meaning. Speakers can be said to know the meaning of the word only by first understanding the background frames that motivate the concept that the word encodes. Within such an approach, words or word senses are not related to each other directly, word to word, but only by way of their links to common background frames and indications of the manner in which their meanings highlight particular elements of such frames.* [15, pp. 76–77]".

The core of the FS approach is the notion of Frame that can be defined as a system of different concepts that are related in such a way that in order to understand one of them it is essential to understand an entire structure of knowledge [26]. It is closely related to the notion of frame introduced by Marvin Minsky in the Artifical Intelligence field [28]. The Frame highlights the cognitive aspects of the connection between words, as they are conceived in LS, and concepts. It suggests that concepts are elements of knowledge of human experience essential for understanding the world around us. It can also be referred to as domain, a knowledge structure that affects the characterization of a meaning [13] and is described as a realm of experiential potential that can be conceptualized [29]. In order to explain more clearly what a frame is and how it works we report a worth-noting example about the *commercial transaction* frame from Fillmore and Atkins [15]. The *commercial transaction* frame is characterized by a domain in which a person acquires possession or control of something from another person, in agreement with him/her and after giving him/her a sum of money. This domain involves different packages of knowledge and information, beliefs, pattern of practices [30] that involve a further background knowledge. In fact, it not only necessitates the understanding of what a money economy, a contract, an ownership are, but also shows that for this frame there are specific core categories: a Buyer, a Seller, the Goods that are bought/sold, and Money. These are the essential elements of a commercial scenario. Nevertheless, the FS approach allows us to expand each category in depth: i.e., referring to the element Money we can distinguish among Cost (the price of the goods determined by the seller), Tender (the sum of money the buyer offers) and Change (the difference between cost and tender). We can involve more and more complex members of each category mentioned above (e.g. Bargaining and Discount are linked to the negotiation of the Cost) and so on.

4   A Semantic Frame Analysis of the Management/ Construction Game Mechanics

Using the library of game mechanics defined in Jarvinen [4] as our starting point, we selected the subset of mechanics (Table 1) linked to a specific category of games: the management/construction game (e.g. like SimCity).

Table 1. List of the selected game mechanics [4]

Game mechanic	Definition
Arranging	Arranging the order, assembly, or location of game elements, typically components, into sets
Bidding	Making an offer on a game component or an area of game environment which is possessed by the game system or another player
Building	Assembling constructions to the game environment, often with the help of components and patterns that emerge from components combinations
Buying/selling	Buying or selling component, environment location, or information from or to the game system or another player
Choosing	The player is presented with making a choice between a number of options
Contracting	A contract by two or more players is made through an agreement that is acknowledged by the game system. I.e. informal cooperation is formalised into a mechanic that makes the contract known to the game system
Discarding	Discarding a component or using one to displace another
Placing	Placing a component or a marker on the game environment
Trading	Exchanging a game element (component, environment-of-self, or information) with another player or the game system
Transforming	The players are given an ability to transform the flow of time or space to better their chances of overcoming a challenge, or to find out an outcome of their actions
Upgrading/downgrading	Changing the attributes of a game element, including player role or player contract

As can be seen in the Table 2, the name of the mechanics always makes reference to a verbal lexical unit (LU), while the definitions recall contexts of use describing the dynamics of use. Each game mechanic was researched in the FrameNet ontology[1], using the infinitive form of the game mechanic name, in order to obtain the frame closest to the game mechanic definition.

---

[1] The FrameNet database (https://framenet.icsi.berkeley.edu/fndrupal/), based on the theory of FS, arises from The Berkeley FrameNet project. Starting from examples of use of words in actual contexts it aims to build a lexical database of English human- and machine readable.

Table 2. List of the semantic frames linked the analized game mechanics

GM - LU	Frame
Allocate (Distribute)	**Dispersal:** "An *Agent* or a *Cause* disperses or scatters *Individuals* from the *Source*, a relatively confined space, to a the *Goal_area*, a broader space."
Arrange	**Arranging:** "An *Agent* puts a complex *Theme* into a particular *Configuration*, which can be a proper order, a correct or suitable sequence, or a spatial position."
Build	**Building:** "This frame describes assembly or construction actions, where an *Agent* joins *Components* together to form a *Created_entity*, which is profiled, and hence the object of the verb."
Buy	**Commerce_buy:** "These are words describing a basic commercial transaction involving a *Buyer* and a *Seller* exchanging *Money* and *Goods*, taking the perspective of the *Buyer*. The words vary individually in the patterns of frame element realization they allow. For example, the typical pattern for the verb BUY: *Buyer* buys *Goods* from *Seller* for *Money*."
Bid (Offer)	**Offering:** "An *Offerer* indicates that he or she is able and willing to give a *Theme* to a *Potential_recipient*. In the absence of further qualifications, it is often understood that the *Potential_recipient* accepts the *Theme*."
Choose	**Choosing:** "A *Cognizer* decides upon the *Chosen* (either an item or a course of action) out of a set of *Possibilities*. The *Cognizer* may have an *Inherent_purpose* or a *Larger_purpose* for the *Chosen*. Often an *Explanation*, which serves as the basis of the choice, is given."
Contract (Settle)	**Make_agreement_on_an_action**[a]**:** "Two (or more) people (the *Parties*, also encodable as *Party_1* and *Party_2*) negotiate an agreement. Both sides are construed as making a commitment to assume an *Obligation* the process is understood to be symmetrical or reciprocal. Instead of specific mention of the *Obligation*, a *Topic* expression may be used to indicate the domain covered."
Contract (Contract)"	**Hiring**[b]**:** "An *Employer* hires an *Employee*, promising the *Employee* a certain *Compensation* in exchange for the performance of a job. The job may be described either in terms of a *Task* or a *Position*. In some cases, the *Employee* frame element will also indicate the *Position*."
Discard	**Removing:** "An *Agent* causes a *Theme* to move away from a location, the *Source*. The *Source* is profiled by the words in this frame, just as the *Goal* is profiled in the *Placing* frame."

Table 2. (*continued*)

GM - LU	Frame
Downgrade (Replace)	**Replacing**[a]: "An *Agent* changes the filler of a *Role* by placing a *New_filler* in the position after the *Old_filler* ceases to occupy the position. Often this entails the *Agent* removing the *Old_filler*. In most cases the *Role* is implicit."
Downgrade (Decline)	**Change_position_on_a_scale**[b]: "An *Entity* improves from a less desirable *Prior_state* to a more desirable *Post_state*. (Note that members of this frame marked with the semantic type "*Negative*" indicate deterioration.) In most cases the *Prior_state* and the *Post_state* are implicit, since the most important fact is simply that the *Post_state* is better than the *Prior_state*."
Place	**Placing:** "Generally without overall (translational) motion, an *Agent* places a *Theme* at a location, the *Goal*, which is profiled. In this frame, the *Theme* is under the control of the *Agent/Cause* at the time of its arrival at the *Goal*."
Sell	**Commerce_sell:** "These are words describing basic commercial transactions involving a buyer and a seller exchanging *Money* and *Goods*, taking the perspective of the seller. The words vary individually in the patterns of frame element realization they allow. For example, the typical patterns for SELL: *Seller* sells *Goods* to *Buyer* for *Money*."
Trade	**Exchange:** "Two parties, the *Exchangers*, each give and receive from the other *Themes*. The parties are also construable separately as *Exchanger_1* and *Exchanger_2*, in which case the *Themes* may be construed separately, too, as *Theme_1* and *Theme_2*."
Transform	**Cause_change:** "An *Agent* or *Cause* causes an *Entity* to change, either in its category membership or in terms of the value of an *Attribute*. In the former case, an *Initial_category* and a *Final_category* may be expressed, in the latter case an *Initial_value* and a *Final_value* can be specified."
Upgrade (Replace)	**Replacing:** "An *Agent* changes the filler of a *Role* by placing a *New_filler* in the position after the *Old_filler* ceases to occupy the position. Often this entails the *Agent* removing the *Old_filler*. In most cases the *Role* is implicit."

[a]Meaning defined by Jarvinen.
[b]Meaning according to the management/construction games context.

If the verbal unit was not present in the FrameNet ontology, the wordnet ontology[2] was used [31]. In fact, exploiting the synonyms synset, we searched

---

[2] Wordnet is a lexical database of English. Lexical elements (verbs, nouns, adjectives and adverbs) are organized in different groups (synset) expressing different concepts. These groups are mutually linked through lexical and semantic relations. WordNet, therefore, can be referred to as a large semantic network of words [16].

for a verbal unit with the same meaning as the original one (according to the definition) but present in the FrameNet ontology [16,32]. We consider synonymy as a relation between two words that can be substituted in a given context without altering the meaning of a sentence (contextual synonymy) [33]. The Table 2 shows the links among the subset of analized game-mechanics (GM) and the semantic frames by means of the Lexical Unit (LU). For each game-mechanic/LU, the frame name and its definition by FramNet database is reported. When the GM/LU is missing in FrameNet as lexical entry, it is followed by another LU in the brackets that represents the contextual synonym selected from WordNet and indexed in FrameNet.

Using this approach it was possible to highlight how some LUs (e.g. *Contract* and *Downgrade*) are tied with different frames. As reported in the table, the first occurrence of the *Contract* LU accords with the meaning defined by Javinen [4], while the second one is another sense of LU, that emerged from the frames analysis. Also the latter meaning of the *Contract* LU has to be taken into account in the context of management/construction game design. The same behavior is reported from the *Downgrade* LU. The set of frames thus obtained, composes a graph with not connected sub-networks of frames. The sub-networks can be seen as the contexts of knowledge that is activated throughout the gameplay.

In the Fig. 1 an example of sub-network linked to the *Buying/Selling* game mechanic is shown. The analysis reveals that *Buy* and *Sell* are linked to different

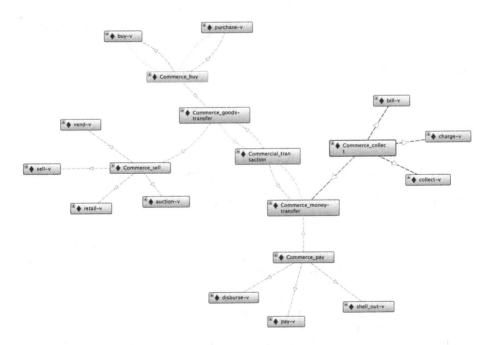

Fig. 1. The *Buy* and *Sell* frames network

but connected semantic frames, and that there are other frames directly linked to them (e.g. *Commerce_pay* and *Commerce_collect*). The frames networks highlights the possibility to specify new game mechanics like *Pay* or *Collect*. Moreover, the identification of these differences among the game mechanics allows us to better specify the actions and their links with the other elements of the game, but also to deepen the knowledge linked to them. In fact, the semantic frame approach allows us to further specify the definition of each game mechanic and clearly highlight not only the actions but also the relationships between the game mechanics and other game elements.

5   Discussion and Conclusion

In this paper we have given some initial steps in the definition of a framework to support the design of Serious Game based on the Frame Semantics approach. Through the exploration of the FrameNet ontology and by adding some nodes to those directly selected we obtained a network of connected frames. The existence of this connected network confirms that the selected game mechanics are semantically linked. The analysis reveals that, defining the game mechanics as verbs, it is possible to link them to their context of use represented by the frames network. The cloud of activated frames is the natural bridge to the educational context. In fact, the semantic frames allow us to tie, with different relations, the previously acquired and the new knowledge, the context of use of the mechanics and the relations between the game elements; moreover, at the same time, they allow the detection of different levels of details in the definition of the game mechanics and then, in their implementation, provide a structured view of the learning spaces connected to them so to be used in defining a software tool to support the design of a serious game.

References

1. Lameras, P., Arnab, S., Dunwell, I., Stewart, C., Clarke, S., Petridis, P.: Essential features of serious games design in higher education: linking learning attributes to game mechanics (2016)
2. Rooney, P.: A theoretical framework for serious game design: exploring pedagogy, play and fidelity and their implications for the design process **2**(4), 41–60 (2012). doi:10.4018/ijgbl.2012100103
3. Arnab, S., Lim, T., Carvalho, M.B., Bellotti, F., De Freitas, S., Louchart, S., De Gloria, A.: Mapping learning and game mechanics for serious games analysis. Br. J. Educ. Technol. **46**(2), 391–411 (2015). http://doi.org/10.1111/bjet.12113
4. Jrvinen, A.: Games Without Frontiers: Theories and Methods for Game Studies and Design. Tampere University Press, Tampere (2008)
5. Mitgutsch, K., Alvarado, N.: Purposeful by design: a serious game design assessment framework. In: Proceedings of the International Conference on the Foundations of Digital Games, FDG 2012, pp. 121–128 (2012). doi:10.1145/2282338.2282364

6. Langacker, R.W.: Foundations of Cognitive Grammar: Theoretical Prerequisites, vol. 1. Stanford University Press, Palo Alto (1987)
7. de Almeida, R.G., Manouilidou, C.: The study of verbs in cognitive science. In: de Almeida, R.G., Manouilidou, C. (eds.) Cognitive Science Perspectives on Verb Representation and Processing, pp. 3–39. Springer International Publishing, Cham (2011)
8. Pinker, S.: Learnability Cognition: The Acquisition of Argument Structure. MIT Press, Cambridge (2013)
9. Levin, B., Hovav, M.R.: Argument Realization. Cambridge University Press, Cambridge (2005)
10. Tomasello, M.: Constructing a Language: A Usage-Based Theory of Language Acquisition. Harvard University Press, Cambridge (2009)
11. Gentner, D.: Why verbs are hard to learn. In: How Children Learn Verbs Action Meets Word, pp. 544–564 (2006)
12. Langacker, R.W.: Investigations in Cognitive Grammar, vol. 42. Walter de Gruyter, New York (2009)
13. Paradis, C.: Lexical semantics. In: Chapelle, C.A. (ed.) The Encyclopedia of Applied Linguistics, pp. 3356–3357. WileyBlackwell, Hoboken (2012)
14. Fillmore, C.: Frame semantics. In: Linguistics in the Morning Calm, pp. 111–137 (1982)
15. Fillmore, C.J., Atkins, B.T.: Toward a frame-based lexicon: the semantics of RISK and its neighbors. In: Frames, Fields, and Contrasts: New Essays in Semantic and Lexical Organization, vol. 103, pp. 75–102 (1992)
16. Boas, H.C.: From theory to practice: frame semantics and the design of FrameNet. Semantik im Lexikon **479**, 129–159 (2005)
17. Pustejovsky, J., Boguraev, B.: Lexical semantics. Lexical Semantics (1996)
18. Baldwin, T.: Lexical Semantics: An Introduction, Lecture Notes from the ACL/HCSNet Advanced Program in Natural Language Processing, Melbourne, Australia (2006)
19. Elman, J.L.: Lexical knowledge without a mental lexicon? Ment. Lexicon **60**, 1–33 (2011)
20. Elman, J.L.: On the meaning of words and dinosaur bones: lexical knowledge without a lexicon. Cogn. Sci. **33**(4), 547–582 (2009)
21. Culicover, P.W., Jackendoff, R.: The simpler sintax hypotesis. TRENDS Cogn. Sci. **10**(9), 413–418 (2006)
22. Jackendoff, R.: Meaning and the Lexicon: The Parallel Architecture 1975–2010. Oxford University Press, Oxford (2010)
23. Van Gelder, T., Port, R.: Beyond symbolic: prolegomena to a kama-sutra of compositionality. In: Honavar, V., Uhr, L. (eds.) Symbol Processing and Connectionist Models in Artificial Intelligence and Cognition: Steps Toward Integration. Academic Press, San Diego (1993)
24. Città, G.: L'asimmetria nominale del primo lessico come tappa iniziale di una conoscenza linguistica softly assembled. Rivista Italiana di Filosofia del Linguaggio **4**, 21–32 (2011)
25. Cruse, D.A.: Lexical Semantics. Cambridge University Press, Cambridge (1986)
26. Fillmore, C.J.: Frame semantics. Cogn. Linguist.: Basic Readings **34**, 373–400 (2006)
27. Petruck, M.R.: Frame semantics. In: Handbook of Pragmatics, pp. 1–13 (1996)
28. Minsky, M.: A framework for representing knowledge (1975)
29. Langacker, R.W.: Essentials of Cognitive Grammar. Oxford University Press, Oxford (2013)

30. Baker, C.F., Fillmore, C.J.: A frame approach to semantic analysis. In: Heine, B., Narrog, H. (eds.) Oxford Handbook of Linguistic Analysis, Oxford, UK (2010)
31. Fellbaum, C.: WordNet. Blackwell Publishing Ltd, Hoboken (1998)
32. Pazienza, M.T., Pennacchiotti, M., Zanzotto, F.M.: Mixing wordnet, verbnet and propbank for studying verb relations. In: Proceedings of the Fifth International Conference on Language Resources and Evaluation, LREC-2006, pp. 1372–1377 (2006)
33. Ježek, E.: The Lexicon: An Introduction. Oxford University Press, Oxford (2016)

The Game Jam as a Format for Formal Applied Game Design and Development Education

Micah Hrehovcsik[1(✉)], Harald Warmelink[1], and Marilla Valente[2]

[1] HKU University of the Arts Utrecht, HKU Games and Interaction,
Ina Boudier-Bakkerlaan 50, 3582 VA Utrecht, Netherlands
{micah.hrehovcsik,harald.warmelink}@hku.nl
[2] Dutch Game Garden, Jaarbeursplein 6, 3521 AL Utrecht, Netherlands
marilla@dutchgamegarden.nl

Abstract. This paper introduces the design and results of an applied game jam integrated in a game design and development curriculum, which took place February 2016 at HKU University of the Arts Utrecht in the Netherlands. The game jam followed a four-phased structure over the course of four days. Forty-five participants shared their demographics, baseline competency, attitude towards game jams, and learning expectations in a pre-jam questionnaire. In a post-jam questionnaire they assessed their collaboration and learning outcomes. Results are generally positive, although some measures of collaboration constructs were unreliable. Nevertheless, a game jam is in principal a format worthy of introduction into formal game design and development education. Several implications and next steps are discussed.

1 Introduction

The game jam has become an established format for rapid and exploratory game design and development. Starting with the Indie Game Jam and Ludum Dare in 2002, and the Nordic Game Jam in 2006, the format proved attractive enough to start holding the annual Global Game Jam since 2009 [1]. The continued growth of the Global Game Jam has greatly helped establish the game jam as a format, in turn leading to local and regional game jams of all sorts all over the world [2–8].

Central to the format is a large group of people coming together to form small teams who design and develop a playable computer game or digital prototype for entertainment purposes or otherwise (e.g., applied/serious games) befitting a prescribed theme or topic spanning a short period of time (typically a 48-hour period). Or put more formally, '[a] game jam is an accelerated opportunistic game creation event where a game is created in a relatively short timeframe exploring given design constraint(s) and end results are shared publically' [9].

Over the past couple of years, several publications have demonstrated the learning potential and benefits of game jams. The most obvious learning outcomes pertain to the format's actual content of game design and development and include the technological

R. Bottino et al. (Eds.): GALA 2016, LNCS 10056, pp. 257–267, 2016.
DOI: 10.1007/978-3-319-50182-6_23

skills involved, as well as participatory design, rapid prototyping and the multidisciplinary of the entire process [1, 8, 10].

The format's social and collaborative processes have also been explored. The format's social setting tends to bring out participants' helpful behaviour towards each other and allows participants to explore each other's highly differing specific design and development competencies, making new friends and having open debates about the (im)possibilities of game design and development along the way [11, 12]. As such game jams have already proven to be informal learning experiences.

At this point some sort of integration of game jams into formal learning is to be expected, i.e., into actual game design and development or other curricula. Preston et al.'s work [13] triggers such calls given the correlation they found between game jam participation and academic performance in game design/development education. Fowler et al. [1] suggested that the Global Game Jam could be the start of, an introduction to, or a prerequisite for an individual student's 'capstone project' or a team-based project. Highlighting learning theories that connect well to game jams, Law and McDonald [14] propose to introduce a game jam in software development curricula, particularly at Glasgow Caledonian University. Meanwhile, Petri et al. [15] propose to use game jams in different high school classes (not just computer science classes) to learn Pocket Code, a platform for learning programming logic.

The nature and implications of integrating the game jam format into a formal game design and development curriculum require further exploration. The study of the collaboration during game jams and their learning outcomes, for both informal and formal learning, is after all still in its infancy. Thus the question remains: if a given game design/development curriculum is to use game jams, which game jam design would fit into the curriculum and what resulting collaboration and learning outcomes could be observed?

To offer a preliminary answer to the aforementioned question, we present the design and measured collaboration and learning outcomes of a first trial of a game jam held over a four-day period in February 2016 at HKU University of the Arts Utrecht (HKU). It was part of the second-year curriculum of students of games/interaction design and development, where students learn more about the intricacies of applied game design and development. The primary purpose of an applied game is not entertainment and intentionally designed for a specific purpose to create a perceivable impact in society, commercial organizations, research, education, healthcare, etc.

We first present the applied game jam's design and placement in the curriculum, and subsequently offer analyses of collaboration and learning outcomes based on the results of questionnaires filled in during the game jam's run in Hilversum, the Netherlands in February 2016.

2   The Applied Game Jam Format

2.1   Designing the Format

The format is built on experiences and perspectives derived from teaching game design, designing applied games professionally and attending game jams. From the lecturer's perspective the format aims to provide game design and development students a meaningful learning experience where students learn about developing applied games. From a professional experience, the game jam aims to provide a structure of best practices. From the jammer's perspective the game jam allows students to experience what makes a game jam meaningful, challenging and fun, but also frustrating.

2.2 Educational Aims

As an educational format the applied game jam aims to provide an intensive practice-based learning experience concerning applied game design theories, co-design, best practices and studio operations related to development. The format values putting students of applied game and development under time and peer pressure, while having them work autonomously in multi-disciplinary teams.

For HKU students, this project-based learning approach comes as no surprise. At HKU, project-based learning is common. Students are expected to find partial or complete solutions to a problem their real-world client has encountered by working towards a tangible outcome [16]. Students are also expected to learn and practice professional conduct for use in future situations.

The main aspects of project-based learning is that it should be (1) Contextually authentic, where students must deliver a product as an answer to a complex and challenging question from a professional domain [16]; (2) Activate independent learning, where students are provided supervision but must depend on themselves to determine what must be researched and analysed [16]; (3) Learn to work together and collaborate in multidisciplinary teams [16]; (4) Learning to learn, where learning is not only about cognitive knowledge, but includes regulating self-learning and self-thinking processes or so called meta-cognitive learning [16].

The applied game jam includes known techniques used to encourage innovation and creative processes. A critical aspect of innovation techniques is to inspire organisations and teams to tackle fuzzy problems. Especially problems that start out seemingly well-defined but where the path to solving the problem is unclear or directly discoverable [17]. Other kinds of problems touched upon by the game jam are those that are vague and only discoverable by experimentation or by redefining the problem. To find solutions to these fuzzy problems, techniques such as brainstorming, prototyping, and frameworks are introduced to help progression through a process characterised by design terms such as: define, discover, develop, and demonstrate [17].

2.3 The Format

The challenge for game jam participants is to develop a playable prototype under time pressure, while considering the needs of the target audience (a.k.a. the players) and the sponsoring organisation(s) (usually treated as a client) in the design of the game. Within the space of the game jam, participants make use of their game development skills, practice articulating needs of clients, ideate game concepts and test game design assumptions. At the end of the game jam, the results are evaluated by judges, and teams are awarded or recognised for their achievements.

Applied game jam participants are students with relevant development skills, i.e. computer programming, video game visual content, sound and music, project management, and game design. Participants work in multidisciplinary teams assembled during the game jam through team building interventions that let students learn how to form teams, network and promote themselves.

Gamification drives the format's learning goals by valuing process and encouraging best practices. During the game jam, "challenges" worth points are given to the teams. When these challenges are completed, teams receive points, which can then be monitored in real-time for the duration of the game jam via an online scoreboard. The challenges, balanced and determined by a lecturer, are implemented in phases during the game jam and designed to stimulate specific competencies and act as didactic interventions. Challenges are always optional and never mandatory. They are meant to continuously test the participant's abilities to organise themselves, communicate internally and externally, cooperate as a team, use their individual skills wisely, and prioritise tasks. Challenges aim to stimulate teambuilding, design research, technology research/choices, cultural/fun activities, best practices, promotion, feedback moments and cultural exchange. For example, participants are rewarded points for testing their design assumptions by pitching concepts, play-testing paper prototypes, and continuous play-testing during the development of their digital prototype. Challenges also include an academic route that encourages knowledge dissemination about the theme and/or about why games can be applied to domains besides entertainment. Participants are not solely judged on the production value of their final artefacts. They are also judged on the process. This is determined by the points earned from completing challenges and their ability to demonstrate the potential utility and greater application of their game.

During the game jam participants are also introduced to applied game design theory so that they can create mental frameworks about what makes an applied game and why applied games are different than entertainments games. The theory emphasises how good game design equals good games, and using approaches such as the Vitruvius Framework for applied games [18] offers designers a way to consider the balance of game-play experience, utility, and sustainability in their games. Participants are also introduced to several tools, e.g. the Applied Game Design Scope Model [19, 20] which helps to articulate the parameters of an applied game's design. Through such a tool participants analyse the context, content and transfer issues surrounding the theme and problem/question.

The applied game jam format consists of activities separated into four phases (see Fig. 1.): (1) Introduction; (2) Teams; (3) Jam; (4) and Results. The format also includes phases that would not typically be included in a game jam format, e.g. the Intro and Teams phase. Within the Jam phase many activities occur as well as some side-track activities (e.g., essay, presentation and communication activities).

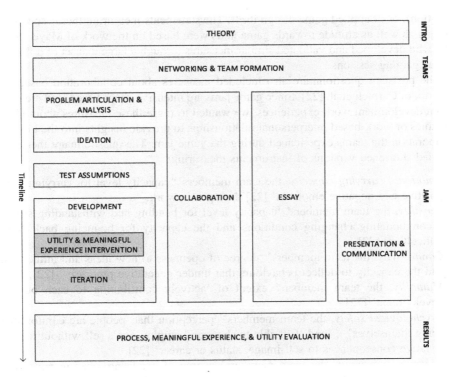

Fig. 1. A schematic of the participant's activities during the four phases of the game jam.

3   Collaboration and Learning Outcomes

3.1   Study Design

To study the collaboration and learning outcomes of this game jam, participants of the game jam's latest run (February 2016 in Hilversum, the Netherlands) were asked to fill in two questionnaires (one pre-jam and one post-jam). Both questionnaires mostly include statements with a 5-point Likert response scale.

In the pre-jam questionnaire, we ascertained participants' basic demographics, baseline competence in game design/development, learning expectations, and attitude towards game jams (including the upcoming one). We also asked how many game jams they had done so far.

In the post-jam questionnaire we asked about the role(s) the respondent had fulfilled in the team, and the amount of team members the respondents had worked with before the game jam. We again measured their attitude towards game jams (including the one they had just experienced), and their perceived learning outcomes, derived from their learning expectations upfront. These statements made a distinction between learning communicative and social skills, professional skills related to game design/development, and expert knowledge related to the domain of applied game design (in this case mental health of adolescents with parents with a psychological condition), or of applied game design itself. The statements measuring these aspects of learning as well as attitude towards game jams were based on the work of Mayer et al. [21], who developed and validated similar measures through a large dataset of different serious gaming sessions.

The post-jam questionnaire also included measures about collaboration based on the work of Carmeli et al. [22]. Since game jams are intensive, team-based, and creative design/development work experiences, we wanted to reuse these measures about team dynamics or work-based interpersonal relationships to provide insights into the kind of collaboration the teams experienced during the game jam. The questionnaire therefore included shortened versions of instruments measuring:

- *Emotional carrying capacity*, the team members' 'capacity level for carrying both positive and negative emotions' [22] during teamwork.
- *Tensility*, the team members' 'capacity level for bending and withstanding strain, accommodating changing conditions and the capacity for bouncing back from difficulties' [22].
- *Connectivity*, the team members' 'degree of openness to new ideas and influences, and the capacity to deflect behaviours that hinder generative processes' [22].
- *Mutuality*, the team members' extent of 'actively contributing to each other's development' [22].
- *Psychological safety*, the team members' 'perception that 'people are comfortable being themselves' ... and 'feel able to show and employ one's self without fear of negative consequences to self-image, status or career' [22].
- *Learning behaviour*, the team members' degree of acquiring, sharing and combining knowledge through e.g. 'frequently seeking new information, speaking up to test the validity of work assumptions and devoting time to figure out ways to improve work processes' [22].

A total of 45 game jam participants of 14 different teams filled in both the pre- and post-jam questionnaires (an average of 3.2 participants per team). Of these participants 27 were male and 18 were female. Their age range was between 18 and 28 years old (mean: 21.3 ± 2.3 years) and participation in prior game jams was between 0 and 5. Just over half of the participants had either never taken part before ($N = 14$) or had taken part once before ($N = 14$). On average the participants had worked with 2.49 ± 2.0 of their teammates on any game design/development project inside or outside school before this game jam (min. 0, max. 7, median 2, mode 0). The statement, 'In general, I receive high marks for courses/assignments related to the content or skills for this game jam' scored an average of 3.40 ± 0.5 (min. 3, max. 5).

Statistical analyses consisted of reliability, descriptive, t-test and correlation analyses. Using Cronbach's alpha we ascertained whether statements reliably measured their corresponding concepts. Only values higher than 0.6 were considered, which led to the conclusion that concerning collaboration the current data only supported the mutuality (0.69) and learning behaviour (0.76) constructs. Learning expectations, outcomes and game jam attitude (both pre- and post-jam) constructs all scored higher than 0.6 on Cronbach's alpha. Paired Samples T-tests were performed to assess differences between attitude towards game jams pre- and post-jam, as well as differences between learning expectations and outcomes. Correlation analyses used Kendall's tau, since the data was (for obvious reasons) not normally distributed (this also limits the validity of the T-tests). Only two-tailed correlations significant at the 0.01 level with a coefficient of at least 0.4 were considered.

3.2 Collaboration

The table below lists descriptives for mutuality and learning behaviour (the two with the best Cronbach's alphas) (Table 1).

Table 1. Mutuality and learning behaviour scores derived from the post-jam questionnaire.

Measurement	Mean	Min	Max
Mutuality	4.17 ± 0.60	3.00	5.00
Learning behaviour	3.60 ± 0.65	2.20	5.00

3.3 Learning Outcomes

The table below lists descriptives for attitude towards game jams (pre- and post-jam), learning expectations and learning outcomes.

T-Tests revealed that differences in attitude towards game jams pre- and post-jam as well as the learning expectations and outcomes (respectively 0.55, −0.23, 0.03, 0.30) are statistically significant, though at differing levels (respectively $p = .000, .000, .001$ and $.052$). It should again be noted, however, that the data is not normally distributed.

3.4 Noteworthy Correlations

The table below shows 15 noteworthy correlations between the applied constructs, which were found using Kendall's Tau (all with $p = .000$).

3.5 Discussion

The results confirm that the constructs of mutuality and learning behaviour, as well as game jam attitude (pre- and post-jam), learning expectations and learning outcomes were statistically valid. The results also show several moderate positive correlations between mostly the learning outcome variables (Table 3). The average game jam attitude scores half a point higher after the game jam, indicating the game jam was a positive experience for participants (see Table 2). Learning expectations and learning outcomes remained similar (see Table 2), indicating that participants were correctly briefed on what they would learn during the jam.

It is noteworthy that other constructs concerning collaboration (Tensility, Connectivity, and Psychological Safety) were not statistically valid. Bearing in mind the limited scope of the sample and the choice to shorten the measures for these constructs, it is interesting to note that these measures are all measuring 'soft' skill-sets which might be less visible or noteworthy to participants, or might be found difficult to express due to cultural differences in the team. With a group of students who are

Table 2. Attitude towards game jams (pre and post), learning expectations and outcomes.

Measurement	Mean	Min	Max
Game jam attitude (pre)	3.51 ± 0.78	1.25	4.75
Learning expectations: communicative and social skills	3.69 ± 0.65	2.00	5.00
Learning expectations: professional skills	3.47 ± 0.79	1.67	5.00
Learning expectations: expert knowledge	3.36 ± 0.63	1.33	4.33
Game jam attitude (post)	4.06 ± 0.73	2.33	5.00
Learning outcomes: communicative and social skills	3.46 ± 0.82	1.33	5.00
Learning outcomes: professional skills	3.50 ± 0.92	1.33	5.00
Learning outcomes: expert knowledge	3.66 ± 0.77	1.67	5.00

Table 3. Noteworthy Kendall's Tau correlations between construct measurements

	Game jam attitude (post)	Prof. skills (expect.)	Expert knowledge (expect.)	Comm. & Soc. skills (outcome)
Game jam attitude (pre)	0.491	0.573		0.447
Communicative & social skills (expect.)	0.466			0.575
Professional skills (expect.)	0.403		0.487	
Expert knowledge (expect.)	0.448			
Communicative & social skills (outcome)	0.507	0.469		
Professional skills (outcome)	0.588			

(p = .000).

already used to practice-led educational methods, reflection concerning their own skills is something which some students find difficult to do as their focus is mainly on the end result of the game jam. The level of experience of jammers was also relatively low, (N = 14, no experience and N = 14, one game jam), which might make reflection on collaboration in hindsight more difficult.

The constructs that were statistically valid (Mutuality and Learning behaviour) are both more concrete in terms of measurable behaviour. This suggests that educational outcomes as well as behaviour which is also in hindsight assessable can be measured more easily than the collaboration process.

4 Conclusions

The results indicate that applied game jams are an effective way of integrating skills/competencies needed as future game designers or in the current work force where innovation, a fast-paced and complex working environment and flexibility are key.

Measuring results of game jam experiences in terms of collaboration and learning outcomes in a quantifiable way is still a challenge. Nevertheless, this paper bridges the gap between design methods used in the games industry and in educational setting by means of a game jam integrated into the curriculum that proves to be a positive experience on several levels.

There are several noteworthy further research opportunities. In a next game jam, the scope and method of analysis could be broadened to include mixed-method approaches such as qualitative results (open-ended interviews) and observations from fellow team members and mentors. This could increase ecological validity and decrease response bias. Adding a cultural measurement scale could also be interesting in terms of whether different values are preferred in cross-cultural teams. If still deemed of interest, measures of the existing constructs could be improved upon to see if a next run will lead to statistically valid results.

The current game jam created 5 internships in Korea and one job offer due to an international game jam participation for a Korean student. This demonstrates the impact an applied game jam can have not just within an educational setting but also in the region. Impact can be measured through means such as cross-over innovation and future collaboration opportunities and can increase networking opportunities and strengthen regional and international partnerships in a relatively short amount of time.

Our efforts organising game jams in the Netherlands and abroad, including in South Korea [23], will continue. JamToday offers a toolkit to facilitate this process [24] for first time organisers of applied game jams. JamToday has illustrated that applied game jams can be organised by all interested parties, whether they are new to the approach or are relative experts in the field. The experiences and lessons learned with the particular game jam analysed in this paper will prove invaluable for next game jams.

References

1. Fowler, A., Khosmood, F., Arya, A., Lai, G.: The global game jam for teaching and learning. In: Proceedings of the 4th Annual Conference on Computing and Information Technology Research and Education New Zealand, pp. 28–34 (2013). http://www.citrenz.ac.nz/conferences/2013/pdf/2013CITRENZ_1_Fowler01-GlobalGameJam_v2.pdf
2. Farhan, E., Kocher, M.: Big team game jams: a framework to emulate big production using game jams with big teams. In: International Conference on Game Jams, Hackathons, and Game Creation Events, Berkeley, CA, pp. 1–7. ACM Press (2016). http://doi.org/10.1145/2897167.2897171
3. Fowler, A., Lai, G., Studios, K., Khosmood, F.: Trends in organizing philosophies of game jams and game hackathons. In: Workshop on Game Jams, Hackathons and Game Creation Events, Pacific Grove, CA, USA (2015). http://ksuweb.kennesaw.edu/~afowle56/pdf/GJ2015_Game_Jam_paper.pdf
4. Kultima, A., Alha, K., Nummenmaa, T.: Design constraints in game design case: survival mode game jam 2016. In: International Conference on Game Jams, Hackathons, and Game Creation Events, pp. 22–29. ACM Press, Berkeley, CA (2016). http://doi.org/10.1145/2897167.2897174

5. Locke, R., Parker, L., Galloway, D., Sloan, R.: The game jam movement: disruption, performance and artwork. In: Workshop Proceedings of the 10th International Conference on the Foundations of Digital Games (Pacific Grove, California, Asilomar Conference Grounds), Pacific Grove, CA, USA (2015). http://ggj.s3.amazonaws.com/GJ2015_submission_5.pdf

6. Pirker, J., Voll, K.: Group forming processes-experiences and best practice from different game jams. In: Workshop on Game Jams, Hackathons and Game Creation Events, Pacific Grove, CA, USA (2015). http://jpirker.com/wp-content/uploads/2013/09/final.pdf

7. Preston, J.A., Chastine, J., O'Donnell, C., Tseng, T., MacIntyre, B.: Game jams: community, motivations, and learning among jammers. Int. J. Game-Based Learn. **2**(3), 51–70 (2012). doi:10.4018/ijgbl.2012070104

8. Shin, K., Kaneko, K., Matsui, Y., Mikami, K., Nagaku, M., Nakabayashi, T., Ono, K., Yamane, S.R.: Localizing *global game jam*: designing game development for collaborative learning in the social context. In: Nijholt, A., Romão, T., Reidsma, D. (eds.) ACE 2012. LNCS, vol. 7624, pp. 117–132. Springer, Heidelberg (2012). doi:10.1007/978-3-642-34292-9_9

9. Kultima, A.: Defining game jam. In: Proceedings of the 9th International Conference on the Foundations of Digital Games, vol. 15 (2015). https://www.researchgate.net/profile/Kultima_Annakaisa/publication/281748266_Defining_Game_Jam/links/55f729d908ae07629dc114bd.pdf

10. Musil, J., Schweda, A., Winkler, D., Biffl, S.: Synthesized essence: what game jams teach about prototyping of new software products. In: 2010 ACM/IEEE 32nd International Conference on Software Engineering, vol. 2, pp. 183–186. IEEE (2010). http://ieeexplore.ieee.org/xpls/abs_all.jsp?arnumber=6062155

11. Reng, L., Schoenau-Fog, H., Kofoed, L.B.: The motivational power of game communities - engaged through game jamming. In: Foundations of Digital Games, Chania, Crete, Greece

12. Smith, P.A., Bowers, C.: Improving social skills through game jam participation. In: International Conference on Game Jams, Hackathons, and Game Creation Events, Berkeley, CA, pp. 8–14. ACM Press (2016). http://doi.org/10.1145/2897167.2897172

13. Preston, J.A.: serious game development: case study of the 2013 CDC games for health game jam, pp. 39–43. ACM Press (2014). http://doi.org/10.1145/2656719.2656721

14. Law, B., McDonald, B.: Game jams: how can they influence software development curricula? In: Workshop on Game Jams, Hackathons and Game Creation Events, Pacific Grove, CA, USA (2015). http://ggj.s3.amazonaws.com/GJ2015_submission_12.pdf

15. Petri, A., Schindler, C., Slany, W., Spieler, B., Smith, J.: Pocket game jams: a constructionist. In: MobileHCI 2015, Copenhagen, Denmark, Approach at Schools, pp. 1207–1211. ACM Press (2015). http://doi.org/10.1145/2786567.2801610

16. Maarse, D.: Meer dan een leuk project: het versterken van projectonderwijs. Hogeschool voor de Kunsten, Utrecht (2011)

17. Silverstein, D., Samuel, P., DeCarlo, N.: The Innovator's Toolkit: 50 Techniques for Predictable and Sustainable Organic Growth. Wiley, Hoboken (2009)

18. Hrehovcsik, M., van Roesell, L.: Using vitruvius as a framework for applied game design. In: Schouten, B. (ed.) Games For Health, pp. 131–152. Springer, Heidelberg (2014)

19. Stubbé, H., van de Ven, J.G.M., Hrehovcsik, M.: Games for top civil servants: an integrated approach. In: Ruggiero, D. (ed.) Cases on the Societal Effects of Persuasive Games. IGI Global, Hershey (2014)

20. Hrehovcsik, M.: teaching "applied" game design: theory and tools. Int. J. Multimedia Ubiquit. Eng. **9**, 243–254 (2014)

21. Mayer, I., Warmelink, H., Bekebrede, G.: Learning in a game-based virtual environment: a comparative evaluation in higher education. Eur. J. Eng. Educ. **38**(1), 85–106 (2013). doi:10.1080/03043797.2012.742872
22. Carmeli, A., Brueller, D., Dutton, J.E.: Learning behaviours in the workplace: the role of high-quality interpersonal relationships and psychological safety. Syst. Res. Behav. Sci. **26**(1), 81–98 (2009). doi:10.1002/sres.932
23. HKU University of the Arts Utrecht: Living Lab Game Jam (2016). http://www.hku.nl/Homeen/Research/ResearchAndInnovationProjects/LivingLabGameJam.htm. Accessed 30 Sept 2016
24. Jam Today: (2016). http://www.jamtoday.eu. Accessed 30 Sept 2016

Analyzing Gamification of "Duolingo" with Focus on Its Course Structure

Duy Huynh, Long Zuo, and Hiroyuki Iida[(✉)]

School of Information Science, Japan Advanced Institute of Science and Technology,
1-1 Asahidai, Nomi, Ishikawa 923-1211, Japan
{duyhuynh,zuolong,iida}@jaist.ac.jp

Abstract. Gamification is the application of game-based elements and game design techniques in non-game contexts. Many learning platforms have applied gamification to increase motivation and engagement. DUOLINGO is a popular language learning platform which has applied gamification. In this paper, game refinement measure is employed to evaluate the gamification of DUOLINGO. The results show that the range of game refinement value of DUOLINGO is reasonable in such as serious environment. By assuming a milestone in a language course as a subgame, it is supposed that the challenges in each milestone could adapt the advancement of learners' skill.

Keywords: Duolingo · Gamification · Language learning platform · Game refinement theory · Attractiveness

1 Introduction

Gamification is a term that refers to the use of game-based elements such as mechanics, aesthetics, and game thinking in non-game contexts aimed at engaging people, motivating action, enhancing learning and solving problem [4,11]. The benefit of game and game-based approaches in education has been investigated since 1980s [7,12,16]. In recent years, there is a growing interest in gamification as well as its applications and implications in the field of education since it provides an alternative to engage and motivate student during the process of learning. While gamification is gaining ground in some fields such as business, marketing, management and wellness initiatives, its application in education is still an emerging trend. In this study, we aim to investigate the attractiveness of DUOLINGO, which is one of the most popular language learning platforms by applying game refinement theory. Due to the lack of research on the gamification in the education domain, numerous questions arise as to clarify how gamification can be used and how it benefits us the most. Therefore, the research question

DUOLINGO[®] and all other trademarks, service marks, graphics and logos used in connection with the Service are trademarks or service marks of DUOLINGO or their respective owners, and certain of them are registered with the United States Patent and Trademark Office.

© Springer International Publishing AG 2016
R. Bottino et al. (Eds.): GALA 2016, LNCS 10056, pp. 268–277, 2016.
DOI: 10.1007/978-3-319-50182-6_24

for this study is "How do game elements make an effect when applying it into an education situation?". To answer this question, we try to quantify the attractiveness of the language course based on the game refinement theory. Specifically, we analyze the game refinement value zone of DUOLINGO.

Game refinement theory has been proposed earlier by Iida *et al.*. [10] to measure the attractiveness and sophistication of games under consideration. A game refinement measure is derived from a game information progress model and has been applied in various games. Classical game theory concerns the optimal strategy from the viewpoint of players, whereas game refinement theory concerns the optimization from the game developer's point of view. The game refinement theory was successfully applied in the domain of board games [10], for Mah Jong [9], and sports games [17]. In fact, there are many challenging questions, especially applying this theory to gamification of serious games.

This paper is organized as follows. Section 2 presents the previous studies in gamification in education and a short sketch of free language-learning platform-DUOLINGO which is our case study in this paper. In Sect. 3, we present the basic idea of game refinement theory and show our analysis using this way. In Sect. 4, we discuss about our experiment and a structure of DUOLINGO language course. Finally, Sect. 5 gives concluding remarks including some future works.

2   Gamification and Education

In this section, we first show the previous study of gamification in education. Then, we give a short sketch of the gamified free language-learning platform DUOLINGO.

2.1   Related Works

We review literatures related to the use of gamification in education. Although some researchers are working on it, there currently is still few works on this subject. Gamification, as a term, was mentioned for the first time in 2008. There are works which have been done, and many papers are written on this topic [1]. Unlike game-based learning which is clearly a game, the essence of gamification is that it occurs in a non-game context; therefore, it would be applied in such a way that would not change the existing practice of learning, and instead focus on making it more engaging and challenging for student [15]. There are increasing number of case studies and researches dealing with gamification in general [8] and in education contexts [2].

Besides, some successful gamification applications, many studies presented a gamification mechanic and its effect when applied into the system. Muntean [13] has shown a theoretical analysis of gamification as a tool to engage users in e-learning platforms. In Fogg's Behaviour Model, gamification mechanics is used to motivate and trigger desired behaviours on learners. He has provided a list of gamification elements and explained how they could apply into an e-learning course. Recently, Scepanovic *et al.* [15] also give a discussion and evaluation of gamification mechanics based on literature review and analysis of implementing gamification concepts in Higher Education learning.

While majority of studies report overall positive results of applying game elements and mechanics into the system, and their effects in motivating and engaging learners. Our study aims at analyzing and measuring the attractiveness of game elements and its effect when combined with a language course's structure. By applying game refinement theory as an assessment method, we could figure out specific factors, which directly make an effect on a platform, and a degree of their effectiveness. By those factors mentioned above, we could adjust them to increase their attractiveness and their making motivation in a platform. Moreover, we could compare the impact between the elements based on a degree of their attractiveness to list elements, which make the most effectiveness in a platform, and enrich them. Those are different points of this study compared to previous works. This contribution will lead to a better understanding of the effects of gamification in learning domain.

2.2 Duolingo

DUOLINGO is a gamified free language-learning platform created by professor Luis Von Ahn and his graduate student Severin Hacker. The system is designed so that users could learn languages, while helping DUOLINGO to translate documents. DUOLINGO became publicly available in 2012 with more than 300000 users. As of April 2016, it offers 59 different language courses across 23 languages [5]. The authors of DUOLINGO skillfully apply gamification into their system in order to engage and motivate their users. They have used some game-elements in their system. They are shown as follows [6]:

- Reward: In DUOLINGO, lingot is a reward. Users can easily collect dozen of lingots by completing their lesson or skill.
- Leader-board: which shows users how they are doing compared to their friends, these are some great motivators to help the users coming back and learning.
- Level-system: providing a way to track users daily activity and compete with their friends, XP (experience point) also determines users language "level", which is displayed on their profile page and above their comments in discussions.
- Badges: DUOLINGO has some achievement tokens which are the skills a user has gained. They are displayed on user's profile. Badges is an excellent tool for making people feel invested in their study.

Although DUOLINGO has used many game elements in their platform, we specifically analyze only "badges" in this study because the important part of successful gamification is content and learning material [15]. Moreover, a main purpose of learners in DUOLINGO is learning a second language, while badges is used to lift up the motivation of learners when they study. Hence, "badges" is an important element in the platform. The game element "badges" is combined in harmony with a learning content to construct the main structure of a language course.

The structure of a language course includes some elements as follows. The core element in a course is its lessons. The lesson is well-designed, drilling skills of user with several different kinds of challenges. They do not get too repetitive, and they are just easy and fun to do [6]. They are categorized into small sets which are called skills by part of speech or lesson vocabulary meaning such as: verb, adjective, sport, food, etc. Each skill has a strength bar, which will be full only when users have passed all lessons in the skill. However, the strength will be decreased overtime to represent "words fading from memory". At the beginning, only basic skill is available, other skills are locked. To unlock other skills, users have to complete all their available skills. The skills in a skill-tree are split into check-points which represent for stages or the milestones of user's study process. Although there is no reward given when users reach each milestone, we could see the expression of milestones in the skill-tree after users have completed the number of skills.

3   Analyzing Gamification of Duolingo

This section presents a basic idea of game refinement theory and a game progress model is figured out with a focus on the course's structure of DUOLINGO to quantify its attractiveness.

3.1   Assessment Method

We show a short sketch of the basic idea of game refinement theory [18]. The 'game progress' is twofold. One is a game speed or scoring rate, and another one is game information progress with a focus on the game outcome. Game information progress represents how certain is the result of the game in certain time or steps. Having full information of the game progress, i.e. after its conclusion, game progress $x(t)$ will be given as a linear function of time t with $0 \leq t \leq t_k$ and $0 \leq x(t) \leq x(t_k)$, as shown in Eq. (1).

$$x(t) = \frac{x(t_k)}{t_k}t \qquad (1)$$

However, the game information progress given by Eq. (1) is unknown during the in-game period. The presence of uncertainty during the game, often until the final moments of a game, reasonably renders game progress as exponential. Hence, a realistic model of game information progress is given by Eq. (2).

$$x(t) = x(t_k)(\frac{t}{t_k})^n \qquad (2)$$

In Eq. (2), n stands for a constant parameter which is given based on the perspective of an observer of the game. Then acceleration of game information progress could be obtained by deriving Eq. (2) twice. Solving it at $t = t_k$, we have Eq. (3).

$$x''(t_k) = \frac{x(t_k)}{(t_k)^n}(t_k)^{n-2}n(n-1) = \frac{x(t_k)}{(t_k)^2}n(n-1) \qquad (3)$$

It is assumed in the current model that game information progress in any type of game is encoded and transported in our brain. We do not yet know the mechanism of information processing in the brain, but it is likely that the acceleration of information progress is subject to the forces and laws of physics. Therefore, we expect that the larger the value $\frac{x(t_k)}{(t_k)^2}$ is, the more exciting the game becomes. Thus, we compute its root square, $\frac{\sqrt{x(t_k)}}{t_k}$, and use the result as a game refinement measure for the considered game. We assign it as R-value, which is short shown in Eq. (4).

$$R = \frac{\sqrt{x(t_k)}}{t_k} \tag{4}$$

The brief results of previous works [14] are shown in Table 1. According to Table 1, we propose a suitable approach for various game types by using the described model. We see that sophisticated games have R-value in the appropriate range, 0.07–0.08. It has been proposed that information acceleration is one of the direct factors of engagement for all game types.

Table 1. Measures of game refinement for boardgames and sports

Game	R-value
Chess	0.074
Go	0.076
Basketball	0.073
Soccer	0.073

3.2   Game Progress Model in Duolingo

DUOLINGO is different from sports and boardgames. It is gamification product, which means that they use game elements to create enjoyment points in learning environment. Therefore, in this study, we highlight a gamification structure in each language course as the main aspect. As we mentioned in Sect. 2, the structure of language course is constructed by some core elements such as lesson and skill. Furthermore, following the basic idea of game refinement theory, game progress is twofold, known as goal and time or steps to archive the goal in sports and boardgames [17]. In a language course, the goal of learners is to complete their study by getting all badges in the skill-tree. To archive a badge, users must complete all lessons in a skill. Therefore, the game progress of DUOLINGO language course can be measured by skills.

Let S and L be the average number of skills and the average number of lessons in the same language courses, respectively. If one knows the game information progress, for example after the game, the game progress $x(t)$ is given by Eq. (5).

$$x(t) = \frac{S}{L} t \tag{5}$$

However, the game information progress given by Eq. (5) is unknown during the in-game period. Hence, a realistic model of game information progress of DUOLINGO language course is given by Eq. (6).

$$x(t) = S(\frac{t}{L})^n \tag{6}$$

Then acceleration of game information progress is obtained by deriving Eq. (6) twice. Solving it with $t = L$, we have Eq. (7).

$$x''(L) = \frac{Sn(n-1)}{L^n}L^{n-2} = \frac{S}{L^2}n(n-1) \tag{7}$$

Therefore, the game refinement value of a language course in DUOLINGO can be described as Eq. (8).

$$R = \frac{\sqrt{S}}{L} \tag{8}$$

4   Data Collection and Discussion

This section presents a gamification analysis of DUOLINGO using game refinement measure and provides some discussions.

4.1   Data Collection

DUOLINGO has 120 million users around the world and currently teaches 19 distinct languages. The most popular courses are available for speakers of a variety of languages: for example, we can learn English from 21 different languages [19]. In order to make the data more objective and reasonable, we collect the statistics by observing a structure of each popular language courses. On the DUOLINGO's website, we go to collect the information of completed language courses and group them by popular learning languages, as shown in Table 2. In each language course, we could get the number of skills by counting a number of badges,

Table 2. Popular languages in DUOLINGO

Language	Number of courses	Total number of enrolment
English	21	181,412,000
Spanish	5	66,199,700
French	6	45,724,000
German	6	28,083,200
Italian	3	18,483,000
Portuguese	2	9,870,000
Others	1	11,532,000

which are displayed on a homepage. Besides, we also get the number of lessons in a skill by adding all number of lessons under each badge icon.

After the data collection step, we calculate game refinement values. For instance, to calculate R-value of English courses, we have to find the average number of lesson L and the average number of skills S of 21 English courses. As a result, R-value were calculated by Eq. (8), which is shown in Table 3.

Table 3. Measures of game refinement for DUOLINGO language course

Language	S	L	R-value
English	55.619	291.958	0.0259
Spanish	64.142	319.571	0.0250
French	72.222	346.333	0.0243
German	89	381.25	0.0243
Portuguese	68	379	0.0204
Italian	66	385	0.0200

4.2   Discussion

In the previous studies (see Table 1), R-values of sophisticated games like sports and boardgames often fall into the range between 0.07 and 0.08. However, we noticed that the results of DUOLINGO show much lower. Here we take English language as an example, there are 55.6 skills and 291.9 lessons on average, so the R-value is 0.0259. To achieve 55.6 skills, learners must complete more than 291 lessons. Moreover, R-value of Portuguese is lower than English for the average number of skills and lessons are 68 and 379. According to Eq. (8), R-value increases when the number of lessons decreases, which means that the goal is easy to achieve. This is similar to increasing the number of skills. R-value falls into the range between 0.020 and 0.025, which shows that the "game" in language course will be too challenging. As we introduced, DUOLINGO is a learning platform, which means that it is a serious environment and game elements are used to increase motivation and engagement of learners, they are not used to make a course become entertaining or relaxing as fun games. Hence, the R-value range is reasonable.

However, with the degree of challenging which is indicated by R-value, the "game" in language course only increases the motivation for advanced users or who learned with a purpose. With novice users or nonnative-language learners, they give up easily their study. There is a reason why DUOLINGO authors have applied a creating milestones technique, as mentioned at the end of Sect. 2, to respond learner's efforts. Like as a game, the skills in course are structured so that learners may have various "levels" of goals. Generally, the requirements of each "level" of goal get increasingly harder from completing the initial tasks until completing the course. This allows learners to learn and practice skills.

We made a brief analysis of the most popular language course *"English for Spanish speakers"* (EFSS) to see the obvious effect of creating "milestone" technique. We assume that each milestone in a course is a sub-game. Next, we calculate R-value in each sub-game in a course, which is shown in Table 4. The R-value of each milestone shows that the milestone is designed for various types of learners. For instance, in the first milestone, R-value is 0.081. This value is higher than the results of the sophisticated sports and boardgames, which implies that the "game" in the first milestone is so exciting and attractive for beginners. The increase in the requirement is to give more challenging and exciting to learners since their skill gets better at every milestone. To prevent the course from getting bored, the number of lessons and skills should be lower, then the performance of learners would be higher. Moreover, after going through many challenges, learners need enjoyments in order to avoid the drop-out from the course. Therefore, in later milestones, the R-value tends to increase to be a higher value such as 0.094, which is shown in Table 4.

Table 4. Measures of game refinement for each milestone in EFSS course

Milestone	S	L	R-value
1	10	39	0.081
2	12	56	0.062
3	15	97	0.039
4	14	79	0.047
5	8	30	0.094

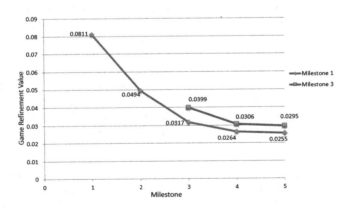

Fig. 1. Game refinement trends when starting from Milestone 1 and Milestone 3

We collected the data of each milestone to quantify the R-value. In general, users usually start from the first milestone and accomplish the final goal. Thus, the trend of R-value for normal players is depicted in Fig. 1. We noticed that the

R-value goes down sharply and maintaining the low value after the 4th milestone. However, for some advanced users, they can start from the third milestone by ignoring the first and the second ones. In that case, we also calculate the R-value for the players who start at the third milestone. An advanced user who starts from the third milestone would not feel entertainment, for the game is maintaining the low value.

5   Concluding Remarks

DUOLINGO is a huge system, we could not analyze all of elements at the same time. In this study, we have focused on a "badge" element, which has been used in the skill-tree to analyze the attractiveness. Badges is an important game element, which is used to boot the motivation of learners when they study. As a result, data analysis has shown that the game refinement value falls into the range between 0.020 and 0.025, which is much lower than other sophisticated fun games. It is reasonable because DUOLINGO is used in the serious environment or non-game context. We also quantified the attractiveness of each milestone, and made a comparison between the players who start at the first and third milestone. It is assumed in this study that every milestone in a course is a sub-game. After the brief analyzing, the game refinement value indicates that the challenges in each milestone could adapt the advancement of learners' skill. The result shows that DUOLINGO is enjoyable for new comers who start from the first milestone, however, less enjoyable for advanced users who start at the third milestone. In this case, it is essential to increase the degree of gamification of DUOLINGO by decreasing the number of lessons or increasing the number of skills in the target courses.

Future works will focus on the analysis of the other game elements which have been applied into DUOLINGO, and perform more experiments to understand the effects of "milestone" technique. Activity theory-based model of serious game (ATMSG) [3] is known as an analyzing framework, which helps users understand in depth the roles of each piece in each happened actions of a game. We will consider to use an ATMSG to figure out the used game elements in the considered game, and understand their goals before measuring game refinement values. Additionally, we will apply game refinement theory in more learning platforms to find the most effective structure from the perspective of gamification.

Acknowledgments. The authors wish to thank the anonymous referees for their constructive comments that helped to improve the article considerably. This research is funded by a grant from the Japan Society for the Promotion of Science (JSPS), within the framework of the Grant-in-Aid for Challenging Exploratory Research (grant number 26540189).

References

1. A brief history of gamification: part III the definitions. http://edulearning2. blogspot.jp/2014/03/a-brief-history-of-gamification-part.html
2. Barata, G., Gama, S., Jorge, J., Gonalves, D.: Engaging engineering students with gamification. In: 5th International Conference Games and Virtual Worlds for Serious Applications (VS-GAMES) (2013)
3. Carvalho, M.B., Bellotti, F., Berta, R., De Gloria, A., Islas Sedano, C., Baalsrud Hauge, J., et al.: An activity theory-based model for serious games analysis and conceptual design. Comput. Educ. **87**, 166–181 (2015)
4. Deterding, S., Dixon, D., Khaled, R., Nacke, L.: From game design elements to gamefulness: defining "gamification". In: 15th International Academic MindTrek Conference: Envisioning Future Media Environments, pp. 9–15 (2011)
5. Duolingo. https://en.wikipedia.org/wiki/Duolingo
6. Gamification Teardown: Duolingo. https://blog.captainup.com/how-gamification-makes-language-learning-even-more-awesome-on-duolingo/
7. Gee, J.P.: What Video Games Have to Teach About Learning and Literacy. Palgrave Macmillan, New York (2003)
8. Hamari, J., Koivisto, J., Sarsa, H.: Does gamification work? A literature review of empirical studies on gamification. In: 47th Hawaii International Conference on System Sciences, Hawaii, USA (2014)
9. Iida, H., Takahara, K., Nagashima, J., Kajihara, Y., Hashimoto, T.: An application of game-refinement theory to Mah Jong. In: Rauterberg, M. (ed.) ICEC 2004. LNCS, vol. 3166, pp. 333–338. Springer, Heidelberg (2004). doi:10.1007/978-3-540-28643-1_41
10. Iida, H., Takeshita, N., Yoshimura, J.: A metric for entertainment of boardgames: its implication for evolution of chess variants. In: Nakatsu, R., Hoshino, J. (eds.) Entertainment Computing. ITIFIP, vol. 112, pp. 65–72. Springer, Heidelberg (2003). doi:10.1007/978-0-387-35660-0_8
11. Kapp, K.M.: The Gamification of Learning and Instruction: Game-Based Methods and Strategies for Training and Education. Pfeiffer, San Francisco (2012)
12. Klopfer, E.: Augmented Learning: Research and Design of Mobile Educational Games. MIT Press, Cambridge (2008)
13. Muntean, C.I.: Raising engagement in e-learning through gamification. In: 6th International Conference on Virtual Learning (ICVL2012), pp. 323–329 (2011)
14. Nossal, N., Iida, H.: Game refinement theory and its application to score limit games. 2014 IEEE Games Media Entertain. (GEM), 1–3 (2014). doi:10.1109/GEM. 2014.7048120
15. Scepanovic, S., Zaric, N., Matijevic, T.: Gamification in higher education learning - state of the art, challenges and opportunities. In: Serbia: International Conference on e-Learning (2015)
16. Shaffer, D.W.: How Computer Games Help Children Learn. Palgrave Macmillan, New York (2006)
17. Sutiono, A.P., Purwarianti, A., Iida, H.: A mathematical model of game refinement. In: Reidsma, D., Choi, I., Bargar, R. (eds.) INTETAIN 2014. LNICST, vol. 136, pp. 148–151. Springer, Heidelberg (2014). doi:10.1007/978-3-319-08189-2_22
18. Takeuchi, J., Ramadan, R., Iida, H.: Game refinement theory and its application to Volleyball. Research report 2014-GI-31(3), Information Processing Society of Japan, pp. 1–6 (2014)
19. Which countries study which languages, and what can we learn from it? http://making.duolingo.com/which-countries-study-which-languages-and-what-can-we-learn-from-it

Mobile Games

Mobile Learning Game Authoring Tools: Assessment, Synthesis and Proposals

Aous Karoui[✉], Iza Marfisi-Schottman, and Sébastien George

COMUE UBL, Université du Maine, EA 4023, LIUM, 72085 Le Mans, France
{Aous.Karoui, Iza.Marfisi,
Sebastien.George}@univ-lemans.fr

Abstract. Mobile Learning Games (MLGs) show great potential for increasing engagement, creativity and authentic learning. Yet, despite their great potential for education, the use of MLGs by teachers, remains limited. This is partly due to the fact that MLGs are often designed to match a specific learning context, and thus cannot be reusable for other contexts. Therefore, researchers have recently designed various types of MLG authoring tools. However, these authoring tools are not always adapted to non-computer-scientists or non-game-designers. Hence, we propose in this paper to focus on five existing MLG authoring tools, in order to assess their features and usability with the help of five teachers, who are used to organizing educational field trips. In the second part of this paper, we present an approach for designing a MLG authoring tool, based on the lacks identified through the analysis, and tailored to the teachers' different profiles and needs.

Keywords: Mobile learning game · Authoring tool · Usability · Assessment

1 Introduction

Mobile Learning Games (MLGs) have proven their efficiency not only for improving students' engagement but also for improving effective learning in certain studies. For example, *Frequency1550* [1], is a MLG designed to learn about medieval Amsterdam History, which helped high-school students get higher scores on the knowledge test than with regular lessons. Other MLGs have also proven their effectiveness for improving engagement (e.g. *TheMobileGame*, designed to introduce a university campus in Berlin to new comers, that students preferred to the classic visiting tour [2]) and creativity (e.g. *skattjakt*, a MLG co-designed with students to promote physical activity while learning a novel [3]).

Now that smartphones are widespread among teenagers and that schools are increasingly equipped with tablets [4], using MLGs in class has never been simpler. Moreover, MLGs can take advantage of mobile devices' assets to enhance learning and gaming experience (e.g. position, orientation and proximity sensors, media capturing and recording, augmented reality on learning objects…). However, very few teachers actually create a MLG for their course. Therefore, we propose in this paper, to analyze the usability and the features offered by current MLG authoring tools, in order to understand this phenomenon. As a second step, we present our work for designing a

© Springer International Publishing AG 2016
R. Bottino et al. (Eds.): GALA 2016, LNCS 10056, pp. 281–291, 2016.
DOI: 10.1007/978-3-319-50182-6_25

MLG authoring tool based on the lacks identified through this analysis and tailored to the teachers' different profiles.

2 Methods

2.1 Screening Set

To outline our screening set, we define the MLGs that we are interested in, as following: a MLG, is a mobile app, combining pedagogic content with a playful scenario to enhance learning, and taking advantage of mobile devices' assets (e.g. location, orientation and proximity sensors, media capturing and recording, augmented reality…).

Consequently, we focused on authoring tools that could be used to create these MLGs, whether they were initially intended to produce MLGs, mobile games or even general mobile apps. As a matter of fact, many interesting Serious Game authoring tools found in literature could not be taken into account in this study, as they do not provide the mobile assets nor do they make mobile apps.

2.2 Selection Method

We chose to focus only on functional authoring tools available on the Internet and usable by teachers who do not have any programming skills or game-design experience. Many MLG authoring tools we found in literature could not be a part of this analysis, since they were still under development or not accessible for public use[1]. Other interesting tools such as ARLearn could not be included since they were not destined to be used by teacher on their own [5]. The five authoring tools we selected are freely accessible online. They were selected on account of provided technical features, essentially the mobile assets needed to create efficient MLGs that we have identified in a previous work [6]. In addition, we took into account the provided assistance to educational and gameplay design (i.e. setting up learning content and provided game mechanics).

2.3 Assessment Method

Our authoring tool assessment is based on a criteria grid[2] regarding two perspectives:

The provided technical features: We identified the features provided by each authoring tool by trying to reproduce existing MLGs that we identified in previous work [6] which proved to enhance learning and engagement. A symbolic score concludes each assessment, in order to obtain comparable results between the five authoring tools.

---

[1] http://perso.univ-lemans.fr/ ~ akaroui/oa_list.htm.

[2] The assessment grid is available here: http://perso.univ-lemans.fr/ ~ akaroui/ot_grid.htm.

The authoring tools usability: In order to measure usability, we firstly used Bastien and Scapin's guidelines for measuring Human-Computer Interfaces (HCI) usability [7]. We then asked five teachers, who organize educational field trips every year, to try to design one of their usual outing activities, with these authoring tools, while adding a few game mechanics that we recommended such as scores and timers. This time, the assessment score was the average between our rating based on the ergonomic criteria cited above and the teachers rating based on their user experience.

3   Authoring Tool Analysis

3.1   ARIS (Augmented Reality and Interactive Storytelling)

The ARIS[3] project started in 2008 at the University of Wisconsin, in order to design an open source tool for creating learning games for iPhones [8].

Feature Assessment. Technically, ARIS incorporates geolocation, QR-codes, uploading media content (photos, sounds), and options for managing teams. The web editor provides a variety of "games objects" to interactively include media content into scenarios. Those "game objects" are created by the designer and then placed on the map representing the game field. For example, *"plaques"* consist in textual tags for showing static information to players. They can be used for tours and for providing narrative events in a game. Additionally, the *"conversation"* object is another way of providing information to players. They combine text and media resources to provide virtual conversations for players to facilitate their progression in the game. ARIS also provides *"quests"* which comprise a notification system to help players focus on what they can and should be doing. In addition to the "game objects", ARIS put to use *"locks"* components, which are triggers defining how players access content by turning the "game objects" visible or invisible during the game. Finally, in order to create coherent game steps, all elements should be held together within *"scenes"* which are abstract units organizing triggers and game objects. Furthermore, ARIS provides a JavaScript API that allows programmers to modify the MLGs in detail. These customizations range from adding interactive mini-games, to complex menu structuring, navigation flow redirection and altering a player's inventory in ways not currently supported by ARIS.

ARIS is surrounded by a large community of users and developers who continuously contribute to the project by adding new features and animating online forums. Considering all the features cited above, we assigned 4/5 to ARIS for its features.

Usability Assessment. From a usability perspective, the major drawback of ARIS is the unusual vocabulary related to the "game objects" presented in the previous

---

[3] http://arisgames.org/make/.

paragraph. Indeed, the five teachers who tested the authoring tools with us, found that terms such as *"plaques, quests, conversations ..."* are completely incomprehensible. Using ARIS is therefore impossible without consulting the online manual and the tutorials that need several hours to be discerned. Three of the five interviewed teachers found that tutorials were "too long" and said that they would have "given up". Finally, the feature customization part is reserved for programmers as it relies on the use of JavaScript programming language. Thus, considering ergonomic criteria and the teachers' feedback for the usability test, we assign 2/5 to ARIS.

3.2   App Inventor 2

App Inventor 2 is an authoring environment for Android mobile apps[4]. It is also very useful for rapid prototyping mobile serious games [9].

Feature Assessment. The App Inventor 2 web editor offers a wide range of pallets, from primary mobile apps components (e.g. buttons, labels, sliders ...), to elaborate data storage components (e.g. storing files, data tables, database ...). Sensors (e.g. position, orientation and proximity sensors), multimedia and connectivity tools (e.g. Bluetooth, SMS, web connectivity ...) are provided as well. All the items can be knit together thanks to the *blockly*[5] library, incorporated within the App Inventor 2 editor. Indeed, blockly is a powerful block programming interface allowing users with a low programming background (e.g. children, programming novices) to easily link and configure items in order to get a functional program. These items could be used as dependencies and triggers for MLG design.

App Inventor 2 is a widely used authoring tool. A large community of designers but also developers, contribute to its content enrichment every day. Considering all the features cited above, we attribute 4.5/5 to App Inventor 2 for its features.

Usability Assessment. App Inventor 2 provides a rich Graphical User Interface (GUI) based on the SPI (*Single Page Interface*) model. Indeed, all the design components are available on the main design page, categorized by type and attainable by *drag-and-drop*. Although, the main design page contains several boxes (e.g. palette, items properties, screen viewer ...) and two main views. The first one is intended for components set up to the mobile viewer box. The second view is intended to coordinate components in order to get a working program via the *blockly* editor. However, this design way, even though much simpler than real programming, is not intended for people without programming background. Indeed, the teachers we interviewed had not any technical background and gave us feedbacks such as "this is for computer-scientists", 'I cannot go through it". Consequently, App Inventor 2 usability score was set to 1.5/5.

---

4 http://appinventor.mit.edu/explore/.

5 https://developers.google.com/blockly/.

3.3   Pocket Code

Pocket Code[6] is an open source authoring tool realized within the Catrobat project [10] for creating and sharing mobile learning apps by children and teenagers.

Feature Assessment. Pocket Code is based on three main components (*scripts, graphics* and *sounds*) that could be highly customized and linked together in order to create playful scenarios. This coordination is feasible by assembling visual programming blocs as same as with App Inventor 2. Thus, Pocket Code incorporates QR-code set up, multimedia content managing (i.e. text, image and sound) and several types of sensors (i.e. location, orientation and proximity). However, Pocket Code is entirely executable on mobile devices and then allows designers to create mobile apps even on their smartphones.

The editor also includes a game scene recorder to easily share created scenes on YouTube. All the projects created by users are open-source and available online in order to be reusable. For example, interesting education-specific resources have been created by the Technology Enhanced Learning (TEL) community and are available online[7]. Pocket Code's large users and developers' community keeps empowering tutorials and creating useful Frameworks such as "Pocket Paint"; a library that enables Pocket Code users to edit images. Hence, Pocket Code's features score was set to 4/5.

Usability Assessment. Although setting the design process on mobile is an original feature for taking advantage of mobiles portability, we believe that this design mode considerably limits the ergonomic comfort required to create MLGs. Yet, the minimized screen size does not provide a full vision of the scenario components (i.e. *scripts, graphics,* and *sounds*). Even these components can be shown on several tabs, a non-complete items view implies memorizing too much data and then would considerably augment memory load especially for novices designers. Indeed, Bastien and Scapin [7] report that this would absolutely worsen the user experience. Besides, some teachers clearly said that they don't prefer designing on mobile as they do not have access to their educational resources, typically stored on their computers. Other difficulties may arise when designing on mobile, such as problems with inaccuracy of touch interactions. Consequently, the average score for Pocket Code for usability is 1.5/5.

3.4   Furet Factory

Furet Factory[8] is an online platform for designing mobile games. It was developed by *Furet Company*[9], specialized in designing cultural heritage games.

Feature Assessment. Several types of games are available (e.g. treasure hunt, interactive tour, quiz). The game stages can also be set up by customizing the challenges:

---

[6] http://www.catrobat.org/intro/.

[7] https://edu.catrob.at/.

[8] http://www.furetfactory.com/.

[9] http://www.furetcompany.com/.

puzzle, multiple choice question, riddle, geolocation. The points earned by players translate into levels of expertise (e.g. Amateur Detective, Chief Inspector, Emeritus Adventurer, etc.). In addition, players can also evaluate the games and assign points to game designers. Score tables are published online and players can invite their friends to play via social networks.

The technical features for Furet Factory are very limited in comparison to the authoring tools analyzed above. Indeed, it lacks features such as QR-code support, including rich multimedia items (e.g. sounds, videos) and configurable triggers. Moreover, it does not handle multiplayer games or provide means of communication between players. Consequently, we attribute 1.5/5 to Furet Factory, for its features.

Usability Assessment. The design process proposed by Furet Factory is instantaneously apprehended. The notions introduced for game items and steps are fully clear and make the design process intuitive even for a first-time user. In consequence, there is no need to go through tutorials to use this authoring tool. In terms of guidance, components information is shown on demand and through pop-up windows in an interactive way. All the teachers participating in the test where comfortable with Furet Factory and gave us positive feedback. In consequent, the average between the resulting score from the ergonomic criteria and the teachers' usability rating is 4/5.

3.5   mLearn4web

mLearn4web[10] is an open-source authoring tool for creating mobile learning activities [11] that can be used for creating MLGs.

Feature Assessment. mLearn4web incorporates the essential features for taking advantage of mobile assets. Then, geolocation, multimedia content management (sounds, videos, images) and QR-code support are provided. The resulting mobile app is generated on a web responsive format, making it compatible with all mobile devices. However, as mLearn4web is not initially intended for MLGs, it does not provide items that could be set up to behave as game mechanics (e.g. scores or timers), as it is possible with App Inventor 2. Similarly, there is no way to alter the linear activities sequences. Consequently, based on a MLG design perspective, we attribute 2.5/5 for its features.

Usability Assessment. The simple design interface does not require specific tutorials to get familiar with. The GUI is interactive and content can be intuitively added by *drag-and-drop*. The design process consist in creating screens (which will contain activities) and gradually adding resources to them.

Although the provided components are not complex to understand, the tool doesn't provide any guidance or help on demand. For this reason, the teachers found mLearn4web less practical than *Furet Factory*, even though it provides an intuitive interface. In consequent, the average between the notation resulting from the ergonomic criteria and the teachers' usability notation is 3/5.

---

[10] http://www.mlearn4web.eu/.

4 Synthesis

4.1 Analysis Summary

According to the analysis detailed above, we notice that the authoring tools which have a top rating for their features, have very low scores for their usability and vice versa. Thus, the analyzed authoring tools can be split into two categories. The first category is composed of the authoring tools that offer rich low-level-item-based GUIs, such as *ARIS*, *App Inventor2* and *Pocket Code*. Even though it is possible to create MLGs with these tools, the effort and expertise required to use them is overwhelming for teachers. Indeed, reading the user manuals and watching the video tutorials to learn how to aggregate low-level items (e.g. text, buttons, media resources) into game mechanics (e.g. game units, scores, timers) demands a considerable effort. This effort was considered unacceptable by three of the five interviewed teachers, while the two others reported that they would prefer easier authoring tools. The second category covers the authoring tools that include few or limited features, but which are relatively simple to use, such as *Furet Factory* and *mLearn4web*. The problem here is that these authoring tools do not provide enough design features to create effective MLGs, such as those cited in the introduction. If the authoring tools in this second category provided more features, would this be the solution? According to HCI specialists, augmenting information density in general, implies augmenting perceptive and cognitive workload [7]. Therefore, we believe that augmenting authoring tools features would make them join the first category and so the usability problem would persist.

4.2 Understanding the Teachers Needs

To explore the previously discussed issues, we sent an online questionnaire to several teachers' mailing lists asking if the teachers would like to try MLGs during their learning outings. Out of the 26 teachers who responded, we selected five teachers to conduct qualitative interviews. We selected these teachers in such a way to have a variety of teaching levels (i.e. middle-school, high-school and college) and field trips (i.e. analyzing landscapes (botany), examining rocks (geology), and observing biodiversity (biology)). Each interview lasted between one and two hours, and consisted in testing a couple of the authoring tools analyzed above. Then we asked the teachers send us their feedback and usability scores for the remaining authoring tools by email. The second part of the interview consisted in co-designing the GUI of a MLG authoring tool that would match their needs (discussed in the last subsection of this paper).

Three of the five interviewed teachers affirmed that they were interested in creating MLGs if it did not take them more than half a day. Actually, they reported that, to start with, they just want to reproduce the pedagogic content of their field trips on mobile devices, and add some game mechanics (i.e. scores, timers, collaboration) to create a playful scenario. The two other teachers affirmed that they already had some experience in learning games design and would probably spend more than half a day in the design process. The analysis of the questionnaire sent out to teachers' mailing also shows this disparity. Out of the 20 answers for this question, 14 teachers said that they were willing to try MLGs and 6 said that it would depend on the required investment level.

Moreover, we do not exclude the fact that teachers' engagement in designing MLGs could vary, depending on their growing experience and also on the authoring tool usability. Thus, this could imply changing in the teachers' investment and have to be taken into account in the design approach that we propose.

Following the five interviews, we notice that teachers are initially divided in two categories. The first one comprises teachers who do not have any game design experience but are quite interested in the topic and would like to try MLG creation, if it doesn't take too much time to be set up. The second category comprises teachers who are motivated for using MLGs and would be willing to put in more effort, if they can create the MLGs they want. In the next section, we propose an innovative approach for satisfying the needs of different teachers' profiles. Indeed, even if we detect two main users' profiles, it could be seen as a continuum and intermediate profiles could exist.

5   Current Work and Proposals

5.1   Authoring Tool Complexity in TEL

Since research on MLG authoring tool usability is lacking, we decided to look for solutions for the authoring tool usability problem in larger areas such as TEL. Even though most of research in TEL focuses on learning environments' usability, there are several works about the usability of learning environment authoring tools. Murray for example, summarized in 2004 [12], the authoring tool design tradeoffs in three categories: power, usability and cost. He proposes a collaborative design with multiple roles as the optimal solution for the authoring tool complexity problem. Given that in this case, the authoring tool would be powerful as each of the designing team members would contribute to the authoring process, and usable as each participant would not face difficulty in handling his/her own part of authoring. In the same context, Ritter [13] adheres totally to the idea that the authoring process should be performed by a designing team. Furthermore, he suggests that different interfaces should be built to support different roles within the designing team "rather than having one huge monolithic authoring tool". Similarly, Oja, in a study for improving usability in complex software systems [14], concludes that systems' interfaces should anticipate the variety of roles and areas of expertise.

Nevertheless, we do not embrace the idea of collaborative design as it implies hiring costly authoring experts. Besides, in his latest research, Murray [15] characterizes the complexity of systems in general terms (such as Complexity Science and Hierarchical Complexity Theory) and updates the tradeoffs that were presented in [12]. In [15], the idea of the collaborative authoring tool does not seem to be retained anymore as it is not brought into discussion again.

Even though, we retain the idea of differentiating interfaces, not for different roles but for the different teachers profiles identified on the previous section. Furthermore, it could be perfectly associated to the Hidden complexity quoted by Murray in [12]. Indeed, the Hidden complexity is a strategy for making tools more usable by hiding the advanced tools and making common and easy tools more salient. We explain our approach of using those insights in the next subsection.

5.2   A Multi-view GUI Based on a Nested Design Process

Based on the teachers' interviews, and to deal with the diversified needs we highlighted in Subsect. 4.2, we aim to design an authoring tool with a multi-view GUI. The several views would not be intended to different roles, as in collaborative design, but rather to match the teachers' various levels of expertise. Because the authoring task requires the ability to conceptualize and structure the concepts from a high level as explained by Murray [15], we propose an authoring tool comprising mainly of three views:

1. A "Standard view" providing a couple of object types that can be slightly adjusted (e.g. gps coordinates of points of interest (POI), learning and questions content). This view will allow the first category of teachers (cited above) to rapidly design a basic playful scenario with preconfigured game mechanics (e.g. a linear game unit order, a standard way of counting scores).
2. An "Intermediate view" allowing designers to go further in details, in order to better adjust their scenarios. This time, the teachers can configure the score mechanisms, the radius of POI, game unit triggers and dependencies …. This view is intended to the second category of teachers (cited above).
3. An "Expert view" allowing the most expert designers to go even further in details. We aim to provide custom component creation at this level and programming features to create the logic between them.

From a conceptual perspective, the underlying data model of our authoring tool is based on mapping high-level components, which are comprehensible by teachers, such as points of interests, activities and clues to low-level executable components (e.g. multimedia resources, buttons, textual items …). From the design process perspective, we intend to provide a nested design process, meaning that views are embedded in each other according to the Hidden complexity theory. The content to be shown in the previously presented three views, was decided by consulting the five teachers. Thus, every view leads to the other as if one chooses to navigate from "standard" to "intermediate", looking for more options to set up. Likewise, navigation in the opposite is necessary if one doesn't feel comfortable with the "intermediate" or the "expert" view.

The three views discussed above have been co-designed with the five interviewed teachers on graphical mockups. Even though, we decided to begin with three levels, this number is not definitive and surely can be adjusted according to intended users, especially if we generalize the use of this approach outside the MLG design field. Then, our next step is to test a first MLG authoring tool prototype, implementing the insights discussed above, with the teachers who answered our online questionnaire.

6   Conclusion and Perspectives

In this paper we analyzed five authoring tools that can be used to create Mobile Learning Games (MLGs). This study identifies the reasons that are slowing down the use of MLGs by teachers, despite the material resources available and the MLGs' potential for learning. Our analysis consisted in assessing the technical features provided by each authoring tool that we tested by reproducing existing MLG scenarios.

The second part of the analysis consisted in assessing the usability of each authoring tool, based on a HCI usability criteria and the feedback provided by five teachers organizing educational field trips.

In the second part of this paper, we presented the main issues that explain why these authoring tools are not used by teachers: either they offer very rich functionalities but are very complicated to use, either they are simple to use but do not offer the necessary functionalities to design MLGs. We therefore propose our approach of a MLG multi-view authoring tool, based on a nested design process. We are currently collaborating with the five teachers to design the mock-up models of three different interfaces: a standard view, an intermediate view and an expert view, which gradually show more and more functionalities.

More generally, authoring tool usability is a persistent problem in the TEL field. As a consequence, our future work will also be focused on generalizing the multi-view model, based on the nested design approach, to TEL systems.

References

1. Admiraal, W., Huizenga, J., Akkerman, S., ten Dam, G.: The concept of flow in collaborative game-based learning. Comput. Hum. Behav. **27**, 1185–1194 (2011)
2. Schwabe, G., Göth, C.: Mobile learning with a mobile game: design and motivational effects. J. Comput. Assist. Learn. **21**, 204–216 (2005)
3. Spikol, D.: Exploring novel learning practices through co-designing mobile games. Presented at the (2009)
4. Johnson, L., Adams Becker, S., Estrada, V., Freeman, A., Kampylis, P., Vuorikari, R., Punie, Y.: Horizon Report Europe: 2014 Schools Edition. New Media Consort (2014)
5. Klemke, R., van Rosmalen, P., Ternier, S., Westera, W.: Keep it simple: lowering the barrier for authoring serious games. Simul. Gaming **46**, 40–67 (2015)
6. Karoui, A., Marfisi-Schottman, I., George, S.: Towards an efficient mobile learning games design model. In: European Conference on Games Based Learning, Steinkjer, Norway, pp. 276–285 (2015)
7. Bastien, J.M.C., Scapin, D.L.: Ergonomic criteria for the evaluation of human-computer interfaces. INRIA (1993)
8. Gagnon, D.J.: ARIS. The University of Wisconsin-Madison (2010)
9. Rouillard, J., Serna, A., David, B., Chalon, R.: Rapid prototyping for mobile serious games. In: Zaphiris, P., Ioannou, A. (eds.) LCT 2014. LNCS, vol. 8524, pp. 194–205. Springer, Heidelberg (2014). doi:10.1007/978-3-319-07485-6_20
10. Slany, W.: Pocket code: a scratch-like integrated development environment for your phone. In: Proceedings of the Companion Publication of the 2014 ACM SIGPLAN Conference on Systems, Programming, and Applications: Software for Humanity, pp. 35–36. ACM, New York (2014)
11. Zbick, J., Nake, I., Jansen, M., Milrad, M.: mLearn4Web: a web-based framework to design and deploy cross-platform mobile applications. In: Proceedings of the 13th International Conference on Mobile and Ubiquitous Multimedia. ACM, New York (2014)
12. Murray, T.: Design tradeoffs in usability and power for advanced educational software authoring tools. Saddle Brook Then Englewood Cliffs NJ **44**, 10–16 (2004)

13. Ritter, S., Blessing, S.B., Wheeler, L.: Authoring tools for component-based learning environments. In: Murray, T., Blessing, S.B., Ainsworth, S. (eds.) Authoring Tools for Advanced Technology Learning Environments, pp. 467–489. Springer, Netherlands (2003)
14. Oja, M.-K.: Designing for collaboration: improving usability of complex software systems. In: CHI 2010 Extended Abstracts on Human Factors in Computing Systems, pp. 3799–3804. ACM, New York (2010)
15. Murray, T.: Coordinating the complexity of tools, tasks, and users: on theory-based approaches to authoring tool usability. Int. J. Artif. Intell. Educ. **26**, 37–71 (2015)

Interest in and Willingness to Pay for Mobile Applications in Museums

Peter Winzer and Tamara Steffen[✉]

Faculty of Design, Computer Science, Media,
Hochschule RheinMain, University of Applied Sciences,
Unter den Eichen 5, 65195 Wiesbaden, Germany
{Peter.Winzer,Tamara.Steffen}@hs-rm.de

Abstract. Mobile applications (apps) are becoming more important for museums. In our research project SPIRIT, we develop a mobile location-based serious game, which enhances museum communications in an entertaining way. By integrating elements of interactive digital storytelling through augmented reality, e.g. interactions with virtual characters, the app converts history lessons into vibrant adventures. By using the app, mobile devices are transformed into "magical equipment", which leads users to the spirit of the past in certain places on site. This paper examines selected economic issues of museum apps, focusing on the potential interest in and willingness to pay for these apps. We present selected findings from two empirical surveys, in which valid questionnaires of over 200 museums and over 1,600 museum visitors were analyzed.

1 Introduction

Given the increasing use and importance of apps the idea of using apps in the context of "serious games" [7] for particular communications in museums and cultural institutions suggests itself. It applies especially for the communication of historical or cultural content that conventional guides, e.g. audio guides, will be replaced or complemented by mobile applications (apps) in the future. Such apps have the potential to reach younger target audiences and museum visitors, who do have a great affinity towards technology.

These topics are currently being examined in an ongoing research project called SPIRIT at the RheinMain University of Applied Sciences in Wiesbaden, Germany [4]. A museum app should facilitate a playful experience while at the same time, gather historical information about the museum or cultural site. This is achieved through interactive stories, which contain the "restless spirits" of historical characters, presenting metaphorical encounters with "spirits of the past", based on augmented reality technology [3]. The current success of the location-based augmented reality app "Pokémon Go" shows clearly that there is a large market potential for augmented reality apps or augmented reality games [10]. Even Apple's CEO Tim Cook announced at the end of July 2016: "We have been and continue to invest in augmented reality in the long run. We'll see whether it's the next computing platform, but regardless it will be huge" [9].

A mobile location-based augmented reality software for dynamic video content has been developed for this purpose in collaboration with an acknowledged historical site and archaeological museum (Saalburg Roman Fort, Bad Homburg, Germany). By

R. Bottino et al. (Eds.): GALA 2016, LNCS 10056, pp. 292–301, 2016.
DOI: 10.1007/978-3-319-50182-6_26

using direction sensors, camera and GPS, location-based information is integrated into the visitor's surrounding. This is why the app is especially suitable for historical outdoor museums. A distinction of similar apps is achieved by the combination of educational and fun elements in a serious game to reshape the experience of a usual museum tour. Therefore, a historical museum app should also be made available for less technophile users.

In this paper, we focus on the economic and marketing aspects of museum apps. To get information about these topics, two empirical surveys with more than 200 museums and over 1,600 museum visitors were conducted in summer 2015.

2   Economic Parameters of Museum Apps

Current literature does not provide specific business models of extensive location-based augmented reality apps and dynamic video content. Previous publications have focused either on basic aspects of app business models but not related to museum apps in particular [1] or general economic analysis in the field of museums but excluding apps based on augmented reality [5].

In this paper the ongoing research project SPIRIT will provide a contribution to fill this research gap. In context of the development of a business model for museum apps, the following topics are of specific interest:

(1) **Individualization of App Content.** What level of individualization is an attractive business model for museums or to what extent should the museum app integrate content which is standardized? These central questions represent a classic economic achievement conflict [2, 6]. On the one hand, a specific content for an individual museum might provide greater acceptance by customers. On the other hand, the associated costs increase with a higher level of individual content. In order to clarify which strategies for the app content the museums prefer, these questions were included in the empirical study.

(2) **Allocation of Entrepreneurial Risk.** A central economic question is, who takes the ownership and entrepreneurial responsibility for the museum app i.e. benefits, e.g. revenue from app sales, and carries the associated costs and risks, e.g. investments or risk of failure. In general, museums do not have the expertise and often not the financial resources to produce a complex museum app. The most likely scenario is that they would rather engage a central marketing organization, who carries all expenses for creation and configuration of the app, including the content production.

Depending on how much entrepreneurial risk the museum is willing to accept, various payment models are possible. In the case of a high level of entrepreneurial involvement, the museum "buys" the app for a fixed sum or licenses the app annually, while collecting the income from the app, e.g. revenue from app sales, increased ticket prices or higher attendance. In the case of rather limited entrepreneurial involvement, the museum would purchase the app free of charge from the "central marketer" or would pay additional costs for content individualization. At the same time, the central marketer would receive income from the sale of the app. Therefore, the museum would only act as a mediator or point of sale. However, in reality, various "hybrid forms" of these two models exist: e.g. the museum could pay a relatively low amount for the app and the revenue from the sale of the app are shared between the central marketer and the museum by a particular allocation key. In the empirical study it was taken into account whether and to what extent museums are able or willing to take the economic responsibility of the commercialization of the museum app.

(3) **Interest in and Willingness to Pay for Mobile Applications in Museums.** Obviously the demand of the customers, museum visitors, and their willingness to pay for such apps has a great impact on the commercial prospects of museum apps. Therefore, these parameters were considered in the empirical study as well.

Because of the restricted scope of this paper, we will focus on last-mentioned parameter, the interest in and willingness to pay for museum apps. The other two parameters will only be considered very briefly.

3   Empirical Analysis of Supportive Apps in Museum Context

This chapter presents an overview of the surveys.

(1) In order to receive an interpretable survey, it was necessary to evaluate the German museum market. Consequently, the first step was to select over 6,000 museums (see Sect. 3.1).

(2) For the online survey over 700 museums were relevant. Overall, 205 museums participated in the survey, which results in a response rate of 29% (see Sect. 3.2).

(3) The survey of museum visitors was implemented in 6 museums. The questionnaire focused on the acceptance of museum apps and the willingness to pay for these apps. Altogether, over 1,600 valid questionnaires were collected (see Sect. 3.3).

When the empirical analysis was conducted, there exists no marketable museum app. Therefore, the current prototype was presented to the respondents in order to explain the principles of playful museum apps and mobile serious games. Thus, the prototype could provide a clear idea of the SPIRIT-app.

3.1   Market Scan of German Museums

Our survey used museum associations and museum directories of the 16 German federal states, depending on the availability, to provide a basis for the inquiry of German museums. Otherwise museum lists from the internet [11] were used as a basis for the investigation. 6,638 museums were identified. The following three criteria were analyzed to estimate the size and relevance of the museums: (a) Annual number of visitors, (b) Opening times, (c) Scope and professionalism of the presence on the internet or in social media.

Museums with less than 50,000 annual visitors were not considered for this survey. If the number of annual visitors was not available, the opening hours were taken into account. If the museum is open less than five days a week, the museum was also not considered. If both previously mentioned criteria were met, the website and social media presence of the museum were additionally evaluated. Museums with a professional web presence or social media presence were also considered.

751 museums were classified as relevant for the empirical study using this method. Additionally, these museums were categorized by content and period, according to the main topics in the following categories based on [8, 11]: (a) Art, Design, Literature; (b) Local; (c) Culture; (d) Nature, Animals, Fossils; (e) Architecture, Housing; (f) Technology, Transportation, Communication; (g) Craft, Industry; (h) Other.

3.2   Online Survey: Museums

Some of the identified 751 museums belong to a regional museum association and therefore, they were combined into a bundle, if associations could only fill out one questionnaire for more than one museum. Finally 707 relevant museums and museum associations were included in the survey. The survey was conducted in June and July 2015 and had a response rate of 205 museums, which is equivalent to 29%.

Major Findings of the Survey.

(1) 18 museums (10%) offer an app that includes "multimedia" content. 19 museums (10%) already provide an app, which can be used as an audio guide. 20 museums (10%) offer an app which has other functions than those mentioned in the survey. In total 26 museums (14%) provide at least one app for their customers. These differences are the result of "multiple mentions", i.e. if museums were offering more than one app. Thus museum apps are not very common in German museums. Especially if we take into account that museums, which offer their own apps tend to have participated in the survey rather than museums which do not offer apps. This is the reason why the percentage of museums with museum apps is probably even smaller.

(2) 55% of the museums classified an app purchase price between 1 to 2 Euros as an attractive offer for their customers (resulting from 32% "1.00 Euro", 7% "1.50 Euro" and 16% "2.00 Euro"). 23% of the museums expect that the museum visitors would not be willing to pay for such an app. Whereas 20 museums (13%) estimate that visitors would be willing to pay an app price over 2 Euros up to 3 Euros. The estimated price average for an app is 1.16 Euros (see Fig. 1).

(3) Most museums expect a medium or high level of individualization of the app content. Furthermore, they are willing to pay a higher price for content that is customized for the museum (see Fig. 2). This means highly standardized content is not an option for a museums app.

(4) The museums, which want to bear a high level of corporate responsibility, have a larger annual number of visitors. Also, they are much more interested in apps like this (see Table 1). In this context the percentage of the preferred corporate responsibility represents the level, the museums wants to participate on all costs or investments and benefits or incomes of the app.

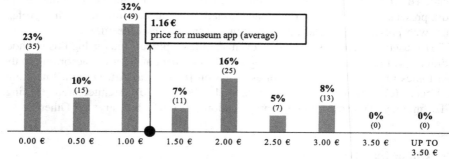

WHICH MAXIMUM PURCHASE PRICE FOR A MUSEUM APP IS AN ACCEPTABLE OFFER THAT YOUR MUSEUM VISITORS CERTAINLY WOULD USE?

Basis: 155 mentions, response rate: 75.61% (not applicable: 50 museums).

Source: Own empirical study, data in parentheses are absolute numbers, deviations from 100% because of rounding.

Fig. 1. Purchase price for museum apps.

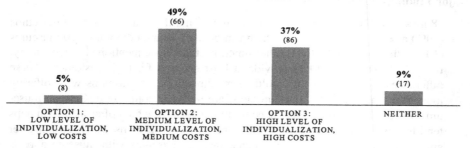

WHICH OPTIONS OF INDIVIDUALIZATION WOULD BE FOR YOUR MUSEUM MOST ATTRACTIVE WHEN YOU CONSIDER THE EXTEND OF APP-CONTENT AND WITH IT THE ASSOCIATED COSTS?

Basis: 177 mentions, response rate: 86.34% (not applicable: 28 museums).

Source: Own empirical study, data in parentheses are absolute numbers, deviations from 100% because of rounding.

Fig. 2. Level of individualization of app content.

Table 1. Preferred corporate responsibility dependent on size of museum.

Preferred corporate responsibility	Mentions (absolute)	Size of museum (annual visitors '000)
0%	5	115
up to 20%	16	61
up to 40%	23	84
up to 60%	14	125
up to 80%	2	175
up to 100%	6	125
Total/average	66	92

Additionally, the following relationship could be detected: The interest of museums to offer such an app depends significantly on (a) how deep the museum "is open-minded about technical innovations" (correlation 0.599; significance 0.000) and (b) to what degree the museum evaluates the app as an "important tool to address young audiences" (correlation 0.597; significance 0.000). The R-squared test shows that the dependent variable "interest of the museums in offering such app" is expounded by "open-mindedness about technical innovations of the museum" (34%) and by an "important tool to address young audiences" (12%).

3.3   Questionnaire: Museum Visitors

Method. First of all, due to practical restrictions, i.e. enabling the interviews, the distance between the museum and the location of the research team at the RheinMain University of Applied Sciences should not exceed more than 1.5 h of travel, in order to have enough time to conduct personal interviews with museum visitors. By this criteria 69 museums were chosen out of 751 museums based on the market analysis which determined museums to include in the survey (see Sect. 3.1).

Because the app is mainly suitable for historical outdoor museums, in a second step, these 69 museums were divided into 3 categories with regard to their relevance to the survey.

- 1st Category: castle museum, which has an outdoor area in addition (9 museums)
- 2nd Category: castle museum (13 museums)
- 3rd Category: all other museums (47 museums)

The museums in category 1 and 2 were contacted to carry out the survey. Finally, five museums from category 1 and one museum from category 2 were selected to conduct the survey of museum visitors: Heidelberg Palace located in Heidelberg, Eberbach Monastery located in Eltville, Saalburg Roman Fort located in Bad Homburg, Open Air Museum of Rhineland-Palatinate located in Bad Sobernheim, Braunfels Castle located in Braunfels and German Pharmacy Museum located in Heidelberg.

Approach During Interviews. In all museums, visitors had been questioned on three different days, except for German Pharmacy Museum which had been questioned on only one day, in order to reach as many different types of museum visitors as possible. These three days had been: (1) a regular business day, (2) a day on weekend and (3) a public holiday. Overall, 1,679 valid questionnaires had been filled out by visitors on 16 survey days: Heidelberg Palace: 520 questionnaires (31%), Eberbach Monastery: 316 questionnaires (19%), Saalburg Roman Fort: 262 questionnaires (16%), Open Air Museum of Rhineland-Palatinate: 222 questionnaires (13%), Braunfels Castle: 193 questionnaires (11%), German Pharmacy Museum: 166 questionnaires (10%).

Major Findings.

(1) Approx. $\frac{1}{3}$ of the visitors use an audio guide when they are visiting a museum (32% resulting from 8% "always" and 24% "often" users). More than $\frac{2}{3}$ of the museum visitors use an audio guide at least occasionally (68% resulting from 8% "always", 24% "often" and 36% "sometimes" users). The average willingness to pay for the usage of an audio guide is 2.51 Euros as shown in Fig. 3.

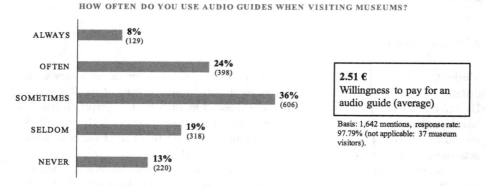

Fig. 3. Usage of audio guides.

(2) ¼ of the museum visitors (25%) had already heard about museum apps and more than ¾ of the respondents are interested or very interested in using museum apps (77% resulting from 26% "very interested" and 51% "somewhat interested") as shown in Fig. 4.

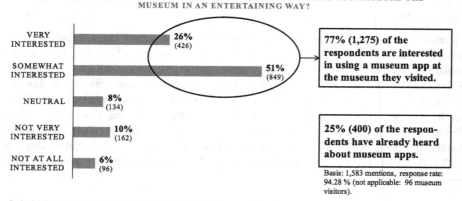

Fig. 4. Interest in using a museum app.

(3) 52% of the visitors are willing to pay between 1 to 2 Euros for a museum app (resulting from "1.00 Euro", "1.50 Euro", "2.00 Euro"). 29% of the visitors would even pay more than 2 Euros (resulting from "2.50 Euro", "3.00 Euro", "3.50 Euro", "more than 3.50 Euro"). 19% of the visitors are not willing to pay 1 Euro (resulting from "0.00 Euro", "0.50 Euro"). The average willingness to pay is 1.75 Euros (see Fig. 5). Visitors who are under the age of thirty, have never visited the museum before or have never used audio guides before, show a lower willingness to pay.

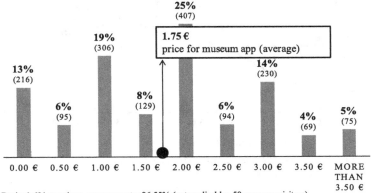

Basis: 1,621 mentions, response rate: 96.55% (not applicable: 58 museum visitors).

Source: Own empirical study, data in parentheses are absolute numbers, deviations from 100% because of rounding.

Fig. 5. Willingness to pay for a museum app.

(4) The R-squared test shows that the dependent variable "willingness to pay for a museum app" is expounded by the "willingness to pay for an audio guide" (25%), see Table 2.

Table 2. R-squared test (dependent variable: "willingness to pay for a museum app").

Variables	R-squared
Willingness to pay for an audio guide	25%
Willingness to pay for in-app purchase of museum	10%
Willingness to pay for paid app	4%
Age	2%
Interest in museums app	1%
In-app purchases	1%
Place of residence	1%
Sum	45%

(5) The strong relationship between the variables (a) the "willingness to pay for an audio guide" and (b) the "willingness to pay for a museum app" can also be proofed by a regression analysis: The correlation coefficient between the "willingness to pay for an audio guide" and the "willingness to pay for a museum app" is 0.533 (significance 0.000). This relation is also illustrated in Fig. 6. Museum visitors, who would be willing to pay a relative low price for an audio guide, would also be willing to pay a relative low price for a museum app.

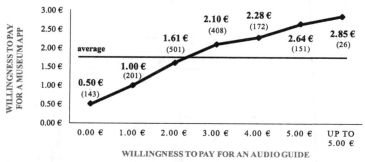

Basis: 1,602 mentions, response rate: 95.41% (not applicable: 77 museum visitors).

Source: Own empirical study, data in parentheses are absolute numbers.

Fig. 6. Relationship between "willingness to pay for an audio guide" and "willingness to pay for a museum app".

4 Summary

This paper presents selected results of two empirical studies, which focus on the acceptance of and willingness to pay for museum apps. In the 1st survey, 205 museums participated with a response rate of 29%. The 2nd survey of museum visitors were carried out in 6 different museums and 1,679 valid questionnaires were collected.

The empirical research of both target audiences revealed these major findings:

(a) 14% of the museums already provide an app for their customers.
(b) The most appropriate price range for a museum app seems to be between 1 to 2 Euros, which is slightly higher than the entry price level for common apps but significantly lower than the typical price level for the usage of audio guides.
(c) Most museums expect a medium or high level of individualization of app content. Furthermore, they are willing to pay higher prices for customized content.
(d) The museums which want to bear a high level of corporate responsibility have a larger annual number of visitors and are more interested in offering museum apps.
(e) There is a high level of interest in using a museum app during a visit to a museum. More than ¾ of the museum visitors are interested in using a museum app.

Acknowledgments. This work has been funded (in part) by the Federal Ministry of Education and Research (BMBF) in Germany (03FH035PA3/B3).

References

1. Aichele, C., Schönberger, M.: App4U: Mehrwerte durch Apps im B2B und B2C, pp. 73–80. Springer Vieweg, Wiesbaden (2014)
2. Angerer, F.: Mobile kontextsensitive Dienste für die Freizeit. In: Egger, R., Jooss, M. (eds.) mTourism: Mobile Dienste im Tourismus, p. 56. Springer Gabler, Wiesbaden (2010)
3. Dastageeri, H., Storz, M., Coors, V.: SPIRIT – Videobasierte mobile Augmented Reality Lösung zur interaktiven Informationsvermittlung. In: Proceedings of DGPF 2015, Köln, vol. 24, pp. 288–295 (2015)
4. Hochschule RheinMain, University of Applied Sciences: SPIRIT. http://spirit.interactive-storytelling.de/. Accessed 28 July 2016
5. Koukopoulos, D., Styliaras, G.: Design of trustworthy smartphone-based multimedia services in cultural environments. Electron. Commer. Res. **13**(2), 137–138 (2013). Springer Science+Business Media, New York
6. Meffert, H., Burmann, C., Kirchgeorg, M.: Marketing: Grundlagen marktorientierter Unternehmensführung, 12th edn, pp. 286–287. Springer Gabler, Wiesbaden (2015)
7. Ritterfeld, U., Cody, M., Vorderer, P.: Serious Games: Mechanisms and Effects, pp. 3–11. Routledge, New York (2009)
8. Segu Geschichte: Zeittafel Geschichte. Historisches Institut der Universität zu Köln. http://www.segu-geschichte.de/zeittafel-geschichte/. Accessed 28 July 2016
9. The Guardian: Apple plans to invest in augmented reality following success of Pokémon Go. https://www.theguardian.com/technology/2016/jul/26/apple-earnings-pokemon-go-augmented-reality-steve-cook. Accessed 27 July 2016
10. Wikipedia [a]: Pokémon Go. https://en.wikipedia.org/wiki/Pok%C3%A9mon_Go. Accessed 28 July 2016
11. Wikipedia [b]: Liste deutscher Museen nach Themen. https://de.wikipedia.org/wiki/Liste_deutscher_Museen_nach_Themen. Accessed 28 July 2016

Gamification of Car Driver Performance

Pratheep K. Paranthaman[(✉)], Gautam R. Dange, Francesco Bellotti,
Riccardo Berta, and Alessandro De Gloria

DITEN, University of Genoa, via opera pia 11A, 16145 Genoa, Italy
{pratheep.paranthaman,gautam.dange,franz,
riccardo.berta,adg}@elios.unige.it

Abstract. The potential of serious games can be used to captivate the road users in exhibiting green driving behavior. Serious games can be an engaging medium in conveying information effectively. We exploited the pervasiveness of smartphone and serious games concept to develop a gamified environment for the road users. Our approach comprises two games that would gamify the driver performance based on the driver performance assessment results. The driver performance will be evaluated using a smartphone-based evaluator and the assessment results will be transmitted through a Bluetooth module to the gamified environment (this happens on real-time basis). The game environment comprises various levels and indicators with the provision of audio feedback on the game status.

1 Introduction

The task of educating or training through a gamified environment unleashes the complexity of a concept. Gamifying mechanism provides an interaction and engagement of users with the gameplay and this could motivate the users in achieving optimal outcomes. The process of gamifying a non-game context, provides a better learning possibilities for the users [1]. Usually the traditional games focus on the engagement of the users with the gameplay by delivering a good amount of interactivity and various properties on the game scene for entertainment. The serious games focus on providing information and training on some context or to instill certain concepts through a gameplay [2, 3]. Designing a serious game is highly challenging as it should seal the information and entertainment in the same box. The core of serious game should be equally balanced between the information and entertainment, if there is an imbalance in this, then the informative content becomes trivial.

Usage of an instructional design (application of technology and multimedia) in crafting a serious game framework can be a significant aspect of a serious game design [4]. The incorporation of instructional design and serious games can enable higher level of learning outcomes, as the design will involve necessary game characteristics (competitions, goals, challenges and etc.) and learning objectives [5]. With all these assets, serious games can be exploited in automotive domain to foster green driving (maintaining optimal driving behavior constantly, without rapid harsh events). The driver behavior has a major contribution in road safety and green mobility aspects. When analyzing the driver behavior, it's important to understand the difference between the

© Springer International Publishing AG 2016
R. Bottino et al. (Eds.): GALA 2016, LNCS 10056, pp. 302–308, 2016.
DOI: 10.1007/978-3-319-50182-6_27

driver behavior and the driver performance, where - the driver performance is referred as the abilities (such as skills, knowledge, and cognitive abilities) of the driver and the driver behavior is the preference of driver from the experiences gained [6]. It's also a mandatory fact to concern about the safety, while developing applications that would captivate driving behavior. These applications should also consider the aspects like driver distraction, immersion on secondary tasks and etc., which could grab driver's attention. Because, the involvement of drivers in secondary tasks while driving can cause on-road hazards [7]. We target to improvise the knowledge of the driver by an infotainment system, which manages to gamify the driver performance. We propose a gamified environment for drivers to promote a green and collaborative driving. The performance of the driver is evaluated using a smartphone-based evaluator and the assessment results are sent to the gamified environment. The game environment allows the player to visualize the performance on the game screen without direct user inter-action to the game. This provides immediate feedback of the performance on game environment and the process of immediate feedback would cultivate a procedural learning [8] and enables user engagement [9, 10]. The immediate feedback also provides an understanding to the user about the driving performance. Especially, when driving behavior is bad with more harsh driving events (such as: harsh brake, high acceleration and etc.), the user can visualize a downfall in the game. Thus the impacts of driving pattern on gameplay helps the users to understand driving performance and improvise the driving behavior. The driver game allows user to advance levels, gain bonuses and win the game, if the performance is good. Incentivizing the user performance provides a motivation for the users to progress and improvise the driving traits from the gameplay [11]. The game provides an audio feedback of the state changes and also for avoiding distraction while driving. The performance gamification enables a broader gaming aspect for the drivers, where the driver can just mount the smartphone on dashboard and game without even interacting or looking on to the game screen.

2   Gamified Approaches for Green Drive

The serious games and community building (SG-CB) application provides scope for gamifying the driver performance and this gamification will spotlight the impact of driving pattern [12]. The driver behavior gets reflected on the game environment and the fluctuations on the game play happens based on the driver performance.

We propose two gamified approaches to encourage the green drive and they are:

- The Driver game
- Snake and ladders.

2.1   The Driver Game

The driver game provides a gamified environment for drivers on a smartphone-based gaming setup. The game involves no interaction with user (driver) and is connected through a Bluetooth module with signal evaluator (Fig. 1).

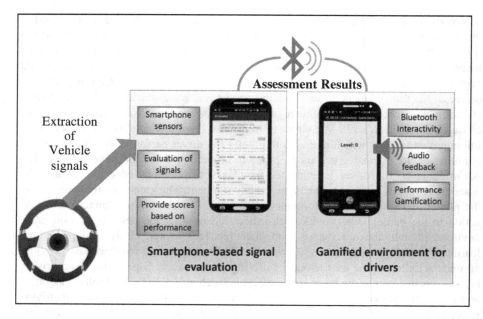

Fig. 1. Driver game architecture and setup

The driver game is housed inside the SG-CB application and the game comprise two phases. The first phase involves the extraction of vehicle signals and this is done using the car evaluator module (A smartphone-based application for assessment of vehicle signals). The second phase involves the representation of driver performance on a gamified environment. The driver game establishes a Bluetooth connection to extract the user performance scores from the signal evaluator module. The user performance results (normally a score ranging from 0–100) are transmitted to the game scene and it's represented on the game environment (Fig. 2).

Fig. 2. Driver game sample scenario

The driver game has a game screen with less number of properties and representations (see Fig. 3(a)). The game screen in driver view comprises a big window with gradient of colors displayed from yellow to green depending on the driver performance. The game starts with the yellow gradient and based on the performance, the yellow gradient will shade towards green. The driver can look for the change in gradient pattern to understand the performance. Additionally, the user gets an audio feedback of the game status and this would allow the user to focus on driving without having need to look upon the game screen for updates. When the user halts the vehicle in a traffic or at any place, there is an option to visualize the game on a detailed view comprising of more visual elements representing levels, lives, score and bonus/malus gauge (see Fig. 3(b)).

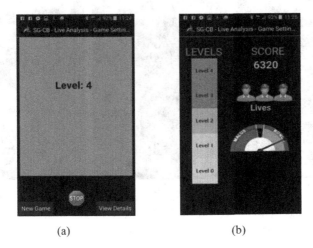

(a)   (b)

Fig. 3. (a) Driver view display with gradient window, (b) Detailed gaming view with representation of various properties of game (lives, levels, score and bonus/malus gauge)

The driver game comprises five levels and each level has a certain threshold value that has to be acquired within the allocated time. If the user completes a level within the allocated time, then the user gets a bonus and will be advanced to another level and if user is unable to complete a level, then a malus is provided and the user gets retained in the same level. The bonus and malus gauge acts as a performance estimator and will predict, whether the user is likely to get bonus or malus based on the current performance. Driver can switch between the views to visualize the performance on a game environment. Thus, the driver game provides a real-time performance display on a gamified environment based on driving events such as brake, acceleration and Steering wheel angle.

2.2 Snake and Ladders

The snake and ladders is a live gaming approach and it's linked to driver performance. The game scene comprises of certain slots, where user's position will be placed and based on the performance the user climbs the ladder and gets advanced to other levels. On the possession of good events, the user gains some points and a dice is rolled virtually and based on the result, the user advances on the slots. The snake and ladders concept in our gaming framework, provides a gamified environment for the users to view the evolution of their performance. In this approach, the users can compete with their peers associated with competition. The game has two levels and the complexity increases as user progresses and winner of the game secures a championship (Fig. 4).

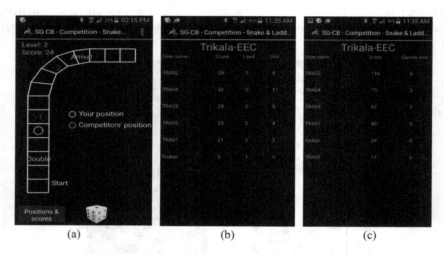

Fig. 4. (a) Snake and ladders game environment, (b) List of user scores and position details, arranged based on performance, (c) Championship screen-list of users, arranged based on scores.

3   Impact on Driver Performance

The two game approaches intend to impact the driver performance through HMI and the user can analyze the performance outcomes during the drive (performance gamification, bonus and malus gauge and evolution of performance on snake and ladders game). Every drive of the user will definitely have something to convey as a part of betterment and eventually, contributes for eradicating the harsh driving behavior. Under the hood, these game approaches convey a mode of feedback to the drivers in the form of incentives, scores and visualization of performance. The feedbacks from the game approaches take a combinational effect on the user performance by inducing the knowledge and comprehensive understanding about the driving behavior in engaging way. The snake and ladders game offers an interactive gaming platform to compete with the peers and progress by acquiring virtual coins. The goal of the user becomes to gather virtual coins and on the pursuit of it, there will be a competitive platform for enhancing the driving performance. The major impact of these game approaches on driver performance would be an emphasis on two attributes, which are the rewards and downfall (Fig. 5).

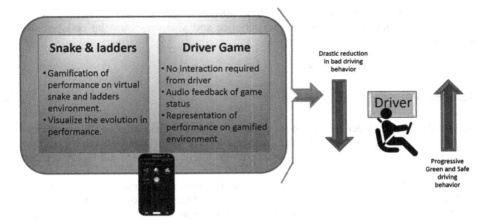

Fig. 5. Driver performance impact based on gamified approaches

The rewards will act as a factor of motivation to improvise the driving behavior and to maintain the optimal performance to earn incentives. Whereas, the downfall in scores and performance would provide an extensive analysis of performance, which enables the users to understand and react towards eradicating the bad driving behavior. The constant exposure to our defined game approaches would progressively increase the driver performance and adheres the driver to stay optimal and also brings down the harsh driving behavior by spotlighting the flaws.

4   Conclusion and Future Work

The game approaches provide a performance gamification that would enable the users to visualize the impact of driving behavior on the game screen. This mechanism would also induce a game based learning traits, as we focus to reflect the driving performance directly on to the game screen. There are certain aspects, which we would like to highlight from our gamified approaches. We aimed to improvise the driver performance and cultivate the green driving traits, but it's more important to make the users to persevere in the state of betterment and keep improvising tenaciously. The gameplay incentivizes the user for good performance and this provides an encouragement. These incentives create motivation and enable the users to maintain an optimal driving behavior at most of the instances. Also, the competitive strategy uplifts the performance of users and peers associated in a game. The strategy is the core of gaming applications and inducing a concept through a gameplay works well in reaching the audience, as it's transmitted through an engaging medium.

As a part of future work, we are planning to reduce the configurational settings for establishing the Bluetooth connection between the smartphone-based evaluator and the game environment. It's also necessary to provide a customizable gaming options for the users to adjust the game parameters on the smartphone UI as per the needs. These concerns are currently on progress for making the gamified environment more user-friendly. Henceforth, the process of performance gamification will provide the users with a competitive self-gaming experience and also promotes the collaborative green mobility.

References

1. Matallaoui, A.: Model-driven serious game development: integration of the gamification modeling language GAML with unity. In: Proceedings of the 2015 48th Hawaii International Conference on System Sciences (HICSS), pp. 643–651, 5–8 (2015) doi:10.1109/HICSS.2015.84
2. Zapušek, M., Cerar, Š., Rugelj, J.: Serious computer games as instructional technology. In: Proceedings of 34th International Convention on MIPRO, pp. 1056–1058 (2011)
3. Deterding, S., Dixon, D., Khaled, R., Nacke, L: From game design elements to gamefulness: defining gamification. In: MindTrek 2011 Proceedings of the 15th International Academic MindTrek Conference on Envisioning Future Media Environments, pp. 9–15 (2011)
4. Kapralos, B., Haji, F., Dubrowski, A.: A crash course on serious games design and assessment: a case study. In: IEEE Games Innovation Conference IGIC 2013, pp. 105–109 (2013)
5. Charsky, D.: From edutainment to serious games. Games Cult. 5(2), 177–198 (2010)
6. Liu, Y.F., Wang, Y.M., Li, W.S., Xu, W.Q., Gui, J.S.: Improve driver performance by experience of driver cognitive behavior model's practice. In: IEEE Intelligent Vehicle Symposium, pp. 475–480 (2009)
7. McGoogan, C.: Pokémon Go gamer crashes car into a tree. The Telegraph (2016). http://www.telegraph.co.uk/technology/2016/07/14/pokemon-go-gamer-crashes-car-into-a-tree/. Accessed 25 July 2016
8. Bellotti, F., Berta, R., De Gloria, A.: Designing effective serious games: opportunities and challenges for research. Int. J. Emerg. Technol. Learn. (IJET) 5, 22–35 (2010). Special Issue: Creative Learning with Serious Games
9. Fogg, B.J.: Persuasive Technology: Using Computers to Change What We Think and Do. Morgan Kaufmann, Burlington (2002)
10. Graesser, A.C., Chipman, P., Leeming, F., Biedenback, S.: Deep learning and emotion in serious games. In: Serious Games: Mechanisms and Effects, pp. 81–100 (2009)
11. Bellotti, F., et al.: A smart mobility serious game concept and business development study. In: De Gloria, A., Veltkamp, R. (eds.) GALA 2015. LNCS, vol. 9599, pp. 385–392. Springer, Heidelberg (2016). doi:10.1007/978-3-319-40216-1_43
12. Dange, G.R., et al.: The absolute and social comparative analysis of driver performance on a simulated road network. In: De Gloria, A., Veltkamp, R. (eds.) GALA 2015. LNCS, vol. 9599, pp. 375–384. Springer, Heidelberg (2016). doi:10.1007/978-3-319-40216-1_42

Posters

Designing Working Memory Games
for Elderly

Antti Koivisto[1(✉)], Antero Lindstedt[2], Sari Merilampi[1],
and Kristian Kiili[2]

[1] Satakunta University of Applied Sciences, Tiedepuisto 3, 28600 Pori, Finland
{Antti.Koivisto,Sari.Merilampi}@samk.fi
[2] Tampere University of Technology, Pohjoisranta 3, 28100 Pori, Finland
{Antero.Lindstedt,Kristian.Kiili}@tut.fi

Abstract. Working memory is of central importance for acquiring knowledge and involved in a variety of complex cognitive tasks and thus the use of working memory training games can lead to a wide range of significant impacts in peoples' life. The aim of this study was to investigate design principles for working memory training games. A game called Brain Farmer was designed and developed as part of this study. Brain Farmer is a working memory game based on n-back working memory training protocol and it is targeted especially for older adults. Users' playing experiences were studied and design principles were identified based on observations, user feedback, and interviews. The most important design principles were found to be the simple and easily understandable game play, adaptation of challenge level as well as clear multisensory instructions and feedback.

1 Introduction

Research on serious games as well as game industry have at some level attempted to address the biggest threats to our society: obesity, ageing, social exclusion and memory diseases. There is an urgent need to develop usable and effective non-medical treatments that can be used to prevent cognitive decline, diagnose memory dysfunctionalities, and promote brain health in different age groups. Serious games, especially working memory games can provide a potential vehicle to deliver controlled brain training interventions and provide diagnostics about players' cognitive functioning.

Previous research has shown that, in general, video game playing can lead to changes in an individual's pleasure, vigilance, dominance, and therefore in the overall state of experienced well-being. Also in the case of older adults, simple and easy to play video games are well accepted and found to create positive feelings and enjoyment [1–4]. Even few minutes regular gaming exercise on daily basis may lead to cognitive benefits such as improving attention and concentration [5].

1.1 Theoretical Foundations for Working Memory Games

Working memory is a brain system that enables us to retain information over a brief period of time, in other words a temporary storage for information. This limited storage

© Springer International Publishing AG 2016
R. Bottino et al. (Eds.): GALA 2016, LNCS 10056, pp. 311–320, 2016.
DOI: 10.1007/978-3-319-50182-6_28

allows us also to manipulate retained information [6]. Working memory is of central importance for acquiring knowledge [7] and involved in a variety of complex cognitive tasks and abilities [8].

It is plausible that working memory plays an important part in everyday life and if trained properly working memory training can support and enhance this brain system that is crucial for acquiring new knowledge and skills [7]. Several empirical studies have demonstrated that working memory training has positive effects on fluid intelligence, reasoning, cognitive control, and reading comprehension etc. [9]. Whereas some other studies have not been able to demonstrate these effects [10]. Nevertheless, the literature on working memory training shows that especially core training of working memory is most promising. Core training studies typically involve tasks that are utilizing sequential processing and frequent memory updating and are designed to target domain-general working memory mechanisms [11].

One very common and successful approach of core working memory training is the "n-back" task. The "n-back" task is a method to assess and to train working memory and requires a continuous monitoring of sequentially presented stimuli. The task of the participant is to give a signal whenever the current stimulus matches the stimulus occurring "n" positions back in the sequence. We have decided to use the "n-back" approach as a core game mechanic in our "Brain Farmer" working memory training game.

Due to the difficulty of the task and the effort participants have to take during working memory training, motivation is a key factor for a successful training. Conventional working memory programs may quickly become boring or monotone, what in turn can lead to decreased training performance. Game elements that can be added to conventional and rather monotone brain training can improve the outcome of the training. Prins and colleagues [12] for example have demonstrated that a game-based working memory training enhanced motivation and training efficacy in children with ADHD. The positive results of previous studies [13] on elderly people with cognitive impairment encourage implementing working memory games also for older adults. Hence, it seems quite promising to combine evaluated psychological methods such as the "n-back" task with games or game elements to increase the efficacy of working memory trainings for older adults.

1.2 Flow Theory in User Experience Optimization

Optimization of subjective playing experience is a crucial part of a game design process. The fun characteristics offered by a serious game is a key factor in determining whether a player will be engaged in a playing/training process and be able to achieve the desired outcomes. We have selected flow theory [14] as a game design framework because flow seems to have a positive influence on performance enhancement, learning, concentration, and engagement [15, 16] that are all important goals of serious games. Furthermore, for example Kiili et al. [17] have shown that Flow framework can be used for analyzing and improving the quality of serious games.

Flow describes a state of complete absorption or engagement in a specific activity in which a person excludes all irrelevant emotions and thoughts [14]. During the optimal experience, a person is in a positive psychological state where he or she is so involved with the goal-driven activity that nothing else seems to matter. An activity that produces such experiences is so pleasant that the person may be willing to do something for its own sake, without being concerned with what he will get out of his action. This kind of intrinsic motivation is very important especially in working memory games that usually require larger cognitive investments compared to entertainment games.

Csikszentmihalyi [14] has distinguished nine flow dimensions that constitute flow experience. These dimensions can be further divided into flow conditions and flow characteristics [18]. Flow conditions are prerequisites of flow and they can be used in optimizing the playing experience. Flow conditions include challenge-skill balance, clear goals, and unambiguous or immediate feedback dimensions. In this paper we use these flow dimensions to back our design decisions of the Brain Farmer game.

1.3 Present Study and the Brain Farmer Game

This paper presents a pilot study in which the usefulness of the Brain Farmer working memory game was studied in an elderly care home. One aim of the study was to investigate game design principles for elderly people and optimize the Brain Farmer game for elderly people.

A farm animal theme was selected to the Brain Farmer game because it became evident that most members of the target group have had some contact to farm and farm animals during their childhood. The gameplay was designed according to n-back training protocol. In the game the player has to recall the location of the animal and answer by pressing one of two buttons indicating either 'true' if the place of the animal was the same or 'false' if the place was different than condition determined by n-back. In level one the player has to remember if the previous (n − 1) animal appeared from the same window as the current animal. Whereas, in level two the player has to remember if the animal before the previous animal (n − 2) appeared from the same window as the current animal (see Fig. 1). Player earns points by answering correctly and suffers damage on wrong answer. The player can freely adjust the game difficulty by selecting number of steps back in the sequence the animal has to be compared to.

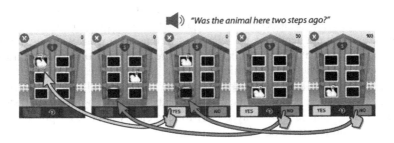

Fig. 1 The implementation of 2-back task in the Brain Farmer game.

2 Methods

The aim of the study was to find out essential game design principles for elderly people and study the effectiveness of the Brain Farmer game as a memory rehabilitation game.

One-hour preliminary test was conducted with three participants before the actual pilot intervention. The idea of the preliminary test was to ensure that the game motivates the target group and the usability of the game is on a decent level.

Participants (n = 22) some of who were diagnosed with memory disabilities played the game for 20 weeks. Participants' were 71–93 years of age. At the beginning and at the end of the intervention a Mini-Mental State Examination (MMSE) and a Corsi Block Tapping test were conducted. MMSE is a simplified test for measuring memory and information processing ability [19]. It contains a set of questions that should be easy to answer correctly for a person with no memory disabilities. MMSE test measures five areas of cognitive function: orientation, registration, attention and calculation, recall, and language with eleven questions. 30 points is the maximum score. A result below 24 points is considered a sign of some memory dysfunction. 17 points or less means a semi-severe memory impairment and below 12 points is a mark of a severe memory impairment. In a Corsi Block test there are nine blocks and the participant is shown a series of blocks that he/she has to remember and repeat afterwards [20]. The series starts with two consecutive blocks, then three consecutive blocks and so on. 14 of the 22 participants completed every part of the pre- and post-test and filled in the questionnaires.

Due to target group's impaired perception and sensation skills, we had to focus on two vital goals over everything else: "One must be involved in an activity with a clear set of goals and progress" and "The task at hand must have clear and immediate feedback". To make this easy to understand one can think of the "worst case playing scenario": despite a frequent playing history the player can forget that he or she has ever played the game before. The right balance between the perceived challenges of the task at hand and participant's own perceived skills was achieved at this point by manual selection of the wanted level from the menu by the user.

Qualitative data and the user experiences were collected by observing the playing situations and with interviews. During the intervention the researchers and the care personnel had mid-term review meetings where they evaluated the current version of the game and provided feedback of the usage. At the end of the pilot study a short questionnaire was given to care personnel (n = 3) and to the participants (n = 22). The questionnaire for participants consisted of questions about the playing device, effectiveness the game, game feedback and clarity as well as team work with care personnel with total of 22 questions. The questionnaire for care personnel consisted questions like how they feel playing helped the participants, how personnel feel games as part of the rehabilitation process and clarity of the game. Interviews were performed by researchers after the test period. Game data was gathered through internet and stored to a data server. The data server displayed easy-to-read charts of player's progress for the care personnel and researchers.

3 Results

Results from the pilot study were generally positive although playing time per participant was lower than we had hoped for. Results for the Corsi Block and MMSE tests are presented in Fig. 2 along with the game data from Brain Farmer. The small number of participants (14) who completed every required part of the study and the total duration of gameplay means that it is not feasible to make any interpretations on the effects on participants' memory improvement or decline over the duration of the intervention. Also possible relations between the results of Corsi Block test, MMSE, and Brain Farmer can be considered unreliable. Because of this we will not concentrate on quantitative data but instead, qualitative user experience data is carefully interpreted.

Participant	Age	Pre-test CBT	Pre-test MMSE	Post-test CBT	Post-test MMSE	N-back level	Total duration
1	91	5	28	4	28	2	14
2	80	4	24	4	24	3	53
3	79	4	26	5	28	3	18
4	87	5	21	5	21	2	47
5	91	5	17	4	14	3	13
6	75	5	30	5	30	4	121
7	71	6	28	4	23	3	19
8	86	4	27	4	30	3	62
9	85	3	23	3	24	2	49
10	86	5	25	4	27	3	35
11	93	5	30	5	30	2	13
12	85	6	30	5	30	6	185
13	91	4	27	5	22	3	11
14	84	3	24	4	24	3	30

Fig. 2 Participants' pre- and post-test data for Corsi Block Test (CBT) and MMSE, the highest N-back level reached and total duration spent (in minutes) on Brain Farmer game.

3.1 General Results

Despite that the complete testing period was fairly long, the participants did not play the game on the regular basis. Only one from the total of twenty-two participants played the game regularly and thus the effectiveness of the game cannot be evaluated in terms of cognitive benefits. The player who played the game the most was experiencing flow and was highly motivated trough the entire game period. Overall playing times were small because the game was played only once a week during an activity hour. So playing the game was only one of the activities on offer. The participants tended to forget the playing instructions due to long breaks between playing sessions and required help from the care personnel. The simultaneous playing was further limited by having only two tablet devices available. One main finding was that even the care personnel are not so familiar with the tablet computers and they encountered a lot of technical problems during the intervention. Tablets could be "stuck" for weeks and nobody really knew how to handle the problem. This supports the findings of our earlier studies [13] indicating that despite of the extremely positive feedback on the game experiences, the implementation in daily practices is often very challenging. The care personnel easily feel that the game interventions are extra work for them while they should consider games as new tools for rehabilitation and recreation.

Although the amount of the playing data was too small we got excellent information about the game design from interviews and observations. In particular usability data was highly valuable. The interviews revealed that although most of the participants were first timers in terms of using tablet PCs, they still found the use of tablets easy and thought that the game suited them well. Moreover, third of the participants felt that their playing skills improved during the intervention. More than half of the players believed that playing Brain Farmer helped them to preserve memory and even improve it. This was however based only on their subjective feeling as the total playing durations were too short to have any actual impact on memory. Still the fact that the game was perceived as suitable and useful would indicate willingness to continue playing the game further if given an opportunity.

According to the care personnel the game was simple and clear. The Brain Farmer game suited well for elderly people and it was found to be good for training their memory functions. Personnel told that some of the participants clearly improved in the game and waited eagerly for next playing session. One of the most valuable feedback was that the participants felt that the game had offered the feeling of success for them and affected positively on quality of their life. This feeling spread from one player to another. Moreover, the participants thought that the game improved concentration skills and increased also collaboration between elderly and the care personnel.

3.2   Redesign of the Game

In this section we discuss our findings and design principles that should be considered when developing games for elderly people. The redesigning implementations that were done to the Brain Farmer game are consistent with flow theory and are usually needed to take into consideration when designing and creating games for special user groups. Care personnel and participants gave all improvement suggestions that are discussed in this section.

Modifications Based on the Immediate and Unambiguous Feedback Dimension. Correct and incorrect answers were presented with a raising text that indicated the gained score or a lost health point. The game characters also had animated gestures for happy and sad that were displayed based on the answer. The participants had trouble following the moving text and the animated gestures were too subtle. Therefore, the participants were often unsure of whether they had answered correctly or not. The text was changed to be stationary. As our previous findings have shown that older adults prefer simple game graphics [21], the animations were still kept subtle but the different expressions were made more distinguished. A spoken feedback was added that commented whether the answer was correct or not. In brief, the researchers found out that the feedback should be shown long enough in order to ensure that player has enough time to process the visual stimuli. Simple audiovisual implementations also seem to work better than visual stimuli.

Modifications Based on the Clear Goals Dimension. At the beginning of the tests participants were given instructions how the game works and how the game should be played. Participants had difficulties to remember the instructions and care personnel had to repeat instructions often. Because of this a spoken guidance was included to the game. Guidance could be turned on/off if needed. The guidance occurred after every event before user interaction was needed. For example, in the first level guidance was following: "Was the animal here?". More specific guidance starting from level two was added as it is important to inform the player what level (current n-back) he/she is playing, for example "Was the animal here two steps ago?".

Modifications Based on the Challenge-Skill Balance Dimension. Participants required a person that helped them to select a level. They wanted to play levels that they master because of the fear of failure and the feeling of security. This decreased the possible training effect. As a solution we developed a treatment mode in which the challenge level is adapted to player's skill level. The game determines on what level the player has ended the last gaming session and starts on one level lower at first to make the player to achieve sense of control. The idea is to start easy to engage the player and then adapt to the current skill level in order to stretch player's mind into its limits.

The adaptive game mode is based on two counters: corrects and incorrects. A correct answer increases the correct counter by one and an incorrect answer adds one to the incorrect counter. The difficulty level rises once the correct counter reaches 10 and lowers if the incorrect counter reaches 6. Additionally, each incorrect answer decreases the correct counter by one and three consecutive correct answers decrease one from the incorrect counter. However neither counter can be negative. This way the difficulty progression requires the player to reach a competence in the ongoing n-back level where most of the answers are correct. The difficulty decrease occurs quicker but still an occasional incorrect answer can be compensated. The exact threshold values might get refined once more game data is recorded.

Figure 3 shows an example of a game where the n-back level changes based on answers. Since the incorrect answers no longer cause a game over, the game length is defined by time. The game offers several options of game lengths (5, 7 and 10 min). Because of this adaptive time-based approach the hitpoint counter become useless and was removed.

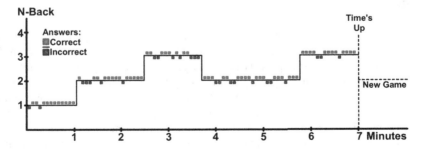

Fig. 3 An illustration of a possible level (n-back) progression in a 7-minutes treatment mode game.

Researchers found also other redesign modifications that could have been useful in this pilot study in terms of extending playing times. These improvements are consistent with the results that we have found in our previous studies with special user groups.

The more familiar and interesting the game elements are the better chance there is to motivate the player. For example, people with learning disabilities may not be able to concentrate on the game so well if it is not very engaging. In the simplest form the engagement is achieved by using avatars or other game elements that are important for the user. For example, instead of the farm animals, flowers could appear in the game, to give a simple example. Although this has been highlighted with people with learning disabilities it could facilitate engagement in case of older adults as well. High score tables could be used to motivate players. High scores are important mainly for players who think that they do well in the game. However, high score table might have reversed effect among users who do not succeed so well. Similarly, too strong indicator (loud sound for example) of wrong answer may decrease the motivation to play, especially when audience is present.

One big issue that we encountered was the player identification. At first it was done by giving each participant an unique ID card with a name and a Quick Response Code (QR-code) which is a two-dimensional barcode. Scanning the QR-code with tablet's QR-code reader launched the game application with the correct user logged in. Nor participants or care personnel were familiar with the scanning process so after a while the game login was replaced with a dropdown name list where one must select the corresponding person. Our previous studies have also shown that Near Field Communication -tag (NFC) is good solution for player identification as the identification progress is simple [22]. NFC can be used to transmit information between two devices or data from a tag by bringing them really close to each others (couple of centimeters).

Finally, when coming back to usability and flow theory, in case of special user groups such as people with memory impairment, people with physical disabilities or people with learning disabilities, the discussion is more on what users are capable on doing instead of personal skills. The definition of usability may have to be extended when dealing with special user groups and various disability conditions. In case of very severe disabilities usability comes closer to accessibility.

The discussion is more on what the user is or is not capable to do.

4   Conclusions

New tools for self-initiative rehabilitation and fighting against cognitive decline are needed. These tools must be motivating in order to have any effect on the user. In this paper, we studied design principles for games targeted for elderly people. A pilot study on working memory training game was presented. The results related to playing experience were very positive especially after some game modifications were implemented. In general, the tested game was experienced pleasant and rehabilitative with respect to subjective measures. The most important design principles in this study were found to be clear goals and immediate multi-channel feedback as well as adaptation of the difficulty level based on the user's skills. The most obvious challenge in the study was the implementation of the game intervention as a part of the daily routines. More generally, it is also the problem with all kind of technology that aims to enhance well-being. Proper training and clear responsibilities are important. Technology training should already be considered when educating the nursing staff, especially in the future. Moreover, a multidisciplinary game design approach is essential when dealing with special user groups. This study also showed that games can be harnessed for self-initiative rehabilitation purpose if they are properly designed. It came evident that elderly people need continuous assistance and designers should take this into account.

Due to the qualitative nature of the study, we only had relatively small test group. The participants of the study were elderly day care clients who are living independently and visiting the daycare activity once a week for an hour or two during which the gaming activity was performed. According to the care staff, in daycare, nursing staff helps elderly with daily tasks such as cutting nails or hair. This means there are many simultaneous activities and only limited time. This is one of the reasons the elderly did not have time to concentrate so deeply solely on gaming. Also lack of knowledge towards the tablets from the nursing staff affected the results and playing time. However, almost all the participants played the game and continued playing during the test period along with the other activities in the day care. We managed to get almost all of the day care clients involved in the study which indicates strong interest on gaming. Although the study only provides limited data about the usability, it is significant basis for further development of serious games for elderly. Research also produced valuable information about how one should design games for memory impaired elderly and in the future how to instruct the staff to deal with unexpected events.

References

1. Khoo, E.T., Cheok, A.D.: Age invaders: inter-generational mixed reality family game. Int. J. Virtual Real. 5(2), 45–50 (2006)
2. Koivisto, A., Merilampi, S., Kiili, K., Sirkka, A., Salli, J.: Mobile activation games for rehabilitation and recreational activities - exergames for the intellectually disabled and the older adults. J. Public Health Front. 2(3), 122–132 (2013)
3. Sirkka, A., Merilampi, S., Koivisto, A., Leinonen, M., Leino, M.: User experiences of mobile controlled games for activation, rehabilitation and recreation of the elderly and physically impaired. In: pHealth Conference 2012, Porto, Portugal
4. Snowden, M., Steinman, L., Mochan, K., Grodstein, F., Prohaskam, T.R., Thurman, D.J., Brown, D.R., Laditka, J.N., Soares, J., Zweiback, D.J., Little, D., Anderson, L.A.: Effect of exercise on cognitive performance in community-dwelling older adults: review of intervention trials and recommendations for public health practice and research. J. Am. Geriatr. Soc. 59(4), 704–716 (2011)
5. Gao, Y., Mandryk, R.L.: The acute cognitive benefits of casual exergame play. In: Paper on The ACM SIGCHI Conference on Human Factors in Computing Systems CHI 2012, 5–10 May 2012, Austin, Texas, USA (2012). http://hci.usask.ca/uploads/256-p1863-gao.pdf. Accessed 3 Dec 2014

6. Baddeley, A.: Working memory: looking back and looking forward. Nat. Rev. Neurosci. **4**(10), 829–839 (2003)
7. Pickering, S.J.: Working Memory and Education. Academic Press, Cambridge (2006)
8. Klingberg, T.: Training and plasticity of working memory. Trends Cogn. Sci. **14**(7), 317–324 (2010)
9. Jaeggi, S.M., Buschkuehl, M., Jonides, J., Perrig, W.J.: Improving fluid intelligence with training on working memory. Proc. Natl. Acad. Sci. U.S.A. **105**(19), 6829–6833 (2008)
10. Redick, T.S., Shipstead, Z., Harrison, T.L., Hicks, K.L., Fried, D.E., Hambrick, D.Z., Kane, M.J., et al.: No evidence of intelligence improvement after working memory training: a randomized, placebo-controlled study. J. Exp. Psychol. Gen. **142**(2), 359–379 (2013)
11. Morrison, A.B., Chein, J.M.: Does working memory training work? The promise and challenges of enhancing cognition by training working memory. Psychon. Bull. Rev. **18**(1), 46–60 (2011)
12. Prins, P.J.M., Dovis, S., Ponsioen, A., ten Brink, E., van der Oord, S.: Cyberpsychology, Behavior, and Social Networking. **14**(3), 115–122 (2011)
13. Merilampi, S., Sirkka, A., Leino, M., Koivisto, A., Finn, E.: Cognitive mobile games for memory impaired older adults. J. Assist. Technol. **8**(4), 207–223 (2014)
14. Csikszentmihalyi, M.: Flow: The Psychology of Optimal Experience. Harper and Row, New York (1990)
15. Csikszentmihalyi, M., Abuhamdeh, S., Nakamura, J.: Flow. A general context for a concept of mastery motivation (2005)
16. Engeser, S., Rheinberg, F.: Flow, performance and moderators of challenge-skill balance. Motiv. Emot. **32**(3), 158–172 (2008)
17. Kiili, K., Lainema, T., de Freitas, S., Arnabc, S.: Flow framework for analyzing the quality of educational games. Entertain. Comput. **5**(4), 367–377 (2014)
18. Swann, C., Keegan, R.J., Piggott, D., Crust, L.: A systematic review of the experience, occurrence, and controllability of flow states in elite sport. Psychol. Sport Exerc. **13**(6), 807–819 (2012)
19. Tombaugh, T.N., McIntyre, N.J.: The mini-mental state examination: a comprehensive review. J. Am. Geriatr. Soc. **40**(9), 922–935 (1992)
20. Corsi, P.M.:. Human memory and the medial temporal region of the brain. Doctoral dissertation. McGill University, Montreal, Canada
21. Koivisto, A., Merilampi, S., Sirkka, A.: Mobile games individualise and motivate rehabilitation in different user groups. Int. J. Game-Based Learn. **5**(2), 1–17 (2015). archive
22. Merilampi, S., Sirkka, A., Leino, M., Koivisto, A., Finn, E.: Cognitive mobile games for memory impaired older adults. J. Assist. Technol. **8**(4), 207–223 (2014)

ACMUS: Comparative Assessment of a Musical Multimedia Tool

Mikel Ostiz-Blanco[1,2(✉)], Alfredo Pina Calafi[3],
Miriam Lizaso Azcárate[3], and Sergi Grau Carrión[4]

[1] Mind-Brain Group, Institute for Culture and Society,
University of Navarra, Pamplona, Spain
mostiz.1@alumni.unav.es
[2] Basque Center on Cognition, Brain and Language, Donostia, Spain
[3] Computer and Math Engineering Department,
Public University of Navarra, Pamplona, Spain
{pina,miriam.lizaso}@unavarra.es
[4] Data and Signal Processing Research Group, U Science Tech,
University of Vic – Central University of Catalonia, Vic, Catalonia, Spain
sergi.grau@uvic.cat

Abstract. In this paper it is described the assessment of the ACMUS (Accessible Music), a multimedia tool that merges sound and colours in order to make music and its benefits more accessible. The aim of the assessment is to clarify the optimal educational field for this tool, either primary education, secondary education or special education through experiences in real context and its evaluation by teachers and students. Based on these data, the conclusion is that special education is the best field for this tool, which provides some useful applications in this context. Besides, the assessment also gives many useful suggestions to improve ACMUS.

1 Introduction

Perception is the fundamental source of information for the world that we have; even though it is not the only source, it is the foundation of all other knowledge [1]. For this reason, perception has a key role in education, specially in young children. It is necessary to correctly address this field in order to strengthen children development. Children should be exposed to colours, sounds, smells and other sensory stimuli, in a motivational way.

Multisensory stimulation is a concept that comes from the 70s although it is a long-established practice. This concept arose together with a multisensory environment called *Snoezelen room* [2]. These spaces have different elements, which are used to stimulate people's senses such as sight, hearing or smell, in addition to proprioceptive and vestibular aspects. *Snoezelen room* have shown benefits for people with autism [3], mental disabilities [4], ADHD [5] and others, and it has been used in education, specifically in children with high support needs [6].

© Springer International Publishing AG 2016
R. Bottino et al. (Eds.): GALA 2016, LNCS 10056, pp. 321–330, 2016.
DOI: 10.1007/978-3-319-50182-6_29

Human perception is multimodal most of the time, so it is mandatory to recreate this condition in sensory activities [7]. The human brain seems to have evolved to learn optimally in multisensory environments.

Music has many beneficial effects in people. First of all, music is art and culture, so learning music is worthy in itself as part of an integral education. Secondly, it has a powerful motivational facet, so it could be a useful mean to achieve other objectives in education, such as emotional or social aspects. Finally, music has a therapeutic role which has been used in different disorders or illnesses, for instance, autism [8, 9], dementia [10], depression [11], ADHD [12], mental disability [13] and others.

This theoretical framework is the basis of ACMUS, which provides a sound experience merged with visual elements and also with a tactile support. ACMUS is a multisensory tool whose main focus is music. In this paper, we explain the experience of ACMUS on education, specifically at primary, secondary and special education.

2 ACMUS Description

ACMUS is an abbreviation of *Accessible Music*, which reflects its main aim: to make music more accessible by using technology. Music has many benefits for everybody (especially for children), however, sometimes it is not easy to practice music because it implies so much knowledge: such as harmony, rhythm and musical theory and other. ACMUS tries to make this process easier through converting some of this knowledge into implicit information. In other words, ACMUS internally manage musical knowledge in order to the make accessing musical benefits easier. It is not just a recreational activity but another example of how serious games could have an important role in education in many ways [14].

ACMUS also uses a characteristic multisensory approach. Aside from touch (it has been designed specifically for touch devices), ACMUS implies sight and hearing trying to merge both in order to achieve a simultaneous multimodal activity instead of just tasks which require sight and hearing separately. In this way, some important connections are made between sounds and colours. For example, there are eight different musical instruments that are constantly linked with colours; the guitar is always linked with red and the piano with the colour cyan. The eight colours have been selected in order to be recognizable and striking. For this reason, the chosen colours are the additive primary colours (red, green and blue), the subtractive primary colours (yellow, cyan and magenta) as well as white and black (see Fig. 1).

In the same way, there is a connection between musical styles and colours. There are six musical styles that try to include the greater part of musical range. They are classical music, jazz and blues, rock, pop, folk and rap/electronic music. The six colours used in this case are selected from the previous collection (see musical styles in Fig. 1). The relationship between colours and sounds has been investigated and it has demonstrated a relevant relationship with emotions [15], which is a very important aspect in education, specially in some disorders such as autism [16].

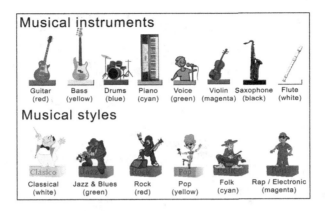

Fig. 1. Musical instruments and musical styles of ACMUS. The colour connection is shown into brackets. (Color figure online)

ACMUS has four activities, each of one focused on a different musical aspect. They have been designed to be complementary and there are some constant elements through all of them such as the musical instrument and the musical style collections. The four activities are *The Composition Workshop, The Musical Scene, The Conductor and The Mixing Studio*.

2.1 Activity 1: The Composition Workshop

The Composition Workshop is a creative activity, which aims to create music and draw at the same time. This multimodality is managed through the connection of visual and sound magnitudes. Specifically, the first connection is between colour (visual) and timbre (sound), which is an intuitive connection. Timbre is sometimes called *the musical instrument colour*; it is the characteristic that allows one to distinguishing between different instruments even if they are playing the same note at the same volume. For example, a trumpet sounds 'brassy or bright' and violin could be described as 'light and delicate'. For this reason, in this activity the instruments are related to colours. When you choose the guitar, the drawing colour would be red, and while you are drawing, the guitar sound will be played. In this way, you can combine colours and sounds at the same time, creating a drawing and a song simultaneously.

The second connection is also very intuitive, because it is made between the drawing thickness (visual) and the volume of the instrument (sound). The bigger the line drawn is, the louder the musical instrument will be played. With these two connections, the player is able to both create music and draw in an intuitive way. Figure 2 shows an example of the activity where the player has created a drawing using five colours of the eight available (the eight instruments). During the activity only the

Fig. 2. The Composition Workshop activity. Different instruments/colours have been used (guitar/red, voice/green, drums/blue, piano/cyan and saxophone/black). In the top there are three tabs to choose instrument (and colour), brush (thickness) and song. There are also buttons to control the different actions that can be used: draw, touch, hear and erase. (Color figure online)

current color (instrument) is played, other ones are muted. When the drawing and the song are finished, it is possible to touch the drawing and reproduce the final result. You can, literally, *hear your drawing*.

2.2   Activity 2: The Musical Scene

The Musical Scene is focused on improvisation. Improvisation is a hard musical skill that is typically associated with jazz and blues, and it implies an intensive training. At the same time, improvisation is one of the most creative musical activities, with many educational benefits [17]. These two statements (the difficulty of improvisation and its benefits) are met but the aim of *The Musical Scene* is to reduce the incompatibility between them, making improvisation an easier activity.

The Musical Scene has a 9-key-piano and six different musical styles for improvisation (Fig. 3 shows the piano in an example). There are three features that made the improvisation easier and adapted to the specific musical style without an advanced training in harmony and musical theory. First, a musical band of the selected musical style accompanies the improvisation. Secondly, the tone of the piano changes with the style: in the jazz style it sounds as a saxophone and in the rock style as an electric guitar. Finally, the most important feature is that the notes associated with the different piano keys are selected from the whole musical scale and they are only "good ones", notes that are appropriated for the style. This way, every note that is played is *in the style* and is a good one; it is not necessary to be thinking on it, just play.

Fig. 3. The Musical Scene activity. In the top there are two tabs to choose the musical style (the rock style is selected) and the song (like a sub-style). There are also the play-pause and the stop buttons to manage the musical accompaniment, and a random button to choose quickly and easily style and song.

2.3   Activity 3: The Conductor

The Conductor is an ear-training activity that consists of a musical instrument recognition game. The aim of the activity is to find the instrument or instruments that are being played. The target is the eight instruments collection (guitar, bass, drums, piano,

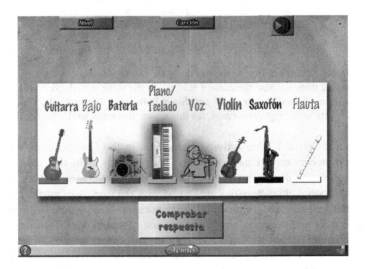

Fig. 4. The Conductor activity. In the top there are two tabs to choose the level (one, two or three instrument played simultaneously) and the song that is played. There is also a button that starts the reproduction of the sound fragment.

voice, violin, saxophone and flute), which is recorded in order to play at the same time and sound harmoniously. The activity has three levels of increasing difficulty, with up to three musical instruments played simultaneously, and which the user attempts to identify (Fig. 4 shown an example of the hardest level).

2.4   Activity 4: The Mixing Studio

The last activity is *The Mixing Studio*, which enables one to mix tracks of real songs just like in a mixing studio. There are various songs (from the six musical styles: classical, jazz and blues, rock, pop, folk and rap/electronic) that can be selected. Once a song is selected, its instruments are displayed as icons in the middle of the screen. These icons represent the tracks that every song has. For example, a rock song usually has a voice track, two or more guitar tracks, a bass track and a drums track (see Fig. 5) and an electronic song mainly has keyboards and synthesized tracks.

Fig. 5. The Mixing Studio activity. In the top there are two tabs to choose the musical style and the song to mix, and there are also the control buttons for the song reproduction. In this example, a rock song has been selected and its tracks are shown in the grid. For example, the drums have a low volume and quite in the right panorama, for this reason it sounds louder for the right channel.

Then, the mix starts. In this activity there is, as in the Composition Workshop, a strong connection between visual and sound characteristics. In this case, the visual characteristics are spatial: they are the vertical and horizontal axes that are shown in a grid. These two spatial characteristics are linked with the two main magnitudes that are handled in a musical mix: the volume and the panorama. The volume is the intensity of how a track sounds, and the panorama is the amount of sound that is heard from the left and the right channel (it makes a track sound from both speakers or more from one than the other). The vertical axis is linked with the volume in an intuitive connection: the higher the instrument's icon is, the louder it plays. The horizontal axis is linked with the panorama in a very transparent way: if the instrument's icon is near to the right limit, it sounds more from the right channel and *vice versa*.

3   Methodology

In order to assess ACMUS in real contexts and to determine the optimal field of application, a comparative assessment was carried out. Different centers and associations from Navarra (Spain) participated in the investigation: *Marqués de Villena* Secondary School, *San Francisco* Primary School, *Virgen de las Nievas* Primary School, *Andrés Muñoz Garde* Especial Education School, the People with Mental Disability Association of Navarra (ANFAS) and *Música sin Barreras* association.

ACMUS was provided to the centers and was used by teachers and students for three months. After the tool was explained and installed, the centers and associations had unrestricted use, in order to discover as many uses as possible. ACMUS was made available for tablets and interactive digital boards (IDB), in order to ascertain individual and group dynamics. At the end of the experience, around 200 students used ACMUS on the three different educational types of schools (primary, secondary and special).

After that, a questionnaire was provided to the centers that used ACMUS and it was completed by six teachers or professionals who were in charge of the evaluation. The questionnaire had three parts: quantitative assessment, qualitative assessment and suggestions. The quantitative assessment had items to be scored from 1 to 10. Those items were related to usability, educational objectives, official educational competences, motivation and others. The second part was complementary to the first one, as it was a qualitative assessment of the same aspects. The third part was very important, because it consisted of suggestions for improving ACMUS. In addition, satisfaction surveys were provided to some of the students that had used ACMUS so that we had a whole panoramic of the assessment.

4   Results

4.1   The Optimal Field for ACMUS

The quantitative data from the different schools and associations were classified by type of schools (primary school, secondary school and especial education). Assessment was based on the general scores for ACMUS and scored for the specific context that it had been assessed (Fig. 6 shows both variables). The less appropriate type of school was secondary school, then, primary school and finally, special education. However, it is also relevant to focus on the differences between the general score and the score in the specific context, which means the suitability of ACMUS of each type of school. The higher difference corresponded to secondary school (3 points), then primary school (1 point) and finally, special education (0 points). These results imply that special education it is the most suitable field of application because it has not only the best score but also the lower difference between the general score and the score in the specific context. Qualitative analysis also confirmed this result, as it can be noticed in these quotes: "I think ACMUS is a tool that offers many opportunities […] for people with mental disabilities or learning disorders" (People with Mental Disability Association of Navarra "We think it [ACMUS] is an interesting tool […] for special education schools" (San Francisco Primary School).

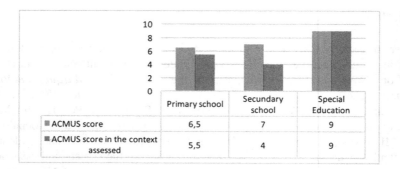

Fig. 6. ACMUS score and ACMUS score in the context assessed in the three fields of applications (primary school, secondary school and special education).

It could be surprising that the general scores for ACMUS differ between centers because it is supposed to be a non-related-to-center score. However, each teacher or professional only used ACMUS in its context so it is difficult to evaluate it in a totally objective way.

4.2 Primary Official Educational Competences Enhanced by ACMUS

In addition, assessment of how ACMUS could help develop some primary official educational competences (measurement only taken in primary schools as requested by the teachers). The primary schools which participated in this investigation assessed the most relevant of those competences in ACMUS, with optimistic results (Fig. 7 shows the score of each competence).

Competence	Score
Social and citizenship competence: Active participation in the classroom	7,25
Social and citizenship competence: Classroom coexistence	7
Artistic and cultural competence: Expression throuhg plastic, visual, musical and corporal language	7,5
Artistic and cultural competence: Imagination and creativity	8
Autonomy and initiative: Interest on challenges	8,5

Fig. 7. Primary official education competences score in ACMUS.

4.3 Improvement Proposals

The main improvement proposals that were suggested by the schools and associations focus on four main aspects. First, there were some specific improvements in each activity such as being able to erase particularly the drawing or have more brushes available in the Composition Workshop activity, could change the number of keys in the Musical Scene activity, a more motivational game dynamic in the Conductor (with a scoreboard, rewards...) or advanced reproduction controls in the Mixing Studio activity. Second, it was suggested to improve the visual style, maybe with a 3D version with more interaction effects. Third, increasing the number of songs and sounds available. Finally, create some new activities as one related with rhythm or other focus on ear training (with task such as differentiate musical notes, compare musical intervals or recognize musical chords).

5 Discussion and Future Work

These results suggest that the most suitable field of application for ACMUS is special education, but also could be helpful on primary school in order to work on some primary official educational competences. Future work should focus on implementing the improvements suggested and examine other possible ways of interactions for ACMUS. Finally, it will be necessary to conduct an experiment to assess the effects of using ACMUS (with the improvements) in special education.

Acknowledgments. This investigation is possible thanks to the scholarship of Foundation La Caixa as well as the support of the European project, Gaviota (JIU-ALA/19.09.01/10/21526/ 245-654/ALPHA 111 (2010)149, http://alfagaviota.eu). We also thank all the schools and associations who have participated in the investigation.

References

1. Goldstein, E.B.: Introduction to perception. Sensat. Percept., 3–20 (2007)
2. McKee, S.A., Harris, G.T., Rice, M.E., Silk, L.: Effects of a Snoezelen room on the behavior of three autistic clients. Res. Dev. Disabil. **28**(3), 304–316 (2007)
3. Hogg, J., Cavet, J., Lambe, L., Smeddle, M.: The use of 'Snoezelen' as multisensory stimulation with people with intellectual disabilities: a review of the research. Res. Dev. Disabil. **22**(5), 353–372 (2001)
4. Singh, N.N., Lancioni, G.E., Winton, A.S.W., Molina, E.J., Sage, M., Brown, S., Groeneweg, J.: Effects of Snoezelen room, activities of daily living skills training, and vocational skills training on aggression and self-injury by adults with mental retardation and mental illness. Res. Dev. Disabil. **25**(3), 285–293 (2004)
5. Lee, S.: Snoezelen therapy: does it work? Dement. Int. J. Soc. Res. Pract. **1**(3), 392–395 (2002)
6. Stephenson, J.: Do multisensory environments have a place in the education of students with high support needs? Spec. Educ. Perspect. **10**(1), 29–39 (2001)
7. Shams, L., Seitz, A.R.: Benefits of multisensory learning. Trends Cogn. Sci. **12**(11), 411–417 (2008)
8. Reschke-Hernández, A.E.: History of music therapy treatment interventions for children with autism. J. Music Ther. **48**(2), 169–207 (2011)
9. Simpson, K., Keen, D.: Music interventions for children with autism: narrative review of the literature. J. Autism Dev. Disord. **41**(11), 1507–1514 (2011)
10. Ahn, S.N., Ashida, S.: Music therapy for dementia. Maturitas **71**(1), 6–7 (2012)
11. Maratos, A., Crawford, M.J., Procter, S.: Music therapy for depression: it seems to work, but how? Br. J. Psychiatry **199**(2), 92–93 (2011)

12. Zhang, F., Liu, K., An, P., You, C., Teng, L., Liu, Q.: Music therapy for attention deficit hyperactivity disorder (ADHD) in children and adolescents. Cochrane Database of Syst. Rev. (8) (2012)
13. Duffy, B., Fuller, R.: Role of music therapy in social skills development in children with moderate intellectual disability. J. Appl. Res. Intellect. Disabil. 13(2), 77–89 (2000)
14. Michael, D.R., Chen, S.L.: Serious games: games that educate, train, and inform. In: Education, pp. 1–95, 31 October 2005
15. Palmer, S.E., Schloss, K.B., Xu, Z., Prado-León, L.R.: Music-color associations are mediated by emotion. Proc. Natl. Acad. Sci. U. S. A. 110(22), 8836–8841 (2013)
16. Dapretto, M., Davies, M.S., Pfeifer, J.H., Scott, A.A., Sigman, M., Bookheimer, S.Y., Iacoboni, M.: Understanding emotions in others: mirror neuron dysfunction in children with autism spectrum disorders. Nat. Neurosci. 9(1), 28–30 (2006)
17. Beckstead, D.: Improvisation: thinking and playing music. Music Educ. J. 99(3), 69–74 (2013)

Serious Games: Valuable Tools for Cultural Heritage

Stavroula Bampatzia[1]([✉]), Ioannis Bourlakos[1], Angeliki Antoniou[1],
Costas Vassilakis[1], George Lepouras[1], and Manolis Wallace[2]

[1] Human-Computer Interaction and Virtual Reality Lab,
Department of Informatics and Telecommunications,
University of Peloponnese, Terma Karaiskaki, 22 131 Tripolis, Greece
{s.babatzia, jbourlak, angelant, costas,
g.lepouras}@uop.gr
[2] Knowledge and Uncertainty Research Laboratory,
Department of Informatics and Telecommunications,
University of the Peloponnese, Terma Karaiskaki, 22 131 Tripolis, Greece
wallace@uop.gr

Abstract. Wishing to connect cultural heritage, games and social networks, the present work describes games to be used within the framework of a European H2020 project. For the purposes of supporting the museum visit, before, during and after, 5 games were designed for social networks to accomplish user profiling, to promote the museum and the application through social network dissemination, to introduce museum items and themes and to also function as visit souvenirs. The games are also presented in a generic framework for games in cultural heritage, which has been used successfully in the past.

1 Introduction

The Horizon 2020 European project "CrossCult: Empowering reuse of digital cultural heritage in context-aware crosscuts of European history" [1] aims at changing peoples' point of view regarding history and to foster numerous interpretations and re-interpretations of the European past through cross-border interconnections among cultural digital resources, citizen viewpoints and physical venues. Moreover, it uses cutting edge technology in order to enhance the visitor's experience with several digital recourses and personalized interactive experiences. In this way, cognitive and emotional responses for vigorous history engagement can be created. Apart from the stimulation of reflection, people have the opportunity to explore historical events and information and to perceive history in an all-encompassing way.

Within the framework of CrossCult a pilot will be implemented for the Archaeological Museum of Tripolis (Greece), a small museum and less known or popular among tourists. This pilot aims to provide guests with an unexpected way of connecting with the museum's historical artifacts, by encouraging crosscutting and transversal viewings of them. Such connections will allow visitors to go deeper than customary method of museum presentations (e.g., type of a statue, construction date, its place of origin). The use of this pilot should facilitate reflections and prospective

R. Bottino et al. (Eds.): GALA 2016, LNCS 10056, pp. 331–341, 2016.
DOI: 10.1007/978-3-319-50182-6_30

interpretations according to the specified topics regarding women in ancient and modern times, including subtopics such as women's appearance, female divinities, ancient female names and meaning, women's status, among many others, all relevant to the museum's physical objects.

Games are a central element in CrossCult used in all project pilots, since they can be highly engaging, attract new visitors and provide cultural content in a way that can lead to long lasting experiences [2]. In particular, for the Archaeological Museum of Tripolis, games were employed as (a) tools for user profiling, (b) mediums to introduce specified thematic topics to the potential museum visitors, (c) an advertising technique to promote the venue, but also the mobile app and (d) a tool for creating souvenirs for the visitors that could be used in social media to remind them of their visit.

2   Related Work

In recent years, gamification methods in cultural spaces play an increasingly important role. Foni et al. [3] assert that serious games are a promising tool in this field. Serious games are able to attract more visitors, unfamiliar with art and history. For instance, serious games have been built to draw the interest of more users to the archaeological places' websites and thus to make these archaeological sites known and possibly to increase physical visits to the sites themselves [2]. Similar studies have been conducted and it has been found that games can successfully promote cultural heritage and tourism [4]. Projects such as Travel in Europe (TiE) [5] and Second China [6] have attempted to make users aware of cultural heritage places. In detail, the Travel in Europe (TiE) application allows users to virtually interact with cultural heritage artifacts (e.g., buildings, artworks) of different European cities through simple treasure hunt games.

In spaces of cultural heritage, contextualization of museum exhibits through serious games will lead people to recognize and appreciate their value, as suggested by Belloti et al. [7]. Serious games can provide player engagement by creating a fun experience for users while also supporting them to achieve learning objectives [8]. Games can also aid in familiarizing young people with unpopular cultural heritage topics, such as art history, and significantly increase their interest levels and engagement [9]. In addition, it has been observed that user participation and contribution towards the creation of digital libraries (e.g., heritage collections) has often been unsuccessful, as low user motivation and participation leads to empty or underutilized collections. To tackle this problem, [10] reports on an experimental platform to build a collection of heritage images through the "SaveMyHeritage" Facebook game. To identify the optimal technique for motivating user participation towards the creation of a heritage collection, two different approaches were compared. Direct user competition through gaming was found to be more effective in motivating user participation when compared to a badge system.

Furthermore, it has been discovered that there an association exists between game playing and personality factors [11]. In recent studies such as EXPERIMEDIA Blue [12] and CHESS [13], user characteristics and preferences have been extracted through games in order to be used for profiling purposes and in particular for museum profiling purposes, since other direct profiling methods might be more time consuming and inappropriate for use in cultural heritage [14]. In this light, games can be used to provide solution to the problem of visitor profiling, in order to maximize the effect of cultural visits through content personalization [15, 16].

According to Antoniou et al. [2], it is important that different types of games with different characteristics and mechanics are designed for the wide range of spaces, which are categorized as cultural heritage sites (e.g. museums of different types, ancient/modern cities, temples of different religions, etc.) due to the fact that they do not shape a homogeneous group. In addition, other researchers also assert that not all games are appropriate for all spaces; for instance De Amicis et al. [17] present a holistic methodology for designing games is applied in three different sites, adjusted to their specific characteristics. The educational potential of the platform approach to gaming has been explored by Apostellis and Daradoumis [18] for dome theatres, and by De Paolis et al. [19] in a variety of different types of sites. Similarly, De Paolis et al. [20] applied a gaming platform approach to assist learning of medieval history. A generic approach for games for cultural heritage is presented by Mikovec et al. [21] based on ten years of experience; in 2012 Bellotti et al. [7] also proposed a holistic model for the design of serious games in spaces of cultural heritage. Finally, Bellotti et al. [5] described the different cognitive elements that games can support which were later incorporated in the framework for the design of cultural heritage games proposed by Antoniou et al. [2], which is also used here to demonstrate the games designed for the Tripolis museum.

3 Descriptive Model for Cultural Heritage Games

The descriptive model for the use of games in cultural heritage, fully explained by Antoniou et al. [2], will be used here to describe the 5 games for the archaeological museum of Tripolis (Table 1). The model is divided into three major categories: (a) game characteristics, (b) player characteristics and (c) organization characteristics.

The game characteristics include: (a) the cognitive skills that the game tries to enhance, (b) the learning objectives of the game which direct to the improvement of player's skills (i.e., knowledge, comprehension, application, analysis, synthesis, and/or evaluation, following Bloom's taxonomy of educational objectives, [22]), (c) the numbers of players, (d) the game's theme (e.g., adventure, strategy, action), (e) the interaction mode (1st person, 3rd person, adaptive, etc.), (f) the target audience (e.g. schools, families, adults), (g) the game flow, (h) the game play, (i) the mechanics, (j) the game aesthetics, (k) the interface design and (l) the technology (e.g., mobile, virtual reality, desktop). Player/visitor characteristics can be divided in situation/visit independent, such as personality factors (i.e., cognitive and learning style, age), and situation/visit dependent, such as visitor type factors (e.g., if the visitor is alone or in a group) and other situational factors (e.g., time of the day, tiredness levels, time constraints). The organization characteristics include (a) information about site/museum type (e.g., archaeological), (b) different organization characteristics and resources (e.g., personnel, budget), (c) the main goals set by the organization for the use of games and (d) the level of *museumness*. Museumness refers to visitors' perceptions on a certain

Table 1. Summary of games, using the descriptive model by Antoniou et al. [2]

			You face on a statue!	Who is your guardian goddess?	Anthroponymy	Your status in the ancient society!	Old-fashion!
Game characteristics	Cognitive skill	Observation	✓				✓
		Reflection		✓		✓	
		Action			✓		✓
	Learning objectives	Knowledge		✓	✓	✓	✓
		Comprehension		✓	✓	✓	
		Application			✓		
		Analysis					
		Synthesis					
		Evaluation					
	Degree of complexity	Mini	✓	✓	✓	✓	✓
		Complex					
	Number of players	Single	✓	✓	✓	✓	✓
		Multiplayer					
	Theme	Strategy					
		Action					
		Adventure			✓		
		Shoot'em up					
		Board					
		Role					
		Knowledge		✓	✓	✓	
		Observingness	✓				✓
	Mode	Interactive games					
	Audience	All users	✓	✓	✓	✓	✓
		Specific target group					
	Game concept	As described above for each game					
	Game description	As described above for each game					
	Scope	As described above for each game					
	Mechanics	As described above for each game					
	User interaction	As described above for each game					
	Technology	Online	✓	✓	✓	✓	✓
		Desktop					
		Mobile	✓	✓	✓	✓	✓
Player characteristics	Players are described in terms of age, cognitive style, whether they visit alone or in a group, etc						
Organization characteristics	Level of museumness	High levels of museumness (archaeological museum)					
	Budget	H2020 European Project					
	Demands on personnel	No demands of museum personnel					

physical or virtual space and whether this space forms a typical museum or not. These perceptions influence the acceptance of different elements in those spaces including games [23].

4   Game Design

The games designed here can be used independently of the museum visit (before or after it) as well as during the visit. As a consequence, the museum experience will be enhanced and in the same time the experience can move beyond the museum walls. To increase the visibility of the games, they will be made available and promoted through social networks such as Facebook, while they will also be made available through the mobile application for the Archaeological Museum of Tripolis. These games are the following: (1) "Your face in a statue!", (2) "Who is your guardian goddess?", (3) "Anthroponymy", (4) "Your status in the ancient society" and (5) "Old-fashion".

It is important to note here that all the games developed will be appropriate for all users and all age groups. Although, they focus on ancient culture themes, the games will not only target museum goers but all interested users, since they can function independently as well. In this light, there are no specific user characteristics to consider other than people accustomed to mobile and/or social network technology, in order to be able to play the game either on social networks or the mobile museum app or both. However, despite the required familiarization with such technologies, the game interface will be user friendly, easy to learn and handle, and will not require high cognitive resources. Finally, the game interface design will respect guidelines for both desktop and mobile applications.

All games described below are mini games for single player that are used for 3 main reasons, to:

1. promote the museum and the application using quick dissemination channels such as social media,
2. acquire sufficient information in order to create user profiles
3. allow users to engage with museum material before and after the visit, offering a continuity of the experience.

In this light, learning was not a main objective in the design of the games, which function rather as an introduction to the museum content. However, some of them have the potential to support learning elements. Using Bloom's taxonomy [22], most of the learning objectives that can be supported are of the lower levels of the taxonomy since learning was not the primary design goal.

The first game "Your face on a statue!" follows the paradigm of online "Face in a Hole" games. In this game, players aim to capture self-portraits and present themselves with the body of an ancient statue of their choice. According to the proposed model of Antoniou et al. [2], "Your face on a statue!" is a mini game. The task of the player is to reassemble an ancient statue by collecting its different parts. When the statue is fully reconstructed, the players can claim a picture with their face on the statue as a reward. Thus, the theme of the game is observingness. This game is designed for players of all ages and it would be a different way of creating souvenirs for the museum visitors.

This particular game is foreseen to function as a social network profile picture and it is believed that will quickly gain popularity with social network users. In addition, since statues from the museum items will be also used, the game can also function as a visit souvenir with a personal twist. This particular game does not have an explicit learning goal, as it rather aims at promoting the application and allow the users to explore the museum content further by using museum items. Having said that, an indirect link to learning is however implied, since the player uses museum content for the game, which could support the further exploration. Since learning though was not a main feature in the design of this game, its learning objectives cannot be further discussed. The game's activity diagram is presented in Fig. 1.

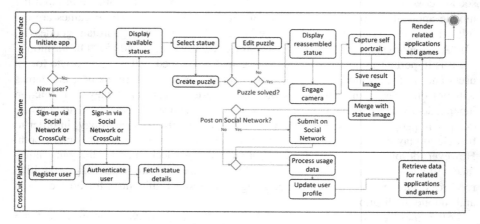

Fig. 1. Activity diagram of the "your face on a statue!" game.

The second game "Who is your guardian goddess?" is a short quiz game, with historical, archaeological and mythological questions regarding the Greek ancient religion and Greek ancient gods. At the end of the game, the player is matched with a goddess as her protector (e.g., Hera/marriage, Artemis/birth, Aphrodite/love). Through this game, cognitive skills such as reflection and low-level learning can be supported, since players learn about the ancient religion and see how this is relevant to their own lives. The target group of this game can be people of all ages. However, this game is designed to also reveal the cognitive style of the player, since while users answer questions to find out their protector goddess, the game collects valuable visitor profiling information to be used later during the museum visit. The quiz questions are based on MBTI (Myers-Briggs Type Indicator) tool for assessing individuals' cognitive styles, which has been successfully used in the past to identify users' personality traits in a game for cultural heritage in social networks [24]. The quiz will assess players cognitive style, by asking questions related to personality preferences (e.g. in the question "What is your favorite animal?", the different possible answers can be linked to specific dimensions in the MBTI tool (for games that reveal personality traits a detailed explanation is presented in [12]. Figure 2 presents the game's activity diagram.

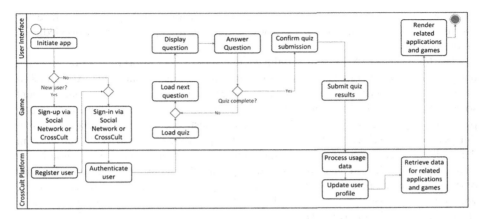

Fig. 2. Activity diagram of the "who is your guardian goddess?" game.

The third game "Anthroponymy" is based on the classic game "PacMan" which is categorized as a maze/action game. The goal of the players is to solve a maze in order to receive the etymology of their name. They can achieve this by unlocking paths inside the maze through anagrammatizing words related to archaeology, within a specific time limit. The faster they find the word, the more points they can earn (Fig. 3). This game targets players of all ages who have to retrieve knowledge regarding word spelling. The game's themes are knowledge and adventure. This specific game will introduce to players terminology used in the area of archaeology and a specific theme of the Archaeological Museum of Tripolis (an important archaeological object is housed at the Tripolis museum about ancient female names) and it is believed to attract Facebook gamers due to its short duration and the personal element that analyzes the name of the gamer. In regards to learning, this game can target the first three levels in

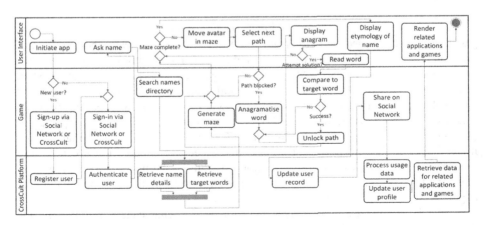

Fig. 3. Activity diagram of the "anthroponymy" game.

the Bloom's taxonomy (i.e. Knowledge, Comprehension and Application), since the user is engaged in anagrammatizing words and trying to apply previous knowledge to unlock game paths.

The fourth game "Your status in the ancient society" is a short quiz game in which players have to answer questions regarding ancient citizens' social status. At the end of the game, players can see their total score and receive extra information about ancient society and the kind of citizen they would be, based on their personalities. This pop psychology quiz, again based on MBTI-targeted questions, will allow users to discover things about themselves and will also collect user profiling information. "Your status in the ancient society" is a mini game which will help us identify the user's profile in the same manner as the "Who is your guardian goddess?" game, with the same learning objectives. It is hypothesized that pop psychology games like the ones described here, will be quickly disseminated through Facebook and will possibly attract new app users and/or museum visitors (Fig. 4).

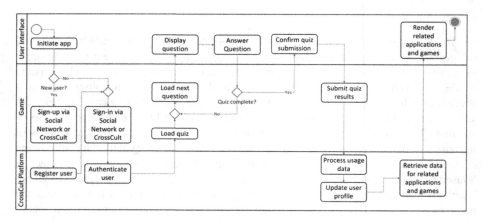

Fig. 4. Activity diagram of the "your status in the ancient society" game.

The fifth game "Old-fashion" is based on the online "Dress-up" games. In this game, the players' objective is to create new fashion styles and learn about fashion of different cultures by selecting low, middle and upper parts of clothes from different eras and areas and combining them. At the end of the game, players can get a digital custom postcard with the outfit they created as a souvenir (Fig. 5). In this way, players will be taught about the alterations of the dresses that occur in various locales, periods or social statuses, which will also introduce an important museum theme (women's appearance) (Knowledge level in the Bloom's taxonomy). The game's theme is observingness, and it can been played from people of all ages and especially children but it can be also used as a design tool for exploring fashion possibilities. Similarly to the previously mentioned games, this one will also function as an advertising tool to promote both the application and the museum.

Table 1 summarizes game, player and organization characteristics, following the descriptive model by Antoniou et al. [2].

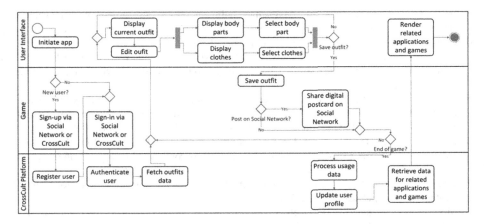

Fig. 5. Activity diagram of the "old-fashion" game.

5 Conclusions

Cultural heritage can be greatly benefited by the use of games. For this reason various frameworks for the holistic design of cultural heritage games have been developed, one of which was used here as a descriptive model for the presentation of 5 games. Currently the authors are also involved in the enrichment of the framework used here to present the 5 games, since important elements (e.g. affective impact of games) are not included in the present version. Affective elements, such as game engagement, triggering emotions, etc. will be studied in detail in our future work and will enhance the existing framework.

All games presented are designed under the scope of the CrossCult project in order to enhance the museum experience. In addition, a small, peripheral museum, like the archaeological museum of Tripolis can use such games to promote the exhibition and the museum visit in social networks and possibly attract new visitors, to introduce the thematic areas of the different exhibitions and to allow the interpretation of the past before, during and after the visit. Hopefully these mini games will become viral on social media and serve the purposes of the project pilot. All the games will undergo an extensive user evaluation and the results will be soon ready for presentation.

Acknowledgment. This research has been performed within the CrossCult: "Empowering reuse of digital cultural heritage in context-aware crosscuts of European history", funded by the European Union's Horizon 2020 research and innovation program.

References

1. http://www.crosscult.eu/
2. Antoniou, A., Lepouras, G., Bampatzia, S., Almpanoudi, H.: An approach for serious game development for cultural heritage. J. Comput. Cult. Herit. **6**, 1–19 (2013)

3. Foni, A.E., Papagiannakis, G., Magnenat-Thalmann, N.: A taxonomy of visualization strategies for cultural heritage applications. J. Comput. Cult. Herit. **3**, 1–21 (2010)
4. Cipolla-Ficarra, F.V., Cipolla-Ficarra, M., Harder, T.: Realism and cultural layout in tourism and video games multimedia systems. In: 1st ACM International Workshop on Communicability Design and Evaluation in Cultural and Ecological Multimedia System, pp. 15–22. ACM (2008)
5. Bellotti, F., Berta, R., De Gloria, A., Zappi, V.: Exploring gaming mechanisms to enhance knowledge acquisition in virtual worlds. In: 3rd International Conference on Digital Interactive Media in Entertainment and Arts, pp. 77–84. ACM, New York (2008)
6. Fishwick, P.A., Henderson, J., Fresh, E., Futterknecht, F., Hamilton, B.D.: Simulating culture: an experiment using a multi-user virtual environment. In: 40th Conference on Winter Simulation, pp. 786–794. Winter Simulation Conference (2008)
7. Bellotti, F., Berta, R., De Gloria, A., D'ursi, A., Fiore, V.: A serious game model for cultural heritage. J. Comput. Cult. Herit. **5**, 1–27 (2012)
8. Mortara, M., Catalano, C.E., Bellotti, F., Fiucci, G., Houry-Panchetti, M., Petridis, P.: Learning cultural heritage by serious games. J. Comput. Cult. Herit. **15**, 318–325 (2014)
9. Froschauer, J., Zweng, J., Merkl, D., Arends, M., Goldfarb, D., Weingartner, M.: ARTournament: a mobile casual game to explore art history. In: 2012 IEEE 12th International Conference on Advanced Learning Technologies, pp. 80–84. IEEE (2006)
10. Havenga, M., Williams, K., Suleman, H.: Motivating users to build heritage collections using games on social networks. In: Chen, H.-H., Chowdhury, G. (eds.) ICADL 2012. LNCS, vol. 7634, pp. 279–288. Springer, Heidelberg (2012). doi:10.1007/978-3-642-34752-8_34
11. Granic, I., Lobel, A., Engels, R.C.M.E.: The benefits of playing video games. Am. Psychol. **69**, 66–78 (2014)
12. Naudet, Y., Antoniou, A., Lykourentzou, I., Tobias, E., Rompa, J., Lepouras, G.: Museum personalization based on gaming and cognitive styles: the BLUE experiment. Int. J. SocNet. Vircom. **7**, 1–30 (2015)
13. Pujol, L., Roussou, M., Poulou, S., Balet, O., Vayanou, M., Ioannidis, Y.: Personalizing interactive digital storytelling in archaeological museums: the CHESS project. In: 40th Annual Conference of Computer Applications and Quantitative Methods in Archaeology (2008)
14. Antoniou, A., Katifori, A., Rousou, M., Vayanou, M., Karvounis, M., Pujol-Tost, L.: Capturing the visitor profile for a personalized mobile museum experience: an indirect approach. In: 1st International Workshop on Human Aspects in Adaptive and Personalized Interactive Environments (HAAPIE 2016), in Conjunction with the 24th ACM Conference on User Modeling, Adaptation and Personalization. ACM (2016)
15. Lykourentzou, I., Claude, X., Naudet, Y., Tobias, E., Antoniou, A., Lepouras, G., Vassilakis, C.: Improving museum visitors' quality of experience through intelligent recommendations: a visiting style-based approach. In: Intelligent Environments (Workshops), pp. 507–518 (2013)
16. Gaeta, A., Gaeta, M., Ritrovato, P.: A grid based software architecture for delivery of adaptive and personalised learning experiences. Pers. Ubiquit. Comput. **13**, 207–217 (2009)
17. De Amicis, R., Girardi, G., Andreolli, M., Conti, G.: Game based technology to enhance the learning of history and cultural heritage. In: International Conference on Advances in Computer Enterntainment Technology, p. 451. ACM (2009)
18. Apostolellis, P., Daradoumis, T.: Audience interactivity as leverage for effective learning in gaming environments for dome theaters. In: Wolpers, M., Kirschner, Paul, A., Scheffel, M., Lindstaedt, S., Dimitrova, V. (eds.) EC-TEL 2010. LNCS, vol. 6383, pp. 451–456. Springer, Heidelberg (2010). doi:10.1007/978-3-642-16020-2_36

19. De Paolis, L.T., Aloisio, G., Celentano, M.G., Oliva, L., Vecchio, P.: A game-based 3D simulation of Otranto in the middle ages. In: 3rd International Conference on Advances in Computer-Human Interactions, pp. 130–133. IEEE (2015)
20. De Paolis, L.T., Celentano, M.G., Oliva, L., Vecchio, P., Aloisio, G.: MediaEvo project: the life in a medieval town. In: 10th WSEAS International Conference on Communications, Electrical & Computer Engineering, and 9th WSEAS International Conference on Applied Electromagnetics, Wireless and Optical Communications, pp. 22–27 (2011)
21. Mikovec, Z., Slavik, P., Zara, J.: Cultural heritage, user interfaces and serious games at CTU Prague. In: 15th International Conference on Virtual Systems and Multimedia, pp. 211–216. IEEE Computer Society (2009)
22. Bloom, B.S.: Taxonomy of Educational Objectives: The Classification of Educational Goals; Handbook I: Cognitive Domain. Longmans, Green, New York (1956)
23. Antoniou, A., Lepouras, G.: Meeting visitors' expectations: the perceived degree of museumness. In: CSEDU, pp. 187–193 (2009)
24. Myers, I., McCaulley, M., Most, R.: Manual: A Guide to the Development and Use of the Myers-Briggs Type Indicator. Consulting Psychologists Press (CPP), Mountain View (1985)

Let's DEsign for MOtivation (DEMO)

Dimitra Chasanidou[✉] and Amela Karahasanovic

SINTEF ICT, Blindern, P.O. Box 124, 0373 Oslo, Norway
{dimitra.chasanidou,amela.karahasanovic}@sintef.no

Abstract. Design for motivation can be defined as a "design practice focused on the activation of human motives, with short or long-term effects, to perform an action" in a context. The paper proposes and develops a design tool called DEMO (DEsign for MOtivation) that aims to address motivation in innovation communities. The DEMO tool is theoretically grounded in motivation theories and based on existing game-like approaches for the development of motivational concepts. The tool incorporates gamification elements, design elements and targets to support multidisciplinary teams in designing for motivation. One application area of the tool is in innovation communities where the design to support user participation and contribution is a complex task, while there is limited understanding how to practically apply motivation. An expert usability evaluation reflected a positive overall experience with the tool. The contribution of this paper lies in its description of the tool and its report on the usability evaluation. Future research in the field should focus on the application of the design tool with various methods in diverse cases.

Keywords: DEMO · Design tool · Innovation community · Motivation · Usability study

1 Introduction

Motivation is widely understood as the activation of a person to do something, while people have different amounts and kinds of motivation [27]. Much research focused on studying what motivates people in various contexts and communities [e.g. 2, 32, 37], in order to understand the people and their motivational drivers to join, participate or contribute to a community, among other issues. Additionally, in the last decade there has been increasing interest in the design of services and systems with a focus on behavioural change [14, 33] and persuasion, as well as gamified experiences with technology [e.g. 8, 11]. These topics are particularly applicable in online communities that depend on the commitment and voluntary participation of their members, for example in innovation communities. Various types of innovation communities, such as brand communities and innovation intermediaries [32], facilitate user interactions who are motivated in doing an activity. Design for such communities to support user participation, engagement and contributions is a complex task due to joint application of motivation theories (e.g. Self-determination theory [27]), design approaches (e.g. persuasive design [14]) and other practices (e.g. gamification). However, there is limited understanding of how to apply theories in designing motivational mechanisms.

© Springer International Publishing AG 2016
R. Bottino et al. (Eds.): GALA 2016, LNCS 10056, pp. 342–353, 2016.
DOI: 10.1007/978-3-319-50182-6_31

Design for motivation can be defined as a *"design practice focused on the activation of human* motives, *with short or long-term effects, to perform an action"* in a context like an online community. It is argued that the design of online communities based on theory can lead to different levels of user participation [26]. However, existing design approaches and tools [e.g. 8, 14, 19] have not yet been explored or evaluated in applied research, and only generic descriptions of these approaches and tools are available. There is, therefore, a need to merge these into a conceptual understanding of how motivation theories and design practices can be applied in the design of motivational services and systems.

We propose a design tool, called DEMO[1] (DEsign for MOtivation), with the aim of filling this gap in the literature. The DEMO tool supports multidisciplinary teams in designing for motivation in innovation communities. The tool is inspired by gamification elements and it seeks to provide a systematic method for developing a design plan for motivation. DEMO is designed for use by multidisciplinary teams comprising designers and non-designers, such as managers, psychologists and other experts engaged in motivation techniques. Usability evaluations of the tool were conducted as a first step to uncover potential issues. The findings indicate that general experiences with the tool were positive. The contribution of this paper lies in its description of the design tool and how this tool could be used in practice by multidisciplinary teams to conceptualise motivational designs during their early stages. A second contribution refers to the report of the usability evaluation.

The next section presents related work, including a review on theories for motivation and existing design approaches. It concludes with the critical review of the design approaches. Afterwards, specifics on the design of the DEMO tool and its components are presented. At the end, the results of a usability evaluation with experts and conclusions are presented and discussed.

2 Related Work: Theories, Tools and Approaches to Design for Motivation

Design for motivation is a highly complicated process because of the involvement of numerous activities and challenges. Each activity can be accomplished by one (or more) designers, each of whom may choose to use different tools. For instance, one crucial activity is to "be creative" and generate ideas especially in early design stages [31]. The challenges refer to, but they are not limited to, how to apply existing theories to design [26, 28], which methods and tools to select [3, 31], and other issues related to the design team and creativity [5, 6, 12].

Motivation to act has been studied in various fields, such as social psychology, educational psychology, and organisational science; however, the application of motivation differs for each of these fields. Across various application areas, two primary types of motivation are used: intrinsic and extrinsic. Motivation is intrinsic if, by engaging in an activity, an individual gains inherent satisfaction. By contrast, in cases

---

[1] Information about the DEMO tool, see here: https://designformotivation.com.

of extrinsic motivation, the activity is an instrument for accomplishing a certain desired outcome of future events [27]. Self-determination theory is a theory of motivation that encompasses both intrinsic and extrinsic motivations on a continuum from internal to external motivation [27]. For instance, intrinsic motivation in innovation communities could refer to a user's need to collaborate and learn through an activity, while extrinsic motivation is often related to virtual goods and monetary compensation. Other theories of motivation can be placed closer to extrinsic (e.g. Maslow's hierarchy of needs [21]) or intrinsic (expectancy value theory [36]) or between extrinsic and intrinsic, such as social-based theories [13]. The application of motivation theories in innovation communities is a common practice for promoting participation [e.g. 2, 34]. Many studies have examined the intrinsic, extrinsic and social motives of user participation in innovation communities. For example, one case study on open innovation communities suggested that monetary rewards are not always the best way to motivate users [2]. Specifically, contributors also value intangible factors, such as community cooperation, learning and fun, particularly when combined with good support and the right cooperation tools [2]. In a second example, a study on a crowdsourcing community showed that intrinsic motivation was more important than extrinsic motivation in inducing participation and suggested a balanced view of extrinsic and intrinsic motivation in order to encourage participation in crowdsourcing [37]. Other studies have produced similar results [e.g. 16, 32].

In practice, the application of motivation theories in innovation communities is discussed within persuasive design [e.g. 14, 33, 34], game design [e.g. 23, 35] and gamification [e.g. 11, 20, 22]. Persuasive design aims to change users' attitudes or behaviours by applying persuasion and social influence through the design of a technology [14, 15]. The design tools of persuasive technology include models, methods, processes and game cards, as well as more traditional methods and tools [4, 14, 15]. It has been argued that design can be seen as inherently persuasive and that objects can be understood as arguments in material form [25]. Motivation theories are applied in games frequently, since games are believed to be capable of changing behaviours both in the game world and in the real world [33]. However, game design uses limited design techniques and tools, meaning design documents and software prototypes as the basic tools for development [1]. Typically, game elements, such as competition, conflict, rewards, resources, time and levels, comprise the motivational elements for game design and beyond. At the intersection of behaviour analysis and game design, we find the widely-used approach of gamification [23]. According to a survey [28], such theoretical foundations as self-determination theory, intrinsic and extrinsic motivation and situated motivational affordance are only few examples of theories currently used to support gamification systems. Gamification is positioned as a "tool that may be used to facilitate extrinsic and intrinsic motivation to accomplish specific tasks through the selective use of game element" [28]. Gamification elements, like game design elements, have been applied and measured in a broad range of fields, such as marketing, learning and health [20, 22, 28]. Deterding argues that "gamification is really a motivational design problem, one that can be best solved with design thinking and design processes" [11].

Design thinking (DT) has attracted the interest of both scholars and practitioners because of the applicability of design methods for promoting innovation and the applicability of DT across many areas [7]. DT shares common methods and tools with service design (SD), interaction design and user experience (UX) design for the development of products and services and is capable of supporting designers in all phases of development. Practical guides for designers [30], online guides for design methods and tools [29], and reviews and case studies on DT and SD tools [e.g. 9] clearly show the wide applicability of DT for both designers and non-designers.

When designing for motivation, another challenge of the early design phases is the selection of tools. Designers and non-designers who are involved in the process have to select from among a broad range of methods and tools. Highly formal methods provide step-by-step instructions or "recipes" to enhance creativity [31], such as in game design [1]. Other designers use un-structured approaches and tools, such as frameworks [31]. In some design fields have well-defined approaches to what constitutes a core set of tools. This is not the case when design for motivation where many of the tools are also commonly found in other design fields.

2.1 Existing Design Tools and Approaches for Motivation

Design approaches from various fields, such as persuasive design, game design and gamification, aim to increase user motivation or target behavioural change by applying motivational mechanisms and creating gamified experiences. Hereafter, we briefly describe a list of design approaches/tools and their phases. It is important to note that this is not an exhaustive list of methods and tools (Table 1); it is representative though:

Table 1. Design approaches for motivation.

Field	Tool/approach	References
Persuasive design	FBM model/process	[14, 15]
	Taxonomy of motivational affordances	[34]
Game design	MDA framework	[19]
Gamification	Player experience design process	[8]
	Player centered design process	[20]
	"Six D's" gamification design framework	[35]
	User-centered framework 'RECIPE'	[24]
	Gamification model canvas	[17]

Persuasive Design: Persuasive design is a model for understanding human behaviour presented by Fogg [14]. The FBM (Fogg Behaviour Model) identifies and defines three factors—motivation, ability and triggers—that control whether a behaviour is performed. In addition, Fogg [15] suggested a process to follow as a best practice in the early stages of persuasive technology design. This process consists of eight steps: targeting a simple behaviour, finding a receptive audience, finding what prevents the target behaviour, choosing a familiar technology channel, finding relevant examples of persuasive technology, imitating successful examples, testing and iterating quickly and, finally, expanding on success. In the field of persuasive design and human-computer interaction (HCI), Weiser et al. [34] suggested a taxonomy of motivational affordances for the design of persuasive technologies. This taxonomy links design components that are typically found in psychological theories on motivation and includes three levels: general design principles, mechanics and elements.

Game Design: The MDA (Mechanics, Dynamics, Aesthetics) framework [19] uses systems thinking to describe the interplay of game elements and apply them outside of games. Mechanics refer to the functioning components of a game, including the various actions, behaviours and control mechanisms afforded to the player. Dynamics work to create aesthetic experiences for the player and describe the run-time behaviours of the mechanics. Aesthetics describe the desirable emotional responses evoked in the player when the player interacts with the game system.

Gamification: The "player experience design" process [8] focuses on players' goals and consists of seven phases: defining the business outcomes and success metrics, the target audience, the player's goals, the player's interaction with the gamified solution, the play space and the player's journey in regards to the provided environment, the incentives and rewards and, finally, the gamified solution, which must be tested and iterated. The "player centered design" process [20] is inspired by the user-centred design philosophy and embeds the concept of engagement. The process consists of five phases: understanding the player and the context of play, defining the mission and the desired business outcome, identifying the human motivation, applying game mechanics with respect to the user interface elements and, finally, managing the mission and metrics and monitoring player motivation. The "Six D's" gamification design framework [35] describes a design process with six phases designed to define business objectives, delineate target behaviour to promote business objectives, describe the players, devise activity loops, embed fun aspects and, lastly, deploy appropriate tools in order to support the alignment of user behaviour and product objectives. The user-centred RECIPE framework [24] targets long-term user engagement and consists of six phases: defining the boundaries of play, exposing the players to the real-world story, the players' choices within the system, the game design and game display concepts, the players' engagement (through encouragement) to discover and learn from others and, finally, reflection, which refers to assisting participants in finding other interests and past experiences that can deepen engagement and learning. Lastly, the "gamification model canvas" [17] is a tool to develop gamified behaviours in non-game environments based on the MDA Framework and the Business Model Canvas. The Business Model Canvas defines nine elements: the implementation platform, mechanics, dynamics, aesthetics, players, feedback components, players' behaviours, related costs of the game and, finally, revenues (i.e. the economic or social return of the solution via the introduction of gamification).

2.2 Summarized Findings

In summary, the related work shows that the challenge in addressing motivation in design are defining links with theory and selecting tools. The majority of existing tools lack of theoretical grounding, especially in gamification-related approaches. Examples, cases and best practices on how to conceptualise design for motivation in practice, with a detailed description from theory to concepts and designs, are also missing. The reviewed approaches (Table 1) have similar phases and provide un-structured ways to design for motivation; yet, their phase descriptions are quite general, without any practical guidance or potential limitations. In addition, there is a lack of description of the use context concerning, for example, what the targeted users may be, whether certain competencies are required to utilise the tools, which development phases should be used when, etc. The reviewed approaches have not been sufficiently explored through applied research and/or evaluated according to usability, performance or other metrics. Lastly, with the exception of the "gamification model canvas" [17], there is a lack of visual representations for guiding the design processes. However, some of the examined approaches and phases have the potential to support future approaches. Therefore, in sum, designing for motivation is a complex activity, and there are several limitations to consider when selecting design tools. Gamification is a promising approach for addressing motivation in innovation communities. Additionally, both intrinsic and extrinsic motivation should be addressed to capture the wide variety of motivation factors, as was suggested in Fogg's model [14] and the taxonomy of motivational affordances [34]. Based on the related work, theories and design approaches, we argue that we need a more structured approach in this field.

3   DEMO - A Tool to Design for Motivation

The idea for developing a tangible tool emerged while working with industrial partners, who wanted to increase user motivation in innovation communities and to ideate about motivation. As discussed, existing work related to design tools shows that existing approaches fail to address important design issues. This gap constitutes the basis for developing the DEMO tool. DEMO is a design tool that supports multidisciplinary teams in the early phases of development to design for motivation. We refer to multidisciplinary groups as groups consisting of designers (e.g. game, interaction and service designers), managers, psychologists, developers and other participants. The tool is theoretically grounded on motivation theories, it incorporates design concepts for motivation, through a stepwise process based on cards. DEMO also uses visual representations as a way of rising communication in multidisciplinary groups during workshops. In particular, we examine the application of the tool in the case of innovation communities. Previous research into design and collaborative teams, participatory design, design and creativity support the design of our suggested tool, as does research on using cards and games as innovation support tools [5, 6, 10, 18].

The DEMO tool consists of three main parts: the template, the cards and the roles. Figure 1 shows an early version of the template and examples of cards. One important advancement implemented in the DEMO tool (compared to previous design tools) is its use of visual representations to guide the design process. The physical artefacts of the tool help teams to build shared understandings and designs. The use context is also suggested, but not limited, to the use of DEMO in the early design phases. Through an iterative process, DEMO uses cards to inspire teamwork in order to produce designs, concepts and other artefacts related to motivation. Roles are optional and should be adopted as necessary to gain a multidisciplinary perspective. The process of utilising

Fig. 1. The DEMO tool with two examples of cards.

DEMO includes, first, a preparation phase, during which the objective(s) to design for motivation (i.e. who is the target user, what should be achieved, why there is a need to achieve it) is set before the workshop. The group also needs time to clarify goals, gather supportive material and become familiar with the functionality of the tool.

3.1   Design of the Template

The design of the template was based on a stepwise process inspired by the reviewed tools (Table 1) and other DT/SD tools. Important and common steps among the previous design approaches, such as the description of the user and experience, were embedded in DEMO template. This template helps the team define the important aspects of the design process: the objective, the user, the experience and the motivation. Participants must describe or clarify the objective to design for motivation, as appropriate; the user is the subject of the design for motivation; experience refers to the general user experience through the innovation platform in relation to the motivation; and, finally, the motivation refers to motivational mechanisms that could be employed by the innovation platform. The flow of the steps and the number of step iterations are be decided by the team. The template is used as a design and information space that supports the collaborative reflection and inspiration through the steps. When printed in a large paper format (preferably A0 or A1), the template and the cards assist the participants in navigating through the process of developing a design plan and help them to include all information essential to the group discussion. As has been shown in related work [5, 6], tangible tools provide collaborative spaces for conceptualising complex concepts with simple, traditional means (e.g. pen, paper).

3.2   Design of the Cards

The cards are inspired by previous card-based design approaches [10, 18] and gamification concepts. Specifically, the cards are designed to inspire the group discussion, with relevant topics and group reflections. Four card categories, namely people, methods and tools, resources and expectations, aim to clarify further each step. The cards for "people" specify who (e.g. industrial partners, users or administration) should be involved in a particular step. The cards for "methods and tools" specify which methods and tools (e.g. personas, qualitative data or surveys) should be used in a step. The cards for "resources" specify which resources (e.g. the platform, policies or points) are needed to complete a step. Additionally, the cards for expectations specify what the expectations (e.g. feedback, learning or new product/service) are for each step. The cards serve as supportive materials for helping the group complete the stepwise process, while the two levels of the cards fit the group's objectives. This means that general-purpose and specific-purpose cards can be sorted according to whether a group's objective is general (e.g. develop a strategy to motivate users) or specific (e.g. develop a user interface component for user motivation). General-purpose cards include more broad concepts, such as users (in category: "people") and qualitative data (in category: "methods and tools"), while specific-purpose cards include more explicit concepts, such as points (in category: "resources") and new product/service (in category: "expectations"). Furthermore, blank cards can be filled with pertinent information and short explanations for some of the cards are included. Let us consider an example to illustrate the role of the cards in the process. A group begins by describing the objective (why to design for motivation). "People" who might be involved in further specifying the objective could include business partners, employees, the IT department, registered users, etc. "Methods and tools" to better describe the objective might include personas, surveys, questionnaires, qualitative methods, interviews, etc. Other "Resources" that are necessary to define the objective could include the innovation platform, related policies and documents, etc. Finally, the "expectations" of this step could be to create a list of requirements or a strategy to proceed with the following steps. For each step, the same set of cards is used (and re-used as needed), without any limitation on the number of cards.

3.3   Roles

The roles are inspired by previous work on design tools [30], DT research [7], participatory design approaches [6], and game-like approaches [5]. The roles have two primary purposes within the process. First, the roles support the participants' engagement in a "gamified" role-playing process, and second, they ensure the participation of several perspectives during the workshop. The roles include: the "facilitator", the "designer", the "developer" and the "manager". The "facilitator" is a process-oriented role that aims to determine the best possible outcome for each step by balancing group dynamics. The "designer" is a design-oriented role that focuses on how to implement the outcome of each step. Designers, who may be interaction designers, service designers or interface designers, need to be able to communicate and define concepts from the other "roles". This means that any given design concept should be visualised in different ways, as necessary, to facilitate the understanding of all participants. Designers usually work with several different tools, most of which are visual, depending on the workflow. The "developer" is a technical role that focuses on how to develop the outcome of each step. Developers have their own tooling needs and usually work with software to test code or build engines or libraries. Lastly, the "manager" is a management-oriented role that focuses on how to organise and deliver the outcome of each step. Managers are characterised by a high level of practice and are comfortable working with a wide variety of different tasks. It is important to note that these roles are not exclusive and that participants may shift between roles depending on the competencies of the group. Other roles that are useful in such workshops could include the roles of "psychologist" and "end user" [28].

4 Usability Evaluation of the DEMO Tool

To ensure the usability of the tool, a group-based expert evaluation method was organised to identify potential usability problems related to the DEMO tool. The evaluation concluded by identifying both overall usability problems and ratings of severity. Potential problem areas related to design, experience with the tool, functionality and interaction with the group were examined. Nine experts, both men and women, with expertise in HCI (median of 17 years of experience), in interaction design and the design of information systems (IS) (median of 12 years of experience) and PhD students in informatics, HCI and interaction design (median of 5 years of experience) were participated in usability evaluation. The evaluation procedure included a short, 15-min introduction to the main goals of the study and the DEMO tool. Then, the groups were introduced to a case scenario. After the general description of the tool, the participants were given some time to familiarise themselves with the tool. The group discussion began with a delegation of roles among participants. The group interacted with the tool and each other following the stepwise process. After one hour of interaction, a short discussion of the process and the tool was conducted. Lastly, the participants were invited to fill in individual evaluation reports, consisting of questions about the stepwise process, the four parts of tool (template, cards and roles), the perceived outcomes of each step and their general experiences with the tool. The evaluation report included open questions, while participants were asked to rate the severity of usability problems using a 5-point scale. No personal data were collected. The total duration of the usability testing session was approximately 2 h.

5 Discussion - Conclusions

The preliminary evaluation of the tool showed that the overall experience with the tool was positive, while some usability issues were uncovered. The expert evaluation was proven to be an effective method for assessing the usability and improving DEMO's design in the early phase of development. The participants, with their different fields of expertise, contributed a diversity of insights into usability problems. Specifically, the experts commented on usability problems and explained their concerns and limitations in detail, either in their reports or in the discussion following the usability session. The majority of researchers went beyond simply pointing to usability problems by suggesting how different problems could be solved in practice. Furthermore, group dynamics played a significant role in the outcomes. Balanced group dynamics can be achieved via roles-in-turn, time-limited discussions or an experienced facilitator who ensures collaborative work.

An important lesson when designing for motivation concerns conceptual models. The concept of motivation is abstract and complex, leaving significant room for misunderstanding. This can be clarified with description of motivation theories, examples of concepts and description of related case studies. In general, the tool incorporates concepts that could be applied to different projects related to design for motivation in or beyond innovation communities. General-purpose and specific-purpose card concepts inspire teams and support group-based discussions and conceptual modelling related to motivation. A good balance of abstract and specific concepts is needed in order for the tool to be flexible and applicable to diverse projects. With two levels of analysis—one at a general level, in which basic conceptualisations of motivations, objectives, users and experiences are described, and one at a specific level, in which more specific conceptualisations of same steps are described—the corresponding cards will have clear roles in the process. Gamification has the potential to be better embedded within the design tool and better connected to motivation theories. Examples from both the practical application of theory and applied gamification elements will support a better understanding. The participants' previous experiences working with their groups helped them to build conceptual models, however they were challenged to build a concept for an artificial scenario within limited time. In the future, more time for preparations is needed, primarily in relation to the concept of motivation, and maybe in combination with other creative methods. In addition, the tool should be more flexible to adopt a group's creativity by embedding relevant creative methods, such as brainstorming, storyboards, mind mapping and many more. Also, the word "steps" is relatively problematic, since this led to the tool being interpreted as a strict, sequential process rather than as a suggested path. Future evaluation of DEMO may involve evaluating the different aspects of the tool separately, sorting out the cards or evaluating the tool's creativity and innovation issues, among others. Furthermore, the expert evaluation of the DEMO could be extended in later evaluations via expert evaluations with multidisciplinary groups of experts (e.g. psychologists, game developers, or innovation managers), as well as evaluations of the design outcomes following the use of the tool.

Design for motivation is a complicated process because of the involvement of many activities and challenges. Thus, it is required to use tested tools and methods that can be applied in diverse projects and employed by multidisciplinary teams. In this paper, a design tool called DEMO was introduced. The main contribution of the paper lies in the presentation of the DEMO tool and its parts. The novelty of DEMO is the fact that it provides a structured and game-like approach to designing for motivation. Potential benefits of using the DEMO tool are twofold: it presents a structured and visual approach involving steps, physical material (cards) and roles (which engage participants in a role-playing activity) within a "gamified" process in designing for motivation; it has been practically tested in usability sessions. A second contribution of the paper concerns the usability evaluation of the tool.

Further work and research should focus on applying the design tool in diverse cases of innovation communities and various application areas. Case studies that report in detail efforts to develop and design for motivation in specific cases are needed. The application of additional methods will reveal more usability and design issues and, thus, inform the design of the tool. Interviews with multidisciplinary groups of participants, observations and surveys with end users are a few examples of additional methods that could be used. Practitioners will find this paper's discussion useful for practice. Practitioners may benefit from design guidelines for how to design for motivation based on this tool. Finally, an online version of the tool might be useful for workshops with remote team members.

Acknowledgments. This research is funded by the Norwegian Research Council through the Center for Service Innovation (csi.nhh.no).

References

1. Almeida, M.S.O., da Silva, F.S.C.: A systematic review of game design methods and tools. In: Anacleto, J.C., Clua, E.W.G., da Silva, F.S.C., Fels, S., Yang, H.S. (eds.) ICEC 2013. LNCS, vol. 8215, pp. 17–29. Springer, Heidelberg (2013). doi:10.1007/978-3-642-41106-9_3
2. Antikainen, M., Makipa, M., Ahonen, M.: Motivating and supporting collaboration in open innovation. Eur. J. Innov. Manag. **13**(1), 100–119 (2010)
3. Bailey, B., Konstan, J.: Are informal tools better? Comparing DEMAIS, pencil and paper, and authorware for early multimedia design. In: Proceedings of the SIGCHI Conference on Human Factors in Computing Systems, pp. 313–320 (2003)
4. Behavior Change Strategy Cards - Artefact. https://www.artefactgroup.com/resources/behavior-change-strategy-cards/. Accessed 2 Oct 2016
5. Brandt, E.: Designing exploratory design games a framework for participation in participatory design? In: Proceedings Participatory Design Conference, pp. 57–66 (2006)
6. Brandt, E., Messeter, J.: Facilitating collaboration through design games. In: Proceedings Participatory Design Conference, pp. 121–131 (2004)
7. Brown, T.: Change by Design: How Design Thinking Transforms Organizations and Inspires Innovation. Harper Business, New York (2009)
8. Burke, B.: Gamify: How Gamification Motivates People to do Extraordinary Things. Gartner Inc., Stamford (2014)
9. Chasanidou, D., Gasparini, A.A., Lee, E.: Design thinking methods and tools for innovation. In: Marcus, A. (ed.) DUXU 2015. LNCS, vol. 9186, pp. 12–23. Springer, Heidelberg (2015). doi:10.1007/978-3-319-20886-2_2
10. Clatworthy, S.: Service innovation through touch-points: development of an innovation toolkit for the first stages of new service development. Int. J. Des. **5**(2), 15–28 (2011)
11. Deterding, S.: Gamification: designing for motivation. Interactions **19**(4), 14–17 (2012)
12. Dorst, K., Cross, N.: Creativity in the design process: co-evolution of problem–solution. Des. Stud. **22**(5), 425–437 (2001)
13. Festinger, L.: A theory of social comparison processes. Hum. Relat. **7**(2), 117–140 (1954)
14. Fogg, B.: A behavior model for persuasive design. In: Proceedings of the 4th International Conference on Persuasive Technology, pp. 40:1–40:7 (2009)
15. Fogg, B.: Creating persuasive technologies: an eight-step design process. In: Proceedings of the 4th International Conference on Persuasive Technology, pp. 44:1–44:6 (2009)
16. Frey, K., Luthje, C., Haag, S.: Whom should firms attract to open innovation platforms? The role of knowledge diversity and motivation. Long Range Plan. **44**(5), 397–420 (2011)
17. Gamification Model Canvas - The Gamification Hub. http://www.gameonlab.com/canvas/. Accessed 2 Oct 2016

18. Halskov, K., Dalsgård, P.: Inspiration card workshops. In: Proceedings of the 6th Conference on Designing Interactive Systems, pp. 2–11 (2006)
19. Hunicke, R., LeBlanc, M., Zubek, R.: MDA: a formal approach to game design and game research. In: Proceedings of the Challenges in Games AI Workshop – 19th National Conference of Artificial Intelligence, pp. 1–5 (2004)
20. Kumar, J.: Gamification at work: designing engaging business software. In: Marcus, A. (ed.) DUXU 2013. LNCS, vol. 8013, pp. 528–537. Springer, Heidelberg (2013). doi:10.1007/978-3-642-39241-2_58
21. Maslow, A.: A theory of human motivation. Psychol. Rev. **50**(4), 370–396 (1943)
22. Mekler, E., Brühlmann, F., Opwis, K., Tuch, A.: Disassembling gamification: the effects of points and meaning on user motivation and performance. In: CHI 2013 Extended Abstracts on Human Factors in Computing Systems, pp. 1137–1142 (2013)
23. Morford, Z., Witts, B., Killingsworth, K., Alavosius, M.: Gamification: the intersection between behavior analysis and game design technologies. Behav. Anal. **37**(1), 25–40 (2014)
24. Nicholson, S.: A recipe for meaningful gamification. In: Reiners, T., Wood, L.C. (eds.) Gamification in Education and Business, pp. 1–20. Springer, Berlin (2015)
25. Redström, J.: Persuasive design: fringes and foundations. In: IJsselsteijn, W.A., de Kort, Y. A.W., Midden, C., Eggen, B., van den Hoven, E. (eds.) PERSUASIVE 2006. LNCS, vol. 3962, pp. 112–122. Springer, Heidelberg (2006). doi:10.1007/11755494_17
26. Ren, Y., Kraut, R., Kiesler, S.: Applying common identity and bond theory to design of online communities. Organ. Stud. **28**(3), 377–408 (2007)
27. Ryan, R.M., Deci, E.L.: Intrinsic and extrinsic motivations: classic definitions and new directions. Contemp. Educ. Psychol. **25**(1), 54–67 (2000)
28. Seaborn, K., Fels, D.: Gamification in theory and action: a survey. Int. J. Hum.-Comput. Stud. **74**, 14–31 (2015)
29. Service Design Tools. http://www.servicedesigntools.org/. Accessed 2 Oct 2016
30. Stickdorn, M., Schneider, J.: This is Service Design Thinking; Basics, Tools, Cases. BIS Publishers, Amsterdam (2010)
31. Stolterman, E., Pierce, J.: Design tools in practice: studying the designer-tool relationship in interaction design. In: Proceedings of the Designing Interactive Systems Conference, pp. 25–28 (2012)
32. Ståhlbröst, A., Bergvall-Kåreborn, B.: Exploring users motivation in innovation communities. Int. J. Entrepreneurship Innov. Manag. **14**(4), 298–314 (2011)
33. Visch, V., Vegt, N., Anderiesen, H., van der Kooij, K.: Persuasive game design: a model and its definitions. In: CHI 2013 Workshop Designing Gamification - Creating Gameful and Playful Experiences (2013)
34. Weiser, P., Bucher, D., Cellina, F., De Luca, V.: A taxonomy of motivational affordances for meaningful gamified and persuasive technologies. In: Proceedings of the 3rd International Conference on ICT for Sustainability, pp. 271–280 (2015)
35. Werbach, K., Hunter, D.: For the Win: How Game Thinking Can Revolutionize Your Business. Wharton Digital Press, Philadelphia (2012)
36. Wigfield, A., Eccles, J.: Expectancy—value theory of achievement motivation. Contemp. Educ. Psychol. **25**(1), 68–81 (2000)
37. Zheng, H., Li, D., Hou, W.: Task design, motivation, and participation in crowdsourcing contests. Int. J. Electron. Commer. **15**(4), 57–88 (2011)

Exploring the Relation Between Game Experience and Game Mechanics for Bodily-Kinesthetic Players

Pejman Sajjadi$^{(\boxtimes)}$, Andreas Lo-A-Njoe, Joachim Vlieghe, and Olga De Troyer

Department of Computer Science, WISE, Vrije Universiteit Brussel,
Pleinlaan 2, 1050 Brussels, Belgium
{Ssajjadi, aloanjoe, Joachim.Vlieghe,
Olga.DeTroyer}@vub.ac.be

Abstract. This paper presents the results of a research on investigating whether tailoring the game mechanics and interaction modality of a game has an impact on the game experience of the player in the case of players with a high bodily-kinesthetic intelligence (with respect to the theory of Multiple Intelligences). For this purpose, we designed and developed a game called LeapBalancer, and evaluated it with a group of kinesthetic and a group of non-kinesthetic players. The results of the evaluation show that considering the intelligences of the players during game design matters and affects their game experience. In addition, we analyzed the players' in-game behavior to explain the results. The finding are also important for learning games, since research suggest that good game experience is positively correlated with improved learning.

1 Introduction

Research [1, 2] has shown that good game experience can lead to the flow state during which an individual would function at his/her fullest capacity [3], enabling more effective learning [4, 5]. One way to achieve a good game experience could be by tailoring the design of a learning game to the characteristics of its players, i.e. through a player-centered game design approach. Several theoretical frameworks on player-centered adaptation [6, 7] have suggested a variety of factors such as *performance*, *playing style*, *level of knowledge*, *affective states*, *history of playing*, *personality* and more, that can be monitored and assessed to be used for personalization/adaptation. Although some of these factors have been the focus of research, more pedagogical-oriented factors like differences in intelligence dimensions of the players with respect to the theory of Multiple Intelligences (MI) [8] have been largely neglected.

In our research we explore the potential of this MI theory for player-centered design of learning games. In [9, 10] we have presented empirical evidence for a relationship between people's strong MI dimensions and their preferences for specific games and game mechanics, The term game mechanic is defined as *"the action invoked by an*

© Springer International Publishing AG 2016
R. Bottino et al. (Eds.): GALA 2016, LNCS 10056, pp. 354–364, 2016.
DOI: 10.1007/978-3-319-50182-6_32

agent (player or AI agent) to interact with the game world, as constrained by the game rules" [11] (Paragraph 25). In this paper, we focus on players that have a high bodily-kinesthetic intelligence. We designed and developed a game, called LeapBalancer, in which the game mechanics and the interaction modality are highly kinesthetic oriented, i.e. using the Leap Motion[1]. Next, we evaluated the game to investigate whether people exhibiting dominance for the bodily-kinesthetic intelligence had a better game experience. The results of the evaluation show that the players who are bodily-kinesthetically intelligent were indeed more immersed in the game and experienced the flow state more than non-kinesthetically players. To better understand the results, they were further explored by analyzing the in-game behavior of the players and by correlating them to their game experience measurements. Although LeapBalancer is not a learning game itself, the findings are also applicable to learning games, as research has shown that a good game experience is positively correlated with higher learning. We chose to first design and implement a simple game to minimize the effects that the learning content or complicated stories, challenges and other aspects could impose on our objective.

The paper is organized as follow: in Sect. 2 we briefly explain the theory of Multiple Intelligences. Section 3 reviews researches related to topic of the paper. Section 4 explains the LeapBalancer game. Section 5 presents the evaluation of LeapBalancer and discusses the results, and Sect. 6 concludes the article.

2 Theory of Multiple Intelligences (MI)

The theory of MI defines the human intelligence as a multi-dimensional concept [8], as opposed to the one dimensional understanding of intelligence commonly referred to as Intelligence Quotient (IQ). Intelligence as "the ability to solve problems, or to create products, that are valued within one or more cultural settings" [8] (page xxviii) is divided into eight distinct dimensions. Each dimension of intelligence represents a different way of thinking, problem solving and learning. According to its developer Howard Gardner, everyone possesses all intelligence dimensions, though with varying strengths. Gardner stresses that all dimensions work together in an orchestrated way and can thus influence each other. The eight intelligence dimensions as defined by the theory of MI [12] [paraphrasing by the authors] are:

- **Visual-spatial** intelligence represents the ability to conceptualize and manipulate large-scale spatial arrays (like a pilot does), or more local forms of spaces (like an architect).
- **Bodily-kinesthetic** intelligence is the ability to use one's whole body, or parts of the body, to solve problems or create products (like a dancer).
- **Musical-rhythmic** intelligence implies having sensitivity to rhythm, pitch, meter, tone, melody and timbre (like a musical conductor). This may entail the ability to sing, play musical instruments, and/or compose music.

---

[1] https://www.leapmotion.com/.

- **Linguistic** intelligence suggests sensitivity to the meaning, order, sound, rhythms, inflections, and meter of words (like a poet).
- **Logical-mathematical** intelligence is the capacity to conceptualize the logical relations among actions or symbols (like done by mathematicians).
- **Interpersonal** intelligence represents the ability to interact effectively with others and being sensitive to others' moods, feelings, temperaments and motivations (like a negotiator).
- **Intrapersonal** intelligence implies being sensitive to one's own feelings, goals, and anxieties, and the capacity to plan and act in the light of one's own traits. Intrapersonal intelligence is not particular to specific careers; rather, it is a goal for every individual in a complex modern society, where one has to make consequential decisions for oneself.
- **Naturalistic** intelligence is the ability to make consequential distinctions in the world of nature as, for example, between one plant and another, or one cloud formation and another (like a taxonomist).

We recognize that there are controversies about this theory. Opponents [13–15] criticize the lack of strong empirical evidence for the existence of the dimensions, while proponents [16] argue that the value of such a theory is rather in the contributions that it could make to understanding and practice in the field. Therefore, we deem researching whether this theory can be used in understanding players' behavior and attitude to be worthwhile.

3   Related Work

The related work of this paper can be divided into two categories. The first category covers studies on the relation between interaction modalities and the theory of MI. The second category covers works related to serious/learning games that use the Leap Motion as their main interaction modality.

With respect to the relationship between interaction modality and the theory of MI, in [17, 18] it is suggested that physical manipulations and interactions are suited for bodily-kinesthetically intelligent players. These suggestions are not empirically validated and are entirely theoretical. On similar grounds, in [19] the bodily-kinesthetic intelligence is mapped to a motion-based interaction modality. The authors claim that playing a game on a Nintendo dual screen that uses a stylus has a positive effect on developing one's kinesthetic intelligence.

With respect to serious/learning games that use the Leap Motion as their main interaction modality, the work of Lotfi et al. [20] presents an interesting case study. The study shows that the game, which aims to teach the Arabic sign language to deaf children using Leap Motion, has significantly improved the learning outcome of the players. Similarly, [21] presents a case study of how Leap Motion is integrated as kinesthetic interaction modality in a serious game focused on rehabilitating stroke patients. One of the most prominent projects that promotes kinesthetic learning and uses the Leap Motion as part of its process is project Geomoto [22]. The project includes a series of learning games aimed at teaching geoscience concepts, all of which employ kinesthetic interaction modalities (including the Leap Motion). This project is based on the hypothesis that "*students would be highly motivated to learn about historically difficult concepts if they were situated within embodied, movement-based learning environments*" (ibid, page 2). Through a pilot study, the different games in the Geomoto project have been evaluated with respect to their effect on learning outcome. Significant knowledge gain from pre-test to post-test among the students has been reported with increases ranging between 5% and 25%. The authors concluded that the games are engaging and educational, and the kinesthetic interaction modality with the games is effective.

4   LeapBalancer

In [9, 10], we have presented empirical evidence that indicates a relationship between people's strong MI dimensions and their preferences for specific games and game mechanics. Furthermore, in [10] we presented a recommendation system[2] that maps the different dimensions of MI to different game mechanics. This mapping indicates positive (appropriate), dubious (uncertain) and negative (inappropriate) relations between MI dimensions and game mechanics. As we aimed for designing a game oriented towards players with a high level of bodily-kinesthetic intelligence, we used this recommendation system to select appropriate game mechanics. We mainly selected game mechanics that were marked as appropriate for bodily-kinesthetic players, but also some game mechanics marked as uncertain. When a game mechanic is marked as uncertain (indicated by the term "dubious") for a certain intelligence dimension this means that positive as well as negative correlations between the mechanic and the dimension were found and that based on the current empirical evidence it cannot be decided whether the mechanic is appropriate or not for the dimension. The game mechanics used in LeapBalancer are listed in Table 1 together with a category that indicates the role the mechanic fulfills in the game. For instance, we selected *Motion* and *Timing* for creating challenge.

Table 1. Employed game mechanics in LeapBalancer

Category	Game mechanic
Challenge	Motion (positive)
	Timing (positive)
Motivation	Pavlovian interaction (positive)
Assistance	Tutorial/first run scenarios (dubious)
Game environment	Gravity (dubious)
Movement action	Directed exploration (no relation)
Object manipulation	Controlling (no relation)

---

[2] http://wise.vub.ac.be/dpl/.

Note that the *Directed exploration* and *Controlling* mechanics are not correlated to the bodily-kinesthetic dimension. This means that in current empirical evidence neither positive nor negative correlations could be found. Thus, although there is no positive correlation it will not harm to use them because there is also no negative correlation. No inappropriate game mechanics for bodily-kinesthetic players were used. The definitions of the mechanics employed in LeapBalancer are as follows:

- **Motion:** The players' bodily stances (postures, gestures, etc.) produce input to the game system or benefit in dealing with its challenges.
- **Timing:** The player has to observe, analyze and wait for the right moment to do something.
- **Pavlovian interaction:** Follows the principle: "Easy to learn, hard to master". This means the game is simple to pick up and play; however it increases in difficulty as the user advances through the game.
- **Tutorial/first run scenarios:** Guided sequence of steps in the beginning for new users.
- **Gravity:** Objects are pulled either in a certain direction or are pulled towards certain objects.
- **Directed exploration:** The player has the capability to explore the environment (browse the area, try different paths and etc.), however, this exploration is constrained by the game and the player is directed by the game through the path in which the exploration can take place.
- **Controlling:** Keeping possession of a component and/or handling/controlling it.

LeapBalancer is a physics-based game that is controlled by the Leap Motion. We chose this device for the interaction, because its highly kinesthetic nature maps well to the *motion* mechanic explained above.

The goal of the game is to navigate a (blue) ball through a maze towards a (green) target by tilting the maze (see e.g. Fig. 1). Tilting the maze is done by only moving both hands, which is detected by the Leap Motion and transformed into a movement of the maze which makes the ball rolling. This allows the player to move the ball towards the target. The player can observe the movement of his/her hands in real-time in the game (see e.g. Fig. 1). If his/her hands leave the detection zone of the Leap Motion, the game will pause and will notify the player that no hands are detected.

The surface of the maze is composed of tiles. As the player traverses through the maze (i.e. rolls the ball over the tiles), the visited tiles will be highlighted, hence forming a colored path that indicates the different tiles the player has already visited on its way to the target (see e.g. Fig. 1). This helps the players observing and remembering the path they have already traversed and explored to reach the target.

The game is composed of 9 levels with increasing difficulty. As the player progresses in the game, the mazes become more complex and include obstacles (red balls). These obstacles can obscure the paths inside the maze when the player tilts the surface because they move in a fashion similar to the main ball. The first three levels are training levels. The next three levels have a medium difficulty. The final three levels have a high difficulty. Difficulty is represented by differences in the size and complexity of the maze (see Figs. 1 and 2). By having 9 levels we assured that the playtime would be at least 15 min. This was necessary for properly measuring the game

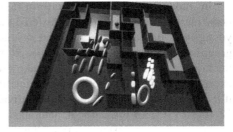

Fig. 1. Medium difficulty level (Color figure online)

Fig. 2. High difficulty level (with obstacles) (Color figure online)

experience afterwards. Note that we did not incorporate any losing condition or time constraint as our goal was not to create a full-fledged game but an experimental environment. Of course, the game does inherently impose a certain level of challenge (see challenge mechanics in Table 1.).

Because we were interested in the performance of the players with respect to moving the ball to the target, we opted to log their movements.

5   Evaluation

The evaluation of LeapBalancer aims to contribute to the answer to the question: *"Can player-centered game design lead to a better game experience?"* More specifically, the evaluation tests the following hypothesis: *"People with a high bodily-kinesthetic intelligence will have a better game experience in a game designed for bodily-kines-thetic players compared to non-bodily-kinesthetic players"*.

Methodology: Two instruments are used to obtain the necessary data for testing this hypothesis: to measure the values of MI dimensions of the players we used the Multiple Intelligence Profiling Questionnaire (MIPQ) [23], and to measure the game experience of the players we used the Game Experience Questionnaire (GEQ) developed by IJsselsteijn and colleagues [24, 25]. In MIPQ, each dimension of MI is measured using 4 statements (rated on a scale of 1 to 5), except for the naturalist dimension which is measured by 3 statements. GEQ has four modules: core, in-game, social presence and post-game. Each module is designed to measure the game experience either at a specific moment of gameplay (in-game and post-game) or focused on certain aspects (core and social presence). We used the core module that contains 33 statements (rated on a scale of 0 to 4), the in-game module (containing 14 statements) and the post-game module (containing 17 statements). The social presence module was not applicable to this experiment, since its purpose is to investigate the psychological and behavioral involvement of the player with other social entities such as in-game characters and other players, which are not present in LeapBalancer. Both the core and the in-game modules measure the game experience based on the following metrics: competence, immersion, flow, tension/annoyance, challenge, negative affect and positive affect. The post-game uses the metrics: positive experience, negative experience, tiredness and returning to reality.

In order to be able to perform a comparison between the kinesthetic and non-kinesthetic players, we administered the MIPQ to 200 people, mostly students and youngsters. Based on the received results (110 people answered), we invited two groups of people: one group with people who showed a dominant bodily-kinesthetic intelligence, and another group who showed dominance in any intelligence dimension except the bodily-kinesthetic one. An intelligence dimension was considered dominant if its value (sum of the scores on the individual questions) was above 15 (out of 20) or 12 (out of 15) in the case of naturalistic intelligence. Each group consisted of 11 players. The players were informed that they would need to finish 9 levels and that the first three were considered training levels. After finishing all 9 levels, the players were asked to fill out the GEQ modules. The differences between the game experience of the kinesthetic and non-kinesthetic players with respect to the different metrics of the GEQ were measured using a two-tailed T-test. The results are given in Tables 2 and 3; the significant differences are highlighted in grey ($P < 0.05$).

Table 2. Comparisons between the core and in-game modules of GEQ between kinesthetic and non-kinesthetic players

	Core Module			In-game Module		
	Kinesthetic	*Non-kinesthetic*	*T-test*	*Kinesthetic*	*Non-kinesthetic*	*T-test*
	Mean	*Mean*	*Sig. 2-tailed*	*Mean*	*Mean*	*Sig. 2-tailed*
Competence	2.76	2.43	0.021	2.59	2.4	0.34
Immersion	2.25	1.9	0.38	2.22	1.63	0.049
Flow	2.29	2.2	0.78	2.4	1.77	0.16
Tension	0.18	0.51	0.12	0.13	0.68	0.01
Challenge	1.47	1.32	0.61	2	2.04	0.88
Negative affect	0.54	0.95	0.017	0.72	0.86	0.68
Positive affect	3	3.01	0.93	2.86	2.63	0.34

Table 3. Comparison between the post-game module of GEQ between kinesthetic and non-kinesthetic players

	Post-game Module		
	Kinesthetic	*Non-kinesthetic*	*T-test*
	Mean	*Mean*	*Sig. 2-tailed*
Positive experience	1.69	1.66	0.92
Negative experience	0.1	0.15	0.6
Tiredness	1.04	0.5	0.24
Return	0.72	0.69	0.93

From the vast amount of logged information, the two measures that proved to be most relevant to our analysis and showed significant correlations with the different game experience modules were the percentage of extra movement made by a player, and the average time spent on a tile. For a player, on each level, the percentage of extra movements was calculated using formula (1) where the *number of tiles visited* represents the number of tiles in the maze touched by the main ball, and *distance to target* represents the minimum number of tiles required to reach the target. The average time spent on a tile for each player on each level is calculated using formula (2) where the *level time* represents the total time it took the player to finish the level.

$$\% \text{ of extra movement } = \frac{\textit{Number of tiles visited} - \textit{Distance to target}}{\textit{Distance to target}} \times 100 \quad (1)$$

$$\textit{Average time on a title } = \frac{\textit{Level time}}{\textit{Number of tiles visited}} \quad (2)$$

We calculated the two measures for every player over all 9 levels. Then we calculated two averages: one using all 9 levels, and one excluding the training levels (first three).

Results and Discussion: On average, all kinesthetic players made *42.9%* extra movements across all 9 levels, whereas the non-kinesthetic players made on average *35.6%* extra movements. However if we compare them without including the training, we see that on average the kinesthetic players made *32.4%* extra movements while the non-kinesthetic made *33.2%* extra movements. We see two possible explanations for this. One explanation would be that kinesthetic players required more practicing to get acquainted to the modality, but once they were, they made less extra movements. Another explanation could be that the kinesthetic players had the tendency to explore the different possibilities of the Leap Motion and the different gestures they could make to roll the ball during the training levels, but once they fulfilled this desire, they made less extra movements compared to the non-kinesthetic players.

Similarly, all kinesthetic players spent on average *0.7* s on a tile across all 9 levels, whereas the non-kinesthetic players spent *0.66* s. If we exclude the training levels, we see that the kinesthetic players spent on average *0.77* s on a tile, and the non-kinesthetic *0.73* s. A possible explanation as to why the kinesthetic players spent more time on average on a tile could be found in Table 2. Kinesthetic players were experiencing more challenge and were feeling more competent during their gameplay compared to the non-kinesthetic, and therefore (and because there was no time limit) were not in a rush to finish the game. The higher in-game flow (only slightly above $P < 0.05$, but nonetheless higher than for non-kinesthetic) and immersion experienced by the kinesthetic players could be testament to this. On the other hand, we see that the non-kinesthetic players are experiencing more tension and more negative affect. Clearly these players are not having a game experience as good as the kinesthetic players, and may therefore be in a rush to finish the game. Their low scores for in-game flow and immersion could be a testament to this.

For each group we also performed a series of two-tailed bivariate correlation analyses using Spearman's rho between the gameplay behavior measures (excluding the training levels) and the game experience modules. The results are shown in Table 4. These correlations help us uncover and interpret patterns between gameplay behavior and game experience. Although the gameplay behavior measures differ only slightly between the two groups, the correlation test indicates that when the percentage of extra movements increases, kinesthetic players experience more challenge and more tension while having a higher positive experience. On the other hand, non-kinesthetic players feel less competence, less positive affect, and have a higher negative experience as the percentage of extra movements increase. In addition, the more time non-kinesthetic players spend on a tile, the more tension and the less challenge they experienced. Moreover, the kinesthetic players are experiencing a good level of challenge, while also experiencing a proportionate level of competence. Thus having a good balance between challenge and competence (as recommended in [3] for experiencing the flow state). On the other hand, the game does not provide a good balance between competence and challenge for the non-kinesthetic players, as the correlations between their gameplay behavior and GEQ indicates. Therefore, we can conclude that a highly kinesthetic oriented game, like LeapBalancer, provides a better medium for bodily-kinesthetic players to experience the flow state.

Table 4. Correlations between game behavior measures and game experience modules. $P < 0.01$ ** and $P < 0.05$ *.

	Kinesthetic		Non-kinesthetic	
% of extra movement	32.4 %	.753** challenge (core) .645** tension (in-game) .741** positive experience (post-game)	33.2 %	−.654* competence (core) −.682* positive affect (core) .636* negative experience (post-game)
Average time on a tile	0.77 s	−	0.73 s	.669* tension (core) −.631* challenge (in-game)

6   Conclusions and Future Work

The work presented in this paper has demonstrated the usefulness of taking players' characteristics into consideration during game design. We have shown that using recommendations based on the different dimensions of MI can lead to a better game experience for bodily-kinesthetic players. Furthermore, we have shown how the gameplay behavior of the players is correlated to some of their game experience measures. This helped us in understanding to some extent the reason as to why the players in each group have certain game experiences.

Our findings are also applicable to learning games, since research has shown that good game experience is positively correlated with higher learning. However, in order to be able to generalize the results, evaluations on a larger scale and with different games targeting different dimensions of MI need to be performed. Moreover, the arguments given by other researchers on the link between a good game experience and effectiveness of learning oblige us to take this research one step further, i.e. investigating whether a learning game adapted to the intelligence of the players will also result in a better learning outcome.

References

1. Millis, K., Forsyth, C., Butler, H., Wallace, P., Graesser, A., Halpern, D.: Operation ARIES!: a serious game for teaching scientific inquiry. In: Ma, M., Oikonomou, A., Jain, L.C. (eds.) Serious Games and Edutainment Applications, pp. 169–195. Springer, London (2011)
2. Poels, K., De Kort, Y., IJsselsteijn, W.: It is always a lot of fun!': exploring dimensions of digital game experience using focus group methodology. In: Proceedings of the 2007 Conference on Future Play, pp. 83–89. ACM (2007)
3. Csikszentmihalyi, M.: Flow: The Psychology of Optimal Experience. HarperPerennial, New York (1991)
4. Webster, J., Trevino, L.K., Ryan, L.: The dimensionality and correlates of flow in human-computer interactions. Comput. Hum. Behav. **9**(4), 411–426 (1993)
5. Craig, S., Graesser, A., Sullins, J., Gholson, B.: Affect and learning: an exploratory look into the role of affect in learning with AutoTutor. J. Educ. Media **29**(3), 241–250 (2004)
6. Vandewaetere, M., Cornillie, F., Clarebout, G., Desmet, P.: Adaptivity in educational games: including player and gameplay characteristics. Int. J. High. Educ. **2**(2), 106–114 (2013)
7. Sajjadi, P., Broeckhoven, F., Troyer, O.: Dynamically adaptive educational games: a new perspective. In: Göbel, S., Wiemeyer, J. (eds.) GameDays 2014. LNCS, vol. 8395, pp. 71–76. Springer, Heidelberg (2014). doi:10.1007/978-3-319-05972-3_8
8. Gardner, H.: Frames of Mind: The Theory of Multiple Intelligences. Basic Books, New York (2011)
9. Sajjadi, P., Vlieghe, J., De Troyer, O.: Relation between multiple intelligences and game preferences: an evidence-based approach. In: 10th European Conference on Games Based Learning: ECGBL2016, pp. 565–574 (2016)
10. Sajjadi, P., Vlieghe, J., De Troyer, O.: Evidence-based mapping between the theory of multiple intelligences and game mechanics for the purpose of player-centered serious game design. In: VS-Games 2016, 8th International Conference on Games and Virtual Worlds for Serious Applications (2016, forthcoming)
11. Sicart, M.: Defining game mechanics. In: Game Studies, pp. 1–14 (2008)
12. The Components of MI. http://multipleintelligencesoasis.org/about/the-components-of-mi/. Accessed 16 Mar 2016
13. Brody, N.: Geocentric theory: a valid alternative to Gardner's theory of intelligence. In: Howard Gardner Under Fire Rebel Psychol. Faces his critics, pp. 73–94 (2006)
14. Waterhouse, L.: Inadequate evidence for multiple intelligences Mozart effect, and emotional intelligence theories. Educ. Psychol. **41**(4), 247–255 (2006)
15. Waterhouse, L.: Multiple intelligences, the mozart effect, and emotional intelligence. Crit. Rev. **41**(4), 207–225 (2006)
16. Chen, J.: Theory of multiple intelligences: is it a scientific theory? Teachers Coll. Rec. **106**(1), 17–23 (2004)
17. McCue, P.: The crucial role of animated children's educational games. In: ACM SIGGRAPH 2005 Educators Program, p. 6 (2005)
18. Katryna, S.: Cognitive behavioral game design: a unified model for designing serious games. Front. Psychol. **5** (2014). doi:10.3389/fpsyg.2014.00028

19. Chuang, T.-Y., Sheng-Hsiung, S.: Using mobile console games for multiple intelligences and education. Int. J. Mob. Learn. Organ. **6**(3–4), 204–217 (2012)
20. Lotfi, E., Mohammed, B.: Teaching Arabic sign language through an interactive web based serious game. Int. J. Comput. Appl. **116**(3), 12–18 (2015)
21. Khademi, M., Mousavi Hondori, H., McKenzie, A., Dodakian, L., Lopes, C.V., Cramer, S.C.: Free-hand interaction with leap motion controller for stroke rehabilitation. In: Proceedings of the Extended Abstracts of the 32nd Annual ACM Conference on Human Factors in Computing Systems, pp. 1663–1668. ACM (2014)
22. Vattel, L., Riconscente, M.: Learning geoscience concepts through play & kinesthetic tracking. In: Games Learning Society Conference, p. 12 (2016)
23. Tirri, K., Nokelainen, P.: Multiple intelligences profiling questionnaire. In: Tirri, K., Nokelainen, P. (eds.) Measuring Multiple Intelligences and Moral Sensitivities in Education, pp. 1–13. SensePublishers, Dordrecht (2011)
24. IJsselsteijn, W., De Kort, Y., Poels, K., Jurgelionis, A., Bellotti, F.: Characterising and measuring user experiences in digital games. In: International Conference on Advances in Computer Entertainment Technology, vol. 620, pp. 1–4 (2007)
25. IJsselsteijn, W., Van Den Hoogen, W., Klimmt, C., De Kort, Y., Lindley, C., Mathiak, K., Poels, K., Ravaja, N., Turpeinen, M., Vorderer, P.: Measuring the experience of digital game enjoyment. In: Proceedings of Measuring Behavior, pp. 88–89 (2008)

To Recall to Play in the Street: A Critical Review of the Transformation of the Game Concept, Importance and Place of Game in Children's World

Pervin Oya Taneri[1(✉)], Mehmet M. Akgunduz[2], and K. Funda Nayir[1]

[1] Department of Educational Sciences,
Çankırı Karatekin University, Uluyazı Kampüsü, Çankırı, Turkey
ptaneri@indiana.edu, fnayir09@gmail.com
[2] Department of Education Management and Policy, Ankara University,
Cebeci Yerleşkesi, Ankara, Turkey
meveme@gmail.com

Abstract. This argumentative study focused on the relationship between children's traditional play cultures and their technology-based play. When the literature examined, it was seen that traditional games contribute children character development, as well as linguistic and communicative development. When children allowed to play outdoor and/or traditional games, they explore the nature, learn democratic behaviors, acquire creative and critical thinking skills, learn how to communicate politely with others, develop muscle strength and coordination, learn sharing and caring, and obtain problems solving skills and self-confidence. In other words, playing traditional games supports the overall development of mind and body of a children. However, nowadays, many children spend too much time indoors, by playing online games, and/or sitting in front of a screen (e.g. television, tablet pc, or smart phone). In contrast to traditional games, online games do not include social interaction. In this study, the significance of game was clarified, and both positive and negative effects of gamification was demonstrated. Consequently, the aim of this study to generate a theoretical framework that display an understanding of theories and concepts that are relevant to the place and importance of games on children's world and disclose a critical perspective about playing games in digital world. Therefore, relevant research studies for theories and analytic models were reviewed and interpreted in order to present two sides of gamification and highlight the importance of games.

Keywords: Play · Traditional games · Digital games · Loose of contact · Contactless games · Importance of games

1 Introduction

There is a continuing discussion about how can playing games can encourage children's interaction, communication, and thinking. There is no commonly agreed description for play, and that most of the behaviors and actions children participate in

© Springer International Publishing AG 2016
R. Bottino et al. (Eds.): GALA 2016, LNCS 10056, pp. 365–373, 2016.
DOI: 10.1007/978-3-319-50182-6_33

can be called as play by one researcher or another [1]. By some experts, game is an aimless action: a kind of entertainment for having fun, with certain rules. They defined game as activities that provides gains (points) and benefits. While others expressed that game is a significant, deliberate, voluntary, enjoyable, purposeful and spontaneous act that concluded with learning. Play is more than just good fun; it is a learning experience. Play is a voluntary act; the power of pleasure or enjoyment from the game allows the continuation of the game. Play is an opportunity for the safe expression of stifled emotions [2]. Consequently, in its broadest sense play could be described as nearly all physical and mental activities that children participate in. These activities allow children to entertain themselves, satisfy free time, and spend good time [3–6].

Modern, fast- paced, and technological societies force children out of childhood too rapidly [7]. Given that, many parents, especially in crowded city centers, are unwilling to permit their children to play outside without and adult's surveillance because of safety issues [8]. In addition, children are living adult-like life. Explicitly, since their parents have really hectic schedule, many children have to start daycare centers, and/or preschool education in very early ages. They have to get up early in the morning, be prepared to leave their house in order to go to the day care center or school, and come back to home after hours. It means that children may not have time to play outside. Therefore, today, many children spend most of their time indoor, generally sitting in front of a screen. As a result of this tendency, the importance of many current societal products and practices such as television programs, computers, infant software, internet, and video games increased. Research studies related to video games are varied in approach and consequences. There are many references to the positive and negative aspects of these current societal products and practices in the literature. In this study the effects of video games were emphasized.

Some researchers asserted that serious games, especially educational games have many confirmed benefits. They offer a valuable service to both children and adults. Since, video games contain various forms of traditional imaginative expression such sculpture in the form of 3D modeling, illustration, narrative arcs, and dynamic music, they are actually an impact of art and science. In her study Sălceanu, stated that according to few of the views of some parents, computer games are beneficial for thinking skills development, observation ability, and creativity of their children [9]. On the other hand, many parents think that computer games cause lack of physical movement, sight disorders and anxiety. Similarly, there are numerous research on negative effects of the electronic games or video games such as video game addiction [10–13], increased aggressiveness [14–19], and medical and psychosocial effect [20]. As said by Elkind, almost all infant software programs, fail to distinguish that infants do not possess critical thinking capacities [7]. Moreover, passively watching TV or playing video games destroy children's capacity for imagination, and cause children obesity.

This argumentative study focused on the relationship between children's traditional play cultures and their technology-based play. This study demonstrates positive and negative sides of gamification, and focuses on the changing meaning of the game in the global world. The aim of this study to generate a theoretical framework that display an understanding of theories and concepts that are relevant to the place and importance of games on children's world and disclose a critical perspective about playing games in digital world. Therefore, relevant research studies for theories and analytic models were reviewed and interpreted in order to present two sides of gamification and highlight the importance of games.

2 Importance of Playing Games in Children's Life

Game gives children the opportunity to show their creativity, and develop thinking skills [21]. Children attain the skills that required in adult life by play [22]. Play also gives pleasure to children, entertains them as well as creates an environment with seriousness, order, conflict, and sharing. Though games defined as a miniaturized version of the world in children's mind, Huizinga stressed that the game is considered as a preparatory stage. According to him, "When living beings play a game, they are dominated by the innate ability to mimic; or they are satisfying a need; or they are making serious preparations for the serious activities that life will demand; or game gives an individual with its own personality" [23]. Generally traditional children's games rarely need equipment or commercial products such as board games. They can be played nearly everywhere with a wide range of ages, abilities and numbers of players. Games provide children lots of learning experiences that are possible in real life. That is, children play through numerous real life situations that reflect everyday life.

Many distinctive theories have been developed to clarify the activities of children throughout the history. In their past study Mitchell and Mason claimed that playing helps children dispose of strong feelings or energy. That is, play can help children to spend their extra energy [24]. On the other hand, Lazarus stated that by playing games children can reinstate their energy levels. "Play is infinitely varied and complex. It represents cognitive, cultural, historical, social and physical interconnections between the known and the unknowing, the actual and the possible, the probable and the improbable. It is a dialogue between fantasy and reality, between past, present and future, between the logical and the absurd, and between safety and risk [25]. Given, this complexity it is hardly surprising that play has defied neat tidy definitions [26]." In the same way, play therapy has a crucial role within current early childhood education [27].

Children try to recognize themselves and their surroundings by playing games from the earliest years of childhood. As a means of expressing emotions traditional games, in which children put themselves in the place of someone else, allow the development of the child's creativity and ability to learn something. Modern educators specify that with this most natural learning style not only the mind of the children but also emotions and bodies are trained and developed [28]. Adıgüzel et al. stated that game is an effective action in accomplishing functions of cognitive, affective, and kinesthetic domains throughout the entire life of an individual. Children as learning subjects investigate what they observe their surroundings, and try to learn the life. The similarities between real life and the roles in traditional games enables games to prepare children for the future as a natural activity [29]. Studies show that games have significant contributions in the language development of children. Specifically, children use deeper, more intellectualist, and precious language when playing with other children than when playing with adults.

Traditional games were played as a form of social interaction and learning. Traditional game process reveals the capabilities of children and influence the development of these skills over time. Children learn to be independent and act freely through play. At the same time children recognize the democratic rules of social coexistence, begin to internalize their place in the society as individuals with equal rights with others. In other words, play is a crucial action in the character development; requires a sharing process with all the people, can be considered as a re-enactment of an event through imitation, and based on living together in a society. Games are collective acts of individuals. They allow a chance to socialize, stimulate the mind and enjoy interesting conversation. They provide an opportunity to spend time with other people and learn about how they thought.

When children were given opportunities to play games their creativity, problem solving skills, social skills, language skills and physical skills expand. Games allow children to develop new ideas, to adapt socially, and to prevent emotional problems. Play is a fundamental component in learning; promotes academic and social learning, allows children to replicate grown-up behaviors, process emotional events, practice motor skills, and learn much about their world [30]. However, many people today believe they can gain a social life from playing computer and video games.

3 The Benefits of Outdoor Play

Researches of children and young people reveal that outdoor play is an essential for health and wellness for children for several reasons. Outdoor plays lead to both a healthy mind in a healthy body. That is, outdoor plays increase the amounts of physical activity in children [31, 32]. They are also a provide exercise, recreation and adventure opportunities. With the outdoor plays allow children to develop communication, problem solving, and creative thinking skills. They help the creation of character, creation of team spirit, the power of organization, altruism and self-confidence [33]. In addition, outdoor plays do not require specific equipment and/or spaces. 'Where children are' is where they play. Most street games are as happily played in the dark as in the light.

Outdoor games require children to move, so they provide opportunities for successful experiences, and it permits interrelationships with other children. Children learn to aware of the others around them, adjusting their movement patterns to avoid crashes. The outdoor games let children can completely and spontaneously experience motor skills like climbing, jumping, running, and leaping; and achiever several manipulative skills as pushing a swing, pulling a wagon, and lifting and carrying movable objects. Moreover, outdoor games help children to burn more calories, thus they hinder obesity, a heart disease risk factor [34–37].

4 Loss of Traditional Children's Games

Though playing outdoors is vital for children to stay active and healthy, and socialize with friends many children today do not spend enough time playing outdoors; they are more inclined to stay indoors and watch television, play computer games, rather than go outside to play [38]. Sanders stated that in the past, in somewhere an idea comes up with a child; or a new game was invented by immediately creating the rules, or the games heard from others were played [38]. A democratic and egalitarian spirit was perceived in most of those games. Indeed, nothing is not fixed or certain in the games based on the imagination. Children would provide a fair distribution when leaving to the teams [38]. Following the entry of into the world of electronic children had to bow to the world's programmed rules. As a result, children began to lose their ability to control and define the rules of their game. Given that performing an action makes one better at it. Many video games children are fighting, killing, hitting, taking drugs again and again. Consequently, children are becoming good at being disgraceful.

Researchers have asserted that western societies have used play to make children adapt and prepare them for their role in capitalism [39]. According to Elkind today's children become consumers of play culture imposed by adults instead of generating their own toys, games, and play culture [7]. Explicitly, nowadays lots of children prefer to play games on their tablets or watching television rather than outdoor or traditional games. Although unstructured outdoor play is critical to the health of children, many children do not know traditional games and they spend much of their time indoors. In similar way, Gill claimed that children are gradually conquered by technology, social media, and academic pressures [40]. Consistent with Senda, although group plays and playing in nature inspire a variety of experience, many children today are not provided outdoor play opportunities. Unfortunately, in many public spaces for playing there are some safety issues such as kidnapping, bullying, violence, accidents, and raping. Therefore, beginning around 1965, children were not allowed to play in the nature such as open lots, rivers, mountains, gardens. Thus, children rapidly lost access to their play spaces. It was known that playing at outside contributes to children's growth in a many ways: they can interact with living things and gain a rich sensitivity. However, hindering to play in nature cause an enormous decrease in opportunities for children to experience nature [8].

In digital (virtual) universe, children's interactions with emptied and simulative objects cause the game ritual detach from the traditional structure. Games identified as a product of the culture industry, their role has been degraded to a commercial product in capitalist production and consumption conditions [41]. At the same time, addressing the concept of the game in the scope of technological developments and especially some social transformations brought about by globalization is important to understand the evolution of the concept of game from traditional to digital (virtual).

5 Today's Children and Play

Children's games have been examined from many diverse standpoints: their influence on children's physical, cognitive, socio – emotional development and language development [3, 42–44], creative learning [45, 46] and socialization [47].

As above-mentioned, currently especially in big cities since the trees have been cut down, the ground levelled, a stream canalized, and the area flooded with asphalt to make an extension to the park, children deprived of play in nature [48]. They could not play real bodily games or participate in sports like climbing, running, jumping, and football as much as they play all these games on digital environment. According to Winter's study, while many parents wish their children played outdoors more often lots of children play outdoors just half as much as their parents did when they were young; children prefer watch TV, play computer games or do inside chores instead of play outside [49]. The study also showed that children undertaking outside for just over an hour each weekday, and fewer than five hours on weekend. As said by Opie and Opie, since the cinema, the wireless, and television had become the focus of their attention, children had lost the power of entertaining themselves [48].

6 Conclusion

With the effect of technological, demographic, and economic forces many aspects of societies and lives have considerably transformed. It is inevitable that children's play and games will not change its appearances in the societies under the influence of globalism. Children turned one of the most important customers in a commercial market, and obtained a culture of consumption. Now digital media culture of children presents a great array of material designed exactly for children. Neoliberal economies take children as their subjects. Consequently, although childhood is culturally specific subject, with the effect of globalization childhood culture becomes more standardized with the same products such as toys, clothes, and games that are accessible everywhere, as well as values, information, and dreams that most children regularly involve. Technology based games generally offers a fairytale like world in which children do not have a fear of losing their gains and focus on to earn/win more of, produce more. In addition, children can purchase extra time/lives to extend the game, extra life, or tricks to win. Especially wait or pay type of online games lead children to behave fraudulently, instead of appreciating patience and falling in line with the rules. That is, although some online games require the act of waiting patiently, and/or struggling forcefully, many children try to find to get extra lives without paying or waiting. As a result, children are beginning to believe that everything can be purchased. Furthermore, they can do most of thing without moving. From this perspective, virtual games may be a significant source of childhood anxiety, and obesity. Therefore, the importance of traditional/outdoor children's games should be considered by game developers, and designers as well as pedagogues, academicians, parents, and teachers.

References

1. Fleer, M.: Universal fantasy: the domination of Western theories of play. In: Dau, E., Jones, E. (eds.) Child's Play: Revisiting Play İn Early Childhood Settings, pp. 67–80. MacLennan and Petty Sydney, Philadelphia and London (1999)
2. Carr, H.H.: The survival value of play. Investigation of the Department of Psychology and Education: University of Colorado (1902)
3. Arslan, F.: 1-3 Yas donemindeki cocugun oyun ve oyuncak ozelliklerinin gelisim kuramlari ile aciklanmasi. C.U. Hemsirelik Yuksek Okulu Dergisi 4(2), 40–43 (2000)
4. Sevinc, M.: Erken Cocukluk Gelisimi ve Egitiminde Oyun. Morpa Kultur Yayinlari, Ankara (2004)
5. Özyeşer-Cinel, N.: Farkli Sosyo-Ekonomik Duzeydeki 3-6 Yas Grubu Cocugu Olan Anne Babalarin Oyuncak ve Oyun Materyalleri Hakkindaki Goruslerinin ve Bu Yas Grubu Cocuklarin Sahip Olduklari Oyuncak ve Oyun Materyallerinin Incelenmesi. Unpublished Master's thesis. Gazi University the Institute of Educational Sciences, Ankara (2006)
6. Colak, F.: Geleneksel Kayseri Cocuk Oyunlari ve Halkbilimsel Incelemesi. Komen Yayinlari, Konya (2009)
7. Elkind, D.: The Power of Play: Learning What Comes Naturally. Da Capo Press, Cambridge (2007)
8. Senda, M.: Safety in public spaces for children's play and learning. Int. Assoc. Traffic Saf. Sci. 38(2), 103–115 (2015)
9. Sălceanu, C.: The influence of computer games on children's development. Exploratory study on the attitudes of parents. Procedia – Soc. Behav. Sci. 149, 837–841 (2014)
10. Griffiths, M.D., Hunt, N.: Computer game playing in adolescence: prevalence and demographic indicators. J. Commun. Appl. Soc. Psychol. 5, 189–194 (1995)
11. Griffiths, M.D., Hunt, N.: Dependence on computer game playing by adolescents. Psychol. Rep. 82, 475–480 (1998)
12. Gunuc, S.: Relationships and associations between video game and Internet addictions: is tolerance a symptom seen in all conditions. Comput. Hum. Behav. 49, 517–525 (2015)
13. Weinstein, A.M.: Computer and video game addiction. A comparison between game users and non-game users. Am. J. Drug Alcohol Abuse 36(5), 268–276 (2010)
14. Anderson, C.A., Shibuya, A., Ihori, N., Swing, E.L., Bushman, B.J., Sakamoto, A., Saleem, M.: Violent video game effects on aggression, empathy, and prosocial behavior in Eastern and Western countries: a meta-analytic review. Psychol. Bull. 136, 151–173 (2010)
15. Ferguson, C.J.: The good, the bad, and the ugly: a meta-analytic review of positive and negative effects of violent video games. Psychiatr. Q. 78, 309–316 (2007)
16. Greitemeyer, T., Mügge, D.O.: Video games do affect social outcomes: a meta-analytic review of the effects of violent and prosocial video game play. Pers. Soc. Psychol. Bull. 40, 578–589 (2014)
17. Griffiths, M.D.: Video games and aggression: a review of the literature. Aggress. Violent Behav. 4, 203–212 (1998)
18. Huesmann, L.R.: Nailing the coffin shut on doubts that violent video games stimulate aggression: comment on Anderson et al. Psychol. Bull. 136(2010), 179–181 (2010)
19. McCarthy, R.J., Coley, S.L., Wagner, M.F., Zengel, B., Basham, A.: Does playing video games with violent content temporarily increase aggressive inclinations? A pre-registered experimental study. J. Exp. Soc. Psychol. 67, 13–19 (2016)
20. Griffiths, M.D.: Computer game playing in children and adolescents: a review of the literature. In: Gill, T. (ed.) Electronic Children: How Children are Responding to the Information Revolution, pp. 41–58. National Children's Bureau, London (1996)

21. Caillois, R.: The definition of play and the classification of games. In: The Games Design Reader: A Rules of Play Anthology. MIT Press, Cambridge, London (2006)
22. Groos, K.: The Play of Animals. D. Appleton and Co., New York (1898)
23. Huizinga, J.: Homo Ludens. Oyunun Toplumsal İşlevi Üzerine Bir Deneme, 4th edn. Çeviren: Mehmet Ali Kılıçbay. Ayrıntı Yayınları, İstanbul (2013)
24. Mitchell, E.D., Mason, B.S.: The Theory of Play. Barnes and Co., New York (1948)
25. Lazarus, M.: Uber die Reize des Spiels. F. Dummler, Germany (1883)
26. Wood, E., Attfield, J.: Play, Learning and the Early Childhood Curriculum. Paul Chapman Publishing, London (1996)
27. Dockett, S., Fleer, S.: Play and Pedagogy in Early Childhood: Bending the Rules. Harcourt Brace, San Diego (1999)
28. Sağlam, T.: Dramatik Eğitim: Amaç mı? Araç mı? Tiyatro Araştırmaları Dergisi 17, 4–21 (2003)
29. Adıgüzel, H.Ö., Üstündağ, T., Öztürk, A.: İlköğretimde Drama. Anadolu Üniversitesi Yayınları, Eskişehir (2007)
30. Hirsh-Pasek, K., Golinkoff, M.R.: Why play = learning. In: Tremblay, R.E., Boivin, M., Peters, R.D. (eds.) Encyclopedia on Early Childhood Development (Summer, 2012 Ed.) (2008). http://www.child-encyclopedia.com/documents/Hirsh-Pasek-GolinkoffANGxp.pdf
31. Baranowski, T., Thompson, W.O., DuRant, R.H., Baranowski, J., Puhl, J.: Observations on physical activity in physical locations: age, gender, ethnicity, and month effects. Res. Q. Exerc. Sport 64(2), 127–133 (1993)
32. Brown, W.H., Pfeiffer, K.A., McIver, K.L., Dowda, M., Addy, C.L., Pate, R.R.: Social and environmental factors associated with preschoolers' non-sedentary physical activity. Child Dev. 80(1), 45–58 (2009)
33. Kapoor, P.: Value of outdoor games. Educational and Informational Articles (2014). http://www.edgearticles.com/55/essays/value-of-outdoor-games/. Accessed 01 Sept 2016
34. Cornell, J.B.: Sharing Nature with Children: The Classic Parents' & Teachers' Nature Awareness Guidebook. DAWN Publications, Nevada City (1998)
35. Gregson, B.: The Outrageous Outdoor Games Book: 133 Group Projects, Games, and Activities. Fearon Teacher Aids, New York (1984)
36. Rockwell, R., Sherwood, E., Williams, R.: Hug a Tree: And Other Things to Do Outdoors with Young Children. Gryphon House Inc., Lewisville (1983)
37. Rivkin, M.S.: The Great Outdoors: Restoring Children's Right to Play Outside. National Association for the Education of Young Children, Washington, D.C (1995)
38. Sanders, B.: A is for Ox the Collapse of Literacy and the Rise of Violence in an Electronic Age. Random House, New York (1995)
39. Sutton-Smith, B.: The Ambiguity of Play. Harvard University Press, Cambridge (2001)
40. Gill, T.: Free range kids: why children need simple pleasures and everyday freedom, and what we can do about it. Dairylea, Cheltenham (2011). http://www.dairyleasimplefunreport.co.uk/pdf/Dairylea%20Simple%20Fun%20Report%20-%20FINAL.pdf
41. Uğurlu, Ö.: Elektronik Dünyanın Çocuk Dünyasına Yansıması: "Temassız Oyun" Kavramı Bağlamında Eleştirel Bir İnceleme. İletişim ve Diplomasi Dergisi 1(2), 51–62 (2014)
42. Gunturkun, E.: Yapi Oyuncaklarinin Tarihsel ve Yapisal Gelisimi (Lego Ornegi Ile). Yuksek Lisans Tezi (Yayinlanmis), Marmara Universitesi, Guzel Sanatlar Fakultesi, Istanbul (2009)
43. Toksoy, A.C.: Yarisma Niteligi Tasiyan Geleneksel Cocuk Oyunlari, Acta Turcica Cevrimici Tematik, Turkoloji Dergisi, II/1, 205–220 (2010)
44. Girmen, P.: Eskisehir Folklorunda Cocuk Oyunlari ve Bu Oyunlarin Yasam Becerisi Kazandirmadaki Rolu. Milli Folklor 24(95), 263–273 (2012)
45. Bishop, J., Curtis, M.: Play Today in the Primary School Playground. Open University Press, Buckingham (2001)

46. Gangadharbatla, H.: Technology component: a modified systems approach to creative thought. Creat. Res. J. **22**(2), 219–227 (2010)
47. Sibireva, M.: Socialization of Children through Play: Socialization of Children through Play (Children as Co-researchers) (2012). https://www.scribd.com/doc/126541380/Socialization-of-Children-in-the-City-Environment-Through-Play. Accessed 01 Sept 2016
48. Opie, I., Opie, P.: Children's Games in Street and Playground: Chasing, Catching, Seeking, Hunting, Racing, Dueling, Exerting, Daring, Guessing, Acting, Pretending. Oxford Clarendon Press, Oxford (2001)
49. Winter, K.: Children today would rather read, do chores or even do HOMEWORK than play outside and they get out half as much as their parents did (2013). http://www.dailymail.co.uk/femail/article-2307431/Children-today-read-chores-HOMEWORK-play-outside.html#ixzz4M2eQR1Pi. Accessed 01 Oct 2016

Towards Computer-Supported Self-debriefing of a Serious Game Against Cyber Bullying

Olga De Troyer[1(✉)], Anas Helalouch[1], and Christophe Debruyne[1,2]

[1] Vrije Universiteit Brussel, Research Group Wise,
Pleinlaan 2, 1050 Brussels, Belgium
{Olga.DeTroyer,Anas.Helalouch}@vub.ac.be
[2] Knowledge and Data Engineering Group, School of Computer Science
and Statistics, Trinity College Dublin, Dublin 2, Ireland
debruync@scss.tcd.ie

Abstract. It is argued that reflecting on the in-game performance in a serious game is important for facilitating learning transfer. A way to facilitate such a reflection is by means of a so-called debriefing phase. However, a human facilitated debriefing is expensive, time consuming and not always possible. Therefore, an automatic self-debriefing facility for serious games would be desirable. However, a general approach for creating such an automatic self-debriefing system for serious games doesn't exist. As a first step towards the development of such a framework, we targeted a specific type of serious games, i.e., games displaying realistic behavior and having multiple possible paths to a solution. In addition, we decided to start with the development of a debriefing system for a concrete case, a serious game about cyber bullying in social networks. In particular, in this paper, we focus on different visualizations that could be used for such an automatic debriefing. We combined a textual feedback with three different types of visualizations. A prototype was implemented and evaluated with the goal of comparing the three visualizations and gathering first feedback on the usability and effectiveness. The results indicate that the visualizations did help the participants in having a better understanding of the outcome of the game and that there was a clear preference for one of the three visualizations.

1 Introduction

For serious games that try to induce attitude or behavioral changes by means of simulations, transfer to reality of what is learned is not obvious, i.e., it is not because the learner performs well in the game that this person will also show the desired attitudes and behaviors in the real world. It is argued in the literature [1–3] that reflecting on the in-game performance is important for facilitating learning transfer. Although they may be different ways to support reflections (e.g., reflection amplifiers [4] and self-regulation [5]), one possible way to facilitate such a reflection is by means of a so-called *debriefing* phase.

Debriefing in serious games can be described as the activity of reflecting on the gaming experience to turn it into learning [3]. Most digital serious games however do not include an explicit debriefing phase. If debriefing is foreseen, it is done by having a human facilitator discussing with the player about his/her results. This is expensive,

© Springer International Publishing AG 2016
R. Bottino et al. (Eds.): GALA 2016, LNCS 10056, pp. 374–384, 2016.
DOI: 10.1007/978-3-319-50182-6_34

time consuming and not possible when the serious game is used in a non-facilitating space (e.g., at home) or when no expert-facilitator is available. Therefore, an automatic debriefing facility for digital serious games would be desirable. However, a general approach for creating an automatic debriefing system for serious games doesn't exist. Moreover, the development of such an approach is complicated by the fact that there are many different types of serious games, which may require different approaches.

Our focus of research is on the automatic debriefing of serious games that use a form of simulation in their gameplay. These games show realistic behaviors that are not too predictable, and have multiple possible paths to a solution. These characteristics can make the outcome of a serious game less transparent, which may actually impede learning when not complemented with an appropriate debriefing. In order to investigate how we can provide computer-supported self-debriefing for this type of serious games, we decide to start with a concrete case, the serious game BullyBook [6], and investigate how to incorporate self-debriefing into this serious game. BullyBook simulates a social network like Facebook, and has the specific didactic aim to let players experience how to behave in case of cyber bullying in daily conversations on social networks by being confronted to realistic cyber bullying cases.

As approach to the debriefing, we decided to opt for providing explanations on the course and outcome of the serious game but without explaining the details of the inner logic used by the serious game. Vig et al. [7] call this *justification*. While *transparency* reveals the mechanism of the algorithm used, justification is decoupled from the algorithm. We opted for justification because, in general, the exact algorithms used may be too difficult to explain, especially to casual users.

As a first step in the research, we decided to focus on experimenting with different visualizations that could be used to explain the outcome of the serious game. Visualizations have the advantage that they allow showing a large amount of information in a compact way. The other advantage is that we can allow the player to interact with them, which will make the debriefing an active process. To provide information about the interactions that took place in the game and to give feedback about how these interactions influenced the outcome, we combined textual feedback with three different types of visualizations, each focusing on a different aspect. A prototype was implemented and evaluated with the goal of comparing the three visualizations and gathering first feedback on the usability and effectiveness. The results indicate that the visualizations did help the participants to have a better understanding of the outcome of the game and that there was a clear preference for one of the visualizations.

The paper is organized as follows. Section 2 discusses related work. Section 3 provides a short presentation of BullyBook game, and Sect. 4 presents the debriefing visualizations devised for BullyBook. In Sect. 5 we present the evaluation. The paper is concluded with a summary, limitations of the work, and further work.

2 Related Work

In (serious) games, we can distinguish two mainstreams of research related to automatically explaining the game outcome. One group focuses on game analytics [8], i.e., analyzing game-related data. Most of these systems have the aim to provide *developers* insight in player behavior for improving the game [9]. In [10–12], examples of visualization tools for this purpose can be found. The tools are in general for a specific game. When the players themselves are targeted as users, it is usually to facilitate community building and to allow players to compare their performances. Analysis of serious game metrics for monitoring the learning process is mostly restricted to a few parameters, such as the average time spent on a task, the average number of attempts, and the scores. An exception is the work in [13] that facilitates data analysis for single player open physics games by logging all basic actions of the player, but the data is used to allow developers to explore possible explanations for students' behavior.

Research in the field of debriefing demonstrates the importance of including debriefing activities to enable the learner using the new knowledge in other settings than the one in which it was acquired [14]. This retrospection usually happens when the game is finished, but in-game or pre-game debriefing is also a possibility. Very few serious games include an explicit debriefing but rather use in-game feedback as a reflection mechanism and an in-game or post-game assessment for monitoring the learning progress. Because this is not our aim, we will not discuss this type of work.

Cleophas [15] provides a framework to design and develop serious games for revenue management. This framework assumes 3 stages: the Briefing of the game and the conditions, the Game Execution, and finally the Debriefing, which includes a descriptive analysis and a casual analysis. In the descriptive analysis, the result indicators are analyzed and compared for all players, while in the causal analysis, the relation between user actions and resulting events are analyzed individually.

Pavlov *et al.* [16], apply structural debriefing for black-box simulations. This (extensive) strategy is based on the Structural Debriefing Protocol, which is a step-by-step description of how to debrief an activity using concepts of System Dynamics. This protocol was tested on LITTLEFIELD, a serious game that simulates a small factory that produces electronic equipment. This debriefing protocol consists of 8 steps and requires the construction of a dynamics model of the black-box simulation.

3 BullyBook

The BullyBook serious game was developed to help youngsters practicing how to behave in case of cyber bullying in a social network like Facebook. To achieve this, the player participates in a fictive social network. The player is represented in the network by the character Angelo who has a number of "friends" (Non-Player Characters (NPCs)). These NPCs interact with each other, as well as with the player, by posting messages on each other's wall or by liking posts. The player can intervene in interactions posted by the NPCs by reacting to a post or he can initiate interactions by posting new messages. Each level of the game gives the player an objective. For instance, for the first level the player has to "befriend" 3 persons (NPCs) from his network, meaning that the player should act as a friend to these people by offering help or support. No indication is given on how to achieve this goal (as this will be part of an accompanied course or serious game). But the game visually shows how the player is progressing towards his objective by means of a progress bar, and a color code shows the player's level of being befriended with the different NPCs.

Figure 1 shows the main screen of the game. In the left most column, the list of NPCs (so-called "friends"), the objective, and the progress bar towards the objective are displayed. As explained, a color code is used as background for the pictures of Angelo's friends to indicate the level of being befriended: green for good; red for bad; and no color for neutral. The second column contains the player's wall and in the third column, we can see the wall of the NPC selected in the first column. On all the walls, the player can post messages or reply to posts by selecting a post from a given (dynamically adapting) list (see Fig. 1). The number of interactions per NPC is limited to avoid that the player is applying a try and error strategy. In the rightmost column newsfeeds are shown to allow the player to quickly navigate to the latest posts.

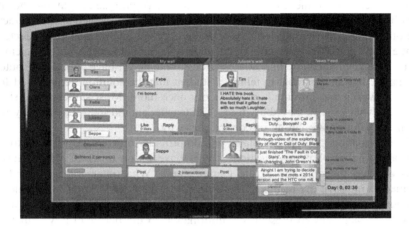

Fig. 1. Main screen of BullyBook (Color figure online)

To realize the simulation of a social network, the iATTAC system was used. iATTAC is a AI-based system for realistic interactions between autonomous game agents in a social network environment [6, 17]. The autonomous behavior of a character is achieved by using the Reiss personality model [18]. This model consists of 16 basic desires, such as "eating", "power", "social contact", and "status". According to the theory behind this model, every human being tries to fulfill these needs, giving priority to the desire with the lowest value. The value for the needs decreases over time. The pace of decreasing is determined by the individual personality of every human being. This personality model is complemented with other components to form a complete personality, for instance rules can be added that can enforce certain behavior, e.g., a rule to express the "not standing up for victims" for a NPC.

To handle social interactions between NPCs, iATTAC uses Berne's transactional analysis [19]. At the core of this framework lies the concept of *social game*, which is a series of interactions that progresses to a well-defined, predictable outcome. An example of such a social game is a greeting. Each such social game has a list of roles (some can be optional), a series of strokes (fundamental units of actions), and a payoff (a social benefit for each participant based on the role he/she played). Social games, also called *rituals*, are used in iATTAC to define how the social interactions will occur, what type of NPCs are involved as well as their roles, and how the interactions affect the personality of these NPCs (i.e., what is the payoff). For instance, in a classical bullying ritual three roles can be distinguished (bully, victim, and bystander) and after being the victim of a bully, the basic desire for safety will increase for the bully.

4   Visualizations for Debriefing BullyBook

Giving insight to the player into the outcome of a game in BullyBook is not obvious. The player can reach the objective in a large number of ways; there is no single correct solution path. Each action can trigger an interaction of other NPCs and eventually lead to a step closer to, or further away from the objective. To provide insight into the effects of the different interactions, i.e., the player's own interactions as well as the interactions of the other NPCs, we should indicate how the different interactions have affected the outcome of the game. Only describing the underlying models used is not sufficient, as it does not give any indication on how the actions of the player have affected the outcome of the game. It is comparable to telling a student that the solution he provided for an exercise is wrong and provide him the theory once more. Most students will still not understand what exactly they did wrong. The teacher should indicate precisely which steps in the solution are wrong or correct, and why.

The information given to the player should provide sufficient information to allow him to answer the following questions: "Why have I won or lost?"; "How have my actions affected the outcome of the game?"; and "What interactions could I have performed to improve my results?". To enable this, we need to know which elements and actions impact the player's success or failure. Next, we have to decide on how do capture them, and how to present this information to the player in a way that (1) is understandable by the player and (2) allows reflection on the past actions. Section 4.1 deals with the capturing of the information and Sect. 4.2 with the visualization.

4.1   Capturing Relevant Data

In BullyBook, different elements, such as time, personalities, and interactions, may influence success or failure in a complex way. To capture the essential elements we have used the concept of game states from [13]. Every time an interaction takes place (either initiated by the player or by a NPC), a state will be logged containing the interaction type and content, the time of interaction, the values for the personality desires of the NPCs and the player, as well as the progress towards objective.

4.2   Visualizing the Data

Three different visualizations, each focusing on different aspect and centering the data on one variable, have been developed. Using an evaluation, we have investigated which one(s) is/are best in the context of the debriefing of a BullyBook game.

The first visualization, called *time-oriented visualization*, puts the focus on the time of occurrence of the interactions. The standard way to do this is to use a time line of events (i.e., interactions) on which the user can click to obtain information about the specific interaction (see top of Fig. 2). On clicking, the content of the interaction is displayed (middle part of Fig. 2). If the action is a "like" or a reaction, the original post is also shown. A feedback message is given to indicate the impact of the interaction (i.e., positive, negative, or no impact). Changes in the values of relevant personality characteristics of the targeted NPC are also displayed in a visual way (using bars - see lower part of Fig. 2). In case of a negative interaction, the player also has the possibility to ask the system what a better action would have been by clicking the "Better Action" button. In addition, a replay button (not yet implemented) could allow the player to return to that specific moment in time and allow him to replay the situation (see further work). The main advantage of this representation is its linearity and the ability to find critical interactions in time. The major drawback is that it does not permit to see the evolution of the personality values of an NPC and how the results of interactions between NPCs and the player influenced the game's outcome.

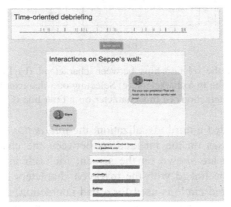

Fig. 2. Time-oriented visualization screen

The second visualization, called *character-oriented visualization*, puts the focus on the characters (player and NPCs) and tries to provide a clear overview of the relation-ships between characters during the game. This is done using a D3 chord diagram (see Fig. 3a). A line between two characters indicates that there were some interactions between these two characters. When hovering over a character name, only the rela-tionships associated with that character are shown. The player can interact with this visualization in two ways. When a relationship between two characters is selected, a list of all the interactions between these two characters is shown (see Fig. 3b; green is a positive interaction, red is a negative interaction). The interactions in this list are clickable to show more information about the interaction. This is done in the same way as described for the time-oriented visualization. Secondly, the name of a character is also clickable, which leads to a screen where the interactions involving that character are shown on a timeline (see Fig. 3c). Below the timeline, the personality values of the character are shown for the selected time. This allows one to see how the personality values evolved over time for a character. The interaction details are shown each time an interaction is selected. This visualization solves the first disadvantage of the time-oriented visualization, but still has the disadvantage of not providing a clear overview of how the interactions affected the characters.

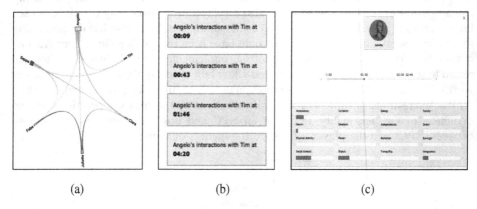

(a)   (b)   (c)

Fig. 3. (a) Overview of the relationships between characters; (b) List of interactions for a selected relationship between two characters; (c) Selecting one character in the character-oriented visualization shows the interactions of this character on a time line (Color figure online)

We therefore provided a third visualization, the *interaction-oriented visualization*. This visualization focuses on the interactions between the characters. The different characters of the game are shown on the screen; for each interaction between two characters, a small circle linked with the involved characters is added to the visualization (see Fig. 4). A red circle is used for a bad interaction, a green one for a good interaction. The circles are clickable to get more information about the interaction

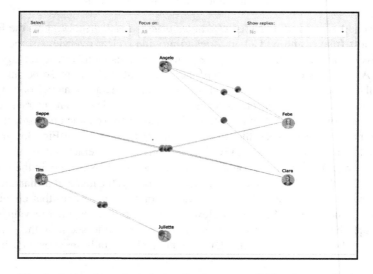

Fig. 4. Interaction-oriented visualization screen (Color figure online)

(in the same way as for the two other visualizations). Because there is a risk that the visualization might be overcrowded (in case of many interactions), filters are provided. These filters allow one to select only good/bad interactions, to focus on a specific character, or to hide the replies and only show the original posts.

5 Evaluation

In order to verify whether the proposed visualizations allow a better understanding of the outcome of a game and to evaluate which visualization(s) was/were most appropriate, we did a pilot study. A pilot study [20] is recommended for a first evaluation of the feasibility of a project, and is done by performing a small-scale experiment. For this purpose, the system was implemented as a web application consisting of three modules, one for each type of visualization. To perform this pilot study, a user experiment with 5 participants between 18 and 27 years old and all frequent users of social networks was conducted, as this is the target audience of the game.

The pilot experiment was performed in a closed setting with the presence of an evaluator and for each participant individually. A participant first received a verbal explanation of the game, but without giving too much information about the debriefing system, as we also wanted to measure the usability of the debriefing system. Next, the participant played the game (one level), after which the participant filled out a post-game questionnaire to evaluate to what extend the player understood the outcome of the game and the effects of the interactions. For this, the player had to rate (on a scale of 1 to 5) statements, such as "I understand the outcome of the game", "My actions had the effect I expected they would have on the characters", "Deciding on my reaction to a bullying post was easy", etc. Then the participant could experiment with the three different visualization modules sequentially (in a random order to avoid that the results were biased by the order in which the visualizations were used). After each module, the participant was asked to answer a number of closed questions about the proposed visualization. For each visualization, the questionnaire was slightly different because some questions were adapted or specific for the type of visualization. We asked how easy it was to obtain a clear overview of all interactions, how easy it was to understand how the interactions affected other characters, how easy it was to understand what the visualizations represented. We also asked questions related to the usefulness of the visualizations for recalling and inspecting the course of the game. The overall usability was evaluated using the System Usability Scale [21].

The average result for the first questionnaire, focusing on the understanding of the outcome of the game and the interactions that took place (but without using any debriefing) was 3.1 (on 5). Although this result is not bad, it is also not good, as we have to consider that only one level was played. This first level is simple and therefore it is likely that participants who had trouble understanding the outcome of the first level will experience more trouble understanding the outcome of next, more difficult levels.

The average score for the time-oriented debriefing module was 3.8 (on 5). We think that this rather good score is mainly due to the simplicity of the visualization. Two aspects, one about the amount of details presented and one about a good overview of the interactions, were not as well received, indicating that although the simplicity of the visualization was an advantage, getting useful information regarding the game was lacking. The character-oriented debriefing received a better score: 4.1 on 5. This can be explained by the used two-step visualization. The first screen only shows the relationships between characters, and only after clicking a relationship the interactions between the two characters are displayed. According to one of the participants, this made the interaction more structured and "fun to use". Finally, the interaction-oriented debriefing received the best score: 4.4 on 5. This visualization provides a complete overview of the interactions and the filters avoid overloading.

The overall usability was evaluated with a score of 78, which indicates that the usability of our system is good (higher than 68 is considered better than average [21]). This result is important because this indicates that the usability of the system did not have a negative impact on the results obtained in the other questionnaires.

Finally, the last questionnaire regarding the understanding of the outcome of the game and the interactions after the debriefing (with similar questions as in the first questionnaire) scored 4.3 (on 5) (while the score before debriefing was 3.1). The participants reported to have a better understanding of the game's outcome after having used the different visualization modules. This result indicates that the visualizations can play an important role in understanding the outcome of a game. On the question "I now feel more secure on how to deal with bullying situations on social networks" most participants replied neutrally. This can be explained by the fact that only one level was played and the context in which the game should be embedded (course material and a game to learn to recognize bullying situations) was missing.

6 Summary, Limitations and Future Work

This paper described the steps undertaken to create an automatic self-debriefing system for a serious games displaying realistic behavior and having multiple possible paths to a solution. We started from a concrete case, a serious game to deal with cyber bullying in social networks, and investigated how to incorporate debriefing into this serious game. We decided to provide explanations on the course and outcome of the serious game but without explaining the details of the inner logic used by the serious game. For this purpose, we first extended the game to capture all relevant data by means of storing game states. After this we investigated how we could present the information to the player in a way that would allow reflection on and understanding of the outcome of the game. We opted to do this by means of visualizations because visualizations allow us to display a large amount of data in a compact way. We developed three different types of visualizations, each focusing on a different aspect: time, the characters, and the interactions. We implemented a working prototype of the system and evaluated it in a pilot study. The results indicated that the visualizations did help the participants in understanding the outcome of the game better and that the interaction-oriented visualization scored best.

We have to note that the pilot study has limitations: the participants played only one level and the number of participants was limited. To evaluate the actual effect on the understanding of the outcome of the game and the impact on understanding how to behave in real life cyber bullying situations, more levels should be played and a larger scale evaluation including quantitative as well as qualitative measures, and over a longer period should be performed.

One feature that was mentioned but not integrated in the current prototype is the replay functionality. This functionality can have a positive effect on the reflection process, as it resituates the player in the context of his decisions. Another extension that we like to consider is the possibility to ask the debriefing system to explain (in words) why a certain interaction occurred. As for the implementation of the prototype, the system is currently a web application that must be used after having played the game. An appropriate integration of the two would obviously be better and might have an impact on a player's overall experience.

References

1. Peters, V.A.M., Vissers, G.A.N.: A simple classification model for debriefing simulation games. Simul. Gaming **35**(1), 70–84 (2004)
2. Fanning, R.M., Gaba, D.M.: The role of debriefing in simulation-based learning. Simul. Healthc. **2**(2), 115–125 (2007)
3. Crookall, D.: Serious games, debriefing, and simulation/gaming as a discipline. Simul. Gaming **41**(6), 898–920 (2010)
4. Verpoorten, D., Westera, W., Specht, M.: Reflection amplifiers in online courses: a classification framework. J. Interact. Learn. Res. **22**, 167–190 (2011)
5. Winne, P.H.: Experimenting to bootstrap self-regulated learning. J. Educ. Psychol. **89**(3), 397–410 (1997)
6. Cebolledo, E., De Troyer, O.: Modelling social network interactions in games. In: Intelligent Narrative Technologies and Social Believability in Games: Papers from the AIIDE 2015 Joint Workshop, pp. 82–88 (2015)
7. Vig, J., Sen, S., Riedl, J.: Tagsplanations: explaining recommendations using tags. In: Proceedings of the 14th International Conference on Intelligent User Interfaces, pp. 47–56 (2009)
8. Medler, B., Magerko, B.: Analytics of play: using information visualization and gameplay practices for visualizing video game data. Parsons J. Inf. Mapp. **3**(1), 1–12 (2011)
9. Wallner, G., Kriglstein, S.: Visualization-based analysis of gameplay data – a review of literature. Entertain. Comput. **4**(3), 143–155 (2013)
10. Medler, B., John, M., Lane, J.: Data cracker: developing a visual game analytic tool for analyzing online gameplay. In: Proceedings of the SIGCHI Conference on Human Factors in Computing Systems, pp. 2365–2374 (2011)
11. Hoobler, N., Humphreys, G., Agrawala, M.: Visualizing competitive behaviors in multi-user virtual environments. In: Proceedings of the Conference on Visualization 2004, pp. 163–170 (2004)
12. Andersen, E., Liu, Y.-E., Apter, E., Boucher-Genesse, F., Popovic, Z.: Gameplay analysis through state projection. In: Proceedings of the 5th International Conference on the Foundations of Digital Games, pp. 1–8 (2010)
13. Harpstead, E., Myers, B., Aleven, V.: In search of learning: facilitating data analysis in educational games. In: Proceedings of the SIGCHI Conference on Human Factors in Computing Systems, pp. 79–88 (2013)
14. Nicholson, S.: Completing the experience: debriefing in experiential educational games. Syst. Cybern. Inf. **11**(6), 27–31 (2013)

15. Cleophas, C.: Designing serious games for revenue management training and strategy development. In: Proceedings of the 2012 Winter Simulation Conference, pp. 140:1–140:12 (2012)
16. Pavlov, O.V., Saeed, K., Robinson, L.W.: Improving instructional simulation with structural debriefing. Simul. Gaming 46(3–4), 383–403 (2015)
17. Cebolledo, E., Troyer, O.: iATTAC: a system for autonomous agents and dynamic social interactions – the architecture. In: Göbel, S., Ma, M., Baalsrud Hauge, J., Oliveira, M.F., Wiemeyer, J., Wendel, V. (eds.) JCSG 2015. LNCS, vol. 9090, pp. 135–146. Springer, Heidelberg (2015). doi:10.1007/978-3-319-19126-3_12
18. Reiss, S.: The Normal Personality: A New Way of Thinking About People. Cambridge University Press, Cambridge (2008)
19. Berne, E.: Transactional Analysis in Psychotherapy: A Systematic Individual and Social Psychiatry. Ravenio Books, Helsinki (2016)
20. Lazar, J., Feng, J., Hochheiser, H.: Research Methods in Human Computer Interaction. Wiley, Hoboken (2010)
21. Brooke, J.: SUS - a quick and dirty usability scale. Usability Eval. Ind. 189(194), 4–7 (1996)

An Approach to Entertainment Tuning in RPGs: Case Study Using Diablo III and Trails of Cold Steel

Shuo Xiong[1], Ying Peng[2], Hiroyuki Iida[1(✉)], and Abu-Bakar Nordin[3]

[1] School of Information Science,
Japan Advanced Institute of Science and Technology, Nomi, Ishikawa 923-1211, Japan
{xiongshuo,iida}@jaist.ac.jp
[2] WISDRI (Wuhan), IT Engineering Co. Ltd., Wuhan, China
cathyhaibara@126.com
[3] Faculty of Computer and Mathematical Sciences,
UiTM Selangor, Shah Alam, Malaysia
nordin-a@jaist.ac.jp

Abstract. This paper proposes a novel method to tune the entertainment impact of Role-playing-game (RPG) with a focus on three bottlenecks of the current RPG: (1) weapon trading system, (2) linear turn-based battle system, and (3) game rhythm and time, i.e., level-up system. We have chosen Diablo III and Trails of Cold Steel as benchmarks, and game refinement measure is employed for the assessment. It reveals that a reliable level up system is the key factor to make the players feel more exciting and adventurous. It then confirms the effectiveness of the proposed method which enables to numerically identify the components that need to be enhanced to improve the game and help creators design a more attractive game by the paradigmatic rules. Future works include the application of the proposed method in other domains such as serious games.

Keywords: Game refinement theory · Role-playing-game · Level-up system · Weapon system · Battle system

1 Introduction

Role-playing game (RPG) is a type of games in which players assume the roles of characters in a fictional setting [1]. Players take responsibility for acting out these roles within a narrative, either through literal acting, a process of structured decision-making or character development. The actions taken within many games deem successful or not according to a formal system of rules and guidelines.

RPGs have been produced by many companies with great quantity and popular around the world. In Console Game area, generally we classify all the RPGs into three types [2,3]: (1) Japanese-style RPG, such as series of Final Fantasy

A.B. Nordin—JAIST Visiting Fellow

R. Bottino et al. (Eds.): GALA 2016, LNCS 10056, pp. 385–394, 2016.
DOI: 10.1007/978-3-319-50182-6_35

and series of the Legend of Heroes, which focus on the weltanschauung, scenario and character setting; (2) Chinese-style RPG, such as series of The Legend of Sword and Fairy, which focus on the love, tragedy and Chinese culture; (3) Western-style RPG, such as series of Diablo and series of The Elder Scrolls, which focus on the operation and play system. Many people are addicted to play RPG. According to the game company Blizzard report about Diablo III, 20 million copies were sold worldwide. So how to make or design an excellent RPG with high playability and quality is worthy of research [1].

RPG is divided into two major categories [1, 4] in the main stream market: ARPG and (half) turn-based RPG. In ARPG, a player does not need to break the game process as all the events and battle scenes will happen in the Big Map; which is similar to real time strategy or MOBA game. For (half) turn-based RPG, the characters move on the Big Map only and the battle will change the stage. It means that the game process will be broken and from the macro's view it seems like chess. It is hard to determine which model is better. ARPG allows the player to get more pleasure, whereas (half) turn-based RPG provides more strategic element to allow the players to easily enjoy the story and scenario [4].

Game designers always pay much attention on the story background or characterization, but the battle system and weapon system are ignored; after a player finishes the game and knows the scenario, they do not want to play again. Therefore, this study explores a novel way to improve the quality of RPG by making a game become more exciting and interestingly long. We put emphasis on the video RPG which is designed on PC or console, and lay emphasis on how to develop the quality of current eastern RPG by utilizing game refinement theory. In the end, this paper will answer the following question: Can entertainment be assessed numerically to set a threshold for excitement? Promising results of RPG entertainment tuning are obtained in this study, which will help game designer improve the quality of games and prolong the excitement period for the gamers to enjoy the game.

2   Three Bottlenecks of Current RPG

There are serious limitations to the RPGs that have hindered players to enjoy the games. These limitations are categorised into three different aspects: weapon system, battle system, and game rhythm and time (or level-up system). In this study we have chosen Diablo III and Trails of Cold Steel as benchmarks.

2.1   Weapon Trading System

The current weapon trading system enforces players to constantly hunt monsters to earn the money, by which equipments and weapons are purchased in the scene shops. However in this way, they meet an irrational phenomenon. Players can only ever buy the lower-level equipment in a shop at an earlier stage (say stage A), after that it becomes possible to buy higher-level weapons in a shop at the later stage (say stage B). When replacing a lower-level equipment with a higher-level weapon, players would feel trapped in an unnecessary obligation because they must repeat buying-and-selling in different scene stores. When considering the story background, it is hard to explain why all the equipments sold in the stage B are much more expensive than the stage A. Moreover, even in the same city, the weapons and equipments in a store can actually develop with cheaper change. Therefore, the current weapon trading system does not only conform to common logic and makes players waste a lot of time, but also lacks the characteristics of weapons. We show, in Fig. 1(a), the traditional weapon trading system, in which a player has no other choices.

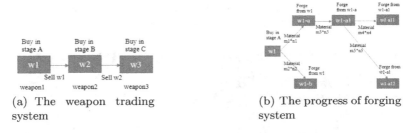

(a) The weapon trading system

(b) The progress of forging system

Fig. 1. Two weapon trading systems compared

2.2 Linear Turn-Based Battle System

The battle system in many traditional RPGs such as "Pokemon" used "linear turn-based", as shown in Fig. 2(a) where one's three characters are marked as $C1$, $C2$ and $C3$ while the opponent's characters are marked as $E1$ to $E4$. Each character and enemy unit can attack, assist or hinder any other unit directly without movement. Such a battle system has been commonly used in *"Final Fantasy (From I to X)"* and many Chinese RPGs such as series of *"Chinese Paladin"*. Under the complete turn-based battle system, players would notice the lack of enjoyment due to many limitations or little uncertainty.

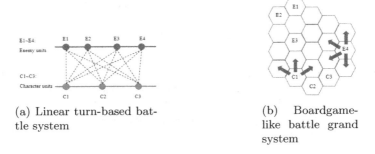

(a) Linear turn-based battle system

(b) Boardgame-like battle grand system

Fig. 2. Two battle systems compared

2.3   Game Rhythm and Time – Level up System

Compared with the other types of games especially like action games or real-time strategy games [5], RPGs lack processing fluency. For example, all the story, non player character(NPC) communication and script triggers are defined in the "Big map stage", the monster and the enemies also move on the "Big map", while players' character hit these enemies, the "Big map" stage will break and change into the "Battle stage" [6] and this is generally called "scene translation", as shown in Fig. 3. Players must break the stage hundreds of times while they move on the big map. Such frequent "times breaks" makes players feel interrupted and destroy the rhythm of game playing; however, fewer breaks would deem the game too easy and worthless. So the current challenge is to know about how many times of breaks for one level up is the best or the most fitting value.

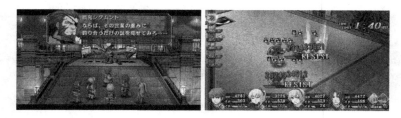

Fig. 3. Snapshots: a scene translation from big map stage (left) to battle stage (right) in "The Trail of Blue"

3   Game Refinement Measure

A general model of game refinement was proposed based on the concept of game progress and game information progress [7]. It bridges a gap between board games and sports games. The 'game progress' is twofold. One is game speed or scoring rate, while another one is game information progress with focus on the game outcome. Game information progress presents the degree of certainty of game's results in time or in steps. Having full information of the game progress, i.e. after its conclusion, game progress $x(t)$ will be given as a linear function of time t with $0 \leq t \leq t_k$ and $0 \leq x(t) \leq x(t_k)$, as shown in Eq. (1).

$$x(t) = \frac{x(t_k)}{t_k} \, t \tag{1}$$

However, the game information progress given by Eq. (1) is usually unknown during the in-game period. Hence, the game information progress is reasonably assumed to be exponential. This is because the game outcome is uncertain until the very end of game in many games. Hence, a realistic model of game information progress is given by Eq. (2).

$$x(t) = x(t_k)(\frac{t}{t_k})^n \tag{2}$$

Here n stands for a constant parameter which is given based on the perspective of an observer in the game considered. Then acceleration of game information progress is obtained by deriving Eq. (2) twice. Solving it at $t = T$, the equation becomes

$$x''(t_k) = \frac{x(t_k)}{(t_k)^n}(t_k)^{n-2} \, n(n-1) = \frac{x(t_k)}{(t_k)^2} \, n(n-1)$$

It is expected that the larger the value $\frac{x(t_k)}{(t_k)^2}$ is, the more the game becomes exciting, due in part to the uncertainty of game outcome. Thus, we use its root square, $\frac{\sqrt{x(t_k)}}{t_k}$, as a game refinement measure for the game under consideration. We call it GR value for short as shown in Eq. (3).

$$GR = \frac{\sqrt{x(t_k)}}{t_k} \tag{3}$$

Game refinement values for various board games such as chess and Go were calculate in [8]. Let G and T be the average branching factor (number of possible options) and average game length (depth of whole game tree), respectively. For the continuous games like sports and video games, it is important to figure out a reasonable game progress model from which game refinement measure is derived. In sports such as soccer and basketball, G and T stands for the number of goals and the number of shooting attempts, respectively [7]. Therefore, in general, GR value for boardgame and sports are obtained by Eq. (4) and game refinement values of major boardgames and sports are shown in Table 1.

$$GR = \frac{\sqrt{G}}{T} \tag{4}$$

Table 1. Game refinement values for board games and sports

	G	T	GR
Chess	35	80	0.074
Go	250	208	0.076
Basketball	36.38	82	0.073
Soccer	2.64	22	0.073

4 Entertainment Tuning

We present an entertainment tuning way with a focus on the three bottlenecks of RPG while using game refinement measure.

4.1 Forging Weapon System

"Forging System" is commonly used in RPGs such as Diablo III and Monster Hunters. Players only need to buy one or a small number of original equipments.

With the game progress past and hunting monsters, players can get a certain amount of "material", after that a player uses these materials and original weapons to forge stronger and more advanced equipment, rather than repeating buy-and-sell. Below we list four benefits, as shown in Fig. 1(b).

- Avoiding unnecessary duplication of operation.
- Players can decide the direction to evolute their weapons and equipments with highlight personality.
- Enhancing the life of RPG. Players want to experience the different weapon systems, so they will try the "New Game Plus" after they clear the story.
- Improving battle system. For example, by forging a weapon with "Water Property", the weapon would have much more effect to monsters with "Fire Property" and less effect to enemies with "Earth Property".

To figure our the game progress model, T is defined as the number of steps from the default equipment to the final equipment in a traditional weapon trading system which is shown in Fig. 1(b). G equals to 1. Therefore, game refinement value of the traditional trade weapon system is given by $GR = \frac{\sqrt{G}}{T} = \frac{\sqrt{1}}{T}$. When transforming the traditional weapon trading system into the forging system, G becomes larger than 1, then GR will be larger. By adjusting parameter G, weapon trading system will be improved or optimized.

4.2   Half Turn-Based and Hexagon Battle System

A new turn-based system called "Half turn-based" has been proposed and established in RPG such as "The Legend of Heroes VI: Trails in the Sky", produced by Falcom company [9]. "Half turn-based" can simulate further the interest and fairness of real-time system, and keep the high strategic factor of turn-based mode, which draw lessons from SLG(Simulation game) and absorbs the advantages of "Military Simulation". Figure 2(b) shows a typical hexagon battle system map of "Half turn-based" which is commonly used in the series of "Civilization" [10]. In Fig. 2(b), from $C1$ to $C3$ is one's character while enemies are marked as $E1$ to $E4$. This is similar to chess-like games. For example, $C1$ can move to the left, right or forward, $E4$ has four directions to move. We can combine the half turn-based system (from traditional RPG) and hexagon map (from SLG) together.

   This game does not imitate the system of board game, but "time concept" can be incorporated into the battle system. It is called "Half-Turn-Based" what can ultimately simulate the real time game as each unit will be assigned a speed value. Now only consider three parameters $C1$, $E1$, $E2$. $C1$ is the fastest which speed value is 3, so every movement cost 3 time units. $E1$ and $E2$ are defined in a similar way as shown in Table 2. This system had been commonly used in several RPGs such as the series of "The Legend of Heroes" or "Chinese Paladin" [9]. The most previous six movement sequence follows as "$C1 - E1 - E2 - C1 - E1 - C1$", where $C1$ is in the front because it can move for three times in six rounds and provide more role properties and features that can also can keep the game in balance. The most important thing is after analysing the half turn-based

Table 2. Time concept in half turn-based battle system

C1	E1	E2	Move piece
3 minimum+3	4	5	C1
6	4 minimum+4	5 5	E1
6	8	5 minimum+5	E2
6 minimum+3	8	10 5	C1
9	8 minimum+4	10 10	E1
9 minimum+3	12	10 10	C1
......	......	......	......

battle system, we can design and set the game parameters much more easily and accurately based on by the game refinement measure.

4.3 Enhanced Level-Up System

We consider the progress of level-up in RPG. To find the game refinement measure, a reasonable game progress model is figured out by two factors: killing monsters to gain the experience and upgrading the levels [11]. Let ΔL and U be the level $n + 1$ minus level n, and the average number of battle times "Unit", respectively. Hence we obtain $GR = \frac{\sqrt{\Delta L}}{U}$. Let us use the score-limited game approach. In RPG, players need to hunt monster to get experience and level up, therefore, each battle is one round. Players cannot lose the battle (if they lose, then game over), so they must win all the battles. Following this idea, ΔL always equal to 1. Now we raise a question: "How many battle time units for one level up will make players feel interesting and comfortable?" Eq. (4) can be changed as the following formula $U = \frac{\sqrt{1}}{GR}$. Here we define a notion called "Battle Time Units", where "Time" has two meanings. First one is the duration regarded as belonging to the present life as distinct from the life to come or from eternity. The second one is the current period or previously present era.

We have chosen two benchmarks – *"The Legend of Heroes: Trails of Cold Steel"* and *"Diablo III"* [12]. In the turn-based or half-turn-based RPG like *"The Legend of Heroes: Trails of Cold Steel"*, a battle breaks the big map and changes the stage, therefore time means the frequency of break. Figure 4 shows the relation between the frequency of break and level-up (level 3 to level 65) and its corresponding game refinement values.

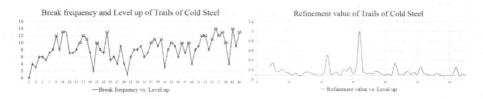

Fig. 4. Frequency of break and level-up (left) and game refinement value and level-up (right) in "Trails of Cold Steel"

Figure 5 indicates that game refinement values are around the dotted line which falls in the range of 0.08 to 0.09. There are six wave crests existed and very 10 levels there is a crest. It corresponds to the "Final boss battle", where plenty of experience are given to the player with a sense of accomplishment.

For ARPG such as *"Diablo III"*, because all the scenes and battle all happened in the same big map without any break, the game progress is clearly defined. In order to describe the concept of "time", we select physical time as the parameter. Figure 5 shows the relation between the time and level-up (level 3 to level 65) and its corresponding game refinement values in Diablo III. Consider Diablo III has a high degree of freedom, hence our statistic is taken from three sample then choose the average time for each level-up.

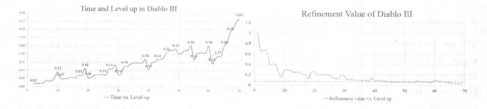

Fig. 5. Time and level-up (left) and game refinement value and level-up (right) in Diablo III

Next, we analyze the "battle time unit". At the beginning of each game, designers provide new players with some incentive to keep them playing the game; thus the character can advance the next level very easily. In Fig. 5, from level 1 to level 2, it only costs 2 mins, so the whole game will follow the same rhythm to adapt the parameter. While 2 mins is "1 unit", then 3 mins will equal to "1.5 unit", therefore, the game refinement value of level 2 to level 3 equal to $GR = \frac{\sqrt{\Delta L}}{U} = \frac{\sqrt{1}}{1.5} = 0.67$. Similarly, we can get all the GR values of each level as shown in Fig. 5.

From Fig. 5 we are aware at the beginning of the game, the game refinement values are higher than the zone value, however, over the time, GR value will decrease very quickly and remains stable at a particular value. After level 35, GR values are all around the dotted line within the range of 0.07 to 0.08.

Upon reviewing the whole equation curve, there are eight wave crests existed. It means that after challenging "Boss battle" or game progress, the character can get new skill or ability, designer also will provide some more incentives and players can level up very quickly. Then by adjusting parameters to make the time period back to normal and make the game become more challenging, the game time progress will be shown as spiral.

4.4 Summary

We have shown, in Figs. 4 and 5, the results in Diablo III and The Legend of Heroes: Trails of Cold Steel. GR values are around 0.08, which is slightly higher than the zone value of sophisticated games. It would attract players more, i.e., they may feel extreme excitement through a challenging battle.

There are some possible ways to adjust GR value of RPG level up system, e.g., reducing the number of monsters where it would be more difficult for each monster to fight, while more times of experience points would be provided. Thus, each battle becomes more challenging but with minimum interruption or progress break. Another possibility is to design or set some reward monsters in a stage where lower skill players would continue their game normally with easy battle breaks, however, experienced players would hunt the reward monsters in a shorter time.

Generally, the work presented here is very fundamental in gaming and would require further studies. Future works in this direction may include the collection of various data in other turn-based RPGs or ARPGs. However, the enjoyment and attractiveness of turn-based RPG does not come from only the battle system, level up or weapon system. It also comes from a good story, interesting background and attractive scenario. Therefore, further research will be initiated to look into game refinement theory in RPG from the other point of view.

5   Concluding Remarks

Game refinement theory utilized in this study has been effectively used in the selected RPGs, with an appropriate game progress model. The entertainment level of RPG was numerically assessed, and a threshold for a comfortable level of excitement was produced. The level-up system in RPG was found to be the key factor that has varied the game refinement values. By enhancing it, the level of excitement can fall within the stipulated range.

A good and interesting storyline with out-of-the-world characters and scenarios will be the main points that keep a player in the game and return to play it all over again. Incessant greed of wealth and power could be laid underneath the battle to pacify serious game players into strategic thinking to win the battle and advance to the next level. Ultimately, game designers could refer to the game refinement values to ensure the level of excitement remains high towards the end of the game and improve the quality of the game. Future works therefore include the application of the proposed method in other domains such as serious games.

Acknowledgements. The authors wish to thank the anonymous referees for their constructive comments that helped to improve the article considerably. This research is funded by a grant from the Japan Society for the Promotion of Science (JSPS), within the framework of the Grant-in-Aid for Challenging Exploratory Research (grant number 26540189) and Grant-in-Aid for JSPS Fellow.

References

1. Bostan, B.: Requirements analysis of presence: insights from a RPG game. Comput. Entertain. (CIE) **7**(1), 9 (2009)
2. Shi, Y.R., Shih, J.L.: Game factors and game-based learning design model. Int. J. Comput.Games Technol. **2015**, 11 (2015)
3. Kanerva, T., et al.: Virtual worlds apart. A comparative study on digital games in Japan and the west. Master thesis of University of Helsinki (2015)
4. Chen, H., Mori, Y., Matsuba, I.: Evolutionary approach to balance problem of on-line action role-playing game. In: 2012 8th International Conference on Wireless Communications, Networking and Mobile Computing (WiCOM), pp. 1–4. IEEE (2012)
5. Xiong, S., Iida, H.: Attractiveness of real time strategy games. In: 2014 2nd International Conference on Systems and Informatics (ICSAI), pp. 271–276. IEEE (2014)
6. Liapis, A., Yannakakis, G.N., Togelius, J.: Towards a generic method of evaluating game levels. In: AIIDE (2013)
7. Sutiono, A.P., Purwarianti, A., Iida, H.: A mathematical model of game refinement. In: Reidsma, D., Choi, I., Bargar, R. (eds.) INTETAIN 2014. LNICSSITE, vol. 136, pp. 148–151. Springer, Heidelberg (2014). doi:10.1007/978-3-319-08189-2_22
8. Iida, H., Takahara, K., Nagashima, J., Kajihara, Y., Hashimoto, T.: An application of game-refinement theory to Mah Jong. In: Rauterberg, M. (ed.) ICEC 2004. LNCS, vol. 3166, pp. 333–338. Springer, Heidelberg (2004). doi:10.1007/978-3-540-28643-1_41
9. Oh, G., Ryu, T.: Game design on item-selling based payment model in Korean online games. In: Proceedings of DiGRA 2007, pp. 650–657 (2007)
10. Rouse III, R.: Game Design: Theory and practice. Jones & Bartlett Learning, Burlington (2010)
11. Xiong, S., Zuo, L., Iida, H.: Quantifying engagement of electronic sports game. Adv. Soc. Behav. Sci. **5**, 37–42 (2014)
12. Finseth, C.: How games work: exploring the instructional design of Diablo III. In: Meaningful Play 2014 Conference Proceedings (2014)

A Generic Model for Emotional AI in Real-Time Multiplayer Fighting Games

Chetprayoon Panumate[1,2], Youichiro Miyake[1,2], and Hiroyuki Iida[1,2(✉)]

[1] Research Center for Entertainment Science,
Japan Advanced Institute of Science and Technology, 1-1 Asahidai,
Nomi, Ishikawa 923-1292, Japan
{panumate.c,iida}@jaist.ac.jp
[2] Square Enix Co., Ltd., Shinjuku Eastside Square, 6-27-30 Shinjuku,
Shinjuku-ku, Tokyo 160-8430, Japan
miyakey@square-enix.com

Abstract. This paper explores a simple generic model for emotional AI in the domain of real-time multiplayer fighting games. The outstanding point of this model is the simplicity. It can be used as a basis model to create a new emotional AI in other domains such as education and psychology. It proposes a notion of emotional component which contains three main factors: personality, memory and mood. All three factors are interrelated and may affect the decision making. For the assessment, a real-time fighting game is used where the proposed model is implemented. The results show the effectiveness of the proposed idea that only three simple factors are enough to show the emotion.

Keywords: Emotional AI · Personality · Mood

1 Introduction

Nowadays, computer games are stronger than humans, for example in chess [21]. However, there are still many remaining challenges which prevent humans and AI from melding together. One of these challenges, the emotion of humans [11,16], is a big issue. While building a strong game AI has been the main stream in the domain of board games such as computer chess [12]. In the game industry, the main focus has been on AI which makes users' experience more enjoyable. This is because a game player usually spends a lot of time interacting with characters which are automatically controlled by AI [20]. This research topic is called *entertainment AI* [19].

Many efforts have been devoted to the study of emotional AI with a focus on different aspects [4,8,10]. In this study, we propose a generic model of emotional AI in the domain of real-time multiplayer fighting games. The outstanding point of the proposed model is its simplicity and it can be used as a basis of emotional AI. Moreover, the proposed idea would be applied in other domains such as serious game and education since it is important to develop AI which can deal

© Springer International Publishing AG 2016
R. Bottino et al. (Eds.): GALA 2016, LNCS 10056, pp. 395–404, 2016.
DOI: 10.1007/978-3-319-50182-6_36

with the emotion. Finally, we implement the model to our simulated game and the evaluation experiments are performed.

The structure of this paper is as follows. We first introduce some background ideas in Sect. 2. Then, in Sect. 3, we describe the details of emotional AI such as the agent structure and the emotional AI model. Next, we implement an emotional AI on our simulated game and an experimental test performed with human subjects is presented in Sect. 4. Finally, the results obtained are discussed in Sect. 5, and concluding remarks are given in Sect. 6.

2   Emotional AI

In order to construct a generic model of emotional AI, we have to look at its foundation. Therefore, this section starts by briefly introducing some background ideas. Then, we try to limit the scope of our work and introduce our model.

2.1   Definition of Emotional AI

We start with a fundamental question: what is emotional AI? There are many attempts to define emotions in various aspects and fields such as in biology, philosophy and psychology [13,23]. While the previous studies give us many definitions of emotions in various aspects, in this study, by simplifying those definitions, we propose our definition of emotions that emotion is a reason why an agent takes a certain action that may not be necessarily taken.

For example, when an agent is angry, some changes would happen in the moving speed, face, voice and speaking style while using impolite words or expressing negative emotions through certain actions. We then see that the reasons behind these actions are emotions. So, we can simply describe emotional AI as an AI containing emotions. It means that it has its own emotion and its actions are controlled by emotion.

2.2   Emotional AI Modeling

Principally, conventional AI will optimize an agent's answer under some limited constraints in order to complete a goal [25]. However, it is likely that emotions do not always make the answer optimized. So, can we conclude that emotions bring about irrational actions? The answer should be no. Our proposition is that emotions bring about rational actions based on an emotional component [15,17].

As the simplest emotional AI, we can use only personality as the whole emotional component [14]. For example, a greedy agent would prioritize money first, a timid agent would go far from a dangerous place and try to avoid any battles. However, human actions are more complex. Sometimes, with the same person and same conditions, the reaction may be different. This is because humans have a mood which may change in time [1]. For example, one's mood today may definitely be different from that of yesterday's. Additionally, various roles of emotions for AI such as action selection, goal management and memory control are discussed in [16]. For example, you remember that you hate a person because the person did something bad to you, so you are biased when you have to do something related to that person. Also, those memories can be deleted depending on time. With these reasons, we propose an emotional component consists of the following three factors: Personality, Memory and Mood.

Nevertheless, emotions are varied in range and it is hard to construct an emotional AI model which can be applied to every domain of games. So, in this study, we focus on a real-time fighting game. We do not focus on more complex emotions such as love, flirt or jealousy, because those emotions are hard to be related to fighting games. Then, in this domain we try to construct a model as general as possible. This means that the model can be applied to every game in this domain by adjusting some factors. Moreover, the model should be simple and easy to implement. So, some rare cases or other cases where the model is hard to understand or implement are not considered.

3   A Generic Model for Emotional AI

In order to implement emotions in AI, we have to add an emotional component [17]. We propose an emotional AI agent architecture based on the concept described in [24]. In this model, the inside of the agent is connected to the outside environment via a sensor, decision making and actuators. Next, we add an emotional component in the agent architecture. We see that sensors receive input from the real world. The input will be sent to the decision making and emotional components. Then, the emotional component will generate its current emotion, and this emotion will affect decision making. Moreover, this emotion also affects actuators. For example, an emotion affects decision making such as choosing what to do next. But, for actuators the emotion affects actuators such as for the walking path, movement speed and shooting speed. We can construct an emotional AI agent structure as shown in Fig. 1. We see that personality affects mood and memory. Also, memory and mood affect each other.

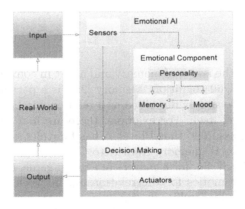

Fig. 1. A structure of Emotional AI

3.1   Personality

Personality is represented by the initialized values that make an agent unique. For example, we may use the real human's classification system like the sixteen personality types [5], the OCEAN model [7,18] or the PEN model [9] for complex games. Personality should be carefully classified depending on the game that is considered. For example, in simple games such as Pokemon, using a limited personality may be sufficient. Moreover, in the human's real life, personality may be changing. For example, one's personality in childhood should be different from one's personality as an adult. However, the change of a human's personality will take a long time. In this study we consider a simple model, so we recognize personality as an initialized constant.

In this study, we consider the following five axes of personality. (1) Calm and Hasty, (2) Mild and Cruel, (3) Timid and Brave, (4) Neat and Naughty and (5) Inattentive and Dedicated. Each agent will have these values in a scale from zero to ten. Zero indicates a personality on the left hand side, while ten indicates a personality on the right hand side. We may add a new axis of personality if necessary in a target game. For example, we may add a Docile and Stubborn axis in a team game which needs teamwork. Also, we may cut some unnecessary axes of personality in the case where the game that is considered does not need the axis of personality. We should make the system as simple as we can, but it should be sufficiently complex in order to create a realistic emotional AI. However, there are some inconsistent combinations. For example, A Calm agent can be timid. A Calm agent can be brave. A Hasty agent cannot be timid. A Hasty agent can be brave. To solve this problem, we add a dependency between the axes of personality. We limit the possible range of each personality axis based on other axes.

Then, personality will affect an agent in many ways because every variable of the agent will be represented as a function of personality; $P(CalmHasty, MildCruel, TimidBrave, NeatNaughty, InattentiveDedicated)$. Also, personality directly affects the decision making.

3.2   Memory

Clocksin [6] explored the issues of memory and affect in connection with possible architectures for artificial cognition. Memory [2,3] is a part for memo events in games. Memory can be simply described as a relationship between an agent and other players including itself. For example, there are four players, say Players A, B, C and D. It is assumed that Player A has four memories which consist of the memory from A to B, memory from A to C, memory from A to D and the memory from A to itself. So, for n players in a given game, each player will have n memories: $n - 1$ memories for the relationship between an agent and other players and 1 memory for itself.

To implement this, memory is a list of events. For example, if agent A kills agent B, agent B simply hates agent A. Also, if agent B can avenge itself on agent A, the hate from agent B to agent A may be decreased. However, it depends on the agent's personality. Moreover, the event will be deleted as time passes. This is the same as a human's memory: when time passes, we forget some events. Furthermore, an agent can remember a good event. For example, you feel good about someone when the person helps you. Memory is affected by personality and vice-versa. For example, the hasty agent and the dedicated agent have a high hate value, while it is hard for cruel agents to forget a hate event. Memory affects the decision making, i.e., whether to decide if the agent kills a given player.

3.3 Mood

Mood is the current feeling of an agent. In contrast with personality, as time passes, mood is changed [26]. It is observed in [22] saying that "Human emotion includes basic emotion and multiple emotions. Basic emotion is a basic element in human emotion while multiple emotions are complicated and changeable". Also, a current mood can be represented as a linear combination of basic moods. To simplify this, in this study we focus on four basic moods: (1) Joy, (2) Anger, (3) Boredom and (4) Fear.

Mood is affected by personality. For example, a hasty agent easily becomes angry, and it will be hard for a brave agent to feel fear, and an inattentive agent easily becomes bored. Mood affects memory. For example, you feel bad and you experience a bad event, even though that event is just a little event, because you are feeling bad, it has more effect. Also, memory affects mood because mood can be quantified by events kept in memory. Mood affects the output of an agent such as decision making. For example, agents which feel fear would try to run away. Angry agents would move fast and try to kill other players. Bored agents would move slowly and not care about the game. However, it depends on personality.

By combining these meaningful factors, we can construct an emotional AI model as a mathematical equation as shown in Eq. (1).

$$O_i(t) = f(RW(t),\ P_i,\ Me_i(t),\ Mo_i(t)) \tag{1}$$

Where $O_i(t)$ is the output of $agent_i$ at time t, f is the emotional AI decision making function, $RW(t)$ is the real world situation at time t, P_i is the personality of $agent_i$, $Me_i(t)$ is the memory of $agent_i$ at time t, $Mo_i(t)$ is the mood of $agent_i$ at time t.

4 Evaluation Experiment

To evaluate the model's effectiveness, we create a suitable game and implement our model as a player in the game. Then, we can see how our emotional AI works by playing with the game or watching its action.

4.1 Test Game

In this game, one can move in four directions by using an arrow keyboard and shoot the bullet by using the space bar button on the keyboard. The goal of the game is to get as many scores as possible. The player who achieves the best score will unquestionably be a winner. To get scores, a player has to destroy given point units. This means that the player does not need to kill other players, but the player has to focus on the point unit and try to collect scores as hard as he can. However, we see that even though the player does not need to kill other players, the player still may do so.

That is our main idea of this test game, which we have proposed before: even though one does not need to carry out such actions as killing, one might do so. That is why we call it 'emotion'.

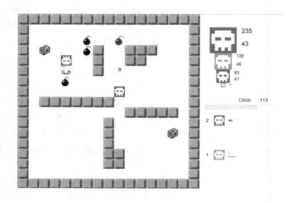

Fig. 2. A screenshot of our test game

Below, we describe the rules of our test game. In Fig. 2, we show a screenshot of the test game.

- This game is a single player mode game. There is no team in this game.
- In order to get scores, a player has to destroy given point units.
- A point unit has seven degrees of hit points (HP). One bullet will reduce one HP.
- A player who gets a last shot, a shot that reduces a point unit's HP from one to zero of point unit, will receive a score.
- The game has the bullet system, which means that the number of bullets is limited. A player can reload a bullet by getting a bullet item.
- The game has initially some basic obstacles (walls) that the bullet and player cannot pass.
- A player can kill other players by shooting.
- A player has no HP. If a player touches the bullet, it will die. When a player dies, it has to wait five seconds before being reborn.
- An agent can display simple emoticons and the agent's mood is shown on the mood bar.

4.2 Experimental Design

We implement our emotional AI in this game and perform an evaluation experiment. For each round, a player has to play with the emotional AI in this game. Next, the player is requested to answer that what the type of personality of each agent is. Then, the results will be calculated using the absolute error for each axis of personality.

However, we wonder whether the 'shown emotion' function such as emoticons and mood bar helps the player to easily understand the agent's emotion. Therefore, we perform this experiment both with the turned on and turned off 'show emotion' function. In addition, we wonder whether the number of agents playing with a tester affects the results. So, we use a different number of agents in different rounds. Furthermore, we wonder, while playing with agents, whether it is hard to recognize the agent. So, we have a replay function which means that, in some rounds, the player does not need to play but just has to watch the replay and provide an answer.

The test is described in Table 1 where R stands for round. In this study, fourteen subjects participated in the test experiment and played six rounds.

Table 1. Detail of each round

R	Human	Agent	Show emotion	Replay	Time (sec)
1	1	1	Off	-	75
2	1	1	On	-	75
3	1	3	Off	-	150
4	Watch 3rd round's replay				
5	1	3	On	-	150
6	Watch 5th round's replay				

Table 2. Average error for each personality and each round

R	Calm-Hasty	Mild-Cruel	Timid-Brave	Neat-Naug	Inat-Ded	Avg error
1	2.14	2.86	4.14	3.71	3.57	3.29
2	2.07	2.29	4.29	2.29	2.79	2.74
3	2.67	1.81	3.86	2.83	3.14	2.86
4	2.74	1.67	3.79	2.81	2.95	2.79
5	2.74	2.60	2.76	2.33	3.10	2.70
6	2.95	2.21	2.17	2.36	3.50	2.64
Avg	2.68	2.14	3.30	2.64	3.17	2.79

4.3 Results

The based error is calculated by fully random's error, an error which is the average of all the possibility errors, which is equal to 3.63. The best error is 2.21, which means that it is better than a random 39.10%. The average error is 2.79, which shows that it is better than a random 23.36%. The worst error is 3.64, which means that it is worse than a random 0.18%.

From Table 2, we see that, as we have wondered, turning on the show emotion function is better than when turning it off as we can see for rounds 1, 2, rounds 3, 5 and rounds 4, 6. Moreover, watching a replay is better than playing as we can see for rounds 3, 4 and rounds 5, 6. However, a high number of agents do not make the error worse, as we can see for rounds 1, 3 and rounds 2, 5. This is because we increase the playing time in rounds 3–6, which have three agents, from 75 s to 150 s. Moreover, the increase of the number of agents leads agents to fight against and interact with each other, so agents will show emotions in this

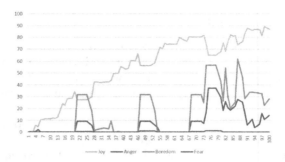

Fig. 3. An example of the change of emotional AI's mood

way. Additionally, Mild-Cruel is the easiest to detect personality. Also, Neat-Naughty and Calm-Hasty are easy to detect. However, Inattentive-Dedicated and Timid-Brave are quite hard to detect.

Figure 3 shows an example of real-time mood change graph which was constructed from one of our experiments. This agent has $P(6, 7, 8, 9, 1)$. We will see that, when joy is increased, anger and boredom decrease simultaneously. Also, when joy is decreased, anger and boredom increase simultaneously. However, it is easier for boredom to increase because this agent is very inattentive. Moreover, it is very hard for fear to increase because this agent is brave.

5   Discussion

For test game, we see that the test game is too simple to show emotion because the output channels of this game are quite limited. The decision-making choice in this game can be simply concluded in three main choices which consist of keeping the bullet item, destroying point units and killing other players. Furthermore, sometimes, we cannot separate the cases between shooting by emotion and shooting by strategy. For example, to win the game, a player needs to collect as many scores as possible, so sometimes players have to kill other players to steal the others' scores even though the players do not hate them. So, it is hard to explain the reason for the shot. Additionally, the test time is quite short. In fact, to understand one human being, we need a long time to learn and understand his/her personality. Also, even though our emotional AI is not complex, more time is needed in order to understand its personality. We can solve these problems by creating a new game which is more suitable and implement our model in that game.

For our model, there is no relationship between moods. For example, occasionally, an agent can feel fully bored and fearful. Even though a real human can experience many moods at a time, for instance, an agent feels joy and fear and a little anger, which means that it feels challenged and excited, but to reach a maximum mood, there should be only one mood. To solve this problem, the mood variable should include a dependency between different moods. When one mood changes, it should affect the other moods.

Apart from this, the scalability of the memory is one of this model's problems. According to our model, we have to use n memories for one agent in an n players game. So, in the case where we have numerous agents, we have to use a lot of memories. We can solve this problem by using the group relationship idea. For example, an agent can remember some events as a group so it can save memory. Furthermore, there should be an agent without emotion for comparison with an agent with emotion. It is hard to understand the emotion of an emotional agent when we do not have an agent without emotion for comparison.

6 Conclusion

We believe that the emotional component can be a significant way to improve the quality of AI for exploring a new player experience. In this paper, we presented a generic model for emotional AI in real-time multiplayer fighting games. We introduced many details about emotional AI and finally proposed an emotional component which consists of personality, memory and mood. Then, we created a simple game for implementing this AI. Next, the assessment test was conducted and the results obtained were discussed. While there are many emotional AI models which focus on different points-of-views, as we have mentioned before, this work is an extension of those previous works by focusing on simplicity. We reduce the complexity of the model by dismissing some factors. The results confirm that only three simple factors: personality, memory and mood, are enough to show emotion, simply. Therefore, the contribution of this work is that, with the simplicity of our model, it can be applied to another game belonging to the present domain and it can be used as a basis model to create a new emotional AI in other domains such as education, psychology and so on.

References

1. Egges, A., Kshirsagar, S., Magnenat-Thalmann, N.: A model for personality and emotion simulation. In: Palade, V., Howlett, R.J., Jain, L. (eds.) KES 2003. LNCS (LNAI), vol. 2773, pp. 453–461. Springer, Heidelberg (2003). doi:10.1007/978-3-540-45224-9_63
2. Atkinson, R.C., Shiffrin, R.M.: Human memory: a proposed system and its control processes. Psychol. Learn. Motiv. **2**, 89–195 (1968)
3. Baddeley, A.D.: Human Memory: Theory and Practice, Revised edn. Psychology Press Ltd, Hove (1997)
4. Li, B., Duoyong Sun, S.G., Lin, Z.: Agent-based simulation of group emotions evolution and strategy intervention in extreme events. Discrete Dyn. Nat. Soc. Article ID 464190 (2014)
5. Cattell, H.E., Mead, A.D.: The sixteen personality factor questionnaire (16PF). In: The SAGE Handbook of Personality Theory and Assessment, vol. 2, pp. 135–178 (2008)

6. Clocksin, W.: Memory and emotion in the cognitive architecture. In: Davis, D. (ed.) Visions of Mind. IDEA Group Publishing (2004)

7. Digman, J.M.: Personality structure: emergence of the five factor model. Annu. Rev. Psychol. **41**, 417–440 (1990)

8. André, E., Klesen, M., Gebhard, P., Allen, S., Rist, T.: Integrating models of personality and emotions into lifelike characters. In: Paiva, A., Martinho, C. (eds.) Proceedings of the Workshop on Affect in Interactions - Towards a New Generation of Interfaces in Conjunction with the 3rd i3 Annual Conference, Siena, Italy, pp. 136–149 (1999)

9. Eysenck, H.: Biological dimensions of personality. In: Pervin, L.A. (ed.) Handbook of Personality: Theory and Research. Guilford, New York (1990)

10. Gratch, J., Marsella, S.: Evaluating a general model of emotional appraisal and coping. In: AAAI Symposium on Architectures for Modeling Emotion: Cross-Disciplinary Foundations (2004)

11. Gross, J.J., Thompson, R.A.: Emotion regulation: conceptual foundations. In: Handbook of Emotion Regulation, pp. 3–24 (2007)

12. Hsu, F.H.: Behind deep blue: building the computer that defeated the world chess champion. Princeton University Press, Princeton (2002). ISBN 0-691-09065-3

13. James, W.: What is an emotion? Mind **9**, 188–205 (1884)

14. Kshirsagar, S., Magnenat-Thalmann, N.: A multilayer personality model. In: SMARTGRAPH 2002 Proceedings of the 2nd International Symposium on Smart Graphics, pp. 107–115 (2002)

15. Ochs, M., Karl Devoogt, D.S., Pelachaud, C.: A computational model of capability-based emotion elicitation for rational agent. In: Proceedings of the 1st Workshop on Emotion and Computing - Current Research and Future Impact, Bremen, Germany (2006)

16. Mariaa, K.A., Zitarb, R.A.: Emotional agents: a modeling and an application. Inf. Softw. Technol. **49**, 695–716 (2007)

17. Martinez-Miranda, J., Aldea, A.: Emotions in human and artificial intelligence. Comput. Hum. Behav. **21**, 323–341 (2005)

18. McCrae, R.R., John, O.P.: An introduction to the five factor model and its applications. J. Pers. **60**, 175–215 (1992). Special issue: The fivefactor model: issues and applications

19. Miyake, Y.: How to use AI technologies to develop digital games. J. Jpn. Soc. Artif. Intell. **23**, 44–51 (2008)

20. Miyake, Y.: The fundamental theory of digital game AI. J. Virtual Real. Soc. Jpn. **18**, 28–33 (2013)

21. Newborn, M.: Kasparov versus Deep Blue: Computer Chess Comes of Age. Springer, Heidelberg (1996)

22. Qing-mei, M., Ai-lian, C.: Artificial emotional interaction model based on EFSM. In: Electronic and Mechanical Engineering and Information Technology (EMEIT), vol. 4 (2011)

23. Reisenzein, R.: What is a definition of emotion? And are emotions mental-behavioral processes? Soc. Sci. Inf. **7**, 26–29 (2007)

24. Russell, S., Norvig, P.: Artificial Intelligence: A Modern Approach. Prentice Hall, Upper Saddle River (2009)

25. Schank, R.C.: What is AI, anyway? AI Mag. **8**, 59–65 (1987). @AAAI

26. Velasquez, J.D.: Modeling emotions and other motivations in synthetic agents. In: AAAI/IAAI, pp. 10–15 (1997)

Gamification and Scrabble

Suwanviwatana Kananat[1], Jean-Christophe Terrillon[2], and Hiroyuki Iida[1(✉)]

[1] School of Information Science, JAIST, Nomi, Ishikawa 923-1211, Japan
{s.kananat,iida}@jaist.ac.jp
[2] Institute of General Education, JAIST, Nomi, Ishikawa 923-1211, Japan
terril@jaist.ac.jp

Abstract. This paper explores Scrabble, scoring boardgames from the perspective of gamification. We propose the swing model, a new measurement based on game refinement theory for an assessment. The result indicates that Scrabble displays a stronger aspect of an entertaining game, compared to that of an educational game. Moreover, the present analysis reveals that increasing vowel tiles would be more appropriate for beginners. Our goal is to generalize game modification to influence a game's usefulness in an educational way.

Keywords: Game refinement theory · Swing model · Scrabble

1 Introduction

Scrabble has been played for a long while in various settings, e.g. as a friendly game among friends or household members, in competitive matches and also as a language learning tool. Our goal is to construct a direction to improve the general setting for the game to become more useful in an educational way. The first step is to qualify the emotional excitement of the current setting of Scrabble for beginners, using game refinement theory [2].

Emotional excitement or mental engagement in games is the subject of game refinement theory. Early work in this direction has been carried out by Iida et al. [1], while constructing a logistic model based on game outcome uncertainty to measure the attractiveness and sophistication of games, known as game refinement theory. Although many efforts have been devoted to the study of scoring sports and boardgames, we could not include Scrabble in any of the models proposed earlier. Instead, we constructed a new model, named swing model based on the original idea.

The structure of the paper is as follows. Section 2 presents some information in Scrabble, including the regulations, popularity, human Scrabble and computer Scrabble. Section 3 describes the basic idea of game refinement theory, in which

---

© Springer International Publishing AG 2016
R. Bottino et al. (Eds.): GALA 2016, LNCS 10056, pp. 405–414, 2016.
DOI: 10.1007/978-3-319-50182-6_37

a new game progress model the so-called swing model is proposed. Section 4 shows the relation between this work and earlier work. Section 5 presents the assessment using the swing model, thus discuss the results of the analysis, and concluding remarks are given in Sect. 6.

2   Scrabble

This section gives an explanation on the basic regulations and the long history of Scrabble. Scrabble is a word anagram game in which 2 to 4 players competitively score points by placing tiles, each bearing a single letter, onto a 15 by 15 grid board. The tiles must form words that are accepted by the standard dictionary, in either the vertical or horizontal direction in a crossword style.

Scrabble is a game with long history, which still maintains its popularity without major changes in its regulations [13]. Scrabble is an imperfect information game, but becomes a perfect information game during the endgame phase. Scrabble is affected by the chance factor during the draw phase [11].

2.1   Regulation

There are 100 tiles in total used for the game, and 2 of them are special blank tiles that can be used as any tile. All tiles points and number distribution are shown in Table 1. The inventor has done this by hand [13].

Table 1. Tiles amount and score distribution

Tile	Points	Number	Tile	Points	Number	Tile	Points	Number
A	1	9	J	8	1	S	1	4
B	3	2	K	5	1	T	1	6
C	3	2	L	1	4	U	1	4
D	2	4	M	3	2	V	4	2
E	1	12	N	1	6	W	4	2
F	4	2	O	1	8	X	8	1
G	2	3	P	3	2	Y	4	2
H	4	2	Q	10	1	Z	10	1
I	1	9	R	1	6	Blank	0	2

Hot spots are located at fixed positions on a board, as shown in Table 2. 2L stands for two times the number of points for a placed letter, 3L stands for three times the number of points respectively, while 2W and 3W give extra points for the whole word. The effect can be triggered only once, multiple bonus effects stack multiplicatively and L takes priority over W. A player is allowed to play word parallells to the existing word if all crosswords that are formed are valid.

Table 2. Scrabble board

3W			2L				3W				2L			3W
	2W				3L				3L				2W	
		2W				2L		2L				2W		
			2W				2L				2W			
				2W						2W				
	3L				3L				3L				3L	
		2L				2L		2L				2L		
3W			2L				2W				2L			3W
		2L				2L		2L				2L		
	3L				3L				3L				3L	
				2W						2W				
			2W				2L				2W			
		2W				2L		2L				2W		
	2W				3L				3L				2W	
3W			2L				3W				2L			3W

Bingo is extra 50 points given to a player who manages to play all 7 tiles in his/her rack. Both pass and tile exchanges are allowed at a cost of a turn. A player can challenge whether the word played by an opponent is acceptable or not. The penalty of losing a challenge is to lose his/her turn and also remove tiles from the board with the corresponding score.

There are 2 general sets of acceptable words, named OCTWL and SOW-PODS. These 2 sets were developed specially for Scrabble so that there are only words of 2–15 characters. OCTWL is generally used in the USA, Canada and Thailand while other countries are using SOWPODS. There are differences in the number of words shown in Table 3.

Table 3. Acceptable words distribution in Scrabble

Set	OCTWL	SOWPODS
Usage	USA, Canada, Thailand	Others
Total word	187632	267751

2.2 Popularity with Educational Aspect

As is so often the case in the game industry, Scrabble struggled to grow during the first 4 years. In 1949, only 2400 sets were made. Then, a year later, the president of Macy discovered the game while on holidays and ordered some for his store. A year after that, Scrabble had become a must-have game and could be found in one out of 3 American homes. Competition increases popularity. Every year, the National Scrabble Championship is held in the USA, and also the World SCRABBLE Championship on an alternate years. In addition, the National Scrabble Association supports over 180 tournaments and more than 200 clubs in the USA and Canada. Scrabble has many tournaments held in the USA and Canada, attracting many intermediate and professional players to join. Scrabble has not only just a competitive purpose, but is also a friendly game among family members, friends and students since the game mechanica is easy to understand. Although Scrabble allows up to 4 players in a game, all participants do not need to focus on the whole game. They can do another job while other players are taking their turn. Players have to aim for a high score move while leaving a good rack evaluation. There are also many advanced techniques, for instance, looking for a hot spot for a chance of a higher score, preventing an opponent from doing so and considering unseen tiles.

Moreover, playing Scrabble makes language more entertaining. A Scrabble player will benefit from vocabulary and its spelling. The score evaluation could also improve mathematical skill [14].

2.3   Computer Scrabble MAVEN

MAVEN [7] is currently the best known computer Scrabble player, presented by Brian Sheppard. MAVEN has 32 wins and 17 losses against a champion caliber position. The statistical record of expert players and MAVEN is shown in Table 4. The statistics show that MAVEN can play significantly better than the expert players. Although many professional techniques were implemented in MAVEN already, there are still several ways to make MAVEN even stronger as mentioned in [7].

Table 4. Scrabble statistic

	MAVEN	Expert player	Intermediate player
Average Bingo per game	1.9	1.5	<1.5
Average tiles played per turn	4.762	4.348	<4.348
Average turns per game	10.5	11.5	>11.5
Chance to play Bingo if exists	100%	85%	<85%

3   Game Refinement Theory

This section gives a short description of game refinement theory. A general model of game refinement was proposed based on the concept of game progress and game information progress [2]. It bridges a gap between boardgames and sports games.

3.1 Game Progress Model

The 'game progress' is twofold. One is game speed or scoring rate, while another one is game information progress which focuses on the game outcome. Game information progress presents the degree of certainty of the game's results in time or in steps. Having full information of the game progress, i.e. after its conclusion, game progress $x(t)$ will be given as a linear function of time t with $0 \le t \le t_k$ and $0 \le x(t) \le x(t_k)$, as shown in Eq. (1).

$$x(t) = \frac{x(t_k)}{t_k} \, t \tag{1}$$

However, the game information progress given by Eq. (1) is unknown during the in-game period. The presence of uncertainty during the game, often until the final moments of a game, reasonably renders game progress exponential. Hence, a realistic model of game information progress is given by Eq. (2).

$$x(t) = x(t_k)(\frac{t}{t_k})^n \tag{2}$$

Here n stands for a constant parameter which is given based on the perspective of an observer of the game that is considered. Then the acceleration of the game information progress is obtained by deriving Eq. (2) twice. Solving it at $t = t_k$, we have Eq. (3).

$$x''(t_k) = \frac{x(t_k)}{(t_k)^n} t^{n-2} \, n(n-1) = \frac{x(t_k)}{(t_k)^2} \, n(n-1) \tag{3}$$

It is assumed in the current model that game information progress in any type of game is encoded and transported in our brains. We do not yet know about the physics of information in the brain, but it is likely that the acceleration of information progress is subject to the forces and laws of physics. Therefore, we expect that the larger the value $\frac{x(t_k)}{(t_k)^2}$, the more exciting the game becomes, due in part to the uncertainty of the game outcome. Thus, we use its root square, $\frac{\sqrt{x(t_k)}}{t_k}$, as a game refinement measure for the game under consideration. We call it R value for short, also call $x(t_k)$ and t_k as G and T respectively, as shown in Eq. (4).

$$R = \frac{\sqrt{G}}{T} \tag{4}$$

In the previous works, the game progress model has been applied to many sport games [3] to confirm its effectiveness. The game progress model has expanded to other domains such as multiplayer card game [4] and video games [5]. We show, in Table 5, the results of measures of game refinement for some games.

3.2 Boardgame Model

Let B and D be the average branching factor (number of possible options) and average game length (depth of whole game tree), respectively. The R value is

Table 5. Comparison of game refinement values for some games

	Successful shoot (G)	Attempt (T)	Game refinement (R)
Soccer	2.64	22	0.073
Basketball	36.38	82.01	0.073
UNO	0.976	12.684	0.078
Badminton	46.336	79.344	0.086
Table Tennis	54.863	96.465	0.077
DotA	68.6	106.2	0.078

obtained by Eq. (5), and game refinement values of major boardgames are shown in Table 6.

$$R = \frac{\sqrt{B}}{D} \qquad (5)$$

Table 6. Measures of game refinement for some boardgames

	Branching factor (B)	Game depth (D)	Game refinement (R)
Western Chess	35	80	0.074
Chinese Chess	38	95	0.065
Japanese Chess	80	115	0.078
Go	250	208	0.076

3.3   Swing Model

A notion of swing (seesaw turnover) is important with respect to a seesaw game or the excitement of games [6]. We give definitions for this study as follows.

Definition 1. Swing *is a state transition during the game progress among some possible states. In this study, we consider two possible states: advantage and disadvantage.*

Definition 2. Scoring game *is a game pattern with an observable score. A turn-based scoring game is a scoring game partitioned by a turn.*

Our newly proposed swing model is based on the game progress model background. Let G, T be the average number of successful shoots and the number of attempts respectively. The $\frac{\sqrt{G}}{T}$ value is used as a measure of the game refinement in the game progress model. In the swing model, we assume that one swing turnover is considered as one successful shoot. Since players try to have score over an opponent in every round, we consider the number of attempts as the game length (Table 7).

Let S, N be the average number of swings and the game length respectively, then we define the refinement in the swing model by Eq. (6).

$$R = \frac{\sqrt{S}}{N} \qquad (6)$$

Table 7. Comparison of the game progress model and the swing model

Game progress model	Swing model
Successful shoot (G)	Swing (S)
Attempt (T)	Game length (N)

4   Related Work

There are many related works on the use of technology that leads to new education trends. Cisic *et al.* [9] conclude that computer games had changed from a worthlessness activity into an important part of the most young persons. Although we could not find an effective language learning game directly, some current popular language learning applications, e.g. FluentU and Duolingo, have integrated a gaming strategy, for instance, leader boards, achievements, time limitation and/or a hit point system.

In this study, we decide to use Scrabble for the following reasons. At this current study, we cannot assure that previously mentioned applications are actually a game or not, but Scrabble is, so we could use game refinement theory. Moreover, Scrabble is also simple, popular and attractive.

By analyzing match data, we could determine the necessary parameters for the game refinement theory equation explained later in Sect. 5. There are also other evaluation methods mentioned in [10], but they depend significantly on various applications, and thus not so suitable for us to obtain data.

5   Assessment and Discussion

Even Scrabble has many variant sets of regulations. 2 players standard tournament rules are considered as a turn-based swing game. We can observe the number of swings via the difference in score, and also the game length via the total rounds. Scrabble looks superficially like a boardgame but also has an aspect of a scoring game. But, the scoring system in Scrabble here has different dimension, compared to that of soccer. One score of soccer is very difficult to achieve, while Scrabble players can score up to hundreds of points per round. We normalize the Scrabble scoring system into an advantage and disadvantage system, i.e., a phase transition. Also, we expect the new model to work properly with the application measured earlier with the game progress model.

We obtained 20000 match records from cross-tables.com [12], then analyzed them with a computer program which we developed. Most players who participated in this study are very skillful. The results are shown in Table 8. We also compare them with previous work [2] in Table 9.

The definition of the swing model itself explains that a match of well-balanced player skills would have an appropriate number of swings, so it seems to be reasonable. Most of the obtained matches are between professional players and the average of those have a computed refinement value of 0.083, which is slightly

Table 8. Game refinement value of Scrabble

Average number of swing turnovers (S)	5.096
Average number of total rounds (N)	27.145
Total data	23164
Game refinement (R)	0.083

Table 9. Game refinement values of various games

Game	Game refinement (R)
Scrabble	0.083
Chess	0.074
Go	0.076
Basketball	0.073
Soccer	0.073

higher than an appropriate value as in other well-refined games such as Chess and Go. This implies that Scrabble has a stronger chance effect, compared to that of well-refined games. However, the obtained matches were played by professional players. According to Table 4, intermediate player usually plays fewer tiles per rounds, thus increases a game length and decreases refinement value. So, we expect that a match of intermediate players should have a lower refinement value, i.e., closer to an appropriate zone. Our expected tendency is shown in Fig. 1.

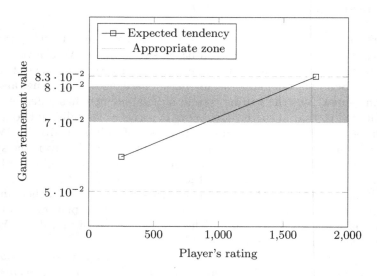

Fig. 1. Expected relation between game refinement values and player's rating

For an educational purpose, the expected relation between the player rating and the refinement value is an inverse variation. A player will notice that once his/her vocabulary pool is increasing, Scrabble would be less chance-related, in other words, more challenging. So, it could encourage players to learn.

From our observations, Bingo makes a swing more difficult to happen since it makes the opponent difficult to catch up. Then, both S and R decrease. We conclude that Bingo has a well-refined rule, since it makes R closer to an appropriate zone. If the number of tile is increased, both S and N will increase since the game will be longer. Even if R may not change significantly, a longer game is usually more boring. The letter distribution can be improved with a newer lexical analyzer [8]. Moreover, we expect that after increasing the number of vowel tiles, Scrabble will be friendlier to a novice player.

The swing model has the following restrictions, it could be applied only to a game with a discrete round since the game length cannot be observed from a continuous-time game without being divided into smaller divisions such as a quarter. This is because the swing model needs a round measurement as its parameter.

As mentioned earlier, Scrabble is luck-dependent during the draw phase. In general, a player cannot predict for a future draw, so it is more effective to play with a local best move (called greedy algorithm). Scrabble has a large branching factor, but only a few of possible moves are meaningful and used by a real player. For this reason, Scrabble is not suitable to use the boardgame model, which requires a plan, and each move may lead to a different outcome. We then conclude that Scrabble is not a boardgame, but a scoring game played on a board.

6   Concluding Remarks

In this study, the game refinement measure was employed to assess the sophistication of Scrabble. For this purpose, we proposed a new model of game progress based on the notion of swing. This is because Scrabble is a game that is different from standard boardgames. Those results show that the game refinement value of Scrabble is slightly higher than that of sophisticated boardgames such as Chess and Go. However, it is supposed that game refinement values of novice or intermediate players would be lower, i.e. become closer to comfortable zone.

Moreover, we were tempted to enhance the original rules of Scrabble based on the game refinement measure to make it attractive and more educational. For instance, one possible change is the rule of Bingo which currently gives 50 points, while seeking for the appropriate point. Another way is to increase vowel tiles, which would make Scrabble more attractive to beginners. When we focus on the educational aspect of Scrabble, it is important to know a suitable relation between game refinement values and a player's skills. Further investigation should be made in this direction in the future. The next step is to obtain data from a wide range of players. Skill-adjustable AI development should be one of the plausible ways since real match data between novice players is difficult to obtain.

Acknowledgements. The authors wish to thank the anonymous referees for their constructive comments that helped to improve the article considerably. This research is funded by a grant from the Japan Society for the Promotion of Science, within the framework of the Grant-in-Aid for Challenging Exploratory Research (grant number 26540189).

References

1. Iida, H., Takahara, K., Nagashima, J., Kajihara, Y., Hashimoto, T.: An application of game-refinement theory to Mah Jong. In: Rauterberg, M. (ed.) ICEC 2004. LNCS, vol. 3166, pp. 333–338. Springer, Heidelberg (2004). doi:10.1007/978-3-540-28643-1_41

2. Sutiono, A.P., Purwarianti, A., Iida, H.: A mathematical model of game refinement. In: Reidsma, D., Choi, I., Bargar, R. (eds.) INTETAIN 2014. LNICSSITE, vol. 136, pp. 148–151. Springer, Heidelberg (2014). doi:10.1007/978-3-319-08189-2_22

3. Nathan, N., Iida, H.: Game refinement theory and its application to score limit games. In: 2014 IEEE Games Media Entertainment (GEM) (2014)

4. Ramadhan, A., Maulidevi, N.U., Iida, H.: Game refinement theory and multiplayer games: case study using UNO. In: The Seventh International Conference on Information, Process, and Knowledge Management, pp. 119–125 (2015)

5. Xiong, S., Zuo, L., Chiewvanichakorn, R., Iida, H.: Quantifying engagement of various games. In: The 19th Game Programming Workshop 2014, pp. 101–106 (2014)

6. Vecer, J., Ichiba, T., Laudanovic, M.: On probabilistic excitement of sports games. J. Quant. Anal. Sports **3**(3), 1–23 (2007)

7. Sheppard, B.: World-championship-caliber Scrabble. Artif. Intell. **134**, 241–275 (2002)

8. Marsha, L.M.: Frequency Analysis in Light of Language Innovation. Math UCSD (2005). http://www.math.ucsd.edu/~crypto/Projects/MarshaMoreno/TimeComparisonFrequency.pdf

9. Cisic, D., Tijan, E., Kurek, A.: Mobile game based learning-Taxonomy and student experience. In: 2007 29th International Conference on Information Technology Interfaces. IEEE (2007)

10. Bernhaupt, R., Eckschlager, M., Tscheligi, M.: Methods for evaluating games: how to measure usability and user experience in games? In: Proceedings of the International Conference on Advances in Computer Entertainment Technology. ACM (2007)

11. Scrabble - Wikipedia, the free encyclopedia. https://en.wikipedia.org/wiki/Scrabble

12. cross-tables.com - SCRABBLE tournaments, statistics, and community. http://www.cross-tables.com/

13. History of SCRABBLE. http://www.scrabble-assoc.com/info/history.html

14. Math and Reading Help - Homework Help, Tutoring and Parenting Advice. http://mathandreadinghelp.org/articles/Scrabble%3A_An_Entertaining_Way_to_Improve_Your_Child's_Vocabulary_and_Spelling_Skills.html

Proposal of a Serious Game
to Help Prevent Dementia

Kiho Kang[1], Eun-Jin Choi[2], and Young-Suk Lee[3](✉)

[1] Smartbig Co., Ltd., Busan, Korea
isakai22@nate.com
[2] The Department of Film Studies, Dongguk University, Seoul, Korea
letresor@empas.com
[3] Institute of Image and Cultural Contents, Dongguk University, Seoul, Korea
tonacoco@dongguk.edu

Abstract. The incidence of geriatric diseases is increasing due to population aging. The present study aims to investigate contents that can be used to prevent, not to treat, dementia. We classified dementia symptoms into different types based on previous studies and applied related factors in our Serious game to design 17 types of mini games. In this study focusing on the prevention of dementia, the necessary contents for a game aimed to help prevent dementia were explored and a medical Serious game was proposed and designed. Consequently, this study enabled the improvement of brain function and physical activity through designing a game composed of 17 mini-games. Our study aims to contribute to preventing dementia in the future.

1 Introduction

As a result of population aging, the world is experiencing numerous adverse effects. In Korea in particular, population aging is progressing rapidly because of decreasing birth rates and the increasing elderly population [1]. According to The Aging World (2015), published by the U.S. Census Bureau on the 28th (local time), Korea will be the country with second highest proportion of elderly people (≥ 65 years old) in the world in 2050 [2]. In 2015, according to the report, the percentage of the population with age over 65 was 35.9% in Korea, which was the second behind Japan with 40.1%. This means 4 out of 10 people are over the age of 65. In Korea, 15.57 million people will be over the age of 65 in 2050, out of a total population of 43.37 million.

In addition, the population suffering from dementia, a major disease of an aging population, is predicted to increase [3]. The word dementia comes from the Latin meaning 'out of one's mind.' It reflects the transition from a healthy lifestyle to having damaged brain function due to various causes and impaired cognitive functions that negatively impact daily life. Cognitive function refers to memory, verbal abilities, visuospatial perception, and judgment. To a certain extent, dementia can be prevented. Currently, with the idea of incorporating games into preventing dementia, medical Serious games are being actively developed.

A Serious game is one with a special purpose in addition to the entertainment elements of typical games. They are an effective medium for delivering clear themes [4, 5].

© Springer International Publishing AG 2016
R. Bottino et al. (Eds.): GALA 2016, LNCS 10056, pp. 415–424, 2016.
DOI: 10.1007/978-3-319-50182-6_38

The world market of Serious games is rapidly growing. It is expected to reach $5,448.82 million in 2020, and predicted to show an annual growth rate of 16.38% from 2015 to 2020. Serious games are largely under development in various fields such as medicine, public education, intellectual training, treatment, and national defense, especially in the U.S. and Europe.

The market for Serious games is also growing in Korea. Domestic sales of Serious games were estimated to be worth approximately 166.6 billion won in 2013 [6]. In Korea, the development of Serious games is mainly focused on education. Recently, the positive effects of medical Serious games have been shown. As the increasing elderly population and consequently skyrocketing national and social costs are becoming apparent, there is a growing need for Serious games to help prevent dementia. In particular, medicine-related development is increasing.

However, previous studies on Serious games have focused on their conceptualization or the analysis of the system structure. This is because Serious games, with their nature as a game, are perceived as a training tool to simply fulfill particular goals. Here, we aim to approach Serious games as a therapeutic tool for in the aging population, rather than a training tool.

Therefore, this study aimed to develop a Serious game for elderly people to help prevent dementia. The study objectives in program development were as follows:

- To incorporate previous studies of Serious games designed to help prevent dementia. The symptoms of dementia will be analyzed and necessary elements for developing a Serious game to help prevent dementia will be established.
- Based on this, a Serious game promoting more effective brain exercises and physical activities will be developed.
- Consequently, a medical Serious game for preventing dementia that induces user's finger stimulation and physical activities will be designed.

2   Related Work

2.1   Research on Aging and Dementia

Recent medical advances have led to educational and preventive approaches with various contents, such as musical therapy and art therapy, being developed. Among them, there have been examples of Serious games for the prevention of dementia.

First, a British Alzheimer's research team developed a mobile game called "Sea Hero Quest" in collaboration with scientists from Deutsche Telekom, University College London, and University of East Anglia. It was seen as a game that changes the perception of diagnosis and therapeutic research of dementia. Dementia patients commonly experience symptoms of losing a sense of direction and becoming lost, but previous studies have not been able to present clear study results or alternatives. However, the "Sea Hero Quest" game diagnoses a loss of a sense of direction in dementia patients and, at the same time, creates a database from the results of the game that can be used in future studies [7]. Therefore, as it is a smartphone game developed to obtain the two aforementioned results, it is clearly distinct from previous games.

In "Sea Hero Quest," a player sails the rough ocean where mysterious monsters appear in various locations. When the player selects the sailing path in the vast tract of ocean, this result can be analyzed by scientists to better understand the 'sense of direction in dementia patients in a 3D environment.' Hilary Evans, from the British Alzheimer's research team, announced that the data collected from this game will be publicly accessible as open source data, and that this is a groundbreaking project in dementia research.

"MindMate" is a mobile platform that can be used by dementia patients [8]. It is a service for dementia patients developed by graduates and professors of the University of Glasgow and Strathclyde University. Detailed information and user reviews of this application can be found on its website, and the application can be downloaded for free on tablets or mobile phones. "MindMate" has three different applications designed for dementia patients, family members of dementia patients, and in-home caretakers. This application provides a service with four large categories (Games, Tools, My Life, My Wellbeing) (Fig. 1).

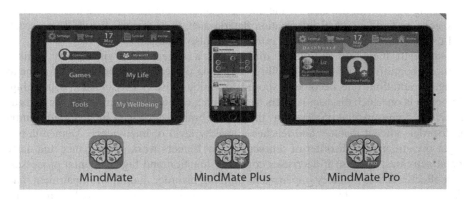

Fig. 1. The composition of MindMate

First, the "Games" section offers interactive games promoting the user's cognitive function based on world-class study results. Second, the "Tools" section provides a notepad function needed for dementia patients in their daily life and various functions that allow the patients to leave daily records to review later. Third, the "My Life" section offers a function to help recover the identity and personal information that can be forgotten by dementia patients. It aids their memory and stores information about themselves, thereby helping doctors and nurses to better understand their patients. Fourth, the "My Wellbeing" section provides physical activities and nutritional advice for dementia patients so they can maintain healthy physical and mental states.

As such, various programs, including games and applications, that aim to supplement treatment of dementia have been continuously developed. With recent increases in the use of mobile instruments, research and development of mobile contents have been very active. We focused on the fact that most dementia-related contents that have been developed thus far mostly target patients that have already been diagnosed with dementia. Instead, we aim to suggest a Serious game that can stimulates the brain in various ways to prevent dementia in middle-aged and older populations that have not been diagnosed with dementia. Dementia is a disease that can arise in everyone; thus, Serious games that can delay the onset as much as possible have become important research topics in medical Serious games. Therefore, the present study aims to suggest a mobile Serious game that can stimulate the brain exercise and induce physical movements.

2.2   Serious Games for Dementia

Aging is part of the developmental process in human, which involves gradual changes of cells and tissues in organisms over time. It is a universal process that all humans go through and varies in each individual. Biological aging refers to changes of physical functions and organs over time. Aging manifests as physical and biological aging, as well as physical features such as a decline in motor memory and movement ability caused by reduced attention, memory, and energy. Intellectual ability also declines with increasing age [9]. In the elderly, the ability to understand new associations or form a new concept and use novel information deteriorates. Furthermore, the ability to recall and use already learned and stored information also declines.

Although there are individual differences, a degeneration of sensory ability, memory, cognitive skill, learning ability, reasoning power, and creativity occurs due to aging. In addition, one becomes exposed to various diseases associated with aging. Dementia is one such disease. It refers to a complex clinical syndrome that manifests as defects in higher mental processes as the human brain is damaged by acquired trauma or disorders after it matures and reaches a healthy level of intelligence. Dementia is a major organic mental disorder of senescence that hinders work performance and daily social activities, because it decreases cognitive function and higher mental processes, with effects such as memory impairment, thinking disorder, judgment impairment, and disorientation caused by brain lesions. Dementia can be accompanied by emotional disorder, character change, and impairment in daily activity abilities. Therefore, dementia is a symptom that can be caused by various diseases that include Alzheimer's disease and vascular dementia [10]. Prevention is the best approach for dementia. Thus, preventive measures are crucial in the approach to dementia in daily life.

Typical dementia symptoms include memory problems; disorientation, which prevents patients from recognizing other people, time, and places; language disorders; apraxia, due to which patients cannot replicate familiar movements; and agnosia, due to which patients cannot recognize particular objects. Moreover, patients also suffer from executive dysfunction as well as visuospatial and perceptual disabilities (Table 1).

The present study does not aim to design games for treating dementia, which require clinical trials; instead, our purpose is to develop games that can be enjoyed by everyone to prevent dementia. In order to investigate factors required for development of such games, we implemented certain factors of dementia symptoms to our game. Dementia, which results in cognitive impairments of brain function, can be prevented with continuous efforts. For this, we divided our mini games into those that stimulate the brain and those that induce physical movements. Brain-stimulating mini games

Table 1. Dementia symptoms and descriptions

	Symptoms	Descriptions
1	Memory impairment	Forgets things that one already knew in the past (different from amnesia)
2	Disorientation	Unable to recognize time, space, and people
3	Speech impediment	Ambiguous, inaccurate, and indirect speech
4	Apraxia	Cannot perform familiar movements
5	Agnosia	Cannot recognize objects
6	Executive dysfunction	Cannot respond properly in daily life
7	Impairment of visuospatial perception	Cannot find one's home or one's own bathroom

aimed to target memory problems, disorientation, language disorders, and agnosia. Mini games that induce physical movements targeted apraxia, executive dysfunction, and visuospatial and perceptual disabilities. In other words, the present study aimed to design a game that can stimulate cognitive brain functions by targeting subfactors of the said two types in our mini games.

3   Proposal of a Serious Game for Preventing Dementia

3.1   Characteristics and Composition of a Serious Game for Preventing Dementia

The contents of this Serious game were designed for the middle-aged and elderly populations. It is a mobile Serious game called Tapbrain (working title). The objective of development was to induce physical activity through brain exercises and finger stimulation. To enable stimulation according to each individual's difficulties, the Serious game was designed to be centered on 17 mini-games and had two main characteristics.

First, for easy manipulation by the elderly, the contents were designed using Tab, without a mobile device environment and extra external devices. Therefore, they are free from device and location-related restrictions. The actual game induces sensory stimulation by asking users to perform easy and simple motions rather than a selective response rate. It was also designed to enhance psychological familiarity in the elderly by using elderly-friendly music in the background and allowing easy manipulation.

The second characteristic is that the adjustment of stages in the game is available according to the game level. In terms of the game level, each stage is set based on the time spent in playing the game. Developing additional items is easy through the selection of an extra mini-game. The game aims to induce physical activity by utilizing various sensors, including the gyro sensor. In addition, by recording and examining the types of finished games and the resulting amount of exercise, guardians can provide assistance.

Thus, this study designed a Serious game for smartphones as a preventive measure against dementia. For this, the game structure was established by the composition of 17 mini-games.

- Game setup for each items
- The game is mainly played through finger tapping and touch.

The game comprised of 13 mini-games to stimulate brain exercise and four mini-games to induce physical activity.

The game is more specifically classified into six categories (four for brain exercise stimulation, two for physical activity induction). The games stimulating brain exercise are divided by memory, attention, problem solving, and response/decision. Mini-games for inducing physical activities are divided by hand motion and upper extremity movement.

Hence, Tapbrain has 17 mini-games that were designed to be suitable for different features (Fig. 2). In terms of the overall construction, the game is composed of seven areas. (Mini game consists of five levels, and tutorial is offered in the first stage of each level). Through our game, we hope to improve players' memory, attention, problem-solving abilities, response, and judgment, while also inducing physical movements.

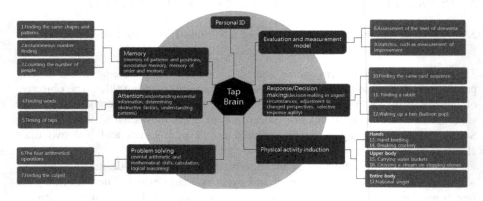

Fig. 2. Diagram of the Tap brain Serious game

3.2 Proposal of a Serious Game for Preventing Dementia

A flow chart and the detailed features of the game are demonstrated below (Fig. 3). This game utilizes a quick response (QR) code or near-field communication (NFC) card to distinguish individuals. Individual identities and their respective data is saved on and loaded from a server. From the given stored identity, the individual data are drawn first, and the level of dementia is assessed through evaluation and measurement models. The mini-mental state examination (MMSE) is conducted as a model assessment for initial measurement of potential dementia, selected as it is the most commonly used

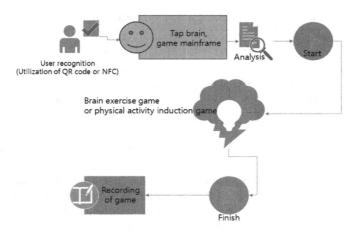

Fig. 3. Flow chart of the game

assessment. Based on the analyzed data, a mini-game customized for each individual is be started. After the game is over, in-game progression is recorded.

There were 60 kinds for all 17 mobile mini-games with 5 stages of difficulty. The first stage in all mini-games acted as a tutorial (Tables 2, 3).

Table 2. Elements of brain stimulating mini-games for brain exercise

Cognitive domain	Game type	Kinds of game
Memory	Memory of patterns and positions Associative memory Memory of order and motion	1. Finding the same shapes 2. Finding the same patterns 3. Finding instant numbers 4. Counting the number of people 5. Order memorization
Attention	Understanding essential information Determining obstructive factors Understanding patterns	6. Finding words 7. Timing of taps 8. Shooting falling squares
Problem solving	Mental arithmetic and mathematical skills Calculation Logical reasoning	9. The main four arithmetical operations 10. Finding the culprit
Response/Decision making	Decision making in urgent circumstances Adjustment to changed perspectives Improvement in agility with selective responses	11. Finding sequences of the same cards 12. Finding rabbits 13. Waking up hens

Table 3. Elements of mini-games for inducing physical activity

Part	Game type	Games
Hand	Touch or Tap	14. Breaking crockery 15. Hand beetling
Upper body	Arms, shoulders, etc. (utilizing the gyro sensor)	16. Carrying water buckets 17. Crossing a stream on stepping-stones

During the shape matching task, the screen displays a simple layout with two or three layers (Fig. 4). The structure of the "shape matching" game, which has three layers, is as follows. It has three large sections: the first item (Fig. 4, area 1) is the presentation of problems, the second (Fig. 4, area 2) is sample problems, and the third (Fig. 4, area 3) is answers. The game consists of brain-stimulating mini games and those that induce physical movements, and can be played as below. For instance, a brain-stimulating mini game involves the use of memory. In the case of the "finding the same shapes and patterns" game, users memorize and find the shapes and patterns of various shapes that were displayed on the screen. Each mini game consists of five difficulty stages, and the first stage offers tutorials.

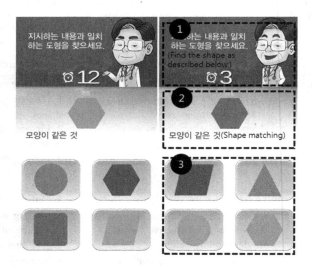

Fig. 4. Shape matching task user interface (UI)

In the case of the "Finding the same shapes and patterns (Table 2, game 1–2)" game, users memorize and find the shapes and patterns of various shapes that were displayed on the screen. Each game offers a sub-mission of distinguishing shapes, rotation, reversal, and colors according to the stage. The "Finding instant numbers (Table 2, game 3)" game consists of memorizing and finding the numbers that appeared in order, and the "Counting the number of people (Table 2, game 4)" task consists of counting the number of people entering and exiting a specific building. In

"Order memorization (Table 2, game 5)," the player touches the order of rectangles shown on the screen; this mini game tests the player's memory. Mini games that require attention include "Finding words (Table 2, game 6)," "Timing of tap (Table 2, game 7)," and "Shooting falling squares (Table 2, game 8)" "Finding words" includes finding of certain words in well-known sayings or writings (well-known novels or essays). In "Timing of tap," the player removes various moving circles at the right timing. In "Shooting falling squares," which tests the accuracy of the player's touch, the player touches and removes rectangles that fall from the top of the screen. "The main four arithmetical operations (Table 2, game 9)", in which the player completes a mathematic formula using arithmetics, and "Finding the culprit (Table 2, game 10)", in which the player finds the suspect using information on surrounding objects, test problem-solving skills. Mini games that test the player's response and judgment include "Finding sequences of the same cards (Table 2, game 11)", "Finding rabbits (Table 2, game 12)," and "Waking up hens (Table 2, game 13)" all these games involve finding characters within the given deadline.

The following mini games induce physical movements in the player. First, "Breaking crockery (Table 3, game 14)" and "Hand beetling (Table 3, game 15)" induce finger movement. Second, "Carrying water buckets (Table 3, game 16)" and "Crossing a stream on stepping-stones (Table 3, game 17)" induce upper body movement through gyro sensors.

4 Conclusion

In this study, the development of a smartphone-based Serious game for preventing dementia was proposed. This game, with a working title of Tapbrain, was designed to be used by middle-aged and elderly populations in daily life.

The development goal was to induce physical activity through the stimulation of brain exercises and finger movements. To allow stimulation appropriate to an individual's abilities, a Serious game composed of 17 mini-games was designed. The games were divided into two categories: brain function enhancement and physical activity induction.

In order to apply various aspects of dementia in our Serious game for dementia prevention, we classified dementia symptoms based on the findings of previous studies. We then identified factors required to develop the game. Next, 17 types of Serious mini-games promoting brain exercise and physical activities were developed. From this, a Serious game comprised of 13 types of games stimulating the user's brain function and four types inducing physical activities was developed. This study aims to help prevent aging-related diseases.

References

1. Kim, I.K., Liang, J., Rhee, K.O., Kim, C.-S.: Population aging in Korea: changes since the 1960s. J. Cross-Cult. Gerontol. **11**(4), 369–388 (1996)
2. He W., Goodkind, D., Kowal P.: An Aging World: 2015, U.S. Census Bureau, pp. 1–165 (2016)

3. Swaffer, K.: Dementia: stigma, language, and dementia-friendly. Dementia **13**(6), 709–716 (2014)

4. Lee, Y.-S., Kim, S.-N.: Design of "TRASH TREASURE", a characters-based serious game for environmental education. Games Learn. Alliance **9599**, 471–479 (2016)

5. Susi, T., Johannesson, M., Backlund, P.: Serious games – an overview. Technical report, School of Humanities and Informatics University of Skövde, Sweden, pp. 1–21 (2007)

6. KOCCA. 2014 Korea Serious Games Business report, KOCCA (2014)

7. Sea Hero Quest. http://www.alzheimersresearchuk.org/our-research/what-we-do/sea-hero-quest/. Accessed 01 May 2016

8. MindMate. http://www.mindmate-app.com. Accessed 01 May 2016

9. Beaver, M.L.: Human Service Practice with the Elderly. Prentice-Hill, Upper Saddle River (1983)

10. Alzheimer's Association. 2015 Alzheimer's Disease Facts and Figures, Alzheimer's & Dementia (2015)

Towards a Human Machine Interface Concept for Performance Improvement of Cycling

Menah El Bastawisy[1]($\boxtimes$), Dirk Reichardt[2], and Slim Abdennadher[1]

[1] German University in Cairo, Cairo, Egypt
{menah.elbastawisy,slim.abdennadher}@guc.edu.eg
[2] Duale Hochschule Baden-Württemberg, Stuttgart, Germany
dirk.reichardt@dhbw-stuttgart.de
http://www.guc.edu.eg/

Abstract. Exercising tends to be tedious and boring. Users search for means of entertainment during their workout. Motivation is an essential factor that inspires a person to maintain physical activity levels. A number of exercise bicycle manufacturers have enabled their equipment to port data signals to computers for the purpose of training logs. However, they all lack the motivational and the fun factors in their system. Many people face obstacles to improve their physical activity due to lack of accessibility to physical activity facilities and physical trainers. Technology can provide immediate personal assistance anywhere and anytime. In this paper, we present a persuasive game environment integrated to cycle training. The system measures the performance of a rider and visualizes a scenario through which the virtual bike trip leads. The players maintain their excitement while riding the bicycle to improve their performance on how to enhance cycling skills.

Keywords: Test environment · Android · Persuasive technology · Exergaming

1 Introduction

It is commonly known that users who exercise on bicycles and other fitness devices, watch television or listen to music so as not to become bored during their workout. In addition, motivation is an essential factor that can help maintain and increase physical activity levels. With the introduction of computer systems, home and gym fitness enthusiasts began seeking solutions for electronic motivational workouts. A number of exercise bicycle manufacturers have enabled their equipments to port data signals to computers for the purpose of interactive training logs. None, however, provides gaming environment, which allows the virtual cycling simulation to be experienced with excitement. There have been many types of exercising devices developed that replicate the leg and body movement of riding a bicycle and are grouped into so called stationary or exercise bicycles. Many people face obstacles to improve their physical activity due to various reasons; such as lack of accessibility to physical activity facilities and

© Springer International Publishing AG 2016
R. Bottino et al. (Eds.): GALA 2016, LNCS 10056, pp. 425–434, 2016.
DOI: 10.1007/978-3-319-50182-6_39

physical trainers. Technology can aid in facilitating physical activity by providing immediate personal assistance anywhere and anytime. The Duale Hochschule Baden-Wrttemberg (DHBW) Intelligent Interaction Lab in Stuttgart, Germany provides a Cycle Trainer system, which measures the performance of a rider and visualizes a scenario through which the virtual bike trip leads. Power and cadence measurements are taken from both pedals and the heart rate will be monitored as well. The aim is to develop a persuasive HMI system for the riders, which influences their behavior in order to improve their performance, through using persuasive computing [3]; by embedding the training into a game environment. The game should be intriguing and interesting to the extent of keeping the motivation of the bike rider up and their performance gains should be improved. However not so overwhelming not to distract the user from the main purpose of the exercise. The game should be captivating and absorbing to keep the user going for a long period of time without getting bored. Nonetheless, it should be as challenging as well to trigger the sense of adventure of the user and the need to go on with the exercise. The Human Machine Interface HMI was tested with a reasonable number of candidates at the end. The interface was be carried out on an appropriate percentage of different mindset of users to verify the quality and the success of the research done. This paper is organized as follows, in Sect. 2, a discussion of the related work done in cycling applications and exergaming is introduced. In Sect. 3, an overview of the system, explanation of the project approach and the game description is given. Section 4, introduces the user study and the results of this work. Finally, Sect. 5 concludes and provides insight into future work.

2   Related Work

Cycling Application. Bolton, Lambert, Lirette and Unsworth [1] presented PaperDude, a Virtual Reality cycling based exergame. Users bike down a virtual street using the Oculus Rift, pedaling on a physical bicycle attached to a power trainer and throwing virtual papers using a gesture through a Microsoft Kinect camera. Another related study with similar setup to our project was done by Hirose and Kitamura [2]. In their work, they used an indoor cycling system but instead of displaying virtual reality routes; they used Google Street view to display Street view images with a route map. They did not provide the users with pedaling speed information. The participants were asked to ride the bike twice, once without anything displayed on the screen and a second time with different assigned tasks. The average speed of both rides where compared to evaluate their system. Their findings concluded that the group who did the exercise with Street view had higher significance in their average over those who did the exercise with no display [2].

Exergaming. There is a large body of work done in utilizing games in general exercises to make it more interactive. In the work of Gardiner [5], the viability of physical interfaces to impose exercise using computer interaction was explored. Exercising in general enforces tediousness and tends to be unexciting; thus integrating the exercises with game interface may change the conceptual idea behind exercises. Many physical game interfaces are in existence using several means like dancing, punching bags, virtual drums and guitars and many more. Following to the several means of exercising, is the exercise bike, Atari Puffer in 1982 was the first to prototype a game controller using the grips of the exercise bike to connect the exercise bike and the game console. Another example is using the snake mobile game in a location-based application that encourages walking. Chatter and Sioni [6] show how using the methodology exergaming, which is video games that combine exercise and play, could encourage physical activity by adding the enjoyment factor to it. Additionally, Lin et al. [7] wrote a paper about an application called FishnSteps, which combines the use of the pedometers, small electronic devices that monitor individuals step counts, with the engagement of social computing games. The application would match the count of steps the user did with the growth and emotional state of a virtual pet that was given to each user.

3   System Design and Implementation

3.1   Technology

In this section, a system overview of the tools and the gears used in this project is presented. The entire project revolves around indoor cycling and bike system. The system setup was built inside the Intelligent Interaction Lab at DHBW Stuttgart. The LCD screen is mounted on the wall plugged to a PC. The PC is connected to the Tacx cycling trainer system using the Genius Smart tool via Bluetooth Smart. In the meantime, the Android tablet is mounted at the front of the bike. The rider's movement while cycling were tracked via Garmin Vector sensor which measures the power output at the pedals. It can independently measure power from each leg and report total power as well as the balance between the right and left leg. Vector 2 records cadence and a variety of power metrics. Mio VELO is a heart rate sensor that tracks the heart rate with peak accuracy from the wrist. With built-in Bluetooth Smart and ANT+ connectivity, Mio VELO easily connects and shares fitness data in real-time with smart fitness apps, GPS watches, and bike computers. Android acted as the host platform for the monitoring and feedback system, which was deployed on an android tablet. All the sensors along with the game graphics were aligned together and integrated on to the android device. Android is starting to add ANT+ support in their newer devices to cover the wide range of sensors using ANT as a communication protocol (Fig. 1).

3.2　Gamification

The Android application and libGDX are communicating together and the user is going back and forth between both entities smoothly; thus having the entire application responsive to all changes applied by the user. Cycling Trainer Game is an Android application that embeds persuasive technology by adding a simple interactive game to the basic android sensor application.

Game Design. For the game to deploy the persuasive technology techniques; the users need to have a sense of accomplishment. Accordingly, the user was awarded with a score whenever the game goal is achieved.

Cycling Trainer Game aims at improving the cyclist riding experience by monitoring and providing feedback on the cyclists balance on the pedals as well as the cyclists pedaling frequency. Each unit needed to be gamified differently. Hence the application includes two distinctive games. The first game objectifies improvement in the cyclist's balance on the pedals while the latter objectifies maintaining constant frequency (cadence). In the meantime the user's heart rate was monitored for health assurance.

Fig. 1. The entire project setup

According to Tanaka et al. [10] findings, the adequate equation for estimating the maximum heart rate is $208 - 0.7 *$ age in healthy adult humans. The equation calculation was done on the age of 30 giving a maximum heart rate of 187. Due to the physical nature of the game, the maximum heart rate was reduced to 160 since the medical background of the participants was unknown. If the user reaches the maximum heart rate while cycling a counter feedback system would initiate. The findings of Mok et al. prove that music improves significantly the patients anxiety levels, heart rates, and blood pressure over patients who did not listen to music [9]; thus a slow soothing rhythm music would initiate playing once the user reaches the maximum heart rate threshold. In addition, the display of nature scenery which was provided by Tacx's virtual reality system. The first game, the balance game as shown in Fig. 2, is a seesaw game where the cyclist targets the state where the board is perfectly horizontal. The seesaw methodology was used for its familiarity thus not putting on the cyclist extra overhead of getting accustomed with the game. The cyclist attains the horizontal state once the feet's pressure on the bikes pedals are equally distributed between the left and the right pedals. As for the second game, the cadence game as shown in Fig. 3, the cyclist is required to maintain constant frequency through the entire exercise, the cyclist needed to receive a motivational scheme to preserve consistency in frequency while completing the exercise. Subsequently, the game mechanism was

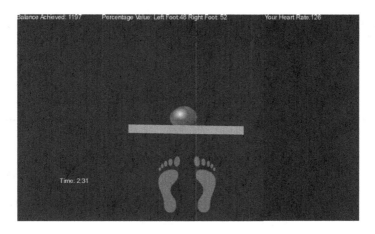

Fig. 2. The balance game, seesaw game

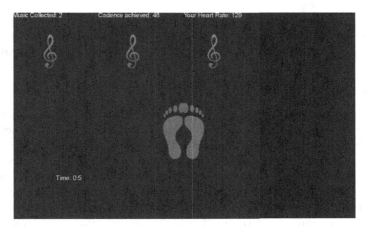

Fig. 3. The cadence game, catch the notes

designed aiming to encourage cycling as well as maintaining constant frequency. For this task, a game of catch the notes was implemented where once the cycling starts the cyclists feet start to move up the screen aiming at catching the flying music notes at the top of the screen. The game has two modes, speedy mode and relaxed mode, accommodating to the variation of users' physical state. The game session would last with time interval of the users input, the time counter is displayed at the bottom left of the screen. In the meantime, displayed at the top of the screen is the metric's value recorded by the sensor along with the heart rate of the user. The user's score is updated and shown at the top left of the screen. When time is up the user is transferred to the scoring screen with some animated fireworks and the score is displayed. Finally, the users can generate a graph presenting visual progress of their cadence throughout the entire workout.

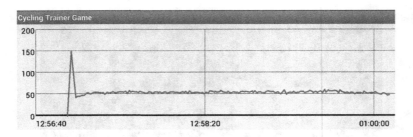

Fig. 4. The output graph at the end of the workout

This graphical visualization helps the user monitor their progress for the entire exercise. A graph example is displayed in Fig. 4.

4   Study Design

In this section, we discuss the user study and evaluation procedure which was conducted at the Intelligent Interaction Lab at DHBW Stuttgart, Germany.

4.1   User Study

The experimental design was as follows: The user group was split equally between four permutations of the following four exercises; Balance Game, Cadence Game, Data Application and Cadence Challenge. The Data application is where the user follows the progress using the ANT+ data while the Cadence Challenge is where the user is asked to maintain the same frequency without any aids. For each participant the user study would be a workout for ten minutes. Each participant carried out only three exercises from the four. Each exercise took three minutes in addition to a minute to warm up. The three minutes time-spam was adequate to retrieve the needed data for analysis. Next, the user group was divided equally into two groups. The first group started with the Balance Game then the Data Application exercise while the other group started vice versa. Consequently each sub user group was again subdivided equally into two groups; one group did the Cadence Game in the meantime the other subgroup did the Cadence Challenge.

User Evaluation. The users' feedback about the system and its features were gathered through quick survey conducted at the end of the experiment. The survey included a list of questions evaluating the users' interpretation of the system, its features and benefits. Each question in the survey targets specific criteria in the evaluation. Most of the questions were answered using the Likert Scale [11], the rating scale of five points.

User Group Profile. The user group was total of 20 participants. The group consisted of both males and females with 70% of the population were males. The biggest age group was between the ages of 20 and 25 years as shown in Table 1. The physique of the participants differed among the user group as well as being accustomed to riding a bike in their daily life. More than half the user group, about 55%, rarely rode bikes, while about only 15% rode bike daily and only 5% never rode a bike before. The users' familiarity with bike riding is displayed in Fig. 5

User Evaluation Feedback. More than half the user group, 65%, disagrees that they were mentally pressured when using the application, whilst, 20% were neutral on how mentally pressured they were, with the remaining user group agreeing to being pressured when playing the game. The users were asked after the experiment about the post-effect of the application on their cycling skills, three criteria were examined for that purpose. First, the

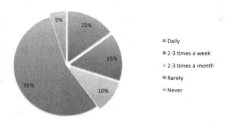

Fig. 5. Users' bike riding demographics

users were asked if they thought they were successful in achieving the goal of the experiment. From the total user group, 75% believed they were successful with the experiment goal while 20% were impartial and only 5% thought they were unsuccessful.

Table 1. Users' demographics

Age	# Females	# Males
<20	0	1
20–25	5	9
26–30	0	2
>30	1	2

4.2 Data Analysis

Cadence Data Processing. For each user, the data values for the cadence from the data task and the assigned task, the game and the challenge, were retrieved and mined. To calculate the cadence consistency; the percentile values were calculated for the two datasets for each user. Cluster analysis was computed on each percentile dataset into 8 clusters. A random user was selected from among the user group to illustrate the Data Mining process carried out. User 7 was assigned to the Game Task and had no physical background. User 7 achieved consistency in the Game task of a value of 73 from cluster 7, 4 and 1, while achieved a value of 64 in the Data task from clusters 7, 4 and 8. The summation of the three clusters was calculated and recorded for each user twice, once for the Data task and once for the Assigned task. These numbers represents the ability of the users to maintain their consistency through out the experiment and were used to carry out the rest of the data analysis.

Each related group was gathered separately for investigation. The participants of each assigned task, the Challenge Task and the Game Task, were grouped together and further split according to their physique nature. This further splitting was needed to distinguish between the outcomes of the participants according to their physical capabilities, since the experiment is dependent highly on their physical background. Four Paired Sampled T-Test were computed, first, for participants with cycling background two paired t-test were calculated. One between the Game and the Data task that the statistics showed that there was a significant difference between the data (M = 80.50, SD = 5.00) and game (M = 66.00, SD = 4.69); t = 7.17, p(0.006) < 0.05. These results suggest that the Data Task affects the participants with physical background more consistent with their compared to the game task. The second test was between the Challenge and the Data task. The statistics showed that there was no significant difference between the data (M = 71.00, SD = 7.57) and challenge (M = 76.00, SD = 3.91); t = 1.132, p(0.340) > 0.05. The same was carried out for participants with no cycling background. For the Challenge-Data test, the statistics showed that there was no significant difference between the data (M = 69.83, SD = 10.28) and challenge (M = 66.50, SD = 5.12); t = 1.055, p(0.340) > 0.05. As for the Game-Data task, the statistics showed that there was a significant difference between the data (M = 63.83, SD = 3.18) and game (M = 69.00, SD = 2.68); t = 3.893, p(0.011) > 0.05, this can be summed up in Table 2.

Balance Data Processing. For each user, the data values for the pedalling balance from the Data task and the Game Task were retrieved and mined. The pedaling balance was evaluated according to how many times the participants were able to achieve complete equilibrium, reaching a value of **50**, retrieved from the vector sensor whilst cycling. Therefore, for each participant the number of occurrences for the value **50** was computed twice, once from the data values retrieved from the data application task and once retrieved from the game application task. The statistics showed that there was none statistical significance between the game (M = 13.00, SD = 11.07) and data (M = 11.65, SD = 9.54); with a pvalue(0.388) > 0.05.

Table 2. Paired sample T test results

Type		P-value	Significant <0.05
With cycling background	game-data	0.006	Yes
	challenge-data	0.340	No
Without cycling background	game-data	0.011	Yes
	challenge-data	0.340	No

5   Conclusion and Future Work

In this paper, an introduction of a persuasive HMI exergame was embedded in a cycling trainer. A user study was conducted to test the system. From the users' evaluations, we gathered that they prefer the gaming environment while exercising more than the usual dull data application. Cyclists agreed to performing better while using the game application and stated they were not mentally pressure nor felt any difficulty imposed by cycling while using the game. They appreciated being provided with a feedback system to follow up on their progress on their own without the need of the help of a personal trainer. Finally, almost all users enjoyed their cycling activity due to having the gaming environment embedded in it. The data analysis that was carried out on the data retrieved from the sensors that tracked the performance of the user for the entire workout, had some limitations. First, due to the permutation of the experiment the data were not consistent on all users. Furthermore, the tiring nature of the user experiment could have influenced the data with some unavoidable noisiness. The data analysis showed that there were significant results in the cadence game over the data application while there was no significance between the data application and the cadence challenge. In the meantime, the balance game did not show significant difference from the data application. However, for participants, who performed better with the game application, had an overall better performance over those who performed better with the data application. This shows a higher probability of the success of the balance game but with some counter measurements; such as, all users should follow the same sequence, who have the same cycling background and with higher number of participants. The challenge task showed that the users require some visual aid that facilitates the monitoring of their progress. From what we gathered from previous work done in this field; is that exergaming could highly affect the population positively and encourages them to exercise while influencing them with a fun factor. However none of the mentioned monitoring the user's exercise progress or gave the user any feedback whilst exercising. We can conclude from this analysis that the addition of visualization and HMI system does have a positive effect on the population. This field has many promises to the exercising world and could benefit from the wide range of opportunities it might provide.

There are few areas which require further investigation. Professional cyclists could highly benefit the analysis with their input to the system. In addition, long term testing is encouraged to monitor the progress of the cyclists after using the system for a longer period of time. Finally, the permutation of the user study could be altered to foresee the resulting analysis.

References

1. Bolton, J., Lambert, M., Lirette, D., Unsworth, B.: PaperDude,: a virtual reality cycling exergame. In: CHI 2014 Extended Abstracts on Human Factors in Computing Systems, pp. 475–478. ACM (2014)

2. Hirose, S., Kitamura, Y.: Preliminary evaluation of virtual cycling system using Google street view. In: MacTavish, T., Basapur, S. (eds.) PERSUASIVE 2015. LNCS, vol. 9072, pp. 65–70. Springer, Heidelberg (2015). doi:10.1007/978-3-319-20306-5_6

3. Kurniawan, S., Walker, M., Arteaga, S.M.: Motivating teenagers physical activity through mobile games (2010)

4. Consolvo, S., Klasnja, P., McDonald, D.W., Landay, J.A.: Goal-setting considerations for persuasive technologies that encourage physical activity. In: Proceedings of the 4th International Conference on Persuasive Technology, p. 8. ACM (2009)

5. Gardiner, M.A.M.: Physically healthy game interfaces. The University of Auckland, viewed 1 (2012)

6. Chittaro, L., Sioni, R.: Turning the classic snake mobile game into a location–based exergame that encourages walking. In: Bang, M., Ragnemalm, E.L. (eds.) PERSUASIVE 2012. LNCS, vol. 7284, pp. 43–54. Springer, Heidelberg (2012). doi:10.1007/978-3-642-31037-9_4

7. Lin, J.J., Mamykina, L., Lindtner, S., Delajoux, G., Strub, H.B.: Fish'n'Steps: encouraging physical activity with an interactive computer game. In: Dourish, P., Friday, A. (eds.) UbiComp 2006. LNCS, vol. 4206, pp. 261–278. Springer, Heidelberg (2006). doi:10.1007/11853565_16

8. Fogg, B.J.: Persuasive technology: using computers to change what we think and do. Ubiquity **2002**, 5 (2002)

9. Mok, E., Wong, K.-Y.: Effects of music on patient anxiety. AORN J. **77**(2), 396–410 (2003)

10. Tanaka, H., Monahan, K.D., Seals, D.R.: Age-predicted maximal heart rate revisited. J. Am. Coll. Cardiol. **37**(1), 153–156 (2001)

11. Likert scale. https://en.wikipedia.org/wiki/Likert_scale. Accessed 30 Dec 2015

Development of a Serious Game for the Elderly (Title: 'Paldokangsan4')

KyungSik Kim[✉]

Department of Game Development, Hoseo University,
Hoseo-ro 79 Beon-gil 20, Baebang-eup, Asan-si, Chungnam, South Korea
kskim@hoseo.edu

Abstract. Old people are prone to get weak in their physical bodies as well as their memorizations. We have developed a serious game for the elderly named 'Paldokangsan4' which is a walking game strengthening legs as well as the ability of memorization with the interface of motion capture using Kinect2, the next version of 'Paldokangsan3'. This game machine has been installed in the show 'PlayX4' in Korea, last May and got responses from 40 visitors. They showed good subjective satisfactions in their responses that we could go on the project further to expand its applications to the elders.

1 Introduction

The societies of the whole globe have increasing numbers of old people living longer with medical and scientific help. However old people are prone to get weaker in their muscle and power with their bodies receding, hence easy to get sick by little activities. Also the abilities of memorization are decaying with their ages. Therefore they need repetitive performance and trials to maintain their vitalities on their physical bodies as well as their mental activities [1].

Computer games are useful bidirectional media which have features of repeating something with fun [2]. There are serious games with special purposes such as for educations or for trainings, not just for amusements [3].

This research is to utilize serious games to improve the life of the old people. We have developed a serious game 'Paldokangsan3' recently which is a walking game to strengthen their bodies with memorizing to help their memorization abilities for that purpose [4–7].

Games for the elderly has been developed and utilized in Japan first where the ratio of old population of more than 65 years old is one of the biggest countries in the world. Their games are 'Taiko Drum Master' to move both arms following the music [8], 'Hebi Hebi' to strengthen the muscles of the leg for the elderly not to be fallen down [9], and recently 'Sit-up' by Kyushu rehabilitation center [10].

There have been several researches on games related to the old person's physical and mental problems: applications for entertainment and information retrieval could compensate for age-related physiological and cognitive shortcomings [11]. Serious games are not only useful for healthy behavior, but generally for cognitive learning (knowledge and skills), motor skills, affective learning (attitude change, motivation) and communicative learning [12].

© Springer International Publishing AG 2016
R. Bottino et al. (Eds.): GALA 2016, LNCS 10056, pp. 435–443, 2016.
DOI: 10.1007/978-3-319-50182-6_40

Recently domestic researches for the elderly are active for the improvement of physical movement and rehabilitation [13]. Some of them are the personal training system for exercise and rehabilitative training [14], game with Wii-mote to improve cognition with activities [15], and game by motion capturing with 3D depth camera to help exercise and rehabilitation [16].

The aim of this paper is to describe the latest development of 'Paldokangsan4' comparing it with 'Paldokangsan3' [7] as well as the usability test with experiment through questionnaire. 'Paldokangsan4' has features focusing on walking in a shopping street with full attention of memorization to buy some designated items. It has the concept of mall walking which permits the player with visional fun as well as physical exercise. It is dealing with five common diseases of the elderly (Dementia, Depressions, Osteoporosis, Diabetes Mellitus, and Hypertensions). The mission of the game is to buy the items walking the shopping street or a mall which are good for the selected disease. 'Paldokangsan4' is using Kinect2 as its interface of motion capturing of the player with intuitive gestures. The expected effect is the improvement of walking, memorization, concentration to find out something in the vision and mental health through entertainment.

The experiment was done with 40 volunteers of all ages in the show 'PlayX4' in Korea in May in 2016. They were all focused on the game to remember the mission and to make correct decision with the gestures walking inside a small area to be captured by Kinect2. The results showed good adaptation of the game for the period.

2   Development of 'Paldokangsan4'

2.1   Design Concept of the Game

In the beginning of this research in 2008, we had collected the survey of the old people about their leisure activities and analyzed that (1) elder generation prefers leisure activities such as mountain climbing, yoga, golf, walking and travel, etc., for health, interest, the development for oneself and relieving stress; (2) they don't prefer game activity for leisure, but prefer to use serious game for health, simulation, medical treatment and sports than middle generation [17]. We started to make a walking game for the elderly in 2010 [18].

We focused on the useful field of view (or UFOV) to make our new serious game for the elderly. By the repeated reaction on UFOV, we thought their bodies and mental abilities could be improved much better [20, 21]. We have decided to develop a walking game with vision giving the scene on the screen just as seen by the walker (Table 1). So the movement of the scene should be adjusted with the steps of the player. Also to control the scene and the steps, we needed a useful and comfortable interface for the elderly.

'Paldokangsan3' [7] and 'Paldokangsan4' has the game concept of 'mall walking' to give walking action with visional pleasure as well as memorization. Walking to buy something in the mall or shopping area could help the player to concentrate on the game with little exhaust and longer play time. Its intention is to raise memorization, concentration, vitality by strengthening UFOV [22]. According to the player there

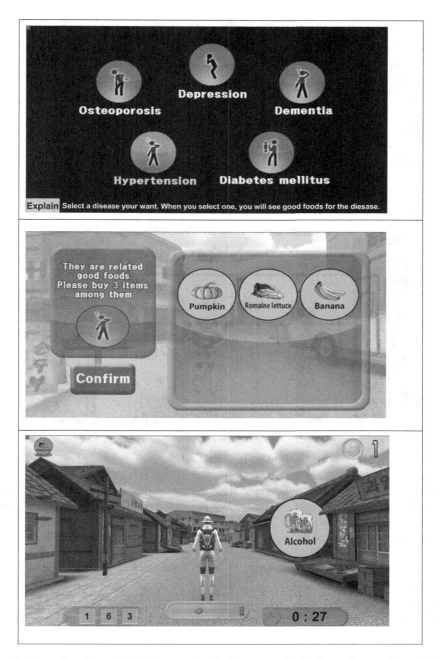

Fig. 1. Game Interface of 'Paldokangsan4': (1) the screen of selecting a disease, (2) a mission screen for target items to buy in the market street, (3) a play screen showing the avatar and the item of the store in the market street in level 1 & 2, (4) new background of the game in level 3, (5) a score page of each level to show the last score and average score of this level as well as daily ranking and weekly ranking.

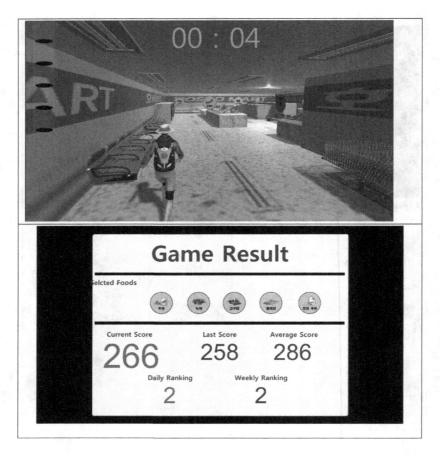

Fig. 1. (continued)

should be several levels of difficulties. Also the game should give feedbacks to the player if the choice was right or wrong. We put different sound effect with color on every selection of the item in the game following the choice. And let the player know the ranking with the score for his or her accomplishment in the game [7].

Table 1. Overview of 'Paldokangsan4'

Objective	Senior entertainment and welfare	
Controller	Kinect2	
Target user	Main	50's and later who want to walk and to improve memorization ability
	Sub	All who want to walk with vision attentions
Expected effects	1. physical exercise (walking)	
	2. memorization abilities of good foods for senior diseases	
Player	1 player	
Play time	5–10 min (3 levels)	

2.2   Game Play

Figure 1 shows 5 screens of the game 'Paldokangsan4'. The game starts with identification to accumulate the personal game data. Next selecting a disease is required to get a mission that is to buy some items in the market. Level is asked from 0 to 3 where 0 is for tutorial for the game. Number of levels stands for difficulty, so that the player can repeat the designated level.

The mission screen shows good foods for the selected disease. After confirming the mission by the player, the walking starts in the screen of the market street with stores at its both sides. Each store shows a sign board of an item it's selling. The player should decide to buy or not by raising hand of each side. At the end of each level, the player gets the score which is produced based on how correctly the player has collected and how fast the player has finished the mission.

The game has three levels. The first level is to remember three items with half round, and the second level is to remember four items with another half round. And the final level is to remember six items in a shopping mart nowadays which is added in 'Paldokangsan4'. The average time to finish the mission would be about 2 min for each level. The player may forget what to buy: then a chance coin can be used to show again the mission on the screen for five seconds.

2.3   Development

'Paldokangsan4' has been developed using unity3D with Kinect2, motion sensing interface by Microsoft. Its base is the last version 'Paldokangsan3' with Kinect.

'Paldokangsan3' had almost 3 years of testing period with several experiments by old people. In the process of experiments we had found several problems of inconvenience in 'Paldokangsan3' [6, 7]. This version 'Paldokangsan4' covers those problems with following features:

(1) Kinect2 has been adopted to have better sensing than Kinect. Many people complained wrong sensing of motions.
(2) Identification (ID) system has been added for the players to keep their personal in-game records such as scores, number of steps and duration time in each level, automatically. The score page (ex. Fig. 1 (5)) shows the score comparing with the last score and its average value with rankings. If the player doesn't remember his or her ID, then the player should key in the name to look for it.
(3) Tutorial level (level 0) has been added for unskilled players to learn how to play the game by themselves. And also players can select a level to start playing, from level 0 to level 3 as they want.
(4) Another background map of recent shopping mall has been added for the players of the game to give them a change in the environment of walking.

3   Experiments

3.1   Participants

We have installed the game machine of 'Paldokangsan4' in the game show 'PlayX4' in May in 2016 and invited 40 visitors for the survey. Table 2 shows their general

Table 2. General reviews of the participants (40 persons)

Area	Element		Average	Ratio (%)
Population and social variables	Sex	Female	26	65.0
		Male	14	35.0
	Age (10–19)		9	22.5
	Age (20–29)		14	35.0
	Age (30–39)		6	15.0
	Age (40–49)		8	20.0
	Age (50–59)		2	5.0
	Age (60–)		1	2.5
	Health	Healthy	34	85.0
		Unhealthy	6	15.0

reviews. They were in different ages but they understood this game was intended for the elderly and they gave their answers on their expectations of the effects to the elderly. Because there were little old people in the game show.

3.2 Usability Test

Usability elements has been classified in 8 areas [19]: if control is easy (easiness), if it's not hard to learn how to control it (learnability), etc. as in Table 3. Those were all the

Table 3. Questionnaire for usability evaluation

Area	No	Contents
Easiness of game control	Q1	Has the walk recognized well?
	Q2	Has the arm motion recognized well?
	Q3	Was the game good to control as you want?
	Q4	Could you see if your choice was correct or not?
Learnability of game play	Q5	Was it easy to understand how to control the game?
	Q6	Could you remember easily to the method to control the game?
Remembrance	Q7	Was the game helpful to remember good foods for a specified disease?
	Q8	Was the game helpful for your normal memorization ability?
Challenge	Q9	Did you think you would like to the game do better next time?
	Q10	Did you feel to continue to play the game for the next level?
Efficiency	Q11	Has it got easier to play the game as you repeat the game?
Tension	Q12	Could you be concentrated on the game in the process of it?
Familiarity	Q13	Was the background of the game familiar to you?
	Q14	Did you feel the avatar just like you in the game?
Satisfaction	Q15	Was the game good enough to play next time for you?
	Q16	Was the game interesting for you to play?
	Q17	Was it all right to have audience when you played the game?

same as the questions of 'Paldokangsan3' which were done with old people [7] except the last question Q17 to look the difference between two age groups. Q17 has an intention of checking sociability effect of the game.

3.3 Result of Usability Test

Each question of Table 3 has Likert scale of 5. The average score of each question is shown in Table 4. It showed the values were varying a little bit according to age groups. We had the result of the old people with 'Paldokangsan3' [7]. So the new results which come out from all the generations can be compared to those of the old people.

Table 4. Result of usability test

Area	Question no	Average						
		All ages	10–19	20–29	30–39	40–49	50–59	Over 60
Easiness of game control	Q1	3.67	3.77	3.35	3.33	4.25	4.00	4.00
	Q2	3.42	3.33	3.07	2.83	4.50	3.50	4.00
	Q3	3.47	3.44	3.14	3.66	3.75	4.00	4.00
	Q4	3.77	4.11	3.57	3.66	4.12	2.50	4.00
Learnability of game play	Q5	4.42	4.55	4.50	4.33	4.37	4.00	4.00
	Q6	4.35	4.55	4.35	4.16	4.25	4.00	5.00
Remembrance	Q7	3.62	3.44	3.07	4.00	4.37	3.50	5.00
	Q8	4.12	4.00	4.07	4.16	4.37	3.50	5.00
Challenge	Q9	3.77	3.77	4.14	3.66	4.37	3.50	5.00
	Q10	3.65	3.66	3.64	3.00	4.12	3.50	4.00
Efficiency	Q11	4.02	3.55	4.21	4.00	4.37	3.50	4.00
Tension	Q12	3.80	3.77	3.64	3.33	4.50	3.50	4.00
Familiarity	Q13	3.05	3.44	2.78	2.66	3.37	2.50	4.00
	Q14	2.77	2.55	2.57	2.00	3.75	2.50	5.00
Satisfaction	Q15	3.65	3.77	3.71	2.66	4.00	3.50	5.00
	Q16	3.70	3.88	3.78	3.00	3.75	3.50	5.00
	Q17	3.52	3.66	3.35	3.50	3.87	2.00	5.00

Learnability of the game (Q5, Q6) was excellent to most age group that means the game was easy to understand and remember how to play. Efficiency of the game (Q11) was good also that means the score would grow with the more playing but got a gap between age groups. Remembrance (Q7, Q8) of this game showed the players' interest. Young people had little interest about 5 common diseases for the elderly but they agreed the concentration on memories in the game would help normal memorization ability. Tension (Q12) and Challenge (Q9, Q10) showed good score as in old people in 'Paldokangsan3' [7]. Satisfaction (Q15, Q16, Q17) were good also but we couldn't see the proudness (Q17) which was common to old people with 'Paldokangsan3'.

Familiarity (Q13, Q14) was in the middle as we expected because the avatars were in the middle ages.

Most participants showed good subjective satisfactions in their interviews also.

4   Conclusion

In this research, we have developed a serious game for the elderly, 'Paldokangsan4' that is a walking game with memorization by motion capture interface using Kinect2. Advanced features from the last version 'Paldokangsan3': (1) Kinect2 for better recognition of motions, (2) ID system to accumulate in-game scores of the players, (3) tutorial level with better user interface, (4) new background of recent shopping mall.

The game has been tested by a survey from 40 visitors of all ages who were asked to expect the game for the elderly. The questionnaires were nearly the same as those of 'Paldokangsan3'. Their response showed the game were working well and valuable to go on with old people of more than 65 year old.

Acknowledgments. This project was supported by Hoseo University (no. 2015-0344).

References

1. Jeon, H.K., Kim, M.Y.: The benefits of aquatic exercise programs for older adults. J. Coaching Dev. **5**(2), 69–76 (2003). (in Korean)
2. 2014 White Paper on Korean Games Guide to Koran Games Industry and Culture. Korea Content Agency (2014)
3. Abt, C.C.: Serious Games. Viking Press, New York (1970)
4. Kim, K.-S., Oh, S.-S., Ahn, J.-H., Lee, S.-H., Lim, K.-C.: Development and analysis of a walking game using controllers of armrests and footboards (title: Paldokangsan). J. Korea Game Soc. **11**(6), 43–52 (2011). (in Korean)
5. Kim, K.-S., Oh, S.-S., Ahn, J.-H., Ahn, J.-H.: Development and analysis of walking game using controllers of hand buttons and footboards (title: Paldokangsan2). J. Korea Game Soc. **13**(3), 95–104 (2013). (in Korean)
6. Kim, K.-S., Lee, Y.-J., Oh, S.-S.: Development and analysis of walking game 'Paldokangsan3' using kinect. J. Korea Game Soc. **14**(1), 49–57 (2014). (in Korean)
7. Kim, K.-S., Lee, Y.-J., Oh, D.-N.: Development and testing of a serious game for the elderly (title: 'Paldokangsan3'). In: Proceedings of International Conference on Games and learning Alliance (GALA), Serious Game Society (SGS) (2015)
8. http://taikopsp3.namco-ch.net/
9. http://www.namcobandaigames.com/
10. Tach, D.: Video Game Uses Kinect to Help Stroke Patients Walk. Kyushu University, Asahi Shinbun, 27 November 2012
11. Gerling, K.M., Masuch, M.: Exploring the Potential of Gamification Among Frail Elderly Persons, Vancouver, BC, Canada (2011)
12. Wouters, P., Van der Spek, E.,Van Oostendorp, H.: Current practices in serious game research: a review from a learning outcomes perspective. In: Games-Based Learning Advancements for Multi-sensory Human Computer Interfaces: Techniques and Effective Practice, pp. 232–250 (2009)

13. Seo, J.-M.: A design consideration element and serious game for disabled person. Korea Soc. Comput. Inf. **16**(1), 81–87 (2011). (in Korean)
14. Ryu, W., Kang, H., Kim, H.: Development of personal training system using serious game for rehabilitation training. J. Korea Game Soc. **9**(3), 121–128 (2009)
15. Ok, S., Kim, D.: Serious game design for rehabilitation training with infrared ray pen. J. Korea Game Soc. **9**(6), 151–161 (2009). (in Korean)
16. He, G.F., Woong, J., Kang, S., Jung, S.: Development of gesture recognition-based 3D serious games. J. Korea Game Soc. **11**(6), 103–113 (2011). (in Korean)
17. Lee, Y.-J., Ahn, J.-H., Lim, K.-C.: Analysis of the needs of middle and elder generation on serious game for the elderly. J. Korea Contents Assoc. **9**(10), 1–27 (2009)
18. Kim, K.-S., Oh, S.-S., Ahn, J.-H., Lee, S.-H.: Development of a walking game for the elderly using controllers of hand buttons and foot boards. In: Proceeding of the 17th International Computer Games Conference (CGAMES), Louisville, pp. 158–161 (2012)
19. Nielsen, J.: Designing Web Usability: The Practice of Simplicity, Indianapolis. New Riders Publishing, Indiana (2000)
20. Ball, K., Wadley, V.G., Edwards, J.D.: Advances in technology used to assess and retrain older drivers. Gerontechnology **1**(4), 251–261 (2002)
21. Sekuler, A.B., Bennett, P.J., Mamelak, M.: Effects of aging on the useful field of view. Exp. Aging Res. **26**(2), 103–120 (2000)
22. Wikipedia (2014). http://en.wikipedia.org/wiki/Useful_field_of_view

A Neuroscience Based Approach to Game Based Learning Design

Nikesh Bajaj[(✉)], Francesco Bellotti, Riccardo Berta,
and Alessandro De Gloria

Elios Lab, DITEN, University of Genoa, via opera pia, 11a, 16145 Genoa, Italy
{nikesh.bajaj,franz,riccardo.berta,adg}@elios.unige.it

Abstract. In recent years designing a game for education has become very popular. Neuroscience has developed many theories of learning, based on how brain learns. We discuss a design approach for conventional teaching methods. The proposed approach illustrates the opportunities to exploit the concept of neuroscience and combine it with game for educational purpose. The pedagogies based on neuroscience and psychology have been adapted in teaching very well and the same is expected to work well with Game Based Learning (GBL).

1 Introduction

Pedagogies for educational learning have been improved over a time due to change in behavior of learners. Education sector is experiencing the change in learners' attitude and motivation towards learning [1], which is a driving force to change the ways of teaching. Studies claim that computer games may be used for teaching [2–4], specifically these games can enhance learners' cognitive abilities and understanding of topics [5–7]. Nowadays, games are being designed for many other aspects such as education, healthcare, defense, training, advertisement, politics and social problems, such games developed for training purpose are termed as serious games [8]. Yet serious games are not meant to replace the traditional teaching methodology, they mean to support learning. On the other hand, neuroscientist and psychologist have been supporting to develop pedagogical tools for education and learning, using the concepts of cognitive psychology and neuroscience. Educational Psychology is a branch of psychology that deals with human learning based on cognitive and behavior prospective. Most of teaching practices used in classrooms are supported by educational psychology. Considering games as effective pedagogy for teaching, it can be further improved by combing it with neuroscience. There are many studies that show different approaches for designing games [9, 10]. In this paper we propose an approach to design a Game Based Learning (GBL) system using concepts of neuroscience of learning. In next section, the concepts of neuroscience which are related to learning are discussed and in subsequent sections a procedure of Game Based Learning with neuroscience is discussed.

© Springer International Publishing AG 2016
R. Bottino et al. (Eds.): GALA 2016, LNCS 10056, pp. 444–454, 2016.
DOI: 10.1007/978-3-319-50182-6_41

2   Learning and Neuroscience

Learning is most effective aspect of life, which changes personality with skills and knowledge. From neuroscience point of view there are some aspects which should be taken care while designing any learning module or procedure [11] and they are as follows:

1. Learning Cycle (Zull's Model)
2. Neuroplasticity (Neural Connections)
3. Social Brain (Engaging with others)
4. Emotions (Flow)
5. Attention and Memory
6. Sensory (Engage Senses)

Among above six aspects, Learning Cycle is a complete process of learning and other are more related to each stage of cycle or flow of cycle. This section will discuss these aspects with enough details to relate with Game Based Learning design for educational purpose.

2.1   Learning Cycle (Zull's Model)

Learning cycle is based on Zull's Model [12] as shown in Fig. 1, according to which there are four stages of learning: Concrete experience (Gathering), Reflective observation (Reflection), Abstract hypothesis (Creation) and Active Testing. Each stage is related to sensory cortices, temporal lobe, pre-frontal cortex and motor cortices respectively. A simplified Zull's model can consider as Learning Cycle as shown in Fig. 2.

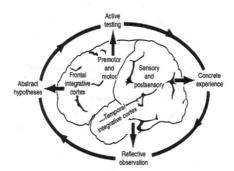

Fig. 1. Zull's model

(i) Gathering: Learning starts from gathering phase, which involves collecting information. Information is collected by the senses of body such as vision, auditory, touch, position, smell and test. This phase engages sensory cortices of brain [11].

(ii) Reflection: The time duration is termed as reflection phase in which collected information is digested. Insight formulation and connecting information to other information is part of the reflection. This duration of reflection varies from person to person. This process involves temporal lobe of brain [11].

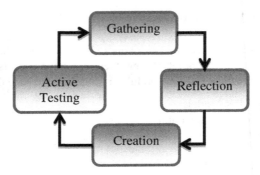

Fig. 2. Learning cycle

(iii) Creation: After insight formulation, learner needs to create his own understanding by creating idea and plan based on information gathered and processed. This part of cycle engages the pre-fontal cortex of brain [11].

(iv) Active Testing: Active testing is a physical process involving motor cortices. It requires any physical activity related to idea formed in creation process. As per Zull's model any action inspired by idea qualifies as active testing [11].

2.2   Neuroplasticity

Neuroplasticity is the most important aspect of learning, as it refers to neurological changes in brain by creating neurons or reorganizing neural pathways for tuning the brain for particular task. As per Hebb [13], Neural Network and connections becomes more effective when associated neurons are used repeatedly. Brain is affected in two ways by learning, either by creation of new neural connections or altering the existing connections. In both cases brain gets modified to observe new information and retain it, if it's useful [11] and this occurs in reflection stage of learning cycle. For quick learner it takes less time as they have more neural connections and they can correlate new information with existing knowledge. Whereas for slow learner it takes more time [11].

For facilitating brain to observe the information and form insight, it should be given enough time for reflection process. This can be fastened by providing extra information and correlation of new information to old information, which learner has acquired already. This can be made effective and strong by repetition. In summary, by providing relation of new knowledge to prior knowledge and giving information repeatedly, the learning process can be enhanced.

2.3   Engaging with Others (Social Brain)

As per UCLA social cognitive neurologist Lieberman and Eisenberger [14], brain learns quickly and effectively when it interacts with others. The contribution to learning because of engaging with others is termed as collaborative learning [15]. Because of interaction with others, brain gets forced to absorb useful information out of new knowledge and try to make sense of it. This works very well in classroom teaching such as group/team work, online discussion forums. Learning becomes faster and effective when learner interacts with other people in same context [16, 17].

2.4 Emotion and Learning

Psychology and neuroscience agree on role of emotions in learning. Virtually all mental activities involve both emotion and cognition [18, 19]. A memory researcher Richard Cytpwic [20] says; *"it is an emotional calculus more than a logical one, that animates us"*. For moving through learning cycle, the right amount of emotion is required. Less arousal makes learner to drop in between of cycle due to lack of interest and more arousal affects learner's ability to focus. Just right balance of emotion is required in order to move through learning cycle and it's known as 'FLOW' in games research [8].

2.5 Attention and Memory

In order to engage learner in learning cycle, not only emotion but attention is also required. Brain always pays attention to something; the only question is on what? [21]. Brain pays attention and remember only things that are relevant and important, rest it drops and forgets easily. Attention is not only required in beginning but in entire learning cycle, It's important to engage attention in start and manage it throughout [11].

For learning process, the information that brain attends needs to be stored in long term memory. The stored information can be retrieved when it's needed. This process has three stages, encode, store and retrieve. Studies show that more attention is required to encode the information rather than retrieval. Encoding is done in working memory, which is effected by cognitive overload [22]. Cognitive load is defined as total efforts being used in working memory and overload is a situation when brain is given more tasks than it's at most capacity. By maintaining cognitive load with attention, brain is expected to go through life cycle smoothly [22].

2.6 Engaging Senses

Deeper learning can be induced by engaging more number of senses. Theory of multimedia learning shows visual stimuli has more impact than audio and others [23], Yet including more senses increase the richness of learning [24]. However same can be argued as engaging more senses increases cognitive load, which can affect the working memory and attention. Consequently affects the flow of learning cycle. So there should be balance among number of stimuli.

3   Game Based Learning Design Procedure

As it was discussed that game alone is not a replacement of complete educational learning experience but a system based on game can be designed. In proposed design, game is incorporated with pre-game and post-game stages. The learning cycle, as discussed in Sect. 2.1, is expected to be valid independent of medium. The idea is to apply learning cycle to serious game with proper design procedure. In rest of our discussion, *User*, *Student* and *Learner* will be used interchangeably, because a student is a user of a system and learner for a learning task, similarly knowledge and information will be used interchangeably.

Design Procedure: As shown in Figs. 3 and 4, Learning cycle is divided into three stages; Pre-Game (PrG), Game Activity (GA), and Post-Game (PoG). Figure 3 shows the procedure of Game Based Learning and Fig. 4 shows the flow of Game Based Learning. The actions of each stage for learning cycle are categorized for three different entities User/Student, Teacher and Designer. User is subjected to a learning task with a

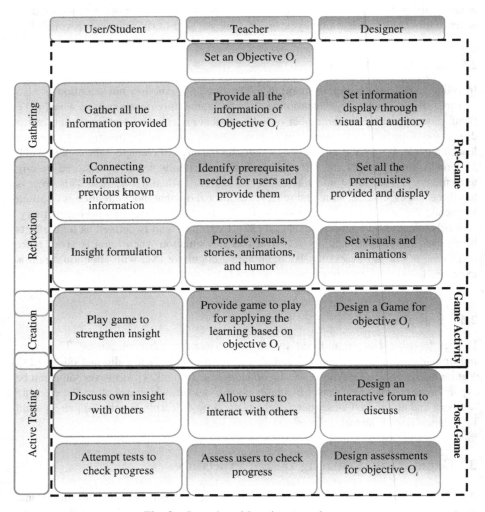

Fig. 3. Game based learning procedure

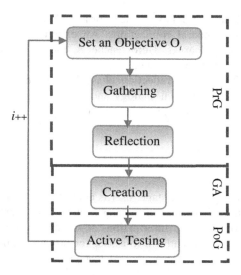

Fig. 4. Game based learning flow

learning objective; teacher provides all the required resources for entire learning cycle and designer is to design pre-game, game, and post-game stages for particular objective. Teacher and Designer need not to be two distinct entities, they can be same, but we will discuss their role distinctly. The collection of objectives can be from single syllabus of a course or from distinct.

3.1 Pre-game

In Pre-game stage, the teacher sets an objective O_i. An objective can be adding two numbers or solving the complex equations. Teacher and a designer both are required to decide the objective considering audience, level and system complexity. Once the objective is set, teacher is required to provide all the information of objective O_i with help of designer who facilitate teacher to use video, animation, and audio. Student is expected to gather all the information provided. This is a *Gathering* phase of learning cycle.

After gathering all the information, *Reflection* phase is required, in which user needs to connect given information to prior knowledge and form insight about the information. Though reflection is defined as a time gap, in which user forms insight, such time gaps are not so feasible in ongoing procedure. Instead an alternative approach can be used to serve the purpose of reflection. This can be done by providing stories, videos or animations related to the objective. In addition, proving prerequisite will avoid the confusion and increase the likelihood of understanding and reduce the time duration of building insight. As in conventional classroom teaching, an ideal teacher asks questions to students for identifying their level of knowledge and give perquisite as per requirement so that student can relate new information to prior knowledge. As all students do not have same prior knowledge, this time duration varies between students to form neural connections. An expert learner forms neural connection quickly than slow learner. Here teacher's role is to identify and provide appropriate prerequisite, where designer needs to have all plausible prerequisites available to be used. The part of reflection phase is to form insight of information, where each student builds their own analogy and imagination to understand the concept. Here teacher along with designer can accelerate this by including animations, stories and humor.

3.2   Game Activity

Once insight is formed in pre-game stage, user is ready to use information provided for Objective O_i. This is *Creation* phase of leaning cycle; where user/student is supposed to create ideas based on gathered information. A suitable design for a game with a particular objective can give a platform to a user for utilizing skills and to strengthen the understanding of concepts. Designer and teacher should decide and design the game to fulfill the need of objective O_i. Using game for learning is the most effective feature of proposed learning system, which distinguishes it from conventional pedagogical classroom teaching.

Game Design: Every game has some basic elements, such as; game plot, target, reward, penalty and game controller [9]. First these basic elements are discussed for game based learning and then other elements of game supporting learning system from neuroscience point of view are discussed.

Basic elements of Game Design:

- *Game Plot:* For maintaining the balance between fun and learning, the game plot does not need not to educational. Game plot can be chosen to make it interesting and engaging. It can be same for all the objectives or can be different for each objective, which teacher and designer can decide. Let's consider an example of teaching projectile motion, the game plot can be killing birds or hitting enemies with missiles or stones.
- *Target, Reward and Penalty:* Target, reward and penalty in the game should be chosen very carefully, as these will compute score of player which will show performance and this is the only way to quantify the learning progress of player. Targets should be achieved by aimed skill for accomplishing the objective and score should be high if skill acquired is high. For example, in projectile motion, target birds should be at many distinct positions to see if player can hit them by calculating right angle and right force. For maintaining fun in game, reward and penalty might not be strictly on skills but roughly it should be.
- *Game Controller:* Though all computer games include at least some motor cortices for example using keyboard, mouse or joystick. This serve the partial purpose of active testing on learning cycle as it involves motor movement. Rest of the purpose of active testing is served in post-game stage. For enhancing learning, game controller can be chosen such that it needs more motor movement [11]. One of the

factor of popularity of *'pokémon go'* game is that it includes more motor movements than usual mobile games [25, 26].

Learning oriented elements of Game Design:

- *Multiplayer:* As Mattew Lieberman suggested [14] brain learns faster when it interact with other people [11], this can be achieved in game by making a multiplayer game. Other players in game can be opposite players or supportive players. In both the cases, players will have interaction, which makes learning deeper and stronger [11].
- *Maintaining the Flow:* For a serious game designer, maintaining the flow in game is perhaps the most important and challenging task. In any game for maintaining flow, the difficulty of gameplay is dynamically adjusted according to player's performance and this is called as Dynamic Difficulty Adjustment-DDA [27]. Many approaches have been proposed for DDA [27]. Approaches of DDA using EEG signal also show the ways to adjust game difficulty according to state of brain [28–31]. Similar DDA approach can be applied in educational games to maintain the flow. DDA in GBL will allow expert learners to move fast and slow learners to learn at their own pace. It will ensures the users engagement.
- *Possibility Space:* As in game, the players will be able to use the information to complete some tasks of game. There should be many possibilities to use skill for objective, for example in case of projectile motion; player should be able to use any combination of angle and force. That range of possibilities is a *possibility space* for a user. As Zull's model suggests that *'learners create their own understandings based on the unique ways that their brain operates'* [11]. Learners need to be given the opportunities to make meaning in their own ways. This can be provided by creating larger possibility space for a learner in ongoing game.

Though Zull's model shows reflection, creation and active testing as three isolated phase of learning cycle, but they are not necessarily isolated. In reflection phase, user connects new knowledge to prior knowledge and forms insight about it, which is also done in creation phase. In creation phase, use of provided information in different ways, not only creates new ideas but also strengthens the insight of information [11]. Similarly, playing game serves partial purpose of active testing, as defined by Zull's model and discussed in Sect. 2.1. Figure 3 shows partial overlapping of reflection and active testing over creation.

3.3   Post-game

In this stage of GBL, user is subjected to physical activities such as; group discussion, assessments and participating in online forums, which are specifically designed for objective O_i. The teacher should allow users to interact with each other. This can be done as group discussion or online forums. Group discussion and online forums should be designed in such a way, which reinforce users to participate actively. For example of projectile motion, discussion can be on designing a launcher for a particular target. Such discussion serves the whole purpose of active testing; however it's challenging to design such discussions for each objective. After discussion, an assessment can be scheduled to check the progress and performance of students. Assessment can be a test or a quiz. Design of test and quiz are solely depended on teacher however the same can be designed with online assessment model with performance bar.

4 Discussion and Challenges

Educational psychology has been using neuroscience findings as pedagogical tools for classroom teaching for long time. Though many of findings and approaches are strictly applicable to classroom teaching where teacher can interact with students and act accordingly. Due to increasing technological development, these approaches are being shifted to virtual classroom. Table 1 concludes the neuroscience aspects and its implication in Game Based Learning design. Designing a game, which interests target audience and has high objective of learning is a challenging task. There is always a trade of between fun and learning, in games. By adding too many learning components fun is lost and for making a game very entertaining, clear learning objectives are lost. Yet there are games well balanced between fun and learning. Proposed approach to design Game Based Learning exploits educational game design and neuroscience concepts and it's expected to be valid for an effective learning system.

Table 1. Key aspects from neuroscience to game based learning designing.

Neuroscience aspect	Implications in GBL design approach
Gathering	Engage reasonably more senses: vision, auditory, touch, position, smell and taste
Reflection	Time break is not very suitable to games, so provide stories, animations, humors etc., to help relate objective with prior knowledge and insight formulation
Neuroplasticity	Connecting new knowledge to prior knowledge and repetition of same task are keys to strengthen the insight. Thus providing prior knowledge might not be required for an expert learner or a quick learner. So teacher has to identify the appropriate prerequisite and provide accordingly. Game can provide repetition of task
Creation	Provide large possibility space or workspace i.e. Many possibilities of using skills of objective
Social brain	Making game as multiplayer or interactive on social media helps learner
Active testing	Engage appropriate motor cortices;
Emotion	Keep measuring the engagement of player and adjust complexities accordingly by using DDA algorithm

One of the recent studies in GBL [32] has proposed a design for learning technology based on neuroeducation. This study reports that reward signal generated in brain with uncertainty, tends to release more dopamine and this supports learning.

The study [32] described five design cycles for the game-based teaching, out of them the four design cycles are based on Microsoft PowerPoint and last one is a web based app. The first four design cycles demanded a teacher to conduct class (roughly as a game show) and last one is online, where the teacher creates a task and students attend it as a game. The design proposed is solely based on reward system combined with the uncertainty of a game.

5 Conclusion and Future Scope

Approach to design game based learning discussed in this paper is based on neuroscience. As game solely cannot replace all the aspects of teaching, a properly designed learning system based on game with pre-game and post-game activities conducted by a teacher can be very effective. A system designed with this approach is expected to satisfy the procedural requirement of brain to lean new knowledge but as discussed challenges remain in designing appropriate game for different objectives.

References

1. Prensky, M.: Engage me or enrage me. Educ. Rev. **40**(5), 61–64 (2005)
2. Scientists, F.: Harnessing the Power of Video Games for Learning. Summit on Educational Games (2006)
3. Gee, J.P.: What video games have to teach us about learning and literacy. Comput. Entertain. (CIE) **1**(1), 20 (2003)
4. Prensky, M.: Digital Game-Based Learning. McGraw-Hill, New York (2001)
5. De Aguilera, M., Mendiz, A.: Video games and education: (education in the face of a "parallel school"). Comput. Entertain. (CIE) **1**(1) (2003)
6. Tang, S., Hanneghan, M., El Rhalibi, A.: Introduction to games-based learning. In: Games Based Learning Advancements for Multi-Sensory Human Computer Interfaces, pp. 1–17. IGI Global, New York (2009)
7. Jenkins, H., Klopfer, E., Squire, K., Tan, P.: Entering the education arcade. Comput. Entertain. (CIE) **1**(1), 8 (2003)
8. Michael, D.R., Chen, S.L.: Serious Games: Games That Educate, Train, and Inform. Muska & Lipman/Premier-Trade, Boston (2005)
9. Hunicke, R., LeBlanc M., and Zubek R.: MDA: a formal approach to game design and game research. In: Proceedings of the AAAI Workshop on Challenges in Game AI, vol. 4. (2004)
10. Fullerton, T.: Game Design Workshop: A Playcentric Approach to Creating Innovative Games. CRC Press, New York (2014)
11. Hendel, R., Oughton, K., Pickthorn, T., Schilling, M., Versiglia, G.: The Neuroscience of Learning: A New Paradigm for Corporate Education (2011)
12. Zull, J.E.: The art of changing the brain. Enriching Teaching by Exploring the Biology of Learning, pp. 14–29. Stylus Publishing, LLC, Sterling (2002)
13. Hebb, D.O.: The Organization of Behavior: A Neuropsychological Theory. Psychology Press, New York (2002)
14. Lieberman, M.D., Eisenberger, N.I.: The pains and pleasures of social life: a social cognitive neuroscience approach. Neuro-Leadersh. J. **1**, 1–9 (2008)

15. Howard-Jones, P., Ott, M., Van Leeuwen, T., De Smedt, B.: Neuroscience and Technology Enhanced Learning. FutureLab, Bristol (2010)
16. Dillenbourg, P.: What do you mean by collaborative learning. Collab.-Learn. Cogn. Comput. Approach. 1, 1–15 (1999)
17. Gokhale, A.A.: Collaborative learning enhances critical thinking. J. Technol. Educ. 7 (1995)
18. LeDoux, J.E.: Emotion circuits in the brain. Annu. Rev. Neurosci. 23, 155–184 (2000)
19. Goleman, D.: Emotional Intelligence: Why It Can Matter More Than IQ. Bantam, New York (1995)
20. Cytowic, R.E.: The Neurological Side of Neuropsychology. MIT Press, Cambridge (1996)
21. Wolfe, P.: Revisiting effective teaching. Educ. Leaders. 56(3), 61–64 (1998)
22. Baddeley, A., Hitch, G.J.: Working memory. Scholarpedia 5(2), 3015 (2010)
23. Mayer, R.: Multimedia learning. Psychol. Learn. Motiv. 41, 85–139 (2002)
24. Kim, R.S., Seitz, A.R.: Shams. L.: Benefits of stimulus congruency for multisensory facilitation of visual learning. PLoS One 31, e1532 (2008)
25. McCartney, M.: Game on for pokémon go. BMJ 354, i4306 (2016)
26. Serino, M., Cordrey, K., McLaughlin, L., Milanaik, R.L.: Pokémon Go and augmented virtual reality games: a cautionary commentary for parents and pediatricians. Curr. Opin. Pediatr. 28(5), 673–677 (2016)
27. Missura, O., dynamic difficulty adjustment. Dissertation, Bonn, Rheinische Friedrich-Wilhelms-Universität Bonn (2015)
28. Bellotti, F., Kapralos, B., Lee, K., Moreno-Ger, P., Berta, R.: Assessment in and of serious games: an overview. Adv. Hum.-Comput. Interact. 2013, 1 (2013)
29. Plotnikov, A., Stakheika, N., De Gloria, A., Schatten, C., Bellotti, F., Berta, R., Fiorini, C., Ansovini, F.: Exploiting real-time EEG analysis for assessing flow in games. In: 2012 IEEE 12th International Conference on Advanced Learning Technologies, IEEE (2012)
30. Berta, R., Bellotti, F., De Gloria, A., Pranantha, D., Schatten, C.: Electroencephalogram and physiological signal analysis for assessing flow in games. IEEE Trans. Comput. Intell. AI Games 5(2), 164–175 (2013)
31. Ninaus, M., Kober, S.E., Friedrich, E.V., Dunwell, I., De Freitas, S., Arnab, S., Ott, M., Kravcik, M., Lim, T., Louchart, S., Bellotti, F.: Neurophysiological methods for monitoring brain activity in serious games and virtual environments: a review. Int. J. Technol. Enhanc. Learn. 6(1), 78–103 (2014)
32. Howard-Jones, P., Holmes, W., Demetriou, S., Jones, C., Tanimoto, E., Morgan, O., Perkins, D., Davies, N.: Neuroeducational research in the design and use of a learning technology. Learn. Media Technol. 40(2), 227–246 (2015)

Author Index

Printed in the United States
By Bookmasters